West's Law School
Advisory Board

FUNDAMENTAL PRETRIAL ADVOCACY

A STRATEGIC GUIDE TO EFFECTIVE LITIGATION

By

Charles H. Rose III

Assistant Professor of Law
Director, Center for Excellence in Advocacy
Stetson University College of Law

James M. Underwood

Associate Professor of Law
Baylor University Law School

AMERICAN CASEBOOK SERIES®

THOMSON
WEST

Mat #40612179

American Casebook Series and West Group are trademarks registered in the U.S. Patent and Trademark Office.

© 2008 Thomson/West
      610 Opperman Drive
      St. Paul, MN 55123
      1–800–328–9352

Printed in the United States of America

ISBN: 978–0–314–18131–2

TEXT IS PRINTED ON 10% POST
CONSUMER RECYCLED PAPER

Professor Rose's Dedication:

"For my children Laura & Charlie. You are the completion of the promise I found within your mother's eyes."

Professor Underwood's Dedication:

"For my caring wife Carol and my beloved boys, Travis, Tyler & Tanner. You are my life's joy."

"In seeking wisdom, the first step is silence, the second listening, the third remembering, the fourth practicing, the fifth—teaching others."

Ibn Gabirol, poet and philosopher (1022–1058)[1]

---

[1] The Painter's Keys, http://www.painterskeys.com/auth_search.asp?name=Ibn+Gabirol.

Summary of Contents

Acknowledgments

Writing a book is a herculean task, one that is frankly impossible without the assistance of more people than one can possibly mention, but I must take a moment to express my gratitude to those that truly made this text possible. First, last and always is my wife Pamela. I am blessed to have found someone who listens when I dream out loud and then helps to make those dreams reality. My world begins and ends in the circle of her arms.

My efforts on this text were made possible by Stetson's generous summer scholarship grant program, and I wish to thank Dean Darby Dickerson for her support and mentorship. Darby has created an environment where reaching for the stars is not only expected but supported, and all of us at Stetson reach higher because we stand on her shoulders. I also wish to thank Associate Dean Ellen Podgor who has been a mentor and friend to a "rough around the edges" new law professor. Ellen is a true scholar who understand the connection between practice and doctrine, and more importantly, that this is a people business and one should never lose sight of humanity when teaching law. I only hope that my small efforts reflect her commitment to excellence in scholarship. I also wish to express my deepest thanks to Ms. Lindsey D. Granados, my research assistant who has edited every page of this text.

Finally I must thank my co-author Jim Underwood. A fine scholar and good friend, Jim listened when I called and asked him to join me on this project. He has made all the difference when it comes to the quality of the text that you will find within these pages. The rough edges are mine, the brilliant analysis and good common sense are rooted in his ready wit and generous spirit.

It is my hope that this text speaks to students and attorneys in a new way, combining the when, the how and the why into a seamless advocacy experience. The mistakes within, and I am sure that there are many, are of course my own.

Enjoy!

Charles H. Rose III
Fall 2007

Acknowledgments

I could not have written this book without the aid and encouragement of numerous people. The book's purpose is to help inexperienced advocates understand why they undertake certain actions during the pretrial life of a civil case–a strategic appreciation for the dynamics of real-world advocacy. Much of the inspiration for this strategic focus comes from having worked with one of the finest and most effective lawyers–Bill Hankinson. Bill was a senior partner at Thompson & Knight's Dallas office when I first entered practice approximately twenty years ago. It was my pleasure to work for Bill as a young associate and later with him as a partner, both at Thompson & Knight and later at Akin, Gump, Strauss, Hauer & Feld. Bill–who I now consider to be a friend–is enjoying retirement in Denver. No matter how complex the matter, Bill showed me that by breaking down a large problem into bite-size pieces, an advocate could find their way through any legal labyrinth. He also demonstrated daily the most important attribute of any advocate–courage.

I am deeply indebted to my co-author and friend, Charlie Rose, for calling me during the spring of 2007 and asking if I would like to collaborate on a pretrial practice book. I had taught a course on pretrial practice eight semesters in a row at Stetson University and had spent considerable time daydreaming about writing such a textbook–but this book would not become a reality without Charlie. I could not find a better person with whom to work on a daunting project. Charlie is a real, emerging star in the legal academy and a prolific author. Call me anytime you want to do another book, Charlie.

I would, finally, like to express my gratitude to Dean Toben and my other faculty colleagues at Baylor University Law School in Waco, Texas for their support and encouragement. Baylor is a unique law school that is wholeheartedly dedicated to instructing law students on how to become exceptional lawyers who can change the world through providing quality representation of clients. It is a joy to teach at an institution with such an important mission. "Sic 'em Bears."

James M. Underwood
Fall 2007

CHAPTER ONE
WHY A PRETRIAL
ADVOCACY BOOK?

"A great part of courage is the courage of having done the thing before."[1]

> When you finish with this book you will be able to *"do the necessary"* when representing clients.

An anxious young lawyer, Jim, having successfully passed his state's bar examination and arriving at the rather large, metropolitan law firm to report for his first day on the job, goes into the office of a senior partner and takes an empty seat. Jim was separated from the partner by a massive oak desk and about forty years of practice experience. The seasoned lawyer finished his phone call, finally making eye contact with Jim and announced in a very authoritative voice: "Jim, welcome to the firm. I've got an important client that has just been sued in county court. My secretary has set up the file and you can get it from her. Make sure you treat this client right and *do the necessary.*"

After very few other pleasantries were exchanged, Jim left the corner office, retrieved the file from the secretary and began to review its contents - in his much smaller office. The file contained a state court petition and a letter from the partner to the client thanking the client for the new matter and promising a good outcome. The petition was filed by a local businessman who apparently had a problem with a leaky roof on a commercial office building - the roofing system in question was manufactured by the firm's client (now Jim's first client), a large out of state corporation. As he read through the factual allegations contained within the petition, a nagging question racked his brain–"what is the 'necessary'"? Indeed.

---

[1] Ralph Waldo Emerson.

Despite an exceptional legal education and a year clerking for a federal trial judge, the young lawyer was uncertain how to proceed with the defense of this new lawsuit. Jim had a vague sense that his job was "to win"–buttressed by the partner's promise to the client in the initial letter. But what does it mean "to win" a lawsuit in a world where most civil cases settle without a trial? What should be done first to begin the defense of a new lawsuit? How does the young advocate know what may be a good

> Defining "victory" is one of the most important parts of civil practice, and one that is rarely taught in a law school environment.

settlement and how to go about obtaining that result? What if the case is one of those cases that doesn't settle? How will the advocate get the case ready for trial? Who should be the one to answer these questions–the client or the advocate–and how does one know when they have arrived at the right answers?

As a result of the leaky roof the plaintiff alleged damages initially of $15,000. Jim, unsure of the answers to the questions above, started doing what he thought lawyers involved in such cases were supposed to do. He prepared and filed an answer, sent out written discovery requests, took several depositions, and even did some legal issue-spotting which resulted in the filing of a motion to dismiss based upon the jurisdictional limits of the court being lower than the damages disclosed by the plaintiff during his deposition (The county court granted this motion, without opposition, and the plaintiff walked down the street and re-filed the case in a state district court having no maximum jurisdictional limits.).

> **To "do the necessary" you must be able to:**
> ► Handle cases from start to finish
> ► Practice unimpeded by fear
> ► Learn the tools of the trade
> ► Think both strategically and tactically
> ► Know the role of ethics

Jim performed these tasks not because the actions were designed to advance the litigation ball strategically toward a specific goal but because Jim was vaguely aware that advocates did these kinds of things. After following this path toward an uncertain destination, the case somehow managed to settle–for an amount in excess of the original demand. As he sent the closing letter to the client, the thought dawned on Jim that, after more than a year of time and thousands of dollars in legal expenses, his client might have achieved a better result by ignoring the claim and suffering a default judgment. Surely, Jim thought with some chagrin, this could not be considered a "win."

So what is "the necessary?" The answer to this question comes from the synergy that is created when common sense, practical knowledge, and legal acumen combine to create representation that is greater than the sum of its parts. This book is designed to assist advocates in bringing these concepts together within the confines of a practical structure that produces results for the client. When you have finished with this book you should be able to identify and "do the necessary" in most situations. In order to reach the point where you can "do the necessary" you will have to develop some specific skills, including: (1) handling cases from start to finish on your own, (2) handling cases unimpeded by fear, (3) learning the tools of the trade (4) thinking both strategically and tactically, and (5) understanding

"Lawyers know life practically. A bookish man should always have them to converse with."

Samuel Johnson

the role of ethics. Litigation is a scary place where the client relies upon you to guide them. When we are done with this course of study you will have the requisite tools to serve as the trusted guide for a client that is lost in a complex and dangerous situation - our goal is to give you the tools to bring the client to the best outcome possible.

It is not unfair to assume that new advocates have a broader knowledge base of the law upon just completing their bar examination than at any other point in their legal careers. They have not yet begun to specialize, and their level of knowledge, while it may be a mile wide and an inch deep, is quite impressive. They also come equipped with energy that only age can appreciate and boundless enthusiasm to become successful lawyers. These are wonderful attributes, but they are not enough. What these lawyers lack at this point is sufficient practical knowledge of how to move a case through the civil adjudicative process and the sound judgment that comes from experiencing actually handling civil lawsuits from start to finish. Until one has done it, it is impossible to fully appreciate this unique process. Nevertheless, this text is designed to help guide the advocate through the litigation thicket for the first time in the hope that the trail will be more familiar to the advocate when the new client calls.

"As our case is new, so we must think anew and act anew."

Abraham Lincoln

A common impediment to an advocate making a judgment about which path to take in handling a litigation matter is the fear that she will choose wrongly and that bad things will happen to her and her client. At least one reason for procrastination is perfectionism or fear of making a mistake. A good advocate must not be bound by such fears and is liberated by the realization that pretrial practice does not involve making cookies but, instead, coming up with creative and non-formulaic solutions for difficult problems. It is much more effective to have Eighty percent of the correct solution on the date it is needed than one hundred percent of the correct solution long after the deadline for action has passed.

This text presupposes that the skills courses taught in law school must be combined with the doctrinal knowledge taught in law school to create an effective and holistic approach to civil litigation. A litigator without sufficient grasp of the substantive law is dangerous, and a litigator without the requisite practical skills is useless. Most law school civil procedure classes introduce the student to some of the tools of litigators but do not begin to educate the students on how, when and why they should use a particular procedure in a given circumstance. This is akin to pointing out to an inexperienced cook the location of the spice rack without offering any actual cooking tips or providing any recipes. When should an advocate file a Rule 12 motion to dismiss[2] and when should the advocate instead wait until after some discovery and instead pursue a motion for summary judgment? Which type of discovery device is best used to inquire about theories underlying the opponent's claim? When is formal mediation better than informal settlement discussions and who should be the first to broach the subject? Knowing how to use the tools of the trade and why you might want to use a particular tool for a specific situation are paramount skills for an effective and efficient pretrial advocate.

This book's subtitle–"A Strategic Guide to Effective Litigation"–emphasizes what will be a common theme throughout the various

---

[2]Federal Rule of Civil Procedure ("FRCP" or "rule ___") 12 can be found in Appendix II to this text.

chapters. To be effective as an advocate you must always be able to explain to yourself why you are doing any particular task on behalf of the client's case. What is the goal of taking this witness' deposition? What are you really seeking in sending out another set of interrogatories? In deciding to add a tort claim to your client's breach of contract lawsuit, what you are trying to accomplish?

> A litigator without sufficient grasp of the substantive law is dangerous - a litigator without the requisite practical skills is useless.

Are you filing a motion to dismiss just because you can or do you really intend for the motion to achieve some objective? While this book cannot supply *per se* answers to all such questions in specific contexts–we are not making cookies after all–hopefully by the time you have finished reading through this text you will be accustomed to asking yourself such questions and having a systematic approach for finding answers. Training yourself to think and plan strategically is one of this book's chief aims and is the thing that will help you not only to be efficient as an advocate, but effective in maximizing the opportunity to achieve your clients' goals.

There are very few topics discussed in this book that do not implicate issues of ethics and professionalism. Advocates do not always agree on what the rules of ethics or a sense of professionalism dictate for a particular circumstance, but advocates are well advised to think about such issues as they work their client's claims through the process of adjudication. While some issues are fairly subtle and not easily anticipated, others simply do not pass the smell test and are generally accepted as the way to do, or not do, things. This book will help advocates discern these issues and will provide practical suggestions for how to avoid inadvertently stepping into ethical and professional pitfalls. Ethics permeates the true practice of law. As attorneys you sell your legal abilities, and an advisor that cannot be trusted is less than useless to the client. The only currency you have that you control is your integrity; once sacrificed, it is extremely difficult to regain.

These skills are something that advocates might, over time and with much anguish, achieve on their own without the assistance of this book–as the authors did themselves during their respective legal careers. But such an arduous path is not necessary. Why should an advocate have to take a client along on a wandering through the wasteland of ignorance? What sane advocate would desire such a journey for herself? That journey is neither preordained nor a worthy pursuit. This text will, therefore, seek to help advocates learn the detailed process of civil pretrial advocacy, understand the major dynamics of civil practice that will shape the details of their case handling and develop a framework for approaching pretrial advocacy in a strategic and systematic fashion.

> One of the most difficult tasks a civil litigator faces is breaking out of the "triangle of despair."

By some estimates, civil advocates will typically spend more than 90% of their professional time involved in pretrial practice. How you handle the pretrial phase of your practice of law will likely dictate how you live your life. If you do not manage the pretrial process it will manage you. An inability to properly focus on the task at hand limits the ability of an attorney to effectively represent their client, creating a maelstrom of activity that does not move the litigation forward. Will you constantly be in a reactive mode bouncing from one situation to the next? Will you be disorganized and in a frenzied state of worry? Will you procrastinate from indecision and suffer from the stress of potentially missing deadlines? Will your apprehensions about exercising judgment in difficult and new scenarios impair your ability to represent confidently your clients' best interests? Or will you act with the confidence of someone who knows how to prepare a case and actually follow through on that knowledge by implementing into practice these valuable skills and, thereby, taking charge of your case? Practicing law is a demanding profession and being an advocate is the most stressful form of law practice. The civil advocate has the potential to suffer much grief from a rather unique potential conspiracy of three sources–opposing counsel, courts and clients–the triangle of despair.

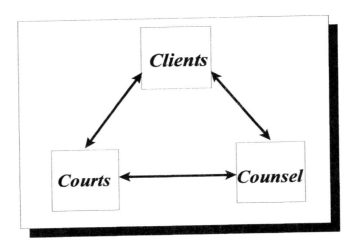

Many other professions offer stress. Doctors face life and death decisions concerning treatment for their patients.   Engineers must design bridges to withstand earthquakes.   Middle school teachers must find a way to instruct students while teaching them discipline.   Real estate agents wonder when the phone will ring with another good listing.   Yet the life of the advocate takes on a singularly unique feature–the specter of another advocate getting paid to undermine the work of the other, often by setting traps and hoping to catch the other in it. It can be daunting for an advocate sitting in her office to think about the fact that, at any given moment during the day, multiple other lawyers around town are plotting against her. Opposing counsel can be untrustworthy, mean-spirited, and unnecessarily contentious.   They can easily ruin the advocate's weekend simply by faxing a Friday afternoon letter threatening to seek sanctions for some perceived failure to produce a document in a timely manner. At least in some law firms, even an advocate's partner might be tempted to try to steal her client to make his year-end revenues look better than hers. The legal profession is comprised of people and people, unfortunately, sometimes behave poorly.

"The reason why worry kills more people than work is that more people worry than work."

Robert Frost

At least at a subconscious level, one reason clients hire the advocate is so the client can take their legal worries and hoist them onto the shoulders of the advocate. In this sense, advocates are professional worriers. Clients can be demanding, unreasonable in their expectations, and they can take advantage of the advocate particularly if the advocate makes the unwise decision to provide her home phone number to the client. Clients can also second-guess those tough judgment calls you make that turn out poorly and wonder why you recommended against accepting a settlement offer when the jury later rejects your claims. Clients can make these demands while paying your fees late, complaining about your fees regardless of the terrific results you achieve, and threatening you when things begin to sour in the life of your lawsuit. Because almost all lawsuits have both high and low moments as they wind their way through the pretrial process, there tend to be ample opportunities for these negative traits to manifest themselves in your clients.

Judges are sometimes quick-tempered, indecisive, wrong about either the law or the facts, arbitrary, lazy, biased, and long on memory of your past mistakes in their presence. Judges sometimes appear to be friends with your adversary and, even when being even-handed, it is often tough to predict how they will rule on any given issue.

Given all of the potential for distress from this unique combination of opposing counsel, clients and the courts, the advocate is often left feeling a sense of uncertainty and apprehension. Such reaction breeds worry in the advocate which can, in turn, manifest itself in many self-destructive behaviors. Advocates sometimes suffer from generalized anxiety disorders, ulcers, and negative addictions. These addictions can take various forms including overindulgence in things as diverse as alcohol or work. Any advocate reading these words who has practiced for any significant length of time can immediately call to mind images of colleagues who have succumbed to these pressures of the practice. Is there a way to avoid or escape this despair? Absolutely.

"Character is like a tree and reputation like a shadow. The shadow is what we think of it; the tree is the real thing."

Abraham Lincoln

While opposing counsel, the courts and clients can be significant sources of stress they can also make the practice of law an immensely rewarding and enjoyable vocation. When you learn to treat other counsel with respect, courtesy and honesty you will frequently find them reciprocate. Those who do not tend to develop a negative reputation that follows them the remainder of their careers. Good advocates know how to vigorously seek their clients' aims while treating their opposing counsel appropriately. Clients likewise can be the source of inspiration for much of the good that you may accomplish during your career as an advocate. Clients not only pay our fees, they also provide us with causes to undertake and the opportunity to serve people most in need of help during a time of crisis in their lives. Clients give us a chance to see justice sometimes served. No legal doctrine or rule of civil procedure ultimately matters except to the extent that these legal constructs impact the lives of people. When an advocate learns to take a sincere interest in the well being of her clients, clients can be the most appreciative people in the world. When a

> No legal doctrine or rule of civil procedure ultimately matters except to the extent that these legal constructs impact the lives of people.

client senses her advocate really cares, such client can even overlook a mistake made by the advocate working hard and acting in good faith. The advocate is, for many clients, their personification of the law and this gives the advocate great power and influence to impact the clients' lives. Finally, most judges are hard-working, strive with all of their power to be fair and achieve just results in the cases they decide, and are quick to show mercy to advocates who have given the court respect and acted professionally.

But how does the advocate encounter the good in these three sources rather than the destructive? We have already alluded to part of the answer–simply by obeying the golden rule and treating others as the advocate would like to be treated, the advocate can foster the good in others they encounter in their pretrial practice. This book will discuss and offer examples of such professionalism throughout the text. But there is so much more that the well-trained advocate can do to make their practice rewarding and a cause for celebration rather than despair. Being organized, strategic, efficient and diligent as an advocate will help to minimize the stress, anxiety and uncertainty associated with pretrial practice. Little choices have a way of defining the character of the advocate and of transforming the advocate's practice. These things include matters such as calculating deadlines appropriately and placing them on your calendar, answering client phone calls and returning phone calls promptly from your opposing counsel, minimizing uncertainty and procrastination by having a strategy for pursing your client's litigation goals and never making ethical choices that cause you to look over your shoulder. The back pages of state bar publications are filled with examples of advocates who failed to learn to practice strategically, effectively and ethically and have received public reprimands and suspensions. But many more advocates have taken the other route–the path advocated and illuminated by this text.

If you are using this text as part of a law school course on pretrial practice you should consider the unique place that such a course has in your law school curriculum. A course on pretrial practice, perhaps more than any other single law school course, combines in a very practical way the lessons you have

> Being organized, strategic, efficient and diligent as an advocate will help minimize the stress, anxiety and uncertainty associated with pretrial practice.

hopefully learned in other courses such as civil procedure, evidence, and professional responsibility, providing a curricular capstone to your law school experience. This is the course where you will learn how to actually practice law on a day-to-day basis. This will hopefully also be the course where you gain self-confidence concerning your ability to practice law the day that your state bar examiners authorize you to begin practice–a day hopefully not far-off at this point. If you have recently entered the practice of civil litigation, congratulations, because you have chosen well. The life of the advocate can be both meaningful and exciting. In either case, this text is designed to enable you to handle a lawsuit on your own from the very inception until the moment the voir dire commences at trial.

Our young advocate who we began with, Jim, closed the file on that first experience with civil pretrial advocacy with mixed feelings. He was glad to wrap up the representation of his first client but dissatisfied with how he had allowed the pretrial process to direct his steps rather than for him to steer the case in a manner that was strategic, efficient and effective. Even in this recognition of failure, Jim was already beginning to learn to be a better advocate. May your path be more precise and measured. Now let's turn to an overview of that pretrial process that awaits you.

Points To Ponder . . .

1. Reflect on what motivates you to consider pursuing the role of advocate in our civil litigation system. How can this motivation help you to achieve success without suffering some of the pitfalls of the profession?

2. Describe the type of advocate that you envision yourself being. What attributes are most important to you? Why?

3. Imagine yourself as a client with a civil claim that needs to be prosecuted. What type of advocate would you want to find to handle your claims?

CHAPTER TWO
THE PRETRIAL PROCESS

"O, what men dare do!
What men may do!
What men daily do,
  not knowing what they do!"[1]

A.   *A PROBLEM, A PRIZE AND THE PROCESS*

This book is designed to lead you on a journey to discover how our system of civil adjudication works, to develop your pretrial advocacy skills, and to then combine your knowledge of the law with your persuasive skills - making you a superior advocate for your client. The ultimate goal is to enable you to put your clients in the best possible position to reach their litigation goals. Regardless of your level of expertise you should find this book a practical and insightful analysis into the dynamics of pretrial advocacy. We combine this practical outlook with analysis that offers an appreciation of, and discussion about, the broader issues that matter to advocates everywhere. These broader issues arise under the topics of ethics, professionalism and the major policies implicated by pretrial adjudication in the United States. This broader perspective helps light the way and uncover the traps waiting for the unwary litigation traveler.

> Pretrial Advocacy is one component of the advocacy experience. Superior Advocates will consider where pretrial advocacy fits into the adjudicative process - using it to complement and support the representation of the client.

To appreciate pretrial advocacy, you should reflect upon where the pretrial process fits into civil adjudication. Every civil matter begins with a client having a legal *problem* that requires the expertise and guidance of an advocate. These legal problems are as diverse as the

---

[1] WILLIAM SHAKESPEARE, MUCH ADO ABOUT NOTHING, act 4, sc 1.

permutations of human behavior. They spring forth as issues based in large part upon human nature, and the human story underneath the surface of the legal issue is often the most persuasive issue that a jury will have interest in. While this type of persuasive issue is often not controlling during the pretrial litigation, advocates would be well-advised to remain sensitive to the issue behind the issue. If and when the case becomes a trial, those human issues become an integral part of case analysis and the development of legal theories, factual theories and moral themes.[2]

Consider the legal problems that enter through the front door of a law firm each day. They are the kinds of issues you learned about in law school courses and by living life. Clients get hurt or lose possessions, suffering personal injuries or property damage, because of the intentional or accidental misconduct of others. In law school, those others are called tortfeasors; although clients usually have more colorful words to apply to those they believe have wronged them. Clients enter into contractual relations and sometimes the other party fails to fulfill a promise made in their contract. Clients own real property upon which others trespass or lay claim. Clients are the victims of misconduct by government officials who have trampled upon their civil rights. Clients have been unfairly treated, perhaps by being terminated without cause or passed over for a promotion by their employers. Other clients have been falsely accused of misconduct by third parties and seek to vindicate their name and reputation in the courts.

> Counseling clients to develop realistic litigation goals is one of the most frustrating and rewarding parts of pretrial advocacy.

Each of these situations involves some client who is, or at least perceives, that he is aggrieved and is interested in prosecuting a civil claim to obtain some type of relief–perhaps seeking damages, an injunction to stop the wrongdoing or even a declaration of their own innocence or of the other party's wrongdoing. But the concept of a legal problem-for our purposes, is broader than these scenarios. For a pretrial advocate, just as frequently the client's problem is not that they have been harmed and thereby own a cause of action; rather, the client's problem may be they have been named as a defendant in a lawsuit. While the attitudes of the claimants, on the one hand, and the defendants on the other, may differ in their initial appearance at the advocate's office, the truth is that both types of clients

---

[2]For an in depth analysis of case preparation and planning see CHARLES H. ROSE III, FUNDAMENTAL TRIAL ADVOCACY. (Thomson/West Publishing Company 2007). This issue will also be discussed in Chapter Four of this text.

face a legal problem and are in need of an advocate–someone like you.

At the opposite end of the continuum from the problem is the *prize*–the goal sought by the client. Often the client's goal is clear to the advocate. Perhaps the client has suffered a broken leg due to someone's careless operation of their car. This client seeks to recover as much money as possible to compensate for their suffering and expenses. Another client has just been served with a summons and complaint for failing to pay royalties contemplated by a contract. This client seeks to defeat any recovery by the plaintiff. These goals may be clear but they are not always realistic. The personal injury client may desire millions of dollars because they have heard reports on television about million-dollar jury verdicts for coffee burn cases. The client who has failed to pay royalties may be under the impression that a good lawyer can get someone off-the-hook in almost any situation. Both clients will require serious counseling by the advocate to adjust their expectations or goals for the representation. There are other situations where the client is concerned or upset about some situation or occurrence but is not sure what they are seeking. Maybe the advocate needs to make the client aware of their options. Perhaps the advocate needs to sort through the convoluted tale to ascertain whether there is any problem for which the law affords any remedy at all. Client counseling by the advocate will similarly be needed in this instance as well to determine whether any goal is feasible.

In between the problem and the prize lies the *process* of adjudication–the primary focus of this text. How does the advocate most effectively move her client from the problem to the prize? What is "the necessary"? This inquiry forms the guts of the study of pretrial advocacy and will be the primary focus of this book. Of course, there are alternatives to the type of pretrial process utilized at this time in the United States. There is another model, found frequently in certain European systems, that does not rely so much upon a litigant-dominated adversarial system of discovery trial presentation but one that is instead conducted chiefly by the active conduct and inquiry of a neutral judicial officer. Some trial lawyers have been known to suggest that a better method of dispute resolution would involve flipping a coin between the adversaries–the model utilized by children around the world. After spending many

> *"What we lawyers want to do is to substitute courts for carnage, dockets for rockets, briefs for bombs, warrants for warheads, mandates for missiles."*
>
> George Rhyne
> Wall Street Journal June 27, 1963

thousands of dollars on attorney's fees only to be told that there is a "50-50" shot of winning at trial, many clients may wonder if the coin-toss might not yield predictable results with much greater efficiency. There is also another possible method of dispute resolution involving guns and squaring off on Main Street.

Anyone who has been involved with modern pretrial advocacy could well argue that it is not necessarily the most efficient form of dispute resolution. Yet this formal system of advocate-dominated pretrial practice offers a process that is peaceable, arguably fair to the combatants, is designed to reach a resolution on the merits, and perhaps most importantly, offers litigants a chance to feel that justice through the law is achievable for any given controversy. The chart below may be useful to you in visualizing how the major phases of pretrial advocacy generally fit into the broader picture of dispute adjudication in the United States.

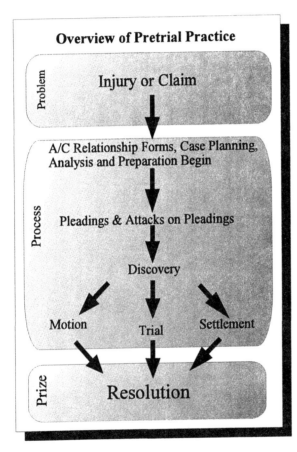

As this chart illustrates, the end-point of contested litigation almost always occurs through one of three routes– the ruling on a dispositive motion (e.g., a motion for summary judgment), settlement or trial–each of which is typically made possible as a result of effective discovery practices. This book details the pretrial process of litigation through the filing of pretrial motions and settlement. Additionally, this book considers trial preparation issues including the preparation and filing of a joint pretrial statement, the use of motions in limine and the preparation of proposed jury instructions. It is impossible to describe the intricacies of trial advocacy sufficiently in this text. That is unfortunate because pretrial advocacy done correctly requires a complete understanding of the trial process - it is after all the ultimate destination of litigation that cannot be resolved through other means. You must understand trial advocacy in order to become a more effective pretrial advocate. While a complete discussion of trial advocacy is far

> **The end-point of contested litigation is either:**
>
> ▸ A ruling on a dispositive motion,
> ▸ Settlement, or
> ▸ Trial

beyond the scope of this book, we have addressed it in the companion book to this text titled "Fundamental Trial Advocacy."[3] Many of the ideas and constructs present in this text can also be found there.

Finally, one other part of the process deserves mention for completion: post-trial advocacy. When a case has been resolved by any means other than settlement, litigants will frequently engage in pursuing post-trial motions at the trial court level and then on appeal. These topics also require a degree of specialized knowledge that is beyond the ambit of pretrial advocacy and deserve separate treatment. These three phases–pretrial, trial and appeals–comprise the entire spectrum of advocacy.

While the flow-chart description addressing pretrial practice is an accurate portrayal of how most issues generally tend, such is not always the case. The real world is never quite that tidy and one caveat must be offered before we discuss each pretrial phase in depth. Sometimes a litigant will file a motion for summary judgment without conducting any discovery–for example, a government-defendant might move for summary judgment on grounds of sovereign immunity concurrent with filing its answer. Or in another case, even after filing a motion for summary judgment the parties may continue with discovery up until close to the eve of trial itself. A party may also re-urge a previously denied summary judgment motion during trial itself. Parties also routinely seek leave to amend their pleadings in response to facts uncovered during discovery. While the general phases of litigation illustrated in our chart are fairly accurate, their real edges tend to be blurred. You must remember this when practicing pretrial advocacy so you do not lock yourself in to a process that does not completely reflect reality. Finally, this chart does not account for the many cases that are uncontested and resolved by entry of a default

---

[3]Id.

judgment following a served defendant's failure to file a responsive pleading. These uncontested cases do not tend to be ones where the pretrial advocate needs much assistance from a text such as this. Our focus in this text is on real, disputed cases where the advocate's need for judgment and discretion are most pronounced.

B.   *THE PRETRIAL PROCESS*

Pretrial advocacy begins with the initial presentation of the prospective client to the advocate for consultation and possible representation. The would-be client already has a legal problem at this time and is looking for help in resolving that problem. The process involves a number of intermediate steps once the attorney-client relationship has been formed and the pretrial portion of advocacy concludes in one of three ways--with a (1) court ruling on a dispositive motion, (2) a voluntary agreement to settlement the dispute, or (3) the commencement of a trial. While each step is covered in considerable detail throughout the remaining chapters of this book, a brief overview of these stops along the path to resolution is an excellent place for us to begin.

> *"Lawyers [are] operators of the toll bridge across which anyone in search of justice has to pass."*
>
> Jane Bryant Quinn
> (Newsweek Oct. 9, 1978)

1. Formation of the Attorney-Client Relationship

Lawyers generally represent clients. Almost every case begins with a prospective client making an appointment to see an advocate. This is a vitally important meeting that determines whether any actual representation takes place and, if so, it tends to set the tone for that relationship for the duration of the case. Special care must be taken by the advocate to gain the necessary information from the client and to convey the appropriate advice to the client. At this meeting both the client and the advocate will need to consider whether they desire for this representation to occur, taking into account a variety of both legal and practical considerations. Should the parties mutually desire for representation to occur, the advocate will need to set the parameters for that representation in the form of a retainer or fee agreement. Fee agreements are sometimes required by law but always recommended. If the fee agreement is properly prepared and executed, both the advocate and the client will have a fairly clear idea what is expected from the representation and possible future misunderstanding between the client and advocate can be minimized. This is the seed of a healthy relationship. Of course, other related activities also promote such a healthy informal working partnership, such as the timely and appropriate recording of time by the advocate showing her activities undertaken for the client, as well as effective on-going mutual communications between advocate and client.

2. *Initial Case Analysis, Planning & Preparation*

Case analysis is a necessary, fundamental and continuing task at all stages of pretrial, trial, and appellate advocacy. This task takes on a heightened importance during the early planning stages of litigation and we will consider it separately at that point in this text. Case analysis involves a systematic approach that allows the advocate to combine law, facts and morality into a coherent approach that achieves the client's objectives. Such rigorous and thoughtful activity should be manifest in each of the advocate's pretrial actions even including the way the advocate organizes her case file. The advocate must use the preliminary factual information gleaned from the advocate's informal investigation and discovery of relevant information about the client's case. Such activity, undertaken outside the lines of the rules of civil procedure, is an aspect of pretrial advocacy most often ignored in the law school curriculum yet of incredible importance in real-world advocacy. Most advocates gain more case information from informal discussions and interviews than they do from formal depositions or use of interrogatories. The fruit yielded by this informal investigation will be abundant in many cases, and can be case dispositive.

> **Seven Steps to Superior Case Analysis & Preparation:**
>
> - Create, Investigate & Organize the Case File
> - Identify Legal Issues
> - Identify Factual Issues
> - Connect Facts to Law
> - Identify your Moral Theme
> - Backwards Plan your Presentation
> - Verify Evidence

It is always of vital importance when approaching the daunting task of identifying a persuasive theory of the case to identify the issue behind the issues- the problem that drives the jury's sense of injustice and motivates them to decide the case in the advocate's favor if it goes to trial. For our purposes here it should be used to assist the advocate in identifying the issues that can be used to induce settlement or otherwise dispose of the case in a fashion that meets the client's goals.

After obtaining as much information as possible about the factual

> **Legal issues for plaintiff's attorneys include:**
> ▸ joinder
> ▸ personal jurisdiction and venue
> ▸ subject matter jurisdiction

underpinnings of the new claim, the advocate has some serious case planning and preparation to tackle. If the case involves the representation of a plaintiff, the advocate will need to consider fundamental questions such as: who the parties to the litigation should be (issues of joinder), where the case can and should be filed (issues of personal jurisdiction and venue), which type of court is appropriate for hearing the case (issues of subject matter jurisdiction), and other practical considerations. A review of the applicable law will prove useful in this text as we consider these various pre-filing considerations.

3. Pleadings and Attacks on Pleadings

The pleadings crafted and filed by the advocate become the blueprint for the duration of the litigation. Both claims and defenses are framed by the pleadings and nothing else that happens in the life of the case happens without reference to these claims and defenses. Careful consideration as to what, when and how various claims and defenses should be pled is required of the prudent advocate. As we will find, the rules of civil procedure provide a mere baseline for the drafting of pleadings, but the art of pleading compels consideration of much more than these bare essentials because the effective advocate wants to accomplish more than to avoid dismissal of their pleading. We will also adopt the defendant advocate's perspective as well and consider attacks that can be leveled at the plaintiff's complaint, including the various Rule 12 defenses and objections and possible changes to the forum that the defendant might be able to effectuate. Battles over the forum for the lawsuit can be just as important as the facts and law underlying the merits of the parties' dispute.

4. Formal Discovery: Written and Oral

Although informal fact investigation is perhaps one of the most important tasks of the advocate, much attention is paid in most cases to various formal procedures for obtaining discovery from one's adversary–things like initial disclosures, interrogatories, requests for admission and requests for production of documents. Each of these tools is governed by separate rules and separate considerations. Each type of formal written discovery has strengths and weaknesses, advantages and disadvantages and the advocate needs to carefully choose from among this arsenal of weapons when going through the discovery phase of a lawsuit. One of the most useful, though expensive, forms of discovery will also be separately considered–the oral deposition. The advocate might depose her own witnesses as well as those of the adversary and even seemingly neutral third parties not named in the lawsuit. There are different styles, methods and variations on oral depositions. Both the law and the art of taking and defending depositions will be the focus of its own chapter. Taken together, these various forms of formal discovery will become the gateway through which every possible resolution of the case will typically flow because such discovery is what generally facilitates disposition of most cases by either motion, settlement or trial.

5. *Motion Practice*

Motions for summary judgment play prominently in most civil lawsuits. These motions can be used to weed out the meritorious claims from those lacking substance. They can be a sword used to establish a plaintiff's claim without need for trial–or a shield–to obtain dismissal on the merits of all or a portion of the plaintiff's claims by a defendant. At one time, motions for summary judgment were frowned upon by most judges and rarely used or granted. Due to many different factors the utility and the occurrence of motions for summary judgment have risen to the point that a typical case does not go to trial without some attempted motion for summary judgment being heard by the court. For many defendants, the filing of a motion for summary judgment is the last-ditch attempt to avoid paying money to the claimant either through settlement or a possible adverse judgment at trial. For this reason, many plaintiff advocates view summary judgments as something to be avoided while many defense advocates fall asleep at night dreaming of grounds for asserting such motions. The primary focus of this chapter will be understanding when and how these motions should be utilized, prepared and argued. We will also pay special attention to the various strategies for responding to summary judgment motions in order to defeat them.

6. *Settlement*

Often the last exit on the litigation"highway" to trial is the voluntary settlement, either through informal and private settlement negotiations or mediation conducted by a neutral mediator. This chapter will consider the timing for such discussions, when mediation makes the most sense, and how to analyze the settlement value of a case prior to engaging in these negotiations. We will also explore the reasons why some cases do not settle. Particular focus will be paid to the unique position of the advocate at mediation and the roles that she plays in the dynamics of such settlement discussions. Additional information will also be provided on the documentation of a settlement. Most cases that have survived a motion for summary judgment will end up settling prior to trial. For this reason, consideration of issues that arise in settlement are of utmost importance for the pretrial advocate.

7. *Trial Preparation*

> *"si vis pacem, para bellum"*
> *- if you want peace, you*
> *must prepare for war.*

While trial advocacy may be beyond the scope of this text, trial preparation is not. Most activities undertaken by the pretrial advocate should be done with an eye toward proceeding to trial. A sentiment shared by many experienced advocates is "si vis pacem, para bellum" - if you want peace, you must prepare for war. Good pretrial advocacy puts one's client in a position to win at trial. From this position of leverage the advocate is also able to negotiate for a favorable settlement should they so choose or, perhaps, move for judgment as a matter of law. While in one sense all of pretrial advocacy is a form of trial preparation, at the end of this text we will consider trial preparation in a narrower sense. Assuming that one's case has not been resolved by pretrial motion as a matter of law and that the parties are not inclined or able to reach a compromise settlement of their dispute, how should the advocate get her case ready for trial? What final steps must be undertaken, what final case analysis should occur, and what additional motions and pleadings must be prepared for presentation to the court? We will return to an important discussion of case analysis again with this trial focus. As the citizens walk into the courtroom for voire dire, this text will close. At that point, the advocate should, with hindsight, be able to look back and conclude that she has, indeed, done "the necessary" to put her client in the best position to win.

Now that we have at least gleaned what pretrial advocacy entails, let us turn to the starting point of pretrial advocacy–the creation of the attorney-client relationship.

Points To Ponder . . .

1.Reflect on the possible various ways for a society to resolve disputes between its citizens. Which type of system of dispute adjudication is best?

2.Which aspect of pretrial advocacy do you think is most important? Which do you believe to be the most difficult? Time-consuming?

3. Looking forward to a career as an advocate, is there one aspect of pretrial activity that you believe will be most enjoyable for you? Do you believe this is the most valuable pretrial activity?

CHAPTER THREE
THE ATTORNEY-CLIENT RELATIONSHIP

"The ideal client is the very wealthy man in very great trouble."[1]

A. *INITIAL CLIENT INTERVIEWS*

Advocates sometimes struggle with what exactly it is they are supposed to do with this client in their office. Most spent little time developing interviewing skills in law school, focusing instead on the development of legal acumen. Being competent in the law is an important step to effective representation, but it is not the only step. While you may be comfortable focusing on legal issues, your client is focused on their problems. Discovering the legal issues in the stories of your client is often like panning for gold - you know it when you see the glitter in the bottom of the pan, but sometimes you have to go through a lot of sand first. Discovering that valuable legal information requires a slightly different skill set than what is learned in most law schools.

Law school teaches analysis of the law, identification of issues, and resolutions of conflict. It rarely teaches the advocate how to actually deal with the client. This chapter applies a logical construct to the attorney client relationship in a way that allows the advocate to guide the process for the client's benefit. It is necessary for the lawyer to develop strategies allowing them to effectively communicate with their clients because the client is not only your initial source of knowledge, however you will actually spend more time with the client than you might imagine based upon the focus of your legal

> The initial client interview transforms a prospective client into a current client.

---

[1] John Sterling.

education. This text combines the legal acumen developed in law school with a practical approach that utilizes your hard-won legal knowledge to the client's best effect.

Legal representation requires, as a *sine qua non*, both an attorney and a client. The presence of the client turns an academic exercise into a real world situation with consequences tied directly to each decision made by the advocate. Without the client all we have is a mock trial competition. The first thing necessary in the formation of the attorney client relationship is consent. The client must assent to representation by the attorney. The initial client interview is the place where the attorney client relationship is normally formed. The client is transformed by their consent from a prospective client into a current client. The legal significance of that transformation ensures that the starting point in pretrial practice is the initial meeting or interview between the advocate and the prospective client. Advocates must approach that meeting with a structure in place to insure that certain fundamental questions are answered. Those include (1) What should happen at this meeting? (2) How should the advocate plan for the meeting? (3) What fruit should this meeting bear? These are the primary questions upon which we will place our initial focus in this chapter.

Initial Client Interviews:

- Identify Goals
- Plan for the Meeting
- Set Benchmarks

This may seem to be a rather pedestrian topic with which to start the first substantive chapter of this text, but do not be deceived. Assuming that working well with clients occurs easily and naturally is incorrect, and reflects a common misperception as to the relative importance of an advocate's activities. Television often depicts a typical lawyer's day involving the discovery of a smoking gun, the delivery of a tear-inducing closing argument after lunch, and a celebratory drink or cigar on the deck of the law offices in the evening.[2] The life of a real civil lawyer is actually much different. One survey of attorneys found that they spent 16% of their time in client conferences–second only to time spent in discovery (16.7%). By contrast, attorneys stated that they

---

[2]For some excellent examples one need only turn to episodes of *L.A. Law, Ally McBeal* or *Boston Legal.*

spent on average only 8.6% of their time in the courtroom.[3] This is not to diminish the importance of courtroom skills–after all, it is the threat of what may happen in the courtroom that drives most cases to settle. Rather the experiences of those who actually practice law indicates that client conferences are an important part of case preparation, analysis and planning.

Clients come into the office in a variety of ways, depending upon the size of the firm, the nature of their practice and advertising strategies employed. Frequently the first contact between the prospective client and the advocate may be a telephone call or,

> **Initial Contact Should Discover:**
>
> *W ho* - is Involved (Potential Conflicts)
> *What* - is the Legal Problem (Competency)
> *When* - Potential Timing Issues (SOL)
> *Where* - It Happened (Jurisdiction)

reflecting our current technology, an email in which the prospective, current or former client contacts the law firm about a problem and seeks to speak with a lawyer. Whether this initial conversation is with the advocate or her office staff, there are some useful, if not essential, things that can be accomplished during this brief exchange. Advocates should create systems within their office to maximize information-gathering from that first contact. For example, it is extremely helpful to obtain at this time (1) a very rough idea of the nature of the legal problem (i.e., has the client suffered a personal injury or are they trying to avoid being evicted from their home?), (2) the names of other prominent players in the potential representation (i.e. who are the "bad guys"?), and (3) an indication of whether there are any important timing issues (i.e. is the client about to suffer some devastating harm?).

> Well prepared advocates are always concerned about possible conflicts of interest when dealing with prospective clients.

The advocate will be better prepared for the meeting if she has some idea what area of law might be applicable to the client's problem. Either the advocate can spend a few minutes to acquaint or reacquaint herself with that area of law prior to the meeting or perhaps to consider inviting additional counsel to sit in who are already familiar with that type of litigation. This

---

[3]Trubek, Sarat, Felstiner, Kritzer & Grossman, *The Costs of Ordinary Litigation*, 31 UCLA. L. Rev. 72, 91 (1983).

advance preparation not only makes the attorney look knowledgeable in the eyes of the client and instills confidence, but it also tends to make the actual interview more efficient because the advocate's attention will be focused on obtaining the information germane to analyzing that certain type of lawsuit. It is important to note, however, that a myopic focus on an assumed legal issue can create problems if the subsequent interview reveals other issues that the attorney misses because they have assumed away certain legal issues. The ability to focus but remain open to other possibilities is important when meeting with clients. Advocates also use information about the other possible litigants' identities to check for conflicts of interest before getting too deeply enmeshed in obtaining privileged information (which could result is being disqualified from representing either side) as well as to begin forming an impression about the merits of either the claims or of the practical benefits of proceeding with litigation (i.e., does the target defendant potentially have assets?).

Finally, information about whether the litigation presents some legal emergency will be needed to decide when to schedule the interview and to permit the advocate to begin clearing the calendar for work that will be initially time-consuming. Examples would be where the client has claims that are about to expire due to application of a statute of limitations (commonly referred to as stale claims), or where the client needs to immediately stop some threatened misconduct such as a former employee who has stolen corporate records and taken them to a competitor. However, even if a prospective client fails to identify any urgent timing issue necessitating an immediate interview, the advocate should still make scheduling the initial conference a priority. Clients are the life-blood of an advocate and the prospect of taking on a new client presents an advocate with a

---

Sample Preliminary Questions:

1. Why do you need a lawyer?
2. Please tell me in just a few words what the problem is that you're calling about?
3. Are there any other people or companies that are involved?
4. Tell me who it is that did this to you?
5. When did this event (e.g. accident) happen?
6. Is anything else bad about to happen to you that requires urgent help?

chance to provide representation that might be the defining case in the advocate's career. A prospective client who feels as though they are not important to a law firm may not hesitate to look up another lawyer's name and phone number in the local Yellow Pages. In any event, a few simple questions on these few topics either over the phone or via e-mail can provide answers that will make the scheduling and conduct of the initial interview appropriate and meaningful.

> **Key Objectives of the Initial Client Meeting:**
>
> 1. Build a bridge to the client.
> 2. Obtain essential facts.
> 3. Obtain documents.
> 4. Identify client's goals.
> 5. Finish well - Answer what we will do next.

How you conduct the face-to-face initial interview or conference obviously varies somewhat depending upon the circumstances, personalities and time constraints of those involved. However, it is essential to keep certain objectives in mind to make the meeting fruitful and to avoid doing things that will be detrimental to the budding attorney-client relationship.

1. Build a bridge

One goal of this meeting is to begin the process of forging a relationship of trust between the new client and the advocate. This is important because a relationship of trust will promote better communication, ease client anxieties over whether to disclose information harmful to their legal position, make the advocate's job more pleasant, and make the new client less likely to consider suing the advocate for malpractice if anything goes wrong in the representation. To build this bridge the advocate needs to get to know who the client is. Time permitting, the advocate needs to show interest in the client as a human being (even if the client is a corporation, it is run by human beings, notwithstanding the suspicions of many plaintiffs' attorneys) and find out about the client's personality, likes and dislikes and style for work and discourse. Is the client comfortable with litigation or will they require much hand-holding while their case proceeds down the potentially long and winding litigation road? If the client is a professional of some sort, the advocate should try to obtain a *curriculum vitae* from the client but in any case the advocate should begin the process of getting to know the client as a person. Obviously the advocate will need contact information to facilitate getting in touch with the client at different times.

The other aspect of building this trust is demonstrating to the new client that the advocate actually cares about them and their legal problem. The advocate must show empathy with their body language (i.e. looking the client in the eye and acting interested no matter how many similar cases the advocate has handled) and with the advocate's questions. In this regard, there are competing thoughts on things such as how and when the advocate should engage in note-taking during this interview session. Certainly, some form of note-taking (or recording if the client is comfortable with this) is necessary so long as the advocate does not become a scrivener instead of a counselor. The advocate might consider having a secretary or legal assistant sit in on the meeting for the purpose of taking the notes to free up the advocate's attention and keep it focused upon the client. These techniques can send a powerful message of concern to the client and instill trust. Building this bridge will not be done in a single meeting but the potential for this effective and positive relationship of trust can easily be destroyed in a single meeting if not a single moment.

2. Obtain essential facts

One of the most important goals of the interview is for the advocate to begin the process of finding out what the facts of the potential case may be. The advocate needs to hear the client's story. A good technique is to ask the client to state why they need help and "what happened?" This will elicit a narrative recounting by the client which will never include all of the pertinent information and will never include information that is harmful to the client's case. As part of the trust building process, the advocate must remain patient and let the client tell their story. While the client is telling the story, the advocate should focus upon the client, giving verbal and non-verbal indicators for the client to continue (e.g. nodding the head) while beginning to organize her thoughts about what additional information will be needed to begin some initial case analysis.

> Remember - clients will never tell you everything the first time, and they will rarely tell you anything that does not support their position.

When the client is through, the advocate should offer some words of encouragement or compassion and then proceed to ask detailed questions to elicit additional facts, both helpful and harmful to the client's position. It is sometimes helpful to explain how confidentiality works at this point so that the client feels at least slightly more comfortable in beginning to trust the advocate with information that they view as either embarrassing or hurtful to their situation. This initial question and answer format can be conducted in a variety of ways, but chronologically ("let's walk back through the sequence of events so that I can be sure I completely understand what happened") or by subject matter ("let's go back to the events concerning your actual termination") are usually most effective at this point. You should choose the method that seems most appropriate under the particular circumstances. The advocate has to balance between asking enough probing questions to gain the information needed while avoiding the unpleasant and damaging specter of cross-examining her own prospective client. Specific information that is usually important to obtain during this portion of the interview might include:

Questions Designed to Produce Potential Essential Facts:

☐ Who else was there? (a list of all possible witnesses to the key events)

☐ Who else is involved? (a list of other potential parties to the litigation)

☐ What did they do to you? (why the client believes the other side has done something wrong)

☐ Have you spoken with any of the involved persons or witnesses about this matter? (whether or not the client has done any of their own fact investigation)

☐ When and how have you contacted the person/entity you have this dispute with? (details concerning every communication between the client and the potential opposing litigants concerning the dispute)

☐ How has this hurt you? (information about the client's damages incurred or potential future harm to the client)

☐ Has anyone accepted responsibility for any of this? (confessions of wrongdoing from anyone connected to the dispute)

☐ Have you talked with any other attorneys about this? (whether or not the client has already spoken with any other legal counsel)

☐ What facts are you most worried about? (Get out the bad facts)

The final item mentioned–"bad facts"–deserves particular discussion. The last thing a new client wants to tell the attorney is a "bad fact." The relationship is only beginning and it is human nature not to expose information that reflects poorly on yourself when you are just meeting a person for the first time. Clients are humans, and they usually want to make a good impression on the advocate. They are not inclined initially to expose their weaknesses, bad character traits or skeletons in their closet. To a certain extent, it is only good salesmanship by the client to leave out the bad information. Right now they are trying to sell their case to you.

> **Reasons a Client Might Not be Candid Include:**
>
> ▸ Fear that bad facts will reflect poorly on them personally
>
> ▸ Fear that bad facts might undermine the desirability of taking the case
>
> ▸ Client does not realize the significance of certain bad facts to their claim
>
> ▸ Client fears advocate will not take case on a contingent fee if it is not a strong enough case

The client wants to be represented and desires you to take the case. They generally fear that you will not represent them once you learn the "bad facts" that either embarrass them or make the case more difficult.

This is true to a certain degree even where the client is anticipating paying the attorney by the hour for their help. It is even worse when there is a potential contingency fee basis for the relationship. In those cases the client truly is in a position of trying to buy the advocate's time in exchange for a piece of the case. This creates a great deal of pressure on the client to "sell" the case to the advocate. The client not only *wants* the advocate to believe that the client's case is a good one - they *need* the advocate to believe that the client's case is a good one. These circumstances further buttress our normal tendency to try and look our best when meeting someone for the first time. It can also make it extremely difficult to discover negative information during an initial interview.

Nonetheless, discovering facts that might reveal a fatal flaw in the case is imperative. The quicker such facts are brought to light the more able the attorney is to deal with them. The advocate's job in this initial interview is to probe for such information without appearing to be trying to dig up such dirt, at least initially. If proper rapport is established during the initial interview it will greatly increase the chances of the client disclosing "bad facts" in the near future.

After the advocate believes that she has done a good job obtaining all necessary information, the advocate should also ask a transparent question about whether there is any information, either about the case or the client, that the other side would either know or try to discover. The advocate should explain that it is better to have this information come out during a confidential session with the advocate than to burst into view during the middle of trial or a deposition. Obviously, if this has not already been done, this would be an appropriate time to explain the basic contours of the attorney-client privilege–which attaches even to a "prospective client" under the ABA Model Rules[4]–and to assure the client that the advocate is "on their side" and only needs to hear such facts in order to help them obtain their goals.

3. Obtain documents

The advocate needs to begin identifying and obtaining the documents that help reveal what happened to the client. Many clients will bring some documents to this interview even without being asked, but few will realize what documents are essential on their own. Part of the interview must include the advocate asking about what documents exist that show the information the client has been discussing. Inquires include whether or not there is a contract between the parties? Is there correspondence? What e-mails have been exchanged between the client and the opponent or other witnesses? Was there an accident report prepared at the scene? Have any insurance reports or claims been submitted to anyone? Were photographs taken by anyone? Does the client have copies of their medical records? Were notes taken during any meetings that may have occurred between the parties? The list is as endless as the subject matter of litigation and the means of communication utilized within the client's world.

> Documents have a strange way of objectively showing past events in a way that litigants often cannot.

The client will not have all of these documents when they come to the advocate's office. After discussing potential documents that may be relevant to the case the advocate should prepare a list of the documents identified and give this list to the client as the client's first "homework" assignment. This gets the client involved in the representation, gives them something to do to feel useful in

---

[4] Ethical Rule 1.18(b) states that "[e]ven when no client-lawyer relationship ensues, a lawyer who has had discussions with a prospective client shall not use or reveal information learned in the consultation . . . ."

the process and will also provide the advocate with an effective tool to gauge the client. If the client does not provide the documents or has difficulty doing so it should clue the advocate into the existence of potential issues beneath the surface. Careful review of documents obtained from the client goes a long way towards shedding the most accurate light on the client's predicament. Documents have a strange way of objectively showing past events in a way that litigants often cannot.

4. Client goals

One area of difficulty for many advocates is in accurately separating the client's goals from their own perceptions of how the case should proceed. Most ethical codes give the advocate the authority to decide upon the tactical means of representation, but they place in the client's hands the strategic decision making process - they decide upon the goals of the litigation, subject to the limitations placed upon the advocate by their own ethics. This creates tension between the advocate and the client, and the manner in which you deal with this tension is crucial in developing not only client confidences but effective litigation strategies.

Under most state's ethical rules, the client has the right to dictate the goals of the litigation, assuming that the goals are ethical. Ethical Rule 1.2(a) states that a lawyer is to abide by a client's wishes concerning the objectives of representation. Further, Disciplinary Rule 7–101(A)(1) requires an advocate to seek to further the lawful objectives of the client. In addition to these ethical mandates, a more practical incentive to discover the client's goals is to turn the client into a "client for life" which is only possible if the advocate understands what the client desires from the representation for two reasons. First, the advocate may undermine the client's goals by wrongfully assuming what the client really wants. The advocate may start working toward a damage recovery when the client really just wants their job back. This can end up being a significant waste of the advocate's time and, worse, can make it impossible for the client to ever achieve their goals. The practical question when faced with this inherent tension is how to begin? The advocate should consider simply asking if the client has any ideas as to how specifically they would like to see their dispute resolved. In other words, the client's goals should not be left unstated no matter

> Explaining in practical terms what is realistically possible is one of the most difficult jobs an advocate has - the ability to do it effectively creates long term satisfying relationships between advocates and their clients.

how obvious it may seem that they are to the advocate.

Second, many clients have an unrealistic idea of what is possible to achieve under the law. They may, for example, believe that they are entitled to punitive damages for a simple breach of contract. Or their view of the damages they can obtain may not mesh with legally cognizable remedies for their type

> You must determine the scope of representation prior to the end of the first meeting with the client!

of claim. The advocate needs to identify such lofty though unrealistic goals and begin the process of educating the client on what is possible with a view toward re-orienting the client to a more realistic set of expectations. The advocate at this stage may be tempted to simply play the role of cheerleader in order to win over the client, but this approach never leads to a good end.

5. Finish well

While an advocate may want to accomplish several things at the end of the interview, determining the status of the possible representation is a crucial question that must be answered. Does the advocate want to take the client's case and does the client want to hire the advocate? Sometimes this cannot be resolved at the initial interview. Indeed, an advocate may want to encourage a prospective client to go home and "sleep on it" before committing to the legal representation. In either event, the advocate should be clear where things stand. If the client is interested in hiring the advocate, some discussion of fees and a fee agreement will be needed. This is discussed in more detail below but the would-be client must understand that until they sign a retainer agreement that they have not yet established an attorney-client relationship. The advocate may also want to have a pre-prepared form with contact information prepared for the client to fill out and turn in at the end of the session. There should be some, however rough, idea for follow-up. Any "homework," such as additional documents or information the client needs to obtain, should be clarified with the client. Finally, the advocate needs to indicate some enthusiasm for the opportunity to help the client resolve their legal problem whatever that problem may be. This can also take the form of some expression of concern–"I know you've been through hell and I'm going to

> Assigning "homework" for the client involves them in the representation while giving you a way to measure their commitment and level of knowledge.

help you get through this and help see that some justice is done."

6. Common mistakes

Doing a thorough and successful client interview takes practice and preparation.[5] When an advocate gets some experience doing these interview and relaxes into their own personal style, they can find such interviews to be an exciting and productive part of their practice of law. Helping people with their legal problems can be a rewarding and fulfilling part of the practice of law, and that process begins with such interviews. Even though this is an enjoyable area of the practice, many advocates make some fairly common mistakes when conducting these interviews. Those mistakes range from the egregious to the mild, depending upon your point of view.

Perhaps the worst mistake is making unrealistic promises to the client. Such promises exacerbate a client's tendency to have expectations that cannot be met under the law. Often the advocate's reason for offering unrealistic promises may be benign– examples include a desire to make the client feel better and to offer "hope". Sometimes though the reason is more sinister – to obtain the engagement at all costs. While the motivations may be different the results are unfortunately the same. Clients fed such dreams end up disappointed, angry and often wind up filing a grievance or malpractice claims against the advocate who initially promised them things they could not produce. On the other hand, advocates should be careful not to immediately dismiss out-of-hand client expectations that, while not likely to be achieved, are possible. Sometimes it is necessary for the advocate to think more creatively to find a path that might remotely lead to where the client wants to go with their case. It is imperative that advocates not think small but instead think realistically and have some frank conversations with the client about the client's goals and whether some alternative goals should at least be considered. If a prospective client senses that you actually care about their predicament,

> Client-focused interviews establish rapport, identify issues and allow the advocate to not only represent their clients, but to also counsel them. When the lawyer is speaking he is rarely learning.

---

[5] Remember the old chestnut "To fail to plan is to plan to fail" that is often attributed to Benjamin Franklin, see JOHN MARKS TEMPLETON, DISCOVERING THE LAWS OF LIFE. (The Continuum Publishing Company, 1995).

they are more likely to accept some disappointing news from you about certain unrealistic hopes they had for the representation.

> *"[I]t is a less inconvenience to listen to what is superfluous than to be left ignorant of what is essential."*
>
> Quintilian, quoted in L. Stryker, *The Art of Advocacy* 7-8 (1954)

Other less severe, though still negative, mistakes are often made during these initial interviews. One such error is for the advocate to be impatient with the client. The press of practice and a desire to get to the bottom line is an occupational hazard that often spills over into many facets of an advocate's professional and personal life. Many a litigator's spouse has complained about being cross-examined by the attorney in the family when trying to tell a simple story and taking too long. The fact is that some clients take longer than others to tell their story. These long-winded clients might need a little more guidance than others during the initial interview but the advocate has to be careful not to cut them off abruptly at the risk of either offending the prospective client or missing out on some important bit of information. Some degree of self-discipline by the advocate in exercising patience is required to avoid creating a chilling atmosphere that creates a fear or other disincentive for the client to volunteer helpful information.

An advocate should always take the time to make the client feel comfortable physically and emotionally during the interview. Failure to do this can either result in losing the client or, at a minimum, make the meeting less productive. Many different ways exist to establish rapport with the client, including having a comfortable chair for the client to use, offering the client some coffee or other appropriate beverage, and taking the time to ask if there is anything they need. The physical location of the interview is also important. Rather than hiding behind a huge desk, the lawyer should come out and sit opposite the client or conduct the interview at a table with the client. Making the client feel comfortable can even start with little things like the advocate coming out to the reception area to greet the client upon their arrival rather than having the client ushered back to the meeting room by a subordinate. The small touches of humanity separating those who care from those who don't are just as important in the law office as they are in other segments of society - perhaps more.

> Never forget that clients are the currency of the legal profession.

Finally, the advocate should consider whether the client really needs a lawyer. Not every instance of a person being upset or disappointed is appropriately handled in our civil courts. People need to vent and get something off of their chest and, occasionally, be directed back from the litigation cliff toward sanity. Sometimes the best advice to the prospective client is to take some alternative route. This advice may cost the advocate in the short term but may still be the right path. A good advocate should be prepared to spot such instances and to act appropriately.

7. Following the initial interview

Often either the client or the attorney determines that there will be no legal representation. Your duties as an advocate do not end simply because you have decided not to represent someone. Your ethical responsibilities to prospective clients[6] require that you ensure the prospective client understands the current situation. The advocate should send a short letter memorializing the fact that no representation is being undertaken. This will help to avoid any possible confusion on that subject later should the client's memory differ on this score. Such a letter might look something like the one below.

September 15, 2007

Dear Bill Smart:

It was a pleasure meeting you yesterday concerning your interest in pursuing legal claims for your injuries incurred while riding your bicycle. Although I would like to be in a position to help you concerning your possible claims, I have concluded that I will be unable to accept your case or to otherwise provide you with any legal representation.

You may still wish to pursue your claims. If so, I urge you to contact another attorney as soon as possible because the law imposes strict time limits on asserting claims such as yours. You may lose your right to sue if you wait too long. If you have trouble finding another attorney, I would suggest that you call the local bar association for assistance.

I am sorry that I will not be able to represent you but I wish you

---

[6] See Appendix I, Ethics Rule 1.18, which addresses this issue.

all the best.

Sincerely,

Jane Aikman, esq.

If, on the other hand, the prospective client and the advocate both desire to enter into an attorney-client relationship there are three additional and immediate tasks the advocate should undertake apart from reducing the representation to writing. The first is to take a moment and be truly thankful and somewhat humble in the face of another person placing their legal life in your hands. A senior partner of Professor Underwood once confided that "clients are the currency of the legal profession. No matter how much people like you, the only real job security in this profession is to have loyal clients." Do not fail to appreciate what trust is being communicated to you by a new client willing to put what may be the most stressful event in their lives in your hands.

After expressing thanks you should reduce to a short memo the information you have learned during the initial interview. This can help you retain focus as to what you should be doing next and it provides a useful reference for you in the future as you go forward with representation of the client. For example, when you begin the process of drafting a complaint (or answer)–discussed in more detail in Chapter 5–for your new client, this

---

Topics for Client Interview Memo:

- ☐ Client biographical and contact information
- ☐ Nature of client problem and stated goals
- ☐ List of other possible parties to the anticipated litigation
- ☐ Impressions of client
- ☐ Summary of facts
- ☐ Identification of other fact witnesses
- ☐ Identification of any documents provided by client
- ☐ To-do list (for client and advocate)
- ☐ Possible course of action and remedies

memorandum will be a useful repository of the facts you know about the case. It will also be helpful to have when you are preparing to take depositions or to answer written discovery–two additional subjects discussed in Chapters 7 and 8. Also, a well organized and maintained file that includes such memoranda will be helpful to a colleague who picks up your file when asked to provide coverage for a hearing, conference or deposition during the life of the case. Finally, the advocate should enter into a fee agreement with the new client.

B. DEFENDANT INTERVIEWS.

The advice above is equally applicable to initial interviews of prospective claimants as well as to interviews of just-served defendants.[7]   But initial interviews of "those unjustly sued" have a few wrinkles deserving of specific mention here before we move on to discuss fee agreements. For starters, it is more common for defendants to have been sued more than once in the past. This has several ramifications. The first is that repeat litigants may already have some litigation philosophy of which you may not be aware. The advocate needs to understand where the defendant-client is coming from in terms of a preferred path for defending the litigation. Some of these clients are interested in extricating themselves from the lawsuit as soon as possible, and early overtures toward settlement will be part of the litigation plan. Others believe that paying a dime in the face of "frivolous litigation" would be tantamount to criminal activity, and for such defendants any early settlement overtures would be a sign of treason by their advocate. The advocate needs to discover during the interview if the client has extreme views on the subject of how best to respond, generally, to litigation.

> Take the time to identify your client's preferred litigation strategy.

These type of clients frequently have strong opinions on how they like their counsel to operate. Larger corporations, for instance, frequently have litigation "guidelines" for their outside counsel to adhere to and can be cited as grounds for refusing to pay bills when violated. It is not uncommon for such guidelines to prohibit counsel from undertaking significant legal research without the client's advance approval or to use courier services or overnight mail for routine matters. In practice, many such clients are much more flexible if the advocate is aware of these guidelines and addresses a need for some different

---

[7]Otherwise known as the "unjustly sued."

> Time is often the enemy when dealing with defendant clients. You must manage filing issues to effectively represent such clients.

rules in the context of a specific, important piece of litigation. But counsel ignore such guidelines at their own peril. Finally, clients who have been involved in litigation in the past often need less hand-holding than clients facing the daunting prospect of being a litigant for the first time. This does not mean that you need not bother showing any empathy for such clients, but rather just that you will often find that you need to spend less time dealing with the emotional needs of the client.

In addition to the fact that the defendant-client might have been a litigant in the past, the initial interview of the defendant requires a different focus in order to be truly effective. *There is typically a very short deadline in which to prepare and file a responsive pleading such as an answer to the original complaint*. The advocate must find out exactly how and when the defendant was first served with a summons. Under the Federal Rules of Civil Procedure, the defendant has only twenty days to respond by either filing an answer, filing certain other specified Rule 12 motions to dismiss or both. The advocate must immediately ascertain and memorialize these deadlines with some calendar system. Because of these looming deadlines, the initial interview of the defendant is frequently followed closely in time by follow-up meetings to help in the final preparation of an answer, a possible counterclaim or other motions to dismiss. Consideration of these possible pleadings necessarily translates into greater urgency than is typical of the initial plaintiff's interview.

In some instances, the defendant's initial urge, often fueled by fear, is to hide the evidence of wrongdoing. For this reason, another objective of the initial interview of a defendant is to take steps to ensure that material evidence is not destroyed, tampered with or otherwise made inaccessible by the misguided intentions of the defendant. The advocate will need to explain to the defendant that, even though formal discovery requests may not yet have been received, the defendant (and its counsel) is already

> Advocates must discuss client responsibilities regarding preservation of evidence in light of claim early in the representation of defendant clients.

under an obligation to preserve evidence in the light of a known claim.[8] The advocate should inquire into the status of certain classes of documents, including e-mails, that might shed light on the plaintiff's claims. The advocate should insist that the client preserve these items and begin to make them available for review by the advocate. Another aspect of evidence preservation involves the advocate interviewing at the earliest time possible other witnesses under the control of the defendant that might have personal knowledge of material information concerning the claim or defenses to it. If the defendant is a business, the advocate will want to interview the client's key employees who had dealings with the plaintiff or who were responsible for the actions of the defendant-business called into question by the plaintiff's complaint. These interviews might either occur at the advocate's office or, more commonly, take place at the defendant's place of business in a conference room. The advantage of doing these early interviews at the defendant's place of business is that the advocate can get a feel for the defendant by touring the defendant's facilities and finding out more general background information about the defendant's industry. This provides invaluable insight for the advocate in understanding the claims in the case, knowing the client better and also demonstrates the advocate's strong desire to be of assistance.

The interview of the defendant will also necessitate consideration of the possible counterclaims that the defendant may have against the plaintiff. These counterclaims typically are required to be filed with the defendant's original answer so, again, time is of the essence in identifying such claims and analyzing whether it makes sense strategically for such claims to be asserted. We will take up consideration of counterclaims again later in this book when we learn about pleadings.

Finally, to the extent that the defendant is a corporate business entity, the advocate should use the opportunity of the initial interview to obtain a clear idea of the corporate hierarchy and to gain some appreciation for the members of the entity's control group who have the power to make decisions for the company during the litigation. A simple request for a corporate chart with some brief questions asked during the initial interview is usually sufficient to gain this understanding.

---

[8]Ethics Rule 3.4(a) states that a lawyer shall not "unlawfully alter, destroy or conceal a document or other material having evidentiary value. A lawyer shall not counsel or assist another person to do any such act."

C. FEE AGREEMENTS

Arriving at an appropriate representation and fee agreement requires consideration of law firm economics and choosing the right type of fee arrangement, setting the amount of the fee, and drafting a good fee agreement.

1. Economics and fee arrangements

Although the law is a profession, law firms are generally for-profit businesses albeit still bound by applicable rules of professional conduct. Different fee arrangements have predominated within the legal profession at different points in time. Long ago, the predominant custom in the United States was for a lawyer to bill a client on a flat fee basis–for example, a lawyer might charge $100 for filing a

Attorney Billing Options:

- Flat Fee
- Hourly
- Contingency
- Hybrid methods

personal injury claim or obtaining a divorce for a client. Over time this flat-fee billing arrangement began to give way to lawyers either charging by the hour or taking a piece of the cause of action in the form of a contingency fee arrangement. Today law firms continue to consider the best way to remain competitive and profitable in terms of creatively devising appropriate fee arrangements. These can consist of any of the above three options or hybrid billing relationships. For example, a firm might agree to handle all of an insurance company's personal injury litigation in a certain geographic locale on a "fixed fee" arrangement (say $10,000) regardless of how many hours it might take the resolve the case and, in the event the case goes to trial, switch to an hourly billing arrangement for all trial and post-trial time. Or a law firm might agree to represent a claimant on a tort claim for a reduced hourly fee of $100 per hour while also taking a reduced contingent fee of 20% on the proceeds of the representation.

Which type of fee arrangement makes the most sense depends, obviously, upon the particular circumstances. While some lawyers might cynically deride hourly fee billing as "selling your soul by the hour," the benefit of this arrangement is that it tends to produce consistent cash flow into the firm's coffers, thereby helping to ensure that the advocate's children receive nice birthday presents every year. For the risk-averse advocate, the hourly billing method may be the most superior method, assuming such advocates have enough potential clients with the assets to pay in this form. Some clients might prefer this billing approach as well if they can afford to pay regular monthly invoices because this billing approach is most similar to how many business pay for other goods and services. From the client's perspective, one downside to this approach is that it rewards the inefficient advocate. That is, a lawyer who spends more time achieving the same end has higher billings and revenues than a more efficient lawyer. In a sense, this relationship can place the attorney and client in a practical conflict. This potential problem is arguably exacerbated by the current practice among many medium and large-sized law firms of rewarding associates (and even partners) with year-end bonuses or distributions contingent on achieving certain minimum billable hours during the year. Thus, the legend of the billing lawyer with the "heavy hand" on the ink pen is born. Of course, clients can and do scrutinize lawyers' monthly invoices to ascertain and complain about questionable billing practices.

> *"If I had only one wish for our profession from the proverbial genie, I would want us to move toward something better than dollars times hours. We have created a zero-sum game in which we are selling our lives, not just our time. We are fostering an environment that doesn't provide the right incentives for young lawyers to live out the ideals of the profession. And we are feeding misperceptions of our intentions as lawyers that disrupt our relationships with our clients. Somehow, people as smart and dedicated as we are can do better."*
>
> Scott Turow
> (ABA Journal, August 2007, "The Billable Hour Must Die.")

Some clients under particular circumstances might prefer either a flat fee or contingent fee billing arrangement, for different reasons. The benefit of the flat fee is that the client knows in advance exactly what their total outlay will be for the attorney's fee. A client can set a legal budget much easier if they are being charged a flat fee for each item of work (case) given to a law firm. This approach can also be lucrative for the advocate if she can handle a legal matter efficiently. If the client is paying the advocate $10,000 to dispose of a lawsuit, the advocate can maximize their revenues by devising ways to bring the matter to a satisfactory conclusion as soon as possible and only doing those tasks that directly lead to that resolution.

The type of billing relationship most often discussed in the media is the contingency fee. This method involves the advocate foregoing a fee on the front end of the litigation for, typically, a higher recovery in the end contingent upon a successful recovery. Many proponents of tort reform attack personal injury trial lawyers for being willing to undertake representation of any so-called "frivolous" lawsuits in order to blackmail the defendant into paying something, out of which the lawyer derives her fee. On the other hand, for many citizens of ordinary or below ordinary means, the only way that litigation of a civil case might be affordable at all is through the contingency fee. Further, this rather unique billing arrangement certainly has the potential to foster a true "team" atmosphere between the client and the advocate because their economic interests coalesce.

Comparing Fee Arrangements

	Good	**Bad**
Flat Fee	Easy to budget	Can be arbitrary
	Rewards efficiency	Might appear unfair in hindsight
Hourly Fee	Easier to set at outset	Poor clients unable to afford retention
	Seems intuitively fair even in hindsight	Lawyer not rewarded based upon results
		Rewards inefficiency
Contingency Fee	Promotes access to legal system by poor	Creates cash flow problems for lawyer
	Creates real team approach by attorney and client	Might seem unfair in hindsight
		Viewed from a policy perspective to impact negatively on the costs of litigation and of business
	Attorney earns fee based on results	

Figure 1 - Comparison of Potential Fee Arrangements

From the advocate's perspective, a contingency fee is a dual-edged sword. On the upside, an advocate has the chance for a much larger ultimate recovery by taking a lucrative percentage of the proceeds of the client's possible recovery than through hourly or flat fee billing, particularly if the client's injury is significant. On the downside, such an advocate risks obtaining no fee whatsoever despite spending several years dedicated to the task of pursuing the client's claims in the courts. Further, during the interim period of time the advocate may face serious economic crises due to not having any cash coming in the door to pay for office salaries, utilities, malpractice insurance, paper, cell phones and fancy lunches. In recognition of these economic realities, some law firms try to handle different matters using different billing methods so that they can share in some clients' recoveries while continuing to receive regular fee payments from other clients. Or on a particular case, using a hybrid method of charging a somewhat reduced hourly rate combined with obtaining a somewhat reduced contingency fee interest allows the client and lawyer to experience the benefits of both the hourly and contingency billing methods.

The bottom line for the advocate is to try to select a billing method that works not only for the advocate but also for the client under the particular circumstances that exist. A client who feels cheated will not be the advocate's "client for life," will not refer other business to the advocate and will not include the advocate on their holiday card distribution list. In order to decide what fee arrangement works best, the advocate should obviously consider the nature of the case, the possible and likely recoveries, the client's financial condition, and the law firm's financial condition. Obviously, the anticipated fee arrangement can impact the focal points of the initial client interview. If the client can only afford a contingency fee arrangement, one would expect the advocate to ask particularly probing questions at the initial interview concerning the factual merits underlying the lawsuit before, in effect, buying a percentage of the client's claim by agreeing to undertake legal representation. By contrast, the advocate who knows she is going to bill by the hour may not feel as compelled to make a correct assessment of the likely outcome at the initial meeting because that advocate will, at least theoretically, collect fees regardless of the outcome.

2. Setting the amount of the fee

There are two primary types of considerations for a lawyer in setting the amount of the fee for undertaking new representation, regardless of which method of compensation the attorney and client have selected. These considerations are ethical and practical. In terms of ethics, the ABA Model Rules and most states have a general prohibition on setting, charging or collecting any attorney fee that is "unreasonable"–presumably this limit only applies to those fees that are unreasonably *high*. But how does the young lawyer decide what amount is too high? Specific rules are hard to come by though they do exist in certain circumstances and the advocate should be aware of such specifics. Florida ethical rules, for example, cap the maximum percentage contingent fee that can be agreed to for any tort case involving "personal injuries," though Florida provides no absolute caps on contingency fees in other classes of cases, nor do they prescribe any arbitrary specific cap on hourly rates or flat fees in personal injury cases.[9] One lesson from this example is that the inexperienced advocate must consult their applicable ethics rules to be sure they are not about to enter into a fee arrangement which is void or voidable. While short on specifics about the appropriate amount for fees, the ABA Models Rules do give a multi-factored list of considerations for evaluating whether a particular fee is "unreasonable." This list includes the following:

1. the time and labor required, the novelty and difficulty of the questions involved, and the skill requisite to perform the legal service properly;

2. the likelihood, if apparent to the client, that the acceptance of the particular employment will preclude other employment by the lawyer;

3. the fee customarily charged in the locality for similar legal services;

4. the amount involved and the results obtained;

5. the time limitations imposed by the client or by the circumstances;

6. the nature and length of the professional relationship with the client;

7. the experience, reputation, and ability of the lawyer or lawyers performing the services; and

8. whether the fee is fixed or contingent.[10]

In other words, a long list of potential factors can be used to decide if the

---

[9] *See* Florida Rule of Professional Conduct 4–1.5(f)(4)(B)(i).

[10] Ethics Rule 1.5(a)(1)-(8). See Appendix I.

advocate is charging her client too much.

Beyond the obvious desire not to charge an unethical fee, how else should the advocate go about setting the ideal rate to charge the client? The most helpful resource is to talk with other lawyers in the community to get a feel for prevailing rates taking into account primarily the experience level of the advocate and the type of work contemplated. Complex securities class action work tends to demand a higher fee than uncontested divorces, in part because there is a shorter supply of attorneys that are qualified for the former than the latter and also because those attorneys handling the former category of cases tend to have superior qualifications and experience. Regardless of the method chosen for the fee arrangement, information about the prevailing rates in the local market will be the best resource. If one is setting a flat fee, the advocate will also need to predict the likely investment of time in resolving the lawsuit. For an inexperienced advocate, therefore, a flat fee is subject to the greatest risk unless the advocate either receives good information from other similarly situated lawyers handling similar work or is very accurate about making predictions concerning the future. In the case of contingency fees, the most important additional factors would include an accurate early assessment of the likely outcome of the case, the amount of time to reach resolution (taking into account the litigation philosophy of the anticipated defendants), and the extent to which the defendant is likely to be able to pay a judgment–information that may not be readily transparent at the time of the initial interview.

Before we leave the topic of setting your fee, a brief illustration is in order to demonstrate how hourly rates tend to drift increasingly higher. Let us say that you are a solo practitioner four years out of law school. Your standard hourly rate is $150 and you plan to do billable work approximately 1,500 hours annually, which assumes six billable hours per day and two weeks of vacation or sick days. This results in your achieving revenues of $225,000. Be careful not to get too excited by this hypothetical because it makes an unrealistic assumption and only uses gross revenues. The unrealistic assumption is that all of the time you spend practicing law will be billed to your clients and that all of your clients will pay all of your bills. It would be more realistic to factor in what lawyers refer to as a "realization rate" which takes into account that you sometimes have to write off some of your time and that some clients cannot or will not pay your invoices. A realization rate that would be considered very good is approximately 90%. The other problem with our hypothetical figure is that is does not include expenses typically involved in operating even a small law office. These expenses include rent on your office, the cost of furniture, computers and printers, utilities, salaries and benefits of a secretary and legal assistant, and legal malpractice insurance premiums.

What happens if you decide that you need to earn more than $225,000 in gross revenues and you typically bill by the hour? You have two options–increase the number of billable hours (assuming the extra work is available) or increase your hourly rate. If you decide that you need an extra $15,000 in revenues, you would need to work an additional 100 hours to achieve your goal. This might not seem too significant except that these 100 extra hours are heaped on top of the 1,500 you have already worked. And it typically takes closer to eight hours in the office to bill six hours of time. So either the lawyer works consistently every weekend or takes no time off for vacation. There is another option. The advocate could work the same number of hours and simply increase her hourly rate by $10 per hour–shifting it up to $160. This simple change in rate results in the same $15,000 increase. Given that lawyers are typically already working pretty hard and perhaps already taking every case that comes through the door, you should be able to appreciate that option number two–increasing hourly rates–is how most advocates increase their earnings when they bill by the hour. This phenomenon is not something that most clients enjoy, particularly not when the advocate needs to explain to an existing client why she is charging more than she used to charge.

3. The fee agreement

After your new client accepts your offer of representation, agrees to the the nature of the fee arrangement and the amount of the fee, what else needs to be done? Although most states' ethics rules only require the fee agreement to be reduced to writing in cases involving contingency fees, this is certainly the preferable practice in all situations. A written fee agreement avoids unnecessary disputes between the advocate and her client, it helps to resolve disputes that inevitably arise, and it is a sound business practice. The type of information that should go into the fee agreement depends somewhat on the nature of the arrangement, but as a general matter the Ethics Rules offer the following suggestions concerning the contents and the time for obtaining this fee agreement:

> t]he scope of the representation and the basis or rate of the fee and expenses for which the client will be responsible shall be communicated to the client, preferably in writing, before or within a reasonable time after commencing the representation.

Ethics Rule 1.5(b).

While both the form and the content of the fee agreement may vary according to the circumstances, and are frequently not strictly prescribed by law, it is essential that any written fee agreement clearly answer the following three questions:

(1) Who is the client?

You might think it would be obvious who the client is the advocate has agreed to represent but this is not always the case, consider the following examples:

♦   If Herman comes into your office with a broken leg from a traffic accident and wants to hire you, have you implicitly also agreed to look out for the interests and claims belonging to his wife? Or his children?

♦   If Margaret comes into your office and seeks your help in incorporating her new business venture, are you precluded from later suing her on behalf of a different client when she has personally guaranteed a debt of the new corporation?

Serious problems can arise if the fee agreement does not offer specifics as to whom the advocate is representing and who is not being represented. What if the claims of the related parties are not filed before the statute of limitations has expired? What if the claims are filed, but the related parties deny the advocate's right to a contingency fee for the result? Or, what if in subsequent litigation, a related party who is now adverse to the advocate claims the advocate is barred from bringing a claim against the related party due to a conflict of interest? Resolution of these important and potentially stress-inducing, nasty questions can either be resolved through simple and quick interpretation of a clear and complete fee agreement or, in the absence of such a provision, through sworn testimony by hostile witnesses with the result turning on the fact-finding of a judge or jury. You make the choice.

(2) What is the scope of legal representation?

You might think that the answer to this question would also be obvious, but the following examples show how easily the matter could be confusing and problematic:

♦   If Samantha comes into your office having been served with a summons for a civil case of battery, have you also implicitly agreed to look out for Samantha's potential criminal exposure?

◆   If Carl comes into your office and seeks your help in connection with his purchase of a software company, have you also implicitly agreed to handle any copyright or patent issues arising out of the sale?

Problems could arise in several respects if the scope of representation is not clarified in the fee agreement. For example, if some legal task is not accomplished because you did not realize the client expected you to handle it, this can not only upset the client but can result in legal malpractice if your fee agreement is not clear as to the limited scope of your retention. Or let us assume that you have undertaken representation pursuant to a flat fee billing arrangement. If the client claims that you also agreed to handle another related matter for the same flat fee, your practice might have just become unprofitable. The scope of representation need not necessarily require great elaboration. A relatively short sentence or two in the fee agreement might suffice: "Advocate hereby agrees to represent Client in pursuing civil claims through final resolution for Client's personal injuries arising out of the accident that occurred on September 1, 2007. Advocate has not undertaken to represent Client on any other matters."

a. How much does the client have to pay?

Both the type of fee arrangement (i.e., flat, hourly, contingent or hybrid) and the manner of calculation should be clear. If you have agreed on an hourly fee, does this amount vary according to timekeepers in your office? What about legal assistant time? Do you have the right to increase the hourly fee on an annual basis should the litigation last more than one year? Further, the fee agreement should consider how expenses of litigation (e.g., filing fees, copying costs, expert witness fees, court reporters) will be borne both initially and ultimately. If the agreement is for a contingent fee, is this percentage calculated before or after expenses are deducted from the recovery? Does the percentage vary depending upon the point in time the recovery is obtained (e.g., 25% if settled before filing a complaint,

> "Be prepared, be sharp, be careful, and use the King's English well. And you can forget all the [other rules] unless you remember one more: Get paid."
>
> Robert N. Nix, Jr.
> Chief Justice,
> Pennsylvania Supreme Court

33% if settled after the case filing but prior to a trial, and 40% if recovery is obtained any time during or after a trial)? Does the fee cover the advocate's fees in the event of an appeal or will there be a separate and additional fee for that work? And what about a client who does not timely pay their monthly invoice (assuming monthly billing will occur)? Is there a late fee imposed as a penalty? Does the advocate automatically retain a right to immediately cancel the agreement and seek to withdraw from representing the client?

In addition to answering the above three essential questions, the prudent advocate should at least consider possible additional clauses such as the following:

♦ *Retainers*: One way to avoid the possibility of doing free legal work due to a client's failure to pay your first bill is to require the client to pay a "retainer" or advance payment. Many firms now require this for new clients as a method of avoiding the unintended, forced *"pro bono"* work.

♦ *Arbitration of disputes*: One way to avoid the unpleasantness of litigation against a current or former client is to include an appropriate clause requiring any disputes arising out of the fee agreement to be subject to mandatory binding arbitration.

♦ *Obligations of the client other than payment of fees*: Advocates should expect and be entitled to something more from the client than simply paying the fees of counsel. These things are best stated explicitly, even if only generally, in the fee agreement so that the client understands the informal partnership contemplated by the representation. For example, it is advisable to consider adding a simple clause whereby the client acknowledges their obligation to provide timely and truthful information to counsel, to cooperate fully with the handling of their claims, to notify counsel if they have a change of address or phone numbers, to refrain from settling the case without the notification to the advocate, and to be present at any depositions, hearings or trial of the matter as requested by the advocate.

Tips to Avoid Working for Free:

☐   Informally investigate client's credit worthiness at the outset, through internet searches or credit checks.

☐   Require a "retainer" up front as an advance payment on future fees earned.

☐   Keep accurate time and submit invoices to client monthly on time.

☐   Follow up promptly with the client on unpaid invoices.

☐   Include a clause in fee agreement requiring payment of interest on unpaid fee and/or giving advocate the right to immediately

---

♦   *Identity of Attorneys*: Is the client expecting a particular advocate to work on their case or will they be satisfied to have any of a law firm's lawyers show up at an important hearing or deposition? Particularly in larger firms, the risk of needing a lawyer to assist, with whom the client has never met, is high. For this reason, the larger the firm the more it is a good idea to include some language in the agreement indicating the possible need for additional lawyers at the firm to assist, unless the client has indicated that this is unacceptable. Either way it is a useful for the advocate and client to be on the same page in this regard. Another related and perhaps more likely issue, at least with respect to smaller-sized law firms, is the possible need by the original advocate to associate another lawyer from a different firm in the event that extra horsepower or expertise is needed as the lawsuit progresses. This possibility might be mentioned in the agreement and provision made for working out an acceptable fee for that new advocate or, in the case of contingency fees, for acknowledging the possible need for some fee-sharing arrangement.

What follows are two samples of generally appropriate formats for different fee agreements. Of course, the advocate must always check her own particular jurisdiction's ethics rules to ensure that a form is appropriate. One of the agreements is in the form of a somewhat less formal letter agreement while the other looks more like a formal contract. Either way, the advocate should be sure to let the client read the document carefully, discuss the agreement with another lawyer of their choosing if they so desire, and sign and date the document and

transmit back to the advocate
with any initial payment or
retainer that may be required by
the agreement's terms.

> *"The defendant who pleads their own case has a fool for a client, but at least there will be no problem with fee-splitting."*
>
> Anonymous

b. Sample contingency fee letter agreement

September 15, 2007

Dear Bill Smart:

I am pleased to offer you legal representation as set forth in this letter. Please read this letter carefully and, if it is acceptable to you, please sign the letter where indicated and return it to me as soon as possible. Once you have done this I will immediately undertake legal representation of you.

I agree to represent your interests in pursuing any and all claims that you may have arising out of your bicycle accident of June 1, 2006 to seek recovery of your damages. At this time, you are not seeking, and I am not agreeing to represent anyone other than you with respect to this matter. As I mentioned to you in our meeting, I cannot guarantee you any particular result in this representation. If I am unable to obtain any recovery for you, you owe me no legal fees whatsoever. In the event I do obtain a recovery for you, then you agree to pay me a fee as follows:

- If recovery is obtained before a trial, the fee shall be 30% of the amount recovered.
- If recovery is obtained during or following trial, the fee shall be 35% of the amount recovered.
- If recovery is obtained during or following an appeal, the fee shall be 40% of the amount recovered.

These percentages shall be calculated based upon the gross amount of the recovery prior to any deduction for costs and litigation expenses.

You understand that you will be ultimately responsible for payment of any and all costs and litigation expenses incurred in the prosecution of your claims. I agree to advance funds for the initial payment of all costs and litigation expenses with the understanding that you will reimburse me at the conclusion of my representation regardless of whether or not there is any recovery obtained.

You also understand that I may need to associate other counsel to assist me in your representation. You agree to permit me to associate any such other counsel at no additional cost to you. If I engage such other counsel, I will work out an arrangement with that other counsel to share in a portion of the fees that you have agreed to pay to me.

You also understand that by retaining me you have also agreed to cooperate fully with my efforts to prosecute your claims, to make yourself available to me when requested, to be present at any depositions, hearings or trial when I have indicated that you should be present, and to keep me fully informed of any change in your circumstances that might impact your claims. You also agree not to make any settlement with any parties in compromise of your claims without notifying me in advance.

I appreciate very much the trust you have placed in me and I look forward to working with you on this matter. Please sign this letter and return it to me as soon as possible. If I do not hear from you or receive this executed letter within thirty (30) days, I will assume that you have chosen not to retain me pursuant to the terms of this letter.

Sincerely,

Jane Aikman, Esq.

Agreed: _____

Bill Smart, date: _____

---

c. Sample hourly fee agreement

Attorney Representation Agreement

1.   This attorney representation agreement ("Agreement") is entered into as of the _____ day of _____, 20__, between Bill Smart ("Client" hereafter) and Jane Aikman, Esq. ("Attorney" hereafter). Client retains Attorney to represent him in the prosecution of any and all

claims arising out of Client's bicycle accident of June 1, 2006. Client is not asking Attorney for any other legal work at this time other than as described above.

2.   Client agrees upon execution of this Agreement immediately to pay Attorney a retainer in the sum of $5,000. Client understands that the total fees could likely exceed this retainer.[11] If not, Attorney agrees to return any remaining portion of the retainer to Client immediately upon the conclusion of the work undertaken pursuant to this Agreement. If the hourly fees incurred in connection with the prosecution of Client's claims do exceed the amount of this retainer, Attorney will bill Client monthly for such additional time at the hourly rate of $200. Any associates utilized by Attorney will be billed to Client at the hourly rate of $100 and any legal assistants will be billed to Client at the hourly rate of $75. If Attorney anticipates a need to bring in additional counsel from outside Attorney's law firm to assist, Attorney will contact Client and reach an understanding concerning the fees of such other counsel prior to formally retaining them.

3.   If this matter is not concluded within one (1) year from the date of this agreement's effective date, Attorney has the right to request an adjustment of the foregoing rates. Client also agrees to reimburse Attorney for any other costs or expenses of litigation reasonably incurred by Attorney, including but not limited to filing fees, witness fees, depositions costs, copy costs, courier fees, postage and other overnight mail, travel expenses, legal research expenses, phone charges and court reporter charges.

4.   Client agrees to pay within thirty (30) days of receipt, all monthly invoices submitted by Attorney for fees and any costs or expenses of the litigation incurred by Attorney. Should any such invoice remain unpaid after sixty (60) days, Attorney may withdraw from representation.

5.   Client also agrees to cooperate fully with Attorney's efforts to prosecute the Client's claims, to make himself available when requested, to be present at any depositions, hearings or trial when indicated, and to keep

---

[11] Typically any sums held in trust, such as a retainer, must be placed by the advocate in a separate interest bearing account–called IOLTA ("Interest On Lawyer Trust Account"). Each jurisdiction has rules governing such accounts and the advocate must comply with these rules.

Attorney fully informed of any change in Client's circumstances that might impact the claims.

6.   Client may terminate this Agreement upon thirty (30) days' written notice to Attorney and paying to Attorney any sums still outstanding for fees and expenses incurred.

7.   Attorney may terminate this Agreement at any time by notifying Client in writing and refunding any portion of the retainer still remaining, unless such termination is forbidden by a court or by the applicable Rules of Professional Conduct.

8.   Client and Attorney agree that should any disputes arise concerning the terms of this agreement or any fees or expenses charged by Attorney to Client, the parties will submit the dispute to binding arbitration through the local bar association.

9.   Client understands and agrees that neither Attorney nor anyone associated with Attorney has made any representation, promise, guaranty or warranty regarding the expected outcome in this matter. Client acknowledges that the outcome of any legal matter is highly uncertain and that Attorney is not in any position to make any such representations, promises, guarantees or warranties.

10.   Client agrees that this Agreement will be enforced pursuant to the laws of the State of _____. Client further agrees that this document embodies the entire agreement between Client and Attorney and that any modifications of the terms of this Agreement must be in writing and signed by both Attorney and Client.

Executed this ___ day of _____, 20__.
Attorney: Client:

D. TIME-KEEPING

Advocates hate to record their time for a variety of reasons and yet timekeeping remains an indispensable part of pretrial practice. Lawyers switching to an alternative career path–teaching for example–commonly list the fact that they no longer have to record their time as a chief benefit of their job change. Recording your time is a chore because, if done contemporaneously, it requires you to stop your real work while you make notations on a pad of paper or type an entry into your computer. It is also a hassle if you do not do it contemporaneously because then you have to try to remember all of the details of your past work and how much time you spent doing that work. It can also be a depressing exercise because the advocate can begin to realize how much time they have spent without always having advanced the ball in their case very far. Let's face it–nobody goes to law school so that they can divide up their life into six-minute increments of time, which is a typical way advocates record their time.

So why does the advocate have to record time? Getting paid seems to be a primary reason but there are other reasons to record time. It is worth reviewing some of these reasons because knowing the audience that will be reviewing the advocate's time sheets is important to understanding the proper way to record the time. Clients obviously are most likely considered the primary audience for an advocate's time entries. Lawyers who are billing by the hour typically send their clients a monthly bill that breaks down the time they spent working on a particular matter, indicating the hourly rate and assigning a total dollar value for the time being charged to the client. But there are other audiences for the advocate's time sheets. Judges are frequently asked to review time sheets, or at least summaries of time sheets, when they are ruling on a request for an award of attorney's fees. In this context, judges are typically ruling on whether the fee request is for time that was "reasonable and necessary" to achieve the advocate's purpose. Senior partners also review time sheets both to decide whether to "write off" any of an associate's time before billing the client and also when reviewing the quantity of the associate's work, perhaps at an annual review. Grievance committees or juries are also sometimes involved in reviewing advocate's time sheets for purposes of determining if the advocate acted competently in representing the interests of a client. Much to the surprise of many young advocates, opposing counsel are sometimes afforded the opportunity to review an advocate's time sheets–typically as a form of discovery when the advocate is seeking an award of attorney's fees. And more recently, clients are engaging legal fee auditors to review in detail the time entries of advocates for the purpose of determining if any monthly invoices contain entries that might be

> **Your Time Sheets Can Be Reviewed By:**
>
> - Clients
> - Judges
> - Senior Partners
> - Grievance Committees
> - Juries
> - Opposing Counsel
> - Legal Fee Auditors

argued to be questionable. In fact, some fee auditors are paid a commission based upon the amount of legal fees they succeed in writing off of a client's bill.

The information an advocate records in her time sheets may, therefore, depend to an extent upon the likely audience for that information. Certainly if the advocate is anticipating making a claim for attorney fees the advocate should understand the possibility of opposing counsel being granted access to those records. This likely activity should influence the degree of detail that the advocate places in the entry. For example, in such a context, consider which of the following two entries would be better:

Entry A:

September 15, 2007   1.5 hrs–Legal research to determine if client's claim may be subject to affirmative defense of fraud.

Entry B:

September 15, 2007   1.5 hrs–Legal research on possible affirmative defenses to client's claim.

Obviously both entries are accurate summaries of the advocate's work but the former could be problematic if the advocate is required by a court to disclose to opposing counsel when the opponent has not yet asserted the defense of fraud. In other words, *the advocate must be careful not to disclose litigation secrets in their time sheets in this circumstance.*

By contrast, in the context of clients as the audience, different concerns are raised concerning both the level of detail and to what extent the advocate can bundle multiple activities with a single time entry. If you were the client, for example, what problems might you have in reviewing the following time entries?

Entry C:

September 15, 2007   1.5 hrs–telephone conferences

Entry D:

September 15, 2007   1.5 hrs–drafted interrogatories; telephone conference with opposing counsel; reviewed letter from client; drafted witness statement.

With Entry C, the client has no idea to whom the advocate was speaking–her spouse perhaps? And Entry D may be a problem if the client has communicated to the advocate that the client is unwilling to pay for time spent having internal conferences because this entry does not demonstrate how much of the total time was spent on that activity. Entry D is an illustration of "lump billing" where the advocate simply records next to a single time entry all of her activities undertaken on that date for the client. Many advocates prefer to bill this way because it is simpler and does not require them to stop each time they pick up a different document on behalf of the client to make a new time entry. Clients are increasingly wary of this practice, however, because they may be suspicious that the advocate is running up the bill and hiding the actual time spent on various activities–sort of the legal equivalent to the advocate "clocking in" and "clocking out" on their file.

Another example would be where the advocate who was sanctioned by the court for not turning over certain documents in a discovery pursuant to a court order is now is facing a grievance by the former client in that case. Which of the following two entries would be better for the advocate to have in her file regarding a key conversation with the client in which the advocate told the client of these obligations?

Entry E:

September 15, 2007   .3 hr–phone conference with client

Entry F:

September 15, 2007   .3 hr–phone conference with client regarding obligation to produce documents in response to court order.

While a nice memo to the file would also help the advocate in this circumstance to win the swearing match with the former client, having recorded their time as in Entry F would doubtlessly provide more restful sleep for the advocate. As each of these examples illustrate, the advocate needs to consider her circumstances and likely audience when recording her time.

> **Time Keeping Principles:**
>
> - Don't lie
> - Don't double-bill
> - Don't nickel and dime

Even when the advocate is getting paid on a contingency fee basis recording time can be very important if the advocate is planning to make a request for reimbursement for their attorney's fees against the opposing party because courts (and juries) are asked to consider whether the fee is "reasonable and necessary" and the amount of time spent pursuing the client's claims is a very important factor in this regard. In addition, even for advocates working on a flat fee arrangement, the only way the advocate can determine whether their billing arrangement is fair is by reference to the time spent on such matters. Because it is always fairly impossible to accurately guess the amount of time spent working on a case, keeping accurate time records is an essential good business practice for such advocates.

> **Fair Billing Procedures are:**
>
> - Inclusive
> - Timely
> - Efficient
> - Honest

1. *Inclusive*

Advocates early in their legal careers are often unsure when they should record time spent working on their client's case. This happens for several reasons. One reason is that the advocate feels guilty because the time quickly adds up and the advocate is uncomfortable with the escalating fees incurred on a matter. A common tendency is for younger advocates to edit their own time-keeping to resist these growing monthly bills. But this practice can

> *"When a young lawyer writes off their own time, they are stealing from me and this law firm."*
>
> Anonymous senior partner at a ridiculously large law firm

hurt the law firm if associate time is not being billed. While it is possible the time needs to be written down, that is typically the job of the billing attorney. Also, younger lawyers tend to bill at lower hourly rates which already takes into account their inexperience and possible inefficiency in handling a case themselves. Further, if there is ever any question raised about whether the advocate provided competent legal representation, having recorded at least initially all of their activities in their time sheets is obviously going to more accurately show the advocate's actions.

Another reason, besides guilt, that advocates are unsure about recording time is because being a lawyer involves the application of skills in many different environments. What if the advocate spends fifteen minutes analyzing a client's legal issue while taking a shower in the morning? Is that time appropriately billed to the client? The answer should be resolved by asking whether the advocate "advanced the ball" during those fifteen minutes. Just because the analysis is done in the shower makes it no less billable. Likewise, just because an advocate is sitting at the client's offices does not make fifteen minutes of daydreaming an activity for which the advocate should bill the client. We should be clear, however, that the advocate should in no instance appear to "nickel and dime" the client by recording time spent on inconsequential matters, such as having a .2 entry show up on a time sheet when the advocate bumped into the client at the shopping mall and reminded the client about an upcoming deposition. An advocate who nickels and dimes a client is an advocate whose short-term approach will never engender client loyalty.

2. Timely

Because advocates are drawn more to preparing closing arguments than recording time, filling out time sheets is a task the advocate may be tempted to perform "tomorrow" rather than at the end of a long day in the office. Of course, tomorrow morning the advocate may get an important phone call followed by the need to prepare for a hearing at the courthouse right after lunch. The recording of time can easily be put off, and, obviously, the resulting time sheets will never be as accurate as if the advocate filled them out contemporaneously with doing the work reflected in the time sheets. For the many reasons outlined above, it is worth recording time and doing so as accurately as possible. This is only possible when the time sheets are prepared now and not later. This is not only a good practice for purposes of keeping the client happy but also for making sure that the advocate it not cheating herself. On Wednesday, it is easy to forget the many small tasks the advocate performed on Monday.

3. *Efficient*

Common experiences tell us that advocates who work on a few large cases have an easier task keeping track of their time than advocates who work on a large volume of small cases. When an advocate is constantly shifting from one client's matter to another during the course of a day, it is almost impossible to prevent some billable time from slipping through the cracks. Obviously this is one reason advocates like to work on big cases, but that is a luxury not all advocates will have. If you are facing the daunting task of handling many small litigation files at the same time, the best way that you can increase your efficiency, and keep your billable time from falling through the cracks, is to do as many tasks at one time on each case file as possible. For example, this approach might mean waiting a few days to draft the case update letter until you have time to draft some discovery requests on the same case.

4. *Honest*

Being honest and accurate in recording time has been alluded to earlier but it bears repeating directly. There is no instance and no audience that justifies an advocate being dishonest in recording their time. For most ethical advocates this will not be a difficult problem. But there are some subtle situations that arise in billing contexts that require careful application of this principle of honesty. For example, if an advocate is on a flight to Detroit to take a deposition for one client and simultaneously drafts a complaint for a different client while en route, may the advocate bill both clients for that same period of time? Is double-billing ever appropriate? Most large firms have legends of particularly aggressive and unscrupulous lawyers billing more than twenty-four hours in a day. Unfortunately, some of these stories are true. The real problem with double-billing is that it is ultimately a dishonest, and therefore, unethical practice. When the advocate submits a bill to one client for time spent on that flight to Detroit, she is implicitly representing to that client that this period of time was spent on behalf of that client alone. Making that implicit representation to two clients for the same period of time is therefore dishonest to both clients. Such a practice may never come to light–but the ethical advocate sleeps better than the advocate who spends her career looking over her shoulder to see if her lies are catching up to her.

While filling out time sheets is never likely to rank in any advocate's top ten list of favorite things about being a lawyer, it is a necessary and important reality of the modern practice of law. Timekeeping does not have to be a cause of unnecessary anxiety or stress, however, if done honestly, timely and prudently.

E. TAKING THE CASE

Before committing to undertake representation of a client on a new matter, the advocate should consider a number of things that relate to the client, the advocate and the case. It is always easier to take on a new case than to dispose of an old one. The advocate needs to remember she is about to make an important and possibly enduring professional and business commitment when she tells the new

> "No other profession is subject to the public contempt and derision that sometimes befalls lawyers . . . the bitter fruit of public incomprehension of the law itself and its dynamics."
>
> Irving R. Kaufman
> United States Court of Appeals,
> Second Circuit

client that she will take their case. The circumstances that should be considered can be summarized by the advocate asking herself the following three questions:

1. Do I want to take the client's case?

At least in the world of civil law, advocates are not required to take a client's case. It is something the advocate chooses to do. Whether the advocate wants to take the client's case may depend, in part, upon the fee arrangement chosen. If the client is paying by the hour or through a flat fee arrangement, the merits of the client's claims are not generally an overriding consideration–assuming the advocate is not being asked to do something unethical, such as advancing groundless theories. But when the advocate is considering taking the case on a contingency fee arrangement, the likely outcome of the case is a paramount and legitimate consideration. The biggest hurdle to this early type of case analysis is that the advocate has less information than she will at any other point during the litigation, and yet needs to make a decision on taking a case–an issue that is arguably the most important one the advocate will make. Nevertheless, the advocate using whatever information is available from the client and other readily available sources of information (e.g., the internet, police reports, client documents, etc) should at least mentally consider the positives and negatives of the case. For example, in a case involving a client who broke his leg after being hit by a car while riding his bicycle, a simple chart might include the following rough observations.

Positive	Negative
Objective, undisputed injury	No serious, permanent or life-threatening damage
Client fairly sympathetic and likeable	Client has been involved in prior personal injury litigation and has one criminal conviction for smoking marijuana.
Car's driver could have easily avoided client on bicycle	Client could have easily used sidewalk rather than riding along the side of road. Possible comparative fault.
Driver has insurance and possible additional liquid assets to pay a judgment	Insurance company has reputation for fighting hard and taking many claims to trial rather than settling

While the advocate's early assessment of the merits of the case will likely change during the course of representation, often these early evaluations are not too far removed from the truth. In any event, the advocate must make an early attempt to at least consider the positive and negative characteristics of the case and the client at this stage.

In addition to the case merits, the advocate has other factors she may wish to consider. Does the advocate desire to handle family law disputes or get into the business of bringing asbestos claims? How does the advocate feel about representing this particular client or taking the legal position necessitated by the client's case–for example, being asked to challenge a city's placement of the Ten Commandments on the courthouse door? Or being hired to challenge a law prohibiting internet child pornography? Certainly the law recognizes that the advocate's "representation of a client . . . does not constitute an endorsement of the client's political, economic, social or moral views or activities."[12] But the public media and your relatives may not share this enlightened distinction between the advocate and the client. Further, it is quite possible that at some point the

---

[12] Ethical Rule 1.2(b). Of course, as Charles Dickens once stated "[i]f there were no bad people there would be no good lawyers."

disagreement may become so profound as to negatively impact the advocate's ability to provide the zealous representation that the ethics rules contemplate.[13] The ethical rules understand this reality and expressly bless the advocate's right to withdraw from representation when "the client insists upon taking action that the lawyer considers repugnant or with which the lawyer has fundamental

---

Issues Raising a Red Flag:

Problem Clients

- Client has had prior attorney who was fired or withdrew
- Client has obvious personality or character defects
- Client has suspect motives for litigation
- Client has unrealistic expectations
- Client believes there is "no way" he can lose

Problem Cases

- Statute of limitations has, or is about to, expire
- Little value at stake yet, client's emotions run high
- Little likelihood of success
- Large counterclaims loom on horizon
- Case beyond your expertise

---

disagreement."[14] But any such effort to withdraw will have to be balanced by possible prejudice to the client from an untimely withdrawal[15]; in this instance, a court may well deny a motion to withdraw representation. The advocate should, if possible, make a realistic assessment of any such issues at the conception of the relationship.

---

[13]Ethical Rule 1.1 requires advocates to provide "competent representation to a client" which the rule further defines as the "legal knowledge, skill, thoroughness and preparation reasonably necessary for the representation."

[14] Ethical Rule 1.16(b)(4).

[15]"When ordered to do so by a tribunal, a lawyer shall continue representation notwithstanding good cause for terminating the representation." Ethical Rule 1.16(c).

2. Should you take the client's case?

Even if the advocate desires to handle the requested representation, she should also ask whether she can take the case due to practical or legal considerations. At the practical level, an advocate may not have the experience or expertise necessary to handle a certain lawsuit. A brand new lawyer has no business attempting to file a complex class action lawsuit and attempting to do so will likely lead to the case not being certified as a class action by the court and the client being disappointed or angry at the lawyer. The advocate also has to consider the time requirements for the anticipated case and ask whether she has the capacity to take on a case with those particular time demands. The case may require emergency relief such as obtaining a temporary injunction against a party that has the finances and incentive to vigorously fight back. Such a case will require the advocate to push aside most if not all other legal matters for several weeks or months. This type of case may also require additional counsel that may not be available to the advocate.

In addition to these practical considerations are issues concerning legal conflicts of interest and business conflicts. With regard to the former, the advocate must be acutely aware of her jurisdiction's rules regarding conflicts of interest and also needs to be aware of the other likely parties impacted by a new lawsuit in order to spot potential conflicts of interest. The worst case scenario is the advocate suing someone against whom the ethics rules preclude the advocate from taking an adverse position and thereby being disqualified from the new case and antagonizing another former or current client. One additional consideration is whether taking on the requested case might alienate another client of the advocate or her firm despite the absence of any legally recognized conflict of interest. For example, if a firm's bread and butter work is medical malpractice defense, the associate in that firm had better think twice before agreeing with a new client to file such a claim against a local doctor.

3. Should the client pursue the matter?

A final consideration is whether the client, who has come to your law office eager to institute a lawsuit, needs to receive counseling against pursuing the matter rather than cheerleading on the way to the court clerk's office. While a client able and

> "People are getting smarter nowadays; they are letting lawyers, instead of their conscience, be their guide."
>
> Will Rogers

willing to pay the advocate's hourly rate might seem like a wonderful new client, this does not mean that it makes sense for the client to pursue every legal remedy conceivably available to that client. Advocates do not want to take on work that is likely to result in an unsatisfied client. For example, if a small business owner had a potential breach of warranty claim against its primary vendor for important parts needed by the business, pursuing the technically-feasible cause of action may come at the expense of an important business relationship. The advocate who wants to be a good counselor, and have satisfied clients, needs to help the client recognize these situations and offer good advice. A lawsuit is a major disruption to a client's life or business. The enthusiasm and zeal held by the client at the inception is likely to wane during the typical two-year period it takes to litigate their claims. One other extremely important consideration is whether filing the new claim will provoke an otherwise dormant counterclaim from the defendant. In some states, even a counterclaim otherwise barred by the statute of limitations may be revived by the filing of a related claim against them. It is not unheard of for the plaintiff who initiated the lawsuit to end up on the defensive and offering to pay money to the defendant as a result of not anticipating a legitimate potential counterclaim before filing suit. The advocate can help the client by spotting such potential issues before they have grabbed the tiger by the tail.

E. RULES MATRIX

This table serves as a starting point for additional inquiry into the potential professional responsibility issues that are implicated at the inception of, and continuing with, the attorney-client relationship.

Issues Arising During the Inception or Continuation of the Attorney-Client Relationship	Applicable Rule of Professional Responsibility*
Advocates must provide "competent representation to a client" which the rule further defines as the "legal knowledge, skill, thoroughness and preparation reasonably necessary for the representation."	**Rule 1.1**
The fact that an advocate finds a client's cause repugnant does not prevent her from representing them.	**Rule 1.16(b)(4)**

"When ordered to do so by a tribunal, a lawyer shall continue representation notwithstanding good cause for terminating the representation."	**Rule 1.16(c)**
Fee arrangements–factors to consider in assessing the reasonableness of a fee	**Rule 1.5(a)(1)-(8)**
Prospective clients are owed a duty of confidentiality by the advocate.	**Rule 1.18(b)**
Lawyer must abide by client's wishes.	**Rule 1.2(a)**
Advocates "shall not counsel or assist" clients to "unlawfully alter, destroy or conceal a document . . . ."	**Rule 3.4(a)**
Suggested contents of a fee agreement	**Rule 1.5(b)**

Table 1 - Potential Rules Applicable to the Attorney Client Relationship

* Unless otherwise indicated all rules referenced in this chart are taken from the Delaware Supreme Court's professional responsibility rules. Those rules are almost identical to those promulgated by the American Bar Association and are public domain documents. Copies of the pertinent rules are provided in Appendix I.

Points To Ponder . . .

1. How does the advocate best decide what the goals of the anticipated case should be? What is the right response of the advocate when the client's desires seem overly optimistic?

2. Is it really necessary to believe in what you are advocating for? How do you effectively represent a client whose goals you find personally repugnant? Should you?

3. At certain points the advocate's interests may not be perfectly aligned with the client–for example, when drafting the fee agreement how does the advocate reconcile her desire to maximize her fees with achieving the best recovery for the client?

CHAPTER FOUR
INITIAL CASE ANALYSIS,
PREPARATION & PLANNING

"When shall we three meet again
In thunder, lightning, or in rain?
When the hurlyburly's done,
When the battle's lost and won."[1]

A. INTRODUCTION

In this chapter we will learn how to perform case analysis and conduct initial preliminary case preparation and planning. These are some of the most important tasks for an effective advocate. Doing these things–and doing them well–often is what separates the extraordinary from the merely competent in pretrial advocacy. To accomplish the first of these tasks–case analysis–you must choose an organizational construct that processes information, prioritizes the value of that information and then identifies crucial legal and factual issues applicable to the case. The choice for how to do this is as varied as the Advocates who analyze cases. Many different types of organizational techniques exists that allowing you to get a handle on this process, but not all techniques are created equally. This is an important step, because the way you conduct case analysis has long-term consequences. It effects the clarity and persuasiveness of your position throughout the litigation, and either assists you or prevents you from identifying potentially case dispositive issues at a point where they can be properly addressed.

A superior case analysis (1) assists advocates in understanding the relevant legal and factual issues, (2) brings clarity and focus to the issues the advocate wishes to emphasize, and (3) provides a moral theme for the duration of the pretrial phase of litigation with a view toward enabling a jury to decide the case in the client's favor in the event trial becomes necessary. The Rule of Threes[2] provides a superior template to handle case analysis, organize case files,

---

[1] WILLIAM SHAKESPEARE, MACBETH, act 1, sc. 1.

[2] Michael Eck has created the most complete internet portal on this subject. *See The Book of Threes: A Subject Reference Tricyclopedia*, http://threes.com.

and prepare for trial in a way that allows an advocate to start on the right foot and be immediately successful. Every attorney must develop the ability to properly perform these tasks. While this skill is not normally taught in a law school environment, it can be learned. The use of logical constructs such as the Rule of Threes,[3] in conjunction with an attorney's heightened ability to logically reason, will assist advocates in creating persuasive trial presentations through a synergistic combination of the practical and the theoretical.

While case analysis is important at all phases of litigation we will focus on trying to understand the way the case will most likely ultimately present itself to the judge and jury at trial. Even if our client is motivated to settle and we have no reason to suspect the case will linger to the point of trial, analyzing the case in terms of its trial potential benefits the client by posturing the case in the strongest possible position for resolution by any means. By planning the case all the way through we are better able to identify decision points in the development and preservation of evidence, as well as those procedural decision points that we must address as we move toward trial. Case analysis manifests itself– and proves valuable–in virtually all pretrial activity you undertake on behalf of your client beginning with your preparation of initial pleadings all the way through the filing of your joint pretrial statement and appearance for the final pretrial conference.

Case analysis is certainly the starting point for the advocate's planning and preparation of the new case and it is an undertaking that will necessarily continue throughout the entire course of the proceeding as it permeates virtually every aspect of pretrial advocacy. Yet it is only one part of the preparation and planning for litigation. The advocate will need to undertake additional tasks and face other key issues at the beginning of the case. This is, for example, where the advocate will perform much of the informal fact investigation into the merits of both the possible claims and defenses that have been or might be raised. If the advocate represents the claimant she will need to address other vital concerns at the outset such as considering what claims to join together and determining what other persons or entities should be made a party to the anticipated lawsuit either because of strategic importance or legal necessity. The advocate should

> "If I had six hours to chop down a tree, I'd spend the first four sharpening the ax."
>
> Abraham Lincoln

---

[3] Mark Twain referenced trilogies in his own inimical way in *The Autobiography of Mark Twain, see* http://www.twainquotes.com/Statistics.html, stating "Figures often beguile me, particularly when I have the arranging of them myself; in which case the remark attributed to Disraeli would often apply with justice and force: There are three kinds of lies: lies, damned lies and statistics."

7 Steps in Preparing and Planning for Litigation:

- Case Analysis
- Informal Fact Investigation
- Joinder of Claims
- Additional Parties
- Subject Matter Jurisdiction
- Personal Jurisdiction
- Venue

also ask where the best forum would be for the lawsuit and then, taking into account issues such as subject matter jurisdiction, personal jurisdiction, and venue, the advocate should try to craft the lawsuit to permit filing in such locale. Sometimes these goals–joining the most advantageous parties and filing the case in front of the most attractive court–can conflict with one another as the joinder of a certain desirable litigant may hurt the plaintiff's ability to file the case in a particular court. The new advocate may be chomping at the bit and eager to simply get the lawsuit on file, but thoughtful deliberation at the outset can be worth more than an abundance of activity later on. This chapter will discuss these considerations, providing both an outline of the applicable law and suggesting strategic considerations appropriate for the advocate's weighing of these options. This chapter will close with a practical discussion on establishing and organizing your case file–the fruits of your labor–to enable you to maintain your effectiveness and focus as your case progresses toward resolution.

B. CASE ANALYSIS

1. Introduction

During case analysis you organize information, apply specialized knowledge to that information, and then view the results of that process in light of your personal understanding of the moral values existing within the community where the case is tried. This is the point in the practice of law where an attorney melds her legal knowledge with her common sense and world experience. At times this process can overwhelm a new attorney. Particularly when they are not even sure if the case will ever make it to trial. She is not quite sure where to start, or how in-depth her initial effort should be. The advocate often wanders aimlessly through the case file, attempting to generate sufficient activity to feel as though she is accomplishing something. This is rarely, if ever, successful, and even when it is, it is not efficient.

> Thoughtful deliberation at the outset of case analysis is worth so much more than an abundance of activity later on. In other words - *Work smart, not hard.*

The more successful and practical approach addresses each case by applying an overarching structure. An old chestnut often attributed to Benjamin Franklin is "to fail to plan is to plan to fail."[4] This adage definitely applies to case analysis. The only way to overcome what appears to be an overwhelming project is to begin. It is a lot like eating an elephant—you do it one spoonful at a time. There are many different contextual models for analyzing cases. Talk to others and you will quickly learn that each of them has a process, some of it quite idiosyncratic to the individual, that allows them to become comfortable with the case. While we realize that over time you too will develop your own personal approach, you must start somewhere. We recommend that you begin with the Rule of Threes. This concept provides a common sense template to assist you in "eating the elephant"[5] of case analysis. This text uses the Rule of Threes as an

---

Seven Steps to Superior Case Analysis & Preparation:

- Organize the case file: use chronologies, time lines and topics
- Identify the procedural and substantive legal issues
- Identify the factual issues: separate facts into the good, the bad and the downright ugly
- Connect the facts to the law
- Identify the moral theme: the sense of injustice, or "the most appalling thing"
- Plan your presentation in reverse: from closing argument through the case-in-chief to opening statement (consider your opponent's case as well)
- Verify the evidence: ensure that you have the witnesses to admit sufficient evidence to support your legal theory, factual theory, and moral theme.

---

overarching structure for case analysis and suggests a series of common sense checklists applicable in most situations. There are seven generally accepted areas where initial case analysis and preparation occur. In each of these discreet sections the Rule of Three can be applied. However, before asking you to apply the Rule of Threes to case analysis we should first provide an overview of how

---

[4] Often Attributed to Benjamin Franklin, see JOHN MARKS TEMPLETON, DISCOVERING THE LAWS OF LIFE. (The Continuum Publishing Company, 1995).

[5] BILL HOGAN, HOW DO YOU EAT AN ELEPHANT? ONE BITE AT A TIME! (Llumina Press 2004).

it works. Keep the seven steps of case analysis in mind as your review the discussion concerning the Rule of Threes. You should begin to see connections between the concepts fairly quickly.

2.   *The Rule of Threes*

The Rule of Threes is an organizational construct used to communicate ideas through the written or spoken word. It posits that when information is organized in triplets human beings are more likely to accept and internalize the messages contained within those three pronged packages. This three part harmony view of communication is a powerful tool if you accept its basic premise. Communication is the primary weapon of the advocate, whether at trial or during pretrial, and learning to use this weapon effectively puts your client in the best position to achieve a successful result.

"Hatred paralyzes life;
Love releases it.
Hatred confuses life;
Love harmonizes it.
Hatred darkens life;
Love illumines it."

Dr. Martin Luther King, Jr.

The Rule of Threes is so ubiquitous in Western society that attempting to uncover the origin of the rule is a difficult if not impossible process. It is possible however, to apply your powers of observation to great moments in communication. We would suggest that in deciding whether or not to use the Rule of Threes you should consider examples of communications recognized and accepted as instances of superior communication. Both western civilization[6] and Asian   Heritage[7] provide many opportunities from which to choose when looking for effective examples of the Rule of Threes. In fact you need look no further than the rich history of the United States for instances where the use of the Rule of

---

[6] Examples from western civilization include Greek philosophy, Judaism, and early Christianity.

[7] Classical Hinduism dates back to at least 500 B.C. with roots extending to 2000 B.C. The Hindu doctrine of divine trinity is called Trimurti(from Sanskrit "three forms") consisting of Brahma, Vishnu, and Shiva. Brahma is the Father or Supreme God, Vishnu is the incarnate Word and Creator, while Shiva is the Spirit of God. Hindus view them as an inseparable unity and worship them as one deity. See "trimurti," Encyclopedia Britannica, 2006, Britannica Concise.

Threes delivered a message that resonated in the hearts and minds of the American people. Consider the words of Dr. Martin Luther King, Jr. Note his use of both the Rule of Threes and parallelism[8] in the organization of two complementary triplets dealing with the twin themes of hatred and love. The message he delivered is powerful, controlled, and ultimately uplifting. Dr. King touched the emotional core of his audience by using the Rule of Threes to arrange his message in a manner that ensured acceptance by the audience. He spoke to us in a way that we could understand. The strength of his message resounded from the depths of a jail cell in Birmingham, Alabama to the steps of the Lincoln Memorial in Washington, D.C. Advocates who use the Rule of Threes to conduct case analysis will begin to develop skills that ultimately will increase their persuasive ability at trial.

    The Rule of Threes has been used to create belief systems and memorable phrases that are part and parcel of the tapestry that forms our daily lives. The philosophy of the ancient world focused on *logos, pathos,* and *ethos* as a way of living, with an intrinsic understanding that who an advocate was mattered nearly as much as what they did.[9] Trilogies teaching others how to live as a member of society exist within many great written works, including The Bible, where messages such as "When I was a child, I spake as a child, I understood as a child, I thought as a child: but when I became a man, I put away childish things" are easily found.[10] As noted previously, Hinduism believes in the Trimurti form of the divine trinity reflected in the gods Brahma, Vishnu and Shiva. The existence and use of the Rule of Threes in cultures separated

"Do what you can,
    with what you have,
    where you are."

President
Theodore Roosevelt

by not only beliefs but time is striking from an organizational perspective and

---

[8] The Catholic Encyclopedia defines parallelism to mean "The balance of verse with verse, an essential and characteristic feature in Hebrew poetry. Either by repetition or by antithesis or by some other device, thought is set over against thought, form balances form, in such wise as to bring the meaning home to one strikingly and agreeably. In the hymns of the Assyrians and Babylonians parallelism is fundamental and essential." *See* http://www.newadvent.org/cathen/11473a.htm.

[9] *See* ARISTOTLE, THE ART OF RHETORIC, (H.C. Lawson-Tancred trans., Penguin Books 1991).

[10] 1 *Corinthians*, 13:11.

supports the argument that the Rule of Threes works because it is intrinsic to the human condition.

This connection exists across cultures and evidence of it can be found in Judea-Christian traditions, the mythology of ancient Greece[11], and the tenets of Hinduism. Beyond issues of faith however, the Rule of Threes is also grounded in our physical ability to perceive the world around us. It is part and parcel of how we think and communicate. Consider for a moment the world surrounding you. Your senses view the world from a three dimensional perspective. These three dimensions form the boundaries of your physical world. When our world does not accurately reflect all three dimensions our physical comfort is compromised. In the same way, words and thoughts that do not reflect a Rule of Threes organizational construct ring less than true in our minds, impinging on our ability to accept as true the message being presented.

Applying the Rule of Threes creates an internal sense of believability and acceptance on the part of any audience whether that is the opposing party, the judge, or ultimately a jury. Noted advocates have lectured on the use of this rule, including Terrence McCarthy, a successful and famous Chicago defense attorney and Thomas Singer, a respected member of the National Institute for Trial Advocacy and the Notre Dame Trial Advocacy faculty. When properly applied, this rule serves as a template for organizing, analyzing, and presenting a case.

> Your view the world in three dimensions. Words and thoughts that do reflect a Rule of Threes organizational construct will ring true in the minds of others. Failure to properly organize your thoughts impinges on the ability of your audience to accept as true the message you are presenting.

The doctrine of primacy and recency is an excellent common sense example of an application of the Rule of Threes. For example, advocates use the doctrine of primacy and recency to (1) tell the judge or jury what they are going to tell them (e.g., opening statement), (2) tell them (e.g., case-in-chief), and (3) then tell them what they told them (e.g., closing argument). Primacy and recency is also used to make certain that advocates start and finish strong. They are taught to put their best facts first and last, with a filling in the middle of their weaknesses. There is persuasive power

---

[11] Apollodorus, *Library and Epitome (ed. Sir James George Frazer)*. "[F]rom the drops of the flowing blood were born Furies, to wit, Alecto, Tisiphone, and Megaera."

in this type of organizational structure, but advocates should be careful to not focus on "hiding" bad facts and instead work on how to either neutralize them or turn them to their advantage.

You will use these tools throughout the advocacy process, including in drafting pleadings, arguing motions for summary judgment, making mediation statements,

". . . [W]e can not dedicate—we can not consecrate—we can not hallow—this ground. . . .The world will little note, nor long remember what we say here, but it can never forget what they did here. . . .[T]hat government of the people, by the people, for the people, shall not perish from the earth.

Excerpts from the Gettysburg Address
President Abraham Lincoln

explaining your case to the judge during final pretrial conference, and certainly planning your possible trial presentation. Before taking those next steps in your development as a successful advocate you must first learn more about how to understand and analyze those materials that you will ultimately form your case file. The Rule of Threes will serve as an excellent tool for breaking the case file down into its component parts, with the goal of fully answering three primary series of questions.

3.   *Initial Case Analysis*

As your lawsuit progresses several things will happen that permit your case analysis to become more refined. You will obtain not only your client's documents but those important documents possessed by others, including your opposing party. You will have access to more witnesses to interview or depose. Amended pleadings will be filed and motions for partial summary judgment may dispose of certain factually unsupported claims or defenses that were originally pled. By the time of your final pretrial conference, your case analysis should be complete and your weaving of the facts, the law and moral theme should be coherent and convincing. But on the precipice of litigation, much of these sources will not yet be available. Using even the limited information that will be available to you prior to the filing of your client's original complaint or answer, however, your initial case analysis must begin if you are to ultimately prevail.

You should understand that in today's legal arena much of the business of case analysis and preparation will involve documents. You must begin to develop expertise in handling them from the outset of your legal career. At the beginning of the lawsuit, you will almost certainly have available the information obtained from your initial client interview and any documents provided by your client. As a part of your initial case analysis, you will need to review and begin to

> **Doctrine of Primacy and Recency:**
>
> - Tell them what you are going to tell them
>   *(e.g., opening statement)*
> - Tell them
>   *(e.g., case-in-chief)*
> - Tell them what you told them
>   *(e.g., closing argument)*

digest information in these client documents that pertain to the claims and defenses in the case. Likewise, although perhaps limited at this point in the process, you may have available certain documents from other sources such as public records (e.g., accident reports), the internet, newspapers, and third-party witnesses. Documents are particularly important in case analysis because of their great evidentiary value placed on them by many jurors. The advocate should read through these documents and then take a moment after this first reading to jot down her initial impressions of the information just received. *What questions are in your mind? Is there something else you need to know? Have you made some initial judgments about the people involved?* These are the same types of questions that other advocates will be asking your client during the client's deposition. Now would be a good time to ask these questions to your client. If the case goes to trial, the jurors will be asking these same kind of questions when the case is presented to them. It is at this point in the process that you are as close as you will ever be to thinking about the case the way a juror would. Once you've done this, set those observations aside in a safe place where you can later come back to them.

Your goal at this early point is not necessarily to obtain an immediate and comprehensive view of the entire facts surrounding the case, but rather to get a handle on what you have before you. It is this process of gathering and organizing all of the relevant documents and other information in a systematic way that you can begin the process of seeing the "conceptual whole" of the case. This big picture understanding will allow you to identify strengths and weaknesses and potential moral themes and legal theories for your case. You must not lose sight of this big picture at any time during the pretrial phase of the case. The ability to correctly identify the underlying moral themes is crucial. Morality, right and wrong, black and white, good guys and bad guys—this is the language

> **The Three Primary Steps in Case Analysis:**
>
> - Identify and analyze the legal issues.
> - Identify and analyze the factual issues.
> - Develop a moral theme that encompasses your legal and factual theories

of the jury. It comes from our shared culture and is reflected in the societal vehicles that teach us about the law. Think in terms of the many television shows, movies, and books dealing with legal situations. The public is fascinated with the process of assigning moral blame and imposing legal judgment. If your client's story falls into an archetype that the jury understands you will benefit immensely from an advocacy perspective when you harness that archetype and make it part of your moral theme.

The initial step in analyzing and understanding these early sources of information is to identify factual and legal issues and how they relate to one another. *Organization in a systematic fashion is the key to successfully analyzing a case.* Once you have organized the information you have gathered you can begin to analyze the contents using the three main steps of case analysis.

The three primary steps in case analysis are used at various pretrial and stages of a lawsuit. You should apply these three steps independently to each of the component parts of a pretrial proceeding to ensure that your case analysis is complete. Examples of where to do that include identifying the proper claims or defenses to assert, preparing and responding to written discovery, conducting depositions, drafting a mediation statement, and preparing dispositive motions and preparing your final pretrial statement. This list is not exhaustive, but does provide a sense of the various portions of the pretrial process to which you can and should apply the three main steps of case analysis. Each of these activities undertaken should reflect your case analysis and provide another step toward resolution of your case.

As you perform each such pretrial task consider the moral theme and legal theory of your case. Your theme and theory provide coherence

> **You should apply the three primary steps to:**
>
> - identifying the proper claims or defenses
> - preparing and responding to discovery
> - conducting depositions
> - drafting a mediation statement
> - preparing dispositive motions
> - preparing your final pretrial statement.

and continuity to the facts gathered and organized for presented at motion, mediation or possible trial and connect those facts to the legal issues you choose in a way that demands success for your side. If dissonance exists between the theme and theory and the facts or law of your case, you must adapt. Discover additional facts or law that support your position, modify your theme and theory, or settle the case. Whenever the theme and theory changes you must go back and reevaluate your case analysis in light of those changes.

A systematic approach is necessary to ensure that you cover all of the possible legal issues. To identify the appropriate legal issues you must understand not only the law, but the specific area of the law that applies to your particular case. Procedurally you should identify admissibility issues as you examine documents or witnesses while substantively looking for strengths and weaknesses where the law intersects with the facts. Always look for both substantive and procedural legal issues because either can be case dispositive.

> **Identify & Analyze Legal Issues:**
>
> 1. List the legal elements for the claims and defenses.
>
> 2. Analyze the legal principles and questions of law.
>
> 3. Develop a legal theory for each persuasive question of fact.

It is imperative that you develop the skill of identifying and analyzing those facts that are case dispositive. Dispositive facts are much more easily identifiable after you have developed the appropriate legal issues presented in the case. The facts of the case will determine whether the law that your predict may be applied by the judge assists or hurts your theme and theory. You must fully develop the relationship between the facts and the law. *Your ability to identify the ruling legal precedent, develop case dispositive facts, and then explain their relationship using an appropriate moral theme and legal theory is the essence of advocacy.*

We have identified three primary areas of case analysis that continuously shift in importance depending upon who you represent and the issues at hand. You must develop the ability to "sense" which is most important for a particular case.

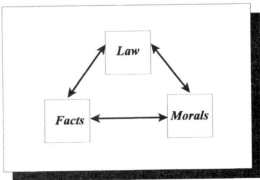

Some of that ability to find the best path will develop through experience, but a great deal of it is centered in the type of person you are and in the way you personally prefer to view the world. You may have a preference for factual analysis, legal analysis, or moral issues. If you lean towards one of these areas then begin your case analysis from that perspective, taking care to ensure that you do not allow your personal predilections to prevent you from seeing issues in areas that may not be your strongest suite. Others have referred to this technique as "mind mapping," and have presented it as a conceptual tool for case analysis.[12] There is a good deal of common sense and practical wisdom in this concept.

At a minimum, starting from a perspective that ensures you are engaged in the process and can see relationships between categories is important. In order to find your best starting point some degree of personal introspection is helpful. Excellent tools exist to assist advocates in this process, including the Myers-Briggs test[13] and the Kiersey Temperament Sorter.[14] The methodology you choose is not important, taking the time to know yourself before you represent others, on the other hand, is not only important but vital to a developing trial advocate, from both a competency and ethical perspective. Once you have identified your starting point and analyzed the case you will have identified certain facts you want to develop further through discovery and to highlight for possible use in guiding the claims toward resolution through motion, settlement or possible trial. With regard to factual weaknesses in your client's case, whether they take the form of harmful documents or testimony from an important witness, you should begin to compile a list of possible topics for inclusion in a motion in limine to present to the court should the case go to trial. We will discuss further these concepts of trial preparation in the last chapter of this book.

A proper case analysis assists the advocate in choosing the correct moral theme and legal theory in light of the available facts. Failure to accomplish this results in a cognitive dissonance in the minds of the fact-finder. What comes out of your mouth or your pleadings does not match the facts in the case. Anyone who reads your pleadings or listens to your arguments will conclude that you or your client are either incompetent or lying. Either way you lose. The goal is to have a coherent and consistent strategy for pursuing each pretrial activity in the case

---

[12] HUGH SELBY & GRAEME BLANK, WINNING ADVOCACY pages (Oxford Press 2d ed. 2004).

[13] NAOMI L. QUENK, ESSENTIALS OF MYERS-BRIGGS TYPE INDICATOR ASSESSMENT pages (John Wiley & Sons, Inc. 2000).

[14] DAVID KIERSEY & MARILYN BATES, PLEASE UNDERSTAND ME: CHARACTER & TEMPERAMENT TYPES pages (Prometheus Nemisis 1984); DAVID KIERSEY, PLEASE UNDERSTAND ME II: TEMPERAMENT, CHARACTER, INTELLIGENCE pages (Prometheus Nemisis 1992).

and to help you maintain your focus on achieving the client's goals.

The theory is the application of the relevant law to the specific facts of your case. It forms the basis for the legal or procedural reasons that you should win. The theory is how, at the end of the day, the judge or jury that might ultimately hear your case would go about deciding the case your way and is derived from a complete case analysis discussed above. Considering each legal element of

> Your ability to identify the ruling legal precedent, develop case dispositive facts, and then explain their relationship using an appropriate moral theme and legal theory is the essence of advocacy.

offenses and potential defenses will quickly identify possible legal theories. A case based solely on legal theories can be difficult from a persuasive standpoint. The shipwrecked crew adrift in a rubber raft that kills and eats the weakest member of their group and is then later rescued is a classic example of the difficulties with a purely legal defense. A murder occurred, but a potential defense of necessity exists. That legal defense however, may not have a moral theme that supports it. In the shipwreck case a good argument could be made that the strongest members of the party had a duty to protect the weaker ones, not a duty to eat them. Conversely, it could be argued that the weakest member was going to die anyway, and killing him saved the lives of the others. It is often possible for valid legal theories to run into a lack of credibility when they require the jury to adopt an unpopular moral theme or to reject a cherished community belief. In either instance you may find yourself with an excellent legal theory that will never carry the persuasive burden. Jurors are not lawyers and most advocates would do well to remember that fact. *Legal theories must be combined with a solid moral theme to succeed.*

The theme is the moral reason that you should win. Some scholars refer to this as the persuasive theme. While that may be an adequate way to describe it, calling this portion of case analysis a persuasive theme is not a completely adequate description. Persuasion means many things to different people - but simply identifying one third of your case analysis as this persuasive thing is insufficient because it does not provide an advocate with tools to identify and choose what is or is not persuasive. Advocates need more than that to adequately analyze a case. We posit that they should not shy away from looking into the realities of life, good and evil, just and unjust, right and wrong - in those themes lie moral tales of power and glory. They are the stories of which life is made, and the moral themes that will resonate with finders of fact.

Finding the moral theme, the action for good that the jury can take is more powerful. It is persuasive because everyone recognizes it as the right thing to do. We are called to support moral themes from our own internal sense of what is right and our certain knowledge of what is wrong. The persuasive power of aligning yourself with the cause of right is an incredible agent for change. A good moral theme identifies an injustice that is being committed against your client and empowers the jury to right that wrong. Themes are as varied as the people, places, and situations they are designed to capture and represent. The theme provides the moral force that brings the case to life. A good theme not only gets the jury on your side, it creates a feeling of comfort within them about deciding things your way.

If you cannot find a theme within your case that will resonate with the jury, try to determine what sense of injustice exists in the case. Is there a wrong that has been committed against your client that you can use to energize the jury to decide for you? Perhaps the government rushed to judgment because your client is a minority. Or the man who committed an egregious tort is walking around healthy and free while your client's exemplary life has been destroyed through the incompetence, stupidity, carelessness, or malfeasance of the opposing side. Other examples include the destruction of a way of life or the health of an individual through the greed of a soulless corporation. Or a plaintiff who caused her own injuries but is trying to drag down an innocent actor by making irresponsible accusations. The storylines are as varied and complex as the tales of humanity that surround us each day. They exist in your shared experiences as a member of the collective society that is represented by the fact finder. Stay in touch with these perennial themes of life. They are the vehicle through which you can persuasively explain your case to others. Coming up with such a powerful message for your client's case is like preparing fertile soil for an abundant crop. Where can you find this information - why in discovery of course. It is during the process of pretrial investigation that these themes become apparent.

C. INFORMAL DISCOVERY

1. Introduction

In order to really understand (analyze) her client's case, the advocate must necessarily engage in a fact-finding investigation. This comes in two forms: (a) formal discovery conducted under the applicable rules of civil procedure that is compelled from others; and (b) informal discovery conducted completely

> *"Lawyers may reason powerfully, but power settles most issues."*
>
> **Mason Cooley**

outside the ambit of any rules of civil procedure and mostly that which is voluntarily given to the advocate by others. Why is such investigation needed? Because in the prior section you learned that facts make up a primary portion of the advocate's case analysis. Indeed, many lawyers espouse the theory that cases are won and lost based mainly upon the facts. There is some truth to this because it is the application of the law to the facts that determines outcomes. If the advocate's job involves getting her case ready for a possible trial, one must remember that the sole purpose for having a trial is so that disputed questions of *fact* can be determined by the judge or jury. As you will be reminded in Chapter 9, where significant facts are not essentially disputed, courts typically enter judgment by motion rather than trial. But even in motion practice, before an advocate can determine what the facts are and whether they are disputed, the advocate must uncover the facts. The facts empower the advocate to obtain her client's goals.

While we treat formal discovery in three consecutive chapters (6-8) later in this book, now is the right time to talk about the significance of informal discovery. In a sense, informal discovery can be defined by what it is not. It is not generally governed by any rules, scheduling orders, or official approved techniques. Unlike formal

> **Informal Discovery is Used to:**
> - Perform case analysis
> - Garner supporting evidence
> - Discover adverse information
> - Reveal additional sources of information

discovery, informal discovery may begin at any time the advocate is considering a possible lawsuit and requires no court permission or supervision. Informal discovery is a short-hand description for the unregulated fact investigation undertaken by an advocate, or under the supervision of the advocate, in order to perform case analysis, garner evidence in support of a client's claim or defense, discover adverse information that might defeat the client's claim, or simply to reveal additional sources of information that might bear on the client's claim. Advocates engage in some degree of informal discovery on virtually every case and, in most cases, advocates perform such investigation *before* the case is filed, *after* it is filed, and *continue* it up until the eve of trial. It can reveal information more profound than that procured under the rules of civil procedure and yet can be much more cheaply obtained. The strategic use of informal discovery can also be critical because it occurs under your opponent's radar. Although informal discovery is almost universally ignored in civil procedure courses, it is worthy of discussion for real advocates planning to win actual cases–people like you.

2.   *When to seek*

Formal discovery almost always comes after the filing of a lawsuit and, at least under the Federal Rules of Civil Procedure, after a required meeting of the attorneys to discuss and plan coordinated discovery. By contrast, informal discovery can happen at any time with or without a pending lawsuit. When the new client comes to meet with the advocate, informal discovery is taking place. The newly hired lawyer as part of the initial case analysis will normally want to find out what other witnesses there are, what documents exist, and whether any other information relevant to the possible claims can be uncovered at that time. Time spent engaged in such informal discovery is time well spent. The advocate wants this information before filing a lawsuit to be sure that there is a good faith factual foundation for the claim as part of complying with her rule 11 obligations,[15] to ensure that the advocate is not wasting her time pursuing the claims, and to help define and refine the appropriate causes of action to allege and the best remedies to seek. Given these purposes, the initial informal fact investigation should be undertaken as soon as possible. Failure to engage in such investigation can lead to inefficient representation by the advocate or, worse, to a loss of important evidence needed to establish the client's case. The passage of time makes it possible for (a) witnesses to move, die, or change their minds about what they experienced, (b) documents to become misplaced, and (c) for tangible physical evidence to be corrupted or for its condition to materially change.

In addition to using informal discovery before filing a lawsuit, advocates continue to use informal discovery while the lawsuit is being prosecuted. Before taking the deposition of a third-party witness, advocates commonly contact the witness to get some advance idea as to whether the witness has any important information and to at least obtain a summary of the substance of that information. This informal interview may obviate the need for the deposition–thereby saving time–or it may at least help to prepare the advocate to do a better job taking the deposition–thereby making the deposition testimony either more useful to the advocate or at least less harmful to the advocate's client. Any new potential sources of information that arise during a lawsuit should be considered a possible fertile ground for additional informal discovery.

> Attorneys must perform informal discovery if for no other reason than to develop the good faith factual foundation for the claim in compliance with their rule

---

[15]Federal Rule of Civil Procedure 11 provides that the advocate's signature on a pleading represents an implicit representation that the allegations contained in the pleading "have evidentiary support . . . ." This rule is discussed in more detail in the next chapter.

3. *What to look for*

It may be difficult for a brand new advocate to decide where to look for information about a new case. The starting point though is usually with the leads given by the client. The client may have some idea of the identity of other witnesses or involved parties. The client can give the advocate information about where the occurrence in question took place to permit a viewing of the scene by the advocate. The client may also turn over documents that reference other documents in the possession of third parties that might be obtained on request. Beyond these client-directed sources, the advocate should generally think in terms of finding relevant people, documents and tangible evidence using her common sense and any real-world experiences.

How does the advocate know what information might be relevant? Case analysis, which we just discussed, is going to be your guide. To this end, the advocate should consider preparing some type of "Proof Chart" which will be

---

Proof Chart

Negligence Elements	Evidence	Source
Duty	Defendant driving car	Client + Police rept
Breach	Too fast	Witness X
Causation	Car hit Client	Witness X
Damages	Client broke leg	Client + Doctor

---

helpful in providing organizational structure to the advocate's intuition. This proof chart, which may be very rudimentary at the outset of the case, will essentially help the advocate determine where their client's anticipated case has evidentiary strength and weakness. From this analysis the advocate can focus upon shoring up the areas of strength (corroboration)and trying to find evidence to fill in the gaps or weak areas of the case (substantiation). This proof chart essentially consists of acquiring basic information on the elements that the law prescribes for the cause of action (or defense) and then applying facts to those elements with a note as to the source of that proof–whether it be from a particular witness or a document or other tangible exhibit. Such a proof chart is simply a visual aid that should illustrate the careful thinking of an advocate. As we will discuss in this book's final chapter on trial preparation, the actual preparation and review of such a tangible display of the advocate's analysis will help to keep the advocate on track and make what could be an enormously complex process much simpler and easier to understand for both the advocate and her audience.

To perform this analysis for purposes of guiding the fact investigation, the advocate first needs to ascertain the elements of any contemplated cause of action as soon as possible in order to help guide the inquiry. This is the "Law" portion of the advocate's case analysis. Th instructions should not be the end point of your legal research on a case but your beginning. If your jurisdiction has no applicable pattern jury instructions for your client's e easiest way to do this is to put your hands on the applicable pattern jury instructions where you practice to obtain a quick feel for the basic contours of the claim, as it will likely be explained to a jury in the future at a trial. Pattern jury claim (or defense), then consider other treatises for your jurisdiction that generally describe the cause of action you are thinking of pursuing. These resources should be enough to get you started in at least outlining the elements of the law for purposes of your proof chart. Then the advocate should fill in the evidence already acquired from the client and other information brought by the client to the advocate. Using this proof chart as a resource and by asking simple questions of your client and following those leads, the advocate can frequently find out the identity of relevant witnesses and documents–potential evidence whose relevance is demonstrated by the proof chart.

The advocate can also consider things such as hiring a private investigator to help locate witnesses or take out an advertisement in a local newspaper. Furthermore, you should consider all public sources of information. If the client was in an accident, the advocate should inquire into accident or police reports that may have been made. In today's information-filled world, the advocate can discover an incredible amount of information simply by logging on to a computer and surfing the internet. For example, if a new client comes to your office considering a personal injury lawsuit after a ladder they were using collapsed, what might be some good sources of information to discover? Just by going to her computer, the advocate can likely uncover much relevant information, frequently from the target manufacturer's own website. The

> ### Public Sources for Informal Discovery:
>
> - Police Department
> - Department of Motor Vehicles
> - Telephone Directories
> - Public Universities
> - Credit Reporting Services
> - County Tax Records
> - Libraries
> - Newspapers
> - Federal Government Offices
> - Internet
> - Post Office

advocate, in this example, can likely find out the characteristics of the ladder, the advertised uses and characteristics of the product, what other alternate designs for that type of product the manufacturer produces, whether other manufacturers make similar products, whether there has been any recalls of the products, where the manufacturer is located and what corporate affiliates it may have. The advocate can also discover other lawsuits that may already have been filed against that manufacturer and, if the company is publicly regulated, information about the company's net worth. The advocate can discover all of this information without sending a single interrogatory to the defendant or waiting for the appropriate time to file the lawsuit, sending the interrogatories to the defendant and awaiting responsive information. Most importantly, the advocate can discover this information while undergoing initial case analysis and deciding whether to sue, who to sue, and what claims to assert.

Beyond witnesses, documents and publicly available information sources, the advocate should also consider investigation of tangible places and things, as well as the preservation of existing evidence and the creation of additional powerful evidence. If the client has been hurt in a public place, the advocate can visit that locale as soon as possible to gather information and document the accident site. For example, the advocate could hire a consulting expert–an accident reconstruction expert–to visit the scene, take measurements, and to take photographs or videotape of the scene. In some cases, the necessity to act on these information sources quickly is extremely high. In addition, to the extent that client's claims involve some tangible personal property that is involved, the advocate should secure

> **Physical Evidence:**
>
> * Photographs
> * Results of Laboratory Tests
> * Measurements
> * Demolished Vehicles
> * Accident Scene
> * Personal Injuries
> * Computer Drives
> * Drawings

that property for safekeeping and to avoid any suggestion of permitting the spoliation of material evidence. If the client is involved in a car accident and there is some consideration given to a product liability suit against the car's maker for defective brakes, the advocate will want to contact immediately the operator of the lot where the car has been towed to make arrangements for its preservation and possible immediate study by a consulting expert.

4.   *Witness interviews: Importance*

Perhaps the most important type of informal discovery is an advocate's interview of witnesses. This particular part of informal discovery requires the advocate to use skills that may have been sufficiently developed during their legal education. This is unfortunate, because interviewing witnesses has the possibility of informing the advocate of possible trial testimony, helping to locate and identify additional document sources, providing elaboration or corroboration for the client's story, disclosing harmful information that will need to be dealt with, revealing additional potential parties, and helping to show other causes of action, defenses, or informing the advocate's analysis of damages. The saying that "ignorance is bliss" does not apply to pretrial advocacy; rather, ignorance is a terrific thing for embarrassing the advocate or her client and causing a case to be lost. With all of the good to be accomplished through witness interviews–or the bad to avoided–should the advocate plan to interview every witness identified as a possible source of relevant information? The answer is yes, with a couple of caveats.

First, with an unlimited budget the advocate would probably choose to interview every possible witness. Unfortunately there are few civil cases with unlimited budgets and none of those are cases where a new advocate will have the primary responsibility for handling witnesses. In most other cases, particularly those you will be handling early in your career, advocates will have to weigh the possible benefits of any given witness interview against the time and cost of locating the witness and then scheduling and conducting the interview. For example let's imagine you are prosecuting a civil negligence claim. Your client was struck by a defendant that you believe ran a red light. You plan to assert the defendant's negligence per se in running a red light at an intersection. At the scene of the accident, the target defendant apologized to your client and admitted to an investigating police officer at the site that he was responsible for running the red light and causing the accident. You now hold a copy of the police report in your hands and notice that it reveals the names and addresses of two eye witnesses. Should you contact them to set up a witness interview? The witnesses are local but you can still plan on several hours of time to set up and carry out an in-person interview of them. On the other hand, it does not appear that liability is going to be seriously contested in the case.

In light of these factors, there are probably two appropriate approaches the advocate might take. One approach focuses on the timing of the witness interviews. This approach would be to hold off on contacting the eye witnesses until you have filed the lawsuit and the defendant has answered. If the defendant denies negligence, then you will definitely want to contact the witnesses. The other approach focuses upon the manner of the interviews. Instead of waiting to interview the eye witnesses, you interview them now but do it over the telephone in a few minutes to get the thrust of their recollection and to let them know that you might need to visit with them again in more detail in the future should the "defendant choose to lie" and recant his original confession. The advantage of this approach is to give you greater confidence in filing your lawsuit that the merits are very good, to shore up the witnesses' recollection that might otherwise fade with the passing of time, and to set up the defendant as the "bad guy" who will be responsible if you have to take up more of the witness' time. This is just an example of the thought process you should employ in determining whether and when to interview a fact witness taking into account your client's budget. All of this must done professionally, leading to our second caveat.

The second caveat is ethical. Ethical Rule 4.2 forbids an advocate from speaking to someone who the advocate "knows to be represented by counsel" without the consent of their lawyer. The idea behind this prohibition, generally followed in most states, is that when one hires an advocate they should be insulated from opposing counsel by that advocate. Obviously, in light of this provision, you would not call the opposing party and begin to question them after being informed of their legal representation. But what if the target defendant is a corporation–say Wal-Mart for example–and your client was injured in a "slip and fall" in the produce aisle of that store? Can you go to the store to interview an employee who was working in that produce section the afternoon of the incident? Wal-Mart is surely represented by counsel, but does that apply to the employee as well? Comment 4.2 helps to answer this question by clarifying that an advocate may *not* speak with the following type of employees for a represented organization:

a. any person having "managerial" responsibility
b. any person whose act or omission may be imputed to the company (through *respondeat superior*)
c. any person whose statement may constitute an admission against the company

If the Wal-Mart employee might have been responsible for keeping the produce aisles free of eggplants, then it is clear that you should not contact that employee for an informal interview. If the employee was the produce manager, you similarly should not contact him. If the employee has recently quit working for Wal-Mart, this does not necessarily resolve the issue because many states apply these prohibitions equally to a company's former employees. If it is unclear in your case whether these prohibitions apply, the safest course is to avoid any potential unethical conduct. You do not want to have a grievance filed against you and, further, the tainted fruits of an improper interview will likely not be admissible at a trial anyway. In fact, it is possible that if the court found your interview to be improper, it might instruct the jury that you engaged in improper conduct.

> ### Reasons to Forego Informal Witness Interview:
>
> - Client budget limited and witness' value minimal
> - Witness represented by counsel
> - Witness bound by privilege (physician-patient)

There is at least one other similar scenario where you may run into a legal obstacle in your desire to interview all witnesses–physicians. In many states, the physician may not speak to third parties (such as you) about their diagnosis and treatment of patients without the patient's express authorization. This does not mean that you should forget about obtaining relevant information from the opposing party's treating physicians, it just limits your options. Rather than call the physician over the telephone, you will instead have to use formal discovery methods, such as obtaining the doctor's medical records through a subpoena and possibly scheduling the doctor's oral deposition. Obtaining the medical records often gives you a pretty accurate idea of the thrust of the physicians' views regarding the patient's condition and will be useful not only in analyzing whether to depose the physician but also will be helpful to you in preparing to depose your opposing party. The particulars regarding these discovery devices and their strategic usages are taken up later in Chapters 6 through 8.

5. *Witness Interviews: Scheduling*

What efforts you must undertake to get a witness interview scheduled will depend to a large extent on what type of witness you are interviewing. There are willing witnesses, some of whom have favorable information for you and some unfavorable. There are also unwilling witnesses and while they may tend to have unfavorable information this is not necessarily true. With regard to the former–witnesses who have no problem with you interviewing them–the main issue will be to find a time convenient for the witness and you. You need to remember that they are not getting paid for their time 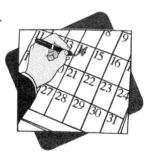 but that you are, in one form or another. What this means is that you need to make the scheduling of their interview as flexible as possible to accommodate their schedule. Depending upon the nature of the witness' job you may have to offer to meet the witness for lunch during the day, for coffee before or after work or sometime on the weekend. For your own sanity, we would recommend against the weekend unless it simply cannot be avoided. For example, call the witness and explain who you are, who you represent and the reason for your call–that you have a few questions on some background information pertaining to your client's case and you would like to meet them at a local café for a cup of coffee to discuss the matter in person. The witness may suggest just doing the interview over the telephone but normally you should resist this easy way out for two reasons: (1) in-person interviews tend to permit more in-depth questioning; (2) in-person interviews allow you to obtain better information, perhaps by showing photographs, having the witness make a drawing, or simply from the fact that you can make eye contact; and (3) the in-person interview allows you to visualize and then to evaluate the witness as a potential trial witness. You can assure the witness that you will be brief but that the questions will be brief and that this is an important matter to your client.

How do you go about convincing someone to meet with you for an interview when they are unwilling initially? Here the answer depends on the source of the witness' attitude. It may be that the witness identifies strongly with your opposing party and does not want to do anything to help your side. Even if this is true, it does not usually hurt to make an attempt to visit with such a person. You are going to have to deal with them anyway during the litigation, so you should begin early to develop strategies that allow you to approach those whom would rather not be approached. You want honesty and fairness. Everyone will usually promise to be honest and fair, even if they intend to be neither.

You can explain that you are just trying to understand what happened to help facilitate a quick resolution of the case and even promise that you will not try to get them to change their mind. If this still does not work, do not badger the individual but instead put them high on your deposition list–such a witness is likely to appear at trial for your opponent. Others may not be reluctant due to any strong affiliation with your opponent, but rather may simply be very busy, wary of any lawyers, or anxious about getting involved in a lawsuit and winding up sitting in a courthouse hallway for days during a possible trial. In these instances, your best approach to the witness when they express their initial hesitancy, is to advise them that the only alternative to a quick, informal chat is an extended, multiple-hour, on-the-record deposition with a court reporter and other counsel taking turns asking questions. You should try to avoid having this sound like an overt threat–in fact, it merely expresses the reality that before a case goes to trial one of the counsel is likely to want to discover the witness' knowledge regarding the occurrence. Between these techniques of explanation and willingness to schedule the interview at their convenience, counsel can enjoy much success in obtaining the witness interview.

6. *Witness Interviews: Techniques*

You are sitting down across a table from a potentially important fact witness. How should you begin the witness interview? What type of questioning technique should you employ? Let's consider some different circumstances and issues.

As a starting matter, it is generally a good idea to again explain who you are, who you represent and what is happening that necessitates an interview–that there is a lawsuit pending between your client and the opponent concerning a certain event or dispute. This is not only ethical but it helps to avoid a claim later on by the witness that you tricked them into saying something that was not true. Explain why you believe the witness might have

> **Beginning the Witness Interview:**
> * Introduce self, explain your role
> * Tell witness why you have contacted them
> * Let the witness know why you think they can "help"
> * Decide whether or not to explain your side of the case before interviewing
> * Choose your questioning techniques

knowledge concerning this event as this will encourage the witness to speak instead of claiming ignorance or feeling like they have nothing important to say. Most witnesses psychologically like the idea of being useful to one side or the other. Finally, before you begin your questions it is often useful to explain to the witness your side's perspective on the dispute. Offering your "spin" first can be a very useful way to influence how the witness recalls the event. People often have a desire to please others at a subconscious level. If the witness understands that your client believes the opposing party was driving "recklessly", was speeding, or was deceitful in a transaction, the witness' recollection will be more likely to be consistent with your client's perspective. This technique, of course, is not guaranteed to lead to only favorable testimony but it can frequently help shade the facts toward your client's position when those facts are in a gray area to begin with. This technique should also be distinguished from telling the witness what to say or trying to distort their testimony–practices that are questionable at best and not fruitful in the long run.

Once you are done with your preliminary statements, often the best technique is to begin with open-ended questions to elicit the witness' basic memory of the incident and then to follow up with more directed or even leading questions to seek clarification and to refine the witness' position clearly. The following dialogue shows an example of some of these techniques:

Scenario 1: Advocate representing victim

Attorney: Alright, now that I've told you a little bit about what is going on in my client's lawsuit, I'd like to see what information you have about the car accident. Can you tell me about it?

Witness: Well, it all happened very quickly. I was walking my dog when I heard tires squeal like a car was applying its brakes. Then I turned my head around toward that noise and when I looked I saw this red car go up over the curb and knock down your client–the kid–who was on his bicycle. I ran over to help and I could tell the boy was hurt, he was bleeding pretty bad and looked unconscious. So I called 911. The paramedics arrived about two minutes later. That's about it.

Attorney: That must have been awful for you to witness. My client is still in pretty bad shape too. Can you remember anything else that you saw?

Witness: Only the smoke from the car's tires. I guess the driver was really stomping on the brakes because there was smoke coming from the tires before he hit the boy.

Attorney: With all of that smoke, that car must've been going pretty fast huh?

Witness: Well, I didn't see it going until he had already hit the brakes but he did run over the curb pretty fast so I'm guessing he was moving pretty good.

Attorney: I've checked and the speed limit in that neighborhood is 25 m.p.h. Do you think the car was going faster than that from what you observed?

Witness: Oh definitely. He had to be going faster than that when he hit the curb even after applying his brakes.

Attorney: So you're telling me that you saw the red car speeding real fast–too fast for the neighborhood–going up over the curb, and hitting my client hard on his bicycle?

Witness: Yes, sir that's about right.

The foregoing was an example where the witness' testimony was favorable to the advocate's client. How might the interview look different if you were representing the car's driver rather than the injured boy but interviewing the same witness?

Scenario 2: Advocate representing tortfeasor

Attorney: Alright, now that I've told you a little bit about what is going on in the lawsuit against my client, I'd like to see what information you have about the car accident. Can you tell me about it?

Witness: Well, it all happened very quickly. I was walking my dog when I heard tires squeal like a car was applying its brakes. Then I turned my head around toward that noise and when I looked I saw this red car go up over the curb and knock down the kid who was on his bicycle. I ran over to help and I could tell the boy was hurt, he was bleeding pretty bad and looked unconscious. So I called 911. The paramedics arrived about two minutes later. That's about it.

Attorney: Well, obviously this was an unfortunate accident. Like you, my client is also very upset about the boy being hurt. I'm just trying to figure out exactly what you saw. Is it fair to say that you were not paying attention to my client driving his car until just about the moment the accident happened?

Witness: Yeah, I guess that's right.

Attorney: So you probably could only guess about my client's speed right? You don't really know that for sure do you?

Witness: No, I guess I don't know his speed, I just know he applied his brakes and then hit the boy.

Attorney: That's right and it is going to be important to not guess but simply to state your observations. That's all I'm ever going to ask you about. I mean you weren't in my client's car and you weren't monitoring his speed were you?

Witness: No I wasn't so I would have no way of knowing that information.

Attorney: What I'm hearing you say is that all you saw was my client applying his brakes pretty hard to do his best to avoid hitting that boy–but unfortunately this did not work. Does that pretty much sum up what you saw?

Witness: I think that's about right. I sure do feel sorry for that boy, just like your client.

In this second scenario, the advocate has likewise begun the interview by explaining the basics of the lawsuit and then asking an open-ended question. Unlike the first interview, by the boy's advocate, in this example the advocate is trying to remind the witness about the limits on what he actually observed and how those observations are consistent with the defendant trying to avoid the accident. Getting the witness to buy into this perspective may do much to help limit the witness' potentially damaging testimony at trial by corralling the witness into not wanting to venture a guess about things like the speed of the car. It's a scenario that calls for damage control. Unless the witness has also seen some misconduct by the victim, all the advocate can hope to do is to minimize the potential harm to the defendant from this eye witness testimony. In both scenarios above, however, the advocate upon hearing the open-ended answer immediately has to exercise judgment about whether this witness is likely to be helpful or harmful and then employ directed, leading questions to either get the witness to expound on their observations or to limit them and gain admissions about the witness' ignorance of disputed facts regarding the matter. The advocate has to be flexible enough in interviewing witnesses to go down either road without unnecessarily antagonizing and alienating the witness. The advocate never wants to give the witness additional motivation to cause harm through their ability to either recall or forget detailed observations. In both instances, the advocate also makes an attempt to empathize with the witness and to get the witness to see the advocate's client as a real person rather than the villain.

7. *Witness Interview: Objectives*

Advocates interview relevant witnesses for a variety of reasons. The types of questioning techniques you use is based in large part upon the reason for the interview. Before beginning to interview all of the relevant witnesses, you should stop for a moment and consider what your actual goals are. Advocates often interview witnesses in order to educate themselves about the facts that they believe are relevant to analyzing the client's case. When this is your primary objective then it is often a good idea to begin the interview with open-ended questions.

> **Three Basic Questioning Techniques:**
>
> **Headlines**
> - Basic Introductory Phrases
> - Transitional Phrases
> - Looping or Coupling Phrases
>
> **Open or Non-Leading Questions**
> - Wide Open Questions
> - Directive Open Questions
> - Probing or Testing Questions
> - Coupling Questions

If the advocate only shows up with certain narrow questions to ask, you risk missing out on other valuable information the witness might be prepared to offer. For this reason you should be prepared to linger with the witness for some length of time even if the witness' initial responses appear to be unhelpful. Remember that you can also use witness interviews to obtain information about other sources of evidence, even from uncooperative witnesses. The witness you are interviewing today might not be very helpful but they may know of another person who has much better knowledge of the facts, and perhaps a more reasonable attitude. If nothing else, your witness interviews should be designed to ask about other sources of proof–other witnesses, documents and tangible items of proof. Additionally, witness interviews can be useful for limiting or pinning down the particular witness for possible cross-examination at trial. If the witness is unfavorable you will want to spend time focusing upon all of the admissions you can obtain from that witness that demonstrate the lack of import of their observations. Many of the advocacy techniques that we will discuss in the chapter on depositions are applicable during witness interviews. As an advocate you must develop those interviewing skills just as you developed your trial and legal writing skills.

8.   *Witness Interviews: Recording or Documenting*

What record should the advocate make of the witness interview? At a minimum, the advocate will want to take some notes from the interview, including the advocate's impressions of the witness as a possible trial witness, and reduce these to some form of memorandum to put in the case file under the name of that witness. This need not be a grueling drafting exercise–dictating a short list of the top three points from the witness along with a conclusion as to the potential usefulness or harm from the witness' anticipated testimony should ordinarily suffice in a simple case. These mental impressions are generally shielded from discovery as the attorney's work product and can be very useful in updating the advocate's proof chart, in considering the need for possible deposition of the witness later on, and for preparation of either direct or cross-examination for the witness at trial. Thus, there is no good reason to fail to make such a memorandum

> **Federal Rule of Civil Procedure 26(b)(3) expressly states that:**
>
> Upon request, a person not a party may obtain without the required showing [of good cause] a statement concerning the action or its subject matter previously made by that person. If the request is refused, the person may move for a court order. . . . For purposes of this paragraph, a statement previously made is (A) a written statement signed or otherwise adopted or approved by the person making it, or (B) a stenographic, mechanical, electrical, or other recording, or a transcription thereof, which is a substantially verbatim recital of an oral statement made by the person making it and contemporaneously recorded.

of the interview.

The other major consideration is whether to create some kind of formal witness statement–either an audio or video recording of the interview or a written statement of the witness' knowledge displayed during the interview. Unlike the attorney's work product memorandum, these kind of recordings can be obtained by the witness upon request from the advocate and given to whomever the witness wants to share it with. Once the recording or transcription of the witness' statement is given to the witness, the rules give the witness absolute freedom to share this with anyone, including your adversary. Thus, the downside to these recordings is that they are, in this sense, discoverable by the adversary potentially. They should be undertaken with the assumption that your opponent will see this witness statement during the litigation.

If there is nothing good in the statement, or at least nothing you can use to impeach or limit the harm from the statement, there is little to be gained from recording it for the benefit of your opponent. On the other hand, if the witness has told you anything helpful, having the interview either recorded or summarized (and having the witness adopt it by signature) can help you to lock in that favorable testimony such that you can count on it at trial. If you are not sure which way the interview might go, you can also just do the interview first. If you decide you would like to lock in the statements, go ahead and prepare a summary and transmit it to the witness to adopt by signature (including any changes the witness desires). If you go this route, one helpful technique can be to insert at the very

---

Statement of Peter Parker

At 10:00 a.m. on September 1, 2007, I was walking my dog on the sidewalk along Elm Street in Grovedale, Ill. I heard a loud sound of a car applying its brakes and turned toward that sound. As I looked I saw a lot of smoke coming from the tires of a red Ford Mustang as it jumped over a curb. The car continued toward the sidewalk and struck a small boy riding his bicycle.

I ran over to immediately assist the boy. He was unconscious and was bleeding severely. I called 911. I later found out his name was Tyler Stewart, the plaintiff in this matter.

I also spoke to the driver of the Ford Mustang at the scene while awaiting the ambulance. He told me his name was John Gabriel, the defendant in this case. As I spoke with him, I detected the scent of alcohol on his breath. He told me that he "sure was sorry" for hitting the boy. Then he got in his car and drove off.

I have carefully read this statement and it is true and complete.

Signed this ___ day of September, 2007.

_____
Peter Parker

beginning a very obvious mistake for the witness to correct in their own handwriting. This correction, coupled with the witness' signature, will be useful later on to establish that the witness carefully reviewed it for accuracy–in case the witness tries to change their testimony.

D. *JOINDER OF CLAIMS AND PARTIES*

An integral part of an advocate's civil case analysis and case planning is the issue of joinder–which claims should be joined together and who should be made parties to the anticipated lawsuit? These issues of joinder have legal components, strategic considerations and practical ramifications and require careful thought by the advocate. These concerns permeate the advocate's initial case analysis and planning, the drafting of the pleadings to be filed with the court and, ultimately, her preparation for trial. We will begin that discussion here with an overview of some applicable legal principles and considerations. We will also take up some related issues again in the next chapter on Pleadings and Attacks on Pleadings.

1. Joinder of Claims

Rule 18 is the primary rule of civil procedure governing the joinder of claims by a litigant. It is a permissive rule in that it does not require the joinder of any claims with leaves that choice up to the advocate and her client. Rule 18 can be stated in fairly succinct fashion: "A party asserting a claim to relief . . . may join . . . as many claims . . . as the party has against an opposing party." What this means is that, from a purely *procedural* perspective, if your client John has a negligence claim against Sarah, in filing your negligence lawsuit you can also include a battery claim against Sarah or even a completely unrelated breach of contract claim arising out of a different event than the negligence claim. The civil procedure rules permit such joinder because of reasons of efficiency and finality–if you are going to war against a particular litigant, you should face no procedural barriers to bringing all potential grievances at your disposal against that opponent and settling all quarrels in one proceeding. If rule 18 were otherwise, John might have to file piecemeal lawsuits against Sarah before having complete resolution of their differences. Rule 18 on its face seems quite broad in two respects: (1) it seems to endorse the joinder of any and all claims no matter how unrelated; and (2) it seems to never require the joinder of any claims no matter how related. These propositions are true looking exclusively at this procedural rule; however, other considerations modify these broad conclusions. These modifications are important to understand in order to avoid being mislead by the simple language of rule 18.

The first check on this seemingly broad permission to join unrelated claims against a litigant comes at the jurisdictional level–just because a court may have territorial power (personal jurisdiction) against Sarah or the jurisdictional power to hear one type of claim (subject matter jurisdiction) against Sarah, this does not necessarily mean that the additional claim can survive either jurisdictional scrutiny. These jurisdictional matters are discussed separately below. For purposes of our consideration of rule 18, we are only speaking of permission to join claims under the rules of civil procedure.

The other check on rule 18's failure to compel joinder of all related claims is the judge-created doctrine of *res judicata* or claim preclusion. The claim preclusion doctrine essentially holds that when a litigant's claim has been finally adjudicated, that litigant's other related claims against the same party are considered to have been merged into the original claim and their relitigation is barred. There are other nuances on this doctrine but the above fairly summarizes its basic operation. What this means is that when John sues Sarah for negligence, once a final judgment has been entered in that suit–whether by motion, trial, or settlement–John may not sue Sarah for battery if that claim is considered to have arisen out of the same transaction or occurrence as the negligence claim. This "one bite at the apple" doctrine promotes finality because Sarah should not have to suffer multiple lawsuits from John arising out of the same incident before she can have peace of mind. The practical ramification for a claimant is that, while rule 18 does not require John to assert a battery claim along with the original negligence cause of action, the claim preclusion doctrine says that if he fails to join the two claims, he will be precluded from attempting to take that second bite of the judicial apple in a subsequent lawsuit.

From a strategic perspective, what are the advantages and disadvantages to filing multiple claims instead of just one? The advantages seem fairly straightforward. One of these is that if one of the claims fails another might still succeed, so adding as many claims as possible to your lawsuit increases your chances of prevailing on something. Just because either the law, facts or moral theme surrounding one cause of action do not seem to apply very well does not mean that the defendant's same conduct must also suffer the same fate under a different legal theory. The substantive law provides for different causes of action because either judges or legislators believed that certain circumstances justified a recovery. Many different causes of action have been recognized, each having their own separate elements, legal application and even remedies. Another advantage to combining different claims against the same party is to overwhelm the defendant into submission. It can be daunting to be sued on multiple claims and it can make the effort to extricate oneself from a lawsuit seem more difficult. If a court is hesitant to dismiss as a matter of law any claim, will not the court be even more reluctant to dismiss many claims? Perhaps. Asserting multiple claims also increases the litigation expenses for the defendant, all other things being equal, because doing so causes the defense advocate to spend more time engaged in legal research and obtaining discovery to try to defeat those theories. Finally, because the limits of discovery are tied to the pleadings, the broader the allegations and the greater the claims, the more discovery becomes available to the plaintiff. It can also increase the chance that a jury at trial might find some legal theory persuasive in a particular factual context.

Given these advantages and the *res judicata* risk of not asserting all possible claims, what would be the reason to refrain from stacking multiple claims together against your adversary in a lawsuit? Actually there are several. We will discuss three primary potential disadvantages here. First, surrounding one good claim with many weaker claims does not enhance the quality of the lawsuit or create any leverage for settlement. In fact, it has the opposite effect. If your client's circumstance

> **Potential Disadvantages of Multiple Claims:**
> - Weak claims hurt strong claims
> - Focus is sacrificed by multiple claims
> - Costs of litigation increase for both sides

gives rise to only one relatively strong claim, then focus on that claim and do not bother with other weaker claims. There are three primary audiences for your assertion of claims—opposing party and counsel, the judge and (someday) the jury. Each audience will be unimpressed by your lawsuit if you disguise your one meritorious claim with claims of questionable value. Your opposition will be less inclined to pay you top dollar to settle, the judge may be more inclined to dismiss the entire lawsuit if there are too many unsound claims attached, and a jury might just conclude at trial that your efforts to stretch signify a frivolous lawsuit. Second, the more claims the advocate asserts the easier it is for the advocate to lose focus and begin diverting her attention to the non-essential claims. The advocate working on a contingency fee can end up spending much time and other resources thinking about and pursuing claims that may not really add any value to the litigation. Third, just as asserting more claims increases the cost of defense for the defendant, this practice can easily increase the cost for the plaintiff or plaintiff's counsel (depending upon the nature of the fee arrangement). It may not cost much to dictate an additional count when drafting your complaint, but each new count may cause the advocate to respond to a motion for summary judgment or other motion attacking the claim's merit, will almost certainly increase the scope of discovery and may make formal discovery tools more expensive in their application. A plaintiff's deposition, for example, in a case with one count tends to be shorter than a plaintiff's deposition in a case asserting six counts.

Since there are both advantages and disadvantages to stacking multiple claims together, one approach will never fit all circumstances - there is no one right approach. The advocate should consider all of these factors when deciding in the context of her specific case which approach is better for her client and worse for the opposing party. Finally, due to the fact that complaints can be amended, as we will discuss in the next chapter, counsel is not stuck with the original conclusion as a vehicle exists to add or delete claims after the original case filing.

The only other rules of great general significance concerning the joinder of claims are those that govern the filing of counterclaims, cross-claims and third-party claims. As these are options for a defendant to consider asserting in response to a complaint, we will wait to discuss these particular joinder rules in the next chapter.

2. *Joinder of Parties*

A Seemingly more complicated task than the issue of joining claims is determining who should be made a party to a lawsuit. The difficulty is multi-faceted. First of all, adding another party increases your adversaries and takes the significance of your case filing to a qualitatively higher level than does merely adding another claim against the same opponent. Second, the decision whether to join another party opponent is fraught with greater practical significance because the addition of the other party can change the dynamics of the litigation in a way that makes the job of the claimant's advocate either easier or more difficult. The additional defendant you have chosen to add to your planned lawsuit, for example, may either attack the primary defendant and assist you in prevailing or may join forces with the other defendant and take a particularly aggressive stance toward your client resulting in a greater burden prosecuting the claims. Anticipating the impact on the practical dynamics of the litigation is difficult and important. Third, the law concerning the joinder of parties is more complex than the straightforward approach of rule 18 governing claim joinder. Finally, the stakes on the party joinder question can be greater because of a greater potential urgency to name all of the potentially responsible parties at the outset due to the possible running of the statute of limitations. This concept will be discussed more in the next chapter when we consider amendments to pleadings. But for now you should at least appreciate the fact that amending your complaint to join another defendant a year after filing the initial case does not mean that such claim will be considered timely. These various factors can make the initial choice of the parties more daunting for the advocate.

Let us consider the primary rule governing the joinder of parties under the Federal Rules of Civil Procedure. Rule 20 is the governing rule for most instances of joining additional parties. Even though the rule speaks in terms of "joining" it is the applicable rule whether the joinder takes place at the outset by joining multiple parties in the original complaint or when the joinder takes place thereafter by the filing of an amended complaint. In operation, rule 20 permits a claimant to join as an additional defendant anyone when the plaintiff's claim against that party (i) arises out of the "same transaction or occurrence" as the plaintiff's claim against the other defendant and (ii) involves at least one common question of law or fact as the claim against the other defendant. In other words, joinder of multiple defendants is permitted when the plaintiff's claims against those defendants are sufficiently related so that the joinder promotes efficiency without causing the unfairness that might result from forcing a litigant to be involved in a lawsuit with unrelated claims involving other parties. These twin concerns–efficiency and fairness–are the impetus behind rule 20's two-part test for joinder. Joining a co-plaintiff invites the exact same scrutiny under rule 20–the analysis asks whether the co-plaintiff's claim arises out of the "same transaction or occurrence" as the main plaintiff's claim and whether it involves any common question of law or fact? In either scenario, whether adding an additional defendant or co-plaintiff, both tests of rule 20 must be satisfied or else the claims must be severed and proceed separately as two cases.

A simple example should help you visualize rule 20 in operation. Imagine that your client, Jack, is hurt in an automobile accident suffering some personal injuries. At the time of your initial visit with Jack he is accompanied by his wife, Jill. As a result of your careful interview, you discover that Jack's injuries have compromised the quality of their marital relationship as Jack can no longer perform many of the functions he traditionally carried out and can no longer offer the same emotional and sexual support for Jill. When you file Jack's claim against the other motorist, can you join to that claim the loss of consortium claim possessed by Jill under rule 20? With regard to the fairness concern of the rule–do the claims of the two different parties arise out of the same transaction or occurrence–courts would find this satisfied using one of two possible tests for applying this standard. Some courts focus on the degree of evidentiary overlap between the claims of Jack and Jill while other courts consider the degree of logical relationship between the two claimants. In this case, you would expect most of the same witnesses to testify if the two claimants' claims were brought separately. In both cases, you would need to offer proof of (i) fault for the underlying accident, (ii) the physical consequences to Jack from the accident, and (iii) the impact of Jack's injuries on the marriage relationship of Jack and Jill. Thus, Jack and Jill's claims arise out of the same transaction or occurrence because the evidence proving or negating the two claims is very similar. You would also conclude that the two claimants' claims are logically related. Indeed, Jill's claims is actually derivative of Jack's–if Jack cannot prevail on liability against the motorist neither can Jill.

The second part of rule 20's test is also easily satisfied in this hypothetical lawsuit. Part two asks whether there are any questions of law or fact shared in common between Jack and Jill's respective claims. Whether or not the other motorist was at fault is one common question of fact. But other common questions exist–were Jack's injuries severe enough to impact on the

> Rule 20 joinder analysis requires the advocate to consider two underlying concerns: (i) does the joinder promote efficiency? and (ii) is the joinder fair to the defendant(s)?

marital relationship between Jack and Jill? There might be common legal questions too–for example, can the other motorist's failure to have a valid driver's license give rise to a negligence per se conclusion? Or does the jurisdiction's limit on punitive damages apply to this case? All it takes is one of these kind of questions to exit between the claims of Jack and Jill in order to satisfy the efficiency concern of rule 20. If the claims belonging to Jack and Jill satisfy this two-part inquiry, joinder of the claims under rule 20 is proper and you may file suit on behalf of them together.

Some observations are in order concerning rule 20. First, like rule 18 this is a rule of permissive joinder rather than one requiring a claimant to join additional parties. No matter how fair and efficient it might be for you to add Jill's claims to those of Jack in the same lawsuit, rule 20 does not require you to bring them together. Because rules 18 and 20 are the two joinder juggernauts of the civil procedure rules, it is fair to say that the rules recognize and promote the inherent value in party autonomy to decide who to sue and what claims to bring. There are some exceptions to this principle of party autonomy, both as to the joinder of claims and parties, but they are few. Further, so long as Jack and Jill are in fact separate parties with their own claims, there is no principle of res judicata or claim preclusion that practically compels their joinder in the same suit. Additionally, there is little downside to an advocate attempting to join parties even where rule 20 is not so easily satisfied. Rule 21 specifies that the consequence of "misjoinder"–filing a pleading joining together party plaintiffs or defendants that do not satisfy rule 20–is not dismissal but rather severance of the claims involving the misjoined party into a separate lawsuit. Finally, it should be noted that rule 20 only addresses the *procedural* propriety of joining multiple parties. Just because the rules of civil procedure allow such joinder does not mean that the court has the jurisdictional power–subject matter jurisdiction–to entertain all of the claims. This will be a separate consideration taken up below.

Even if rule 20 procedurally blesses your decision to join multiple plaintiffs or to sue multiple defendants in the same lawsuit, the careful advocate needs to consider the joinder issue from a strategic perspective. What are the practical implications of joinder and how will this impact upon the advocate's ability to prevail in the lawsuit? In terms of joining multiple claimants the primary advantages of joinder are to provide relief in the same lawsuit for multiple clients in as efficient manner as possible. Why try to establish liability against the other motorist in two separate proceedings? If the advocate is getting paid on a contingent fee basis, the greater the total recovery the greater the attorney's fees. Another reason to join multiple claimants might be to bolster the merits of the claims. For example, in a case of employment discrimination where the defendant is accused of failing to promote employees due to their race, would it play better to a jury to have one minority claimant who was denied advancement or to have five such claimants joining together complaining of similar treatment?[16] Under the assumption that "where there is smoke there is fire", the advocate can appeal to juror's assumptions that there is more likely to be race-based discrimination when they are seeing as claimants in the same case similarly situated employees treated unfairly by the defendant employer. Further, if there is one claimant with a particularly strong evidentiary basis–perhaps a memorandum in that employee's file mentioning his race as a basis for his treatment–this will likely make the proof of mistreatment against the other employees easier. So for both reasons of litigant and advocate efficiency and increasing the likelihood of success, there can be strong practical and strategic rationales in support of the advocate's use of rule 20's relatively easy requirements for joinder.

Similarly, in the case of joining multiple defendants to a lawsuit, the greater the number of defendants sued, the greater the chance of prevailing against at least one potential wrongdoer. Likewise, by suing more defendants the advocate is more likely to achieve full recovery by increasing the total assets of the defendants to recover against in the event of obtaining a favorable judgment. If one defendant does not have enough to pay the entire judgment, one of the other defendants joined under rule 20 might be able to make up the deficiency.

Even aside from issues of obtaining a judgment against a particular additional defendant, another consideration for joinder may be how this may impact the advocate's ability to utilize formal discovery tools or to obtain useful

---

[16]A frequently cited example of this type of multiple-claimant joinder in an employment discrimination context is *Mosley v. General Motors Corp.*, 497 F.2d 1330 (8th Cir. 1974).

testimony from a party joined. As we will discuss later in the Chapter on formal discovery, some formal discovery tools can only be used to compel disclosure of information from a party to the lawsuit rather than a mere witness. Also, there are instances where a plaintiff's counsel joins a potential joint tortfeasor, who many not have the resources to pay a judgment, in order to give that litigant incentive to provide deposition testimony blaming another target defendant. After the damaging testimony is given, the plaintiff's counsel might well consider dropping that party from the lawsuit. One final major reason to consider joinder is in order to help to fix the location or the type of court that where the lawsuit will be heard. This will be discussed more in the next section. These practical considerations must be evaluated by the advocate.

Are there some negative consequences to consider in exercising rule 20 joinder? The answer, of course, depends on the situation faced but certainly there are some reasons not to join a party even though the rules might permit it. Obviously if the joined claimant's claim is very weak it might serve to cast a cloud over the stronger claims of the other plaintiff(s). Or if you are considering joining as an additional defendant a party against whom your client has very little chance of succeeding against, you risk making your client's entire case look weaker and spending precious time and other resources pursuing this weak claim. You might also risk alienating someone for whom your client might have some possible future interest in keeping as an ally rather than an adversary. The one other important reason to consider not joining an additional party is if the joinder of that party might hurt your ability to pick a particular court as the chosen forum for your lawsuit by changing the venue or subject matter jurisdiction analysis in your case.

When in doubt, the logical decision at the outset is often to go ahead and name as many parties as possible to the lawsuit, assuming a valid evidentiary and legal basis for doing so.[17] This is because it is easier to join a party defendant at the outset than later on for two reasons: (1) joining the additional claimants or defendants today helps to avoid possible statute of limitations concerns tomorrow; and (2) it is easy to join a party to your initial pleading than it is to wait and seek permission to join them at a later date by court-authorized amendment to your pleadings under rule 15. The statute of limitations concern is fairly self-evident in that the sooner the claim against a defendant is brought the less chance there is for that claim to be legally stale. With regard to the issue of joinder through amendment, you must consider the possibility that you will be disrupting a lawsuit after discovery has been ongoing. This is because the newly joined defendant has will have the right to take depositions that may have previously been taken by the

---

[17]We will talk about the ethical limitations on this practice in the next chapter.

other parties and to engage in their own initiated formal discovery. These rights, obtained by the new party upon being joined to the lawsuit, will either be a good ground for the original opponent to oppose joinder or, even if the amendment is permitted, adding the new defendant after significant discovery has already been completed will drive up the time and costs of plaintiff pursuing the lawsuit. It will also almost always result in a delay in getting the case ready for trial or settlement discussions. These potential problems with joining a party later in the life of a lawsuit are practical reasons to join the additional parties in your initial pleading.

On the brink of filing a lawsuit, there are a few other joinder rules that the advocate should at least bear in mind as the new lawsuit is planned. The first of these is found in rule 17's requirements that (a) the "real party in interest" be the one named in the pleading and (b) the requirement that only parties having the"legal capacity" to sue or be sued should be made parties to a lawsuit. The real party in interest requirement is designed to prevent a lawsuit from being pursued by or against someone who does not have the authentic interest in the dispute. This provision, however, expressly permits those having a proper representative capacity to pursue litigation on behalf of others. Such representatives include court-appointed guardians, executors, administrators and trustees. With regard to the issue of capacity, this is most likely to be a problem with regard to a business entity that has not followed a state's corporate formalities for formation or continued existence (e.g., through non-payment of certain fees and taxes). This suggests that if your client is sued by such a questionable legal entity, it might be worthwhile to check the applicable state's corporate records to determine the current legal status of the opposing party. If the defunct corporate entity is a target defendant, the advocate should consider the possibility of suing the principals of that entity directly who may no longer be protected by the corporate shield from individual liability.

In addition, another joinder provision that should at least be considered by the advocate is the compulsory joinder provision of rule 19. Unlike rule 20, rule 19 requires the joinder of a "necessary" party and, further, declares that if such a party is not only "necessary" but "indispensable" and cannot be joined due to reasons of venue or personal jurisdiction restrictions, the entire lawsuit should be dismissed rather than proceed in their absence. The implicit idea in that latter situation seems to be that justice dispensed in the absence of the indispensable party is so flawed that it is better for the court to withhold its adjudicatory hand altogether. So the first consideration of rule 19 when planning a lawsuit is whether there are any potential parties plaintiff or defendant who might be considered necessary. When rule 19 applies, the necessary party must be added as either a plaintiff or defendant regardless of the fact that none of the existing parties may actually desire their joinder and the missing party may not desire to be joined.

Check-List for Joinder:

☐ Are there other similarly aggrieved clients or possible clients who might want to join in filing the lawsuit? (Rule 20 plaintiff joinder)

☐ Can you think of any other potentially responsible parties who may have contributed to causing your client's harm? (Rule 20 defendant joinder)

☐ Can you think of any other valid claims, whether related or not, to add to the claims already being contemplated against the target defendants? (Rule 18 joinder of claims)

☐ Are there any additional potential plaintiffs or defendants whose presence might be so important to be considered essential to the lawsuit? (Rule 19 compulsory joinder)

☐ Has the target defendant acted in such a way as to similarly injure so many others, like your client, that their individual joinder might be practically impossible? (Rule 23 class action joinder)

☐ Do the parties named have capacity to sue and be sued?

Because Rule 19 represents a departure from the valued principle of party autonomy discussed above, courts apply rule 19's express provisions rather narrowly. In fact, it is common for law students studying rule 19 for the first time to see rule 19 application where it does not really exist. For example, one might consider the situation of multiple joint tortfeasors. Some litigants have tried to argue that a plaintiff is required to join all potential tortfeasors under rule 19 because not joining them might prejudice those tortfeasors who are named. For example, you might imagine that when Jack is hit by the other motorist, there might also be potential blame placed on the local municipality that recently repaired a traffic signal that malfunctioned at the time of the accident. If Jack chooses to only sue the other motorist, can that defendant point to the city and argue for their compulsory joinder under Rule 19? Courts have uniformly rejected this argument–effectively exorcizing such potential phantom application of the rule–holding instead that joint tortfeasors are *appropriate* for voluntary joinder under rule 20 but are not necessary parties required to be joined under rule 19.[18] If a joint tortfeasor is not considered necessary, when might a missing litigant receive this characterization?

Rule 19's language describing "persons to be joined if feasible" offers many words but little clear guidance. Rule 19(a) provides for the compulsory joinder of a person if:

> (1) in the person's absence complete relief cannot be accorded among those already parties, or (2) the person claims an interest relating to the subject of the action and is so situated that the disposition of the action in the person's absence may (i) as a practical matter impair or impede the person's ability to protect that interest or (ii) leave any of the persons already parties subject to a substantial risk of incurring double, multiple, or otherwise inconsistent obligations by reason of the claimed interest.[19]

While an in-depth analysis of this language is beyond the intended scope of this text, for our purposes it should be sufficient to describe the most usual scenarios where a rule 19 necessary party has been identified. These situations primarily consist of the following situations:

- Claims where a limited fund is available to satisfy the competing claims of others–the idea behind rule 19 status is that other claimants who do not sue quickly enough are frozen out of any recovery. What constitutes a true limited fund is an issue subject to much case law discussion and analysis.

- Claims involving disputes as to the ownership of property where some of those claiming an interest are not joined–the idea behind rule 19 status here is that the only way to fairly and effectively quiet disputes as to title is to get all of the competing interests before the court.

---

[18] In *Temple v. Synthes Corp.*, 498 U.S. 5 (1990), the United States Supreme Court rejected a defendant medical device manufacturer's argument that the plaintiff was required to join the surgeon who implanted the device as a necessary party because of his status as a potential joint tortfeasor. Neither this holding nor any other provisions of Rule 19 or 20, however, preclude a defendant from considering the joinder of the missing joint tortfeasors directly through the filing of a third-party complaint pursuant to Rule 14. Rule 14 is discussed in the next chapter as part of a defendant's options in responding to a lawsuit.

[19] Fed. R. Civ. P. 19(a).

- Claims involving contractual disputes among joint obligees or obligors–the idea behind Rule 19 status in this situation is that complete and effective relief might not be possible without the joinder of all such parties.

If a missing potential party is considered to be necessary under Rule 19(a), the court should order that party's joinder. Of course, in these scenarios there is more often than not sufficient litigant interest to join the missing party so that a motion is unnecessary. Where Rule 19 gets really interesting, though, is when that missing party cannot be joined because of venue or personal jurisdiction limitations. In this scenario, Rule 19(b) advises the court to consider whether or not to simply dismiss the entire case due to the impossibility of joining the indispensable party. This Rule 19(b) determination hints at the real utility of Rule 19–this provision enables a litigant to seek dismissal of the entire lawsuit on a true technicality regardless of the underlying merits of the existing claims between the present parties. If you are representing a defendant and you can identify someone beyond the jurisdictional powers of the forum court whose presence is sufficiently important, you now have at your disposal a tool for having the case dismissed. Such dismissal will not preclude the re-filing of the lawsuit elsewhere, but it can be a powerful weapon to force the plaintiff to file the lawsuit in a different forum perceived to be more hospitable to the defendant. This is the scenario where real advocates are most interested in rule 19's application.

The truly upwardly mobile plaintiff's counsel interested in "super-sizing" her lawsuit should remember the most dramatic joinder rule of all–rule 23 class actions. Entire courses–entitled "Complex Litigation"–in law school are devoted to an in-depth study of this one joinder rule. Rule 23 contemplates representative litigation brought by a named party, the class representative, on behalf of similarly situated absent class members against a wrongdoer. Rule 23 is an example of incredible efficiency as it permits the adjudication of the claims of many hundreds, thousands or even millions of claimants without them even being made a party to the lawsuit. Because of the potential unfairness of adjudicating someone's claim in their absence, rule 23 class actions have fairly strict prerequisites and other built-in devices designed to protect absent class members' interests. As a prerequisite for any class action, the proponent must demonstrate a well-defined class that has so many members in it to preclude, as a practical matter, the possibility of joining all members using rule 20. In addition, the class representative must demonstrate that, for purposes of efficiency, there are questions of law or fact shared in common by the class, and that the class representative's claims are similar to, or "typical" of, the absent members and that the representative, and their advocate, are likely to be "adequate" representatives to bring the claims. These last two features of the rule are designed to demonstrate some baseline of fairness before further consideration of a class action will be undertaken by the court. Once these prerequisites are met, in order to achieve class "certification"–a court order declaring the class to be officially represented–the representative must also show that the case involves one of the few scenarios described in Rule 23(b). These scenarios can be described as follows:

- when the defendant has acted similarly toward the entire class such that injunctive or declarative relief is requested and might be appropriate;

- when there is a limited fund held by the defendant and there are so many competing claims against it that many class members will be deprived of a meaningful remedy otherwise;

- when the threat of multiple lawsuits against the defendant might subject the defendant to the risk of inconsistent or varying adjudications; or

- when damages are sought on behalf of a class whose claims are so similar that the common questions of law and fact "predominate" over individual issues and the class action device is found to be "superior" to other more traditional forms of litigation.

Class action procedures are so complex that inexperienced counsel should proceed cautiously before filing such a proposed case. Further, the court at the time of certifying a class action is empowered by the rules of civil procedure to appoint class counsel–who may be someone other than the original lawyer who filed the case–and is expressly authorized to consider counsel's "experience in handling class actions." For any new advocate, the best advice would be to consider associating with other more experienced counsel if a class action were deemed to be an appropriate way to conduct the litigation. When a case proceeds as a class action, there is tremendous upside for the advocate and the client because a defendant facing a class action has enormous incentive to attempt settlement rather than face a "bet the company" trial. Even a seemingly trivial claim of $2.50 for overcharges to a consumer can take on monolithic proportions when converted into a class action on behalf of tens of millions of such consumers. Further, attorney's fees in class actions are frequently approved by courts in enormous sums based upon the relief obtained by the class counsel. At this point in your career, you should just be on the lookout for such a case and prepared to spot an opportunity to do justice on a large scale.

E. FORUM SELECTION

In addition to analyzing *who* should be made parties to the lawsuit and *what* claims should be asserted, the advocate should analyze thoughtfully the issue of *where* the claims should be asserted. A layperson probably assumes that if they have a lawsuit to file, they should simply go to the nearest courthouse to do so. This is not only incorrect as a legal proposition but may prove

> *"Every trial lawyer . . . would agree that [where] the case is to be tried is, without question one of the most significant factors, perhaps the most significant factor, in the outcome of the case."*
>
> Prof. Louis Muldrow (testimony before Texas legislature during hearings on possible venue reform)

unwise as a strategic proposition. Anyone who has ever been a child (most of us?) recognizes that the identity of the one who will resolve a dispute–mom versus dad–can be critical to the outcome of a particular controversy. The same is even more true of lawsuits. The identity of the judge, the make-up of the jury, and other geographic, demographic, and legal issues highlight the importance of picking the best forum for your lawsuit. This inquiry has two primary components–horizontal considerations (personal jurisdiction and venue) and vertical considerations (subject matter jurisdiction).

At each choice the advocate should analyze the issue from both the strategic and the legal perspective. Consider, by way of simple example, that a new client of yours located inOhio has a potential claim against an adversary located in New York. You should be asking yourself, at a minimum, (a) whether you should file the lawsuit in Ohio or New York (horizontal issue) and, (b) whether it would be better to file in state court or federal court in either of those states (vertical issue). Which would be a better choice (the strategy)? Do you actually have all of these choices available (the law)?

1. Horizontal Inquiry

Horizontal inquiry refers to the attempt by the advocate to determine where in the United States a lawsuit may be filed in accordance with the U.S. Constitution, long-arm statutes and venue restrictions. We will address each of these briefly, but first we should pause to consider the significance of this forum choice. Just because your law office is located in Orlando, Florida and your new client retains you in this fair city does not mean that your new lawsuit for that client must or should be filed in Orlando. Is that the best place for the lawsuit? Consideration of this issue normally involves asking yourself three questions: (1) where would be the most convenient place for you and your client to pursue the litigation? (2) where would be the worst location for your opponent to face litigation and a possible trial? and (3) what is the outlook for the possible judge and jury in each forum under consideration? Perhaps Orlando will be the preferred destination for your new lawsuit, but perhaps not. Where does your client reside? What is the nature of the lawsuit? Where did the claims arise? Who are the target defendants and where are they located? Where are the most favorable witnesses located? What will the local citizens think of your client's claims? Do you know any of the local judges and their styles, preferences, attitudes and judicial philosophies? It may be that you live in a part of the state where there is only one local district judge so you know for certain the identity of your judge if you file the suit there. If you live in a larger area where there are multiple judges, and a random method is utilized for selecting the judge on any new case

> **The horizontal analysis of forum selection considers:**
>
> - personal jurisdiction by the court over the defendant
> - the applicable state's long-arm statute
> - venue statutes

filing, you will have less certainty regarding the traits of your anticipated judge if you file locally. These are all very important considerations as you engage in case planning and preparation for filing the new lawsuit.

But significant limitations exist on where a lawsuit can be filed. At the outermost reaches of the inquiry lies the due process clause of the U.S. Constitution which limits the territorial power or reach of courts over litigants dragged into their courtrooms. The classic case of *Pennoyer v. Neff*[20] is likely where you began your law school study of the doctrine of personal jurisdiction but the law has changed enormously since that opinion was issued. It would be difficult to provide an exhaustive survey of more than a hundred years of Supreme Court case analysis to furnish an accurate historic survey of personal jurisdiction. Fortunately, you don't need this kind of information to analyze your possible forum choices in most cases. We can break down this discussion into two parts–general jurisdiction and specific jurisdiction.

2. *General Jurisdiction*

General jurisdiction is the concept that, in certain situations, a court can exercise jurisdictional power over a litigant regardless of the connections–or lack thereof–between the forum and the facts giving rise to the lawsuit. General jurisdiction typically exists in four different situations. As you consider the possible places to file your new lawsuit, you should determine what states are feasible fora based upon the defendant's home, tag jurisdiction, the doctrine of waiver, and maximum contacts.

Practical Considerations of Where to File Include:

- Where would be the most convenient place for you and your client to pursue the litigation?

- Where would be the worst location for your opponent to face litigation and a possible trial?

- What is the outlook for the possible judge and jury in each forum under consideration?

a. Defendant's Home

Courts consistently hold that you can always sue a defendant in its home court without offending the "traditional notions of fair play and substantial justice" dictated by the due process clause. When the defendant is a person, home means the state where the defendant is *domiciled* at the time of the lawsuit. Domicile is not necessarily the same thing as "residence" but rather requires both physical presence and the intention to remain there indefinitely in order to create a domicile

---

[20]95 U.S. 714 (1877).

in a state. Once created, the domicile remains unchanged until those two conditions are established elsewhere. When your defendant is a corporation, home refers to both its state of incorporation and its principal place of business. General Motors, for example, can never lodge a due process objection to being sued in Michigan regardless of how unrelated the case is to any events that transpired there. While a litigant might not generally think that suing the defendant on its home turf makes the most sense, other considerations outlined above may outweigh this initial assumption in certain cases.

b. Tag

When the defendant is a person, and not an artificial entity such as a corporation, the Supreme Court has recognized "tag" jurisdiction as appropriate to give a court personal jurisdiction. Tag refers to serving the defendant personally with a copy of the summons while the defendant is located within the borders of the forum state. Even if the defendant is only in the forum state on vacation, say in Florida at the beach, if the plaintiff's counsel arranges for service on that defendant while he is present in that state, there can be no due process challenges to any court in that state exercising jurisdiction over the defendant. In other words, the defendant's presence at the time of service, even in a very transient sense, qualifies to confer general jurisdiction. This may seem arbitrary and absurd, but the Supreme Court has embraced this conclusion and shows no sign of retreat: "Among the most firmly established principles of personal jurisdiction in American tradition is that the courts of a State have jurisdiction over nonresidents who are physically present in the State." The only recognized exceptions seem to be where the plaintiff engaged in some fraud or unlawful duress to secure the defendant's presence within the state to obtain service. So you may not kidnap your defendant, drive him to the forum state, and then serve him with process. Actually you *can* do this but it will not suffice to provide the local courts with personal jurisdiction and you will likely be prosecuted for a crime.

c. Waiver

Because the Supreme Court has held that personal jurisdiction is more about the defendant's personal rights than the courts' power, personal jurisdiction is something that may both be waived after the filing of the lawsuit or consented to in advance of the lawsuit. Waiver usually occurs when a defendant makes an appearance in court, either in person or through a filing in the clerk's office, without initially asserting an objection to a lack of personal jurisdiction. When the defendant does assert this initial objection they are said to have made a "special" appearance. But filing a pleading without such an objection, or appearing in court without initially making such objection, constitutes a "general" appearance and waives any personal jurisdiction issues. A different form of waiver recognized as valid can be where a court strikes a defendant's special appearance as a discovery sanction for failure to abide by a court's lawful discovery order.[21] At the other end of the spectrum, courts will enforce contractual provisions that are "fundamentally fair" where a potential litigant agrees or "consents" to being sued in a particular state or forum for some future lawsuit. Fundamental fairness seems to include actual notice of the consent provision and no evidence of fraud or bad faith in picking the choice of forum. This waiver in advance permits someone transacting business with another to provide a measure of predictability for where a possible lawsuit may be filed. By the same token, litigants can not only provide for consent to jurisdiction in particular courts but can also go further and require that any contemplated litigation be filed in a particular locale.[22] You need to know if the contemplated parties to your lawsuit have signed any such consent to jurisdiction.

d. Maximum Contacts

In the next section, under "specific jurisdiction," we will remind you of *International Shoe* and the "minimum contacts" analysis for personal jurisdiction. The Supreme Court has declared that where the defendant has engaged in such continuous and systematic contacts with a particular forum state, the defendant may be sued in that state even on claims that may be unrelated to the defendant's contacts with the forum.[23] This is considered a type of general jurisdiction in that the jurisdiction is not tied to the particular facts giving rise to the instant claim. Case law application of this type of general jurisdiction is scarce because defendants do not tend to assert personal jurisdiction defenses when their contacts with the forum are so extensive, but examples are easy to come by. Businesses with significant, on-going presence within a state would appear to be likely subject to general jurisdiction in those states, like Wal-Mart, McDonalds, 7-Eleven, Publix, Kroger, based upon such extensive and continuous physical contacts. This does not mean that every lawsuit can be filed in any state where such business operates a store (don't forget about venue and long-arm statutes discussed next) but it does suggest that the constitutional doctrine of personal jurisdiction should not be a significant bar to planning a suit there.

---

[21]*Insurance Corp. of Ireland v. Compagnie Des Bauxites De Guinee, 456 U.S. 694 (1982).*

[22]*Carnival Cruise Lines, Inc. v. Shute,* 490 U.S. 585 (1991).

[23]*International Shoe Corp. v. Washington,* 326 U.S. 310 (1945)("[T]here have been instances in which the continuous corporate operations within a state were thought so substantial and of such a nature as to justify suit against it on causes of action arising from dealings entirely distinct from those activities.").

2. *Specific Jurisdiction*

> The U.S. Supreme Court has made it clear that the minimum contacts sufficient to bestow personal jurisdiction are those that show the defendant purposely availed themselves of the forum and that exercising jurisdiction *over the defendant in the particular case* would be fair.

Specific Jurisdiction is the subspecies of personal jurisdiction where a forum court is recognized to have power over the litigant based upon those particular "minimum contacts" the defendant has with the state that gave rise to the litigation. This analysis began with the seminal *International Shoe* case involving the state of Washington's attempt to obtain overdue tax payments from a company based in St. Louis but doing business in Washington through traveling shoe salesmen, each carrying a bag of shoes around the state and obtaining shoe orders. The constitutional application of the due process clause in this area has evolved considerably since then. What counts today as sufficient minimum contacts in order to justify a court's power over a particular litigant so as not to offend traditional notions of fair play and substantial justice depends very much on the circumstances and the type of case. Fortunately for you, there has developed a fairly substantial body of case law that takes at least some of the constitutional guess-work out of the equation. Most advocates, after all, are not trying to make new due process precedent for law school professors when preparing a new case for filing but are simply trying to pick an advantageous forum and get the lawsuit moving.

In terms of specific principles and tests, the Supreme Court has offered some helpful guidance. The Court has made it clear that the minimum contacts sufficient to bestow personal jurisdiction over the defendant are those that show "purposeful availment" by defendant of the forum and facts that show that the exercise of jurisdiction over the defendant *in the particular case* would be fair.[24] Although the due process principles remain the same from one type of case to another, the framework of analysis can differ. For cases arising out of contractual relationships, for example, the Supreme Court has indicated that four specific factors should be considered in performing this search for purposeful availment and fairness, which include: (a) prior negotiations between the parties; (b) contemplated future consequences; (c) the actual terms of the parties' contract; and

---

[24]*Hanson v. Denckla*, 357 U.S. 234 (1958).

(d) the parties' actual course of dealing.[25] Thus, a nonresident of the forum state who chooses to do significant business with a forum resident may very well subject themself to being hailed into court in that remote state.

With regard to intentional tort cases, the Supreme Court has authorized an "effects test" which asks whether the nonresident defendant intended conduct toward a specific person or class of persons knowing the conduct would lead to adverse effects within the forum state.[26] And for personal injury negligence and product liability claims, at least a considerable portion of the Supreme Court's justices have considered as particularly significant the extent to which the defendant could have foreseen their contacts having a potential impact within a state, although the details of such requirement is still a matter of some debate on the Supreme Court.[27] The Court has been nearly unanimous though in holding that even apart from indications of minimum contacts showing some degree of "purposeful availment" in such cases, that courts considering personal jurisdiction objections need to separately analyze whether the jurisdictional exercise would be "fair" using the following additional factors: (a) the burden to the defendant of litigating in the forum; (b) the forum state's interest in the dispute; (c) the plaintiff's interest in obtaining relief in that particular forum; and (d) notions of judicial efficiency and effectiveness. While not being specific enough as to prescribe results for every disputed exercise of personal jurisdiction, these factors go a long way toward helping advocates consider possible fora for their planned lawsuits.

A uniquely modern personal jurisdiction problem is also worth mentioning at this point concerning internet contacts as a way of demonstrating sufficient minimum contacts. For example, if a defendant posts actionable content on its website which causes injury to the plaintiff in a state where defendant has never had any physical contacts, can suit against the defendant in that remote forum occur consistent with the due process clause? As more and more human activity occurs in the virtual world of the internet, this is much more than just an academic inquiry. Although the Supreme Court has yet to answer this question, the prominent test being used by lower courts currently is the *Zippo* "sliding scale" analysis:

---

[25]*Burger King Corp. v. Rudzewicz*, 471 U.S. 462 91985).

[26]*Calder v. Jones*, 465 U.S. 783 (1984).

[27]*Asahi Metal Industry Co. v. Superior Court*, 480 U.S. 102 (1987).

At one end of the spectrum are situations where a defendant clearly does business over the Internet. If the defendant enters into contracts with residents of a foreign jurisdiction that involve the knowing and repeated transmission of computer files over the Internet, personal jurisdiction is proper. At the opposite end are situations where a defendant has simply posted information on an Internet Web site which is accessible to users in foreign jurisdictions. A passive Web site that does little more than make information available to those who are interested in it is not grounds for the exercise of personal jurisdiction. The middle ground is occupied by interactive Web sites where a user can exchange information with the host computer. In these cases, the exercise of jurisdiction is determined by examining the level of interactivity and commercial nature of the exchange of information that occurs on the Web site.[28]

Even this useful sliding scale analysis does not explain whether these factors should still be used in cases of intentional torts, for example, to the exclusion of the "effects test" mentioned above.

While the pretrial advocate may not be able to obtain absolute predictions from these principles and factors on anticipated disputes over personal jurisdiction issues, the advocate can at least engage in case planning and analysis knowing the relative strengths of different fora's personal jurisdiction capabilities over the target defendant. Obviously if the two fora in question are relatively close in terms of their desirability then the advocate might opt for the forum where the planned case faces no considerable jurisdictional barriers.

3. Long-Arm Statutes

In terms of our horizontal inquiry, thus far we have focused on the U.S. Constitution's limits for forum selection. The horizontal analysis–where in the United States may the suit be filed–is not, however, limited to engagement at such a lofty plane. Each state can decide whether and to what extent it wishes to *exercise* personal jurisdiction within the parameters dictated by the due process clause. In other words, just because Oregon may constitutionally be permitted to exercise jurisdiction over a nonresident who is personally served (or "tagged") within Oregon's borders does not mean that Oregon has chosen to do so. To determine how aggressive a state has chosen to exercise its territorial jurisdiction,

---

[28]*Zippo Mfg. Co. v. Zippo Dot Com, Inc.*, 952 F. Supp. 1119 (W.D. Pa. 1997).

the advocate must put their hands on the applicable state's "long-arm" jurisdictional statute.

Some states have chosen to exercise their jurisdictional powers up to the very edges of the due process clause by enacting long-arm statutes that either expressly or implicitly provide for any exercise of personal jurisdiction that is consistent with the U.S. Constitution. For example, in 1987 Louisiana modified its original statute that only provided for personal jurisdiction in specific factual situations to authorize its courts to "exercise personal jurisdiction over a nonresident on any basis consistent with the constitution of this state and of the Constitution of the United States."[29] Alabama and Texas have statutes that are not quite this clear in their adoption of the due process standard but yet have been judicially interpreted to apply to whatever extent the due process clause permits.[30] In other states, there are specific statutory provisions stating when personal jurisdiction exists that are not held to be as far reaching as the U.S. Constitution. Florida is an example of such a state: "Generally speaking, Florida's long-arm statutes are of a class that requires more activities or contacts to allow service of process than are currently required by the decisions of the United States Supreme Court."[31] In states like Florida, there is in effect a two-pronged inquiry for the advocate trying to determine a possible forum for the anticipated lawsuit: (1) does the state's long-arm statute provide for the exercise of personal jurisdiction by the courts of that state? and, if so, (2) is this exercise consistent with the due process clause of the U.S. Constitution?

With regard to each forum being considered as a possible filing place for her new lawsuit, the pretrial advocate needs to check the state's long-arm statutes to see whether it is coextensive with the U.S. Constitution. If it is not, then the advocate needs to satisfy herself that the contemplated lawsuit is authorized by the statute and is constitutional. If the long-arm statute is as broad as the Constitution permits, then the two-part inquiry will collapse into the single constitutional question discussed above.[32]

---

[29]La. R.S. 13:3201.

[30]"The reach of [Alabama's rule of civil procedure], Alabama's equivalent to a long arm statute, has been held to extend the jurisdiction of Alabama courts to the permissible limits of due process." *Duke v. Young*, 496 So.2d 36, 39 (Ala. 1986).

[31]*Gibbons v. Brown*, 716 So. 2d 868 (Fla. Dist. Ct. App. 1998).

[32]Although there are theoretical reasons for believing that any given federal court's personal jurisdiction should be analyzed in terms of the entire borders of the United States–since the U.S. is defined by its total borders and is not limited by a particular state's borders–such discussion is

4.   *Venue*

There is one more stopping place for the advocate prior to finishing the horizontal inquiry into the possible fora for the new lawsuit. The personal jurisdiction and long-arm analysis discussed above answers the questions of "within what U.S. states may a contemplated lawsuit be filed?" The issue of venue asks, within any particular state, "has the legislature offered any further limits on what counties are appropriate filing places for the suit?" Thus, while Ohio may have no constitutional or legislative limits on an Ohio court exercising personal jurisdiction over a particular California tortfeasor, the advocate needs to consider which Ohio courts are appropriate for hearing the case.

> **Horizontal Inquiry**:
>
> - Does the proposed forum state have the constitutional right (due process) to exercise jurisdiction over the defendant? (personal jurisdiction)
>
> - Has the forum state authorized such exercise of personal jurisdiction? (long-arm statute)
>
> - Has the forum's legislature dictated any particular counties/districts within the state for this lawsuit? (venue)

Federal courts similarly have venue restrictions provided by Congress with the difference that venue is limited according to federal districts rather than counties, as most relatively populous states are divided into more than one federal district. Venue statutes provide the answer to the question of where within a particular state a case may be filed, and they differ from state to state and from state to federal court as to the details of the answer. The primary federal venue statute, 28 U.S.C. Section 1391, for example, generally permits venue in any federal district where the defendant "resides" or where a "substantial part of the events or omissions giving rise to the claim occurred." One should note that the definition of "resides" for a corporation means any district where the defendant has sufficient minimum contacts to exercise personal jurisdiction if the district's boundaries were treated as the state's borders. This definition frequently helps an advocate to find venue in more than one district within a state when federal court

---

entirely academic. Federal Rule of Civil Procedure 4(k)(1)(A) has been interpreted to provide a general long-arm equivalent for most federal cases that is the same as the host state where the particular federal court in question sits. Thus, a federal court in Oklahoma City can exercise personal jurisdiction to the same extent as an Oklahoma state court. This simplifies the analysis somewhat for the advocate choosing between state and federal courts.

is contemplated as the chosen forum. State venue statutes frequently provide for venue based upon these or other factors, such as where the plaintiff resides or, in particular types of cases, other considerations. For example, venue over actions to quiet title might be provided for in the county where the real estate is located. Or actions against the state government might be required to be filed in the state's capital city.

Although venue statutes often offer an advocate more than one forum choice for filing the lawsuit, the advocate must be aware of the applicable venue statute and apply its provisions carefully to avoid filing a lawsuit in a county or district where venue does not lie. Choosing among the possible places of permissible venue will also be an important consideration for the advocate planning the new case. Lawyers perceive that there are considerable differences between different geographic locales within particular states sometimes based upon urban versus rural considerations and sometimes tied to different demographics of the local citizenry.

5. *Vertical Inquiry - State or Federal Court*

Senior law students and newly licensed lawyers often find themselves in a state of residual confusion over the first-year topic of subject matter jurisdiction, and it is not entirely their fault. We could spend the next 500 pages pouring over the details of a topic that can be extraordinarily complex and continues to evolve. Most advocates have a relatively simply question -- "Does my case belong in federal court, state court, or whether do I get to choose?"--the vertical aspect of forum selection. Advocates must be able to synthesize this topic into a usable analytical model that takes into consideration the lwhat might appear on the surface to be the rather mundane decision about which clerk's office to send your legal assistant with your complaint. We will focus upon a practical understanding of the three statutory pillars of federal court jurisdiction, 28 U.S.C. §§ 1331, 1332 and 1367–federal question, diversity and supplemental jurisdiction. Understanding the scope of these statutory grants of jurisdiction is important because federal courts are courts of limited jurisdiction. Unlike state court systems, which generally provide for some court of general jurisdiction able to hear virtually any type of lawsuit, federal district courts are limited by both Article III of the U.S. Constitution and congressional statutes as to the type of cases they may entertain.

It is relatively easy to appreciate naturally at least some of the significant reasons why a Minnesota plaintiff might prefer to file her lawsuit in her home of St. Paul, Minnesota rather than Waco, Texas. But assuming the plaintiff has chosen to sue in Waco, perhaps because that is where the accident occurred that gave rise to her lawsuit and the defendant is only amenable to suit in Texas, does it really matter that much whether the plaintiff files her suit at the state district court or the federal district court in Waco? They're both in downtown Waco after all, just a few blocks from one another.

Potentially there are a number of significant distinctions between a state and federal court that may be critical. These differences include the fact that dissimilar judges preside over each court. The federal judge, you may recall, has lifetime tenure due to Article III of the U.S. Constitution. The state judge does not and may hold an elected position making her much more sensitive to local partisan influences and current public opinions on volatile subjects. Even if not subject to partisan elections, the state judge might at least have to face regular retention elections or re-appointment by an elected official. If you are choosing to attack a local ordinance against sexually oriented businesses, do you really want to have a popularly elected (or retained) judge ruling on the issue? On the other hand, if your case involves the interpretation of a disputed contract provision this distinction may not be particularly important on your case. The judges likely will have some differences in their educational and vocational backgrounds. What if the federal judge, prior to being appointed to the bench, was an insurance defense lawyer and you are preparing a personal injury case for filing? As will be discussed in later chapters, judges can impact the outcome of cases in many subtle and not-to-subtle ways. Whether actual bias exists or not, the advocates' mere perception of bias will impact settlement discussions. The judges also have different staffs–most state trial judges do not have professional law-school educated law clerks helping them perform legal research, reading long legal briefs and helping resolve disputed motions for summary judgment while every federal judge does have these law clerks (often who have graduated near the top of their law school class). If you are considering filing a suit that faces some tough uphill battles on possible technical legal defenses that are likely to be incorporated into a motion for summary judgment, do you prefer a judge who will have the matter well researched or one who will not? This will depend upon whether you think you have the better arguments under the law or not. Each of these distinctions between particular federal and state judges can be important.

Other significant differences exist between the federal and state court options apart from the judges and their staffs. While the Waco example offered above involved a state and federal court in the same city, this is often not the case. The typical county has a state trial court of general jurisdiction but most counties in the United States do not have a sitting federal district judge. Most federal districts include multiple counties with the judge sitting in one courthouse usually located in the biggest city in that region. So the choice between state and federal court may involve driving to a different county if you choose the federal route. The broader border for the federal district court also means that it is drawing its jury pools from a larger geographic area and this will likely impact the type of jury that your client may face. Further, while the federal district courts choose potential jurors from the voter's registration rolls, the state court may use a different base such as drawing from the list of those citizens holding a driver's license. Conventional wisdom says that the demographics of the former are more conservative than the latter. Finally, state courts tend to have more cases filed each year than federal courts and, thus, may have larger dockets and slower average times to trial. This is not always true and there are published statistics that advocates can check for their jurisdiction that will reveal how long the wait for adjudication (resolution through motion or trial) may be.[33] Usually the plaintiff wants a shorter time to trial, all other things being equal. Defendants are often more content with the status quo being maintained as long as possible.

One additional layer of difference may exist between the federal and the state option and that is differences in the law or at least the judges' views on what the law may be. You may recall that the *Erie* doctrine[34] dictates that the "substantive" law to be applied in a federal diversity jurisdiction lawsuit is supposed to be the same law that a state court sitting in that state would apply to the action, such that differences in substantive law should no longer motivate forum shopping my

> You can accurately assume that any rule dictated by the Federal Rules of Civil Procedure or Federal Rules of Evidence will certainly be applied to your lawsuit if it is filed in federal court notwithstanding any different rule in your state court system.

litigants. While this is certainly true, one has to be careful not to get too ivory-tower about the actual application of this principle. After all, the substantive law from the applicable state is not always entirely clear leaving the federal court to make an "Erie guess" as to the right legal principles to be applied. While a state trial court may have to, in effect, make the same guess as to what the law is, once again a particular state trial judge's view of the law may not be the same as a particular federal district court judge's view. The same principle applies in federal question disputes—cases where federal statutory or regulatory law provides the rule of decision. Because of the Supremacy Clause in the U.S. Constitution, both the state and federal trial judge should be applying the same law to the advocate's

---

[33]The Administrative Office of the United States Courts, for example, annually publishes statistics with this kind of information entitled "Federal Court Management Statistics." The information is broken down by Circuits and Federal Districts.

[34]*Erie Railroad v. Tompkins*, 304 U.S. 64 (1938).

case. Yet their interpretation and approach to that law's application may differ. Finally, the *Erie* doctrine in no way mandates or supports a federal court applying state rules of civil procedure or rules of evidence to a federal lawsuit. And despite Supreme Court precedent suggesting, at least at one time, an "outcome determinative" test for divining when a particular federal rule is one of substance or "mere" procedure, the fact is that you can accurately assume that any rule dictated by the Federal Rules of Civil Procedure or Federal Rules of Evidence will certainly be applied to your lawsuit if it is filed in federal court notwithstanding any different rule in your state court system. There are some significant differences between federal and state courts' rules of civil procedure and evidence, many of which might actually result in a different outcome in your lawsuit. As an advocate, you should be aware of such differences in your jurisdiction and consider how these differences might impact your lawsuit at both the pretrial and trial stages.

Because meaningful distinctions exist between federal and state courts, due to variations in judges, staffs, dockets, geography, jury pools, and the law, your job as an effective advocate is not to take the forum choice lightly. For any potential lawsuit, in addition to deciding (horizontally) where you would like to file your lawsuit, you must also consider (vertically) whether a choice between federal and state court exists for your contemplated legal action and, assuming you get to decide where to file, you need to exercise your best judgment as to whether a federal or state court is best for the resolution of your client's legal problem. Now let's engage in a practical review of some important jurisdictional principles that will help illuminate whether you have a vertical choice to make.

> After more than a century of interpretation and application, the U.S. Supreme Court has still failed to clearly state a bright-line rule that allows for a certain application of the standard found in 28 U.S.C. § 1331.

6. Federal Question Jurisdiction

Although other very narrow and specific federal statutes exist that provide for federal court jurisdiction, by far the most important congressional grant of federal question jurisdiction is that contained within 28 U.S.C. § 1331: "The district courts shall have original jurisdiction of all civil actions *arising under* the Constitution, laws, or treaties of the United States." These twenty-two words seem so simple that many law students are surprised to find that, even after more than a century of interpretation and application, the U.S. Supreme Court has still failed to clearly state a bright-line rule that allows for a certain application of this standard. Congress first provided for general federal question jurisdiction during the aftermath of the Civil War because of a fear that state courts would refuse to apply correctly important new federal statutes. Prior to that post-war grant, most federal cases were diversity lawsuits brought between citizens of different states or countries. Today the concept of federal courts applying federal statutes is accepted as such a natural condition that advocates sometimes need reminding that most federal causes of action can still be filed in state court as well as federal court–the concept of *concurrent jurisdiction.* Only the exceptional federal statutory grant of a cause of action provides for *exclusive* federal court jurisdiction, such as the Federal Tort Claims Act which lifts the protection of sovereign immunity for negligence-based claims against the U.S. government on non-discretionary matters but requires all such claims to be brought exclusively in federal courts.[35]

Many issues that have been raised about the scope of the phrase "arising under" contained within § 1331 have been clearly resolved by the Supreme Court. There is the *"well-pleaded complaint"* rule that dictates that for a case to arise under federal law, courts must confine their analysis to the plaintiff's complaint and ascertain the nature of the claims asserted.

> "[E]xisting doctrines as to when a case raises a federal question are neither analytical nor entirely logical."
>
> Charles Alan Wright

This rule means that any federal defenses asserted, or possibly to be asserted, by the defendant are irrelevant.[36] If a plaintiff asserts a common law defamation claim (state law) it does not matter if the primary dispute in the case concerns the defendant's contention that the First Amendment protected his defamatory speech. This claim only arises under state law and may not be filed in federal court under federal question jurisdiction.[37] The result does

---

[35]28 U.S.C. §§ 2674, 2680 and 1346(b)(1).

[36]*Louisville & Nashville R.R. v. Mottley*, 211 U.S. 149 (1908).

[37]You may recall the "federal ingredient" test from *Osborn v. Bank of the United States*, 22 U.S. 738 (1824) which indicated that any federal issue arising anywhere in the parties' dispute is sufficient for the U.S. Supreme Court to exercise its Article III appellate jurisdiction powers. But this broad standard has no application under Congress' narrower grant of jurisdiction to the federal district courts in § 1331.

not change even if the plaintiff anticipates the federal defense in her complaint. Students in civil procedure or federal courts classes might find these principles worthy of vigorous debate as neither this analysis nor result seem preordained. For our purposes, you may let go of the analytical objections that are undoubtedly available to assail these holdings, consider this debate closed, and simply apply the rule to your potential lawsuit. The net effect of the well-pleaded complaint rule is to narrow the breadth of the statute and limit the number of cases that can be filed in federal court, or removed to federal court, based upon the idea that federal issues are raised by the lawsuit.

Another matter fairly well settled about § 1331 is understanding how to determine when the plaintiff's claim actually arises under federal law by looking at the well-pleaded complaint, . Justice Oliver Wendell Holmes articulated long ago the "creation" test that courts still generally apply today–a suit arises "under the law that creates the cause of action."[38] As Professor Joseph A. Glannon so succinctly states about the beauty of this creation test: "The vast majority of cases brought under the arising-under jurisdiction fit neatly within the Holmes test, and consequently there is no question that the federal court has jurisdiction under 28 U.S.C. § 1331."[39] So if your client has a claim created by the federal discrimination laws that you are interested in asserting in your complaint, your client's claim arises under federal law and may be filed in federal court. Simple enough–and this analysis will answer the vast majority of potential questions you have in practice about possible federal question jurisdiction.

On the edges, however, lurks one very fuzzy issue about the scope of § 1331 which will, for explanation, necessitate a brief discussion of two cases. Is there federal question jurisdiction when your client's potential lawsuit involves the scenario of a state-created cause of action that depends, for its resolution, upon the interpretation and application of some federal-law based standard? Two leading Supreme Court cases exist on this issue and they reached different conclusions without the latter overruling the former. In *Smith v.*

> If your client has a state-created cause of action that has embedded federal issues in its proof, whether or not federal question jurisdiction exists is debatable and worthy of further in-depth research.

---

[38]*American Well Works v. Layne,* 241 U.S. 257 (1916).

[39]Joseph A. Glannon, *Civil Procedure: Examples & Explanations* 68 (5th ed. 2006 Aspen).

Kansas City Title and Trust Co.,[40] the Supreme Court found federal jurisdiction on a claim created by state law–a claim to enjoin a corporation from exceeding its investment powers under state law–but its resolution required a determination of whether a federal statute under which certain bonds were created was constitutional. Despite the creation test not being met here, the Court still found that because this substantial federal issue was necessarily embedded within the state law claim (and not a defense to the claim), the case arose under federal law. This is still good law[41] though certainly limited perhaps by the more recent decision in *Merrell Dow Pharmaceuticals Inc. v. Thompson*.[42] In this case the plaintiffs filed a personal injury case alleging state tort claims against a drug manufacturer. Plaintiffs alleged that proof of negligence could be found in the defendant's failure to provide warnings on the drug's label as required by the Federal Food, Drug and Cosmetic Act. Once again, here was a case that was clearly created by state law but resorted to federal law to prove the plaintiff's claim. Yet the Supreme Court found that no federal jurisdiction existed primarily because it interpreted the FDCA statute as embodying congressional intent not to create any implied ability to sue for damages for violation of the statute. Undoubtedly this precise issue will undergo further evolution at the hands of the Supreme Court. In the meantime, if your client has a state-created cause of action that has embedded federal issues in its proof, whether or not federal question jurisdiction exists is debatable and worthy of further in-depth research if you believe a federal forum is worth considering. Even if you do not and simply file in state court, there is a very good chance your defendant will consider removing the case to federal court. This specter of removal, an attack on your forum choice, will be considered further in the next chapter.

If you believe that you have a potential case that arguably arises under federal law, you must consider the practical decision about whether to file the case there. Strategically, there are two main reasons to assert a federal cause of action: (1) because there is an attractive federal claim available that is appropriate to provide your client the relief that she desires and you believe that federal court provides the best forum for its resolution; or (2) even though your non-federal claims are much more important to you, you so desire a federal forum that you may want to assert the federal claim to provide a jurisdictional anchor to gain you

---

[40]255 U.S. 180 (1920).

[41]*Grable & Sons Metal Products Inc. v. Darue Eng. & Mfg.*, 545 U.S. 308 (2005)("[A] federal court ought to be able to hear claims recognized under state law that nonetheless turn on substantial questions of federal law."). [Update cite.]

[42]478 U.S. 804 (1986).

access to the federal court. This latter rationale will be explained below under the topic of Supplemental Jurisdiction. But first we will consider the more controversial jurisdictional juggernaut–diversity jurisdiction.

7. Diversity Jurisdiction

Diversity jurisdiction is the red-headed stepchild in the world of federal court jurisdiction despite being the primary original form of federal jurisdiction. The popularity of this form of jurisdiction has waxed and waned throughout the preceding two centuries. During the 1970s and 1980s calls for the legislative abandonment of this type of jurisdiction were pronounced and the U.S. House actually voted in favor of its demise. The thrust of the criticism seemed to be that federal courts were too busy to continue messing around with deciding state law disputes and that continuing to do so was an affront to federalism. The truth is that many federal judges do not like hearing diversity lawsuits and eagerly look for reasons to dismiss them on jurisdictional grounds. This phenomenon is particularly accentuated when a defendant sued in state court attempts removal to federal court on diversity grounds. Special consideration of diversity-based removals will be discussed in the next chapter.

Yet diversity jurisdiction not only continues to survive but actually thrives and may be entering a new golden era of expanded use. Rather than discard diversity jurisdiction, as its critics assumed would happen, Congress has in the last two decades, and particularly recently, legislatively increased the number of cases that can be heard in federal court on diversity grounds.[43] This is good news for plaintiffs who prefer a

> "To me, a lawyer is basically the person that knows the rules of the country. We're all throwing the dice, playing the game, moving our pieces around the board, but if there is a problem the lawyer is the only person who has read the inside of the top of the box."
>
> Jerry Seinfeld

---

[43]Through three enactments, Congress has not only preserved diversity jurisdiction but expanded its application, through the Supplemental Jurisdiction Statute discussed next (28 U.S.C. § 1367), the Class Action Fairness Act's adoption of a minimal diversity standard for class actions (28 U.S.C. § 1332(d)), and the Multi-Party, Multi-Forum Jurisdiction Act's minimal diversity standard for mass accident cases (28 U.S.C. § 1369). See James M. Underwood, *The Late, Great Diversity Jurisdiction*, 57 Case Western Reserve L. Rev. 179 (2006) for a discussion of the historical development of diversity jurisdiction.

federal forum for their interstate disputes. More often than not, however, it is the defendant who prefers the federal forum. This means that the plaintiff's lawyer needs to be acutely aware of diversity principles to consider crafting the lawsuit to avoid diversity jurisdiction so that the case filed in state court stays in state court.

The main statutory provision granting diversity jurisdiction is contained at 28 U.S.C. § 1332 (a) which provides in part:

(a) The district courts shall have original jurisdiction of all civil actions where the matter in controversy exceeds the sum or value of $75,000, exclusive of interest and costs, and is between

(1) Citizens of different States;
(2) citizens of a State and citizens or subjects of a foreign state;
(3) citizens of different States and in which citizens or subjects of a foreign state are additional parties; and
(4) a foreign state, defined in section 1603(a) of this title, as plaintiff and citizens of a State or of different States.

You will notice that while analysis of federal question jurisdiction under § 1331 focuses upon the nature of the claims alleged by the plaintiff, diversity jurisdiction analysis under § 1332 focuses primarily upon who the parties are in the litigation. Concerning this grant of jurisdiction there are two primary issues to grasp–(1) when do we have the right type of diversity of citizenship to satisfy the statute? and (2) how do we analyze the "matter in controversy" to determine if the case is big enough to get into federal court?

Most diversity cases are between U.S. citizens and in these cases only provision § 1332(a)(1) has application–a suit between "Citizens of different States." In an important yet poorly analyzed opinion, the Supreme Court long ago interpreted this to require *complete diversity* as between all those who are named as plaintiffs and those who are named as defendants.[44] The justification for this requirement was recently explained by the Supreme Court as follows:

---

[44]d*Strawbridge v. Curtiss*, 7 U.S. 267 (1806).

The Court, nonetheless, has adhered to the complete diversity rule in light of the purpose of the diversity requirement, which is to provide a federal forum for important disputes where state courts might favor, or be perceived as favoring, home-state litigants. The presence of parties from the same State on both sides of a case dispels this concern, eliminating a principal reason for conferring § 1332 jurisdiction over any of the claims in the action.[45]

In terms of analyzing the potential for having a federal forum for your case, you must first determine the citizenship of all of the contemplated parties (including any that might be considered "necessary" under Rule 19) and then look to see if there are any of common citizenship looking across the "versus." We have already discussed in the earlier section on general jurisdiction the concept of "domicile" and this is the same concept and test utilized in analyzing diversity of citizenship. A litigant can have only one domicile at a time and this is based upon where the litigant most recently established concurrently both residence and an intention to remain there indefinitely. The critical point of time in this analysis is the time of filing the lawsuit–meaning that a litigant can actually change the diversity analysis simply by establishing a new domicile between the time of the claim arising and the lawsuit's filing.

Once you have determined the citizenship of each party,[46] it is rather easy to determine if complete diversity exists under § 1332(a)(1), as shown on the following page:

---

[45]*Exxon Mobil Corp. v. Allapattah Services, Inc.,* 545 U.S. 546 (2005). Recently Congress amended § 1332 to add subpart (d) which provides for minimal diversity jurisdiction in class action cases where at least $5 million is being claimed, in aggregate, by the class. In such cases, so long as one member of the plaintiff class is diverse from one of the defendants being sued, diversity jurisdiction exists subject to a few statutory exceptions. This enactment was part of the controversial Class Action Fairness Act designed to sweep more significant, interstate class actions out of state courts and into federal courts.

[46]The party invoking federal court jurisdiction bears the burden of demonstrating any facts upon which jurisdiction is based. If there is any objection raised to diversity jurisdiction based upon the citizenship of the parties included in the suit, the party that filed (or removed) the case to federal court will need to be able to offer proof of the citizenship of each litigant. Of course, courts frequently permit the litigants to obtain formal discovery on this matter once the suit is filed so an advocate can get the lawsuit on file in federal court based upon the mere appearance of having complete diversity of citizenship.

Does Complete Diversity Exist?			
Plaintiffs	vs.	Defendants	Conclusion
WA	vs.	SC	Yes
GA	vs.	GA	No
TX, GA, WY	vs.	IN, MI, WI	Yes
MN, VT, ID	vs.	CA, OR, VT	No
OK, NV, CO	vs.	NH, WY, CO	No

The "alienage" provisions contained within § 1332(a)(2)-(4) can be a little more difficult to understand and apply. While these do not have as frequent application as (a)(1), in these days of an increasing global economy it is likely that advocates will encounter these alienage situations more frequently in the future. Subsection (2) contemplates a case with one or more U.S. citizens on one side and citizens or subjects of a foreign state only on the other side. Thus, the presence of foreigners on both the plaintiff and defendant side of the "versus" destroys diversity. Subpart (a)(3) involves a case with completely diverse U.S. citizens on

both sides of the "versus" with foreign citizens added in the mix–here it does not matter that the case may involve foreigners on both sides of the versus because you still have completely diverse U.S. citizens. Subpart (4) involves a U.S. citizen suing or being sued by a foreign government and is fairly straightforward. In case any of these explanations still seem paint a somewhat murky image for you, try utilizing the following chart to assist you in your analysis of this issue.

Does Complete Diversity Exist?			
Plaintiffs	vs.	Defendants	Conclusion
FL	vs.	TX	Yes– § 1332(a)(1)
FL	vs.	TX, Mexico	Yes– § 1332(a)(3)
FL, Japan	vs.	Mexico	No
Mexico	vs.	Japan	No
FL	vs.	Japan, Mexico	Yes– § 1332(a)(2)
FL, Mexico	vs.	TX, Japan	Yes– § 1332(a)(3)

In addition to satisfying § 1332's requirement of complete diversity, a litigant seeking to claim a federal diversity forum must also demonstrate that the requisite $75,000 minimum amount in controversy is met. The language of the statute indicates that a plaintiff alleging diversity must show she is seeking an amount greater than $75,000–even a penny more is sufficient. Also, whether the plaintiff actually recovers this sum does not impact the federal court's jurisdiction. It is only whether a good faith claim for this sum exists that matters. Courts have also determined that if a defendant seeks to challenge jurisdiction based upon the amount in dispute, the defendant must show "to a legal certainty" that plaintiff cannot recover more than $75,000 in order to prevail in seeking dismissal.[47] These principles are fairly straightforward.

Two issues have arisen over application of the amount in controversy requirement that can impact your forum choice. The first is to what extent different claims can be added, or aggregated, in order to satisfy this minimum amount in controversy requirement. The Supreme Court has held that, in effect, each plaintiff must ordinarily have their own large (in excess of $75,000) claim(s) to support federal diversity jurisdiction and that a co-plaintiff with a small claim cannot ride the coattails of the other under § 1332(a).[48] Thus, Paul's $100,000 claim against Deborah meets the statute's amount in controversy requirement but Mary Beth's related claim against Deborah joined in the same lawsuit for $50,000 would not satisfy this statute. Further, if Paul has two claims against Deborah, each for $50,000, joined together under Rule 18, Paul has satisfied § 1332.

[47]*St. Paul Mercury Indemnity Co. v. Red Cab Co.*, 303 U.S. 283 (1938).

[48]*Clark v. Paul Gray, Inc.*, 306 U.S. 583 (1939).

However, if Paul has one $50,000 claim against Deborah and Mary Beth joins Paul pursuant to Rule 20 asserting her own $50,000 claim against Deborah, the two litigants cannot aggregate their claims–neither claimant can be in federal court under § 1332. The only exception to this rule of non-aggregation of different claimants' claims is when the two claimants are pursuing a damage remedy that is considered undivided and joint, which is not normally the case. These principles are demonstrated for you in the chart below.

Amount in Controversy Satisfied?			
Claim			Conclusion
Paul $100,000 claim	vs.	Deborah	Yes
Paul claim #1 $50,000	vs.	Deborah	Yes
claim #2 $50,000			
Paul $100,000 claim	vs.	Deborah	Yes
Mary $25,000 claim	vs.	Deborah	No
Paul $50,000 claim	vs.	Deborah	No
Mary $50,000 claim	vs.	Deborah	No

The second issue of note relates to valuation of the amount in controversy. When your client is primarily seeking monetary damages, application of these amount in controversy principles is fairly straightforward. How do you figure the amount in controversy, though, if your client is seeking injunctive relief instead of damages? The courts have not resolved this; some courts suggest valuing the injunction from the perspective of the defendant (what it will cost to comply with the requested court order), some valuing the injunction from the plaintiff's perspective (the amount of the loss avoided by the injunction) and others say that valuing the injunction from either perspective is appropriate in order to satisfy the amount in controversy requirement. If your contemplated case involves such relief, you will need to research the law of the circuit where you are thinking of filing suit to determine the approach likely to be taken in your case.

8. Supplemental Jurisdiction

The final jurisdictional principle you need to include in your analysis is the supplemental jurisdiction statute, 28 U.S.C. § 1367, which since 1990 has taken the place of what used to be called ancillary and pendent jurisdiction. (If you see a complaint referencing "pendent" jurisdiction, you should realize that a lawyer educated prior to 1990 has drafted the pleading.) Supplemental jurisdiction is a necessary doctrine if the federal courts are to remain a viable forum option.

Because of the limited jurisdiction of federal courts, traditional subject matter jurisdiction analysis requires that each and every claim filed in federal court have a jurisdictional grounding. That is each claim either needs to be a part of a sufficiently large dispute (over $75,000) between completely diverse parties (§ 1332) or needs to "arise under" federal law (§ 1331). The problem is that a great many lawsuits that have one claim that qualifies for federal jurisdiction also involve other claims that lack such jurisdictional pillar yet are so related to the other claims that are permitted in federal court that it would only seem to make sense to allow them to be heard together. The doctrines of ancillary and pendent jurisdiction were created by the U.S. Supreme Court in recognition of this fact. Failure to do so would result in the federal courts not being of much utility because litigants wanting to resolve *all* of their related claims would go to state court instead. After the Supreme Court, in 1989, issued an opinion suggesting that these court-created doctrines might be illegitimate in the absence of congressional approval,[49] Congress came to the rescue the following year by passing the Supplemental Jurisdiction Statute. The statute mostly codified the prior doctrines although it clearly resulted in some changes, both intentional and unintentional[50]–meaning that you need to be careful when researching this topic to distinguish between case law before and after 1990.

Both in its structure and function, there are three major components to supplemental jurisdiction, as reflected by § 1367–paragraphs (a), (b) and (c). The initial component is the very generous grant of supplemental, or extended, jurisdiction. Section 1367 begins as follows:

> (a) Except as provided by subsections (b) and (c) or as expressly provided otherwise by Federal statute, in any civil action of which the district courts have original jurisdiction, the district courts shall have supplemental jurisdiction over all other claims that are so related to claims in the action within such original jurisdiction that they form part of the same case or controversy under Article III of the United States Constitution. Such supplemental jurisdiction shall include claims that involve the joinder or intervention of additional parties.

In essence, this grant says that so long as there is an anchor claim in the case over which the federal courts have original jurisdiction (under the federal

---

[49]*See Finley v. United States,* 490 U.S. 545 (1989).

[50]For further explanation of the history behind this statute and its unintended consequences, you might refer to James M. Underwood, *Supplemental Serendipity: Congress' Accidental Improvement of Supplemental Jurisdiction,* 37 Akron L. Rev. 653 (2004)(Complex Litigation Symposium Issue).

question or diversity statutes), the additional or supplemental claims may also be heard by the federal court so long as they are "so related [to the anchor claim] that they form part of the same case or controversy under Article III of the United States Constitution." The standard test for the requisite relationship between the claims necessary to be considered part of the same constitutional case is the same "transaction or occurrence" test we saw when reviewing Rule 20 joinder of claims for convenience. The Court has also previously described this test as a practical one where the court can consider whether the claims are so related that it would "ordinarily expect" an advocate to bring the claims in one proceeding. Let us consider two different examples of such supplemental claims.

First let us say your new client has an employment discrimination claim alleging liability against her employer for permitting a hostile work environment (a federal question anchor claim) arising out of co-workers' taunts and innuendo. Your client's state-law defamation claim arising out of those same communications could be heard in federal court despite lacking its own independent jurisdictional legs. On the other hand, if the additional claim were for unreimbursed travel expenses, this seemingly unrelated claim could not be brought in the same federal lawsuit unless there were complete diversity of citizenship between the employee and employer and the client's total[51] claims exceeded $75,000.

Second, if your client files a breach of contract claim against a former business partner (who has since moved out of state and taken up a new diverse domicile) for $100,000 (a diversity anchor claim), that business partner can file a counterclaim for $25,000 alleging a breach of the same contract by your client despite the fact that it would be too small to bring by itself in federal court. On the other hand, if the counterclaim seeks $25,000 in damages for an unrelated auto accident, it could not be asserted in the same federal proceeding as it would not be considered part of the same constitutional case. These examples show a basic application of the relatively broad grant of supplemental jurisdiction in § 1367(a)–all the litigant claiming the federal forum need show is a jurisdictional anchor claim and that all other claims are part of the same constitutional case. Upon this showing the federal court can hear the entire dispute.

The second major component of the statute is subpart (b)'s limitation of the broad grant just discussed. In other words, what subpart (a) giveth, subpart (b) partially taketh away. This provision states:

> (b) In any civil action of which the district courts have original jurisdiction founded solely on section 1332 of this title, the district courts shall not have supplemental jurisdiction under subsection (a) over claims by plaintiffs against persons made parties under Rule

---

[51]You may recall that a single claimant may aggregate all of her claims against a single defendant for purposes of calculating the amount in controversy.

14, 19, 20 or 24 of the Federal Rules of Civil Procedure, or over claims by persons proposed to be joined under Rule 19 of such rules, or seeking to intervene as plaintiffs under Rule 24 of such rules, when exercising such supplemental jurisdiction over such claims would be inconsistent with the jurisdictional requirements of section 1332.

This subsection has been the focal point of much hand-wringing by courts and scholars over whether to interpret this language literally–which results in some changes to preexisting doctrines–or to interpret it the way many believe Congress really meant to legislate. The Supreme Court adopted the literal approach,[52] which makes our discussion somewhat simpler–we can focus on the language of the statute instead of reading tea leaves for unexpressed desires. Under this approach, if your client has at least one claim over which the federal courts have jurisdiction but the other claims arose out of the same transaction or occurrence, you would check for a possible subpart limitation by asking the following three questions:

> (i) is jurisdiction over the proposed supplemental claim grounded solely on diversity of citizenship?

> (ii) is the proposed supplemental claim being brought by a "plaintiff"?

> (ii) is the proposed supplemental claim being asserted either (a) by a plaintiff joined of necessity under rule 19 or by one who has intervened under rule 24? or (b) against a party joined under rule 14 (third-party defendant), 19 (necessary party), 20 (for convenience) or 24 (intervenor)?

If the answer to all three questions is "yes," then no supplemental jurisdiction exists. If any of the three questions is answered "no," then subpart (b)'s limit on supplemental jurisdiction does not apply and the proposed supplemental claim may be added to your planned federal action. In sum, what Congress has done is limited supplemental jurisdiction in diversity cases on many–but not all–claims asserted by plaintiffs. Because most counterclaims, cross-claims and third-party claims tend to be asserted by people sued–defendants–rather than plaintiffs, subpart (b)'s limitations generally do not limit the exercise of supplemental jurisdiction on such related claims. One other example of the application of this tripartite analysis under subpart (b) should further demonstrate a major unintended extension of prior jurisdictional doctrine.

Let's assume that you have two clients, Ringo and Paul, who are both citizens of North Dakota. They were both hurt by John, an Idaho citizen, when

---

[52]*See Exxon Mobil Corp. v. Allapattah Services, Inc.*, 545 U.S. 546 (2005).

John was visiting North Dakota for spring break and ran his car into them. Paul was driving his car and suffered property damages to the car of $13,000. Ringo was Paul's passenger and suffered personal injury damages estimated to be approximately $100,000. Complete diversity of citizenship exists and Ringo's claim against John satisfies the amount in controversy requirement for a diversity action. Thus, Ringo's claim against Paul provides a jurisdictional anchor in federal court. Paul's smaller claim, however, does not meet § 1332's amount in controversy requirement on its own and aggregation–as we just learned–is not generally permitted. However, because the claims are so related, arising from the same event, subpart (a) indicates that a federal court could hear the supplemental claim against Paul. Now we have to consider the three-question application of subpart (b)'s limitation. The answer to the first question is "yes" the anchor is a diversity only one because no federal claim is involved. The answer to the second question is also "yes" because the supplemental claim is one brought by one of your clients, a planned co-plaintiff in the planned litigation. The final question, however, is answered "no" because the claim is being brought by a plaintiff joined merely for convenience under rule 20 which is not on subpart (b)'s hit-list of prohibited exercises of jurisdiction. Accordingly, § 1367 would permit the filing of both claimants' claims against John in federal court, should you choose a federal forum as the most advantageous. In this way, supplemental jurisdiction has expanded the instances in which a diversity case can be brought in federal court even though one plaintiff joined under rule 20 has a claim too small to satisfy § 1332 on its own.

Finally, the third major aspect of § 1367, subpart (c), provides a federal district court approval to exercise its discretion to choose not to hear a supplemental claim. It provides:

> (c) The district courts may decline to exercise supplemental jurisdiction over a claim under subsection (a) if–
>
> (1) the claim raises a novel or complex issue of state law,
>
> (2) the claim substantially predominates over the claim or claims over which the district court has original jurisdiction,
>
> (3) the district court has dismissed all claims over which it has original jurisdiction, or
>
> (4) in exceptional circumstances, there are other compelling reasons for declining jurisdiction.

This aspect of the statute has not been seen as a significant departure from prior case law recognizing that there might be instances where a federal trial judge should decline to hear a pendent or ancillary claim.[53] The typical instances where this discretion has been invoked are either when the non-federal tail is wagging the federal dog (an insignificant federal claim is the only anchor) or where the federal anchor claim has been dismissed or dropped during the pretrial stages of the lawsuit and all that is left for decision is the state claim. Principles

---

Jurisdictional Inquiry

- Is there any claim in your client's case that is created by federal law? In the alternative, is there any claim that requires significant application of federal law to be proven? (§ 1331)

- Who are the anticipated parties and what are their domiciles (states of citizenship)? Are each plaintiff's claims worth more than $75,000 independently valued? (§ 1332)

- Are there any other claims your clients desire to make that are outside of the federal court's original jurisdiction?

- If there are any anchor claims over which subject matter jurisdiction exists, based upon the above, do each of the other claims you desire to file arise out of the same transaction or occurrence as the anchor claim? (§ 1367(a))

- Are any of the related other state-law claims within the exclusion of subpart (b) based upon the three questions raised by that subsection? (§ 1367(b))

- Are there any discretionary factors present that might cause the federal district court to decline to hear the additional claims? (§ 1367(c))

- Do you want your client's case in federal court?

---

of federalism, in both instances, support the idea of dismissing the case and allowing the claimant to take their state law dispute to state court. If you are trying to stay in federal court on the basis of a federal claim, this means that you should work your hardest to keep that claim in the lawsuit at least through the beginning of trial or else risk having to start the process over in state court–a particularly bad

---

[53]*Gibbs v. United Mine Workers*, 383 U.S. 715 (1966) is the modern seminal case addressing pendent jurisdiction and the district court's discretion to exercise it. Both § 1367(a) and (c) reflects its principles.

procedural miscue for your client. It also means that if your only federal anchor claim is either relatively insignificant in terms of the remedy sought or is legally or factually weak, you might need to reconsider your attempt to invoke a federal forum.

The point of the foregoing discussion is to emphasize to you that the choice of forum should not be an after-thought or something that is otherwise taken for granted. Indeed, the motive to find the best forum for your anticipated lawsuit may very well drive your decision as to what claims to bring or who you should plead as a party to the lawsuit. Understanding of the applicable law, awareness of the appropriate strategic considerations and appreciation for the possible impact of forum selection on your ability to achieve your client's prize are invaluable to the effective pretrial advocate.

F. THE CASE FILE

For the pretrial advocate, a complete case file does not typically just appear in your hands. Recognition of this fact provides a major distinction in the law school curriculum between a course on pretrial practice and one on trial advocacy. For the pretrial advocate, the case file is something you create through your own planning and perspiration. The case file for the pretrial advocate will include the fairly mundane (e.g., letters to clients and invoices), the case blueprints (e.g., all pleadings filed with the court), court schedules and other orders, the evidence that has been gathered informally and through discovery (e.g.,client documents, depositions, answers to interrogatories), and the results of your creative thought processes (e.g., demonstrative exhibits you are preparing for hearings or possible trial, cross-examination outlines, etc). All of the best work of the pretrial advocate is for naught if it is not captured in a workable case file in an organized manner that makes the fruit of the advocate's labors readily retrievable. Accordingly, establishing and maintaining an organized case file is an essential, though admittedly not very sexy, part of an advocate's case planning and preparation.

If you work at a law firm of significant size, you may well encounter a preferred system for setting up case files. Certainly if you work with very many other lawyers you will discover differences among those lawyers in terms of the nuances of their file organization. As a new advocate, it is vitally important that you use some system for organizing your case file and that you (and anyone else who will be accessing that file) understand that system so that you can find the information and materials you need when you need them. The young advocate will feel empowered by having her file organized in such a way. Further, if the advocate has an older associate or partner look at the file, perhaps to help out on

```
╔══════════════════════════════════════════════╗
║          Contents of a Typical Case File       ║
║                                                ║
║  I. Communications                             ║
║  1.1 Contact Information                        ║
║  1.2 Correspondence                             ║
║       a. Client                                 ║
║       b. Courts                                 ║
║       c. Counsel                                ║
║  1.3 Billings and Invoices                      ║
║                                                ║
║  II. Pleadings, Motions, Orders                 ║
║  2.1 Plaintiff Complaints                       ║
║  2.2 Defendant Answers                          ║
║  2.3 Defendant M/Partial Summary Judgment       ║
║  2.4 Plaintiff Response to Defendant MSJ        ║
║  2.5 Court Order Overruling MSJ                 ║
║  2.6 Scheduling Order                           ║
║                                                ║
║  III. Discovery                                 ║
║  3.1 Plaintiff Interrogatories and Responses    ║
║  3.2 Plaintiff Document Requests and Responses  ║
║  3.3 Plaintiff Request for Admissions and       ║
║      Responses                                  ║
║  3.4 Plaintiff Deposition Notices               ║
║  3.5 Defendant Interrogatories and Responses    ║
║  3.6 Defendant Document Requests and Responses  ║
║  3.7 Defendant Request for Admissions and       ║
║      Responses                                  ║
║  3.8 Defendant Deposition Notices               ║
║  3.9 Motions to Compel and Responses            ║
║  3.10 Motions to Quash and Responses            ║
║  3.11 Client Documents                          ║
║  3.12 Documents Produced by Defendant           ║
║  3.13 Documents Produced by Third Parties       ║
║                                                ║
║  IV. Research                                   ║
║  4.1 Case Evaluation for Client                 ║
║  4.2 Research on Statute of Limitations         ║
║  4.3 Research on Fraud Claims                    ║
║  4.4 Research on Motion for Summary Judgment    ║
║                                                ║
║  V. Misc.                                       ║
║  5.1 Order of Proof for Trial                   ║
║  5.2 Trial Exhibits                             ║
╚══════════════════════════════════════════════╝
```

some matter, they will gain confidence in the abilities of the associate when they see such an organized method being utilized. These are both important aims for a new advocate.

In a sense, effective advocates actually have two files. They have the comprehensive case file that is typically maintained by some combination of legal secretaries and legal assistants. This should contain the original copies of all important documents relating to the case. Additionally, the advocate should consider maintaining a "trial notebook" which will be small enough for the advocate to carry to all important pretrial events (meetings, depositions, hearings). This is kind of a ghost file which will contain only the most critical copies of documents from the original case file. Isn't it premature, you might ask, to call such a notebook a "trial" notebook when we have not even filed our lawsuit? Absolutely not, because the advocate will be utilizing this notebook not only to have ready access to the most critical information and documents but also to maintain a *trial perspective* at all junctures of pretrial.

As shown from the example above, there can be numerous categories of information within a case file and this highlights the need for a capable staff to assist the advocate. You might also be able to think of categories of documents that might be logically included within more than one folder. There is nothing wrong with some such redundancy for more important materials. What is essential about the case file is that it be the absolute resting place for all information important about your case and that it be readily accessible by being organized, indexed, up-to-date, and accurate. Sloppy filing can not only be inefficient, it can cause and advocate to go into an important hearing or deposition unprepared because certain key information was not readily available to the advocate when preparing for the event.

By contrast with the comprehensive case file, the advocate should consider keeping a trial notebook for everyday use and access when out of the office. A typical organization of such a trial notebook is illustrated for your possible use. There is nothing magical about this organization or contents–that is something that you should necessarily alter to suit your own preferences. But the idea of maintaining such a notebook–the smaller the better–is something that most effective advocates adopt. You will also notice that, unlike the case file, the trial notebook does not attempt to hold every scrap of paper. For example, while your case file should contain every pleading ever filed in the suit, your notebook only needs to contain those that are "live" and not superceded by a subsequent pleading. While the case file contains all of the documents exchanged in discovery, the notebook typically only contains an index of those documents that are likely to be utilized at a trial. While the case file should contain all documents relevant to a particular witness, the notebook only needs to contain a condensed copy of the witness' deposition or other written statement (e.g. affidavit filed in support of a motion).

Many of the items listed in the trial notebook will evolve as the case

---

Contents of a Typical Trial Notebook

Miscellaneous
1. Scheduling/Deadlines
2. To-do List

Live Pleadings
3. Plaintiff's 2nd Amended Complaint
4. Defendant's Answer
5. Joint Pretrial Statement

Evidence
6. Chronology
7. Discovery Needs
8. Answers to Interrogatories
9. Responses to Requests for Admission

Witnesses
   Plaintiff
10. Plaintiff John Sherman
11. Dr. Kenneth Marshall
12. Sylvia Morales
   Defendant
13. Donna Meza
14. Cynthia Harper
15. Dr. Allen Godsey

Trial
16. Order of proof
17. Exhibit Lists
18. Proposed Jury Instructions
19. Motion in Limine
20. Directed Verdict Points
21. Opening & Closing Ideas

progresses. While your initial case analysis should have revealed some possible moral themes, it is probably not worthwhile to even begin thinking too seriously about your opening statement or closing argument when the case is newly filed because much will change about the case before trial. But as the pretrial phases of the case move forward, it is helpful when the advocate (perhaps sitting in a deposition) thinks of a possible theme, phrase or argument that might be persuasive to a jury to immediately jot this idea down in the trial notebook where it can be remembered and possibly utilized later. When you are planning to take a witness' deposition, your notebook should contain a topical index for your anticipated examination (much more on this will be forthcoming in Chapter 7). After the deposition, a condensed and indexed deposition transcript (in small font with multiple pages of text per page, to keep it thin) should be placed behind that tab perhaps with a short memo to yourself outlining the most important portions of the testimony. Further, as the advocate is defending a deposition of her client and certain inflammatory testimony is extracted by opposing counsel's brilliant and thorough questions, rather than sit and suffer through mere unproductive sweating, the advocate might also pull out the trial notebook and, under the topic of "Motion in Limine", simply scribble a note to seek exclusion of that item at trial. This may not obviate the sweating, but at least the advocate can ease the stress somewhat by actively dealing with the bad evidence instead of simply worrying about it. Documenting these important but sometimes random thoughts in your trial notebook will make your final trial preparation much more efficient and effective. Think of the trial notebook as an organic document that changes during the pretrial portion of the case and which will be helpful to have at your side during any significant case activity.[54]

Having engaged in careful case analysis, preparation and planning, you have now laid the foundations for a successful lawsuit. It is time for the advocate to begin the work of drafting her client's initial pleadings. It's time to get this party started. We shall now turn to that subject.

G. RULES MATRIX

This table serves as a starting point for additional inquiry into the potential professional responsibility and civil procedure issues that are implicated at the initial stage of case analysis, preparation and planning.

---

[54]Of course, those that do not need a tangible piece of paper at their disposal might be inclined today to simply carry a laptop computer with all of this same information easily indexed and accessible. Documents that the advocate has not created can be scanned into the system.

Issue Arising During Initial Case Analysis, Preparation & Planning	Applicable Rule of Professional Responsibility, Federal Rule of Civil Procedure, or U.S. Code
Good faith factual and legal basis requirement for any claim	**FRCP 11**
Prohibition on contacting witnesses represented by counsel	**Ethics Rule 4.2**
Witness entitled to copy of their own statement	**FRCP 26(b)(3)**
Permission to join in one lawsuit all claims against a party opponent	**FRCP 18**
Permission to join in one lawsuit additional plaintiffs or defendants on related claims	**FRCP 20**
Requirement to name the real parties in interest	**FRCP 17**
Requirement to join all necessary parties	**FRCP 19**
Permission to file class action representing a plaintiff or defendant class	**FRCP 23**
Federal general venue requirements	**28 U.S.C. § 1391**
Congressional grant of federal question jurisdiction	**28 U.S.C. § 1331**
Congressional grant of federal diversity jurisdiction	**28 U.S.C. § 1332**
Congressional grant of federal supplemental jurisdiction	**28 U.S.C. § 1367**

Table 1 - Potential Law Applicable to Initial Case Analysis, Preparation and Planning

Points To Ponder . . .

1. What should the advocate do when her case analysis suggests that pursuing the client's claims is unlikely to be a success? Are some claims so important that they are worth pursuing against all odds? What can the advocate do to enhance any chance of prevailing in such dire situations?

2. Case analysis might appear to be a rigorous and time-consuming activity. Is this necessary even for the smaller cases? To the same extent?

3. Is it wrong for an advocate to sue someone solely for the purpose of obtaining discovery useful against another party? Is it wrong for the advocate to select a court that she believes will be biased against her opponent? How does that promote a search for truth and justice?

4. How can an advocate still be effective despite not having a personality that values the skill of organization?

CHAPTER FIVE
DRAFTING, RESPONDING TO, &
ATTACKING PLEADINGS

"My words fly up, my thoughts remain below: Words without thoughts never to heaven go."[1]

A. INTRODUCTION

Before you are prepared to initiate your client's lawsuit you must first perform a careful case analysis, informal factual investigation and preliminary legal research. There are two common approaches the vast majority of advocates use in drafting pleadings. The first one is to grab a lawyer's form book, look in the index to find the general type of lawsuit you are planning to file and then fill in the blanks in the form document. After this thirty minute exercise, you then dial the country club to schedule your afternoon

> **The Superior Pleading:**
> - Furthers your client's strategic objectives
> - Sends the right message to your adversary
> - Anticipates and avoids any procedural issues
> - Places your client on the winning path

tee time and forget about the matter. This is not only good for your golf handicap but it *might* suffice as a technical matter in terms of getting your new lawsuit underway. Or it might not. The second approach is to carefully and thoughtfully construct a document that furthers your client's strategic objectives, sends the right message to your adversary, anticipates and avoids any procedural kinks in the case armor and places your client on the winning path with the very first step in the pretrial process. We advocate this latter approach and will describe it thoroughly

---

[1]William Shakespeare, Hamlet Act 3, sc. 3.

in this chapter. Exploring the best way to draft the pleading embodying your client's claims is important and constitutes a major step in "doing the necessary" but you must also consider separately preparing a client's primary response to her adversary's claims–the answer. After we have addressed these two tasks we will finally consider other ways that a responding litigant can attack the claimant's pleading at the outset, using various Rule 12 objections and motions and by changing the

> **A Complaint's 3 Essential Ingredients**
> - Jurisdictional Justification
> - Claim Articulation (weaving facts & law)
> - Wish List

plaintiff's forum selection through removal of the case from a state to a federal court or via transfer to another venue of the defendant's choosing. These defense maneuvers are important to understand both for defense counsel as well as for plaintiff's counsel. The ability to appreciate and anticipate possible moves by your adversary makes the advocate much more effective and efficient.

B. DRAFTING A POWERFUL, BULLET-PROOF CLAIM

This section will first consider the various rules an advocate should bear in mind while drafting her client's complaint and then we will consider strategies for drafting a goal-oriented complaint. Following these two discussions, we will actually walk through some basic considerations you will encounter in the context of a specific hypothetical lawsuit. In other words, we will cover the law, the art, and the skill of drafting pleadings.

Types of Pleadings:		
Affirmative Pleading		*Responsive Pleading*
Complaint	☞	*Answer*
Counterclaim (versus an opposing party) [Rule 13(a)-(b)]	☞	*Reply*
Cross-Claim (versus a co-party)[Rule 13(g)]	☞	*Answer*

```
┌─────────────────────────────────────────────────────────────┐
│                                                               │
│   Third-Party Complaint                                       │
│     (versus a non-party)         ☞        Third-Party Answer   │
│        [Rule 14]                                              │
│                                                               │
└─────────────────────────────────────────────────────────────┘
```

Rule 7(a) actually defines what documents constitute "pleadings" under the civil procedure rules. These include the "complaint and an answer; a reply to a counterclaim denominated as such; an answer to a cross-claim, if the answer contains a cross-claim; a third-party complaint, if a person who was not an original party is summoned under the provisions of Rule 14; and a third-party answer, if a third-party complaint is served. No other pleading shall be allowed, except that the court may order a reply to an answer or a third-party answer." In other words, a pleading is a legal document containing either a claimant's claims or a defending party's direct response to such claims. Pleadings consist of both factual and legal assertions. Our focus in this chapter will be upon complaints and answers, as well as certain related documents used to attack pleadings. To the extent that a claim may be located in another type of pleading–such as a counter-claim, cross-claim or third-party claim, most of the same pleading principles apply with equal force.

> A pleading is a a legal document containing either a claimant's claims or a defending party's direct response to such claims.

To the extent these other types of pleadings invite different considerations, we will discuss these other matters later in this chapter.

1. The Law

There are several sources of law that both directly and indirectly govern how an advocate should go about preparing a pleading stating a claim and we will briefly discuss each. The procedural rules of primary importance to consider in drafting your client's initial pleading will be Rules 8-12. Of these rules, the rule most directly pertinent to your task and which expressly provides for the requisite contents of a litigant's complaint can appear to be disarmingly simple. In essence, Rule 8(a)[2] indicates three bare essentials of a complaint: a statement of why the

---

[2]Federal Rule of Civil Procedure 8(a) provides that:

"[a] pleading which sets forth a claim for relief, whether an original claim, counter-claim, cross-claim, or third-party claim, shall contain (1) a short and plain statement of the grounds upon which the court's jurisdiction depends, unless the court already had jurisdiction and the claim needs no new grounds of jurisdiction to support it, (2) a short and plain statement of the claim showing that

federal court has subject matter jurisdiction, an explanation of the claimant's claims and a prayer for relief listing what the claimant wants the court to order.

The court expects you as the claimant's advocate to expressly state in your complaint why the court has the power to hear the claims you are raising. Failure to demonstrate the court's jurisdictional power over the case can result in the court, on its own, dismissing the case or will at the very least draw a motion to dismiss from your adversary. Of the three requirements of Rule 8, this jurisdictional justification is the one item courts tend to be most demanding about in terms of the complaint's contents. Although the jurisdictional statement does not usually require great elaboration, it does require the advocate's attention and planning to be sure the federal forum is available. There is an official Appendix of Forms attached to the Federal Rules of Civil Procedure that provides officially sanctioned illustrations of the pleading principles contained with the rules, such as

---

A Form-Pleading's Circle of Life

Step 1: A thoughtful advocate pleads certain Allegation for a good legal or strategic reason in a specific case.

↓

Step 2: Advocate shares pleading with other, perhaps younger, attorneys in the office.

↓

Step 3: The pleading is shared by with a friend working in a different law firm.

↓

Step 4: A different advocate, perhaps at a different firm, and certainly working on a different case, comes across the original pleading containing the Allegation. This advocate is unsure how to plead her case and decides to include the same Allegation (just to be safe).

↓

Step 5: The Allegation begins appearing in lots of different pleadings, prepared by different advocates on different cases, perhaps with different applicable law and certainly with different applicable facts.

↓

Step 6: Usage of the Allegation becomes so widespread that its usage is assumed to be essential. Nobody seems sure of the origins of the Allegation, what it means, or why it must be included. But isn't it safer to follow this well worn path than to blaze a new trail?

↓

Step 7: Some judges and advocates wonder why form-books in their jurisdiction contain a pleading reciting the mysterious Allegation (perhaps something such as "Defendant demands strict proof thereof and throws himself upon the country.")

↓

Step 8: Another effective and thoughtful advocate strikes the inapplicable and, by now, non-sensical Allegation from the answer. The advocate uses a different Allegation instead.

---

the pleader is entitled to relief, and (3) a demand for judgment for the relief the pleader seeks. Relief in the alternative or of several different types may be demanded."

the following:

Diversity Jurisdiction Allegation

(a) Jurisdiction founded on diversity of citizenship and amount. Plaintiff is a [citizen of the State of Connecticut] . . . and defendant is a corporation incorporated under the laws of the State of New York having its principal place of business in a State other than the State of Connecticut. The matter is controversy exceeds, exclusive of interest and costs, the sum specified by 28 U.S.C. § 1332 [currently $75,000].

Federal Question Jurisdiction Allegation

(b) Jurisdiction founded on the existence of a Federal question. The action arises under . . . [the Act of _____, _____ Stat. _____; U.S.C., Title _____, § _____] as hereinafter more fully appears.

These examples demonstrate the ease by which one can articulate succinctly the jurisdictional basis for a federal court lawsuit and come from Form 2 of the rules' Appendix. Although the Rules' Appendix does not offer an example of a pleading in a non-diversity case where there is a federal question anchor claim and related state law claims, an advocate needs to remember to include a jurisdictional allegation to demonstrate why a federal court can hear such additional claims. A statement such as the following would suffice: "In addition to the federal cause of action that arises under [federal statute], plaintiff also asserts state law causes of action for negligence, gross negligence and strict products liability against defendant. Jurisdiction for these state law claims is founded upon this Court's supplemental jurisdiction in that these claims arise out of the same transaction or occurrence as the federal claim and are, therefore, part of the same constitutional case. 28 U.S.C. § 1367(a) provides for this Court's jurisdiction over these state law claims and subsection (b) of that statute is not applicable." By remembering that each claim presented to a federal court needs some jurisdictional legs, the advocate can avoid the embarrassing dismissal of all or a portion of their client's case.

By contrast, the "short and plain statement" showing that your client is "entitled to recover"–the second requirement of Rule 8(a)–reflects the federal courts' embrace of "notice pleading"–a departure from the common law and code pleading days where precise detail was required to be in the pleading to demonstrate the validity of your claim or risk dismissal. But what is expected from the advocate pleading the "short and plain statement" of her client's claim?

A cause of action is essentially a legal construct applicable to certain factual scenarios by which either the court (common law claims) or legislature (statutory claims) has declared entitles the claimant to recover some relief from a defendant. So a short and plain statement of someone's claim will weave some degree of facts and law together sufficient to demonstrate possible entitlement to relief from the named defendant. Rule 8(e) is helpful to understanding this requirement. It confirms the implicit notice-pleading mandate of Rule 8(a) in its declaration that "[e]ach averment of a pleading shall be simple, concise, and direct. No technical forms of pleading . . . are required." The official examples of pleadings contained in the Rules' Appendix of Forms shows how extremely simple it can be to plead a client's claim:

Form 4. Complaint on an Account

1. Allegation of jurisdiction.
2. Defendant owes plaintiff _____ dollars according to the account heretofor annexed as Exhibit A.
Wherefore, [plaintiff demands judgment against defendant for the sum of _____ dollars, interest, and costs.]

Form 9. Complaint for Negligence

1. Allegation of jurisdiction.
2. On June 1, 1936, in a public highway called Boylston Street in Boston, Massachusetts, defendant negligently drove a motor vehicle against plaintiff who was then crossing said highway.
3. As a result plaintiff was thrown down and had his leg broken and was otherwise injured, was prevented from transacting his business, suffered great pain of body and mind, and incurred expenses for medical attention and hospitalization in the sum of one thousand dollars.
Wherefore plaintiff demands judgment against defendant in the sum of _____ dollars and costs.

What do the two above official examples from the rules drafters have in common? They both reference a specific factual transaction or occurrence (e.g., a traffic accident), expressly or implicitly latch on to a particular cognizable legal theory (e.g., negligence) and briefly state why the defendant should be liable to the plaintiff. In other words, by brief reference to both facts and law each complaint gives the defendant fair notice of why the plaintiff has sued that defendant. Each complaint could, obviously, have gone into greater detail regarding the factual circumstances that gave to the cause of action. Neither complaint is particularly dramatic or offers any hint of a potential moral theme for the case. They are both sort of a Vulcan-like logical recapitulation of the bare essence of the reasons why the claimant feels entitled to relief from the particular defendant. Imagine Spock playing the role of advocate giving an opening statement. Accurate. Efficient. Sufficient. Not terribly exciting. Yet each example points the defendant to a particular incident and informs the defendant of the legal theory plaintiff attempts to invoke to justify the requested relief. In this limited regard, these official form complaints satisfy Rule 8(a), withstand the minimal scrutiny of Rule 12(b)(6) and get the case officially started–the claims survive for now. As we will discuss later, discovery can be utilized by the defendant served with such a complaint in order to flesh out additional factual details within the plaintiff's knowledge. The complaint provides enough information to at least facilitate this additional activity.

If boring, bare-bones allegations are not a problem, what type of deficiencies might get a plaintiff's claim into pleading difficulty? The deficiencies typically fall into two categories. First, courts sometimes dismiss complaints that fail to allege facts supporting each element of the alleged cause of action. It is debatable whether such dismissals technically are consistent with the *Conley v. Gibson*[3] standard, which mandates that "a case should not be dismissed pursuant to Rule 12(b)(6) 'unless it appears beyond reasonable doubt that plaintiff can prove no set of facts in support of his claim which would entitle him to relief.'"[4] But courts still frequently cite such a failure as a ground for dismissal. As the drafting advocate you simply need to be informed as to the applicable elements of the claim you are stating and make sure that you do allege facts supporting each such element. Subtlety is not the goal here–you can explicitly list the elements and in fairly conclusory fashion inform the court that facts have transpired meeting each such element. Second, courts also frequently dismiss complaints where the claimant's own allegations affirmatively negate the cause of action often by admitting facts that constitute an affirmative defense to the cause of action. For example, if the applicable statute of limitations on your client's contract claim is four years and your facts alleged reveal that the breach occurred more than four years prior to the filing date of the lawsuit, you have just pleaded yourself into a dismissal. Thus, the advocate needs to not only know the elements of the claims being alleged but also the potential defenses to each such claim. Drafting with these two things in mind can typically avoid dismissal of your new lawsuit or at least drive you toward pursuing a different claim.

---

[3]355 U.S. 41 (1957).

[4]*Clark v. Amoco Production Co.* 794 F.2d (5th Cir. 1986)(quoting from *Conley v. Gibson*).

You also need to be aware that the above pleading principles are sometimes heightened by rule, statute, local rule or simply judicial invention for particular classes of cases that are suspect or actually disfavored. Rule 9, for example, requires pleading "the circumstances constituting fraud or mistake" with "particularity" because, the thinking goes, it would otherwise be too easy to convert any contractual dispute into a fraud claim involving punitive damages.[5] Courts interpret this rule to require a fraud plaintiff, for example, to allege specifically what misrepresentation was made, the identities of the speaker and recipient, and the time and circumstances of the communication–the type of information a litigant accused of fraud would need to try to defend themselves. Importantly, the defendant accused of fraud need not flesh out the particulars of the accusation during discover but is entitled to this detail up front in the complaint or else may seek dismissal of the claim on the pleadings. In some instances, other portions of Rule 9 actually minimizes the pleading burden by, for example, not requiring either capacity of a litigant or the specific occurrence of conditions precedent (in a contract case) to be plead specifically.[6]

Other types of claims–generally disfavored or abused causes of action–are often accompanied by similar requirements to be pled with specificity. During the heyday of civil litigants use of the federal racketeering statute–RICO–to gain access to a federal forum and treble damages for their common law fraud claims, some federal districts' local rules required extensive pleading of the prerequisites for such claims in the original complaint. A statutory example of such heightened pleading requirement would be The Private Securities Litigation Reform Act of 1995 which, along with other requirements, requires the complaint to "specify each statement alleged to have been misleading, the reason or reasons why the statement is misleading, and, if an allegation regarding the statement or omission is made on information and belief, the complaint shall state with particularity all facts on which that belief is formed."[7] Such details go far beyond the concept of mere notice pleading embodied by Rule 8(a). The point of this discussion is not to try to highlight every cause of action that comes with such heightened pleading requirements but simply to underscore the importance of the advocate's preliminary legal research into her client's causes of action to be aware of any such requirements imposed by law in your particular jurisdiction.

---

[5]Fed. R. Civ. P. 9(b).

[6]Fed. R. Civ. P. 9(b)(c).

[7]15 U.S.C. § 78u-4(b)(1)(B).

Finally, Rule 8(a) requires that the claimant include a "demand for judgment for the relief the pleader seeks." This final ingredient will be your prayer for relief at the end of your pleading. Form Complaints 4 and 9, set forth above, show such prayers in the final paragraph of each beginning with the magic term "Wherefore". Many unofficial form books

Plain Language Substitutes:	
Traditional Language	**Plain Language**
"Wherefore premises considered"	"For this reason" or "Because"
"Hereinafter referred to as [ABC]"	("ABC")

begin the prayer with the phrase "Wherefore, premises considered . . . ." Some plain language advocates now simply substitute the more modern phrase "For these reasons . . . " before launching into their relief wish list. From your client interview you should already have some good understanding of the client's goals which your preliminary factual and legal research have (hopefully) confirmed are realistic goals for the litigation. If not, you need to communicate further with your client to reassess some goals for the litigation that are consistent with what the facts and law appear to warrant.

Your research of the substantive law should reveal the type of damages or other remedies available to you for the applicable cause of action you are pleading. The general categories for your consideration will be actual damages, punitive damages, declaratory relief, injunctive relief, attorney's fees and court costs. The prevailing party typically recovers their taxable court costs (e.g., filing fees, court reporter costs, copying charges) but the substantive law varies as to whether you will be entitled to attorney's fees. You should remember that the default position in the United States is the so-called "American Rule"–that each litigant bears its own attorney's fees. Many young advocates plead for attorney's fees only to look dumbfounded at a pretrial conference when the presiding judge inquires as to the source of their right to receive such fees. With respect to this item, in addition to checking the substantive law concerning your client's entitlement, you also need to determine if the parties to the suit have a contract governing their relationship and, if so, whether that contract provides for the recovery of attorney's fees to the prevailing party in the event of a lawsuit arising out of the agreement.

Terms of actual damages, in some jurisdictions the claimant is supposed to plead a specific amount and in others the claimant is told to only plead the categories of actual damages without alleging particular dollar amounts. You will need to consult local pleading rules for your jurisdiction on this point. Further, Federal Rule of Civil Procedure 9(g) requires that items of "special damage" be "specifically stated." Special damages refer to quantifiable economic losses such as past and future wages and medical expenses and can be distinguished from general damages such as pain and suffering, physical disfigurement or other types of hedonic damages. This is not an appreciable burden because it often makes sense strategically for the claimant's advocate to specify all damages desired whether such specificity is technically required or not. We will discuss such considerations further under the next section. You should also be aware that, with respect to claims for punitive damages, some jurisdictions (though not the Federal Rules of Civil Procedure) require a claimant seeking punitive damages to file a motion seeking leave of court before pleading a claim for punitive damages or to plead with greater specificity. Florida, for example, requires this in any all cases in which punitive damages are desired.[8] California only requires this "Mother may I" procedure in medical malpractice cases.[9]

If you are stating something in your pleading that does not at least indirectly relate to one of Rule 8(a)'s three requisite topics–subject matter jurisdiction, the claim and the relief sought–you should ask yourself why you are including such matter in your pleading. There may be a good reason for the inclusion. Under the "Art" of pleading, we will discuss some such reasons. However, blind adherence to ancient allegations found in a form book–"throwing yourself upon the country"–is not such a good idea.

Rule 10 governs the "form of pleadings" and is not exactly a lightning rod for controversial Supreme Court opinions, but it is helpful for the new advocate. Rule 10(a) states that every pleading should have a case caption indicating the identity of the court (including the district and division), the name of the parties, the file number and an indication of the name of the particular pleading ("Plaintiff's Original Complaint"). Rule 10(b) reveals that a pleading should be broken down into numbered paragraphs that are logically organized. And Rule 10(c) permits a party adopt certain statements by reference and to simply attach

---

[8]*Citron v. Armstrong World Industries*, 721 F. Supp. 1259 (S.D. Fla. 1989)(discussing Florida's statutory rule requiring court approval before pleading for punitive damages and holding that the Erie doctrine did not require the federal court to apply this "procedural" rule).

[9]California Code of Civil Procedure § 425.13(a)(Deering 1995).

pertinent documents without continually reciting all of their contents. This is pretty practical stuff that you will quickly take for granted once you have filed a few pleadings.

Before moving past the legal background governing complaints, we should pause to consider two other very important provisions in the Federal Rules of Civil Procedure (and in most states' procedural rules) an advocate must keep in mind when drafting a claim–Rules 11 and 12. Rule 11 imposes certain quasi-ethical obligations upon all counsel who sign for filing in federal court a "pleading, written motion, and any other paper." Of course, Rule 11 simultaneously requires that all such documents be signed by counsel so you may not avoid Rule 11 obligations by failing to sign the document–the district court clerk will simply reject the document and send it back to you. Rule 11 operates upon a legal fiction–that the signatory counsel is deemed to implicitly make certain representations to the court about the pleading through affixing her signature upon the instrument. Specifically, counsel is representing, with respect to the document being filed, that "to the best of [counsel's] knowledge, information, and belief, formed after an inquiry reasonable under the circumstances":

(1) it is not being presented for any improper purpose, such as to harass or to cause unnecessary delay or needless increase in the cost of litigation;

(2) the claims, defenses, and other legal contentions therein are warranted by existing law or by a nonfrivolous argument for the extension, modification, or reversal or existing law or the establishment of new law;

(3) the allegations and other factual contentions have evidentiary support or, if specifically so identified, are likely to have evidentiary support after a reasonable opportunity for further investigation or discovery.

In essence, Rule 11 requires the allegations of your complaint to be well grounded in law and fact and requires that your pleading only be filed for a proper purpose. Filing a pleading solely to cause delay or to harass your opponent are not considered proper though there are relatively few instances where

> "My word is my bond."
>
> Robin Williams (as Peter Pan in *Hooked*).

Rule 11(b)(1)'s prohibition on a poor motive are called into play. For most advocates preparing a complaint there are two chief concerns: (a) are your allegations of fact reasonably warranted by what information you and your client know or believe to exist?; and (b) does your invocation of the law accord with accepted legal principles? If so, you should have no Rule 11 problems in signing and filing your pleading.

Rule 11 is an example of a rule that is well intended but still abused by many advocates. The rule provides for various sanctions, applicable in certain instances to both client and counsel, and unfortunately many lawyers decided that they could use Rule 11 as an offensive weapon to attack their opposition. In too many instances, counsel would file motions for Rule 11 sanctions in the face of a pleading or motion that they found disagreeable. Rather than simply oppose the claim or motion on the merits, counsel would invoke Rule 11 and ask the court to sanction the lawyer who signed the original document. As a consequence, courts became besieged with so-called "satellite" litigation–that is, the resolution of Rule 11 disputes having little to do with the merits of the case. In response, Rule 11 was revised to contain the current "safe harbor" provision that requires counsel spotting a Rule 11 violation to bring it to the attention of the offending counsel and to give that counsel 21 days to voluntarily retract or modify the offending statements before being permitted to file a motion seeking sanctions with a court.[10]

This revision coupled with many judges' increasing hesitancy to suffer the hearing of Rule 11 arguments has helped somewhat to reduce the offensive use of Rule 11 in litigation. But advocates must still be careful to not run afoul of Rule 11's implicit representations because Rule 11 has significant teeth and courts are not bound by the safe harbor provisions–any judge spotting a possible Rule 11 violation by counsel can act immediately without affording the signatory counsel time to recant a questionable allegation of fact or law. If you remember nothing else about this discussion, please recall when you are drafting your pleadings that your signature upon a document filed in court is more than a formatily. There are consequences to affixing your signature onto a legal document, and this realization should impact your legal research, factual investigations, client counseling and strategic considerations.

Rule 12(b) offers a defending party a smorgasbord of objections and motions to assert against a claimant. Plaintiff's counsel is well advised to consider and avoid through careful analysis and pleading of her allegations the various matters listed in Rule 12(b). Some of these matters we have already discussed, such as the Rule 8(a) requirements to state a valid basis for the court's exercise of subject matter jurisdiction and to articulate a basis for a valid cause of action against the defendant through pleading facts and law. Rule 12(b)(1) and (b)(6)

---

[10]Fed. R. Civ. P. 11(c)(1)(A).

indicate that a failure by plaintiff to plead adequately on either of these matters give rise to a possible ground for dismissal. Rule 12(b)(2) similarly provides a defendant the right (in fact an obligation will be explained below) to object to a lack of personal jurisdiction. Rule 12(b)(3) provides a basis for dismissal if the plaintiff has filed suit in a forum not supported by the applicable statutory venue provisions. As to both personal jurisdiction and venue, the best practice for the plaintiff's counsel is to affirmatively plead why the court has personal jurisdiction (including citation to the appropriate state long-arm statute) and why venue is proper in the district chosen by the plaintiff. This demonstrates to the court and defense counsel that plaintiff has considered these matters carefully and can justify maintenance of the suit in the forum chosen. Rule 12(b)(4) and (5) support dismissal where either the summons is drawn up improperly (e.g., misstating the identity of the defendant) or the manner of service on the defendant is improper under the appropriate rules. As issuance and service of the summons take place in time *after* the filing of the complaint, there is usually little to be gained from referencing service in the body of the pleading. Finally, Rule 12(b)(7) motions allow a defendant to complaint about the absence of a so-called "necessary" party pursuant to Rule 19–a type of motion rarely raised but at least requiring plaintiff's counsel to consider whether she has named all important parties to the dispute in the complaint. Thus, while Rule 12(b) does not by its terms dictate the contents that should be included in a plaintiff's initial pleading, an advocate who wants to file a bullet-proof complaint should consider it as a check-list for possible problems while still drafting the complaint.

One other important source of legal authority for the drafting advocate to consider before hitting the "save" icon on her computer is the Local Rules for the district in which the suit is being filed. Every federal district has its own published local rules of court often separated into different sections governing general civil cases, bankruptcy cases and criminal cases. At the state court level, many counties are similarly beginning to adopt local rules in many jurisdictions. With respect to the federal districts' local rules, these are not intended–nor authorized by Congress–to deviate from the applicable provisions of the Federal Rules of Civil Procedure but rather are supposed to provide additional guidance on specific issues where the FRCP do not provide a specific answer or to help effectuate the purposes behind the FRCP. For example, Rule 56 (discussed in an in significant detail in Chapter 9) provides for the filing of motions for summary judgment and responses but does not indicate any deadline for filing of a response. By local rules, each district has the authority to set a deadline–often 10 or 20 days–for the filing of a response to a motion. Local rules often also provide for related things like a pre-filing conference between opposing counsel prior to submitting a disputed matter to the court by motion. Obviously any counsel handling a case in such a district will need to be intimately familiar with all of the provisions of the local rules. Included in this text at Appendix III are the Local Rules for the United States District Court for the Middle District of Florida ("Local Rules") intended to serve as a good representative sample of such local rules. These particular local rules govern all federal lawsuits pending within that district's various divisions, including cases filed at the federal divisions in places as diverse as Jacksonville, Orlando, Ft. Myers and Tampa. This text will refer to these particular Local Rules as a reference point. Obviously, because the local rules may significantly differ from district to district, you will need to obtain a copy of your own home-district's local rules as you enter practice.

The attached Local Rules are quite specific about certain matters related to the drafting and filing of a pleading. Local Rule 1.05(a) indicates the precise physical dimensions for the paper, typeface, margins and spacing. Local Rule 1.05(c) requires in the first pleading filed by a party to designate which counsel (in cases where more than one counsel appears for the party) is the "Trial Counsel" with ultimate responsibility for the case. Local Rule 1.05(d) also requires the pleadings to be signed "personally" by the named counsel rather than, for example, by counsel's secretary on her behalf. Under these local rules, the chief judge for that district has struck a pleading filed by a party when the counsel attempted to have her secretary sign the pleading, thus indicating how seriously judges take their local rules. This makes sense because the local rules are adopted by these particular judges. Local Rule 1.06 requires that in any pleading in which a demand for a jury trial appears (as required by Rule 38 to perfect such a demand) that included in the case caption must be the phrase "Jury Demand" as well as an indication when injunctive relief is set forth in a pleading's demand. Local Rule 4.04 is an example of local rules requiring extra pleading detail for certain types of cases–in this instance, the local rule requires in any pleading of a putative class action that the elements for class certification (set forth in FRCP 23(a) and (b)) be alleged separately and specifically. Wouldn't it be embarrassing to file a fancy class action lawsuit only to have the judge dismiss it at the outset for failure to abide by such a local rule?

2. The Art

The procedural rules prescribe the contents of a pleading as well as provide other important considerations to avoid an early dismissal of a claimant's lawsuit. Adherence to these rules will permit you to successfully initiate a lawsuit and, assuming your legal research demonstrates accurately a viable cause of action, to keep that lawsuit from suffering a dismissal before you even have the chance to obtain formal discovery to gather evidence supporting the elements of your client's cause of action. But what other considerations should an advocate bear in mind when her fingers are upon the keyboard and she is deciding how to describe the facts giving rise to the claim and how much detail to include? Does it matter if the pleading is persuasive or internally consistent? The answers to these questions depend upon the circumstances and what the secondary purposes are for filing the pleading.

Obviously the primary goal in drafting a complaint is to initiate a lawsuit. But what other secondary objective might an advocate consider achieving with this pleading? In one not infrequent scenario, the goal might seem quite modest. It is quite possible that your client's claim is growing stale as the statute of limitations looms near on the horizon and you just need to get a complaint against the defendant on file and served to stop the clock from running. You may, therefore, consider the drafting and filing of the complaint to be a necessary evil to preserve and prosecute your client's claim. In this scenario, pulling out the form book and writing as little as possible in support of the claim seems to be a pretty safe route to take. However, with the statute of limitations looming you may have to consider drafting the dispute as broadly as possible in order to be able to later amend your complaint to add other related causes of action without them being time-barred. This is discussed in more detail later in this chapter under the subject of Rule 15 amendments.

In other instances, there are more aggressive secondary goals you might have in mind when drafting your complaint. When you think about it, your complaint is directed more to your opponent than it is to the court where it is filed. In fact, unless prompted to review your pleading by a motion, hearing or trial setting, most judges do not have the time or inclination to sit in their chambers reading over freshly filed complaints as if they contained the morning news. But you can be sure the defendant you have named in your complaint, as well as the defendant's retained counsel, will pour over your pleading in great detail. Whether you intend it or not your pleadings send a message about your client, and you, to your adversary. What will your message be? That you practice law out of form books? That you are not careful and sometimes refer to the wrong client's name in your pleadings? That you do not take the time to proofread your work and leave typographical errors in your work product? Your authors have seen many examples of such messages coming from opposing counsel's pleadings. These type of messages do not inspire much admiration, respect or fear from one's adversary. Without such reactions from your opponent, you are starting your case from a disadvantaged position of leverage.

Another consideration in pondering *how* you should construct your initial pleading is what type of story your pleading is telling. Will the media pick up on your complaint and provide coverage of your lawsuit to the public (your potential jury panel)? Do you desire such coverage or would your client benefit from keeping the public out of the dispute? Will your opponent upon hearing your complaint's message react with an initial desire to settle the case or instead to dig in their heels and fight? Your complaint tells a story and your client benefits if the story is not only accurate (as Rule 11 implicitly requires) and compelling but also designed to effectuate your strategy for resolving the case on the best terms possible. If you look at the pleadings of some of the best plaintiffs' advocates you will see as a common denominator that they understand the importance of telling an important story in their pleadings. By the time they file their initial pleading, they have already thought ahead to their likely trial themes and this is made plain in the story their pleading exclaims. Pleadings that fail to do this and present a dry, cookie-cutter recitation of some basic facts (as with the sample forms in the FRCP's Appendix of Forms) miss out on a great opportunity to motivate the defense to come to the settlement table or to motivate the public to cry out at the injustice caused by the defendant's misconduct. Such sterile messages do not typically drive the defense team to their checkbooks to make significant settlement offers. Starting a case by showing the opposition how weak your effort will be is one of the worst offenses you can commit as a pretrial advocate. Most civil cases settle before trial and counsel's perceptions of the parties' relative strengths and weaknesses are directly related to the amount of settlement demands and offers. This principle relates to other pleadings and written motions filed in a case but because first impressions are vitally important, taking care to put your best foot forward in your initial pleading is a particularly valuable use of your time and resources.

Another context that should impact how you draft your initial pleading relates to the relief requested. In some cases, the entire dispute is likely to be resolved in a rushed manner because the outcome hinges on whether the court is going to provide emergency injunctive relief in the form of a temporary restraining order or preliminary injunction. These cases are often resolved in weeks rather than seasons or years and the entire pretrial process is typically truncated into a very compacted time frame. Not only does your complaint have to tell a compelling story, this pleading needs to alert the court to the idea that irreparable harm is likely to result to your client in the absence of an immediate court order directed at the defendant. Further, jurisdictions have specific rules related to the issuance of such orders and these frequently include heightened pleading requirements that are made by someone with personal knowledge of the facts alleged and verified by affidavit or other sworn declaration as to their truth.[11] Because of this verification requirement, the advocate must balance a fine line between having a convincing story in the pleading yet not overstating the personal knowledge of the affiant or declarant. Judges will not only fail to issue emergency temporary or preliminary injunctive relief in the face of a hint of exaggerated allegations but they may even consider referral of the matter to the local district attorney for perjury charges. Thus, in these instances particular care and strategy must be poured into the drafting endeavor by the claimant's advocate.

3. *The Skill*

a. *Drafting the Pleading*

There is no substitute for improving one's skills than through the practice of your profession. As we have already covered a number of topics related to the drafting of pleadings, it would be helpful to walk together through the drafting of a complaint in a straightforward hypothetical case. This exercise will help to demonstrate and summarize many of the principles we have already covered as well as to provide a concrete illustration of additional suggestions for your consideration.

Imagine your clients are John and Susan Robinson. Susan was involved in a traffic accident when her car was rear-ended by a 18-wheeler driven by David Berning, an employee-driver for Paulson Breweries, Inc. Berning did not have a commercial driver's license because he had failed the vision examination on two separate instances. Berning's supervisor did not know about the poor vision or the lack of license but had failed to ask for a copy of Berning's license when he was first hired as Paulson's company policies require. On the day of the accident, Berning was on the interstate headed toward his next delivery, according to the statement Berning gave the police and reflected in the accident report. The report also noted that Berning failed to control his vehicle by maintaining the proper distance between his truck and your client's Volvo. The traffic just ahead of

---

[11]For example, in federal court Rule 65(b) provides for issuance of *ex parte* temporary restraining orders only in limited circumstances and requires, among other things, the pleading of specific verified facts demonstrating that "immediate and irreparable injury, loss or damage will result to the applicant" in the absence of emergency relief. These orders typically expire within ten days with the rule contemplating the immediate setting of a preliminary injunction hearing. Illuminating the idea of speed in cases involving injunctive relief, Rule 65(a) even authorizes district judges to consolidate the final trial on the merits with the preliminary injunction hearing. Obviously, in such instances the pretrial phase of the lawsuit will uncharacteristically be over very quickly.

Susan's car had slowed due to some construction on the interstate and Berning failed to see the slow down in time to stop his vehicle. Berning's truck hit the Volvo at approximately 50 miles per hour while the Volvo was stopped, causing the car to go through the median, flip over several times and crash into a guardrail along a bridge. Unfortunately, Susan is now paralyzed from the waist down. She can no longer perform her job as a certified public accountant. She was alone in the car. She has been married to John for five years and they have no children. With these background facts in mind, let us walk through the drafting of your original complaint. As we go through this exercise, we will first begin each section of the complaint with our draft for that section followed by a short discussion of our thoughts related to that portion of the pleading. Let's begin with the case caption.

Case Caption

****

In the United States District Court
For the Middle District of Florida
Tampa Division

Susan Robinson &	§	
John Robinson,	§	
	§	
Plaintiffs,	§	
	§	
vs.	§	Civil Action No. _____
	§	
Paulson Breweries, Inc. &	§	
David Berning,	§	
	§	
Defendants.	§	

Plaintiff's Original Complaint

For their original complaint, Plaintiffs Susan Robinson and John Robinson (the "Robinsons") state the following:

****

Every pleading must have a case caption as per Rule 10(a). This only makes sense so that the court and parties know what they are reading and to give context to the remainder of the document. This caption begins with the identification of the court where the pleading will be filed, including the designation of the specific district and division of the court. In state court this might include the specific county and district number or type of court (e.g., 62nd District Court of Travis County or Probate Court for Jefferson County).

The pleading next identifies each of the parties to the litigation specifically. Both plaintiffs John and Susan Robinson are mentioned. In subsequent pleadings, it is typical to only refer to the first plaintiff or defendant by name followed by "et al." though you may have reasons to want to refer to all the named parties specifically in the caption of other pleadings. That is up to you. We have listed Susan Robinson as the first plaintiff not in a bow to equal rights but because she is the primary victim of the defendants' misconduct. Her husband's claim is a derivative claim for loss of consortium. Again, we could list the plaintiffs in any order that makes sense or, in the absence of any logical listing, an advocate could simply list them in alphabetical order (this happens frequently in complex litigation with many parties). You will also note that even though you might consider the driver, David Berning, to be the primary defendant this pleading lists his employer as the first defendant. This is a conscious strategic decision to start planting the seed that the Brewery has direct culpability for causing the accident. To the extent that punitive damages are going to be sought, it will be important for the jury to view the employer has the chief offender because most punitive damage claims against truck drivers are not going to be worth as much as a large claim against a corporation.

Because this is the initial pleading establishing the case, at the time of drafting there is no civil action number yet known to the plaintiff's counsel but a blank in placed on the document for the clerk to stamp the new case number. In all subsequent pleadings, counsel can place that number on their pleadings themselves. This draft also includes a title for the particular pleading, omits any unnecessary verbiage ("To the Honorable Judge of said Court"), and immediately demonstrates an efficient use of abbreviations ("Robinsons") for future references in this instrument.

Introduction

****

I. Introduction

1.1   The Robinsons bring this action against Defendants to recover for the severe and permanent injuries suffered by Susan Robinson in a tragic accident on August 15, 2007 when the 18-wheel tractor-trailer unlawfully driven by

Defendants smashed into Susan Robinson's vehicle from behind at a high speed. Susan Robinson suffered permanent and disabling physical and emotional injuries in this accident. Her husband, John Robinson, joins her in this suit to recover for the serious harm to his marital relationship with Susan that this unnecessary accident caused.

****

Some effective advocates find it useful to offer a brief overview or introduction at the beginning of their complaint. To the extent that you are trying to articulate a persuasive story in your pleading, this can be a useful writing tool. Such a short paragraph can immediately set a tone for the remainder of the pleading that can strike fear in the heart of your opponent. You need not do this in any pleading but there is certainly no rule that prohibits the inclusion of such a statement. It can also be useful if a presiding judge reviews out your pleading for any purpose. Further, if you desire for the press to pick up on the significance of your lawsuit, it can also be a good way to get some attention for your case. The media typically have a reporters check new case filings at local courthouses to spot new cases worthy of the public attention. You will also note the numbering of the paragraphs as contemplated by Rule 10. Numbering the paragraphs not helps you with organizing your thoughts in drafting the pleading but it makes it easier for the defending party on the claim to draft an answer responsive to your specific allegations.

The Parties

****

II. Parties

2.1   Plaintiffs Susan and John Robinson are individual citizens of Florida residing in St. Petersburg, FL. They have been married for five (5) years.

2.2   Defendant Paulson Breweries, Inc. ("Brewery") is a foreign corporation incorporated in Delaware and having its principal place of business in Madison, Wisconsin. Brewery is authorized to do business in Florida. Its registered agent for service of process is [include name and address of local agent, typically available from public corporate filings].

2.3   Defendant David Berning ("Driver") is an individual citizen of Georgia who resides at [list street address] Macon, Georgia. Drive was at all times related to this accident an employee of Brewery and acting in the course and scope of his employment with Brewery.

****

Although the procedural rules do not expressly discuss identifying the parties further in the body of a pleading, it is customary to list each party in separate paragraphs of a pleading. In addition to identifying the local of a party, it is often useful in this early portion of the pleading to indicate the basic involvement of each party (e.g., the driver or the employer or the spouse of the injured plaintiff). You might also observe that rather than simply use a portion of a defendant's name as an abbreviation for that party, you can apply a more useful descriptive term ("Brewery" or "Driver" or, in another case, "Drunk Driver"). The defending party may not approve of this practice but it's not their pleading. Even in these seemingly benign paragraphs we begin to paint a sympathetic picture of a happily married couple aggrieved by the conduct of a brewery and its employee. We also provide addresses to assist a process server in locating the defendants to obtain service of the summons and complaint. You can provide such information independent of the pleading but it can be useful to also list the address in the body of the pleading.

Jurisdiction and Venue

****

III. Jurisdiction and Venue

3.1   Plaintiffs are citizens of the State of Florida. Brewery is a citizen of the States of Delaware (its place of incorporation) and Wisconsin (its principal place of business). Driver is a citizen of the State of Georgia where he is domiciled. This matter in controversy greatly exceeds, exclusive of interest and costs, the sum of $75,000. Accordingly, this Court has subject matter jurisdiction over this matter in accordance with 28 U.S.C. § 1332.

3.2   Defendants are each subject to personal jurisdiction in Florida because they engaged in tortious conduct in Florida that was the cause of the Robinsons' harm for which they seek relief in this matter. Further, Florida's applicable long-arm statute provides for this Court's exercise of personal jurisdiction over the Defendants [add statutory citation].

3.3.   Venue is appropriate in this district and division pursuant to 28 U.S.C. § 1391(a)(2) because the tragic accident that gave rise to this lawsuit occurred in Tampa, Florida.

****

As discussed previously, Rule 8(a) requires a statement of the federal court's subject matter jurisdiction and this is provided in paragraph 3.1. In a state court of general jurisdiction, such an allegation should be unnecessary. Even though Rule 8(a) does not require a statement of the court's personal jurisdiction or justifying venue of the matter in the chosen forum, because such matters may be raised by objection or motion of either defendant under Rule 12(b), it is helpful to address these matters up front and to demonstrate that plaintiff has carefully analyzed these issues already. It demonstrates competence and careful attention to detail.

Facts

****

IV. Background Facts

4.1   John and Susan Robinson were high school sweethearts who married on June 1, 2002 in their hometown of St. Petersburg, Florida. Susan is a highly qualified certified public accountant and John is a public elementary school math teacher.

4.2   On the fateful afternoon of August 15, 2007, as Susan was driving north on I-275 on her way to do charitable work, the traffic ahead of her slowed due to construction on the freeway. Susan noticed this slow-down and appropriately reduced her speed. In fact, her car came to a complete stop as a result of the construction work. Within seconds of stopping, however, her car was smashed from behind at a high rate of speed by a fully loaded 18-wheel tractor-trailer driven by Driver on behalf of Brewery.

4.3   At the time of the accident, Driver had recklessly disregarded construction signs posted along the sides of the freeway and had either refused to slow down his vehicle or had failed to observe the obvious slow-down of traffic on the roadway. Upon information and belief, Driver's conduct either reflected his indifference to the safety of others or was due to a visual impairment that he had throughout his employment with Brewery.

4.4   At the time of the accident, Driver was driving Brewery's 18-wheel tractor-trailer unlawfully in that he failed to possess a valid commercial driver's license as required by Florida law [cite appropriate statute]. Upon information and belief, Brewery either was aware of Driver's failure to have such license or failed to obtain verification that he was properly licensed prior to permitting him to drive on its behalf.

4.5   Through no fault of her own, Susan Robinson was seriously injured in the accident fracturing her lower back. She is now permanently paralyzed and has suffered and continues to suffer extreme pain and anguish, physical disability and disfigurement, and lost enjoyment of life. She has incurred lost wages and, because she can no longer perform her prior duties as a certified public accountant, has a significantly diminished earning capacity in the future. As of this time, Susan has incurred over $500,000 in past medical expenses and is expected to have significant expenses for her health care and nursing assistance for the duration of her life.

4.6   As a consequence of the permanent and severe injuries suffered by Susan Robinson, the Robinsons' marriage has undergone tremendous upheaval and injury. Susan Robinson can no longer perform many of the important functions she previously committed to the marital relationship. John Robinson sues for this loss of consortium.

****

The recitation of "facts" or "background facts" in your pleading helps to not only establish a cause of action but to lay a predicate for the case themes that will drive your litigation of the dispute. The facts are the guts of the pleading. Most cases are won, or lost, on the facts. Here is where your case analysis plays an important role in helping you to marshal the facts that help to support your client's claims. If this is done well, the remainder of the pleading should be relatively easy and concise. You should remember that you can attach documents to your pleading and incorporate their contents by reference. Please do not try to attach all of your foreseeable trial exhibits here. Only key documents, such as a contract, should be considered for possible attachment to the pleading. You should also remember that it is permissible to plead in the alternative, particularly since formal discovery has not yet begun and the rules recognize that you may not have yet figured out exactly what actions the defendant took. For example, until you depose a defendant accused of misstating certain facts you may not know whether the misrepresentations were made carelessly or intentionally. It is alright to plead both in the alternative.

The facts set forth above provide significantly greater detail than, for example, Form 9 from the Appendix of Forms in the FRCP, yet these facts are not unnecessarily long. They help to provide a glimpse of an emerging powerful story of two innocent individuals whose lives were devastated by the callous misconduct of the defendants. The facts might include an introduction to who the parties are–a happily married couple or a greedy, callous mortgagor–and contextual background information that adds color to the specific incident in question. The extent to which you will plead such details will vary based upon your secondary motives in filing the pleading, the availability of factual knowledge concerning the incident in question, your strategy plans for resolving the case (i.e., quick settlement or a likely trial) and the characteristics of the defendants (how they might react to the pleadings). You *may* also wish to avoid using in your background facts certain adjectives such as "recklessly." As you will see in the next section on Answers, use of such terms makes it easier for the defendant to avoid having to admit unsavory facts in the complaint in preparing their answer. On the other hand, you may be more interested in showcasing the strength of your case and less interested in using the pleading as an opportunity to obtain admissions. If that is true, adding some colorful language to the complaint may be a positive approach to take. You will also note that certain allegations that plaintiff's counsel believes will likely be established after the receipt of additional discovery are made "upon information and belief" as is authorized by Rule 11. If your pleading is filled with such allegations it may signal that you need to engage in additional information factual investigation before filing the lawsuit. But it is common to include some allegations upon information and belief in order to help fill in the details of a complaint to paint a complete portrait of the events. You should also be sure to plead the plaintiff's damages in the general facts if these same items of damage will be sought under the various causes of action. This will enable you to avoid needless repetition of the same allegations under each claim.

Your Claim(s)

****

Causes of Action

V. Negligence

5.1   The Robinsons incorporate by reference each of the prior allegations contained within ¶¶ 1.1 through 4.6 above.

5.2   Both Defendant Brewery and Driver owed duties of ordinary care to the Robinsons. These duties were breached and such breaches were the proximate cause of the Robinsons damages. The Robinsons sue for recovery of all of their damages.

5.3   Driver was negligent in that he failed to observe or respond to construction signs and the slow-down in traffic, in failing to control the speed of the truck he drove, and in driving the truck into the rear of Susan Robinson's automobile at a high rate of speed. Driver was also negligent *per se* in driving the truck without the required commercial driver's license.

5.4   Brewery was negligent because under the doctrine of *respondeat superior*
       Brewery is vicariously liable for Driver's acts of negligence. Further, Brewery
       was independently negligent in permitting an unlicensed employee with poor
       vision to drive an 18-wheel tractor-trailer on the public highway in the course
       and scope of his employment for Brewery.

VI.   Gross Negligence

6.1   The Robinsons incorporate by reference each of the prior allegations contained
       within ¶¶ 1.1 through 5.4 above.

6.2   In permitting its employee with poor vision and no commercial driver's license
       to drive a fully loaded 18-wheel tractor-trailer on the public highway, Brewery
       was grossly negligence. Brewery had subjective awareness of a high probability
       of significant harm yet consciously disregarded this risk when it permitted
       Driver to drive its truck.

6.3   As a result of Brewery's gross negligence, the jury should be permitted to make
       an appropriate award of punitive damage to deter such misconduct and to
       punish Brewery. The Robinsons request that such an award of punitive
       damages be assessed against Brewery.

****

Because Rule 10(c) permit the claimant to refer to other allegations of the
pleading by reference, the plaintiff certainly need not be redundant in repeating the
same facts under each cause of action. For this reason, or in an abundance of
caution, advocates almost always begin the recitation of a cause of action by
incorporating the prior allegations by reference, as we have done above.
Sometimes lawyers may lump more than one cause of action together in the same
portion of the pleading, particularly if it involves related causes of action such as
for negligence and gross negligence. However, by separating out each cause of
action into its own section of the pleading, the advocate makes it easier to keep the
claims organized and to be sure to plead the appropriate elements of each claim
separately. Where the different causes of action have different remedies, it is
important to make the pleading clear as to what relief is requested under each
claim. When multiple claims are being presented you might consider listing first
either the strongest claim, the claim most applicable to the facts, or perhaps the
federal cause of action when the case is filed in federal court and involves both
federal and state causes of action. Again, this is up to you.

Relief Requested

****

VII.   Prayer

7.1   For the reasons stated above, the Robinsons pray that this Court enter judgment on their behalf as follows:

- Actual damages in the sum of $10,000,000, plus interest as permitted by law;
- Taxable costs of court;
- Exemplary damages as determined by the jury; and
- Any such other relief to which they may be justly entitled.

****

Jurisdictions vary as to whether it is appropriate or necessary to plead for specific damage amounts in the pleading. Federal courts do not require that a claimant plead the precise amount sought, though as you will see later, disclosure of such information in discovery, will be required. Even if this precis pleading of a dollar amount is permitted, you need to ask whether the claims are reasonably capable of being quantified so as to commit you and your client to a specific figure at this early stage. You also need to remember that even though you may obtain permission later from the court to amend your pleading, your opposing counsel may be allowed to show your original pleading to the jury.

Most important in drafting your prayer for relief is to make at least some mention of every category of relief for which you are suing the defendants-failure to even mention a category of damages can waive your client's entitlement to such recovery. You will also notice the catch-all provision listed at the end ("Any such other relief"). This is also a fairly universal practice of lawyers although it is of questionable actual value. If you show up for trial, for example, never having pled for lost earning capacity damages, never having itemized such damages in your formal discovery responses and never listing such damage in your joint pretrial statement as relief you seek, it is unlikely a judge will permit you to seek this additional item for the first time at trial no matter your reliance on this catchy mysterious phrase at the conclusion of your pleading. On the other hand, it is a relatively benign, short phrase to include and it may arguably be used to help support a motion for leave to amend later to formally seek additional damages. In the final analysis, you should use it or not depending upon how much you want your pleadings to conform to pleadings traditionally filed by other advocates.

Signatures

****

Respectfully submitted,

          _____

Jane Aikman, Esq.
State Bar No. 123456789
Trial Counsel

Aikman & Associates
315 Central Avenue
St. Petersburg, FL 33602
Telephone (727) 710-4396
Facsimile (727) 710-9944
Jaikman33602@yahoo.com

****

As discussed, Rule 11 requires a signature by at least one counsel for a party. The applicable Local Rules (Appendix III) require that this signature be personally affixed by counsel as well as the inclusion of a designation of "Trial Counsel" for the matter. The local rules in this jurisdiction, and generally, also require other information as to counsel's firm affiliation, mailing address, phone number, bar number, fax number and email address. Always check your local rules to see what specific information must be included on items filed with the clerk of your court. Also, for all pleadings you file after the initial complaint, you will need to also include a "Certificate of Service" at the end demonstrating whom you served, how you served the pleading and the date of service. This obviously is not applicable to your original complaint because it is not served by counsel but through formal service of process. A return of service prepared by the process server and filed with the court will provide proof of service of the original complaint.

To enable you to fully visualize the final work product,[12] the final draft of our original complaint would look like the following:

In the United States District Court
For the Middle District of Florida
Tampa Division

Susan Robinson &	§	
John Robinson,	§	
	§	
Plaintiffs,	§	
	§	
vs.	§	Civil Action No. _____
	§	
Paulson Breweries, Inc. &	§	
David Berning,	§	
	§	
Defendants.	§	

Plaintiff's Original Complaint

For their original complaint, Plaintiffs Susan Robinson and John Robinson (the "Robinsons") state the following:

I. Introduction

1.1   The Robinsons bring this action against Defendants to recover for the severe and permanent injuries suffered by Susan Robinson in a tragic accident on August 15, 2007 when the 18-wheel tractor-trailer unlawfully driven by Defendants smashed into Susan Robinson's vehicle from behind at a high

---

[12]Though not strictly a pleadings matter, it is worth noting here the good practice of making your demand for jury within the body of the original complaint. Rule 38(b) requires the jury demand to be made "not later than 10 days after service of the last pleading directed to such issue." In most cases, this ten days would begin to run with the service of the defendant's answer (the last pleading directed to the plaintiff's claims). Because many other distracting things can begin to happen after filing a new lawsuit, rather than take the chance of forgetting this important deadline, if you are inclined to make a jury demand you should simply do it sooner rather than later. A jury demand is particularly simple in federal court. All that is necessary is a one sentence demand for jury made in writing, served on opposing counsel and filed with the court. The rule even says that this demand "may be indorsed upon a pleading of the party" meaning that you can simply add this one-sentence demand at the end of your complaint. In some state court systems, a jury fee must be paid before any jury demand is effectuated.

speed. Susan Robinson suffered permanent and disabling physical and emotional injuries in this accident. Her husband, John Robinson, joins her in this suit to recover for the serious harm to his marital relationship with Susan that this unnecessary accident caused.

II. Parties

2.1   Plaintiffs Susan and John Robinson are individual citizens of Florida residing in St. Petersburg, FL. They have been married for five (5) years.

2.2   Defendant Paulson Breweries, Inc. ("Brewery") is a foreign corporation incorporated in Delaware and having its principal place of business in Madison, Wisconsin. Brewery is authorized to do business in Florida. Its registered agent for service of process is [include name and address of local agent, typically available from public corporate filings].

2.3   Defendant David Berning ("Driver") is an individual citizen of Georgia who resides at [list street address] Macon, Georgia. Drive was at all times related to this accident an employee of Brewery and acting in the course and scope of his employment with Brewery.

III. Jurisdiction and Venue

3.1   Plaintiffs are citizens of the State of Florida. Brewery is a citizen of the States of Delaware (its place of incorporation) and Wisconsin (its principal place of business). Driver is a citizen of the State of Georgia where he is domiciled. This matter in controversy greatly exceeds, exclusive of interest and costs, the sum of $75,000. Accordingly, this Court has subject matter jurisdiction over this matter in accordance with 28 U.S.C. § 1332.

3.2   Defendants are each subject to personal jurisdiction in Florida because they engaged in tortious conduct in Florida that was the cause of the Robinsons' harm for which they seek relief in this matter. Further, Florida's applicable long-arm statute provides for this Court's exercise of personal jurisdiction over the Defendants [add statutory citation].

3.3.   Venue is appropriate in this district and division pursuant to 28 U.S.C. § 1391(a)(2) because the tragic accident that gave rise to this lawsuit occurred in Tampa, Florida.

IV. Background Facts

4.1   John and Susan Robinson were high school sweethearts who married on June 1, 2002 in their hometown of St. Petersburg, Florida. Susan is a highly qualified certified public accountant and John is a public elementary school math teacher.

4.2   On the fateful afternoon of August 15, 2007, as Susan was driving north on I-275 on her way to do charitable work, the traffic ahead of her slowed due to construction on the freeway. Susan noticed this slow-down and appropriately reduced her speed. In fact, her car came to a complete stop as a result of the construction work. Within seconds of stopping, however, her car was smashed from behind at a high rate of speed by a fully loaded 18-wheel tractor-trailer driven by Driver on behalf of Brewery.

4.3   At the time of the accident, Driver had recklessly disregarded construction signs posted along the sides of the freeway and had either refused to slow down his vehicle or had failed to observe the obvious slow-down of traffic on the roadway. Upon information and belief, Driver's conduct either reflected his indifference to the safety of others or was due to a visual impairment that he had throughout his employment with Brewery.

4.4   At the time of the accident, Driver was driving Brewery's 18-wheel tractor-trailer unlawfully in that he failed to possess a valid commercial driver's license as required by Florida law [cite appropriate statute]. Upon information and belief, Brewery either was aware of Driver's failure to have such license or failed to obtain verification that he was properly licensed prior to permitting him to drive on its behalf.

4.5   Through no fault of her own, Susan Robinson was seriously injured in the accident fracturing her lower back. She is now permanently paralyzed and has suffered and continues to suffer extreme pain and anguish, physical disability and disfigurement, and lost enjoyment of life. She has incurred lost wages and, because she can no longer perform her prior duties as a certified public accountant, has a significantly diminished earning capacity in the future. As of this time, Susan has incurred over $500,000 in past medical expenses and is expected to have significant expenses for her health care and nursing assistance for the duration of her life.

4.6   As a consequence of the permanent and severe injuries suffered by Susan Robinson, the Robinsons' marriage has undergone tremendous upheaval and injury. Susan Robinson can no longer perform many of the important functions she previously committed to the marital relationship. John Robinson sues for this loss of consortium.

Causes of Action
V. Negligence

5.1   The Robinsons incorporate by reference each of the prior allegations contained within ¶¶ 1.1 through 4.6 above.

5.2   Both Defendant Brewery and Driver owed duties of ordinary care to the Robinsons. These duties were breached and such breaches were the proximate cause of the Robinsons damages. The Robinsons sue for recovery of all of their damages.

5.3   Driver was negligent in that he failed to observe or respond to construction signs and the slow-down in traffic, in failing to control the speed of the truck he drove, and in driving the truck into the rear of Susan Robinson's automobile at a high rate of speed. Driver was also negligent *per se* in driving the truck without the required commercial driver's license.

5.4   Brewery was negligent because under the doctrine of *respondeat superior* Brewery is vicariously liable for Driver's acts of negligence. Further, Brewery was independently negligent in permitting an unlicensed employee with poor vision to drive an 18-wheel tractor-trailer on the public highway in the course and scope of his employment for Brewery.

VI.   Gross Negligence

6.1   The Robinsons incorporate by reference each of the prior allegations contained within ¶¶ 1.1 through 5.4 above.

6.2   In permitting its employee with poor vision and no commercial driver's license to drive a fully loaded 18-wheel tractor-trailer on the public highway, Brewery was grossly negligence. Brewery had subjective awareness of a high probability of significant harm yet consciously disregarded this risk when it permitted Driver to drive its truck.

6.3   As a result of Brewery's gross negligence, the Robinsons request that punitive damages be assessed against Brewery in an amount sufficient to deter such misconduct and to punish Brewery.

VII.   Prayer

7.1   For the reasons stated above, the Robinsons pray that this Court enter judgment on their behalf as follows:

- Actual damages in the sum of $10,000,000, plus interest as permitted by law;
- Taxable costs of court;
- Exemplary damages as determined by the jury; and

- Any such other relief to which they may be justly entitled.

Respectfully submitted,

_____

Jane Aikman, Esq.
State Bar No. 123456789
Trial Counsel

Aikman & Associates
315 Central Avenue
St. Petersburg, FL 33602
Telephone (727) 710-4396
Facsimile (727) 710-9944
Jaikman33602@yahoo.com

b. Other Filing Tasks

In addition to preparing your original complaint for filing there are several other tasks you must complete in order to successfully get your new lawsuit underway. First, if you are in federal court you must fill out a civil cover sheet form. This form asks you basic information about the new case such as to identify the parties, counsel, to provide basic information about the type of case being filed, the relief requested, whether a jury is being demanded and the jurisdictional basis for the suit. This is not an essay exam but mostly fill in the blank and multiple choice. Below is the current version of the official civil cover sheet being utilized at federal courthouses today. You can obtain a current version of the applicable civil cover sheet by going to the website of most district courts.

Although the issue does not come up often, where a litigant has tried to take advantage of discrepancies between the substantive information provided by plaintiff's counsel on the civil cover sheet and their complaint, courts have said that the allegations of the complaint govern. The civil cover sheet's purpose, therefore, is not primarily for reliance by the opposing party but for statistical purposes by the courts and by the media which is given access to a copy of all the civil cover sheets filed in the clerk's office. This may seem like a trivial document to prepare, but clerks will refuse to file your new lawsuit without this document filled out and signed by counsel. If your suit is being filed on the last day before limitations runs, you do not want to risk having your filing rejected.

Second, you will need to prepare a summons for each defendant that you are planning to serve with the complaint. The summons form is contained in the FRCP Appendix of Forms as Form 1. You simply have to supply the case caption, the name of the defendant and the identity and mailing address of plaintiff's counsel. The clerk of court will supply the case number, date the summons and affix the clerk's official seal. At this point, the summons is ready to be served upon the defendant along with a copy of the complaint.[13] You can generally either pay a service fee for the court to obtain personal service or you can rely upon other approved methods of service of process, including retaining your own private process server.

Original Complaint Filing Checklist:

☐ Complaint form per Rule 10(a) (e.g., caption, numbered ¶s, court ID)?

☐ Complaint satisfies Rule 8(a) criteria (jurisdictional statement, the claim & remedy)?

☐ Any heightened pleading requirements applicable (e.g, fraud claim)?

☐ Complaint signed per Rule 11?

☐ Complaint satisfies local Rules (e.g., double-spaced, correct font and paper)?

☐ Consider any possible Rule 12 objections?

☐ Civil cover sheet prepared and signed?

☐ Summons prepared for each defendant?

Third, unless you represent an indigent, plaintiff must pay a filing fee to initiate a new lawsuit. Each court has a published list of filing fees for various

---

[13]Rule 4(f) provides for the various methods for serving complaints upon different types of defendants, such as individuals, corporations and foreign parties. Often even though your case may be in federal court, you are authorized to use methods of service available under the state law where the federal forum is physically located. Methods of service may include such things as personal service on the defendant, leaving the summons and complaint and the usual residence of the defendant, mailed service, or service upon the secretary of state for some foreign corporations.

pleadings and services and often the amount varies by the number of defendants you are suing. Like the civil cover sheet, you must tender a check to cover the cost of the filing fee upon presentation of your original complaint. Many pleadings and most motions have no filing fee but fees are generally required for things such as original complaints, counterclaims, cross-claims and third-party claims in many courts. It is not a bad idea to have your secretary check on the current rates either online or by placing a telephone call prior to finalizing your original complaint.

c. Amendment of Pleadings

Okay, you may be asking yourself how it is that we haven't even yet finished the chapter on drafting pleadings and already we have bumped into a topic heading dealing with amending these pleadings of ours. This is because most advocates in most disputed civil cases file amended pleadings commonly if not frequently. Indeed, because the civil procedure rules are set up in such a way as to contemplate the parties' receipt of significant factual information following the initial volley of pleadings through formal discovery, it should come as no great surprise to you that attorneys may need to amend their pleadings during the pretrial life of their lawsuits. The good news is that courts usually have no problems with counsel needing to amend their pleadings so long as the amendment is sought in a timely manner.

Rule 15 governs the filing of amended pleadings (those that supercede prior pleadings) and supplemental pleadings (those that complement or update prior pleadings). Rule 15(a) sets forth a very liberal standard. First, it indicates that a party "may amend the party's pleading once as a matter of course at any time before a responsive pleading is served or, if the pleading is one to which no responsive pleading is permitted and the action has not been placed on the trial calendar, the party may so ament it any time within 20 days after it is served." This provision gives counsel one quick shot at amending a pleading to correct a mistake or omission if done promptly. Few amendments are filed in this time period as a matter of course. Otherwise, the party may amend its pleading through one of two methods: (a) stipulation of opposing counsel; or (b) leave of court. If you decide to file an amended pleading your next step should be to contact opposing counsel to see if it can be done by agreement. If not, then you need to seek the court's permission. Rule 15(a) helps you this regard, though, by adding that "leave shall be freely given when justice so requires." The amount of time that has passed and the reason for not having pled the matter otherwise in your prior pleading are the critical focal points in this analysis. If you are seeking leave to plead a matter that you only recently became aware of during discovery, courts will be very accommodating to you in permitting amendment. If the allegation was something you knew about originally and you have waited to replead until after the discovery cut-off in your case and on the eve of trial, the court will be much less hospitable to your motion. The point is that you should act quickly once you are aware of the need to amend, either to add additional allegations or to delete allegations that no longer make sense or are warranted by your current knowledge of the facts or law.

Another portion of Rule 15 worth mentioning briefly is the relational back doctrine set forth in Rule 15(c). This states that certain amended pleadings can be considered to have been filed with the original pleading. Typically this is permitted when the "claim or defense asserted in the amended pleading arose out of the same conduct, transaction or occurrence set forth" in your original pleading. This means that if you sue a defendant for breach of contract and later discovery the party never intended to perform their promise–a type of promissory fraud recognized in many jurisdictions–the fraud claim will relate back in time to the filing of the original complaint. Why does this matter? If the fraud claim would otherwise be barred by the applicable statute of limitations, the relation back doctrine might rescue your cause of action. The broader the scope of the transaction or occurrence complained in your original petition, the easier will be your subsequent task of trying to assert an additional claim and claim the relation-back benefits from this rule.

Finally, Rule 15(d) permits supplemental pleadings to be filed upon motion on "such terms as are just" when the supplemental pleading desires to set forth a transaction or occurrence or event which has transpired since the filing of the original pleading. Note that both amended and supplemental pleading rules govern all types of pleadings–complaints, answers, counterclaims, cross-claims, third-party complaints, etc set forth in Rule 7(a).

These provisions are examples of the grace that is sometimes available to counsel under the rules of civil procedure. It is, of course, better not to have to ask for such grace but it is still somewhat reassuring to know that sometimes the court can give counsel a break.

C. RESPONDING TO & ATTACKING A COMPLAINT

Twenty days. Thirty days. At some stages of life–such as a high school student waiting for the beginning of the summer break or a new attorney waiting for bar results–these time periods seem to last an eternity. Even as a law student, this may seem like a long time to have to accomplish a task. But when your client has been served with a complaint, the clock is ticking and you have much to think about and important tasks to perform. And you must remember that, hopefully, you will have many clients and cases with different pretrial deadlines approaching nearly every day of the week. At the outset of the litigation, the defending party is typically in a reactive mode and does not have the luxury of time that many claimants possess to engage in lengthy investigations and analysis prior to filing a pleading. This may be heresy to admit, but some of the initial tasks of the defendant not be accomplished perfectly at the outset. We have already seen, for example, the grace afforded by the Rule 15 amendment procedure. But other potentially important rights possessed by your client have a short shelf life and, like Cinderella's carriage, will vanish at the appointed hour if not acted upon correctly.

Up until now, we have often focused upon the advocate's job representing a claimant. But for many of you, your first litigation experience will be representing a defendant in a new lawsuit. The goal of this section is to fix your eyes and thoughts on what you need to accomplish in the very early days defending against a claim. We will begin with the answer to the complaint.

a. Answers

Just as the plaintiff's advocate must file a pleading in order to preserve and prosecute her client's causes of action, so you as the defendant's advocate must respond to that complaint with a timely filing of an answer and/or a Rule 12 motion or else forfeit your client's defenses. Failure to file one or both of these documents within the prescribed time period from the date of service of process on your client–generally 20 days under the FRCP–results in the plaintiff's right to immediately obtain entry of default against your client under Rule 55(a).[14] This can land you in the office of a senior partner under bad circumstances as well as result in a very uncomfortable phone call to your malpractice insurance carrier.

---

[14]Rule 55(a) states that when a defending party has "failed to plead [answer] or otherwise defend as provided by these rules [Rule 12 motion] and that fact is made to appear by affidavit or otherwise, the clerk shall enter the party's default." Default judgment practice is beyond the intended scope of this text but our hope is that your first experience with it is as a plaintiff's counsel and not a defense counsel. It is worth noting that for "good cause" a defendant held in default can still obtain a court order setting it aside under Rule 55(c), but the recognized circumstances for application of this rules-based grace are limited and often require counsel's admission of error. One of your authors worked at a firm where rumor existed of a prior associate who kept a form affidavit on his computer that explained why he had missed an answer deadline–in apparent recognition of his many unfortunate encounters with default judgments.

Avoiding a default judgment, we suppose, is one minimal goal behind the preparation and filing of your answer. Yet from a strategic perspective, the initial appearance of the defendant in the lawsuit is the time to begin effectuating the defense advocate's case analysis and to start guiding the case toward the resolution desired by the defense client. From a slightly more technical perspective, there are three primary tasks associated with filing an answer–(i) responding to the plaintiff's allegations, (ii) stating affirmative defenses; and (iii) adding certain of the defendant's own claims to the litigation party. We will explore each of these tasks and then consider various attacks on the plaintiff's pleadings that the defense advocate can employ at the outset.

1. Responding to the claimant's allegations

Rule 12(a)(1)(A) provides that a defendant generally shall have "within 20 days afer being served" to serve an answer.[15] Rule 8(b)-(d) governs answers and these provisions contemplate the defending party doing one of three things in response to each factual allegation of the complaint or other pleading setting forth an affirmative claim for relief–admit, deny or say you don't know (or any combination of these three). Rule 8(b) provides that:

> A party shall state in short and plain terms the party's defenses to each claim asserted and shall admit or deny the averments upon which the adverse party relies. If a party is without knowledge or information sufficient to form a belief as to the truth of an averment, the party shall so state and this has the effect of a denial. Denials shall fairly meet the substance of the averments denied. When a pleader intends in good faith to deny only a part or a qualification of an averment, the pleader shall specify so much of it as is true and material and shall deny only the remainder. Unless the pleader intends in good faith to controvert all the averments of the preceding pleading, the pleader may make denials as specific denials of designated averments or paragraphs as the pleader expressly admits; but, when the pleader does so intend to controvert all its averments, including averments of the grounds upon which the court's jurisdiction depends, the pleader may do so by general denial subject to the obligations set forth in Rule 11.

---

[15]Rule 12 has always seemed an odd place to stick the answer deadline since Rule 12 governs various objections and Rule 8 governs answers. This placement underscores, however, the interplay between answers and Rule 12 motions.

Under Rule 8, a failure to deny is the same as an admission of an allegation's truth. Rule 8(d) says that "[a]verments in a pleading to which a responsive pleading is required, other than those as to the amount of damage, are admitted when not denied in the responsive pleading." The effect of these provisions is to transform simple words written in a pleading by the plaintiff's counsel into little time-bombs set to go off unless defused within the twenty days through a proper denial. Any pleading response which does not deny an allegation is treated as an admission. Also, unless the plaintiff's counsel has done such an awful job as to misstate every single factual allegation–including the identity of the parties or benign jurisdictional facts–you must parce through each and every allegation and determine whether to admit, deny or claim ignorance of the allegation's merit.

      Why not simply deny categorically the entirety of the plaintiff's complaint under the theory that you want to create as many barriers to the plaintiff's success as possible? Rule 8(b) specifically incorporates Rule 11's implicit representations to the court. Rule 8(b) states that unless you can comply with Rule 11 in denying every single allegation in a complaint, including such benign things as the party's name or jurisdictional facts, a so-called "general denial" is not permitted. We looked at most of the Rule 11 obligations earlier when we discussed the drafting of a claim. But at that time we did not consider one additional provision of Rule 11 applicable specifically to responsive pleadings. Rule 11(b)(4) instructs that in signing an answer (or other responsive pleading), the advocate's signature represents an implicit representation to the court that "the denials of factual contentions are warranted on the evidence or, if specifically so identified, are reasonably based on a lack of information and belief." Unless you or your client is aware of factual information suggesting that a factual allegation is incorrect, denying that allegation outright is not acceptable. You may still deny the allegation, in effect, when you are ignorant as to the truth of an allegation but you accomplish this result not through a denial but by affirmatively stating your ignorance. The effect of these provisions is to require you as the advocate to walk through each specific allegation of the complaint with your client and to determine which facts you agree are true, which are false and which you simply cannot determine to be true or false at that time without further investigation or discovery. But unlike some state courts that still permit the filing of a general denial, even when you know some facts to be true, defense advocates in federal court have to take care in only denying certain of the complaint's allegations or else risk running afoul of Rules 11 and 8.

In addition to adhering to Rule 11, another practical reason for being careful about what you deny, in preparing your answer, is because the denial of a fact your client *should* know can make your client look like a liar or fool under cross-examination either in deposition or

> Denial of a fact your client should know can make your client look like a liar or a fool under cross-examination.

at trial. When the corporate president is on the witness stand at trial having testified to her "hands-on" management approach, being challenged by the company's answer professing ignorance of a pleading alleging basic information about the corporation's structure does not bode well for the witness' credibility. One mistake, in other words, is not choosing your battles at the pleading stage. You may fear making the plaintiff's job easier by admitting to an alleged fact but you must remember that the case may actually be tried one day and surely you will not be contesting every material fact about the dispute in front of the jury. This is yet another reason why careful case analysis and early informal factual investigation (including thorough client interviews) are critical even at the early stages of pleading. These tasks will help you to master the basic factual overlay for the litigation and to understand the significance of each allegation in the plaintiff's pleading and the impact on the case of your admission or denial of such facts.

The federal rules' official Appendix of Forms offers a very simple example of the type of response required of an answer. It shows an example of a complaint and an answer to it, as follows:

Form 8. Complaint for Money Had and Received

1. Allegation of jurisdiction.

2. Defendant owes plaintiff ____ dollars for money paid by plaintiff to defendant by mistake on June 1, 1936, under the following circumstances: [here state the circumstances with particularity–see Rule 9(b)(1)].

Form 21. Answer to Complaint Set Forth in Form 8

Defense

Defendant admits the allegations stated in paragraph 1 of the complaint; and denies the allegations stated in paragraph 2 to the extent set forth in the counterclaim herein. [Counterclaim omitted.]

Some answers are as simple as that set forth in the above example but most filed in the real world are not. In fact, in the official example the seemingly broad denial of the second paragraph was actually made easier only by virtue of the pleading incorporating a counterclaim into the same document that offered additional explanation of the facts related to the original payment of money–otherwise the broad denial of the entirety of the factual support for the claim would seemingly have been too broad under Rules 8 and 11.

For another more real-world example, let's consider the complaint we drafted together in the previous section from the hypothetical case involving the 18-wheeler hitting plaintiff Susan Robinson's vehicle from behind. One paragraph of the plaintiff's complaint we drafted stated as follows:

4.3   At the time of the accident, Driver had disregarded construction signs posted along the sides of the freeway and had either refused to slow down his vehicle or had failed to observe the obvious slow-down of traffic on the roadway. Upon information and belief, Driver's conduct either reflected his indifference to the safety of others or was due to a visual impairment that he had throughout his employment with Brewery.

Imagine now that you have been hired to represent the driver. During your interview he admitted hitting the plaintiff from behind but denies that it was at least wholly his fault. He told you that he was momentarily distracted by looking to a map to locate his next exit when he looked up, saw the plaintiff's car stopped in the middle of the highway and was simply too late to avoid hitting her. He saw some construction signs and said the traffic was slow but stated that the plaintiff need not have come to a complete stop. He also admits to not having a commercial driver's license because of his past vision problems. (After the accident he had admitted this to the highway patrol officer and this was mentioned in the accident report you obtained.) Nevertheless, the driver inform you that last year he had surgery to correct his vision but he has not bothered to go apply for his commercial driver's license. He believed this was not a big deal because he already had a job for the Brewery and was a safe driver who never got pulled over by the police. With this information at hand, how should you draft the Driver's answer to this paragraph of the complaint? Consider the following possibility:

4.3   Defendant admits that he was involved in a traffic accident with Plaintiff Susan Robinson on the date in question. However, Defendant denies disregarding any construction signs or traffic conditions and denies any act of recklessness concerning the accident. Defendant further denies that his conduct was improper and, specifically, denies any indifference for safety or that he has had vision problems throughout his employment with the Defendant Brewery.[16]

Go back and compare this answer to the allegations from the complaint. Have we adequately responded to each allegation? A simple admission or denial in this circumstance would not have been realistically feasible because some of the facts alleged or referred to in the plaintiff's complaint are obviously true. Surely the defendant cannot deny the accident altogether–remember you do not want to represent at trial a fool or a liar and, further, Rule 11 would not permit denying this information. Because your client in apparent good faith takes issue with some of the circumstances of the accident and its causes, you can and should deny some of the other allegations in paragraph 4.3. Remember, it is not your job as the advocate to admit facts that you client disputes just because your opinion is that the jury will find the other side's story more credible. So long as you can deny the facts in good faith, you have satisfied Rule 11. (Your opinions, however, will be critical during settlement negotiations.) What about the denial of the vision problems? There is some truth to this allegation even by your client's own admission. However, your client informs you that he no longer has vision problems. Is this a scenario, contemplated by Rule 8(b) where "the pleader shall specify so much of [the allegation] as is true and material and shall deny only the remainder"? If so, you must admit that the driver previously had a vision problem but deny that it has continued. Most defense counsel in this scenario, however, would interpret the complaint to allege that the driver has *always* had a vision problem while driving for the Brewery and that unless this precise allegation is true, a simply denial of that entire allegation is warranted. Technically this approach seems sound; this example though demonstrates that application of Rule 8(b)'s seemingly simple dictates is often not very simple at all in a world of gray circumstances.

Three additional observations are available from this example. First, the more convoluted and colorful the language of the complaint, the easier it is for the defending party to simply deny an entire paragraph of allegations. The more the pleader uses adjectives to describe a factual allegation (e.g., "defendant improperly represented the status of the loan . . .") the greater the opportunity for

---

[16]You should note his this answer is numbered to correspond to the numbered paragraph in the complaint to which this response relates. Use of numbered paragraphs, as directed by Rule 10, thus makes the task of comparing the answer to the complaint easier for court and counsel.

the defendant to deny the allegation altogether. This bears consideration when you are drafting the allegations of a pleading. Are you more interested in telling a compelling story or in gaining admissions to basic facts to streamline your proof process later in the litigation? Depending upon your goals, your approach to the drafting problem may vary. Second, you should also be able to see how the task of answering a complaint can be very tricky and time-consuming. Yet this is too important a task to take lightly and your time invested in this process now will certainly pay dividends later in the case. Third, there may be some allegations that offer a legal conclusion that is mixed with a factual allegation implicit or mixed with the statement of law. For example, in our example the reference to the defendant "recklessly disregarding" the construction signs is neither purely a factual allegation nor a statement of law. You might consider it to be a mixed observation of fact and law. For this reason, the defendant must respond to this allegation–presumably by denying it in its entirety as we have done with our draft response. A purely legal allegation, such as that "this court has subject matter jurisdiction over this case" or that "Title VII applies equally to sexual and racial discrimination" would technically not require an admission or denial. When in doubt if an allegation is of law or fact, however, certainly the safest approach is to treat it as a factual allegation and respond to it accordingly.

2. Stating all affirmative defenses

Beyond responding directly to the factual allegations of the plaintiff's complaint, the party responding to a pleading asserting a claim has the obligation under Rule 8(c) to affirmatively plead in response all "any . . . matter constituting an avoidance or affirmative defense." The goal of this pleading requirement, perhaps as is true with virtually all pleading requirements, is to avoid unfair surprise at trial. The rules drafters were nice enough to include within the text of this rule a non-exhaustive list of such defenses, including "accord and satisfaction, arbitration and award, assumption of the risk, contributory negligence, discharge in bankruptcy, duress, estoppel, failure of consideration, fraud, illegality, injury by fellow servant, laches, license, payment, release, res judicata, statute of frauds, statute of limitations, waiver . . . ." This rule seems fairly straightforward, at least where your client wishes to assert one of the foregoing defenses. You simply must raise this in your answer (usually a fairly conclusory listing of such under the title "Affirmative Defenses" after the admissions and denials) or else risk waiving it. The only caveat here to the waiver principle is that the court might subsequently permit you to file an amended answer adding an affirmative defense previously omitted from your pleading, particularly if later-acquired discovery only made you aware of the defense.

The only significant litigation dispute concerning Rule 8(c) arises in situations where it is unclear if a certain defensive allegation that was not mentioned in an answer constitutes an affirmative defense and has been waived. Characterization of something as an affirmative defense or not is undoubtedly an area for substantive law to resolve and so resort to state law in a diversity jurisdiction case is often needed to supply the answer to this procedural inquiry. Some matters are not entirely clear. Take for example the concept of a plaintiff's failure to mitigate damages. This might sound like an affirmative defense yet at least some courts have ruled that it is actually an "inferrential rebuttal"–that is, something that argues against one of the elements of the plaintiff's claim (proximate causation of harm)–rather than a true defense. As the defense advocate, you should be well informed on what the substantive law controlling the disputed claims recognizes to be defenses to each claim and you need to know whether any of these "defenses" are considered to be an affirmative defense. Affirmative defenses are often described as matters of "confession and avoidance." You might think of such defenses as implicitly saying in response to the plaintiff's allegations "yes, but . . . ." In other words, "yes I may have been negligent in performing surgery on you, but that was ten years ago and you have waited too long to sue me under the statute of limitations." When in doubt as to whether some defensive argument or doctrine you may rely upon must be pled affirmatively or not, it is much better to go ahead and plead the questionable matter rather than to inject a trial dispute into your pleadings. After all, do you really want to have plaintiff's counsel at trial object to your evidence as beyond the scope of the pleadings and irrelevant at trial because of your failure to plead it under Rule 8(c)? Because trial courts' rulings are not always easily predictable, it would be far better to have pled the matter in your answer. It is not the goal of this book to advocate that you habitually do certain things solely to "cover" your behind, but when there is no significant upside in undertaking a procedural risk, the "safe" approach truly is the better approach.

3. Asserting the defendant's own claims

The final item for consideration in drafting your client's answer is the assertion of the defendant's own causes of action. In the case of compulsory counterclaims, including this claim within your answer is essential in order to avoid waiving the claim. With respect to other claims–permissive counterclaims, cross-claims and third-party claims, it may simply be good litigation strategy or efficiency to plead them with your client's answer. The rules governing the drafting of original complaints apply with equal force to each of these three additional varieties of claims. Rule 8(a) provides for the same three essential ingredients we already learned about earlier, Rule 11 applies equally (as it does to any written document filed with the court and signed by counsel), Rule 10 contemplates the same general organization and even Rule 12(b) applies to such claims permitting courts to consider their early dismissal on technical grounds.

b. Counterclaims

Some say that there is no good defense like a good offense. If that is your philosophy for dispute resolution you will love to file counterclaims. Rule 13 divides counterclaims into two varieties, those that must be asserted with the answer ("compulsory") or else are waived and those that may be asserted by the defendant at its pleasure ("permissive"). Counterclaims are claims that a litigant asserts against someone who has already sued them first. That is, counterclaims are asserted against those already considered *opposing parties*. The difference in definition between compulsory and permissive is whether the counterclaim is related to the plaintiff's claim(s) set forth in the complaint. If the counterclaim "arises out of the same transaction or occurrence" as any claim set forth in the plaintiff's complaint, then the counterclaim would be denominated as compulsory under Rule 13(a). This definitional test is the same test we previously saw in Rule 20 governing joinder of additional claimants or defendants to a lawsuit and, in fact, is the test for relatedness used in many procedural and jurisdictional rules governing civil cases. Courts will typically consider the degree of evidentiary overlap as well as the extent to which the counterclaim is logically related to the plaintiff's original claim in analyzing whether the counterclaim would be considered compulsory or permissive.

Where there is any chance that your client's counterclaim would be considered compulsory, you and your client must decide during the initial twenty day answer period whether the client should assert this claim or waive it. Obviously, spotting the existence of such a claim is part of the goal of your initial defense client interviews. You must always remember to step back from the hand-wringing associated with focusing upon your adversary's original complaint long enough to consider possible counterclaims. As between compulsory and permissive counterclaims, spotting the compulsory counterclaims is a relatively easier task since, by definition, they must relate to the plaintiff's original claim. At every interview of the defense client you should also inquire about any other disputes your client has with the plaintiff however unrelated. While the unrelated counterclaims need not be asserted with your original answer it might be a wise litigation strategy to do so. It is not unheard of at all for the counterclaim to end up exceeding in importance, focus and pretrial activities the original claim–the tail wagging the dog you might say. There is also incredible efficiency and finality achieved when two opposing parties air all of their grievances in one proceeding rather than engaging in piecemeal legal attacks upon one another. This is the rationale behind the procedural rules' tolerance for the filing of unrelated counterclaims. If nothing else, a counterclaim might be useful for leverage in negotiating a settlement of the plaintiff's claim or as a legal offset for a portion of the defendant's possible liability to the plaintiff.

In state courts, the procedural inquiry—whether the rules require or permit the filing of the counterclaim—is the end of the legal analysis. But in federal court, because each claim must have jurisdictional legs upon which to stand, the advocate must also consider whether the federal court has subject matter jurisdiction over a contemplated counterclaim. With regard to compulsory counterclaims—those arising out of the same transaction or occurrence as the plaintiff's original claim—the jurisdictional analysis is pretty easy. Even if there is no independent subject matter jurisdiction for the counterclaim, because it is neither arises under federal law nor meets the diversity requirements for jurisdiction, there should almost always be supplemental jurisdiction for such counterclaims under 28 U.S.C. § 1367(a) which uses virtually the same test as 13(a) for relatedness. In other words, this supplemental jurisdiction statute contemplates subject matter jurisdiction for related claims asserted by defendants; compulsory counterclaims are so related. Where the defendant's counterclaim might stumble jurisdictionally is with regard to permissive counterclaims. By definition, these will not satisfy the § 1367(a) test for supplemental jurisdiction because they are unrelated to the federal anchor claim. Therefore, any permissive counterclaim either needs to arise under federal law or meet the diversity requirements (complete diversity and more than $75,000 in controversy) to be asserted in federal court. If it does not, such counterclaim will have to either be saved for another rainy day or filed elsewhere.

In terms of helping to spot possible counterclaims for your defense client, one other interesting legal phenomena is worth observation here. Some states have what have been referred to as "revival" statutes for compulsory counterclaims.[17] A claim that might otherwise be considered stale or time-barred under the applicable statute of limitations, can frequently be asserted anyway if brought as a compulsory counterclaim within a certain period of time. This is another reason why, as a plaintiff's counsel, you need to consider possible counterclaims that your original complaint might draw because, in opening the doors to the

---

[17][Insert a couple of example statutes here.]

courthouse and inviting in the defendant, you might also be resuscitating a claim that the plaintiff had presumed to be dead.

c. Cross-claims

A cross-claim is a claim asserted by a litigant against a *co-party*. More often than not, cross-claims tend to be claims for contribution or indemnity filed by one defendant against a fellow defendant jointly sued by the plaintiff but the rules do not limit cross-claims to such narrow confines. Rule 13(g) does, however, limit the scope of permissible cross-claims to claims that are closely related to either those claims asserted in plaintiff's original complaint *or* those claims asserted in a counterclaim filed in the case. To this extent, cross-claims might somewhat resemble compulsory counterclaims because they must logically relate to another claim already in the case. But unlike compulsory counterclaims, cross-claims are *never* required to be filed in the same action. It's one thing for the procedural rules to require enemies (i.e., opposing parties) to bring their related claims against each other in the same suit, but the procedural rules are not designed to create enemies out of co-parties. You are not required to assert a cross-claim by any procedural rule.

Interestingly, this same principle must be borne in mind when you are analyzing the possibility of asserting a cross-claim against your client's co-party. Do you want to make a potential enemy out of someone who may be "on your side" at the present? Every relationship is different so there is no rule of thumb for when to assert such a cross-claim and when to refrain from doing so. You should consider the impact of the filing on your client's relationship (personal, business and litigation) with the co-party as well as the impact of such filing on your client's ability to defend against the plaintiff. How will the jury view your allegations and proof against the co-party? Does this same evidence also tend to incriminate your client on the plaintiff's claim? These kinds of concerns prompt many advocates to hold off on filing a cross-claim, often deferring such disputes until after the plaintiff's claim is resolved. As with compulsory counterclaims, because cross-claims must be related to another claim already before the court, they are usually within the court's supplemental jurisdiction even if there is no independent federal jurisdiction for the claims.

d. Third-party claims

The final variety of claim that a defendant might consider injecting into an existing lawsuit is a third-party claim against a *non-party* for contribution or indemnification. These claims are governed by Rule 14 and are the narrowest category of claims permitted to be filed by a defendant.[18] Rule 14 describes the scope of permitted third-party claims to be those that are against a "person not a party to the action who is or may be liable to the third-party plaintiff [the defendant] for all or part of the plaintiff's claim against the third-party plaintiff." In application, this refers to claims that a defendant might have if found liable to the plaintiff against a non-party to help satisfy or reimburse for all or a portion of that defendant's liability to the plaintiff–in other words, only claims for contribution or indemnification. While many cross-claims are for contribution and indemnity, third-party claims by definition are limited to such scenarios. Most jurisdictions that recognize joint and several tort liability permit one tortfeasor to sue another joint tortfeasor to help contribute (reimburse) to the judgment. Recognizing such a right ameliorates the harshness of the common law joint and several liability doctrine. Indemnification can arise by contract (e.g., an indemnity agreement) or by law (e.g., many jurisdictions permit one held vicariously liable for another's misconduct to seek indemnification from them). If your defendant-client advises you that the plaintiff has simply made a mistake and sued the wrong party this does not give rise to a third-party claim because, if true, your client would have no liability to the original plaintiff. Without such possible exposure to the plaintiff, there is no third-party claim possible. Given the very narrow scope of permissible third-party claims, it is hard to envision one that is properly made procedurally that would not be within a federal court's supplemental jurisdiction because third-party claims are intrinsically related to the main claim.

Strategically, a third-party claim may be a valuable way to get another possible wrongdoer before the jury as well as to bring another party into the settlement talks so that your client is not left paying for the plaintiff's entire damages initially. The primary countervailing consideration is whether your defense client would be better off at a trial against the plaintiff pointing to the "empty chair" and blaming the entire incident on the non-party who may not even make an appearance at trial to argue otherwise.

---

[18]Technically, both cross-claims and third-party claims can be asserted by plaintiffs as well as defendants but this is much rarer. For example, during discovery a plaintiff might discover that a co-plaintiff's negligence might have been a cause of the accidental injuries and file a cross-claim against that co-plaintiff. Likewise, if a plaintiff's complaint has drawn a counterclaim from the defendant, the plaintiff may file a third-party claim against a non-party for contribution or indemnity on that potential liability arising out of the counterclaim. Things can get complex in terms of diagraming out the various claims that can begin to expand from the roots of the original complaint.

As long as a third-party claim is filed (either in the same pleading as the answer or in a separate pleading entitled a "Third Party Complaint") within ten days of defendant's service of its original answer, no permission from the court is required. After this initial ten day window, a motion for leave to file the third-party complaint must be presented to the court. Obviously, the more time that has passed in the pretrial life of the case the more potential prejudice there would be to other parties to the litigation from the untimely assertion of the third-party claim. The sooner you and your client can decide whether to assert such a claim, the better.

e. Rule 12 objections/motions

We have previously looked at the Rule 12(b) objections that can be lodged against a complaint–things going either to the court's jurisdictional power over either the case or the defendant (12(b)(1)-(2)), the plaintiff's filing of the case in the wrong venue (12(b)(3)), the plaintiff's bungling of service (12(b)(4)-(5)), the plaintiff's failure to satisfy Rule 8(a)'s elements by accurately pleading a cognizable claim (12(b)(6)) or filing a lawsuit and leaving out a necessary party (12(b)(7)). Any of these matters, according to Rule 12(b), can be asserted either by simply reciting a short objection within your answer or raising the matter by separate motion to dismiss. Of course, merely listing such an objection in your answer might very well preserve the matter but it hardly brings the issue before the court for resolution. If you actually want to obtain a ruling on any such matter, you should file a motion to dismiss (complying with your local rules governing motions) and seek a ruling on it. Other than serving as an attempt to bring a speedy resolution to a lawsuit, Rule 12(b) is also used by defense counsel for purposes of delay in having to file an answer. This is because filing any Rule 12 motion effectively stays any obligation to file your answer until ten days after the court has ruled upon the motion.[19] Rule 11 does not condone filing a motion for purposes of delay,[20] and counsel should be cautioned against filing frivolous motions for any purpose. But the truth is that often defense counsel do see this

---

[19]Rule 12(a)(4) states that service of "a motion permitted under this rule" alters the time period for the filing of answers until 10 days after the court has denied the motion. Of course, if the court grants the motion no answer is needed anyway. Often, with respect to Rule 12(b)(6) motions to dismiss for failure to state a claim, a court in granting the motion will give plaintiff's counsel leave to file an amended complaint seeking to cure the pleading deficiency unless the court determines that such opportunity would be futile.

[20]You may recall that the first implicit representation made by counsel filing any motion is that it is "not being filed for any improper purpose, such as . . . to cause unnecessary delay . . . ." Rule 11(b)(1).

automatic extension of time as an additional motivation for filing a possible Rule 12 motion. As we went through the preparation of an answer, you could appreciate how time-consuming the process can be particularly if the complaint is fairly lengthy and there is significant factual history alleged. Apparently any motion made under Rule 12, whether to dismiss or for a more definite statement, provides this pleading extension.

In addition to the Rule 12(b) motions to dismiss, Rule 12 offers a party defending a claim three other possible motions. Rule 12(e) provides for a "motion for a more definite statement" whenever the responding party is unable to frame a responsive pleading due to the "vague or ambiguous" nature of the claim pled. If granted by the court, the claimant must replead their claim or face dismissal. At the opposite end of the spectrum, Rule 12(f) offers a "motion to strike" when the claimant has pled any matter that is "redundant, immaterial, impertinent, or scandalous."[21] This motion is of rather dubious value because, physically, even when a matter is ordered "stricken" the original pleading is still on file and may be reviewed by any member of the public no matter how scandalous the original allegations may have been. In practice, district judges disdain Rule 12(e) motions because the defending party can utilize formal discovery to obtain a more definite statement of the claim. They likewise disdain Rule 12(f) motions because they actually accomplish very little. Use these two motions sparingly and only when there is a valuable strategic objective sought to be achieved.

The one other motion possible under Rule 12 is the motion for judgment on the pleadings. Rule 12(c) provides that "[a]fter the pleadings are closed but within such time as not to delay the trial, any party may move for judgment on the pleadings." This rule is treated by courts as roughly equivalent with a Rule 12(b)(6) motion except that it is filed after an answer has been filed rather than in a pre-answer motion. Also, Rule 12(c) reiterates that it only deals with legal deficiencies evident on the face of the pleadings as any such motion relying upon matters of proof extrinsic to the pleadings should instead be treated as a motion for summary judgment under Rule 56. We will discuss summary judgement practice in considerable detail in Chapter 9.

What we have not yet discussed is *when* Rule 12 objections/motions need to be asserted and the consequence of failing to assert such objections in the

---

[21]Rule 12(f) also suggests that when a defending party's answer has pled something that constitutes an "insufficient defense" the claimant can similarly seek an order striking the matter from the answer.

defendant's original answer or concurrent with the answer in a motion. The answer to both inquiries varies depending upon the particular objection being discussed. A basic understanding of how Rules 12(g) and (h) work together is needed to appreciate the deadlines associates with Rule 12 motions. Rule 12(g) states that a party who makes a Rule 12 motion must include within it all other Rule 12 objections available to the party or else the other non-included matters are waived. This waiver principle expressly *does not* apply to motions referenced in Rule 12(h)(2)–chiefly 12(b)(6) and (b)(7) motions. But the wavier concept runs deeper than this rule of mandatory coupling of all Rule 12 motions together, for you can waive Rule 12 matters by not making any timely motion as well. Rule 12(h) provides this broader waiver principle and breaks the rule down into three scenarios:

> (1) objections to personal jurisdiction (12(b)(2), improper venue (12(b)(3)), and service of process objections (12(b)(3)-(4)) are all waived if not made in the defendant's answer or by motion filed concurrently with the answer;

> (2) objections for failure to state a claim (12(b)(6) and failure to join an indispensable party under Rule 19 (12(b)(7)) may be made in any pleading, in a motion for judgment on the pleadings (Rule 12(c)) or even at trial on the merits;

> (3) an objection to the court's lack of subject matter jurisdiction (12(b)(1)) may be asserted by "suggestion of the parties" at any time.[22]

What sense can be made of these distinctions? The first category deal with problems that might cause unfairness to the defendant's ability to litigate the matter, such as being sued in an improper geographic location or not receiving legally adequate notice of the lawsuit. As the Supreme Court has stated, venue is "primarily a matter of convenience [for] litigants and witnesses."[23] As these

---

[22]You may recall covering the case of *Louisville & Nashville R.R.Co. v. Mottley* 219 U.S. 467 (1911) in your first year civil procedure class. In that case, even though no parties ever brought up a problem with the trial court's subject matter jurisdiction, on appeal the U.S. Supreme Court raised it for the first time in the court's opinion vacating the judgment. That case demonstrates that so long as the case still has a breathe of life to it, problems with subject matter jurisdiction can be asserted. Only after the final appeal is exhausted is it too late to raise such an objection.

[23]*Denver & Rio Grande Western R.R. Co. v. Brotherhood of Railroad Trainmen*, 387 U.S. 556, 560 (1967).

constraints are more designed for the benefit of the defendant, there is little hesitation to find waiver when that defendant has chosen not to assert the matter initially. At the other end of the spectrum, problems associated with subject matter jurisdiction go to notions of federalism which are not a matter that an individual defendant ought to be allowed to subvert through waiver. So long as the case is still pending, even at the highest level of appeal, subject matter jurisdiction issues can be raised. In the middle category are objections (12(b)(6) and (b)(7)) that might impair the ability of the court to work efficiently and effectively. Therefore, it makes some sense for a defendant to be able to assert problems with plaintiff's failure to state a claim or to join an indispensable party at a later time, even at trial. However, as a strategic matter, even when Rule 12 permits the raising of a certain Rule 12 matter at a time after the filing of the defendant's answer, this does not mean that it is wise for a defendant to tarry in raising such issues. The sooner the better is the rule of thumb and certainly before the trial judge (and your client) has invested considerable time and energy in resolving the dispute. For example, if you truly believe that a questionable claim asserted by the plaintiff may not be legally cognizable even assuming the facts as alleged by plaintiff to be true, why would you not raise this matter as soon as possible? The alternative is to waste much time and money doing discovery that logically should make no difference in the case outcome. Rule 12 is full of opportunities for the defense advocate to bring to an abrupt halt many a lawsuit filed without either adequate case analysis or proper pleading.

f. Changing the Forum

The last topic for this chapter concerns what might be most accurately described as not so much a direct "attack" on the plaintiff's pleading but more of an end-run around what is often the most important strategic decision the plaintiff can make in a lawsuit–the plaintiff's choice of forum for the suit. You may recall our earlier discussion from the prior chapter on how important the forum selection can be on the perceived likely outcome of a lawsuit. In the world of litigation, most cases are disposed of by settlement and settlements are driven by perceptions of what the likely outcome would be at trial. Thus, perception becomes reality. And there is increasing empirical evidence that this perception of the important role that forum selection plays in case outcomes is grounded in fact. Recent scholars researching this phenomenon confirmed the common sense conclusion that the "forum matters" to case outcomes.[24] If this is true, then wouldn't it make sense as the defense advocate that if you could upset the plaintiff's forum choice that you would gain tremendous leverage in the litigation? Research reveals that the role of forum in influencing case outcomes may be strongest when a plaintiff's choice of a forum is denied by the defendant's legal maneuvers such as, for example, whe a defendant removes a case from state to federal court. One researcher looking into this precise situation observed that "a plaintiff's ability to avoid removal [from state to federal court] could mean the difference between winning and losing."[25] Because trial lawyers know that the forum is so important, both plaintiff and defendant advocates spend much time and energy in civil pretrial litigation focused upon forum issues. We will provide an overview of several methods available to the defendant to shift the momentum in the case away from the plaintiff's forum through both direct and indirect attacks on the plaintiff's forum choice.

4. Venue

We have previously discussed one direct attack on the plaintiff's forum selection and that is through the Rule 12(b)(3) motion to dismiss for improper venue. The substantive inquiry under such motion is whether the plaintiff has complied with the applicable venue statute, typically 28 U.S.C. § 1391.[26] In the last chapter we already provided you an overview of this venue statute which focuses most venue choices on either the district where a substantial portion of the actions that gave rise to the claim arose or where the defendant resides. If the plaintiff has filed the case in a district not authorized by the venue statute, the

---

[24]Kevin M. Clermont & Theodore Eisenberg, *Do Case Outcomes Really Reveal Anything About the Legal System? Win Rates and Removal Jurisdiction*, 83 Cornell L. Rev. 581, 598 (1998).

[25]Allyson Singer Breeden, *Federal Removal Jurisdiction and Its Effect on Plaintiff Win-Rates*, Res Gestae 1 (Sept. 2002) (finding that the plaintiff win-rate in removed federal civil lawsuits is 36.7% compared to a overall win-rate in federal civil cases of 57.9%). Professors Clermont & Eisenberg, *supra*, found a win-rate in original diversity cases of 71% but only a 34% win-rate for cases originally filed in state court but removed to federal court.

[26]While § 1391 is the general federal venue statute, many other specialized venue statutes exist. A few examples can be found in 28 U.S.C. §§ 1392, 1397, 1400-1402. Part of the advocate's initial legal research of the substantive law should focus upon whether any specialized venue provisions apply to the claims raised by the facts. In fact, the opportunity to take advantage of a specialized venue provision might even influence the choice of claims to be asserted in the plaintiff's original complaint.

defendant actually has two options. First, the defendant may file a Rule 12(b)(3) motion to dismiss. This is often the less potent of the two options. The other option derives not from the procedural rules but from 28 U.S.C. § 1406(a) which provides, in part:

> The district court of a district in which is filed a case laying venue in the wrong division or district shall dismiss, or if it be in the interest of justice, transfer such case to any district or division in which it could have been brought.

The advantage of this statute is that it gives the defendant the opportunity to divest the venue choice from the plaintiff when the plaintiff has been too sloppy or aggressive with its original choice. If the defendant simply asks for dismissal under Rule 12(b)(3), the plaintiff then has the chance to choose again when she refiles her lawsuit in another forum. The venue statutes are often broad enough to provide multiple districts as candidates to host the lawsuit, particularly after prior language from § 1391 pointing to the district where the claim "arose" was modified to the current language which points to any district where a "substantial part" of the events giving rise to the dispute occurred. As you might imagine, there are a great many causes of action that involve facts that occurred in more than one district. Imagine a simple fraud case that occurs over a telephone call placed in New York and received in Los Angeles. The fraud claim would like be deemed to arise in both of those districts. Dismissal under 12(b)(3) simply puts the matter back in the hands of the plaintiff to select another forum of the plaintiff's choosing. Section 1406, however, allows the defendant to suggest an appropriate venue choice to the court when the plaintiff's first choice is improper. In effect, the plaintiff who made the original bad venue choice is penalized by placing the court in the position of blessing an alternative venue picked by the defendant instead. In this way, § 1406 is a powerful tool for the defendant.

Even if the plaintiff's original venue selected was authorized by a venue statute, that choice is still not necessarily absolute. Section 1404 allows the defendant to request that the district court transfer the case to another district where the case could have been filed to promote convenience. This section provides in part: "For the convenience of parties and witnesses, and in the interest of justice, a district court may transfer any civil action to any other district or division where it might have been brought."[27] This means that any case pending in a federal district court (even those that arrived there upon removal from a state

---

[27] 28 U.S.C. § 1404(a).

court) may be transferred to any other district in the country where it could have been filed originally, so long as the district court concludes that for reasons of convenience and justice the proposed forum is a superior choice. How far superior the other district has to be is not always clear. Courts often say that they give great deference to the plaintiff's original selection but even this principle is not applicable when the plaintiff has chosen to file the suit originally in a forum other than the plaintiff's own home.

In application, courts say that this provision requires consideration of public interest factors and private interest factors. The former considers as between the original forum and the proposed forum matters such as the relative time to trial, the forum's interest in resolving the issues, the relative access to sources of proof, and each forum's familiarity with the likely substantive law to be applied in the case. With regard to the so-called private factors, the most significant considerations are the location of key witnesses and documents and the amenability to subpoena for witnesses beyond the control of the parties.

The burden of demonstrating that the proposed transferee district is far superior to the original district lies with the defendant moving for transfer. In reality, district courts have great discretion in ruling on a motion to transfer venue and in different cases the relative importance of particular considerations may vary widely. Defense advocates preparing a motion to transfer venue for convenience must plan to support the arguments balancing the public and private factors with affidavit proof demonstrating specifically the facts that show the proposed district to be superior. Conclusory allegations in support of such a transfer typically lead to a prompt denial of the motion. The movant must plan to be specific as, for example, listing the witnesses in the proposed district and explaining the importance of their likely testimony to a resolution of the case.

Defendants considering the filing of such a motion should also consider whether a Rule 12(b)(2) attack on the forum's personal jurisdiction over the defendant is warranted because many of the same private interest factors that argue in favor of transfer frequently also suggest a lack of minimum contacts between the existing forum and the defendant. For this reason, motions to transfer for convenience are often coupled with a Rule 12(b)(2) motion to dismiss for lack of personal jurisdiction. If you find yourself preparing a motion to transfer for convenience, you should be sure to pause and analyze whether there is any valid objection to the court's exercise of personal jurisdiction as well.

One other different though related procedural device is a motion to dismiss for *forum non conveniens*. This is a judicially created doctrine that allows a court–state or federal–to dismiss a case despite being filed in a proper forum because there is a far superior forum for the lawsuit. As with § 1404 motions, a motion to dismiss for forum non conveniens also considers generally the same public and private interest factors discussed above and the movant is likewise considered to bear a heavy burden of demonstrating that the other forum is far superior to the original forum.[28] The biggest difference in scope is that forum non conveniens is applied when the proposed forum is not part of the same judicial system as the original forum. Thus, a case filed in Georgia state court cannot be transferred to another court in California because that is a foreign system. A case filed in Georgia state court could only be transferred to a sister Georgia court. Further, even a case filed in federal court cannot be transferred to a court outside of the U.S. federal court system. So a case filed in federal district court in Minnesota cannot be transferred to Brazil. In both of these examples, however, the defendant in Georgia state court can move for dismissal in favor of a California forum and the defendant in Minnesota federal court can move for dismissal in favor of a Brazilian forum. Another major difference between forum non conveniens and dismissal and § 1404 transfer is that the former permits the subsequent forum to apply different substantive law (Brazilian law over Minnesota law) than the original forum would have, assuming the ultimate forum's choice of law rules dictate such a result. However, when cases are transferred under § 1404, the transferee court is supposed to apply the same choice of law principles as the original court and, at least theoretically, the transfer should not impact the substantive law to be applied to the case.

Each of these venue-centric devices can be used by the defendant to effectuate a horizontal movement of the case from the original forum to one more desired by the defendant. Doing so can have great impact on both pretrial matters and the anticipated trial of the case.

5. Removal to Federal Court

Federal removal procedures permit defendants in certain instances to remove a case from state court to the federal district court in the district embracing the place where the state court is located.[29] For example, a state court action filed in St. Petersburg, Florida (Pinellas County) would be removed to the United States

---

[28] *Piper Aircraft Co. V. Reyno,* 454 U.S. 235 (1981).

[29] 28 U.S.C. § 1441(a) sets the general standard for the removal of cases.

District Court for the Middle District of Florida, Tampa Division located in nearby Tampa, Florida (Hillsborough County).[30] Often this results in the case being shifted to a different court in the same city. Other times, as with our example, the removal results in the case being moved to an adjoining county. Most significantly, the defendant gains a new judge, new federal procedures, different rules of evidence, a new docket, a different jury, different appellate judges, the possibility for the application of different substantive law[31] and certainly the prospect for a different perceived outcome for the case. Not bad for an afternoon's work at the computer for defense counsel. For many defendants sued in remote and undesirable locations–perhaps one of the so-called "judicial hellholes"[32]–the chance to remove a case to federal court may be much more important to it than any of the lawsuit's underlying facts or applicable law. Obviously plaintiff's counsel want to narrow if not eliminate removal prospects in such cases and and defendant's counsel wants to be sure to spot the right to remove and act on it effectively. We will first explore the scope of removal jurisdiction in the federal courts and then discuss removal procedures stopping along the way to provide tips to both plaintiff and defense counsel.

a. Scope of Removal Jurisdiction

The scope of cases that can be removed to federal court is governed by 28 U.S.C. § 1441 and is somewhat more limited than those cases that could have

---

[30]Title 28 lists for each federal district and division the state court counties (or parishes) that comprise that district and division. This takes all of the guess-work out of the practitioner's analysis of where to remove a state court case. In a sense, this acts as an alternative venue provision for federal court cases that arrive at the federal courthouse through removal processes rather than as an originally filed federal case.

[31]If you paid attention in your civil procedure class, you will of course object to this statement as being inconsistent with *Erie Railroad v. Tompkins*, 304 U.S. 64 (1938), which taught that in diversity cases the federal court should apply the same substantive law as the state courts. This principle is all well and good but ignores the fact that when the controlling state law is unclear, the federal court must make an "Erie guess" as to what state law is and how state law applies to the particular case before the court. For a good discussion of this phenomenon, see Benjamin C. Glassman, *Making State Law in Federal Court*, 41 Gonzaga L. Rev. 237 (2005/06).

[32]The American Tort Reform Association annually publishes a list of the "most unfair jurisdiction in which to be sued" on its website located at http://www.atra.org/reports/hellholes. As an example, the ATRA identifies as a regular member of its list the "Rio Grande Valley and Gulf Coast, Texas" which it describes as having a "reputation as a 'plaintiff paradise' . . . where extremely weak evidence can net multimillion dollar awards . . . ." An out of state corporation sued in such a state court frequently views removal as its only chance to avoid paying a huge settlement driven by fear of remaining in such a hostile forum. Removal is a very real lifeline for such a client.

been filed originally in federal court. This narrowing of the class of cases suitable for removal relates only to diversity jurisdiction cases. For cases filed in state court having at least one claim that arises under federal law, the scope of removal is the same as with federal court's original jurisdiction. To the extent the case is deemed to "arise under" federal law, even if other related state law claims have been pled, the entire case becomes removable. The only trick on these federal question cases is to follow the correct procedures in a timely fashion and avoid waiver of the right to remove. These concerns are discussed below.

Diversity cases, on the other hand, face some additional roadblocks to removal. As you hopefully recall from the previous chapter on subject matter jurisdiction, diversity jurisdiction requires complete diversity as between each of the plaintiffs and each of the defendants as well as requiring that claims exceed the minimum jurisdictional limits of $75,000 as between the claims by each plaintiff against each defendant. In addition to these requirements for diversity jurisdiction imposed by § 1332, the removal statute also dictates that if any of the "parties in interest properly joined and served as defendants is a citizen of the State in which such action" was originally brought, the case cannot be removed.[33] The thought behind this limit ties into the primary purpose behind diversity jurisdiction–protecting the interests of the nonresident defendant sued in a foreign state. If the plaintiff in a diversity scenario has chosen to bring the lawsuit in at least one of the defendant's home state, federal court protection is no longer needed. Whether you buy into this shaky assumption does not matter. This is the way the statute is written and removal practice is governed by these statutes. If you are a Connecticut corporation facing a suit in Mississippi state court and recognize that even though your co-defendant is from Mississippi you still face a daunting prospect going to trial in that state court, we suggest that you call your Congressman and start your settlement discussions.

b. Removal & Remand Procedures

If you represent a defendant on a new state court suit and believe the case could have been filed in federal court, you have thirty days from the first date of service on *any* defendant to effectuate removal.[34] This sounds like a decent amount of time if your client is the first defendant served and the client calls you immediately. But what if by the time your client has been served, nearly a month

[33] 28 U.S.C. § 1441(b).

[34] 28 U.S.C. § 1446(b).

has already passed since another co-defendant was served? You have little time to react. This suggests two tips. For plaintiff counsel, if you are suing multiple defendants in state court and are concerned about the case being removed, you can consider serving first the defendant you believe is most likely to be unrepresented by counsel, disorganized, etc. You want the clock to start ticking as long before the other defendants are served as possible. If you are defense counsel and your client is sued in a multiple-defendant case that appears to be removable, you had better either contact the other defendants or the court clerk immediately to ascertain when the first service occurred.

What if the case was not removable at the time of its filing but later becomes removable? For example, the plaintiff might amend her complaint to add a federal cause of action or the plaintiff might voluntarily dismiss a local defendant creating complete diversity of citizenship for the first time. When this happens, the thirty day clocks begins to run upon the plaintiff's service of some document that demonstrates that the case is now removable.[35] The caveat, and second major limitation on diversity removals, is that under no circumstances is a case supposed to be removed solely on diversity grounds more than one year from the date the action was first filed.[36] This time limitation on diversity removals was a compromise piece of legislation that came during a period of tremendous congressional animosity toward federal courts' exercise of diversity jurisdiction. This also suggests yet another tactic for plaintiff's counsel–avoid taking actions that make your case removable on diversity grounds until one year has passed. Or stated another way, make sure you sue a nondiverse defendant in your original complaint and keep that defendant in the case for at least a year. There are several limits on this latter tactic however. First, Rule 11 and the ethical rules discourage filing cases against people for improper purposes. Second, for about the last one-hundred years, federal courts have recognized the doctrine of fraudulent joinder–that when a plaintiff sues a local defendant against whom the plaintiff has no chance of succeeding, the court may disregard the citizenship of the local defendant in ascertaining whether diversity jurisdiction exists. Both the application and the standards governing this fraudulent joinder analysis are far from clear as each circuit has adopted different tests and the Supreme Court has

---

[35]28 U.S.C. § 1446(b).

[36]*Id.*

not yet weighed in on the precise fraudulent joinder analysis.[37]

Another part of the process that is not clear at all from the removal statutes is the requirement for unanimity. That is, all defendants named and served must join in the removal papers or provide some other written ascent to the removal. If only part of the defendants join in the removal, grounds for immediate remand back to state court exist. This provides another incentive for defendants sued in multiple-defendant cases to contact one another immediately if the case appears to be removable. If you represent a client who is ambivalent about removal, you can consider trading your client's ascent to removal for some other favor from the other defendants–perhaps a covenant for the defendants to refrain from asserting cross-claims against one another.

Assuming that you have correctly spotted a removable action, gained the consent of all the other defendants, and that the thirty-day deadline has not yet passed, how does you go about removing the case? Section 1446 governs the procedure and the process is actually somewhat more straightforward than in the past but still full of traps for the unwary. The primary document to prepare is the Notice of Removal which needs to set forth in a "short and plain statement . . . the grounds for removal" and attach a "copy of all process, pleadings and orders served upon such defendant or defendants in such action." Next, "promptly" after filing this notice of removal in the federal court, the removing defendant "shall giver written notice thereof to all adverse parties and shall file a copy of the notice with the clerk of such State court, which shall effect removal and the State court shall proceed no further unless and until the case is remanded."[38] Notice to the state court is usually done by preparing a short "Notice of Filing Notice of Removal" which simply advises the state court that the defendant(s) has filed a notice of removal with the federal court–typically a file-stamped copy of the notice of removal filed with the federal court is attached to this state court notice. This second step is critical because until this is filed, the state court still technically has jurisdiction over the case and can proceed to judgment.

As referred to above, there is some history of congressional animosity toward diversity jurisdiction. Most federal judges seem to share this chagrin with many believing that their time is better spent on federal causes of action and trying

---

[37]For a comprehensive survey of the various federal circuits' treatment of the fraudulent joinder analysis and a proposed resolution, you might enjoy reading James M. Underwood, *From Proxy to Principle: Fraudulent Joinder Reconsidered*, 69 Albany L. Rev. 1013 (2006).

[38]28 U.S.C. § 1446(d).

to keep a lid on their busy criminal dockets.[39] Between this underlying hostility and Congress' statutory invitation for federal trial judges to closely scrutinize notices of removal,[40] defense counsel preparing a notice should exercise great caution to prepare the document without any mistakes. Courts have held, after all, that there is a great burden on the removing party to demonstrate clearly that all of the requirements for removal have been satisfied. Some items to pay particular close attention to include the following:

- **Timing**   Defendant must specifically state the relevant dates to demonstrate that the removal was timely–be precise as to when the first defendant was served with process or, in cases that became removable later, when the first paper was served that demonstrated that the case was removable.

- **Citizenship**   In diversity removals, counsel should clearly state the *citizenship* of each party rather than refer to residence. Further, counsel should articulate that this necessary complete diversity of citizenship existed, if applicable, at both the time of the filing of the original complaint and at the time of the filing of the notice of removal. In cases where counsel is attempting to rely upon the doctrine of fraudulent joinder, specificity must be employed to demonstrate why the claim against the suspect local defendant is not possible.

- **Unanimity**   Either have counsel for all named and served defendants sign the notice of removal or indicate how you are otherwise demonstrating their ascent to removal (attaching a letter or email from other defense counsel perhaps).

---

[39]For a greater detailed history and exploration of these attitudes, we would recommend James M. Underwood, *The Late, Great Diversity Jurisdiction,* 57 Case Western Res. L. Rev. 179 (2006).

[40]Section 1446(c)(4) states that the "United States district court in which such notice is filed shall examine the notice promptly. If it clearly appears on the face of the notice and any exhibits annexed thereto that removal should not be permitted, the court shall make an order for summary remand."

- **Amount**   For diversity cases, if the state court complaint does not specify clearly a demand for more than $75,000, counsel must explain to the court what the basis is for believing that plaintiff's claim exceeds this sum (e.g, reference a demand letter).

- **Local Rules**   Counsel must also check the local rules to determine if any additional requirements exist for the district where you are removing the case, such as attaching additional documentation.

- **Waiver**   Courts have held that certain pre-removal conduct by a defendant can be deemed a waiver of a right to removal. A common action held to waive this right involves the defendant voluntarily filing a claim in the state court such as a permissive counterclaim or third-party claim. Other courts have held that engaging in extensive discovery or scheduling hearings on motions in state court might evidence a waiver of the right to remove. Case law is not uniform on these topics and counsel should check precedents from your own circuit for additional guidance when in doubt. Purely defensive pleadings (e.g., answers, compulsory counterclaims, objections to venue, opposition to a preliminary injunction, etc) should not constitute a waiver of the right to remove.

Although courts frequently do remand cases on their own initiative for perceived defects in the removal notice, defendants are free to file amended notices of removal as much as they desire during the thirty day window for removal. If you file a notice and realize you made an important mistake in the papers, you should take advantage of the opportunity and draft an amended notice for immediate filing.

Plaintiff counsel served with a notice of removal should first consider whether a remand is desired. It may be that upon removal the case was assigned to a federal judge that you think would be perfect to preside over the case. This sometimes happens where the removal can bite the defendant hard. However, if you are still desirous of your original state court forum, you obviously want to help the court in its scrutiny of the notice of removal. In this regard, plaintiffs have their own deadline to worry about. Section 1447 governs remands to state court and gives plaintiffs only thirty days from the filing of the notice of removal to move for remand on the "basis of any defect other than lack of subject matter jurisdiction."[41] For defects that go to the federal court's original subject matter jurisdiction, there is no deadline for filing the motion to remand. This is consistent with our earlier discussion of defendants' Rule 12(b)(1) motions–that they can "suggest" a lack of subject matter jurisdiction at any time, even following a trial.[42] What you may find surprising is how this is actually interpreted by the courts. For example, if a defendant attempts to remove a case on diversity grounds more than one year after the case was first filed, the plaintiff must move for remand on this ground within thirty days or else waives this basis for remand. This is true because the one-year limitation on diversity removals does not relate to the federal courts' original jurisdiction for diversity cases under § 1332. The same is true if a defendant attempts a diversity removal even though a co-defendant is a citizen of the forum state–plaintiff must move for remand in this scenario within thirty days.

Time does not permit further discussion of removals but hopefully you get the hint that removal procedures need to be monitored closely by both defense and plaintiff counsel. Your time is worth this undertaking, however, because the ability to move a case away from the plaintiff's original chosen forum can be extraordinary in its impact on the case.

D. RULES MATRIX

This table serves as a starting point for additional inquiry into the potential professional responsibility and civil procedure issues that are implicated when drafting and filing pleadings.

Issue Arising During Pleading and Attacks on Pleadings	Applicable Rule of Professional Responsibility, Federal Rule of Civil Procedure, or U.S. Code Provision
Necessary ingredients in a pleading setting forth a claim for relief	FRCP 8(a)

---

[41] 28 U.S.C. § 1447(c).

[42] Rule 12(h)(3).

Responding to a claim in an answer	**FRCP 8(b)**
Obligation to Plead affirmative defenses	**FRCP 8(c)**
Pleading certain matters with particularity	**FRCP 9**
Form of Pleadings	**FRCP 10**
Having a good faith factual and legal basis for allegations in a pleading	**FRCP 11**
Objections to a claim in a pleading that can be set forth in an answer or by separate motion	**FRCP 12(b),(c),(e) and (f)**
Counterclaims and cross claims	**FRCP 13(a),(b) and (g)**
Third Party Claims	**FRCP 14**
Jury demands	**FRCP 38**
Default judgements for failing to timely respond to a pleading	**FRCP 55**
Pleading for a temporary injunction	**FRCP 65**
Seeking transfer of venue from one federal district to another for convenience	**28 U.S.C. § 1404(a)**
Seeking dismissal or transfer to another federal district when the original venue chosen by the plaintiff was improper	**28 U.S.C. § 1406**
Scope of removal jurisdiction	**28 U.S.C. § 1441**
Removal procedures	**28 U.S.C. § 1446**
Remand procedures	**28 U.S.C. § 1447**

Table 1 - Potential Law Applicable to Pleadings

Points To Ponder . . .

1. Is it worth the investment of time to put a lot of careful thought into the contents of your client's pleadings and in writing the document persuasively? Or should you just include the bare essentials and save your time for other more rewarding pretrial activities?

2. How aggressive should the advocate be in pleading questionable claims, from a strategic and an ethical perspective? Are there any competing ethical objectives in this scenario? Consider the development of the common law and how the recognition of new causes of action or developments in the law might potentially be impeded by rule 11.

3. What does the use of the phrase "upon information and belief" in an advocate's pleading suggest to the adversary and to the court? With this in mind, when should you conclude that your reliance upon such questionable allegations is desirable or needed?

4. If you suspect that a certain affirmative defense or counterclaim may be available to your client but believe that additional discovery will help to establish such defense or claim, when should you plead the matter? Are there risks to pleading the matter now? Are there different risks involved in waiting to plead the matter later? Does rule 15 adequately eliminate this risk?

5. How does the scope of the parties' pleadings impact other aspects of the case, such as discovery and the expenses of litigation? How might an unscrupulous advocate use this relationship to cause harm to her adversary and to the legal system?

6. When does the advocate know when she is ready to move from case analysis and fact investigation to the drafting of pleadings? What about the client who cannot afford to pay the advocate for extensive case analysis?

7. Even with the modern shift toward "notice pleading" the procedural rules governing pleadings can still be somewhat daunting. What does this suggest about the desirability of pre-suit settlement negotiations? When should pre-suit settlement discussions be initiated by plaintiff? Always?

CHAPTER SIX
INTRODUCTION TO FORMAL DISCOVERY

"Though this be madness, yet there is method in 't."[1]

A.   *THE GOOD, THE BAD AND THE VERY UGLY*

Both the bench and the bar have a love/hate relationship with formal discovery conducted under the Federal Rules of Civil Procedure. Formal discovery contrasts markedly with the informal fact investigation and fact gathering activities that occur when counsel is engaged in *informal discovery* previously discussed in Chapter 3. In the informal setting, counsel digs where she desires, generally only taking in new information but rarely dispensing it to others, and does little that she does not desire to do to advance the litigation ball for her client. This activity presents a mostly upside risk, the only possible downside being the discovery of negative information about your client's legal position–and even this is far better than hearing the bad facts at trial for the first time. The sooner you discover unsavory details the better you are able to work around them. Costs are also less of a problem with informal discovery. When the client can afford it, counsel may engage in extensive investigation; when the client cannot, counsel reigns in the information dragnet.

In the world of formal discovery, the dynamics are very different. Formal discovery differs from informal by invoking the compulsory or forced processes of the courts to extract information from others, both parties and nonparties, who often are unwilling to provide the information voluntarily. Duringan earlier period of time, advocates spent more time pleading the factual details of their client's claims and defenses but were given very little if any discovery from their

---

[1] WILLIAM SHAKESPEARE, HAMLET act 2, sc. 2.

opponents. This system has given way in the United States to the current model of notice pleading and liberal formal discovery which has both good and negative consequences.

The advent of formal discovery tools has transformed both pretrial litigation and trials and has given rise to the development of certain types of litigation rarely seen in the past. At the trial stage, the availability to compel your opponent to turn over information concerning the dispute has tended to even the playing field in situations where one party has unique access to information. The rules now actually permit a plaintiff to file a lawsuit based at least in part upon "information and belief" with the good faith hope of acquiring some flesh to apply to the bare- bones pleading through formal discovery directed at the defendant. In prior days, this would not be feasible and such plaintiff's claims would be doomed to dismissal either through an attack on the pleadings or a summary judgment motion. Even if the case was lucky enough to survive attack by motion, a claimant facing the ensuing trial by ambush was not likely to succeed. Such David and Goliath scenarios now can not only survive dismissal but can proceed to a trial where David has a fighting chance to actually prove his claims. Further, trials tend to be conducted in a much more orderly and efficient manner now that both the litigants and the presiding judge are generally well versed on each side's positions and supporting evidence in advance. This advance knowledge, as we will see in Chapter 10 of this book, also goes a long way in facilitating settlements by informing the parties of the relative strengths of their positions. In this sense, the onset of formal discovery mechanisms tend to make trials less common.

> Every contested lawsuit is resolved either by dispositive motion, voluntary settlement or trial.
>
> Discovery is the gateway to all three resolutions.

The availability of formal processes to compel discovery has impacted pretrial litigation through enabling certain types of litigation to develop and flourish. Imagine a minority employee's dismissal on suspect grounds. Without discovery, that single employee may or may not be able to piece together enough personal knowledge to prosecute an employment discrimination claim. With the benefit of discovery, this employee's access to information can not only provide evidence to substantiate the suspicions of bias, but might well enable the employee to serve as a class representative suing on behalf of numerous other mistreated employees whose files might well be available under current rules. Or consider the rise in products liability litigation with plaintiff's counsel now having the ability to obtain access to the product research and development files of manufacturers as well as "smoking gun" internal memoranda showing the callousness of corporate executive's disregard for anticipated injuries caused by their products. The very recent rise in electronic discovery, which we will consider further in the next chapter, serves to highlight the impact of formal discovery on the pretrial process. No longer do counsel and clients have the luxury of only producing tangible

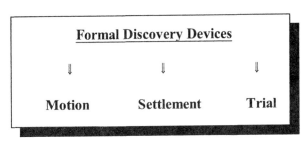

written documentation in response to discovery requests, but today they need to brace themselves for having to produce thousands of informal e-mails the authors and recipients believed to have been "deleted" but, in fact, are still available for prying eyes to view. There are both tremendous costs associated with such production as well as significant ability to shift leverage in civil lawsuits.

Formal discovery methods are best understood as pretrial tools designed to facilitate the resolution of lawsuits through one of three possible avenues. Every contested lawsuit is resolved either by dispositive motion, voluntary settlement or trial. Discovery is the gateway to all three resolutions. The facts learned during discovery, including the possible discovery that your opponent has no evidence to support her alleged claim, may be utilized to support you motion for summary judgment. If the facts discovered do not reveal a fatal weakness on the party of your adversary, these facts will need to inform your case evaluation for purposes of settlement consideration and discussions. Finally, if the case cannot be settled or resolved through motion for summary judgment, the only other destination for your lawsuit is the inside of a courtroom for trial. The facts learned during discovery will guide trial counsel's direct and cross-examinations and will furnish many of the documents that counsel will offer into evidence. Other than utilizing discovery for one or all three of these strategic purposes, there is really no other appropriate reason supporting the use of formal discovery requests. Used strategically for the purpose of aiding in case resolution, formal discovery fulfills a critically necessary role in pretrial practice.

But appreciation for the great and equalizing utility of discovery must be joined with the sober realization of the abuse of discovery devices by many advocates and their clients. Discovery abuse comes in many forms and can be motivated by different desires. Counsel getting paid by the hour might view the utilization of numerous discovery requests as a way to churn the file and increase their revenues. Counsel frustrated with their opposition might transmit discovery requests as a punishment for some perceived slight.

> The greatest threat to open discovery is the abuse of the process by counsel.

Counsel might send unnecessarily burdensome discovery to an opponent as a means of wearing down their resolve in the litigation and to motivate them to settle. Clients wary of allowing an opposing party to discover information harmful to the clients' position might fail to turn over documents responsive to legitimate discovery requests. Counsel preparing a client for a deposition might encourage the witness to be less than forthcoming in answering questions under oath. Counsel taking a deposition might ask mean-spirited and unduly personal questions in an attempt to frighten or intimidate the opposing party into abandoning their claims. Counsel resisting discovery might lodge groundless objections in the hope that their opponent will not have the time or resources to go to the court for an order compelling the discovery responses. As a pretrial advocate, you will encounter each of these forms of discovery abuse and many others as well. You may even be tempted on occasion to engage in similar conduct yourself, if only as a means of self-defense or to placate an unhappy or overbearing client.

Surely, you may ask, this bad behavior is not permitted–is it? Several sources prohibit discovery abuse. The most direct rule governing discovery conduct by counsel and clients is Rule 26(g). This rule provides the discovery counterpart to Rule 11 which governs pleadings, motions and other documents filed with the court. Subdivision (2) of Rule 26(g) sets forth the discovery manifesto and subpart (3) discusses the consequence of violating part (2), as follows:

> (2) Every discovery request, response, or objection made by a party represented by an attorney shall be signed by at least one attorney of record in the attorney's individual name, whose address shall be stated. An unrepresented party shall sign the request, response, or objection and state the party's address. The signature of the attorney or party constitutes a certification that to the best of the signer's knowledge, information, and belief, formed after a reasonable inquiry, the request, response, or objection is:

(A) consistent with these rules and warranted by existing law or a good faith argument for the extension, modification, or reversal of existing law;

(B) not interposed for any improper purpose, such as to harass or to cause unnecessary delay or needless increase in the cost of litigation; and

(C) not unreasonable or unduly burdensome or expensive, given the needs of the case, the amount in controversy, and the importance of the issues at stake in the litigation. If a request, response, or objection is not signed, it shall be stricken unless it is signed promptly after the omission is called to the attention of the party making the request, response, or objection, and a party shall not be obligated to take any action with respect to it until it is signed.

(3) If without substantial justification a certification is made in violation of the rule, the court, upon motion or upon its own initiative, shall impose upon the person who made the certification, the party on whose behalf the disclosure, request, response, or objection is made, or both, an appropriate sanction, which may include an order to pay the amount of the reasonable expenses incurred because of the violation, including a reasonable attorney's fee.

These provisions thus prohibit discovery practices that counsel (or the party) knows, or should know, are inconsistent with other procedural rules. Perhaps more importantly, Rule 26(g)(2) also prohibits discovery requests and responses that are improperly motivated. In Chapter 9 we will explore in more detail the topic of discovery motions and the sanctions available to the courts. For now it is sufficient to note from the above provision that sanctions may be recovered against offending counsel as well as the represented party.

Apart from the rules of civil procedure, there are other sources that condemn abusive discovery practices. The rules of ethics are also called into play when counsel chooses to use discovery for an improper purpose. The preamble to the ethical rules in Appendix I ("Ethical Rule") states at subpart [5] that a "lawyer should use the law's procedures only for legitimate purposes and not to harass or intimidate others." In more concrete terms, Ethical Rule 3.4(d) states that a lawyer shall not "in pretrial procedure, make a frivolous discovery request or fail to make reasonably diligent efforts to comply with a legally proper discovery request by an opposing party." Many district courts, state supreme courts, and state and local bar associations have issued various forms of proclamations exhorting advocates to undertake discovery in a professional manner. As an example, the Middle District of Florida court published a "Handbook On Civil Discovery Practice" which outlines the court's expectations for counsel. Among its many very specific prescriptions, the Handbook offers a few general expectations for counsel engaging in discovery, including the following:

A.   Courtesy and Cooperation Among Counsel

1.   <u>Courtesy</u>. Discovery in this district should be practiced with a spirit of cooperation and civility. The districts lawyers and the Court are justifiably proud of the courteous practice that is traditional in the Middle District. Courtesy suggests that good faith consultation is appropriate before commencing action that might result in disagreement among counsel.

2.   <u>Scheduling</u>. A lawyer shall reasonably attempt to accommodate the schedules of opposing lawyers, parties, and witnesses in scheduling discovery.

Similarly, the Texas Supreme Court issued professionalism guidelines for lawyers practicing in that state under the title of "The Texas Lawyers Creed." These were issued in 1989 by that court in an effort to demonstrate the expectations the court had for practicing lawyers. Among these guidelines are the following important provisions dealing, at least partly, with discovery:

5.   I will notify opposing counsel, and, if appropriate, the Court or other persons, as soon as practicable, when hearings, depositions, meetings, conferences or closings are cancelled.

6.   I will agree to reasonable requests for extensions of time and for waiver of procedural formalities, provided legitimate objectives of my client will not be adversely affected.

     *   *   *

16.   I will refrain from excessive and abusive discovery.

17.   I will comply with all reasonable discovery requests. I will not resist discovery requests which are not objectionable. I will not make objections nor give instructions to a witness for the purpose of delaying or obstructing the discovery process. I will encourage witnesses to respond to all deposition questions which are reasonably understandable. I will neither

encourage nor permit my witness to quibble about words where their meaning is reasonably clear.

18.   I will not seek Court intervention to obtain discovery which is clearly improper and not discoverable.

These are but examples of the profession's reaction to a perceived rising tide of unsavory discovery practices by counsel. Other states have issued similar statements, such as the following representative excerpts:

Oregon

2.6 With respect to discovery, we will not seek information from our adversaries for the purpose of harassment, nor will we refuse to produce information that we know the court will ultimately require to be produced. We will try to schedule depositions informally by mutual agreement for the convenience of parties, counsel, and witnesses before resorting to formal notice procedures.[2]

California

A lawyer should not seek Court intervention to obtain any discovery which is clearly improper, irrelevant and not likely to lead to the discovery of admissible evidence.

A lawyer should refrain from unnecessary, abusive or excessive discovery.[3]

Idaho

9. We will not use any form of discovery or discovery scheduling as a means of harassment, or for any other improper purpose.

10. We will make good faith efforts to resolve by agreement our objections to matters contained in pleadings, discovery requests and objections.

17. We will take depositions only when actually needed to ascertain facts or information or to perpetuate testimony. We will not take depositions for the purposes of harassment or to increase litigation expenses.

18. We will not engage in any conduct during a deposition that is inappropriate under court rule or rule of evidence, including:

(a) obstructive questioning;
(b) inappropriate objections;
(c) irrelevant questioning.

---

[2]Statement of Professionalism, approved by Oregon Supreme Court (January 23, 1991).

[3]State Bar of California Litigation Section's Model Code of Civility and Professionalism (adopted July 20, 2007).

19. Document requests and interrogatories shall be drafted in accordance with court rule, without placing an undue burden or expense on any party.

20. Responses to document requests and interrogatories shall be submitted in accordance with the court rules, fairly meeting the request or question without strained interpretation. We will not produce documents or answer interrogatories in a manner designed to hide or obscure the existence of particular documents or information.[4]

Boulder, Colorado

6. Lawyers should not use information requests or discovery proceedings for any purpose other than legitimate ones. Information requests and discovery should never be used for the purpose of harassment or delay.

7. Whenever possible, lawyers should reach agreement on preliminary procedural and factual matters and enter into written stipulations when appropriate.

8. Whenever possible, lawyers should agree to schedule matters with a view toward accommodating the needs of opposing parties, and generally engage in a spirit of cooperation without abandoning the role of an advocate.[5]

Notwithstanding the proliferation of these kinds of published admonishments, abusive discovery practices still occur across every jurisdiction. Judges are increasingly frustrated with this phenomenon, as witnessed by many notorious court orders that have been shared by lawyers through e-mail exchanges. Below is an example of such an order, issued by a well respect Austin, Texas federal judge. As you read this,

> **Discovery Abuse is Prohibited by:**
>
> - FRCP 26(g)(2) - Discovery Manifesto
> - FRCP 26(g)(3) - Consequences for Violating (2)
> - JudicialRulings
> - Ethics Rules
> - Bar Association Guidelines

remember that the lawyers' conduct was taking place fifteen years after the publication of the Texas Lawyers Creed discussed above:

---

[4]Standards for Civility in Professional Conduct (United States District Court for the District of Idaho and the Courts of the State of Idaho).

[5]Boulder County Bar Association Standards of Professional Courtesy.

**IN THE UNITED STATES DISTRICT COURT
FOR THE WESTERN DISTRICT OF TEXAS
AUSTIN DIVISION**

```
*       *       *
vs.                              Case No. *       *       *

*       *       *
```

ORDER

BE IT REMEMBERED on the 21ˢᵗ day of July 2004 and the Court took time to make its daily review of the above-captioned case, and thereafter, enters the following:

When the undersigned accepted the appointment from the President of the United States of the position now held, he was ready to face the daily practice of law in federal courts with presumably competent lawyers. No one warned the undersigned that in many instances his responsibility would be the same as a person who supervised kindergarten. Frankly, the undersigned would guess the lawyers in this case did not attend kindergarten as they never learned how to get along well with others. Notwithstanding the history of filings and antagonistic motions full of personal insults and requiring multiple discovery hearings, earning the disgust of this Court, the lawyers continue ad infinitum. On July 24, 2004, the Court's schedule was interrupted by an emergency motion so the parties' deposition, which began on July 20, would and could proceed until 6:30 in the evening. No intelligent discussion of the issue was accomplished prior to the filing and service of the motion, even though the lawyers were in the same room. Over a telephone conference, the lawyers, of course, had inconsistent statements as to the support of their positions. . . .

The Court simply wants to scream to these lawyers, "Get a life" or "Do you have any other cases?" or "When is the last time you registered for anger management classes?"

```
        *       *       *
```

If the lawyers in this case do not change, immediately, their manner of practice and start conducting themselves as competent to practice in the federal court, the Court will contemplate and may enter an order requiring the parties to obtain new counsel.

```
        *       *       *
```

SIGNED this 21ˢᵗ day of July 2004.

```
        __/s/ [SAM SPARKS]_____
        UNITED STATES DISTRICT JUDGE
```

Easy solutions to this problem are not readily apparent. It may be that the stakes in litigation are simply too high and client loyalty too low nowadays to reign in such harmful practices by advocates increasingly anxious about retaining their precious client relationships. It is our observation, however, that when judges are able and willing to spend the time discussing discovery issues with counsel practicing before them, and willing to back up their talk with actions, these practices tend to diminish. This is actually a delicate balance–some judges err by simply becoming upset with all counsel and issuing sanctions without carefully investigating which side was truly at fault. But it surely helps when judges spot advocates misbehaving and have the backbone to make it clear that unprofessional conduct will not be tolerated. Do you think the advocates from the foregoing case acted any differently after reading that judge's sharply worded order? One would certainly hope so.

For better or worse, pretrial advocates will spend a significant portion of their days engaged in formal discovery–more time pursuing this activity than any other according to one study.[6] Let's begin the process of understanding this task in more detail.

B. DIFFERENT METHODS

The modern pretrial advocate has a number of different types of discovery tools available. The following chart should be helpful to you in seeing the larger picture.

Type	FRCP	Description	Ltd to parties?	Other Limits
Disclosures	26(a)(1) 26(a)(2) 26(a)(3)	There are 3 types of mandatory disclosures: initial, expert and pretrial. These are designed to provide basic, essential information about the case.	Yes	N/A
Interrogatories	33	Written questions that must be answered under oath.	Yes	Party may serve only total of 25 per each other party
Request for Production	34	Written requests for inspection and/or copying of documents and other tangible items.	Yes	N/A
Subpoenas	45	Used to require attendance at deposition or hearing of a witness and/or to compel production of documents	No	N/A
Physical or Mental Exam	35	Under limited circumstances, may require opposing party to undergo exam when they have injected this issue into the case.	Yes	N/A
Requests for Admission	36	Written statements that receiving party must admit or deny as to truth.	Yes	N/A
Depositions	30-31	Written or oral questions posed to a witness for answering under oath.	No	Limited to 10 per side, each one to be 7 hours or less

---

[6]In Chapter 3 we mentioned a study showing civil advocates spent 16.7% of their time undertaking discovery matters.

Whether you are in federal or state court, most of these methods are typically available, though some variations in a given device may differ somewhat from jurisdiction to jurisdiction. For example, both the federal courts and different state courts have begun to experiment recently with crafting initial disclosures that must automatically be answered at the early stages of discovery as well as creating some arbitrary limits on the number or frequency of certain discovery devices. Both types of innovation serve the similar objective of streamlining discovery.

These tools will be covered in significantly more detail in the next two chapters. As an overview, some are rather automatic as they are activated upon the appearance of the parties and must be responded to by each litigant absent an agreement to the contrary. Most are initiated only by a litigant's service of the appropriate legal document on the other party or witness. In other words, the rules do not compel parties to take depositions or serve document requests. All devices except the oral deposition take written form and involve a written request followed by a written response of some sort. All formal discovery tools except the required disclosures may be the subject of a variety of objections and either motions to compel by the proponent of the discovery or motions for protective order by the responding party seeking to limit or avoid the production of information, documents or witnesses.

Discovery methods have different strengths and weaknesses and different advocates may utilize different discovery techniques to go after the same types of information. In fact, frequently advocates may engage in some redundant use of discovery methods to be sure to capture the information sought. For example, counsel may have already received information about their opponent's witnesses in the initial disclosures. Yet most counsel follow up on this with interrogatories asking for the identities of specific classes of additional witnesses. Counsel also will carefully review documents produced by that same party for the names of other individuals who may have personal knowledge of the disputed transaction or occurrence. And when taking oral depositions in the same case, counsel will almost always ask each witness about the identities of others of whom the witness might have knowledge. This somewhat redundant use of discovery methods is done not only to combat unresponsive or incomplete discovery responses but also because different sources of information might each need to be sought to complete the picture as one source rarely possesses knowledge of all facts on a subject. Part of the art of discovery includes the strategic use of the different discovery tools to achieve the advocate's goals.

C. SCOPE OF DISCOVERY

The permitted bounds of formal discovery have three significant general limitations: (i) All matters sought in discovery must be relevant to the lawsuit; (ii) matters which are privileged are beyond the scope of permitted discovery; and (iii) discovery which is unduly burdensome is not acceptable.

Is it relevant?

Just because the rules of civil procedure allow you to use a certain discovery device generally does not mean that you can seek *any* information or documents with that mechanism. Almost all discovery must be within the confines of Rule 26(b)(1)'s limitation concerning the permitted scope of inquiry:

> Parties may obtain discovery regarding any matter, not privileged, that is relevant to the claim or defense of any party, including the existence, description, nature, custody, condition, and location of any book, documents and other tangible things and the identity and location of persons having knowledge of any discoverable matter. For good cause, the court may order discovery of any matter relevant to the subject matter involved in the action. Relevant information need not be admissible at the trial if the discovery appears reasonably calculated to lead to the discovery of admissible evidence. All discovery is subject to the limitations imposed by Rule 26(b)(2)(i), (ii), and (iii).

This provision thus links the scope of discovery to the search for information that is relevant to the contents of the parties' pleadings. If you have pled a claim for fraud against a defendant arising out of the sale of a used car previously involved in an accident, your discovery seeking to ascertain the truthfulness of certain of the defendant's representations would be within this scope because the truth or falsity of one's representation is considered an element of a common law fraud claim. On the other hand, if in the same suit you send that defendant interrogatories asking whether the defendant ever hit his spouse, this would be improper as irrelevant to any claim or defense pled. You might actually desire to have the information about the abuse more than information about the car, particularly if you planned to threaten the defendant with exposure of this embarrassing incident. But aside from the ethical and perhaps criminal questions raised by such threats, your requests for this very personal information are governed not by the degree of your desire for the fruits of the discovery but by notions of relevancy to the pled claims and defenses in the lawsuit. Thus, questions of the relevancy of discovery are inexorably linked with the substantive law governing the parties' claims and defenses. Your case analysis should, therefore, guide you in terms of drafting your discovery as well as spotting whether your adversary's discovery is within the proper scope.

There are a few other important observations concerning the scope of discovery raised by this passage. First, your plans for discovery need to be reflected by your pleadings. The only way to guarantee your right to engage in discovery on an issue is to plead that issue as a part of your claim or defenses.

Rule 26(b)(1) does permit the court to expand the scope of discovery into any "matter relevant to the subject matter involved in the action" but the proponent of such discovery must show the court "good cause" exists for this discovery. Even if you are successful in making this showing, you have red-flagged for your adversary why you are seeking certain discovery. It is much better to be able to be more subtle in your discovery approach. For example, using the hypothetical car purchase from above, if you are the plaintiff and have sued only for breach of contract, you are not entitled to discovery on issues relating to the truth of the salesperson's representations. Those are fraud issues and you have not pled fraud. You may seek such discovery by filing a motion for leave to obtain this discovery. Yet the defendant will know at that point that you are asking questions (or seeking documents) to try to garner evidence for that element of a fraud claim. There will certainly be no surprises and you can bet the defendant's attorney will craft defendant's discovery responses particularly carefully in light of her knowledge of your intent. On the other hand, due to Rule 11 or other strategic considerations, you may not be prepared (even on information and belief) to plead a fraud claim until you obtain certain discovery.

Second, according to Rule 26(b)(1), discovery might be relevant even though it does not yield admissible evidence. The test is whether it is "reasonably calculated to lead to the discovery of admissible evidence." Imagine you are the defense advocate taking the oral deposition of a non-party nurse in a medical malpractice lawsuit against a surgeon. You ask the nurse this question: "You mentioned speaking with a good friend of the plaintiff's who came by the hospital after the surgery to visit the plaintiff. Did that friend say anything to you about her conversations with the plaintiff?" Now the substance of what the nurse was told by the friend about conversations with the plaintiff might well constitute Hearsay of the Rankest Sort, but is this question still properly asked during a deposition? Of course it is, because such testimony might lead you to find other sources that can verify (or refute) these statements in a form which might very well be admissible—sources like the friend. So long as your discovery is "reasonably" designed to lead you toward your ultimate treasure of admissible evidence, it matters not that the immediate discovery response might not be usable itself at trial. You must remember that the concept of relevancy for purposes of pretrial discovery is broader than at trial.

> "Relevancy" during discovery is a broader concept than during trial.

Is it unnecessarily burdensome?

Rule 26(b)(2)(C) indicates that if discovery is, on balance, too burdensome for the responding party, it may not be permitted even though it meets the test for relevancy. This provision states:

> The frequency or extent of use of the discovery methods otherwise permitted under these rules and by any local rule shall be limited by the court if it determines that: (i) the discovery sought is unreasonably cumulative or duplicative, or is obtainable from some other source that is more convenient, less burdensome, or less expensive; (ii) the party seeking discovery has had ample opportunity by discovery in the action to obtain the information sought; or (iii) the burden or expense of the proposed discovery outweighs its likely benefit, taking into account the needs of the case, the amount in controversy, the parties' resources, the importance of the issues at stake in the litigation, and the importance of the proposed discovery in resolving the issues. The court may act upon its own initiative after reasonable notice or pursuant to a motion under Rule 26(c) [governing protective orders].

Trial courts are bestowed with enormous discretion in ruling on these type of discovery issues, the prevailing thought being that trial judges are much closer to the action and in the best position to rule on discovery matters. In addition, immediate appeals are not typically permitted from interlocutory orders on such matters and, after entry of a final judgment, it is often difficult to find harmful error sufficient to support post-trial appeals on a discovery issue. For all of these reasons, the trial court is effectively the court of last resort for litigants quarreling about most discovery issues in the pretrial context.

The trial judge's power over discovery practically means that as a pretrial advocate you had better take the time to learn about your presiding judge and to be able to gauge when that judge will agree that certain discovery is going too far. This ultimately requires judgment that necessarily relies upon experience. Until you gain that experience first-hand, you should learn to heed the helpful advice of advocates more senior than you who have appeared before your trial judge on discovery matters. You should also be prepared to offer concrete explanations, and perhaps evidence, of why certain discovery you wish to challenge under this provision is unduly burdensome for your client. Specific affidavits discussing estimates for the time and expense involved in producing the requested information, documents or witnesses in response to the challenged discovery request are much more compelling in support of a motion for protective order than conclusory hyperbole attacking the discovery request.

Is it privileged or otherwise exempt?

Rule 26(b)(1) expressly carves out of the scope of discovery any matter which is "privileged." With one exception, however, these rules do not create any privileges. Some privileges have constitutional origin, others have been recognized at common law, and most are currently recognized by state statute. On federal question cases, the federal common law of privileges is applied. Congress chose not to codify these privileges and to simply allow the federal courts to continue to evolve this area of law. In state court, or in federal court on diversity cases, state law of privileges is generally applied.[7] Commonly recognized privileges include the following:

- Privilege against self-incrimination The Fifth Amendment to the U.S. Constitution dictates that one need not be compelled to testify against himself in a criminal proceeding. In a criminal case, the prosecutors may not even hint at the defendant's invocation of this privilege. This privilege extends to discovery (e.g, a deposition) in a civil case so long as the anticipated or on-going criminal case is sufficiently related to the discovery. In other words, the witness may be able to avoid answering the questions during his civil deposition. However, unlike the criminal trial, the defendant's assertion of the privilege may be referenced during the civil trial and the jury may very well be permitted to view a videotape excerpt from the deposition during which the privilege is asserted. You can imagine the ramifications on the witness' credibility in the civil case when this occurs. The lesson here is that if you have an adverse witness in a civil case that has related pending criminal charges, you should consider insisting on taking the witness' deposition and be sure to arrange for a videographer.

- Attorney-client This is a classic privilege designed to protect the sanctity of the important attorney-client relationship through facilitation of trust. All confidential communications pertaining to the legal representation are treated as confidential. The client owns the privilege against disclosure of these communications. This privilege can cover both oral and written communications that occur during the course of representation. While this privilege is broad, there are some notable exceptions to it such as when the attorney and client are in litigation against one another (i.e., legal malpractice or fee dispute) and when the communication is made in furtherance of fraud.

- Physican-patient Patients need to be able to communicate with their physician in an environment that encourages the patients to disclose potentially embarrassing information. This is vital for

---

[7]Fed. R. Evid. 501.

doctors to be able to do their jobs.   To encourage these disclosures, and perhaps out of a sense of simply recognizing the patient's right to privacy over personal matters, courts have long recognized this privilege as well. Most states have also codified the privilege.

- <u>Spousal</u> States generally recognize a privilege within the marriage. This privilege arises out of the intimacy of the marital relationship and actually has two components. One variety of this privilege is owned by a spouse not to be compelled to testify against the other spouse and is owned by the witness-spouse. The other variation is designed to protect the confidential communications made within the marriage ("pillow talk") and this is a privilege owned by both spouses. This privilege has not (yet) been extended to cover quasi-marital relationships such as civil unions between homosexual couples but, in the right setting, a court might be willing to extend the privilege to such non-traditional relationships.

- <u>Work product</u> Since the seminal case of *Hickman v. Taylor*[8] the federal courts, and now the state courts as well, have recognized a quasi-privilege against producing anything that reveals an attorney's mental impressions concerning an on-going case. This work product exemption from discovery is not nearly as absolute as a true privilege. It is now codified at Rule 26(b)(3) and creates a presumption against discovery for matters conducted "in anticipation of litigation" by an advocate or other client representative (e.g., consultants, insurers).   To access such information, a discovery proponent needs to make a "showing that the party seeking discovery has substantial need of the materials in the preparation of the party's case and that the party is unable without substantial hardship to obtain the substantial equivalent of the materials by other means." Even when production is ordered, the rule states that courts are to fashion the order to "protect against disclosure of the mental impressions, conclusions, opinions, or legal theories of an attorney or other representative . . . ."   Under this rule, things such as attorney's drafts of documents, case evaluation materials, research, witness interview notes, etc are presumptively exempted from discovery. The same rule does specify, however, that witness statements (recordings or written statements signed or otherwise adopted by the witness)

---

[8]329 U.S. 495 (1947).

have to be provided to the witness upon the witness' request.

- <u>Miscellaneous</u> There are other privileges recognized across many jurisdictions although these vary significantly from one state to the next. An advocate should always check the applicable law that will apply to her lawsuit, prior to engaging in formal discovery, to be in a position to spot and preserve any potential privilege. Examples of some of these other privileges include the priest-penitent privilege, the psychotherapist-patient privilege, the optometrist-patient privilege, the medical peer review privilege, an accountant-client privilege, the teacher-student privilege and even a scholar's privilege. Further, jurisdictions also recognize a trade secret privilege that protects a business' secret business dealings, product design information, customer lists and other proprietary information. This trade secret privilege, however, normally only gives rise to a protective order that permits the litigant-adversary to obtain such information if it is relevant but protects the materials from disclosure to any other third parties. Each of these privileges reflects a concern by the court or legislature that wide-open discovery of certain information might destroy important relationships or other privacy interests to a degree that is greater than the litigation needs for discovery of such information.

No overview of privileges would be complete without a discussion of the concept of waiver. Waiver is the nemesis of the pretrial advocate. Waiver is commonly understood to be something such as the voluntary surrender of a known right. But the Supreme Court has held that "waiver" is a term that can only be understood in a specific context:

What suffices for waiver depends on the nature of the right at issue. "Whether the [litigant] must participate personally in the waiver; whether certain procedures are required for waiver; and whether the [litigant's] choice must be particularly informed or voluntary, all depend on the right at stake." For certain fundamental rights the [litigant] must personally make an informed waiver. . . For other rights, however, waiver may be affected by actions of counsel.[9]

There are at least three primary ways that an advocate might be held to have waived his client's privilege or exemption against disclosure. First, a claimant might be held to waive a privilege in the so-called "sword and shield" scenario when the claimant affirmatively takes a position that can only be defended against by access

---

[9]*New York v. Hill*, 528 U.S. 110 (2000)(quoting *U.S. v. Olano*, 507 U.S. 725, 733 (1993)).

to the privileged materials. The most obvious example of this is the former client suing her lawyer for legal malpractice. The lawyer cannot be expected to defend herself against such a claim without being able to make use of privileged information. Another classic example is the personal injury claimant's attempt to recover for certain injuries. She cannot expect to avoid the defendant's access to her medical records concerning treatment for that injury while simultaneously trying to recover damages for those same injuries. You simply cannot force the adversary to litigate your claims while withholding key evidence. Second, should you or your client voluntarily disclose the essence of the privileged information you are at serious risk for being found to have waived the privilege otherwise applicable. Third, failure to assert a timely objection in response to the discovery request seeking the privileged information has often been held to have effectively waived the privilege. Courts have even been known to find a waiver despite the party and counsel having only inadvertently disclosingthe information or failing to object in a timely manner. The stakes can be very high and caution must be exercised not to waive a client's privilege through inattention or sloppy lawyering.[10]

In terms of the mechanics for asserting a privilege, Rule 26(b)(5) provides the following specifics:

> When a party withholds information otherwise discoverable under these rules by claiming that it is privileged or subject to protection as trial preparation material, the party shall make the claim expressly and shall describe the nature of the documents, communications, or things not produced or disclosed in a manner that, without revealing information itself privileged or protected, will enable other parties to assess the applicability of the privilege or protection.

If your adversary, for example, serves you with a request for the production of documents you need to indicate in the applicable written response (served timely under Rule 34) that documents are being withheld because of a certain privilege and offer some general description of the nature of the document and circumstances demonstrating its privileged status. Often, at least with regard to challenged documents, the courts expect the objecting party to prepare a written "privilege log" that offers this information with regard to each challenged document. Preparation of this log can be a fairly time consuming project but some such information has to

---

[10]Various courts have reacted differently to inadvertent waivers, such as the accidental production of privileged documents. Some courts strictly find waiver and others offer some leniency at least where it is clear that reasonable efforts had been made (i.e., a thorough procedure for document reviews prior to production) to avoid the accidental production. *Compare Carter v. Gibbs,* 909 F.2d 1450 (Fed. Cir. 1990)(strict approach) *with Amgen, Inc. v. hoechst Marion Roussel, Inc.,* 190 F.R.D. 287 (D. Mass. 2000)(lenient approach). When this happens to you, hopefully you will find the judge in a merciful mood. But practicing law in a prudent manner to avoid such accidents is far superior.

be offered to your adversary for them to be in a position to debate the issue from an informed position. Further, many courts will require you, before upholding the privilege, to tender the documents to the court for a confidential *in camera* inspection. Some advocates have been made to look foolish or dishonest upon submitting obviously non-privileged documents to a court in this context. To avoid such embarrassment (or waivers), you will need to expend the time to engage in a very careful document review and analysis of the possible privileges prior to asserting any privilege objection. When document requests call for the production of hundreds of boxes of files, this task can be herculean. Now perhaps you can understand how discovery can be the most time intensive aspect of a pretrial advocate's practice.

D. *CALCULATING DEADLINES*

Having just discussed the concept of waiver through missed deadlines, this seems to be an appropriate place to discuss how a pretrial advocate should calculate deadlines both in discovery and with respect to other pleadings, motions and responses. The rules of civil procedure, in any jurisdiction, are filled with various time deadlines each of which is keyed to some particular event. Some examples include:

- Answers and objections to interrogatories are due "within 30 days after the service of the interrogatories."
- Responses and objections to document requests are due "within 30 days after the service of the request."
- Regarding requests for admissions, each particular "matter is admitted unless, within 30 days after service of the request . . . [the responding party] serves . . . a written answer or objection addressed to the matter."
- Jury demands must be filed "not later than 10 days after the service of the last pleading directed to the issue."
- Under local rules there is a deadline to file written responses and briefs to contested motions. Under our Local Rule 3.01(b), such responses are due "within ten (10) days after service of the motion."
- A motion for new trial "shall be filed no later than 10 days after entry of the judgment."

Rule 6 is the primary source for guidance on calculating time deadlines under the rules. Under subpart (a) it states that the day of the "act, event, or default from which the designated period of time begins to run" shall not be included in the calculation but that the last day "shall be included unless it is a Saturday, a Sunday, or a legal holiday, or, when the act to be done is the filing of a paper in court, a day on which the weather or other conditions have made the office of the clerk of the district court inaccessible." However, when the time period in question is "less than 11 days" the calculation is markedly different–all intervening weekends and holidays are excluded from the calculation. This means that, as between a deadline of 10 days and one of 12 days, the former will end up giving the litigant more time–under the rules of civil procedure 10 is less than 12. Isn't this a great profession?

Subpart (e) of Rule 6 also provides for an additional modification to the general rules for calculating deadlines. It requires that whenever the deadline in question is triggered by your adversary's service of a document upon you (i.e., a request for production) and the adversary completes this service by such mechanisms as either mail or electronic means (e.g., e-mail or facsimile), you are entitled to 3 additional days to be added to your deadline. With regard to ordinary or "snail mail" this additional time makes sense to ensure that the responding party is not prejudiced in meeting the deadline by virtue of having to wait to receive the instrument. However, the application of this 3 day extension to a method such as e-mail can only be viewed as a punishment on advocates utilizing such a service method.

This 3-day automatic extension also raises one significant, and in many districts unresolved, interpretational dilemma. What if you are facing a 10 day deadline–say a response to your adversary's motion for summary judgment? Under our Local Rule 3.10, your deadline is 10 days from the date of service by your adversary of their motion. As indicated above, normally you would not count the intermediate weekends (and holidays) in counting to 10. But if your adversary served you the motion by e-mail, Rule 6(e) gives you an additional 3 days. Does this new 13 day deadline still get the benefit of the Rule 6(a) provision to exclude weekends from the calculation? If not, your 13 days may be less than the 10 days originally bestowed. Some districts, by local rule, have answered this riddle. Our Local Rule 4.2 provides that, in this instance, you should first calculate the 10 day deadline using Rule 6(a), meaning you exclude the weekends and holidays. Then you add 3 days to this calculation. This two-step calculation ensures that the responding party is not actually hurt by the 3 day automatic extension of Rule 6(e). In the absence of such a local rule or authoritative opinion from your circuit or district, the safer route is to calculate the most conservative deadline or to stipulate in writing with your opponent as to when the deadline will be.[11]

One other caveat also should be noted. The additional 3 days offered by Rule 6(e) only applies when your deadline is triggered by the opponent's service of a document on you. Some deadline are not triggered by service but by the filing of an instrument or the entry of judgment. In these cases, there is no additional 3 day

---

[11]Rule 29 permits the parties through written stipulations to modify the discovery procedures so long as doing so does not negatively impact the court's own docket.

period added to your deadline.

Calculation of deadlines may seem to be a very dry topic until you or an opponent has arguably missed a deadline. When this happens, time calculations will be the most important thing in your world. For this reason it is best to calculate deadlines carefully and early and to keep careful track of all of your case deadlines through a traditional or electronic calendar as well as through help from your legal secretary or legal assistant.

E. CASE MANAGEMENT REPORTS

Prior to being permitted to begin your formal discovery efforts you have one task to complete in federal court. Rule 26(d) states that a "party may not seek discovery from any source before the parties have met and conferred as required by Rule 26(f)." Although this prohibition is stated in very broad terms, it does not apply to any informal discovery. But before any party is permitted to serve deposition notices, interrogatories or any other formal discovery request, this Rule 26(f) meeting must occur.

Rule 26(f) requires the parties to meet "as soon as practicable and in any event a least 21 days before an [initial] scheduling conference is held or a scheduling order is due under Rule 16(b)." The purpose of this face to face meeting is for counsel to discuss any changes to the time, form or content of mandatory initial disclosures, the subjects on which discovery is desired, whether discovery should occur in certain phases, any electronic discovery issues or concerns, any anticipated privilege problems with discovery, and whether any changes to the normal discovery limitations set forth in the rules are appropriate. The parties are to discuss these subjects and then prepare a joint report (often called something like a Case Management Report) for filing with the court "within 14 days" of the meeting and in advance of the initial scheduling conference with the court contemplated by Rule 16(a). This rule requires the court to enter a pretrial scheduling order, usually after meeting with the parties, for the purpose of:

(1) expediting the disposition of the action;
(2) establishing early and continuing control so that the cases will not be protracted because of lack of management;
(3) discouraging wasteful pretrial activities;
(4) improving the quality of the trial through more thorough preparation, and
(5) facilitating the settlement of the case.[12]

---

[12]Rule 16(a)(1)-(5).

In addition to discussing these general topics, counsel attending such an initial conference must be prepared to discuss suggested deadlines that will govern the case and even time estimates for the trial. This seems like a tall order for the initial days of the case but the planning must begin early if the court is going to promote efficient pretrial litigation. Further, most trial judges understand that many things discussed at these early stages are necessarily preliminary and that any of the topics may need to be readdressed in the future as discovery proceeds and issues are narrowed. This rule contemplates and formalizes some of the case analysis that this text endorses for advocates to undertake anyway. Further, many state court judges are beginning to hold initial scheduling conferences that are generally similar to this federal conference required by the rules. The one additional benefit of these early conferences is that it requires opposing counsel to sit with each other and visit in person early in the life of the dispute. For many people, it is more difficult to be obnoxious in these face to face contexts than if all business were conducted over the telephone or through the exchange of correspondence. One can at least hope.

Rule 16 also states that the scheduling order issued by the judge following this initial conference will "control the subsequent course of the action unless modified by a subsequent order."[13]

With these early planning stages behind you, you are now ready to dive into full blown formal discovery in your lawsuit. As we proceed to the next chapter, let's go over the details of this formal discoverybeginning with the various forms of written discovery.

D.   RULES MATRIX

This table serves as a starting point for additional inquiry into the potential professional responsibility and civil procedure issues that are implicated when drafting and filing pleadings.

Issue Arising During Formal Discovery	Applicable, Ethical Rule, Federal Rule of Civil Procedure, or Federal Rule of Evidence
Prohibition on discovery abuse	**FRCP 26(g), Ethical Rule 3.4(d)**
Required disclosures	**FRCP 26(a)(1)-(3)**
Interrogatories	**FRCP 33**

---

[13]Rule 16(e).

Requests for Production	**FRCP 34**
Subpoenas for witnesses	**FRCP 45**
Physical or Mental Exams	**FRCP 35**
Requests for Admission	**FRCP 36**
Depositions	**FRCP 30-31**
Scope of discovery–relevancy	**FRCP 26(b)(1)**
Prohibition on burdensome discovery	**FRCP 26(b)(2)(C)**
Scope of Privileges	**FRE 501**
Work product exemption	**FRCP 26(b)(3)**
Privilege procedure	**FRCP 26(b)(5)**
Calculating deadlines	**FRCP 6(a), (e)**
Timing for commencement of formal discovery	**FRCP 26(d)**
Mandatory pre-discovery meeting of counsel	**FRCP 26(f)**
Permission to agree to different procedures	**FRCP 29**
Pretrial conferences	**FRCP 16**

Table 1 - Potential Rules Applicable to Formal Discovery

Points To Ponder . . .

1. What incentives are there for litigants and their counsel to abuse discovery?

2. Given human nature and the incentives to violate the letter and spirit of the discovery and ethical rules, is it inevitable that lawyers will abuse discovery? If so, is there any alternative to the present system that would be better?

3. Is formal discovery worth the exorbitant cost to the parties? What can you do as counsel to minimize these costs while being a zealous advocate?

CHAPTER SEVEN
WRITTEN DISCOVERY

"Lawyers may reason powerfully, but power settles most issues."[1]

A. MANDATORY DISCLOSURES

Rules 26(a)(1)-(3) prescribe three mandatory disclosures by litigants during the pretrial phase of a case. Each variety of disclosures require litigants to automatically provide certain information and documents to their opponents without awaiting any discovery request. The basic idea behind these three disclosure provisions is to ensure that basic information concerning a party's claims or defenses is provided to the opponent. The first two types–initial disclosures and expert witness disclosures–are properly cast as a type of discovery. The last variety–pretrial disclosures–is less about discovery and more about final trial preparation because there should be no truly new information disclosed at this time. In this chapter, therefore, the disclosures we will concern ourselves with are the initial disclosures and expert witness disclosures. Coverage of pretrial disclosures will occur in the last chapter of this book on final trial preparation.

1. Initial disclosures

Initial disclosures are required by Rule 26(a)(1) in all but a handful of specialized civil lawsuits. The exempted categories are set forth by Rule 26(a)(1)(E) and include matters such as administrative reviews, habeas corpus, prison inmate suits, student loan default cases, etc. Unless you practice exclusively in one of these particular areas, you will find that almost all of your civil cases in federal court require that initial disclosures be exchanged. These disclosures are

---

[1] MASON COOLEY, *City Aphorisms* (Fifth Selection, New York 1988).

of fairly recent vintage being a part of the 1993 changes to the Federal Rules of Civil Procedure. The rules drafters seemed to believe that certain basic information was requested through interrogatories and document requests in virtually all contested cases and that such run-of-the-mill material should not have to await a formal request or be subject to the delays occasioned by unnecessary objections being asserted by counsel. In the eyes of some, the advent of initial disclosures as a form of discovery would be revolutionary and cause changes in the way parties conducted discovery, drafted pleadings and prepared for settlement conferences. As one observer has stated, "[i]nitial disclosures change how lawyers litigate."[2] Most practitioners today, with more than a decade experience making these initial disclosures, would likely respond with a collective yawn if asked about the actual impact of this disclosure obligation on their pretrial practice. The truth is that the initial disclosures required by Rule 26(a)(1) provide very rudimentary information at a somewhat faster pace than before. They serve as a mere starting point for formal discovery and arguably fail to replace any formal discovery traditionally sought by counsel using other means. Some counsel view them as a token gesture that must be made to avoid getting into trouble with the court. In apparent disillusionment with the impact of initial disclosures on pretrial practice, one prominent federal district court judge opined that they "don't help that much. In fact, I think it increases expense."

As an advocate, whether you find meaning in drafting or reading these disclosures, there is a serious downside to not taking them seriously and that is the exclusion at trial of your evidence. Rule 37(c)(1) states that if a party "without substantial justification" fails to comply with their disclosure obligations, the party is "not, unless such failure is harmless, permitted to use as evidence at trial, at a hearing, or on a motion any witness or information not so disclosed." You might think of this as another form of waiver–not disclosing information waives your right to rely upon it later in the case. This is a very severe sanction. Further, coming shortly on the heels of the initial pleadings, your client's initial disclosures will say much to your opponent about the state of your case. Therefore, it is worthwhile to understand initial disclosures and to provide them correctly.

Initial disclosures must be made no later than fourteen days after the parties' Rule 26(f) scheduling conference unless altered by court order, stipulation of the parties under Rule 29, or if the party objects at the conference that stipulations should not have to be made in that case. If this objection is made, the objecting party is excused from making initial disclosures until the court rules on

---

[2] THOMAS A. MAUET, *PRETRIAL* 193 (Aspen 6th ed. 2005).

the objection.[3] In reality, there are very few cases where it would be worthwhile to object to making initial disclosures. Because most courts view the information required to be disclosed as very basic, the courts would view the disclosure obligation as minimal and warranted. Further, counsel might spend as much time preparing for and attending a hearing on the objection as she might preparing the substantive disclosures.

All parties share this same deadline for making disclosures because the deadline is not triggered by service of any request or pleading but by the parties' mandatory joint scheduling conference. Further, the rule expressly states that certain potential excuses to making disclosures are unacceptable:

> A party must make its initial disclosures based on the information then reasonably available to it and is not excused from making its disclosures because it has not fully completed its investigation of the case or because it challenges the sufficiency of another party's disclosures or because another party has not made its disclosures.[4]

So unless you have lodged a formal objection to the application of the initial disclosure obligation to your case, you really have no argument for skipping this assignment. In this regard, disclosures do offer a bit of an advantage over other discovery devices because there is no delay occasioned by boilerplate objections or assertions of unhelpful responses (e.g., "Defendant is still investigating and will supplement at a later date.") that are commonly provided in response to interrogatories.

There are four categories of information required to be included in your client's initial disclosures:

Helpful Witnesses

The rule requires disclosure of:

> the name and, if known, the address and telephone number of each individual likely to have discoverable information that the disclosing party may use to support its claims or defenses, unless solely for

---

[3]Rule 26(a)(1)(E).

[4]Rule 26(a)(1)(E).

impeachment, identifying the subjects of the information;[5]

The disclosing party must briefly identify witnesses–by name, address, phone number and at least make categorical reference to their area of knowledge–for witnesses the party anticipate possibly using at trial. The biggest limitation, only disclosure of witnesses helpful to your case, is one that came about in the 2000 amendments to these provisions. Thus, to the extent that you are aware of witnesses who are hostile to your positions, your disclosure can omit any reference to them at all. What does this limited disclosure accomplish? It gives your opponent at least a starting point for possible witness interviews or depositions of witnesses and perhaps a preliminary view of your possible trial presentation. But the disclosure does not provide details of each witness' personal knowledge and it certainly does not help the opposing advocate to try to isolate potentially helpful witnesses to its own case. For this type of additional information, other formal discovery devices (particularly interrogatories) will necessarily have to be propounded.

An example of the disclosure of some witnesses in response to this requirement might look like the following:

26(a)(1)(A): Witnesses

Plaintiff discloses the following individuals:

Sherry Smith
9201 Dove Meadow Drive
Mansfield, OH
(419) 517-3272
Information concerning the traffic accident

Donald G. Holtzapple, M.D.
703 Hanley Road
Mansfield, OH
(419) 387-4100
Information concerning Plaintiff's injuries

You should note that the disclosing party need not provide any anticipated details of the witness' testimony. The plaintiff in this example need not say what Sherry

---

[5]Rule 26(a)(1)(A).

Smith saw or what injuries Dr. Holtzapple treated. Yet armed even with this very cursory information, the defendant in this case determine to obtain Dr. Holtzapple's medical records (through subpoena) and possibly take his deposition after examining his opinions reflected by his records. The defendant might also decide to make a phone call to the third-party witness, Sherry Smith, in order to ascertain at least preliminarily what she saw. Obtaining her affidavit or deposition to preserve her knowledge might also be a subsequent possible move by the defendant.

It is also worth observing how a party's pleadings might impact their decision as to what witnesses to identify. Let's assume you are the defense counsel in the traffic accident case referenced in our example. You have interviewed a bartender who said that he saw the plaintiff leaving his bar in an intoxicated state a few minutes before the accident. If you have not yet made the decision to plead comparative fault based upon the plaintiff's intoxication, you may not need to disclose yet the identity of this bartender. Of course, once you have amended your answer to include such a defense, you will also have an obligation to supplement your original disclosure. In this regard, Rule 26(e)(1)) states that a party who has made a disclosure must "supplement or correct" its disclosure "at appropriate intervals" if the party learns that "in some material respect the informationi disclosed is incomplete or incorrect and if the additional or corrective information has not otherwise been made known to the other parties during the discovery process or in writing." If the identity of the bartender has already come out during a deposition taken in the case, this rule indicates that no formal supplementation of the original disclosure is needed. Otherwise, the defendant must serve a supplemental disclosure to the plaintiff adding the bartender to the list of possible helpful witnesses.

Helpful Documents

The rule requires disclosure of:

> (B) a copy of, or a description by category and location of, all documents, electronically stored information, and tangible things that are in the possession, custody or control of the party and that the disclosing party may use to support its claims or defenses, unless solely for impeachment;

This provision provides a corollary to the first disclosure obligation. As with the identification of witnesses, the parties must only provide those documents and tangible items (e.g., contracts, correspondence, e-mails, defective steering wheel, photographs, audio recordings, etc) that are helpful to their own cases–those they anticipate possibly using to support their position later in the case. The disclosing party has the option of either making and producing a copy or simply describing the materials and disclosing their location. If the disclosing party chooses the latter, she can immediately expect to receive a request for production of the materials. There really is nothing to be gained from taking this route–description rather than production–other than delay. And if you are acting for delay, you are in violation of at least the spirit of Rule 26(g)'s implicit representation that you are not acting for delay and you are also likely to receive similar treatment from your opposing counsel throughout the case. In other words, unless you have a good reason to do otherwise you should normally plan to just make copies and produce with the disclosures the responsive materials. One good reason to not take this approach would be if the volume of responsive materials was large. As we will discuss below, in such instances it is better to make the material available to opposing counsel for their own inspection and decision about copying.

A disclosure of documents from the defendant in the same hypothetical car accident case we referenced above might look like the following:

26(a)(1)(B): Documents

Defendant provides copies of the following documents:

1. Accident report dated August 15, 2007.
2. Sixteen (16) photographs from the accident scene.
3. Defendant's driver's log.
4. One photograph showing damage to Defendant's truck.

Any time you are making an actual production of documents, you should consider "Bates-stamping" the documents and keeping a log of the documents you have produced. This means assigning a unique number and affixing it to the bottom of each page of produced materials. When you transmit the materials, your cover letter should reference the bates numbers of the documents being furnished (e.g., "I am attaching for production documents numbered DEF001-DEF087."). In this way, you can maintain an accurate record of every item you have produced. This makes identification of certain pages on the record (e.g. during depositions) and also helps to avoid disputes at trial about whether a proposed exhibit was ever previously disclosed.

Damage Calculations

The rule requires that each party asserting a claim for damages to disclose:

(C) a computation of each category of damages claimed by the disclosing party, making available for inspection and copying as under Rule 34 the documents or other evidentiary material, not privileged or protected from disclosure, on which such computation is based, including materials bearing on the nature and extent of injuries suffered;

Plaintiff's counsel may find this disclosure–of damage calculations–somewhat redundant if she chose to include specific numbers in drafting her complaint. If her pleading was more general in merely describing the categories of injuries, this will be an important disclosure. Although disclosures can be supplemented, and thus the damage calculations can be changed up or down, opposing counsel can certainly cross-examine the plaintiff with the original disclosures. Even for general damages that are not easily quantified, such as pain and suffering, counsel needs to be prepared to provide specific dollar amounts being claimed at this point. Courts are reluctant to permit counsel to show up at trial and suggest a damage figure to the jury that has not been properly disclosed in response to this disclosure obligation. The same principle ought to also apply to claims for punitive damages–if counsel plans to suggest a figure to the jury, counsel needs to disclose it here. Further, this disclosure obligation requires counsel to furnish the documents that evidence these damage figures. This would certainly include medical expenses in personal injury cases or receipts for alternate products purchased in a consumer breach of contracts case.

A response to this disclosure responsibility in our hypothetical traffic case might include the following:

26(a)(1)(C): Documents

Plaintiff's current estimate of damages is as follows:

Past medical expenses:	$25,000
Future medical expenses:	$ 5,000
Lost fair market value of car:	$10,500
Pain and suffering:	$100,000
Past lost wages:	$ 17,000
Future lost earning capacity:	$100,000

Plaintiff is producing in support of these calculations the following documents:

1.   Plaintiff's most recent tax return
2.   Hospital and doctor bills
3.   Pharmacy receipts

Defense counsel also needs to be aware that their clients have a similar obligation to disclose damage calculations, and supporting documents, concerning any counterclaim (or cross-claims or third-party claims) by which a defendant seeks monetary relief. This could also arise in a breach of contract setting where the contract specifies that the prevailing party in any dispute is entitled to attorney's fees. In that situation, the plaintiff will insist that defendant disclose the attorney's fees, with supporting documentation, at some point. Obviously this is one situation where the fees will continue to escalate as the case goes forward so that the most meaningful disclosure will likely take place immediately prior to trial.

Insurance Policies

Finally, Rule 26(a)(1)(D) requires that the following information also be furnished with the initial disclosures:

> (D) for inspection and copying as under Rule 34 any insurance agreement under which any person carrying on an insurance business may be liable to satisfy part or all of a judgment which may be entered in the action or to indemnify or reimburse for payments made to satisfy the judgment.

This provision renders frivolous any defendant (or counter-defendant's) argument that it need not produce a copy of its relevant insurance policies. Although technically an insurance policy might not be "relevant" to any issue to be decided in the case, the rule drafters saw the wisdom in requiring disclosure not only of the existence of such policies but of the policies themselves. This serves two very practical purposes: (a) it informs the claimant of whether the case is worth prosecuting in light of the ability of the defendant or its insurer to pay; and (b) it educates the plaintiff on issues of possible insurance coverage for the allegations pled in the case. This information helps the claimant to plead the case properly to invoke insurance coverage (e.g., consider dropping intentional tort claims if such claims are excluded from coverage) and offers much guidance for settlement discussions. Again, any party against whom a claim for monetary damages has been pled has to disclose any insurance policy that might possibly provide coverage. A simple disclosure response indicating that the party is tendering its applicable policy with the disclosure should suffice.

2.   Expert witness disclosures

The next type of disclosure–chronologically and categorically–is expert witnesses. Rule 26(a)(2)(A) says that, in addition to the initial disclosures, a party "shall disclose to other parties the identity of any [expert] witness [who] may be used at trial to present evidence . . . ." In addition to disclosing the identity of such experts, the disclosure "must be accompanied by a written report, prepared and signed by the witness" if the witness is one retained or specially employed to provide expert testimony in the case or one whose duties as the party's employee regularly involve giving expert witness testimony.[6] The rule goes on to specify the requisite contents of the expert report for such specially retained experts, as follows:

(i) a complete statement of all opinions the witness will express and the basis and reasons for them;

(ii) the data or other information considered by the witness in forming them;

(iii) any exhibits that will be used to summarize or support them;

(iv) the witness's qualifications, including a list of all publications authored in the previous ten years;

(v) a list of all other cases in which, during the previous four years, the witness testified as an expert at trial or by deposition; and

(vi) a statement of the compensation to be paid for the study and testimony in the case.

Preparation of this report is a much more onerous task than the initial disclosure of fact witnesses. Just the first category–a statement of all opinions and the basis and reasons–requires careful deliberation and coordination between advocate and

---

[6]Rule 26(a)(2)(B).

expert. The risk is that if you don't disclose one of the expert's opinions you will likely face an objection at trial (or to that portion of the expert's affidavit if a summary judgment hearing) regarding that undisclosed opinion. If you have not yet had the pleasure to work with an expert–and it truly can be an enjoyable part of the practice of law–you may not appreciate how the expert's ultimate opinion (e.g., that the defendant doctor's treatment was below the applicable standard of care) is buttressed by a potentially great many "little" opinions (e.g., that aspirin is a significant medication that a family physician should inquire about the patient taking in addition to the prescription provided by the doctor). Suffice it to say that great care should be made to include in the report all of the ultimate opinions and as many supporting opinions as you and the expert can spot.

The rules contemplate broad discovery from and regarding specially retained expert witnesses. In addition to the fairly comprehensive information in the mandatory aspects of the expert report, the rules provide a right to take the deposition of any such expert following the issuance of their report. Rule 26(b)(4)(a) states: "A party may depose any person who has been identified as an expert whose opinions may be presented at trial. If a report from the expert is required under subdivision (a)(2)(B), the deposition shall not be conducted until after the report is provided." In this deposition, you should expect counsel to go through each item from the expert's file, including all correspondence (and emails) between expert and the retaining counsel, marginal notes made on materials reviewed by the expert, the expert's time sheets, draft copies of reports, etc. If you are the retaining counsel, you need to bear this in mind (and discuss with any expert who does not have extensive testifying experience) when sending any communication to the witness. Nothing exchanged between you and the expert will be considered confidential from the prying eyes of opposing counsel and ultimately the jury. Even seemingly innocuous statements in a transmittal letter–such as "I am sending you these materials so that you can testify concerning the defendant doctor's malpractice"–can be construed as coaching by the advocate and used to undermine the expert's credibility. Or imagine how it might look if the materials the advocate sends to her expert have little Post-It notes all over them with comments from the advocate about the material's significance? Some communications that might be taken out of context are best left in unwritten form.

In terms of the timing of the disclosure, it is usually governed by a court-issued scheduling order following the parties' Rule 26(f) conference and the initial scheduling conference with the court. In the absence of a specific date in a court order (or stipulation of the parties), Rule 26(a)(2)(C) provides that expert disclosures are typically due "at least 90 days before the trial date or date the case is to be ready for trial." A major advantage of a scheduling order or stipulation is that this generic 90-day-before-trial deadline simply makes no sense applied to all litigants. Most scheduling orders, therefore, have staggered deadlines. For example, typically the party with the burden of proof on an issue (i.e., plaintiff) designates their experts first and the responding party has a deadline of 30 or 60 days later to designate their rebuttal experts. This staggering of the deadlines theoretically gives the responding party a chance to determine if they need an expert and, if so, on what topics prior to having to commit to designate someone. In reality, both parties should be consulting with possible experts as long before the designation deadline as possible because the process of forming an expert opinion can often be quite time consuming.

So far we have simply assumed that you have an expert. And you may not have to look very far to find one. If your client is an expert, you have the terrific fortune of having a "built-in" expert–though one whose bias is fairly obvious. In other words, in an accountant malpractice case, the defendant accountant obviously will have opinions supporting her own defense. These are expert opinions that must be disclosed. But in most cases of significant value, even those with built-in experts, resort to possible independent expert witnesses should be a consideration. How does counsel decide when she needs an expert witness and how does she go about locating one? After all, until you have found such an expert and are confident enough in their opinions to have them prepare a report, you have nothing to disclose.

The purpose behind expert witnesses is to assist the jury with understanding something with which they would not normally be familiar. Most jurors do not understand how a trampoline is designed, how to draft an owner's manual for an all-terrain vehicle, whether aspirin is something most doctors inquire about when prescribing heart medicine, how many cameras work best for providing security in a mall parking lot, whether a sprained ankle can lead to impotence, or how to reduce $700,000 in future lost earning capacity over the next twenty years to present value. We hope that jurors are capable of figuring these things out, but frequently expect expert witnesses to provide substantial guidance and context. Your case analysis should go a long way toward spotting some important factual disputes that might suggest a possible need for expert witness testimony.

How do you go about finding a possible expert? After you become a specialist at hot-coffee litigation you will no doubt have a long list of possible experts on coffee temperature or lid design. Until then, there are a variety of sources to consult. Often you can begin by asking your client for some help if your client is involved in a certain industry that has experts. If you represent a stockbroker, your client should have some ideas about prominent people in their field. The caveat here is to avoid hiring professional colleagues or friends of your client. In such instance, you are hardly better off than not having any retained expert. You can also do some literature research, either with your client's direction on simply by warming up the search engine on your computer. If you find some helpful literature that discusses an issue with command (and in a sympathetic manner to your client) you should consider calling the author. Ask your colleagues for tips on good expert witnesses. There are also many experts who advertise their services in lawyer publications and some of these may be just fine. We have just never used any expert who did this and would suggest that this be your last resort because such experts tend to face hot cross-examination.

Random Tips for the Care and Feeding of an Expert Witness:

- If you find your expert's invoice breath-taking, the jury will find it mind-boggling.

- Avoid the funny "P.S." on your correspondence with the expert. The jury may not be amused.

- It is best to know your expert disagrees with your pleadings *prior* to having served your designation of him.

- It is nice if your expert knows more about the substance of the technical issues than you do.

- If your expert mentions a neat invention for detecting alien life on our planet, you might want to keep him as a consulting-only expert.

- If your expert earns 75% of her income from trial lawyers, her independence might be called into question.

- Avoid hiring experts who begin the initial consult by asking "do I need to disclose any prior felony arrests?"

You have found a possible expert. What do you do next? When do you feel comfortable disclosing them? You should first agree on a rate of compensation and perhaps an initial budget for their work, with the client's approval. You should supply the expert the written materials they will need to understand the issues and to have some factual context. Counsel often provide pertinent pleadings (a complaint or a motion for summary judgment) discussing the matter as well as documents gathered informally or through discovery. Often counsel also will provide deposition transcripts to experts if these are already available. You must understand, again, that any materials you provide to the expert are fair game for disclosure and further examination by your opponent. For this reason, you should probably not provide your confidential case notes or client evaluation letters to the expert! After the expert has had time to review the materials and perhaps do some of their own research, normally a telephonic or (better) a face to face meeting to informally discuss their thoughts is appropriate. The issues may be convoluted enough to require a series of such meetings before you know if you have a potential testifying expert. Until then, you should consider this expert as a purely consulting expert. Such experts needs not be disclosed under normal situations under Rule 26(b)(4)(B) unless and until the advocate determines that the expert is "expected to be called as a witness at trial." At this time, it is usually appropriate to consider having the expert begin their drafting of their report required with your disclosure. Just be sure that this process is complete prior to your designation deadline.

B. INTERROGATORIES

1. The Law

Interrogatories, governed by Rule 33, are written questions served upon another party (an opposing party or a co-party) which must be answered under oath within thirty days of service. They may properly be used to inquire about facts, contentions and mixed questions of fact and law but may not be used to inquire about pure questions of law. Rule 33(c) explains the scope of the authorized use of interrogatories:

> Interrogatories may relate to any matters which canbe inquired into under Rule 26(b)(1), and the answers may be used to the extent permitted by the rules of evidence.

> An interrogatory otherwise proper is not necessarily objectionable merely because an answer to the interrogatory involves an opinion or contention that relates to fact or the application of law to fact, but the court may order that the interrogatory need not be answered until

after designated discovery has been completed or until a pretrial conference or other later time.

For example, it would be improper to propound an interrogatory asking "what is the applicable statute of limitations for fraud in Kansas?" because this is a pure question of law. It may be answered solely by reference to statute or case law. But it would be acceptable to instead ask "when do you contend that the statute of limitations began to run in this case and what facts support this contention?" because this question inquires into a contention as well as the application of law to the facts of the case. Of course, interrogatories like other written discovery devices are subject to Rule 26(b)'s exclusion for privileged matters. An interrogatory, for example, that asks "who do you intend to call as a witness at trial" invades the mental impressions and plans of counsel and violates the work product exemption of Rule 26(b)(3).

As with other forms of discovery, interrogatory practice has received its fair share of criticism. Consider the following scholarly attack:

> Interrogatories are the most abused discovery vehicle, and what is more problematic is that their cost generates little value. Attorneys ask questions drawn from a stock reserve and those questions return only objections, vague answers, and very little information. This is due in part to the ease with which one can generate interrogatories, as well as "the proliferation of machine-stored questions." As a result, interrogatories are often "frustrating, costly, and ineffective for both parties." The standard objections of "overly broad," "vague," and "unduly burdensome" provide no substantive content to the sender of the interrogatories. Compounding the problem, adversaries and the courts are normally reluctant to condemn the liberal objector. Courts want to stay out of discovery disputes except in the worst cases, and adversaries themselves are playing similar games with their own objections.

> Put broadly, the problem with interrogatories is that lawyers believe, and the system reinforces, that the exchange and answer of interrogatories is a game. That a lawyer expects an objection causes the sender to wrangle over the form of a question and to hesitate over the proper term with which to define a thought. Historically, "practitioners have used interrogatories as a litigation tactic to harass and to overwhelm an opponent or to delay the resolution of a dispute." In return, an entire body of literature explains how to avoid giving thorough and responsive answers to interrogatories.

At base, the problem with interrogatories is lawyer conduct. Lawyers must somehow be held accountable for their zealous but inefficient use of the device. Burdensome, overreaching, and frivolous questions -- and boilerplate, bad-faith objections in return -- cause delay instead of enlightenment. Any consideration of how to reform the interrogatory device must acknowledge the lack of incentives for lawyers to exchange and to request information from one another in good faith.[7]

At least in part due to such criticisms of the ease by which counsel can pummel their opponents through a few minutes of dictating voluminous sets of interrogatories, the rule drafters have now incorporated an arbitrary limit on their use. A single party is limited to sending to any other one party a total of twenty-five interrogatories throughout the life of the case "including all discrete subparts."[8] The limitation means that an advocate must plan her uses of interrogatories carefully, perhaps sending a small set early in the case but reserving additional interrogatories until later, perhaps as a follow up to some depositions. So long as the advocate does not send, in the aggregate, more than 25 interrogatories to a particular party she does not violate the rule's limitation on the number.

> *"I will study and get ready, and perhaps my chance will come."*
>
> Abraham Lincoln

Further, counsel must be careful to note that the rule counts as separate interrogatories the "discrete subparts" of an interrogatory. This provision means that, in the mysterious world of litigation counting–you might recall our conclusion from the prior chapter that, under Rule 6(a) - (e), 10 days may be longer than 13–the following inquiry might well constitute five interrogatories rather than one:

Interrogatory No. 1:   With respect to the accident in question, please state:

(a) the complete identities of each fact witness to the accident and, for each such witness, provide their address, phone number, and their current employer;

---

[7] Amy Luria & John E. Clabby, *An Expense Out of Control: Rule 33 Interrogatories After the Advent of Initial Disclosures and Two Proposals for Change,* 9 Chap. L. Rev. 29, 30-31 (2005).

[8] Rule 33(a)(1).

(b) your contentions as to each factor that contributed to causing the accident and, for each such contention, all facts supporting your contention;

(c) whether you were under the influence of alcohol or other medications at the time of the accident;

(d) whether you have had any similar accidents during the preceding five (5) years; and

(e) please identify all documents evidencing your knowledge of the facts giving rise to the accident.

This example seems pretty clear because each subpart is set forth separately and seems to inquire about a fairly discrete topic–counting this as five separate interrogatories seems fair. But what about the following interrogatory–is it one or four?

Interrogatory No. 1: With respect to the accident in question, please state the identities of each witness to it, including in the identifying information each witness' full name, address, phone number and employer.

Caveats Regarding Interrogatory Use:

- Remember that your opposing counsel is drafting the answer and not the opposing party.

- Unlikely to extract confessions from interrogatories since opponent has 30 days to deliberate over their answer. Do not expect any Perry Mason moments.

- Understand that lawyers try to minimize the volume and the usefulness of the answers.

- Must draft carefully–there is no immediate follow-up available to you, unlike in a deposition.

- Can be easily evaded by sharp-eyed counsel who will object if the interrogatory is too broad and will fail to give you anything meaningful if you draft it too narrowly.

Although this interrogatory is not broken into separate sections, the key distinction between this example and the prior one is that each bit of information sought here is not discrete. Rather, each aspect of the information sought (i.e., the name, address, phone number and employer) is merely supplying identifying information about certain witnesses. For this reason, courts would properly view this as one interrogatory seeking identifying information about fact witnesses, rather than four interrogatories. But you can easily see how there might be interrogatories that fall somewhere between these two clear examples–situations where it might be very debatable as to how many interrogatories have been served. In these real world scenarios, the best practice is to be reasonable. Don't nitpick your opponent's interrogatories because you might be able to count to slightly more than 25 including discrete subparts. After all, the purpose of this limitation is to hamper abuse of the device not to invite it. But if that same opponent sends you another set of interrogatories, now clearly exceeding the 25 limit, you should properly object to answering any of them.

Rule 33(b)(3) provides that the receiving party must serve its "answers, and objections if any, within 30 days after the service of the interrogatories. A shorter or longer time may be directed by the court or, in the absence of such an order, agreed to in writing by the parties subject to Rule 29." In terms of the answers, Rule 33(b)(1) requires that each interrogatory be answered "separately and fully in writing under oath" unless objected to within this 30 days. The rule goes on to state that there are two ways for a litigant to waive its objections: (i) failure to state an objection with "specificity"; and (ii) failure to state an objection timely unless a tardy objection is excused by the court "for good cause."[9] An objection that would likely be deemed too general to count would be one that asserted in response to an interrogatory that "defendant objects to this interrogatory to the extent that it calls for privileged information." This objection fails to even identify the specific privilege much less explain how answering the interrogatory would require disclosure of confidential information. A better objection might state instead that "defendant objects to this interrogatory because it seeks disclosure of confidential communications between defendant and its counsel in violation of the attorney-client privilege." Two of your most important tasks upon receipt of interrogatories, therefore, are to calculate accurately the deadline for serving your response and helping to spot objections, particularly privileges, that must be asserted no later than that deadline.

2. Drafting Interrogatories and Responses

In terms of drafting interrogatories, effective advocates desire to gain useful information and to avoid creating barriers or at least delays through the sloppy drafting of objectionable or otherwise vague interrogatories. The most

---

[9]Rule 33(b)(4).

helpful interrogatories inquire into matters that can most efficiently be discovered through interrogatories–contentions, the sources that should be pursued through other discovery requests, and for information that supports the receiving party's allegations. In terms of form, interrogatories should be short, clear and inquire into a single topic. In this regard, the best rule of thumb is for drafting counsel to imagine themselves receiving the same interrogatories and asking themselves if they would find their own interrogatory objectionable. This is a particularly good idea because often one litigant receiving interrogatories will immediately send their own interrogatories in response often mirroring some of the same questions. If you first sent the same interrogatory, it is difficult for you to object with a straight face.

Good Uses for Interrogatories:

- Good way to get answers when you don't know which witness for the other side might posses the correct information if asked during a deposition.

- Good way to obtain elaboration on a party's bare-bones allegations. Courts prefer this technique rather than a Rule 12(e) motion for a more definite statement.

- Good way to ask opponent to marshal their proof in support of certain of their contentions.

- Good way to find out what witnesses need to be deposed.

- Good way to find other third-party sources of proof (for possible interview, deposition or obtaining documents through subpoena).

- Good way to be sure you have sued the correct party in the correct legal name and capacity.

In term of the substantive answers, the first thing to realize is that the advocate typically drafts the answers for the client's approval rather than being drafted by the client. Normal practice is for counsel to draft answers and then to meet with the client to go over the draft answers to be sure they are accurate. In some instances, counsel might ask the client to make the first draft of an answer to a particular interrogatory simply because the advocate has no information yet in her file on that subject. But ultimately counsel will be responsible for the form of the answers even though the client provides the verification. This realization should be taken into account by advocates in drafting the interrogatories–you are unlikely to trick opposing counsel like you might be able to trick the opposing party.

In terms of the actual drafting of the answers, advocates must avoid evasive or nonresponsive answers while minimizing the harmfulness of the answers to their own clients. Most courts expect counsel to interpret interrogatories according to their plain meaning and to provide meaningful answers. Failure to do so is "treated as a failure to . . . answer"[10] and typically results in the propounding advocate filing a motion to compel and perhaps seeking sanctions. Courts also expect litigants to answer as much of an interrogatory as possible even in the face of an objection that might, if upheld, excuse provision of a full answer. For example, if an interrogatory asks about a personal injury claimant's "entire life's medical history" plaintiff's advocate might very well lodge an objection that this is overbroad, unduly burdensome and seeks information that is not relevant to any claim or defense pled. But plaintiff's counsel would be well advised to at least provide an answer as to that portion of the plaintiff's medical history that is relevant to the claims pled. Courts are more likely to upheld such an objection if it is clear that plaintiff is not simply using the objection as an excuse for withholding discovery that is clearly relevant and appropriate for inquiry.

One other acceptable way for counsel to respond to an interrogatory other than through objection or answer is by producing business records that provide the answer in lieu of fashioning an answer. Rule 33(d) provides:

> Where the answer to an interrogatory may be derived or ascertained from the business records, including electronically stored information, of the party upon whom the interrogatory has been served or from an examination, audit or inspection of such business records, including a compilation, abstract or summary thereof, and the burden of deriving or ascertaining the answer is substantially the same for the party serving the interrogatory as for the party served, it is a sufficient answer to such interrogatory to specify the records from which the answer may be derived or ascertained and to afford the party serving the interrogatory reasonable opportunity to make copies, compilations, abstracts or summaries. A specification shall be in sufficient detail to permit the interrogating party to locate and to identify, as readily as can the party served, the records from which the answer may be ascertained.[11]

---

[10]Rule 37(a)(3) states that "an evasive or incomplete . . . answer . . . must be treated as a failure to . . . answer . . . ."

[11]Rule 33(d).

Responses to interrogatories actually contemplate two signatures–one for the client's verification of the answers under oath and the second for counsel. Rule 33(b)(2) states that "[t]he answers are to be signed by the person making them, and the objections signed by the attorney making them." The party's signature is verifying the truthfulness of the answers and the counsel's signature is made for compliance with Rule 26(g) implicit representations concerning the good faith basis for the objections asserted. If you represent a single individual there is typically little problem with the verification requirement. When you represent a corporate entity it is often difficult to find one officer or employee who can swear to the truthfulness of all of the answers. Often in this scenarios the responsive information is gathered by a variety of employees working in different offices or divisions of the corporation. One interrogatory in an employment discrimination case may inquire into the company's record of hiring or promoting minorities and will likely be answered by someone in the human resources office. Another interrogatory might ask about past lawsuits against the same company alleging discrimination and this will likely be answered by personnel in the company's legal department. Rule 33(a) contemplates the furnishing of answers in the case of corporations, partnerships and governmental agencies will be furnished by different personnel. In this instance, the acceptable practice of many advocates is to provide separate verification sheets for different signatures governing different portions of the answers. Such a verification might look something like the following:

> David Parsons, vice president of ABC Corp., upon oath states that the answers to interrogatories 5, 6, 9, and 10 were compiled with information he provided and that these answers are within his personal knowledge and are true and correct.

> _____
> David Parsons

> Signed and sworn to before me, the undersigned notary, on this ____ day of _____, 2007.

> _____
> Notary Public, State of Utah

Additional similar verifications would be necessary to cover any remaining answers to the interrogatories.

The requirement for the verification under oath can, at least theoretically, be a cause for concern. What if the truth is that counsel is the one to gather the answers and that the client does not really have personal knowledge of the responsive information? For example, a simple interrogatory inquiring into the identities of all persons to witness the incident may call for information that counsel has gained through informal fact investigation. The actual client has not undertaken this factual research. In practice, courts still expect a verified answer and the custom is to have the client verify even these type of answers rather than counsel. Most counsel are rightfully hesitant about signing any verifications for fear of injecting themselves into the case as a fact witness and possibly requiring recusal under the rules of ethics.[12]

Now let's practice some of these principles by considering some possible interrogatories in a case against a locally owned gas station for selling gasoline that was tainted and cause damage to the engine in plaintiff's car. If you are the defense counsel in this case, what possible problems or objections might you have to the following interrogatories?

Interrogatory No. 1: Please state each and every fact which you plan to introduce at trial to support your contention that you have not engaged in any wrongdoing.

Interrogatory No. 2: Please produce a list of all customer complaints during the preceding ten years.

Interrogatory No. 3: Please identify all customers of your tainted gasoline during the period two weeks prior to plaintiff's purchase of gasoline from you.

Interrogatory No. 4: Name the source of the gasoline you sold to plaintiff.

There are a number of potential problems, and objections, with these discovery requests. The first interrogatory invades counsel's mental impressions by asking about trial plans. It also might be considered unduly burdensome in its request for defendant to state "each and every fact" supporting, in essence, its entire defense of the case. Many courts would say that such interrogatory needs to be more focused and less demanding. The second interrogatory is objectionable for several reasons–(i) it is not really an interrogatory as much as it is a request for defendant to prepare a document perhaps not even in existence and then to produce this; (ii) "all customer complaints" would cover many more situations than selling tainted gasoline and thus is overbroad in seeking irrelevant information; and (iii) the time-period is likely too burdensome or too remote in time. The third interrogatory makes the mistake of injecting an adjective into the interrogatory with which the opposing party will not agree. Defendant's position will likely be that its gasoline is not tainted and, therefore, its answer to this interrogatory might well be "none." Interrogatory number four is poor because it is ambiguous. Is this seeking defendant's immediate supplier, the original producer of the product, the

---

[12]Ethical Rule 3.7.

refiner, or the location of the field in which the product was pulled from the bowels of the earth? Or is the most precise answer simply "defendant" since the defendant sold the gasoline to the plaintiff? The problem with each of these examples, that might look perfectly fine to a layperson, is that the drafting counsel did not draft with precision and failed to consider how she might respond if served with the same questions. Better interrogatories inquiring into these same subjects might look more like the following:

Interrogatory No. 1: Please state the facts that support your contention that the gasoline you sold to plaintiff was not tainted by any contaminants.

Interrogatory No. 2: Have you received any other customer complaints regarding selling tainted gasoline during the past year? If so, please identify such customers by name, address and phone number.

Interrogatory No. 3: Please identify all of your customers for gasoline during the period of August 15, 2007 through August 31, 2007 by name and address.

Interrogatory No. 4: Who was your immediate source of the gasoline that you sold to plaintiff?

These interrogatories are written with greater precision, are less likely to be found objectionable (by either opposing counsel or the court), are not easily evaded through creative interpretation, are reasonable in their scope and will more likely generate useful information being provided in response. These are reasonably good goals for the drafting advocate–propound simple interrogatories that will clarify something about the other side's position or point toward other precise targets for additional follow-up discovery or possibly for inclusion as an additional party to be added to the case. Advocates make a mistake when they draft interrogatories with the unrealistic goal of trying to win the whole case through certain hoped for answers.

a. Local Rules

Any time advocates are drafting written discovery or responding to it, they need to also remember to pull out the applicable local rules to determine if there are any provisions that might modify their conduct. Our model Local Rules, for example, require that:

- Interrogatories shall be "prepared and arranged that a blank space shall be provided after each separately numbered interrogatory." (Local Rule 3.03(a));

- The party propounding interrogatories shall serve an original and one copy on the opposing party with copies to all other parties in the case. Neither the interrogatories nor the responses shall be filed with the court unless accompanying a discovery motion. (Local Rule 3.03(b)); and

- Counsel are encouraged to serve interrogatories (and other written discovery) "with a copy of the questions on a computer disk in addition to the written copy" in order to "utilize computer technology to the maximum extent possible." (Local Rule 3.03(e)).

b. Supplementation and Enforcement

Just because you have answered your opponent's interrogatories and received no complaints in response does not mean that your job is complete. As with initial disclosures, there is a duty on parties to supplement their original interrogatory answers:

> A party is under a duty seasonably to amend a prior response to an interrogatory . . . if the party learns that the response is in some material respect incomplete or incorrect and if the additional or corrective information has not otherwise been made known to the other parties during the discovery process or in writing.[13]

Perhaps you did not disclose a certain fact witness when you answered the defendant's interrogatories because you did not know about the person at the time. Since serving your client's answers the name of another witness came up during a deposition of a third party. You have not interviewed that person and have confirmed that they did see the incident. Must you supplement your answer to add this new witness' name or may you rely upon the fact that the witness' name has already been revealed during discovery? The practical answer, and one that most counsel adhere to, is to avoid any controversy by supplementing your client's answer to add this new name at least if you think you might be interested in using that witness in the case. This supplemental answer, like the original, must also be signed by your client under oath so that your opponent can rely upon its truthfulness.

If you receive some interrogatory answers that you believe to be inadequate what should you do? What courts expect counsel to do is to pick up the phone and talk to your adversary about the matter in a calm and rational manner. Courts expect counsel filing discovery motions to have first engaged in such dialogue–this is based upon the belief that most discovery disputes can be avoided if counsel will

---

[13]Rule 26(e)(2).

simply act reasonably and reach compromise where their client's case will not be hurt. Rule 37(a), governing motions to compel discovery, states that any such discovery motion "must include a certification that the movant has in good faith conferred or attempted to confer with the party not making the disclosure in an effort to secure the disclosure without court action." You need not give up your right to important discovery in order to avoid filing a motion but you should at least consider a reasonable compromise–say accepting responsive information going back five years instead of ten, at least as a starting point. If you cannot reach agreement you have two primary options to deal with the lack of responsive information. First, you can simply do nothing (for now) based upon the realization that any information not provided in response to a proper discovery request to which no objection has been lodged, will not be permitted to be offered into evidence by your opponent. This is the automatic rule of exclusion we already encountered in our discussion of initial disclosures and it applies to other forms of discovery as well.[14] But often the missing answers are things that might be helpful to you rather than your opponent. In such cases, the automatic rule of exclusion does not aid your cause because the last thing your opponent would desire is for the jury to hear this information. In this case, you should consider filing a Rule 37(a) motion to compel. Rule 37(a)(2)(B) authorizes such motions for a party's failure to answer an interrogatory. Rule 37 allows the court the order the opponent to answer the interrogatory and instructs the court to award as a sanction against your opponent your "reasonable expenses incurred in making the motion, including attorney's fees" unless your opponent's refusal to answer was "substantially justified" or "other circumstances make an award of expenses unjust."[15] If your opponent persists by refusing to obey the court order, additional severe sanctions are warranted under the rules including the striking of the party's pleadings and entry of default judgment or dismissal.[16] These provisions underscore the importance of taking your discovery obligations seriously and, even where you disagree, obeying court orders compelling your client to provide discovery.

C. DEPOSITION ON WRITTEN QUESTIONS

1. The Law

Rule 31 authorizes a procedure that is actually a hybrid of a deposition and interrogatories. This rule permits the taking of a deposition on written questions from "any person" whether a party or not. Depositions on written questions share certain characteristics of both interrogatories and oral depositions. Because this

---

[14]Rule 37(c)(1).

[15]Rule 37(a)(4)(A).

[16]Rule 37(b)(2)(C).

procedure uses written questions rather than an interactive live exchange typical of oral depositions it *functions* as the equivalent of interrogatories. Of course, true interrogatories are limited to 25 in number and may only be served on parties. Rule 31, however, has no such limit on the number of questions and may be used to compel non-parties to answer. The absence of such limits is more reminiscent of the oral deposition device. It also resembles an oral deposition because the deponent does not just serve written responses; rather, she sits in front of a court reporter and states the answers orally to the reporter who types them and prepares a deposition transcript.

To initiate a deposition on written questions, the discovering party prepares a list of questions and a notice of the deposition and serves this on all parties to the case. If the deposition is of a non-party (and it typically is) it must be served upon them along with a subpoena authorized by Rule 45 to compel their attendance. Rule 45 also permits the subpoena to include a list of documents the deponent must produce at the deposition. In this manner, you can also say that a deposition on written questions can function like a Rule 34 request for production except, again, it is discovery permitted against a non-party while 34 only permits document requests to be made upon parties. In response to the notice and the list of questions, the other parties have 14 days in which to serve "cross-questions" and then the original party has an additional 7 days in which to serve "redirect" questions; within an additional 7 days the other parties can submit written "recross" questions. This is a fairly cumbersome process that, by definition, takes about a month just in order to get the questions all submitted.

2. The Practice

Depositions on written questions have the same limitations that attach to interrogatories–chiefly that there is no procedure for immediate follow-up on the answers and the deponent has much time to consider the questions and to formulate answers. This means that the device does not typically work well with hostile witnesses or with other parties to the litigation. Also, one must be careful in using this device because it counts as a deposition and witnesses generally only have to give a deposition once in a lawsuit absent a stipulation or a court order upon a showing of good cause. In other words, you would not want to use a deposition on written questions on an opposing party just in order to get around the limit of 25 interrogatories. You would succeed in bypassing that limitation but at the expense of foregoing your right to take your opponent's oral deposition.

Depositions on written questions are best used when your goal is fairly limited and non-controversial. Advocates tend to use it to obtain business records from a non-party while "proving them up"

> *"An ounce of action is worth a ton of theory."*
>
> **Ralph Waldo Emerson**

as admissible business records through the deposition questions. This task works well with this device because no follow-up questions are usually needed to accomplish this goal and most non-parties are perfectly content to produce the documents in this fashion if they can avoid an all-day oral deposition–assuming the records being requested are not privileged. You might also consider using a deposition on written questions if you need a few very focused questions answered in a form that will permit you to introduce the testimony into evidence at a trial. Affidavits are not typically admissible at trial from someone who otherwise offers no testimony before the jury. Yet an advocate can offer excerpts from a deposition on written questions to the same extent as an oral deposition.[17] Used in these few limited instances, depositions on written questions can be considered a useful but mostly non-lethal arrow in your quiver of discovery tools.

D. REQUESTS FOR ADMISSION

Rule 36 permits one party to serve upon any other party requests that the other party admit that certain facts are true or that certain documents are genuine. Some would contend that this is not really a discovery device at all. There is some insight in such views, to a certain extent, because the primary purpose of discovery is to find out information or contentions whereas the chief reason for propounding a request for admission is to confirm, mainly for purposes of trial or motion preparation, certain information that you already know or at least strongly suspect to be the case. Many holding to this view would also suggest that advocates reserve use of this tool until formal discovery is mostly complete and the facts are basically on the table. Yet requests for admission can be an important part of discovery, even early on. Advocates can use requests for admission in order to help narrow the scope of the factual disputes. If utilized in this manner, it makes sense to propound requests for admission early on and prior to expending resources on depositions and document requests. This can make the advocate more efficient and productive in her pretrial practice and also lead to faster resolution of the lawsuit.

1. The Law

Rule 36(a) states that:

> A party may serve upon any other party a written request for the admission, for purposes of the pending action only, of the truth of any matters within the scope of Rule 26(b)(1) set forth in the request that relate to statements or opinions of fact or of the application of law to fact, including the genuineness of any documents described in the request.

---

[17]Rule 32 governs the use of all depositions in court proceedings.

The propounding party sends a written request to another party with each matter upon which admission is sought "separately set forth." If the genuineness of a document is sought to be admitted, that document should be attached to the request unless it has previously been provided–in this latter scenario the request should refer to the document by descriptive label and bates stamp number to avoid all confusion while making the request and response meaningful.

Requests for admission function much like the factual allegations of a plaintiff's complaint. Just as the defendant must answer the complaint by specifically admitting or denying each factual allegation, the party served with requests for admission must similarly admit or deny each matter requested. And admissions also operate like little sticks of dynamite in that each matter requested is deemed to be admitted "unless, within 30 days after service of the request . . . the party to whom the request is directed serves upon the party requesting the admission a written answer or objection addressed to the matter, signed by the party or by thr party's attorney."[18] If the responding party does not wish to admit a matter requested, she must "specifically deny the matter or set forth in detail the reasons why [she] cannot truthfully admit or deny the matter."[19] This also suggests another perhaps less noble utility of requests for admission–they can be used not only to gain confirmation of a known truth but also sent out to your opponent in hopes that they will err in failing to serve a timely denial and thus have some matter deemed admitted against them. Indeed, some lawyers will routinely send out requests for admission asking the opponent to admit that all of the propounding party's allegations in their pleading are correct. The failure to timely deny these requests thus spells doom for the responding party. Again, an advocate must not only know how to calculate deadlines under the rules but be vigilant in meeting such deadlines. This is not an area where being close is good enough.

The admission of a requested fact does not necessarily mean that the responding party believes the fact to be true in any absolute sense–just that they are not going to contest the matter in that litigation. The rule expressly contemplates this limitation:

> Any matter admitted under this rule is conclusively established unless the court on motion permits withdrawal or amendment of the admission.. . . . Any admission made by a party under this rule is for the purpose of the pending action only and is not an admission for any other purpose nor may it be used against the party in any other proceeding.[20]

---

[18]Rule 36(a).

[19]Rule 36(a).

[20]Rule 36(b).

> *"What is truth?"*
>
> Pontius Pilate

It is in recognition of this same principle that the rule does not require a party's response to be signed under oath, as distinguished from interrogatory answers. The party is, after all, not swearing that some requested fact is true–they are just agreeing that the fact will be deemed true for purpose of that lawsuit. This is an important limit on the use of an admission. A party might be perfectly willing to admit some fact in one lawsuit but might view the same admission in a different context to be not only inaccurate but horribly damaging to its legal position. The rule thus makes this discovery device have much greater utility as parties are much more likely to admit a fact with the understanding that the admission will die with that particular lawsuit.

Unlike interrogatories and depositions, there are no arbitrary pre-ordained limits on the number of requests for admission that a party may serve in a case. In fact, some counsel will regularly transmit boxes full of documents to an adversary accompanied by corresponding requests seeking admissions as to the genuineness of each and every document in the boxes; in this way, the party may be propounding thousands of requests for admission and expecting a response within 30 days. This may either reflect a lack of appreciation for the burden created, an obnoxious attempt to wreak havoc on an opponent, or be a calculated attempt to trick an adversary into inadvertently admitting to the genuineness of a suspect document stuck into the middle of the pile. To the extent this causes a burden, particularly given the 30 day window of time granted by the rules, the responding party very well may need to file a motion with the court either seeking more time or some other relief from the burden. If you are inclined to send such voluminous requests, you should consider contacting your adversary in advance and arranging to stipulate to more than thirty days for their response pursuant to Rule 29. This would be an example of something that the rules do not require but an act of professionalism. Such conduct has its own rewards.

2. The Practice

Unless you are preparing requests to serve on someone you are hoping will miss the deadline–in which case you simply ask your opponent to admit the elements of you claim/defense to be true–you will need to draft your requests carefully to be effective. Your goal should be to put your opponent in a position where they will be forced to admit the truthfulness of as many of your requests a as possible. This suggests a couple of drafting techniques. First, you should limit each request to one concise fact. If there are lots of details or facts set forth in one request, it makes it more likely that you will simply draw a response of "denied" which accomplishes little. The rules require the responding party to admit or deny based upon the substance of the request: "A denial shall fairly meet the substance of the requested admission, and when good faith requires that a party qualify an answer or deny only a part of the matter of which an admission is requested, the party shall specify so much of it as is true and qualify or deny the remainder."[21] Nevertheless, the responding party might very well deny an entire request because of one disagreeable component that arguably taints the remainder of the request.

This raises the question, because the response is not verified under oath, what is the incentive for a litigant to admit any fact no matter how certain of its accuracy? Rule 37(c)(2) speaks directly to this, providing for sanctions in certain situations:

> If a party fails to admit . . . the truth of any matter as requested under Rule 36, and if the party requesting the admission thereafter proves . . . the truth of the matter, the requesting party may apply to the court for an order requiring the other party to pay the reasonable expenses incurred in making that proof, including reasonable attorney's fees. The court shall make the order unless it finds that
>
> > (A) the request was held objectionable pursuant to Rule 36(a); or
> > (B) the admission sought was of no substantial importance; or
> > (C) the party failing to admit had reasonable ground to believe that the party might prevail on the matter; or
> > (D) there was other good reason for the failure to admit.

In practice, the primary reason for denying sanctions is where the responding party had reasonable ground to believe the jury might agree with its denial. This is interesting because the inquiry is not whether the responding party denied the fact in good faith but only whether they thought it was possible to convince the jury of their version of the truth. Imagine a simple traffic accident lawsuit. The plaintiff sends a request for admission to the defendant that says "admit that the light facing you at the time you entered the intersection was red." The defendant denies the request but the plaintiff prevails at trial on this issue. Does this mean that the plaintiff automatically recovers attorney's fees on her negligence claim—a result normally not permitted under the American rule in most jurisdictions? The answer depends upon whether there was enough doubt that the court concludes that a reasonable basis existed for the jury to reject the plaintiff's position. Yet a great many matters advocates include in their requests for admission are things that, from discovery, appear to be true with no direct evidence suggesting the contrary. Even though some of these matters may support the discovering party the responding party has some incentive to admit such matters to avoid a possible hefty sanction at the end of the case. When this device

---

[21]Rule 36(a).

functions in this manner it achieves a laudable goal of streamlining the litigation and permitting the judge, jury and even the advocates to fight only real battles.

The second drafting technique you should employ is to avoid using adjectives that, being matters of opinion or style, can be easily denied. For example, a request to admit that "the light was bright red" is much easier to deny than one that simply says that "the light was red." Further, filling your requests with colorful adjectives rarely serves any purpose other than gaining some phrases to use in jury argument.

In terms of the form of your requests, you should simply indicate that you are requesting the other party to admit each of the following facts within 30 days and then separately set forth and number each of the requested facts. This permits the defendant to respond under each request by admitting, denying, objecting or stating why she can neither admit nor deny the request at that time–typically due to a lack of information then available to the party.

From the responding party's perspective, you need to read each request carefully and try to decipher whether there are any unstated assumptions within each request as well as to comprehend any alternative interpretations of each request. In other words, you need to be sure you understand exactly what you are admitting before doing so. If there is any doubt in your mind at all, the proper response is to simply say "denied." For some requests though, you can admit to a portion of it while denying the remainder. For example, consider the following request and response in our simple traffic intersection collision case.

Plaintiff's Request for Admission No. 1: Admit that, with respect to the accident between plaintiff and you on August 15, 2007, the light facing you was red when you entered the intersection.

Response: Defendant admits only that there was a car accident between the parties on the date indicated. Defendant denied the remainder of the request.

As with any other form of written discovery, you are also permitted to assert objections to a request for admission. In addition to any of the possible privileges we discussed in the prior chapter, the most common objections to particular requests for admission pertain to their wording–that the request is "vague" or "ambiguous" and "subject to varying interpretations." Many counsel after stating such objections will add "subject to these objections, denied." Such a denial is probably very plausible in these instances where the request is not clear as to precisely what fact you are being asked to admit.

With these practice tips in mind, consider the following requests and responses from a hypothetical premises liability case involving the plaintiff's exposure to a toxic substance on the defendant's land. As you review these, consider whether you would respond the same way as the defendant. Do the objections seem valid or evasive? Could the requests have been drafted better to avoid any of the objections?

> Plaintiff's Request No. 1: Admit that Defendant had a heightened duty to safeguard Plaintiff from accident or injury while on Defendant's premises.
>
> > Response: Defendant objects to this request as ambiguous due to the vague and overbroad use of the phrase "accident or injury."
>
> Plaintiff's Request No.2: Admit that Defendant took no extra precautions to safeguard Plaintiff from accident or injury.
>
> > Response: Defendant objects to this request as vague due to its use of the phrase "extra precautions" as Plaintiff does not indicate what precautions are presumed to have been taken or what precautions Plaintiff considers to be "extra."
>
> Plaintiff's Request No. 3: Admit that Defendant has refused to offer Plaintiff any amount of compensation for his injuries incurred during the incident.
>
> > Response: Defendant objects to this request because it is beyond the scope of relevant discovery under Rule 26(b)(1) as it only inquires into settlement issues.
>
> Plaintiff's Request No. 4: Admit that Defendant has been properly sued in its correct name in this lawsuit.
>
> > Response: Defendant objects to the vague use of the term "properly." It is Defendant's position that it has engaged in no actionable misconduct and, therefore, the claims asserted against it are not "proper." However, subject to the foregoing objection, Defendant admits that Plaintiff has accurately named Defendant in this action.
>
> Plaintiff's Request No. 5: Admit that Defendant has adequate insurance to cover the damages claimed by Plaintiff in this lawsuit.
>
> > Response: Defendant objects to this request because it goes beyond the scope of relevant discovery under Rule 26(b)(1). Further, any insurance information has already been disclosed by Defendant with its initial disclosures and Plaintiff is equally able to determine the adequacy of the insurance coverage.

Defendant's Request No. 1: Admit that but for the Plaintiff's refusal to comply with posted warnings, he would not have suffered his accidental exposure to toxic substances.

> Response: Plaintiff objects to this request because it wrongly assumes that there were adequate warnings posted on Defendant's premises, which Plaintiff denied. Subject to this objection, denied.

Defendant's Request No. 2: Admit that Plaintiff was convicted in 1985 of indecent exposure.

> Response: Plaintiff objects to this request because it inquires about a matter that, even if it were true, would not be admissible and, therefore, is not within the proper scope of discovery under Rule 26(b)(1).

You might find yourself frustrated with the objections raised in the responses but in practice you will see lawyers assert objections to such imprecise requests or to any matter that may not clearly be relevant to the claims or defenses pled. With regard to the allegedly irrelevant inquiries, counsel could always simply admit or deny the matter requested and plan to object to any use of such admission at trial or seek exclusion by way of a pretrial motion. In other words, a failure to object to relevancy during discovery in no way waives a trial objection as to the inadmissibility of the fruits of the discovery. With regard to certain embarrassing matters, such as the inquired indecent exposure conviction, you can probably understand why the party would not want to have to answer this request.

What is the result if the responding party inadvertently fails to respond to a request within the 30 days, or accidently types "admitted" rather than "denied" under a particular request? The good news is that the rule does contemplate some bestowal of mercy: "[T]he court may permit withdrawal or amendment when the presentation of the merits of the action will be subserved thereby and the party who obtained the admission fails to satisfy the court that withdrawal or amendment will prejudice that party in maintaining the action or defense on the merits."[22] Two matters are important for a party wishing to be allowed to assert an untimely denial: (1) that the party file its motion as soon as possible–the longer the time the admission stands the more opportunity for the opponent to claim reliance upon that admission; and (2) the party demonstrate facts showing a good faith basis justifying the desire to deny the requested fact–such a showing helps to demonstrate that a withdrawal of the admission would "promote the presentation of the merits of the action." As with other provisions in the rules that contemplate mercy, it is

---

[22]Rule 36(b).

comforting to know this possibility exists but advocates should not plan to have to rely upon them. It makes for more restful sleep simply to draft your responses carefully and serve them timely.

In practice, an admitted fact can have terrific value. Unlike other discovery responses, the admission "conclusively" establishes the fact and may not be contradicted by contrary evidence. There is also a significant advantage to counsel, at trial, being permitted to stand before the jury and reading an admission from the other party, perhaps with an instruction or explanation from the trial judge: "Ladies and gentlemen of the jury, defendant XYZ admits to the following fact . . . ." This can be good, powerful stuff at a trial if displayed with the just the right dramatic touch. Thus, whether used at the outset of discovery to streamline the dispute and focus the subsequent discovery or used at the tail end of the discovery period in order to confirm what discovery has already suggested, requests for admission can be a valuable (or dangerous) tool for the advocate.

E. REQUESTS FOR PRODUCTION

Requests for production under Rule 34 have the potential to equalize the litigation playing field more than any other form of discovery. How many times has some adamant denial of wrongdoing or other cleverly crafted story crumbled in the face of a document or tangible bit evidence revealing the lie? Litigants are like other human beings–flawed–but they have an extra incentive to spin, stretch or simply slander the truth in order to gain their highly sought prize or to preserve the status quo. Tangible evidence is hard to dispute and can have a profound impact on resolving controversies. Does anyone need reminding about the power of one stained blue dress to quickly transform "I did not have sex with that woman" to statements or of sorrow, contrition and apology? Regardless of your views of presidential politics, none can deny how the debate was transformed overnight by reports of that dress with conclusive proof of the alleged act. Rule 34 provides the pretrial advocate the opportunity to gain access to proof that can likewise transform the nature of the parties' litigation. The fruits of a Rule 34 request can, and do every day, radically alter lawsuits. Whether you are on the hunt for that smoking gun evidence or are defending against such inquiries, understanding the principles and strategies surrounding this final form of written discovery will be very important to your career as a pretrial advocate.

Concerning each type of discovery, we have tried to highlight both the positive and negative aspects of the device. Requests for production illustrate this duality more so than any other form. As already mentioned, tangible evidence has a uniquely important evidentiary value to juries. And large defendants tend to do business in a way that leaves in the wake of most every decision a trail of tangible evidence for the forensic advocate to investigate for clues of the truth. Meetings are scheduled, minutes are taken, e-mails are exchanged, conferences are videotaped, memos are drafted, notes are jotted down, designs are drawn up, strategies are put into binders, message slips are created, phone calls are logged–each of these actions leaves either a paper or some form of digital or electronic footprint. This stuff provides grist for the advocate's prosecution or defense of a lawsuit. Some cases, often business litigation, involves litigants with equal amounts of such material in their possession that they may be forced to produce in response to a Rule 34 request. Remember, if we were only talking about the items in a litigant's hands that help litigant's case these are already required to be produced with the litigant's initial disclosures. (As you will learn in the last chapter, such items will also be required to be listed as a trial exhibit in a party's final pretrial statement.) So our real focus now is on items in a litigant's possession that help the adversary's case; these are materials that are not covered by the initial disclosures and which would never be revealed voluntarily as a trial exhibit by the possessing party. The only way such items tend to come to light–other than through clandestine informal meetings with disgruntled former employees–is through the Rule 34 device. And in a great many civil cases, the parties do not possess equal amounts of tangible materials subject to discovery. The personal injury plaintiff or the employee fired for reasons of sex or race do not tend to have reams of paper to turn over. Rather, it is often the corporate defendant in possession of this litigation-transforming stuff. Viewed in this way, Rule 34 can do much to change the balance of power in this David vs. Goliath scenarios. From the perspective of everyone except Goliath, this is a good thing both for the plaintiff and society interested in principles of compensation, deterrence and even punishment.

But the wonderful aspects of Rule 34 come at a price. Not every corporate defendant, after all, is really a Goliath. Some are innocent of the accusations with nothing in particular to hide. Yet a plaintiff's advocate armed with a computer and ten spare minutes of time can turn that defendant's world upside down through the simple drafting of comprehensive document requests. These document requests can dominate the life of the corporate defendant resulting in the expenditure of thousands of hours of employees' time trying to locate, isolate, review and organize for production the materials referenced in the "Plaintiff's First Request for Production." In this world of electronic storage of information, even information believed to have been "deleted", these positive and negative traits of Rule 34 requests are magnified geometrically. What is there to stop an advocate from drafting document requests motivated primarily by the desire to disrupt, harass, and intimidate a litigation adversary into offering to settle a case just to stop the bleeding occasioned by the discovery? Of course, the Rules (e.g., Rule 26(g)) we have already mentioned before instruct advocates not to behave this way. But just as litigants are flawed human beings so too are advocates and sometimes they don't play by the rules absent judicial intervention. Of course, advocates develop reputations with other counsel and with judges and those that abuse the rules do not tend to be successful over the long term. But your client needs the case you're handling today to run smoothly and effectively and your job is to know how to make that happen.

With this background, let's learn more about Rule 34 and the strategies for propounding and responding to requests for production.

1. The Law

<u>Generally</u>

Rule 34 permits a litigant to obtain from another litigant for inspection and/or copying documents and other tangible items that are relevant to any party's pled claims or defenses (Rule 26(b)(1)) by making a specific request for the materials:

> Any party may serve on any other party a request (1) to produce and permit the party making the request, or someone acting on the requestor's behalf, to inspect, copy, test, or sample any designated documents or electronically stored information–including writings, drawings, graphs, charts, photographs, sound recordings, images, and other data or data compilations stored in any medium from which information can be obtained–translated, if necessary, by the respondent into reasonably usable form, or to inspect, copy, test, or sample any designated tangible things which constitute or contain matters within the scope of Rule 26(b) and which are in the possession, custody or control of the party upon whom the request is served; or (2) to permit entry upon designated land or other property in the possession or control of the party upon whom the request is served for the purpose of inspection and measuring, surveying, photographing, testing, or sampling the property or any designated object or operation thereon, within the scope of Rule 26(b).[23]

Litigants often begin their Rule 34 requests with an elaborate and all-encompassing descriptive list of everything that might constitute a "document" or "tangible item" covered by the enumerated requests. Their goal is to describe so many categories of things that nothing will slip through the cracks. The forms generated by these advocates tend to grow longer and longer as one thinks of another way to describe an object not already expressly included and so adds this new term to the definition. This is unnecessary–simply state in your document request that you wants all items responsive to the specified categories within the scope of Rule 34(a) definition of documents and other tangible items. Many advocates unnecessarily add many pages of details instructions and definitions to their written discovery requests. These are almost always redundant of what rule

---

[23]Rule 34(a).

34 already provides or a sinister attempt by counsel to try to force their own procedures onto opposing counsel. A better practice is to keep your definitions to a minimum (perhaps only defining simple terms like party names or incidents referenced in the specific requests) and your instructions limited to details like when and where you would like the documents produced.

When you are served on behalf of your client with a Rule 34 request you have 30 days to serve your response which must, for each category requested, either object or indicate that production of the responsive materials will be made. Often there may be no responsive documents to a particular request and you can simply note this in your response. In many situations you may lodge an objection to the request–perhaps to his over breadth or to a possible privilege protecting certain responsive materials–but, subject to the objection, indicate that you will permit inspection and copying of at least a portion of the requested materials not covered by the objection.

Disclosures are limited to the four specified categories, and interrogatories are limited to 25 absent court order or stipulation, and in the next chapter you will learn that the rules also provide for a limit on the number of depositions in a case. But document requests, as with requests for admission, have no preset limit on their number absent action by the district court. You could theoretically serve your adversary with dozens of Rule 34 requests, perhaps one each week for the entire summer, with each written request having hundreds of enumerated categories of materials sought for production. But the more sets of voluminous Rule 34 requests you send the more likely you are to have the court sustain the responding party's objections or grant their motion for protective order. Rule 26(g) requires the advocate's implicit promise not to use discovery requests for improper purposes. Likewise, Rule 26(c) provides that a court may craft a protective order to offer appropriate relief for each unique situation:

> Upon motion . . . and for good cause shown, the court . . . may make any order which justice requires to protect a party or person from annoyance, embarrassment, oppression, or undue burden or expense, including one or more of the following:
>
> > (1) that the disclosure or discovery not be had;
> > (2) that the disclosure or discovery may be had only on specified terms and conditions, including a designation of the time or place;
> > (3) that the discovery may be had only by a method of discovery other than that selected by the party seeking discovery;
> > (4) that certain matters not be inquired into, or that the scope of the disclosure or discovery be limited to certain matters;
> > (5) that discovery be conducted with no one present except persons designated by the court;

(6) that a deposition, after being sealed, be opened only by order of the court;

(7) that a trade secret or other confidential research, development, or commercial information not be revealed or revealed only in a designated way; and

(8) that the parties simultaneously file specified documents or information enclosed in sealed envelopes to be opened as directed by the court.[24]

Given the volatile mix created by the lack of any arbitrary limit on the number of Rule 34 requests and the ability of even a single request to call for the production of millions of pieces of paper, protective orders are sought more often in the Rule 34 context than with any other type of formal discovery. There is a wealth of published case law interpreting and applying these admittedly broad rules of civil procedure to unique factual scenarios. For this reason, it is often impossible to predict accurately exactly how far a trial judge will permit a litigant to go in extracting documents and other tangible items from their adversary. Advocates tend to rely upon their personal experiences in front of particular judges to gain a "feel" for a specific judge's likes and dislikes in discovery and then model their behavior and discovery positions accordingly. Most trial judges certainly apply a rule of reason balancing the rightful needs of a litigant to have wide open and robust discovery with the desire not to cause responding parties to collapse under the oppressive weight of their discovery obligations. And because most discovery disputes are not immediately appealable, as an advocate you had better stay on the judge's good side. Establishing control over your client will be critical to staying out of hot judicial waters. For example, the advocate will need to engage in direct communications with her client detailing the client's discovery obligations and ensuring compliance with discovery requests and any court orders.

One other issue that is frequently litigated by parties concerns when a document or tangible item is considered to be under the "possession, custody or control" of a litigant–for the duty to produce is limited to such information thus held. Courts take a flexible approach in applying this standard. If the responding party has a superior right, relative to the requesting party, to obtain the materials from a third party, most courts will consider this sufficient to trigger the production obligation. Certainly affiliated corporate or partner entities cannot shield relevant documents from production by claiming that one sister corporation is distinct from another. Their common ownership or affiliation is typically considered sufficient "control" for a court to justify an order compelling the responding party to obtain the documents from its affiliate for production.

Of course, by its own terms Rule 34 only applies to obtaining documents

---

[24]Rule 26(c)(1)-(8)..

from parties to the litigation. Rule 34 reminds advocates, however, that ""[a] person not a party to the action may be compelled to produce documents and things or to submit to an inspection as provided in Rule 45."[25] Rule 45 states that a court-issued subpoena can be obtained by a litigant to "command each person to whom it is directed to attend and give testimony or to produce and permit inspection, copying, testing, or sampling of designated books, documents, electronically stored information, or tangible things in the possession, custody or control of that person, or to permit inspection of premises, at a time and place therein specified . . . ."[26] Rule 45 is an important counterpart to Rule 34 by extending a duty to produce materials to nonparties. A nonparty may resist these obligations through service of a written objection served before the earlier of the time specified for compliance or 14 days after the subpoena is served.[27] To a certain extent, Rule 45 imposes less protection for nonparties than Rule 34 does for parties; nonparties only have to be given a "reasonable time to comply"[28] which often may be less than thirty days. On the other hand, in ruling on motions to quash a subpoena or for protective order, courts are in practice much more sympathetic in practice to assertions of burden in complying with a subpoena by a non-litigant.

As with all other forms of discovery under the rules, a litigant has an ongoing duty to supplement their prior Rule 34 production to account for responsive items that come to the attention of the party after an initial production.[29] This is, by the way, not a license for withholding key documents until the last minute before trial. Courts have the right to sanction both client and counsel for knowingly withholding responsive information when it could and should have been produced earlier. On the other hand, it is not uncommon for clients with large warehouses of information to have additional responsive materials come to light months after making the original production of documents. Courts expect reasonable diligence in locating and producing the materials. The more organized your client is, in its ordinary course of business, in storing and retrieving materials the less burdensome this obligation will be in pretrial practice. In terms of supplementation, the sooner the better to avoid the court potentially from issuing sanctions, such as the exclusion of the material (if helpful to your client) from evidence at trial or on motion.

a. Electronic Discovery

---

[25]Rule 34(c).

[26]Rule 45(a)(1)(C).

[27]Rule 45(c)(2)(B).

[28]Rule 45(c)(3)(A)(i).

[29]Rule 26(e)(1).

It is worthwhile to pause here to discuss specifically the concept of requests for electronically stored information under Rule 34. The Federal Rules of Civil Procedure were amended recently to provide specific treatment for such items. Electronic information has always been within the scope of discovery available under Rule 34 and there has evolved a significant body of case law governing this type of data–for the most part dealing with issues of (a) what efforts must be undertaken by responding litigants to produce data that was not easily accessible and (b) who should bear the extraordinary costs associated with such production. The recent amendments to the rules has provided some helpful clarification on these subjects. Rule 26(b)(2)(B) now provides a specific limitation on the responding party's e-discovery obligations:

> A party need not provide discovery of electronically stored information from sources that the party identifies as not reasonably accessible because of undue burden or cost. On motion to compel discovery or for a protective order, the party from whom discovery is sought must show that the information is not unreasonably accessible because of undue burden or cost. If that showing is made, the court may nonetheless order discovery from such sources if the requesting party shows good cause, considering the limitations of Rule 26(b)(2)(C) [limiting discovery that is too cumulative, inconvenient, expensive or where the burden outweighs the needs of the case]. The court may specify conditions for the discovery.

This provision establishes that the burden to resist e-discovery is on the responding party which may avoid discovery upon making an evidentiary showing that the electronically stored information is not reasonably accessible. Upon making this showing, the presumptions effectively turn against production unless the discovering party can demonstrate good cause. Rule 34 also provides that a responding party can articulate an alternative form for producing electronically stored information:

> If objection is made to the requested form or forms for producing electronically stored information–or if no form was specified in the request–the responding party must state the form or forms it intends to use.[30]

Further, Rule 34 provides guidance for the form a document production must take and offers some specifics in this regard when e-discovery items are involved in the production:

---

[30]Rule 34(b).

Unless the parties otherwise agree, or the court otherwise orders:

> (i) a party must produce documents for inspection shall produce them as they are kept in the usual course of business or shall organize and label them to correspond with the categories in the request;

> (ii) if a request does not specify the form or forms for producing electronically stored information, a responding party must the information in a form or forms in which it is ordinarily maintained or in a form or forms that are reasonably usable; and

> (iii) A party need not produce the same electronically stored information in more than one form.[31]

A final word of advice for advocates concerning e-discovery is to have available either on your staff or through as-needed consultation the services of an expert at computer forensics. Most advocates, and many clients, simply do not have the expertise on their own to ascertain what information is readily accessible on their computer hard drives or networks much less how to retrieve such stored data. In fact, many clients are still shocked to discover that e-mails and other electronically stored documents they believed had been deleted are still, in fact, stored in their computer databases. The services of an information technology expert can thus be an important addition to an advocate's litigation team.

2. The Practice

Advocates drafting document requests must "describe . . . with reasonable particularity" each item or category of items to be inspected and specify a "reasonable time, place, and manner" for the inspection.[32] The responding party must within 30 days of service of the request, serve a written response either objecting to each specific request, in whole or to a portion of a request, or indicating whether and how discovery shall be permitted of that item(s).[33] Typical practice is for the discovering party to simply provide a numbered list of the categories of materials sought and to specify each category with as much detail as possible so that the responding party can understand exactly what their obligations may be. In drafting requests, advocates often make the mistake of using such global terms in each request that they draw many otherwise unnecessary objections of "overbreadth", "vague" and "unduly burdensome." Drawing such objections

---

[31]Rule 34(b)(i)-(ii)..

[32]Rule 34(b).

[33]Rule 34(b).

tends to delay discovery of the real materials actually sought; for this reason, advocates should be as specific as possible with each enumerated item. A related type of mistake is to use global terms that, logically, request materials that obviously are not within the scope of discovery due to classic privileges such as attorney-client materials. An example of this a request illustrating these drafting problems would be as follows:

> Request for Production   No. 1: Produce all documents evidencing, referring to, or in any way related to the allegations of plaintiff's complaint.

> Response: Defendant objects to this request because it fails to specify with any reasonable particularly the precise category of documents being requested. In effect, this request seeks production of all documents that might be relevant to the claims or defenses pled but without guidance as to what documents plaintiff is actually seeking. Further, Defendant objects to this request because it expressly seeks documents that are clearly privileged–such as counsel's privileged correspondence with the defendant–as such documents are "in any way related to the allegations" of this case.

Much better examples of precisely worded requests in a hypothetical case involving plaintiff's ingestion of a taco chip tainted by a foreign substance, might include:

> Plaintiff's Request for Production No. 1: Please produce defendant's formula for the Product [as defined above] which identifies the intended ingredients and quantities for each ingredient.

> Plaintiff's Request for Production No. 2: Please produce a list, by ingredient, of each of defendant's suppliers used in the production of the Product during the previous two years.

> Plaintiff's Request for Production No. 3: Please produce a corporate hierarchy chart that illustrates the officers of the defendant corporation.

> Plaintiff's Request for Production No. 4: Please produce the documents evidencing defendant's quality control efforts to prevent contamination of the Product by foreign substance.

> Plaintiff's Request for Production No. 5: Please produce documentation of the volume of sales of the Product during the preceding three years as well as the geographic distribution of such sales in the United States.

> Plaintiff's Request for Production No. 6: Please produce all customer complaints concerning contamination of the Product by foreign substances

during the preceding three years, and also produce defendant's correspondence with such customers on this subject.

Plaintiff's Request for Production No. 7: Please produce documents showing when defendant first became aware that the Product had been contaminated by foreign substances.

In such a case, of course, counsel might literally think of hundreds of requests for equally relevant information. But both sides are well served by such specificity of the requests–the discovering party is more likely to obtain responsive documents and to do so in shorter time and the responding party is in a better position to respond knowingly and with fewer boilerplate objections. Likewise, legitimate disputes concerning the discoverability of specific documents can be more efficiently resolved by the advocates and the court when the veneer of ambiguous requests and boilerplate objections is removed from the equation.

With regard to legitimate items sought for which no objection is made, Rule 34 does not actually call for their immediate transmission on the 30th day after service of the request. Rather, what is due at that time would be the responding party's written statement that it will permit inspection and copying. In practice, if the volume is not too voluminous, responding counsel will go ahead and send bates-stamped copies of the responsive documents with their written response. In fact, in a great majority of cases this is how counsel act. But when the anticipated production is quite large, the response normally just states that discovery will be permitted as to certain categories of materials and then counsel follow up with each other informally to schedule the trip to the warehouse or law firm to do the actual inspection and arrange for the copying. With regard to these voluminous productions, counsel for the responding party still needs to arrange for some pre-production review of the materials to be sure no privileged document slips through inadvertently. When counsel engaged in the review of the materials, often taking days or even weeks in larger scale productions, they will mark which items they want copied and than negotiate with opposing counsel to arrange for a copying service to make the copies, bates stamp them and provide a set to both litigants. There are many minute variations on these logistics but this general description should suffice for our present purposes.

One other matter should be considered at this point in terms of the strategy decision in making production of voluminous materials. The rule states that the responding party has the option to produce the records as ordinarily kept in business or by segregating the documents according to which request each item is responsive. A responding party can thus search its own warehouse and produce only the responsive information or open its warehouse doors and permit the discovering counsel, and a team of legal assistants, to do the search themselves (guided typically by some reference materials showing how the documents are stored). Obviously many clients do not want opposing counsel prying their files.

On the other hand, making the adversary do the search themselves can save money as well as make it more likely that a responsive document gets overlooked in the process. This does not mean that you can ethically remove an item from its normal storage point and hide it in a stack of unrelated records. But the rule does permit litigants to simply produce the documents as they are normally maintained. There is no general right answer for the best strategic approach but this is something worth discussing with your client in each case involving voluminous production of materials.

F.   RULES MATRIX

This table serves as a starting point for additional inquiry into the potential professional responsibility and civil procedure issues that are implicated when drafting and filing pleadings.

Issue Arising During Written Discovery	Applicable Rule of Professional Responsibility, Ethics Rule, or Federal Rule of Civil Procedure
Initial disclosures automatically required of a litigant at the early stages of litigation.	**FRCP 26(a)(1)**
Expert witness disclosures, including requirement for an expert report.	**FRCP 26(a)(2)**
Pretrial disclosures of witnesses and documents required on the eve of trial.	**FRCP 26(a)(3)**
Preclusion from using information or materials at trial or hearing that were not, but should have been, disclosed or produced earlier.	**FRCP 37(c)**
Interrogatories	**FRCP 33**
Evasive or incomplete discovery responses treated as a failure to answer.	**FRCP 37(a)(4)**
Restrictions on counsel serving as a witness.	**Ethical Rule 3.7**
Duty to supplement disclosures and other discovery responses.	**FRCP 26(e)**

Motions to compel disclosure or discovery.	**FRCP 37(a)**
Depositions on written questions	**FRCP 31**
Use of deposition answers in court proceedings	**FRCP 32**
Requests for admission	**FRCP 36**
Sanctions for failure to admit	**FRCP 37(c)(2)**
Requests for production	**FRCP 34**
Obtaining court ordered protection from harassing or burdensome discovery	**FRCP 26(c)**
Electronic discovery protections	**FRCP 26(b)(2)(B)**

Table 1 - Potential Rules Applicable to Formal Discovery

Points To Ponder . . .

1. Of the various written forms of discovery we have discussed, do you suspect that one type is more helpful than another? Does it depend upon the circumstances of the case? How so?

2. How do you feel about the fact that certain discovery tools (e.g., interrogatories) have arbitrary limits but others do not? Should these limits be removed from the rules or should all forms of discovery have some presumptive quantitative limits?

3. How should you go about planning your written discovery in terms of the order? Is it better for you to send out discovery requests first or wait until your opponent sends discovery requests to you?

4. What things can the pretrial advocate do to maintain the credibility of a specially retained (i.e., paid) expert witness? What things can the advocate do inadvertently to undermine such credibility?

5. Given the pleading obligations of Rules 8(a) and (b) (complaints and answers), is there anything to be accomplished from using requests for admission or is this discovery redundant?

CHAPTER EIGHT
ORAL DISCOVERY - DEPOSITIONS

"The man that hath no music in himself,
Nor is not moved with concord of sweet sounds,
Is fit for treasons, stratagems, and spoils . . ."[1]

A. DEPOSITION QUESTIONING TECHNIQUES

There are several different issues that an advocate must consider when preparing to conduct a deposition. They include case analysis and preparation to identify areas of inquiry, the actual schema for conducting the deposition, and the identification of areas of potential impeachment at trial. Your goals for depositions should include pinning the witness down and verifying the evidence that supports you case, identifying the evidence that will potentially hurt your case, and discovering the strengths and weaknesses of the witness. Before we can discuss such issues of strategy you must first master the tools that will allow you to unlock witnesses during depositions. We will begin with the most basic fundamental building block of the deposition - asking questions.

> The most basic and universal skill that an advocate must master is the ability to ask cogent, relevant, and applicable questions while listening to the answers given by the witness.

1. Asking Questions

As advocates the words that we use, the form of questioning that we choose, and our physical presence are the music of our profession. Before you can begin to recognize and make that music, you must first master the use of language with witnesses. In this section we will discuss the most fundamental skill that you must first master before you can conduct superior depositions - the ability to ask

---

[1] WILLIAM SHAKESPEARE, THE MERCHANT OF VENICE, act 5, sc. 1.

questions that help get out information and empower witnesses to both understand what we are asking and to answer it completely. The most basic and universal skill that an advocate must master is the ability to ask cogent, relevant, and applicable questions while listening to the answers given by the witness.

A thorough knowledge and understanding of Basic Questioning Techniques[2] is an <u>absolutely essential skill</u> for any competent advocate attempting to conduct a deposition. All relevant information received by the finder-of-fact begins with a question posed by an advocate.[3] The substantive evidence identified during depositions and later introduced at trial has its genus in the art of asking questions. You must master all of the basic questioning techniques available in order to maximize your effectiveness during depositions. Questioning is the primary means of discovering information from the witness, and the ability to properly formulate and ask questions is a fundamental skill that all advocates must continually develop and practice. We will first develop your understanding and ability to apply each discrete questioning technique, afterwards we will work on the organization of these questioning techniques into a pattern of questioning that will accomplish your intended goals during the deposition.

> ### Three Basic Questioning Techniques
>
> **Headlines**
> - Basic Introductory Phrases
> - Transitional Phrases
> - Looping or Coupling Phrases
>
> **Open or Non-Leading Questions**
> - Wide Open Questions
> - Directive Open Questions
> - Probing or Testing Questions
> - Coupling Questions
>
> **Closed or Leading Questions**

There are three basic questioning techniques for examining a witness that you will learn: (1) Headlines, (2) Open or Non-Leading Questions and (3) Closed or Leading Questions. You must not only know when you are allowed to use each type of question, you must also know why one type of question is superior to another in a given situation. Once you learn these Basic Questioning Techniques you will be able to use them to effectively achieve your purpose or goal in any

---

[2]Professor Rose owes his understanding of these **Basic Questioning Techniques** and the pedagogy involved in teaching them effectively to Professor Jim Seckinger at the University of Notre Dame Law School. Jim's materials on this subject are excellent and we commend them to you.

[3] The Federal Rules of Evidence give the judge the power to control the means of questioning, and also provide guidance on how questioning should occur. *See* Fed. R. Evid. 611.

situation that might arise. We are discussing them here in the context of depositions, but they are just as applicable during witness interviews, direct examination and cross examination. These Basic Witness Questioning Techniques should be a pervasive element in your planning and execution whenever you are questioning a witness.

> **Basic Introductory Phrases:**
>
> - *Let's talk about . . .*
> - *We will now discuss . . .*
> - *Please direct your attention to . . .*
>
> These are just a sampling of possible introductory phrases. You are limited by your knowledge of the English language, common sense, and ability to identify issues relevant to your witness.

An advocate uses these techniques in several different situations. Some are controlled by procedural rules, some by case law, and others by local practice rules. As we discuss the various portions of a deposition where these techniques may be used, we will identify which techniques you should employ and why. Before doing that we must first fully identify each type of technique and discuss ways to employ them. Let us begin with how we introduce questions, through headlines.

2. Headlines

A *Headline* is a statement consisting of two parts: an introductory phrase and a topic. There are three main types of Headlines: (1) basic introductory phrases, (2) transitional introductory phrases, and (3) looping or coupling introductory phrases. It is important to remember that Headlines are statements, not questions. The primary purpose of a Headline is to orient the witness to the area of the witness' testimony you wish to discuss. It also creates a feeling of flow and ease to the examination, providing guidance and clarity to the process. This is of particular importance during depositions, because time is often a factor when questioning. Effective Headlines are succinct and to the point. When Advocates construct long or complex introductory phrases they are creating ineffective headlines that do not accomplish much and waste a great deal of time. Long and complex Headlines defeat the primary purpose of orienting the witness to the specific area or issue. Witnesses who are asked closed ended questions using ineffective Headlines will use these long and complex Headlines to misconstrue the question and respond in a non-responsive fashion or give an out right destructive answer.

Headlines are used in all the various types of witness examination: direct examination, cross examination, redirect examination, impeachment on cross, rehabilitation on redirect, laying foundation for and using exhibits, expert testimony, taking depositions, and even when speaking to the judge, jury, or arbitrator on jury selection, opening statements, and closing arguments. When using Headlines you should always combine their use with the other basic questioning techniques discussed in this chapter. Those include WideOpen Questions, Directive Open Questions, Probing or Testing Questions, Coupling Questions, and Closed or Leading Questions. The Headline by itself does not produce substantive testimony from the witness. Think of Headlines as the signposts along the highway of your deposition. Each Headline is a marking stick that delinates within the depositionthe specific area about which you are inquiring. You want the depositions to be sufficiently clear that if you need to use during trial it will accomplish the purpose for which you have designed it. Headlines will always signal where you are going, and keep you focused and on track, a rare skill for most advocates taking a deposition. Because of this, Headlines are useful in conjuction with both open ended and close ended questions.

Headlines help the witness understand the questions and the issue(s) that the advocate wants to discuss. This creates a degree of comfort on the part of the witness, allowing them to focus on telling the truth as they remember it. For the witness, a deposition is usually not an everyday experience. They are nervous, worried, and sometimes frightened. Tell the witness that the two of you are going to have a conversation during the deposition. All they have to do is listen to your questions and then truthfully answer them. Headlines will allow you to make certain that the witness understands where you want to go and will then help them take you to that location. They assist the witness in testifying comfortably and persuasively, enhancing the witness' credibility. They also allow you to keep the witness on the topic you wish to discuss and provide a ready means to bring them back to the issues at hand if they begin to stray or wander while being deposed.

> **Transitional Introductory Phrases:**
>
> *Let's now talk about . . .*
> *Let's now move to . . .*
> *Now, I want to discuss . . .*
> *We will now turn to . . .*

In addition to assisting the witness in understanding the specific question asked, Headlines allow an advocate to create an organized, easy to follow and understandable deposition. An organized deposition allows the advocate to control the tempo, tenor and direction of the questioning.

When examining an adverse witness, on cross examination or when taking a deposition, Headlines help the examining lawyer control the witness. Headlines keep the witness on the examining lawyer's topic, requiring the witness to answer the examining lawyer's question, regardless of the witness' desires. This allows you to establish control and limit the scope of a witness' testimony. The caveat here is that Headlines also orient the witness being examined as to the subject you wish to discuss. In certain instances you may choose to forgo Headlines in order to ensure the witness does not have time to formulate a "coached" or "untrue" answer to your questions. Finally Headlines serve as road signs for anyone listening to the examination, focusing the inquiry as the advocate chooses, not as the witness might wish.

3. Open or Non-leading Questions

An Open or Non-Leading Question is one that showcases the witness and not the advocate. It invites a complete answer from the witness on a topic chosen by the advocate. It does not, however, suggest an answer to the witness. Instead, Open Questions identify a topic with varying degrees of specificity, allowing the witness to testify fully regarding that topic. There are certain words that are used by advocates when posing Open Questions, and there are also a variety of Open Questions normally used when examining witnesses. The type of Open Questions chosen depends upon the demeanor and knowledge of the witness as well as the specificity of the issue the questioner wishes to discuss. Examples of Open Questions include: (1) Wide Open Questions, (2) Directive Open Questions, (3) Probing or Testing Questions, and (4) Coupling Questions. You arrange these different types of questions depending upon the goal of that particular line of questioning. Sometimes you are searching for information, sometimes you are pinning witnesses down, and sometimes you are fishing. The right type of open ended question helps.

Advocates use Wide Open Questions during depositions to get the witness talking. They are designed to identify a particular topic that the advocate wants the witness to address. Most effective Wide Open Questions are used immediately following a Headline that has oriented the witness to the topic the advocate

Wide Open Questions:
Describe for us . . .
Explain . . .
Tell us about . . .

wishes to discuss. Wide Open Questions normally direct the witness to a specific **time**, **place**, **person**, or **event** identified in an earlier question or Headline.

After identifying the area you want to discuss with Wide Open Questions, you can use Directive Open Questions to narrowly focus the topic the witness should address. Directive Open Questions are normally coupled with a Headline so that the witness understands the scope and direction of the advocate's inquiry. Directive Open Questions, when coupled with a Headline, are an effective and capable means of orienting your witness to a very specific issue you wish to discuss, while also ensuring that the witness is fairly bound by the answer. One of the goals of a deposition is to pin the witness down, sloppy questioning techniques often prevent that from happening. Understanding the true basics of questioning will go a long ways towards avoiding the questions that leave a witness with a place to run once opposing counsel gets the opportunity to try and get the witness out of the box the answer to your question has put them in. Directive Open Questions normally appear after Wide Open Questions. They are often followed by Open Questions that allow the witness to further explain the

---

Examples of Directive Open Questions Used With a *Headline*:

I'd like to draw your attention to the fax you received that day—what did you do with it?

Please direct your attention to the store on the corner of Smith and Wesson—did you or didn't you go into the establishment located there?

Let's now talk about the window of that store—could you see inside the store through the window?

A Follow-Up Wide Open Question Would Be:

What did you see?

---

specific issue you have identified through your Directive Open Questions. They are usually followed up with summation questions that get the witness to agree that the topic has been exhausted and that their answers are true, fair and complete.

Open questions are designed to get out relevant information about a specific **time, place, person,** or **event** that the advocate wishes to discuss in greater detail by allowing the witness to answer with more details. The structure of Open Questions allows for the possibility of maximum explanation by the witness. Open Questions free the witness to answer with greater specificity by throwing open the door for them to answer completely based upon their own knowledge and experience.

Open Questions:
Who . . . ?
What . . . ?
When . . . ?
Where . . . ?

After you have gotten most, if not all, of the relevant facts from a witness you may need to employ a more specific type of Open Question to elicit those last few bits of relevant information. These types of Open Questions are usually referred to as Probing or Testing Questions. While they are narrowly construed, they are still Open Questions. They lead the witness to the specific fact you wish to discuss, but do not suggest the appropriate answer to the witness. These are focused questions that normally begin with a verb or have other elements that either clarify or explain an issue or point in the case. You are leading the witness to a particular issue when you use these types of questions, but you still are not suggesting answers. The test for an appropriate Probing or Testing Question is whether or not it is focused on a specific item about which further inquiry is necessary in order to explain a relevant point for your case.

Once you have wrung every last bit of relevant information from the witness on a specific item, you can then use Coupling Questions to emphasize the testimony of the witness that you wish emphasized. Coupling Questions can also be used to give a flow and

Probing or Testing Questions:
Did you . . . ?
What about . . . ?
How about . . . ?

continuity to the examination. They allow both the witness and anyone subsequently reviewing the deposition to understand where the examination is going. It also mimics normal speech patterns, creating a sense of believability and credibility concerning the examination. A Coupling Question takes a word or words from the witness' answer and then uses it to connect or couple the answer from the last question to the current question.

Open Questions may be used during all portions of the deposition, and must be used by advocates when performing a direct examination of their own witness druing trial. Although Advocates are not allowed to ask Closed or Leading Questions of their own witnesses whenever relating factual information that is disputed in the case during trial, hat restriction does not extend to depositions, and the use of closed ended or leading questions have a definite place in your deposition skills kit bag. Let us move on to a basic discussion and understanding of how to ask leading questions.

Now that we have identified and discussed the primary types of open ended

> ### Coupling Questions:
>
> *Q: Mr. Witness, I draw your attention to what happened immediately after the accident occured—what did you see the defendant do next?*
>
> ***A: I saw the defendant open the door to car, get out, lean over and throw up.***
>
> *Q: After the defendant got out of his car and threw up what did you do?*

questions let us move on to the next tool in your questioning kit bag - leading questions.

4. Closed or Leading Questions[4]

A Closed Question is designed to identify the witness' knowledge of the facts or to challenge the credibility of the witness. The structure of the Closed Question ensures that the witness can only respond with one possible truthful answer which is already known by the advocate posing the question. A variety of techniques are available to formulate Closed or Leading Questions. Some of them include: (1) telling the witness instead of asking, (2) using taglines to force agreement by the witness, and (3) asking one-fact questions.

> ### Telling the Witness Instead of Asking:
> *"You got out of your car."*
> *"You closed the car door."*
> *"You walked across the sidewalk."*

These statements require agreement or disagreement from the witness, nothing more. This technique can be used to great effect during cross examination, but it also a useful tool during depositions. Closed ended questions in depositions tie witnesses down, committing them to one version of events. You can use it to verify information, ensure that the witness is on record as giving the most

---

[4] Most authors of trial advocacy use the terms "closed questioning" or "leading questioning" interchangeably. Advocates should understand that regardless of the terminology used these questions focus the witness and suggest an answer. The attention of the jury should be on the advocate, not the witness, when asking these types of questions.

complete answer possible, and to provide the semblance of fairness in that you are verifying the substance, depth and nature of their testimony during the deposition. When done properly it prevents the witness from wandering during trial testimony into "new" facts that were not disclosed during the deposition. The witness is left with a hobson's choice at trial - no true choice at all. This is a crucial skill if you are going to properly set up witnesses for impeachment at trial based upon their inconsistencies, or unwillingness to admit facts which they perceive hurt them.

Using taglines to force an answer from the witness requires them to either agree or disagree with you. However, the sound and tenor of taglines can become an annoying habit and may invite some witnesses to argue with you. You do not want witnesses or others who may receive the deposition to focus on the various "quirks" in your presentation. An overwhelming use of taglines is distracting and does not do an adequate job of assisting you in controlling a witness. While the choice of using taglines is one of style and demeanor, as well as local practice, we recommend losing them. They tend to become crutches and distract from the power of your questions.

> **Using Taglines To Force Agreement By the Witness:**
>
> *"You got out of the car, didn't you?"*
> *"You closed the car door, correct?"*
> *"We can agree that you walked across the sidewalk?"*

The third tool that ensures your questions will be Closed or Leading Questions is to only ask one fact per question. Think of one-fact questions as the building blocks that allow you to place the witness in a box during depositions that tie the witness down. One senior partner at Littler Mendeleson Law Firm refers to this as "pinning the butterfly." She imagines that the witness is a butterfly and her leading one fact questions are pins that she is using to hold the butterfly down. She is done when the butterfly cannot move anymore. This is an excellent image to keep in mind as you focus on one fact leading questions that are driving towards a conclusion that the witness must accept.

Pin the Butterfly!

Advocates use one-fact questions to control witnesses. It becomes very difficult for a witness to prevaricate when only one factual issue is posed in the question. Closed or Leading Questions are normally used during cross examination of adverse witnesses, when laying a foundation for the admissibility of evidence through any witness, or when the witness' demeanor or nature requires Closed or Leading Questions in order to assist the finder-of-fact in getting to the testimony of the witness. This usually occurs when the witness' ability to communicate is diminished due to their age or status as a victim of a violent crime. All of these situations may arise during depositions.

Always keep in mind that these Closed or Leading Questions are used to control witnesses, to showcase the advocate, and to lay foundations for the admissibility of evidence. The focus for Closed or Leading Questions is on the advocate, not the witness. Closed or Leading Questions allow the advocate to probe for logical weaknesses or fallacies in the witness' testimony, while also providing a vehicle to test the credibility of the witness through the crucible of cross examination.

One-Fact Questions:

"You opened the front door?"
"The front door of your house?"
"You walked through the open door?"
"You closed the door?"
"You locked the door?"
"You left your house?"

We have discussed several important concepts in this chapter on asking questions and have begun to develop a deeper understanding of the decision making process and case preparation that goes into asking questions. However, study of these three basic questioning techniques will never produce mastery. You must practice constructing these types of questions until they become second nature. Every time you question a witness, whether it be an interview, a deposition or at trial you should keep in mind that these encounters can be crubiles of emotion and ego. The struggle between advocate and witness when leading questions are used, particularly during cross examination, is sometimes so frustrating that even seasoned advocates lose their way and ask the wrong question, in the wrong fashion, at the wrong time. This can also occur when using open ended questions when you have not asked focused questions and your witness has not provided helpful answers. You can minimize that possibility by inculcating within yourself these basic questioning techniques, allowing you to immediately adapt your question to the situation and the goal. Let us move on now and discuss how to organize depositions to ensure that you have accomplished the goals you identified during your case analysis and informal discovery.

B. CONDUCTING DEPOSITIONS

1. Taking the Deposition

Having decided to take a deposition there are certain basic practicalities that you must get out of the way before you can get down to the actual questioning process. You must identify the location for the deposition, ensure that sufficient seating is available, arrange for a court reporter, consider the need for food, identify a break area, know how witnesses will be

> **Fundamental Goals for Depositions:**
> - Get commitments
> - Explore for information
> - Test potential legal, factual and moral theories

sworn and decide whether or not you will provide copies of any documents you will reference in the deposition. All of this should be done with an eye to civility and a commitment to reducing distractions so that the fruits of the deposition will hold up when you need to use them later. How you go about accomplishing these mundane tasks is not particularly important, but they must be taken care of so that you can focus on preparing for the deposition. A good place to start is by considering the procedures already in place in your particular firm or agency.

Each organization is different, and you should take the time to ride along with someone else's deposition before you are responsible for doing your own. If your practice does not allow for that possibility then you must take care of the support work before you can begin the intellectual development of your questions. Both are important, one serves as the backbone of the deposition and the other is the brains. A person with a backbone and no brains is useless, and a person with no backbone and a brain is dangerous. Get off on the right foot so that you can focus on what matters, extracting information from the witness that will stand up to scrutiny at trial.

Advocates normally depose witnesses with three fundamental goals in mind, getting commitments, exploring for information, and testing potential legal, factual and moral theories. The questioning technique that is employed by the advocate varies, depending upon the goal of the deposition, but the basic questioning techniques discussed earlier in this chapter form the basic building blocks for all lines of inquiry during depositions. Depositions often have multiple goals, and it is not uncommon for the questioning techniques to vary in order to accomplish all of the stated goals. There is a methodology to this process that can effectively illustrate how it works.. Think of a downward pointing directional

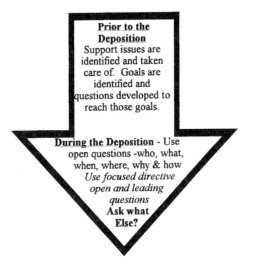

Prior to the Deposition Support issues are identified and taken care of. Goals are identified and questions developed to reach those goals.

During the Deposition - Use open questions -who, what, when, where, why & how *Use focused directive open and leading questions* **Ask what Else?**

From broad to narrow - How to Organize Deposition Questions

arrow pointing towards your goals(getting commitments, exploring information and testing theories). Once you arrive at one goal you can move horizontally to another, finish that line of inquiry and then return to wide open questions or otherwise, depending upon the reason for the deposition and the limitations imposed. Flexibility is the key to this process. In order for it to work properly you must develop the ability to listen to the witness. Listening is not limited to the words coming out of the witness's mouth. You should also pay attention to their body language. An adroit questioner will pick up on the unspoken clues during certain lines of inquiry that indicate additional questioning would be fruitful.

We will discuss how to arrange these questions in a moment, but for now accept on faith that this approach maximizes your time in depositions and increases your chances of getting truthful and complete information. Once you have identified your goals for the deposition, prepared your line of questions, and taken care of the support issues, you should consider how you will actually begin the process of questioning the witness.

a. Beginning at the Beginning-Admonitions

Once all of the niceties have been dispensed with and the witness has been sworn it is time for the deposition to begin. While each advocate has their own style, there are certain issues that should always be addressed at the beginning of the deposition. The initial lines of questions that most seasoned advocates include when beginning depositions are commonly referred to as admonitions. They get the deposition started properly, laying the groundwork for the entire process.

You want to get off on the right foot with the witness, and there are psychological, practical and persuasive reasons for beginning in a certain fashion. Psychologically you want to create the appearance that you are setting the deponent at ease, at least on the surface. Practically you are also closing off potential excuses for changes in testimony at a later date. This is an extremely important point. You want whatever information you confirm, discover or develop during the deposition to be frozen in place, without the possibility of modification between the deposition and the witness's subsequent in court testimony, at a minimum you must ensure that any changes will come at a price for the witness, usually extracted through impeachment. Your initial introductory questions should take care of those excuses that a wiley witness might later use to justify changing their testimony. From a persuasive perspective the appropriate introductory questions can put the honest witness at ease and place the slippery witness on notice. Either way you lay the groundwork for a devastating impeachment if the witness changes their story at trial. While not all witnesses lie, there are many that find themselves mistaken, and one of the job's of a good deposition is to remove issues of uncertainty. This allows for finality in the process and supports proper settlement of cases. A good deposition will get everything out into the light of day where it can be deal with, both the good, the bad, and the downright ugly.

Even though you are putting the witness in a box, there is nothing wrong with beginning in a civil fashion, and continuing in that vein. Questions such as "Could you please tell us your name and where you live?" Followed up by requesting contact information are respectful and let the witness know that this is a professional endeavor. You are attempting to build rapport and guarantee honesty. Once you have begun, you should move right into the admonitions, a series of questions that are fairly standard in nature, if not form. We call them "admonitions" under the theory that you are admonishing the witness to do certain things or suffer the consequences. They are informative questions, designed to pin the witness down as to their current mental and physical state, while ensuring that they agree concerning the purpose of the deposition. Of course they are crafted in a variety of ways, depending upon the witness. Consider the following series of questions. Ask yourself if they cover all of the issues necessary to inform the witness while simultaneously committing them to the process.

The Witness is sworn by the court reporter.

Q.   *Good morning. Please tell us your name and address?*
A.   *My name is Charlotte Johnson. I live at 123 Mockingbird Lane here in Pelican Bay.*

Q.   *Thank you Ms. Johnson. Please provide us with a good phone number and email address that we can use to get in touch with you between now and trial.*
A.   *Sure. My number is 555-1234, my email address is wildflowers@yahoo.com.*

Q.   *Thank you. Ma'am you just took an oath this morning. What does that oath mean to you?*

A.   *I believe it is a promise to tell the truth as best as I can remember it from the day of the accident.*

Q.   **That is part of it. Do you understand that it is a promise to truthfully and completely answer the questions you are asked today?**

A.   *Yes.*

Q.   **Are you willing to do that? It is very important that we have a complete and honest record of what you can remember and your promise under oath makes that possible. Will you be able to keep that promise today?**

A.   *Yes I will. (nods head as well).*

Q.   **I appreciate that ma'am. I noticed that you nodded your head when you answered my last question. Since this is not a video deposition the court reporter cannot record head nods, or other things that we might normally use to communicate an answer. I ask that you speak all answers to my questions so they can be fairly and accurately written down. Will you do that?**

A.   *Yes, I want this to be correct.*

[This takes care of reminding the witness about the oath, getting a commitment to be truthful and complete, as well as the need for oral answers. The advocate now moves on to understanding questions.]

Q.   **Ms. Johnson I will probably ask a question at some point that is not clear. Could you please promise me that you will let me know if there is anything about any of my questions that is not clear and understood by you?**

A.   *Don't worry sir, if I don't understand what you are asking I will be sure to let you know. Can I ask my attorney to explain what you are asking to me if that happens?*

Q.   **Ma'am you are free to discuss anything with your attorney when I do not have a question pending. I am sure you would agree that it would not be fair for him to talk to you if I have asked you a question that has not yet been answered, so if you don't understand the question please let me know and I will rephrase it. After all they are my questions, not his. Will you do that for me?**

A.   *Yes.*

Q.   **Have you taken any medications that would effect your ability to truthfully and completely answer my questions today?**

A.   *No.*

Q.　*Do you have any other health issues that will prevent you from participating completely in this deposition?*

A.　*None that I can think of, other than this broken leg from where your client ran into me.*

Q.　*We will get to that.　What about sleep.　Did you get enough sleep last night?*

A.　*Yes.　I am fine and more than able to understand and answer your questions.*

Q.　*Ms. Johnson let's start by discussing how you prepared for today's deposition.　Please tell me what you did to get ready?*

A.　*Well I got up this morning...*

Q.　*I'm sorry ma'am, let me be more specific.　Did you meet with your attorney to discuss this deposition before today?*

A.　*Yes.*

Q.　*What documents did you look at before coming to testify?*

A.　*Well, I reread my statement to the police and looked at the copy of the accident report that my attorney has on file.　I also talked with my mom, she was in the car with me that day.*

Q.　*Other than your mother and your attorney have you talked with anyone else about the accident that happened July 1st of last year?*

A.　*Well, I talked to the police officer that showed up that day, and I also talked to the station attendant from the gas station who ran out to help me while I was in the street.*

Q.　*Ma'am I understand you are married.　This was a hard thing for you, I'm sure you have talked about it with your husband too?*

A.　*Well, yes, I have, I just didn't think that mattered since he wasn't there when it happened.*

Q.　*I understand.　Let me check one last time, other than your mother, your attorney, the police officer and your husband, you have never talked about the accident that happened on July 1st with anyone else?*

A.　*Just you here today.*

Q.　*So you agree then that those are the only people you have talked with about the accident?*

A.　*Yes.*

Q.　*So if someone else said you had talked to them about it they would not be telling the truth?*

A.   *That's right. I haven't talked about this with anyone else.*

Q.   **Thanks. I'll move on now. I'd like to talk to you about the time
             you spent in the restaurant in the 3 hours immediately proceeding
             the time of the accident.**

A.   *All right.*

And so it goes. A review of these initial admonitions clearly establishes
that you are laying the groundwork for a complete deposition, and establishing
your ability to vitiate any changes in testimony with an effective impeachment
based in large part upon the witness's answers to your initial admonition
questions. This is an important part of the deposition and should not be rushed
through. Use this time to set up the witness that intends to lie for destruction
during cross examination at trial. It will also remind the truthful witness of the
importance of the deposition and the need to do the right thing at all times. You

---

Doing the Necessary - Handling Admonitions in Depositions:

- Get off on the right foot

- Solemnity of the oath

- Purpose of the deposition

- Promise to be truthful and complete

- Handling questions

- Opportunity to revie w testimony before signing

- Need for oral answers

- How did you prepare for this deposition

- Breaks and Refreshments

- When you can talk with your attorney

- Remember Information or Clarification

- How to handle Pending Questions

- Capacity to participate today

- Reiterate they can ask questions at any time if something is
  unclear

---

win either way. From this point on the deposition will begin to get into the
substance of various issues germane to this particular case.

Now that we have broken the ice, let us move on to the structure of the meat of the deposition.

b. How to structure your questions

We will continue to use the the accident scenario found earlier in this chapter for this portion of our discussoin. Having finished with the admonitions you must next decide which topics you want to address and in what order. There is art in this part of the deposition. The topics that you choose, and the order in which you address them will have a definite effect upon the tenor of the deposition. Much like cross examination, it is often helpful to begin inquiring in areas that the witness must agree on. In other words noncontroversial topics as initial subjects set the witness at ease and allow you to get them in the habit of answering your questions. You can then move to more controversial or disputed topics as the deposition proceeds, or when you feel the time is right to bring them up. You accomplish this by organizing your questioning techniques to go from broad topics to narrow topics, with your follow on questions designed to be sufficiently focused to force all possible knowledge from the witness. The techniques follows this general model:

Four Steps to Maximize Deposition Questioning:

1. Open inquiry with newspaper style questions: Who, What, When, Where, Why, How, Describe

2. Continue to prod the witness by asking, "What else…" Please Explain

3. Refresh memory with leading questions, "Did you…"; "Do you…"; "What about…"; etc.

4. Recap by listing all of the responses and asking, "Is there anything else you can tell me."

Broad to Narrow - Effective Deposition Questioning Techniques

The topics that you need to discuss should come from your case analysis to date. In our example here the advocate is concerned about the weather that day, how the accident happened, and the extent of the injuries the witness received. The advocate has decided that each of these topics must be covered in order for the deposition to be successful. The advocate also has to be prepared to listen for any gems that might occur during question that identify other fruitful areas to inquire about. She must then decide whether to chase that issue down immediately or make a note of it and return later. Both methods are acceptable, and the advocate should consciously choose based upon the totality of the deposition and the case itself. consider the following questions and ask youself whether or not the advocate has done a sufficient job in beginning to tease out all of the facts, as well as handling any other issues that arise.

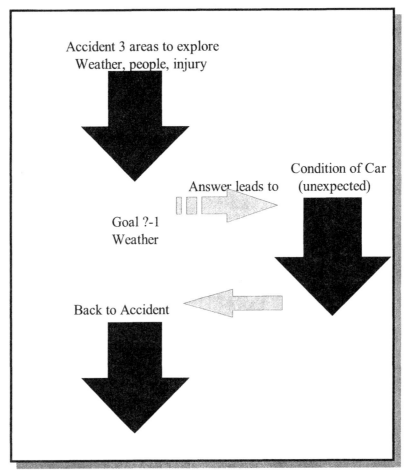

Graphic Presentation of a series of deposition questions, going from broad to narrow as each topic is exhausted. Note how you can shift to a topic when it arises and then come back to your initial line of inquiry.

Q.   ***What was the weather like that morning?***

A.   *Well, I remember that the forecast called for rain, and I had my umbrella with me that day.*

Q.   ***Did it rain that day?***
A.   *Yes. I got wet on the way on the way back from the restaurant to the car.*

Q.   ***Why? I thought you said you took your umbrella with you.***
A.   *Well, I was running late and forgot it.*

Q.   *I see. What was the weather like once you got in the car?*
A.   *It was still raining hard.*

Q.   *What did you do?*
A.   *I waited for the rain to die down.*

Q.   *Why did you do that? Was everything okay?*
A.   *I was worried about being able to see well while driving in the storm. My wipers didn't work that well.*

Our advocate has just discovered that something was wrong with the wipers on the car. She can begin to inquire in that area, or simply make a notation about it and follow up later. Using the arrow concept of large to narrow discussed. she now has to ability to make an informed decision about how to proceed. The beauty of preparing in this fashion is that all the advocate needs to do when an unexpected issue comes up is make a notation to ensure that she covers it when she wants to, not when the witness would prefer to. Advocates must remember that depositions are a series of inquiries, going from the broad to the specific and back again, chasing down lines of questions and series of facts to their inexorable conclusions. The advocate should always control the process, not the witness or opposing counsel. It is through case analysis that the right lines of questions and the proper needed facts are first identified and developed.

     c. *Theory testing*

The examples that we have just discussed deal primarily with deposition questions designed to get commitments and obtain information. The process for these tasks is relatively straightforward and their success depends in large part on the ability of the advocate to properly prepare and properly posit cogent and focused questions. The third goal for deposition questions, theory testing, is not for the faint hearted. Some caution against attempting theory questions, arguing that the witness is not going to agree with you, and that you will expose your theories to your opposing counsel, educating them on the theory of your case. On the other hand, if your theory is strong then exposing that theory to opposing counsel may very well lead to a settlement of the case on terms that are benefical to your client. Remember also, that testing theories can be used to exclude those that do not work so that you may focus on the ones that do. The stakes may be high, but the potential return is immense. This, like many other elements of the art of advocacy, is a judgement call. Sometimes you will gain more than you will lose by testing the validity of your theories. It is much better to discover the weak points of a particular legal, factual, or moral theory or theme in a deposition where you can adjust before trial. A theory that has not been tested is a hot house plant, its hardiness untried. Depositions provide an opportunity to test those hunches that sit in the gut of the best advocates.

If you decide to go about the task of theory testing, preparation is key. You must begin by marshalling all of the necessary facts to support the theory you have chosen. Theory testing presumes that you have performed case analysis in a manner sufficient to identify those theories you believe valid, and that you have identified the facts and have them available

> The goal is to string together a series of leading questions that support and lead to the conclusory question that encapsulates the theory you are testing.

to use at deposition and trial. The challenge is to test the validity of those theories with a witness that is not on your side, and who may in fact be downright inimical to your position. To accomplish this you can rely upon a techinque used during cross examination that is known as impeachment by the probabilities. It is often referred to as following the "logic train" of thought to its logical conclusion. The goal is to string together a series of leading questions that support and lead to the conclusory question that encapsulates the theory you are testing. Using leading questions is key here, because your desire is to control the witness while validating your position. If the witness challenges this, you can always come back with an inquiry along the lines of "Well then how else can you explain this?" At a minimum you will get the witness talking in an attempt to do so, and you may expose some fact or issue that hurts your position that you would not have otherwise learned. While theory testing is not for the faint hearted advocate, on balance the potential benefits far outweigh the possible negative consequences. Let us turn now to using documents in depositions a necessary skill that the untutored advocate ignores at their peril.

d. Using documents during depositions

> **Documents in Depositions are Used to:**
> - Authenticate
> - Obtain discovery
> - Force admissions
> - Impeach

Documents pervade the civil practice of law. They are both ubiquitous and sometimes pernicious, and the ability to properly utilize them during a deposition is crucial. Their is a dance to the art of documents in adversarial proceedings and many of the steps to that dance can be found in the deposition process. They are used to assist in discovery, identify missing documents, prod the witness's memory, test the candor of the witness, organize your questions, obtain admissions, corroborate witness statements, test theories, tie theories to witness statements, impeach witnesses and to convince the witness and opposing counsel that you are in charge and will prevail. When used impropery they show your lack of planning, expose gaps in your logical constructs and eat up a tremendous amount of time during the deposition that could be better spent asking questions and getting answers. You must have a purpose in mind every time you pick up a document and begin to use it in a deposition.

Questions about documents during depositions normally fall into the following categories:(1) authentication, (2) obtaining discovery, (3) getting admissions and (4) impeaching witnesses. You need to identify the purpose for using the document and then carefully craft your questions to achieve that goal.

Suggested Questions Dealing with Documents:

1. When was the document prepared?
2. Why was the document prepared?
3. Who prepared the document?
4. Are there any earlier drafts of the document?
5. Are there any notes pertaining to the document?
6. Where is the original document?
7. Who received the document?
8. Was there anything attached to the document?
9. Is there anything missing from the document?
10. How do you interpret the document?
11. What else can you tell me about the document?
12. Have you told me everything about the document?

Authenticating documents in the deposition can be particularly useful, because it allows you to remove that hurdle from the admission process at trial. Foundations are non-threatening, and they allow you to control the witness in a non-confrontational manner, not a bad way to start when dealing with a document.

Practically speaking, you must organize the documents in order to make certain that the deposition controls the documents. They should be grouped in sets according to the reason for their use. Sometimes these groupings are based upon chronologies, at other times they are founded on the author of the documents in question. The teaching point is to ensure that you have organized them, pre-marked them, and have a system to use them properly during the deposition. When you begin to use a particular document you should identify it by its number and nature, show it to opposing counsel, show it to the witness, ask the witness to identify the document in question(laying foundation), and then include the identifying number in all questions concerning that particular exhibit. This will make the record clear and keep you on track. A beautiful impeachment that ties a witness to a particular theory and exposes a falsehood is nowhere near as effective if you have not properly identified the document in question in the record.

Once the deposition is complete the advocate needs to end it. There are no magical jurisdictional words required to end a deposition. The important point is to ensure that you have covered the topics identified or raised by your questioning. Once that has been accomplished you can close the deposition with a simple "That is all for now." We have discussed the law skill and art of depositions from the standpoint of the advocate taking the deposition. Let us now consider how to best defend depositions.

C. DEFENDING A DEPOSITION

1. The advocate's role

An advocate that is defending a deposition of her client or a witness that is favorable to her client has a much different task in front of her than an advocate taking the deposition. She does not have the control of the deposing side, must deal with the concerns of her witness, and object as necessary to

> *The first step when preparing to defend a deposition is to identify the status of the witness.*

ensure that issues of proper questioning and admissibility are not waived, particularly privilege. The advocate must accomplish all of this while not violating ethical norms, specifically the prohibition against falsifying evidence or coaching witnesses to testify falsely.[5] While doing so she must also protect at every turn the interests of her client. It is important that advocates embarking on this endeavor begin by determining their specific relationship with the witness being deposed. From that realtionship will flow rights and responsibilities that the advocate can rely upon when navigating these issues.

Witnesses usually fall into three categories, client, client's employee or associate, and neutral parties. While these are general categories it is useful to intially sort witnesses into one of these boxes. The reason is simple - the

---

[5] See Model Rule of Professional Responsibility 3.4 in Appendix II of this text.

advocate's responsibilities to the witness is signficantly different when the witness is the client. When it is an employee of the client or an associate a gray area exists that may create ethical issues for the attorney, while the "neutral" witness may have information that cannot be managed for maximum persuasiveness. Each creates different challenges for the attorney defending the deposition. The status of the witness is not, however, the only question that the advocate who is defending the deposition must answer. Once you understand your relationship with the witness you must review what you are and are not allowed to do.

> ### Acceptable Witness Preparation Includes:
>
> - Reminding the Witness to be Truthful
>
> - Allowing the Witness to Review Relevant Documents
>
> - Empowering the Witness to Give Complete, Truthful Answers in the Shortest Form Possible
>
> - Teaching the Witness to Only Answer the Question - No Volunteering
>
> - Allaying Witness Concerns

2. Witness preparation

You can prepare the witness for testifying at trial and in deposition, in fact failure to do this may indicate a lack of due dilligence on your part. You should always begin each session by reminding them that all you need them to do is to tell the truth. This is a true statement, and also provides them with the correct answer if opposing counsel asks them under oath what you told them to do. Advocates are well within their authority to explain the applicable law in any given situation with the caveat that you cannot mistate the law or provide such an explanation with the intent of empowering the witness to avoid the law. It is also proper to review not only your questions, but the questions that you expect the opposing side will ask. This review is allowed so that the witness will be ready for their testimony, not to coach answers. The acceptable goal is one of preparing the witness to present themselves and their testimony in the best possible light - without changing that testimony. In fact failure to prepare a witness for this experience is arguably an indication that the lawyer in question may be either incompetent or insufficiently dilligent in the performance of their duties. Your prefered end state in witness preparation is reached when both you and the witness are confident that the witness can and will testify truthfully and effectively in a poised, confident and persuasive manner - all while keeping firmly in mind the relevant

> *Do not fall into the trap of thinking that the witness has done this before simply because you have.*

facts. You acccomplish this by empowering the witness to provide opposing counsel with the shortest but most complete truthful answer during the deposition. Now that we have talked about what is and is not allowed let's shift focus to the first time the witness meets with the advocate.

When the witness first meets with you they are nervous. They have concerns that must be addressed before you can effectively prepare them to testify. You must take the time during this initial meeting to let the witness decompress and become comfortable with the situation. Small talk, exchanging pleasantries, offering refreshments and slowing down are an important part of the preparation process. You need to get your witness in a receptive frame of mind so that you can maximize your session. Time spent doing these things at the beginning, and during appropriate breaks, are often the most important moments in the preparation process, but they are also the easiest ones for busy attorneys to ignore. Advocates are constantly pressed for time, and after a while the entire witness preparation process becomes old hat. Do not fall into the trap of thinking that the witness has done this before simply because you have. Treat them with dignity, respect and understanding. There is no need to check your humanity at the door in these situations, and in fact you are well served by taking the time needed to set the witness truly at ease.

> ### During the Initial Meeting with the Witness Advocates Should:
>
> - Set the witness at ease
> - Explain your role
> - Give a case overview
> - Explain the purpose of the deposition
> - Explain what to expect
> - Review the do's and don'ts
> - Have relevant documents available

> ### Witness Do's:
>
> - Bring nothing
> - Listen to the question
> - State facts
> - Don't make conclusions
> - Avoid legal terms
> - "I don't recall" is OK
> - If I object stop talking
> - Handle documents

After you have set the witness at ease it is time to explain your role in the process. This explanation varies, depending upon your relationship with the witness. If the witness is not your client you should consider carefully how you advise them. You must at a minimum make certain that they understand that you do not represent them, even though you may represent their employer. This is an important conversation and handling it correctly so that you properly cover your ethical obligations is important. You want to acccomplish this goal without alienating the witness or making them feel that you are prepared to throw them under the bus to save your client - without creating a false impression in their mind about the purpose of your presence at the deposition. It is often useful when explaining your role to discuss it in terms of the case overview. The case overview normally contains the factual information that allows the witness to place their participation in the litigation in context. It also does a great job of further delineating your role in the process. Once you have clearly explained your role you can begin to review the accepted do's and don'ts of witness testimony during depositions. This is an important moment, because what you tell the witness is ultimately discoverable and a good opposing counsel will inquire about the extent of witness preparation. You need to make certain that the witness understands their role and yours. From that relationship and your explanation of the relevant law will you can produce a clear picture of what the witness can expect and what they are, and are not, allowed to do. Once you have accomplished this you can move into the substance of the witness's testimony.

> **Witness Don'ts:**
>
> - Get angry
> - Talk to fill the silence
> - Volunteer information
> - Guess
> - Answer compound questions
> - Answer wouldn't you agree questions

3. Practicing witness testimony

From an ethical perspective this is the most dangerous area of witness preparation. While you have a vested interest in knowing what the witness will say and how they will say it you cannot coach the witness into doing it the way you want. You can observe, practice and suggest, but you cannot force demeanor or substantively change substance. Doing so violates professional and ethical norms and does not serve your client's interests. The purpose of witness preparation is to prepare the witness to testify truthfully in the best light possible, not to modify the truth to fit your particular theory or theme. Advocates are often myopic at this point in the proceedings, and they have a great deal of impact with witnesses. You must be careful to not subliminally coach the witness into doing what you "perceive" is best. You may get away with it occasionally, but in the long run the cost far outweighs any benefits received.

Accepted methodologies for practicing witness testimony include bringing in someone to play the "interrogator" for the other side. While your witness is being questioned listen to both the substance of their answers and the nonverbal communication that occurs. It is helpful during this process to have more than one person available to observe and compare notes with. All of the body language cues that raise concerns at trial are also viable here. You should look for eye contact, blinking, talking to floor, excessive swallowing or any other physical cue

**Problematic Questions
from Opposing Counsel:**

• Is it fair to say..

• Can we agree..

• In other words..

• You wouldn't dispute..

• Would it surprise you…

• Compound questions

• Soooo

• Asking about earlier testimony

that your witness is in distress. You must also judge the ability of your witness to handle compound questions, suggestive questions and other verbal tricks that a sophisticated advocate may use during a deposition. You can discuss these with the witness, but do so through the lens of assuring them that if they are confident in what they remember and simply tell what they believe to be the truth they will be fine. You should then reiterate with them that it is difficult to tell the truth if you do not completely understand the question, and that there is absolutely nothing wrong with asking the attorney to phrase the question properly so that they can understand it. Get them to affirmatively promise you that they will do this, and then have your mock opponent ask questions that you would expect them to request clarification for. How they respond will assist you greatly in determining how much preparation is necessary before the actual deposition.

4. Dealing with objections

One issue that you must discuss with your witness is what happens when you object to the question posed by opposing cousel. Your witness needs to understand that from time to time you will object to the form or substance of the pending question. They should know that when that happens they should stop answering and look to you as to whether or not they should continue. If witnesses adopt this paradigm then you have acheived some important points. First of all you now have the ability to break the flow of the deposition when an advocate is using questioning techniques to place your witness in a unfair position. You can also break up the tenor and flow of the questioning with an objection when you get a sense that your witness needs a break. Finally you can ensure that in those extremely limited circumstances when the Federal Rules of Civil Procedure actually allow you to prevent your witness from testifying,[6] normally dealing with privilege, the witness will not inadvertently let the cat out of the bag. The simple device of asking them to look at you when you object and to wait for your nod to continue will help prevent unauthorized disclosure of privileged information. If you need to assert privilege during a deposition make sure that you take the time to do so properly. Opposing counsel should also make the record clear on this point. They should ask if (1) the witness understands the question, (2) is

---

[6]See FRCP 30(d)(1) in Appendix I of this text.

opposing counsel instructing them not to answer, (3) request the basis for that instruction with supporting documents, (4) ask the witness if they are following opposing counsel's instruction not to answer, and (5) verify that but for that instruction the witness knows the answer and would provide it. After they have asked these questions they should then affirmatively request that the court reporter mark the record at this point for easy retrieval.

5. *Conclusion*

A review of the topics we have discussed in this section should lead you to conclude that witness preparation is a difficult but necessary part of defending a deposition. The greatest danger that you must concern yourself with is placing your knowledge into the witness's head so that they parrot what you want them to say instead of what they actually remember. A good way to avoid this when practicing with the witness is to ask the witness to mentally place themselves back at the scene of what you are discussing. Sometimes it will help if you have the witness close their eyes while doing this. Once they are in that moment begin by asking open ended questions. This will allow them to exhaust their memory, recounting what they know to you without your providing clues as to what you expect they know. As you go through this process watch your witness to see if they modify their story based upon their interactions with you. When memory problems arise, and they always do, fall back on those tested techniques for

---

SEVEN PRINCIPLES OF PAST RECOLLECTIONS:

Witnesses will forget essential facts.

Memorize the foundational elements for refreshing memory and past recollection recorded or know where to find those foundations when your memory fails.

Memory can be refreshed by any document.

Past recollection recorded must be a document made or adopted by the witness when the matter is fresh in the witness's memory.

Documents used merely to refresh memory are not admitted into evidence.

Documents qualifying as past recollection recorded may be admitted but are only read to the fact-finder unless offered by the adverse party.

---

refreshing memory and past recollection recorded that you know the court would accept at trial. When doing so be cautious with your word choice and demeanor so that you do not inadvertently change the witness's recollection. The beauty of

---

Foundation for Past Recollection Recorded:

Witness cannot remember a fact or event on the stand;

Witness had firsthand knowledge at one time;

That knowledge is reflected in a memorandum or record made at or near the time the fact or event occurred, made or adopted by the witness;

Record was accurate and complete when made;

Record is in same condition now as when made; and

Witness still cannot completely and accurately recall the fact or event even after reviewing the record.

---

using these techniques is that it allows you to fairly and honestly address memory issues in a way that cannot be considered unfairly coaching the witness. It also

---

Foundation for Refreshing Recollection:

Witness states she cannot recall a fact or event;

Witness states that a particular writing or other aid could help jog her memory;

Witness is given the writing to read silently to herself;

Witness returns the writing to counsel;

Witness states that the writing has refreshed her memory; and

Witness testifies to the fact or event, without further aid of the writing.

---

allows you to practice a set of skills that you must have available if the case goes to trial. The following page contains the foundational questions that you would be required to use to lay the foundation for either refreshing memory or past recollection recorded. Use them now when your witness has memory problems during witness preparation and then they will be comfortable with the process and understand what you are doing and why you are doing it when you begin to lay the foundation using documents with which they are familiar. Often such familiarity is sufficient in and of itself to spark their memory and they will not need to actually review the document. Let us move on now to the next chapter where we discuss the motion for summary judgment that you can expect after completing depositions.

D.   *RULES MATRIX*

This table serves as a starting point for additional inquiry into the potential professional responsibility and civil procedure issues that are implicated during depositions.

Issue Arising During Depositions	Applicable Rule of Professional Responsibility or FRCP
(a)(1)–(3): A lawyer must not offer false evidence.	**RULE 3.3: Candor Toward the Tribunal**
(e): A lawyer must not "allude to any matter that [she] does not reasonably believe is relevant or that will not be supported by admissible evidence . . ." She must not "assert personal knowledge of facts in issue . . . or "state a personal opinion as to the justness of a cause, the credibility of a witness, the culpability of a civil litigant or the guilt or innocence of an accused."	**RULE 3.4: Fairness to Opposing Party & Counsel**
(a): A lawyer must not illegally "seek to influence a judge, juror, prospective juror or other official." (d): A lawyer must not intentionally disrupt the court and must conduct herself with respect for the court.	**RULE 3.5: Impartiality & Decorum of the Tribunal**
Required conferences	**Rule 26(f)**
Deposing a corporation, designating a corporate witness that binds the corporation	**Rule 30(b)(6)**
Objections should be made in a timely and concise manner	**Rule 30(d)(1)**
Objections as to relevance, hearsay, confusion and competency are never waived	**Rule 32(d)(3)A**

Table 1:The Most Prevalent Rules Concerning Depositions

Points To Ponder . . .

---

1. Can depositions be fairly said to more accurately follow the tenets of the civil law system as opposed to the common law system?

2. Should we allow the same degree of freedom during questioning at trial that we allow during depositions? Why not?

3. Why should the jury receive information that has been strained more than once through lawyers? Would it make sense to do away with depositions completely? What arguments favor this position and which do not? Which one do you find most persuasive? Why

CHAPTER NINE
MOTIONS

"Oft expectation fails, and most oft there
Where most it promises; and oft it hits
Where hope is coldest, and despair most fits"[1]

A. *MOTION PRACTICE*

1. Overview

When an advocate needs to ask the court to do something they usually file a motion. A motion is a request by a litigant to the court, asking them to take some action in a case. As you might guess, some requested actions are more important than others–a motion for a one week extension of time to designate expert witnesses is usually not outcome determinative while a motion for summary judgment often is. Because of the different impact that motions may have on the case some are not opposed while many others are viciously opposed; it is quite frankly impossible to predict in general terms which motions are going to be contested. Just because your adversary wants to the court to do something does not necessarily mean it is a bad thing for your case. Even

> Motions are either oral or written requests to the court to take some action in a case and run the gamut from the benignly mundane administrative request to the Rambo-like "death penalty" motion seeking to strike a litigant's pleadings.

a partially dispositive motion seeking summary judgment against one of your causes of action may be good for you by removing a weak claim so that you can focus your efforts on your better ones. If your on-going case analysis reveals that a claim should be dropped you may not care to invest time resisting a requested partial summary judgment. On the other hand, that additional week extension being sought by your opponent may be critical if it gives them the ability to

---

[1] WILLIAM SHAKESPEARE, All's Well That End's Well, act 2 sc. 1.

designate a new expert witness for trial who otherwise might play no role in the case outcome. The ability to accurately determine the degree to which you should fight opposing motions is grounded in a thorough and ongoing case analysis.

Motions may be either oral or written. During trial and some evidentiary hearings, a good many motions (e.g., to exclude evidence, for directed verdict, for a recess) are made by one advocate standing and making a request to the court. During pretrial, motions take written form and there are some rules in both the civil procedure rules and in most courts' local rules that govern when motions may

---

Seven Fundamental Tasks of Successful Motions Practice:

1. Know the local rules for filing deadlines, both according to the legal issue when appropriate and according to time.

2. Draft sound legal motions in writing when required. Use law, facts and inference to your advantage.

3. Identify the source of your evidence for the motions hearing and have it available in an appropriate form to admit before the judge. Do not forget the effect of Federal Rule of Evidence 104, or its state equivalent.

4. Do not forget to balance your law, facts and moral theme, even when dealing with motions. There is always a reason for the legal protection. Remind the judge of that necessity when necessary.

5. Know whom you are trying to persuade - the judge.

6. Do not argue with opposing counsel, argue to the judge.

7. Know when a ruling is preserved on appeal and when you must raise it again during the case in chief. Understand the tactical and strategic reasons behind any decision to raise such issues at trial.

---

be filed, their form, contents, responses to motions and obtaining a hearing or ruling on the motion. We have previously discussed the law governing certain motions in specific contexts, such as the various rule 12 motions lodged against a pleading as well as motions for leave to file an amended pleading under rule 15.

In this chapter we will begin with an initial focus upon motion practice itself. This discussion will be generally applicable to most pretrial motions, including an examination into the components of a motion, drafting strategies, evidentiary support, the preparation of a response to a motion, and effective advocacy at a hearing on a pretrial motion. Following these topics, we will explore some specific nuances and application of these general principle in the context of perhaps the two most often filed motions–motions for summary judgment and discovery motions.

2. *Strategic Use of Motions*

When should you file a motion? There are a number of different reasons that may inspire an advocate to seek a court order and the particular circumstances of your case will dictate the reasons for seeking pretrial relief. Pretrial motions can be grouped into one of two major categories: (a) case administration; and (b) claim resolution. With respect to the former, sometimes litigants simply need judicial intervention because counsel cannot reach agreement regarding the procedures that govern the case–either

> **Seven Steps of Motions Argument:**
>
> * State your position
> * Present your facts persuasively
> * Present case law consistent with your theory
> * Distinguish adverse case law
> * Apply the law to the facts
> * Restate your position
> * Request relief

because the rules are unclear, the rules invite examination into whether a certain prerequisite for action has been fulfilled or because one party is in need of some modification to the rules' application. Examples of these type of motions might include: a motion for leave to amend a pleading under rule 15; a motion to require the joinder of a necessary party under rule 19; a motion for leave to take more than 10 depositions in a case under rule 30; a motion for protective order to stop burdensome discovery under rule 26; a motion to consolidate two cases for trial under rule 42; any motion for extension of time under rule 6; or a motion for a more definite statement under rule 12. In these situations, one litigant has made the strategic decision that they wish to pursue some course of action (e.g., taking some discovery, adding another party, changing their pled affirmative defenses) but need either the opposing counsel's consent and stipulation or a court order to gain permission for the contemplated litigation step. These are all examples of motions that are expressly provided for in the text of the rules of civil procedure.

Advocates must be careful not to presume that every motion needs to be expressly invited by some civil procedure rule. The rules do not discuss every situation that might requeire a court order; in fact, any time an advocate's conduct is nt clearly permitted by the express dictate of the rules, a motion may be needed

to gain permission to act. Perhaps
you want to ask the court to appoint
a mediator to guide the parties'
settlement discussions. Maybe you
would like an order permitting you to
use a conference room at the
courthouse for a deposition. Perhaps
you have grown weary of your

> *"Common sense is genius dressed in working clothes."*
>
> *Ralph Waldo Emerson*

opponent filing too many motions for summary judgment and you would like to
obtain an order forbidding them from filing any additional motions. Maybe you
believe opposing counsel has an irreconcilable conflict of interest and needs to be
disqualified. There are no specific rules of civil procedure dictating all of the
possible motions counsel might craft, much less providing a certain standard
governing their consideration. These issues may either be left solely to the
discretion of the trial judge exercising some combination of common sense and
individual preferences for how a case should proceed on the docket or perhaps
some other body of law outside the rules of civil procedure–such as the governing
ethics rules an advocate, therefore, do not be put-off from filing a motion just
because there does not appear to be a specific rule that discusses it. So long as
there is a good faith basis for you to ask for the court's time and attention to the
matter, you should feel free to file a motion on any of these administrative matters.

In terms of claim resolution, the other major category of motion, there are
particular rules of civil procedure governing how and when a court may dispose
of a party's pled claim or defense. In many instances, the action of the court
sought consists of the court *rejecting* a claim or defense because either the law or
the facts (or sometimes a combination of the two) demonstrates an unquestionable
lack of merit or due to some other fatal defect in the case (e.g., lack of
jurisdiction). Such actions at the pretrial stage would include any of the rule 12
motions to dismiss we discussed earlier or the granting of a rule 56 motion for
summary judgment. In other scenarios, the motion may be asking the court to rule
as a matter of law in *favor* of establishing the claim or defense. This happens in
the summary judgment context when there is a showing that the facts and law
establish the matter pled with relative certainty or, in the default judgment context
(rule 55) when a party fails to plead timely in response to a claim and the rules
essentially presumes the party to have conceded the truth of the claim pled .

In the default scenario there is not much strategy involved in deciding to
file the motion. Your adversary, properly served with the pleading setting forth
the claim, has simply failed to file a written response (pleading or rule 12 motion)
on time and the rules give you the right to have judgement entered immediately on
the matter. With respect to rule 12 motions to dismiss, as we learned earlier,
many of these are effectively lost or waived if not asserted prior to or with the
defendant's answer. You do not have the luxury of time to defer making the

strategic decision on whether to pursue such a motion. Many counsel believe that, so long as they are not frivolous, filing any possible rule 12 motion is a wise move because it sends a signal to your opponent that you will make their litigation path thorny. Further, even if the motion is not granted counsel often feel as though the motion begin the process of educating the trial judge to possible fatal weaknesses in the plaintiff's claims and, thus, may be the first step toward a possible summary judgment later in the case. Other counsel believe that filing a rule 12 motion that has little chance of being granted sends exactly the opposite signal that an advocate should desire–that filing a weak motion only shows weakness. These are issues you need to consider. With respect to summary judgment motions, there is much more thought required of the advocate to consider before preparing a filing such a motion. Not only does the advocate need to consider whether the motion has enough merit to warrant filing but issues of timing are uniquely embedded in the summary judgment process. These timing issues exist because summary judgment motions may be filed throughout much of the pretrial process and because summary judgment motions can be denied solely because the court believes that additional discovery is needed by your opponent. Summary judgment motions have become one of the most important motions for claim adjudication and will be covered separately later in this chapter.

Dispositive motions also exist that are unrelated to the merits of a claim or defense but can still be employed to resolve a case. Examples of these would be a rule 41 motion to involuntarily dismiss a claim for failure of the plaintiff to prosecute the action (e.g, when the plaintiff fails to appear for a hearing or other conference), or a motion for the severe sanction of striking a party's pleading due to certain significant violations of rule 11 or disregard of another court order (e.g., disregarding an order compelling discovery under rule 37(b)). In these two situations the court has to be sufficiently frustrated with the actions of a litigant or counsel that the court determines that it is only fair to impose such a stiff penalty. Unless an advocate believes that the court has reached this level of frustration, caution should be heeded in bothering to make such an extraordinary request for relief because courts grow weary of advocates asking for sanctions too often and without sufficient grounds. Failure to appreciate the proper time and place for making such a non-merits based dispositive motion can be fatal to the motion and leave you in the court's disfavor. If you interpret this message to suggest that an advocate should hesitate before seeking sanctions against a litigation opponent, you are reading well.

3. Drafting of a Complete Motion

Though the rules of procedure generally governing motion practice are scant, there is some guidance for advocates contemplating the preparation and filing of a motion. Rule 7(b) provides the following mandates:

(1)   *In General.* A request for a court order must be made by motion. The motion must:

        (A)   be in writing unless made during a hearing or trial;

        (B)   state with particularity the grounds for seeking the order; and

        (C)   state the relief sought.

(2)   *Form.* The rules governing captions and other matters of form in pleadings apply to motions and other papers.

These minimum components of a motion are reminiscent of rule 8(a)'s requirements for the pleading of a claim–they each require (i) a statement of the ground for either the "order" sought or of the basis for the "claim" and (ii) a statement of the "relief sought." The major differences are that only complaints and not motions require the statement of jurisdiction and motions are directed at the grounds for the requested court action while pleadings offer the grounds supporting a cause of action. The similarity does not end with rule 8. In addition, rule 7(b)(2) states that other rules regarding "captions and other matters of form in pleadings" also apply to motions. This certainly means that rule 10 "Form of Pleadings" applies equally to any written motion. Further, one must also look to your applicable local rules which typically have specific provisions that govern all written pleadings and motions (e.g., dictating size of paper, line spacing and font size) and often have specific rules for filing and responding to motions. For example, our Local Rules have the following provisions that apply generally to the preparation and filing of motions:

- Motions must be typewritten, double-spaced (except quotations), in at least 12-point font using 8 ½ x 11 "opaque, unglazed, white paper" with certain minimum margins (L.R. 1.05(a));

- Motions must contain a caption that conforms to rule 10(a) and shall state in the title the name and designation of the filing party (L.R. 1.05(b));

- Motions must be "personally" signed by counsel as required by rule 11 and below the signature line counsel must provide their typed name, state bar ID number, firm name, mailing address, phone and fax numbers and e-mail address (L.R. 1.05(d));

- In any motion the moving party must include a "concise statement of the precise relief requested, a statement of the basis for the request, and a memorandum of legal authority in support of the request, all of which the movant shall include in a single document not more than twenty-five (25) pages" (L.R. 3.01(a)).

- Except for a few designated categories of exempt motions (e.g., motions for injunctive relief, for judgment on the pleadings, summary judgment, certification of a class action, to dismiss under rule 12, or to involuntarily dismiss under rule 41), the moving party "shall confer" with opposing counsel in a "good faith effort to resolve the issues raised by the motion" and must certify this conference in writing. If agreement has been reached, the motion's caption must include the designation of "unopposed" or "agreed" (L.R. 3.01(g));

- All dispositive motions must be designated as such in the caption of the motion (L.R. 3.01(h)); and

- Hearings are not ordinarily available for motions. Counsel desiring an oral hearing can make a request for oral argument which shall accompany the motion and estimate the time required for the argument (L.R. 3.01(j)).

Using this combination of rules, let's consider the preparation of a simple motion for leave to amend a plaintiff's complaint.

a. case caption

IN THE UNITED STATES DISTRICT COURT
FOR THE MIDDLE DISTRICT OF FLORIDA
TAMPA DIVISION

Susan Robinson, et al.	§
	§
vs.	§ Case No. A-07-CA-855-JMU
	§
Paulson Breweries, et al.	§

Plaintiffs' Motion for Leave to Amend Complaint
And Memorandum of Law In Support

The case caption in this motion looks similar to the original complaint we drafted in the earlier chapter on pleadings with a few differences. The complaint required that all of the parties' names be set forth but the motion only needs to state the first party designated as plaintiff and defendant with the designation "et al" to signify that other parties have also been named. In addition, with the original complaint there was only a blank left for the case number so that the court clerk could stamp that information not yet available to counsel at the time of drafting. Further, the title for the motion must be contained on this document and, in accordance with our Local Rules, must indicate the name of the party asserting the motion and also must reflect that the brief or "Memorandum of Law" is included within this document. In many federal districts, briefs may be filed as separate documents and may or may not be required to be filed at all depending upon the type of motion asserted.

b. body of motion/brief

The body of this motion complies with both rule 7(b) and the local rules[2] because it states specifically the basis for the motion–the recent discovery of new facts giving rise to a new cause of action–and incorporates a legal memorandum

---

Plaintiffs move this Court for an order granting leave for Plaintiff to file an amended complaint, for the following reasons:

Plaintiffs Susan and John Robinson filed their original complaint in this matter on August 15, 2007 asserting a claim for negligence. Defendants are David Berning–the driver of the 18-wheel truck that rear-ended Susan Robinson's vehicle and his employer–Paulson Breweries, Inc. The accident caused serious disabling injuries against Plaintiff Susan Robinson. As a result of discovery conducted against Defendants, Plaintiffs have recently become aware of additional facts demonstrating that Defendant Paul Breweries was aware that its driver had no valid commercial driver's license at the time of the accident. Such facts give rise to a claim for gross negligence. Accompanying this motion as Exhibit "A" is a copy of the proposed Plaintiffs' First Amended Complaint setting forth the new claim which seeks an award of exemplary damages.

Rule 15(a) provides that leave "should be freely given when justice so requires." Plaintiffs did not allege a claim for gross negligence in their Original Complaint because they were not yet aware of the facts supporting this cause of action. Because recent discovery has just revealed these new facts (*see* attached excerpts from deposition of Defendant Berning as Exhibit "B"), and because this case is still in its infancy with trial not scheduled for an additional year, justice requires that Plaintiffs be permitted to assert this new claim by way of amendment. *See Foman v. Davis*, 371 U.S. 178 (1962), *on remand* 316 F.2d 254 (1st Cir. 1963) (rule 15(a) should be liberally construed and motions for leave to amend should normally be granted absent a showing of prejudice to the opposing party). Defendants can demonstrate no prejudice from the granting of this motion as discovery is still on-going in this matter.

Plaintiffs request an oral hearing on this motion. The hearing should take approximately fifteen (15) minutes.

---

[2]The only exception is that the above example uses single-spacing rather than the double-spacing required by our Local Rules, for the sake of brevity.

supporting the motion. In many instances, particularly for motions of administrative nature like the above example, no greater recitation of facts or law is needed. In this example, the legal memorandum consists solely of citation to the governing rule of civil procedure and one illustrative case interpreting that provision. This motion also offers two attached and marked exhibits, the proposed amended pleading (which many courts expect in this circumstance) and the deposition showing how and when the moving parties obtained the discovery that underlies the proposed amendment. In this way, the moving party has offered evidentiary support for each significant factual assertion contained within the motion and offered legal support for each statement of the law within the motion. Must each factual assertion be proven in a motion? The truth is that it depends on the motion and the circumstances of the case. For an administrative motion such as for leave to amend it might be sufficient to simply recite without proof when and how the plaintiff acquired the new evidence. Yet by offering as an exhibit some factual support for this assertion, the moving party decreases the likelihood of the opposing party taking issue with the assertion and makes the court more likely to be inclined to grant the motion, perhaps without need of oral argument on the matter. For any opposed motion, the moving party may also know the basis for the opposition in advance particularly if the local rules require a conference with opposing counsel prior to filing. Thus, the moving party is often in a position to anticipate and refute the opposing party's arguments. This can obviate the necessity for filing a reply to the response. In many districts, reply briefs are not only discouraged but may be prohibited absent court approval.[3]

Dispositive motions, like motions for summary judgment, would normally be expected to contain a much more detailed recitation of the undisputed facts as well as greater description of the applicable law demonstrating the movant's entitlement to judgment as a matter of law. We will discuss this further in our separate discussion of summary judgments below.

We could discuss at great length generally how to draft briefs but this is better left to your legal research and writing courses. But we should at least remind you that many courts, particularly federal courts, rule on motions based solely on the written submissions. Thus, your brief is your only chance to argue the merits of your motion or opposition. Obviously, it should be organized and persuasive while remaining succinct. Most local rules have some page limit for briefs and rarely is there truly good cause for seeking permission to go beyond the typical page limits. It should also be polished, thoroughly proof-read, and directed to the precise legal issue before the court. Briefs are not an opportunity to engage in hyperbole or personal attacks on the adverse party or counsel. They should not only demonstrate why the court should want to rule in your client's favor but offer

---

[3]Our Local Rules state that "[n]o party shall file any reply or further memorandum" unless leave of court is obtained. (Local Rule 3.01(c).)

sufficient factual and legal support so that the court is confident that the ruling you request will be well grounded and not likely to lead to a reversal on appeal. In this regard, assuming there is no U.S. Supreme Court authority right on point, most advocates desire to rely upon cases from the same circuit, district or local jurisdiction in their brief. A detailed discussion of this case law is only called for if there is a particular case that is on point. You should not require such detailed discussion of multiple cases on each issue raised by the motion except in unique situations. Briefs should also consider addressing how the requested ruling will impact the remainder of the case assuming that the requested order does not result in final judgment. For example, is the requested relief likely to lead to greater delay or expedition in the case resolution? Will it make the trial more or less complicated? Will it result in a need for the inclusion of additional litigants or the expansion of discovery and associated expenses? Depending upon the specific motion under consideration, such matters may go a long way in providing appropriate incentive for the court to rule in a certain way. Above all, do not include any matter in a motion or supporting brief that will undermine the court's confidence that what you see is accurate. Do not overstate the factual or legal support for your position. A candid admission of a gray area can buy an advocate much credibility. Taking liberties with either the facts or law normally results in the court's summary denial of your position and you should assume that your opposing advocate will be motivated to double-check your cited sources.

> *"A lawyer is a person who writes a 10,000-word document and calls it a 'brief.'"*
>
> *Franz Kafka*

A good rule of thumb for the possible organization of a motion with an incorporated memorandum of law might be as follows:

1. **Introduction** It is helpful to tell the court at the very beginning what is the specific nature of the motion and the relief you are requesting. For many motions, some factual and/or procedural context would also be invaluable to the court in understanding your case better. This may be the most important case to you or your client, but undoubtedly it is one of many hundreds if not thousands resting in your presiding judge's docket. Is this a personal injury claim or a contract dispute? Does it arise out of a particular event–if so mention that event briefly. Not only does it make the motion arguably more interesting (again, this is one of hundreds or thousands of cases before your judge)[4] but you can use this short introduction to subtly suggest an emotional basis for why the court

---

[4]One judge remarked at a hearing attended by Underwood, "Oh, how interesting–another breach of contract case."

should want to grant your client the relief requested. In our example, we have referenced a tragic accident caused by a large truck hitting the plaintiff from behind and cause serious personal injuries. A judge reading this introduction might be motivated to grant relief that helps that injured party get all of their claims before the factfinder.

2. **Governing Law or Standard** Is there a specific rule of civil procedure governing this type of motion? If so, reference it and consider quoting it in the text of your motion. If there is a statutory basis for the motion, do likewise. Is there relevant case law where other courts have granted similar motions in similar circumstances? Cite those case and consider discussing briefly one or a handful of appropriate case examples. For example, consider discussing (and quoting) a case that seems to be right on point. Or consider discussing (and quoting) even a case from your jurisdiction even if it is only generally applicable. For many motions there may also be a specific burden of proof or persuasion–"good cause" for example–and you might as well acknowledge what your burden is and then demonstrate how your motion satisfies this burden. The judge deciding your motion needs to understand the legal landscape for the request you are making in order to feel comfortable that she has the power to grant your request. In our example, we have referenced and quoted briefly from the applicable rule–rule 15(a)–and briefly cited to one controlling precedent offering the applicable holding or principle from that decision. No elaboration was offered because motions to amend are fairly common (the judge only needs reminding of the standard and not an education on it) and this motion seems straightforward.

3. **Factual Application** No matter how clear the legal standard governing the motion, there must be some factual discussion demonstrating how the standard applies to the case pending before the court. Where any of the significant facts you rely upon has not been admitted by your opponent (in a pleading) you should consider–and the governing law may require this–attaching as exhibits the evidentiary support for your factual assertions. Rule 43 permits the court to hear evidence in support of a motion through written submission or live testimony, at the general discretion of the trial judge.[5] Remember to stay focused–other than brief background facts, you should emphasize those facts that you can

---

[5]Rule 43 states that "[w]hen a motion is based on facts not appearing of record the court may hear the matter on affidavits presented by the respective parties, but the court may direct that the matter be heard wholly or partly on oral testimony or depositions. In practice, courts routinely consider evidence in many forms when ruling on pretrial motions, including interrogatory answers, authenticated documents, deposition excerpts, and responses to requests for admission.

demonstrate are true and which combine with the governing legal standard to entitle you to the relief you request in your motion. If facts you offer are disputed by your opponent, you gain credibility points by acknowledging this dispute but demonstrating why you are still entitled to relief in the face of that dispute (if this is true).

4. **Anticipating and Gutting the Opposition** Where you know or feel sure you can predict the likely basis for your opponent's opposition of the motion, you should raise these matters and refute them in the body of your motion or brief. This will help to de-fang your adversary's response when it is filed with the court. Be careful, however, not to raise any objections that the other side might otherwise have missed. You do not want to be your own worst enemy. In our example, the only likely ground for opposition to a motion for leave to amend would be some showing of prejudice or delay. Our motion raises and quickly refutes both possible bases for denying the motion.

5. **Wrap-up** After discussing the law and the facts, you should be prepared to summarize again why you are entitled to the relief your motion requests and, perhaps subtly, offer the court encouragement for why this is the best and fairest resolution of the issue either for the parties or the procedural posture of the case. If the grant of your motion somehow eases any burden on the court, this is obviously an observation worth making–but don't suggest the judge is lazy just that, for example, granting of the motion will render moot certain other aspects of the case and ease the court's docket or might promote settlement.

You do not necessarily need to organize your motion using these topic headings although courts do often appreciate some guideposts in a motion, particularly in submissions of any significant length. But the real point here is that you incorporate each of these components into your written submission to make it as complete and compelling as possible.

Finally, you should note that the above example includes a specific request for an oral hearing. Federal courts are increasingly ruling on most motions based upon the written submissions but may still permit a litigant to request an oral hearing on a particular matter. Check your local rules to determine if hearings are normally given as a matter of course and, if not, how to go about requesting such a hearing. Our Local Rules require the written request for a hearing to accompany the motion including a specific statement of the length of time requested for the hearing. When you are asked by a court for such an estimate, you need to take into account both your argument and the anticipated arguments of your opposing counsel. Courts do not like to show up for a ten minute hearing, as requested by counsel, and be confronted by multiple lawyers with many exhibits and perhaps witnesses prepared to testify. Even if the court permits such extensive presentation, it will throw off the remainder of the court's schedule for the day.

In many state courts, the attorneys can expect a hearing on virtually any opposed motion and even on some agreed matters that impact the court's docket (i.e., a motion for continuance of the trial date). In fact, the court may allow you to arrange the hearing date and time over the phone prior to your filing of the motion. In these instances, you may (by local rule or custom) need to reference the hearing that has been set in the body of the motion itself. Even if you are in state court and expecting a hearing on your motion, the written submissions are still important in two respects. First, the submission must include the legal grounds supporting the request for relief and, often, the only evidence that might be considered by the trial or appellate court is that which is included with the submission. Second, if the judge has had the opportunity to review the written submissions prior to the hearing, the judge often walks into the courtroom predisposed to grant or deny the motion before hearing arguments of counsel. A good submission on your part can, therefore, greatly increase your chances of finding a warm reception for your client in the courtroom. We will discuss advice on how to conduct the hearing itself in the next section.

c. request for relief

The rules require that a motion include a statement of the relief requested–this is a benefit for both the court (which needs to know what action you want from the court) and for opposing counsel (to determine whether they wish to oppose the motion or, perhaps, offer some alternative relief to the court as a compromise). If you are uncertain what relief is appropriate, you should still make a specific request but you might consider offering some alternative forms of relief. For example, if you are filing a motion to compel you may consider relief (a) compelling the opponent to answer your interrogatories, (b) awarding you reasonable attorney's fees for preparing and arguing the motion, and/or (c) some other appropriate sanction warranted under rule 37. Just be sure that you have legal support for the relief you are requesting or at least a good faith argument for the, perhaps, unique remedy you are proposing.

For these reasons, Plaintiffs request the following relief:

- That this motion be granted; and
- That Plaintiff be permitted to file the proposed First Amended Complaint within ten (10) days from the grant of this motion.

Respectfully submitted,

_____

Jane Aikman, Esq.
State Bar No. 123456789
Trial Counsel

Aikman & Associates
315 Central Avenue
St. Petersburg, FL 33602
Telephone (727) 710-4396
Facsimile (727) 710-9944
Jaikman33602@yahoo.com

You will also observe the filing counsel's signature which is provided in accordance with rules 7(b), 11 and our Local Rule 1.05(d). You are representing that the motion is not filed for any improper purpose and that the factual and legal assertions are well grounded. If you have doubts about any of these implicit representations, you need to pause and reconsider how important your reputation (and law license) may be. This is only the first of three likely signatures you will place on your motion.

certificate of conference

Certificate of Conference

The undersigned counsel contacted Mr. Randy Smith, counsel for the Defendants, on November 30, 2007 concerning the issues raised by this motion. Counsel were unable to reach any agreement on these issues and, therefore, the matter is being submitted to this Court for resolution.

_____

Jane Aikman, Esq.

As mentioned previously, most non-dispositive motions filed in federal court are required by local rules to contain a certification that counsel have discussed the issues and been unable in good faith to resolve them on their own. In fact, for motions to quash discovery or to compel discovery, and requests for sanctions under rule 37, the federal rules of civil procedure require this conference regardless of any local rules. Some states courts also expect counsel to confer before filing certain motions. The idea behind such expectations or requirements is that, at least on non-dispositive motions, there should be room for good advocates to reach a compromise that accommodates the legitimate concerns of all parties. For example, most reasonable and initial requests for extensions of time should be agreed to by counsel. This is true because courts will typically provide such relief, when forced to rule on the matter, and because you are likely to be in need of a good many extensions yourself–you may as well start operating under the dictates of the Golden Rule. On the other hand, the courts have no expectation that your opposing party will agree to a dispositive motion on the parties' claims or defenses. On these subjects, professionalism does not dictate that a compromise be reached. Compromise on these matters is reserved for mediations and settlement conferences and not in motion practice.

What does an advocate do when your opposing counsel has not returned your phone call? Many courts hold to the view that more than one last-minute superficial attempt at a conference is contemplated. In other words, many judges are not impressed by an advocate calling their adversary to confer on a motion during the lunch hour on the same day the motion is being filed. If you opponent has not returned your call, you should at least make a second attempt and give your adversary reasonable time to respond. If the exigencies of your case truly demand an earlier filing of your motion, you should indicate your efforts to confer with counsel and why you could not wait further before submitting the matter to the court. Also, some judges do not believe that sending a snippy letter to opposing counsel is a sufficient good faith attempt to confer ("Dear counsel: Unless I hear from you by 5:00 tomorrow, I will presume you oppose the attached motion."). Your careful reading of your jurisdiction's local rules and some research into your presiding judge's views on these matters are well worth the investment of time because judges tend to take mandatory conferences seriously as it directly impacts the number of disputes they are require to referee.

1. Certificate of service

Certificate of Service

In accordance with Fed. R. Civ. P. 5, the undersigned served the foregoing motion on Mr. Randy Smith, lead counsel for Defendants, by courier on this 30th day of November, 2007.

_____
Jane Aikman, Esq.

Rule 5(a) requires that "every written motion other than one which may be required to be heard *ex parte* . . . shall be served upon each of the parties." Except in cases where a party is proceeding *pro se*, service under this provision is to be accomplished by making service upon each party's attorney of record.[6] Rule 5(b)(2) offers the methods available for serving each party's counsel, and these methods include handing it to the person, leaving it at the person's office, mailing it to the person, or utilizing other electronic means (fax and e-mail) if that person has consented in writing to receiving service in such manner for that case. These provisions are designed to ensure due process for each litigant and to avoid the ethical quandaries created by counsel, in effect, communicating with the presiding judge without all counsel or parties being privy to the communication.[7] This certification constitutes your third and final signature on the motion.

To help you visualize the entire finished product, consider the full text of our motion for leave to amend on the following two pages:

IN THE UNITED STATES DISTRICT COURT
FOR THE MIDDLE DISTRICT OF FLORIDA
TAMPA DIVISION

Susan Robinson, et al.	§	
	§	
vs.	§	Case No. A-07-CA-855-JMU
	§	
Paulson Breweries, et al.	§	

Plaintiffs' Motion for Leave to Amend Complaint
And Memorandum of Law In Support

Plaintiffs move this Court for an order granting leave for Plaintiff to file an amended complaint, for the following reasons:

Plaintiffs Susan and John Robinson filed their original complaint in this matter on August 15, 2007 asserting a claim for negligence. Defendants are David Berning–the driver of the 18-wheel truck that rear-ended Susan Robinson's vehicle and his employer–Paulson Breweries, Inc. The accident caused serious disabling injuries against Plaintiff Susan Robinson. As a result of discovery conducted against Defendants, Plaintiffs have recently become aware of additional facts demonstrating that Defendant Paul Breweries was aware that its driver had no valid commercial driver's license at the time of the accident. Such facts give rise to a claim for gross negligence. Accompanying this motion as Exhibit "A" is a copy of the proposed Plaintiffs' First Amended Complaint setting forth the new claim which seeks an award of exemplary damages.

---

[6]Rule 5(b).

[7][Add cite to appropriate ethical rule.]

Rule 15(a) provides that leave "should be freely given when justice so requires." Plaintiffs did not allege a claim for gross negligence in their Original Complaint because they were not yet aware of the facts supporting this cause of action. Because recent discovery has just revealed these new facts (*see* attached excerpts from deposition of Defendant Berning as Exhibit "B"), and because this case is still in its infancy with trial not scheduled for an additional year, justice requires that Plaintiffs be permitted to assert this new claim by way of amendment. *See Foman v.Davis*, 371 U.S. 178 (1962), *on remand* 316 F.2d 254 (1ˢᵗ Cir. 1963) (rule 15(a) should be liberally construed and motions for leave to amend should normally be granted absent a showing of prejudice to the opposing party). Defendants can demonstrate no prejudice from the granting of this motion as discovery is still on-going in this matter and this amendment should cause no delays.

Plaintiffs request an oral hearing on this motion. The hearing should take approximately fifteen (15) minutes.

For these reasons, Plaintiffs request the following relief:

- That this motion be granted; and
- That Plaintiff be permitted to file the proposed First Amended Complaint within ten (10) days from the grant of this motion.

Respectfully submitted,

_____

Jane Aikman, Esq.
State Bar No. 123456789
Trial Counsel

Aikman & Associates
315 Central Avenue
St. Petersburg, FL 33602
Telephone (727) 710-4396
Facsimile (727) 710-9944
Jaikman33602@yahoo.com

Certificate of Conference

The undersigned counsel contacted Mr. Randy Smith, counsel for the Defendants, on November 30, 2007 concerning the issues raised by this motion. Counsel were unable to reach any agreement on these issues and, therefore, the matter is being submitted to this Court for resolution.

_____

Jane Aikman, Esq.

Certificate of Service

In accordance with Fed. R. Civ. P. 5, the undersigned served the foregoing motion

d. Responding to a Motion

An advocate faced with a motion filed by an adversary can respond appropriately and effectively by answering the following questions about the motion:

1. Should you really oppose this motion?

As referenced earlier, just because your opponent has requested some action from the court does not necessarily cut against your client's own best interests. Perhaps your opposing counsel conferred with you prior to filing the motion and you would not agree at the time. It is still not too late to reconsider–no judge was ever heard to complain about the need to cancel a hearing–so long as your communicate your agreement with the motion prior to showing up for the hearing. Possible reasons to withdraw your opposition are:

- You anticipate the court granting the motion anyway–unless you need to preserve some error for possible appellate purposes (or to placate a client) you might be better off not waging this battle.

- The relief requested by the motion might benefit your client–even though the motion might seek a continuance of a trial setting, perhaps your client is not too eager for trial anyway or the extra time could help you get better prepared for trial or give you time to attempt an additional summary judgment attack.

- Your agreement might set a good example–consider whether your client might need to ask for similar relief at some point during the pretrial phase of the lawsuit. If so, your agreement with your opponent's current request will help to establish some informal precedent in the case.

- Perhaps the relief requested is not of any significant consequence from your perspective. Given that filing a response in opposition, and preparing for and attending a hearing involves an expenditure of time, energy and money, you may decide that resistance, while not futile, is not worth the effort.

2. Has your opponent misstated any facts or law?

Perhaps the most powerful ammunition in motion practice is utilizing mistakes from within the motion itself to cause it to implode. You should not assume that your opponent's statements of fact or law are accurate. Double-check the evidentiary record to determine if the factual assertions are wrong either outright or through taking some statement or document out of context. You should also read the cases cited by your opponent to see if there are any serendipitous nuggets of law or conclusions that you can pull out of your opponent's own cases. One of the best phrases used in a response to a motion is: "Even the cases cited by movant show that the motion should be denied." Maybe the motion did not correctly state the burden on the movant. Or you might find that a case relied upon by your opponent has been reversed or overruled. Not only does finding such a mistake or misstatement undermine any appeal in your opponent's motion, but it may very well serve as a basis for the presiding judge to favor your client for the remainder of the litigation. And well earned bias in favor of you or your client gives you tremendous leverage in the litigation. Just be careful to only throw in the face of your opponent mistakes that are significant–it probably does not matter, for example, if the motion cited the wrong page number for a published precedent. If you elevate the trivial to the forefront of your response, it may make you appear both petty and desperate.

3. Are there any other facts/law you need to bring up?

Your own careful case analysis, based upon a thorough knowledge of the facts and a comprehensive awareness of the applicable law, will guide you in determining whether there are additional facts or legal principles/authorities that you need to bring to the court's attention. Perhaps your opponent's factual recitation was entirely accurate but incomplete. It is your job to make sure the record before the court paints the full picture. Likewise, if there are other published decisions that demonstrate a lack of unanimity among the courts in ruling on the present issue you will want to cite to these cases so that, at a minimum, you empower your judge by demonstrating that a ruling in either direction is at least plausible. Sometimes an advocate may fail to cite some caselaw that might be instructive on an issue. This is not necessarily wrong although if the court believes the advocate's submission to be misleading it will certainly cause a loss of credibility. On the other hand, if counsel has knowingly failed to disclose to the court controlling legal authority that is adverse to counsel's position, this may well implicate both an ethical violation[8] as well as a violation of rule 11.

4. Do you have any counter-motions?

It may very well be that consideration of your opponent's motion raises the same issue as a motion that you have also been thinking of filing for your client. Or the grant of your opponent's motion may raise a need that your client has for some relief of its own. An example of the first scenario might be the defendant filing a motion for summary judgment raising its sovereign immunity

---

[8] See Professional Responsibility Rule 3.3(a)(3) in Appendix I accompanying this text.

as a defense. If you are the plaintiff opposing this motion, you might consider filing your own cross-motion for summary judgment asking the court to render partial summary judgment against this affirmative defense. Wouldn't that be like hitting a grand slam–not only getting your opponent's motion defeated but getting your own cross-motion granted? An example of the second scenario might be where the plaintiff files a motion for leave to amend her complaint to assert another cause of action. You might oppose this request because the discovery deadline has nearly passed and you feel your client will be prejudiced by the late amendment. In the alternative, you might consider a cross-motion to extend the discovery deadline so that if the plaintiff is granted leave to amend your client will be able to engage in more discovery on the new matters being pled. Even if you refrain from filing a cross-motion now, you may be able to pursue such relief at a later date. But there is certainly efficiency achieved in raising your related issues now and there may very well be strategic benefit to filing the cross-motion now and having it heard at the same time as the primary motion. If nothing else, maybe the court will view denial of both motions as a reasonable compromise of the matter.By considering these four questions, you can be guided in determining whether and how to prepare a response in opposition to the motion. In terms of the actual contents of the response or deadlines for filing the document, the rules of civil procedure of noticeably silent. Of course, any pleading, motion or resonse should have the case caption (rule 10) and be signed by counsel (rule 11) but beyond this the preparation and filing of a response to a motion are matters largely governed by local rule. You will definitely need to consult your applicable local rules for important information on limitations on the page length of your response and to ascertain the deadline for filing your written response. For example, our Local Rules provide:

> Each party opposing a motion or application shall file within ten (10) days after service of the motion of application a response that includes a memorandum of legal authority in opposition to the request, all of which the respondent shall include in a document not more than twenty (20) pages.[9]

As an advocate you cannot afford to miss the deadline for responding because the judge may issue a rule promptly based upon the assumption that you decided not to oppose the motion. If you need additional time, you should contact opposing counsel. If she does not oppose your request, you should promptly file an agreed motion and also consider alerting the judge's law clerk or deputy (by letter or telephone call) that your motion is being filed and that the parties request that the court not rule on the merits of the motion yet.

---

[9]Local Rule 3.01(b).

e. Hearings

For most motions, the rules of civil procedure are silent as to any requirement for a hearing or oral argument before the court. In a few instances the rules reference a hearing but never forbid the trial judge from disposing of the matter exclusively through written submissions.[10] The rules with respect to both summary judgments and preliminary injunctions are examples of this latter scenario. Rules 56 (summary judgment) and 65 (injunctions) make passing reference to a hearing on the motion or application but do not actually state that a live hearing is required. In practice, some federal judges routinely consider the vast majority of the motions filed before them exclusively by written submission. Our Local Rule states that motions will "ordinarily be determined by the Court on the basis of the motion papers and briefs or legal memoranda."[11] But some federal courts still grant hearings on some motions when requested by a party or when the court feels that the motion requires exceptional consideration.

> The rules of civil procedure are generally silent as to any requirement for a hearing or oral argument before the court for most motions. It is important to note that there is a marked difference on this issue between federal and state courts.

Most state courts are at the other extreme by typically conducting hearings with oral arguments on contested motions. Thus, whether you even will have a hearing depends to a large extent on whether your case is pending in state or federal court. This actually makes some sense because all federal district judges have professional law clerks assisting them. These clerks traditionally read the motions and responses and help to draft memorandum orders ruling on pending motions in civil cases. Thus, the federal courts are equipped to handle most motions exclusively on the written submissions. On the other hand, most state trial courts do not have professional law clerks sifting through written motion submissions. For the typical state court judge, the arguments given and evidence referenced at a hearing may be all that the judge has time to consider seriously. In these instances, the written submissions may sometimes serve primarily as a written record for appellate purposes, with the real action taking place in the courtroom. These arguments are still framed by the written motion, the evidence and the parties' briefs but the judge is directly impacted most by the arguments at the hearing.

---

[10]One notable exception concerns class action procedure under rule 23 which explicitly requires a hearing in at least one circumstance–for the approval of a proposed class action settlement rule 23(e)(C) states that the court may approve a settlement "only after a hearing."

[11]Local Rule 3.01(j) located in Appendix III of this text.

Let's say that you do have a hearing scheduled on a motion in your lawsuit. What should you do in anticipation of the hearing and how should you plan to make the best argument possible? Consider the following principles and factors:

1. judge

Not every pretrial motion is heard by the presiding trial judge. In some venues, there may be a motion judge assigned to hear all motions set for hearing regardless of which court is assigned to the case. In addition, some jurisdictions utilize the services of visiting judges who are often retired judges who travel to different venues and fill in for the regular judges hearing motions. You need to be aware of any such possibilities in your forum and be prepared for argument before someone other than the regular presiding judge in your case. In some instances, you may have a right to object to a visiting judge if you know the correct procedures available in that jurisdiction for doing so. In any event, you should take into consideration the personality of the judge that you anticipate hearing your arguments. Individual judges will differ in their levels of patience, the type of argument they find appealing, and their degree of formality. Knowledge of such differences will be extremely useful to you in organizing your arguments. In addition, advance information on your judge will tend to help any advocate by reducing the degree of surprise associated with a hearing and thereby increasing the advocate's confidence. Displaying a confident demeanor can be important in a closely contested argument.

2. location

As a part of knowing your judge, you should also try to ascertain information about exactly where the argument will be held. Some judges make a practice of conducting all hearings in the formal confines of the courtroom with counsel behind a podium or counsel tables. Many judges invite counsel to approach the bench and conduct their arguments from this position of proximity to the judge. Other judges will utilize the courtroom but will conduct hearings by coming down from the bench–imagine Moses returning from the summit of Mt. Sinai carrying the stone tablets–and sitting at counsel table with the advocates. Other judges will invite counsel into their chambers to sit in couches and desk chairs around the judge. As you might imagine, an advocate's dramatic planned presentation for the courtroom simply may not work seated on a floral sofa with the judge's favorite music station playing in the background while everyone sips coffee. Frankly, loud arguments are not appropriate in chambers. In other words, the formality and the simple logistics of the argument can vary tremendously from one court to another. This may impact not only your style but the substance of your arguments.

Finally, one other possibility impacting on the location is the potential for a telephonic hearing. Many judges are open to conducting a variety of hearings over the telephone. Our Local Rule 3.01(i), in fact, states that the "use of telephonic hearings and conferences is encouraged, whenever possible, particularly when counsel are located in different cities." There are some obvious advantages to telephone hearings because it saves the counsel time. Further, if you oppose the motion a telephonic hearing may be good because it suggests implicitly that the matter being heard is not important enough to justify counsel appearing in court. In some instances, the local lawyers may appear live in the courtroom while the out of town counsel appear by telephone usually placed on the judge's bench and utilizing the speaker phone. If you are the out of town counsel, you may already face an uphill battle if the judge knows the other counsel and they have earned the judge's respect. The hill can easily become steeper when you are not even in the courtroom. Often it is difficult to hear what is going on in the courtroom and you never have any visual cues. Is the judge growing weary of the arguments, or is he snickering at you along with some of the other lawyers? This is not ideal but if a telephone hearing is scheduled, it is best for you if all counsel participate by phone.

<u>3. time</u>

It helps you to know in advance how long the court has scheduled for your hearing and whether there are other hearings scheduled immediately before and after yours. Whether you are the movant or the respondent, this information will help you plan to use whatever time you are given most productively. It is a shame when an advocate has prepared tirelessly to give a 30 minute argument only to appear and discover the judge only has 10 minutes to devote to the case. Sometimes this will happen no matter how much planning and advance intelligence you have gathered on the hearing length. You should try to limit the occurrence of such surprises but be prepared and flexible enough to react to a change in circumstances. Even though your half hour presentation is brilliant, is it possible to pick the very best and most important argument to focus upon if the court says you have only five minutes? If not, you may consider asking the court to reschedule the hearing for another time so that the court can spend the time necessary to work through the intricacies of the legal issues presented by the motion.

More important than knowing the length of time is that counsel knows when the hearing is scheduled to start and gets to the court early. Being late is unacceptable unless you are in another court, you are in the hospital or your car is broken down on the side of the road. And even in this exceptional circumstances

> *"There are two kinds of lawyers, those who know the law and those who know the judge."*
>
> *Anonymous*

there is no excuse for you failing to call the court hearing your motion and explain your situation. Most judges are human too and can excuse your tardiness in such situations, if you call. This means as an advocate you must carry a fully charged cell phone when you have a hearing scheduled. Being present on time is a good start. Being early is better. The truth is, particularly in small rural venues, that often the hearing unofficially begins fifteen minutes early over coffee in the judge's reception area or adjacent hallway. This is when counsel engages in small talk with the courtroom personnel, often including the judge. The rules of ethics forbid *ex parte* communications concerning the merits of the matter about to be heard unless all counsel are present, but if you are not there how will you ever know this occurred? The judge may view the banter as innocent and unimportant. But the rapport that may develop between coffee-sipping counsel and the court can tip the balance in a closely contested motion. Not only is it a safe practice to be present early to prevent this from happening, but planning to be there early can at least help you avoid being late in case "a funny thing happens on the way to the courthouse." Even if there is no coffee hour taking place in chambers prior to the hearing, it can be helpful to arrive early so that you can check in with the court bailiff or courtroom deputy. It never hurts to get to know these personnel.

4. argument

Assuming you have filed a good motion or brief already, what are the additional purposes to be served by having oral argument? Is it just to read your submission out loud to the court? Hardly. Most importantly, oral argument gives you the chance to focus the court's attention on the most important points raised by the motion or response. The essence of the parties' dispute arising out of the motion being heard may boil down to one or two critical points. If you can figure out what those key points are and plan a convincing and cogent argument around those points, you greatly increase your chance of prevailing at the hearing. The hearing also gives you a chance to supplement what was already said in the briefs of the parties, particularly since many courts do not permit the filing of reply or sur-reply briefs. If you are the moving party, you may not yet have had any opportunity to address certain arguments (or evidence) raised in your adversary's response.

Finally, a hearing is your opportunity to have a live exchange with the decision maker. This is not an event to be feared, but rather one to embraced. You should eagerly await the opportunity to answer questions posed by the judge during the argument. Too many counsel view questions from the court as some intrusion on the autonomy of their outline for the argument. Instead, when the judge begins asking lots of questions, counsel should be prepared to abandon their outline and just focus on what the thinking is behind the court's questions. Often the judge's questions suggest some level of discomfort with a party's position. You should try to be sensitive to these matters and then fashion your answers and arguments to try to assuage whatever judicial concerns might hinder a favorable decision. Or the court might suggest a weakness in your opponent's case. For example, perhaps you went into a summary judgment hearing convinced that causation was the easiest point of attack. The court keeps bringing up a concern that perhaps your client had no duty to the plaintiff. It's time to reshuffle your argument when this happens. This is the benefit of a live audience that is not possible on written submissions alone.

There are many other tips for oral arguments. Many of these are common sense matters but never hurt being repeated:

- Do be focused upon the few issues or facts of most importance yet be flexible enough to react to other matters that come up.
- Do be organized and do not ramble.
- Do maintain eye contact with the judge so that you can determine if the judge is confused, weary, or accepting of your arguments.
- Don't speak too fast–this is often a sign of either nervousness or trying to cover too much material in too little time.
- Do remind the judge of key phrases or points at the end.
- Don't try to restate everything in your brief.
- Don't be condescending toward the court.
- Don't be rude to opposing counsel.
- Don't speak over the judge–remember what the court is thinking ought to be a main object of your inquiry.
- Do be prepared to show the court highlighted copies of key cases or exhibits that are part of the record.
- Do be prepared to use other demonstrative aids such as chronologies or blown up copies of exhibits or testimony.
- Do keep your evidence (in evidentiary hearings) on point, organized, marked for admission into evidence and have your witnesses available.
- Do try to relax and be yourself even if this means laughing when the judge tells a joke.
- Do stand when the judge comes or goes and every time you address the court–unless the court tells you otherwise.
- Do refer to the court with respect–you can use "your honor" and "judge" interchangeably.
- Do take charge of the hearing, if it's your motion, when the court invites the argument with a statement such as "okay, what are we here for today counsel?" It's important to be the first to cast the nature of the matter before the court. If opposing counsel tries to initiate the hearing by jumping into their responsive argument, interrupt politely and ask the judge if you can present your motion first.

5. ending

Sometimes the hearing ends abruptly when the court is out of time and indicates that she is taking the matter under deliberation. If a ruling needs to be made quickly, you might politely remind the court of these circumstances. On other occasions, the court might simply let the counsel go back and forth arguing indefinitely. After all, motion arguments tend to be more informal and less structured than appellate arguments. There is no red light to tell you to sit down. If the argument seems to be going well for your side, you should delicately try to wrap up the arguments perhaps by offering a simple summation. If the hearing does not seem to be going too well, you might be able to continue the debate perhaps trying out additional arguments or raising alternative issues. Counsel sometimes feel that whoever argues last will win, and there are some judges whose conduct does invite this type of speculation.

But all arguments eventually come to an end and the court may even state whether she intends to grant or deny the motion. Some judges prefer to draft their own written orders, particularly federal judges, but many times they will ask the counsel who has "won" the hearing to prepare a proposed order consistent with the court's announcement of the outcome and to circulate the order to opposing counsel to agree as to its form. Be careful not to be greedy and try to inject matters into the order that were not discussed at the hearing–such conduct might result in an additional hearing where your tentative victory might be reconsidered. Doing this is also unprofessional and may be unethical. If you are the losing counsel be sure that you do not sign off generally on a proposed order. Rather, as the losing party you should sign an accurately drafted order "as to form only" to preserve your right to complain on appeal if necessary about the ruling.

A final note about post-hearing letters to the court. If the court has taken a motion under advisement, some lawyers in some locales will make a habit out of sending additional written arguments to the court in the form of a short letter. They often begin with "At the hearing, opposing counsel mentioned another case. After reviewing this opinion, I wanted to respond further by pointing out to the Court that . . . ." Some judges do not mind receiving these letters. Frankly, when it becomes routine and both sets of lawyers continue the debate in this manner it can get frustrating. It also may tend to delay the court in reaching a decision on the motion under submission. Before you begin this letter writing campaign, you should be sure that both local practice and your judge's individual preferences are consistent with doing so. Our Local Rules prohibit this practice saying that legal arguments belong in motions and briefs only and "unless invited or directed by the presiding judge, shall not be addressed or presented to the Court in the form of a letter or the like."[12]

---

[12] Local Rule 3.01(f).

Top 10 Ways to Have a Bad Trip
to the Courthouse

10. Grundge Is In Style

Be sloppy in drafting your motion and in your attire. First impressions aren't that big of a deal.

9. Lose Credibility

Cite a bunch of cases and don't bother to read them or check to see if they are still good law.

8. Litigation Is Like a Box of Chocolates--Let the Judge Pick Your Relief

Don't think carefully and creatively about the relief you are requesting before you show up.

7. Surprises Are Good

Don't ask anyone about the judge to learn her likes/dislikes/tendencies.

6. Who Needs Friends Anyway?

Go ahead and annoy and offend the judge with your attitude and body language.

5. Show the Judge the Real World

Be rude toward opposing counsel and use course language toward her.

4. Your Voice Sounds Wonderful

You should ramble on aimlessly and at length because the judge has nothing better to do.

3. Style Counts More Than Substance

Don't bother knowing the factual record. Spend your time thinking of a good joke to tell.

2. Who's That Person In the Black Robe?

Direct your remarks at opposing counsel so the judge feels like a useless spectator.

1. Make a Fashionable Appearance

Increase the drama by marching into the courtroom after the hearing has already begun.

B. *Motions for Summary Judgment*

1. Standard

In the past, motions for summary judgment were frowned upon by the courts–trial courts were reluctant to grant such dispositive motions. This reluctance was, in part, fueled by fear of reversal from the appellate courts which were quick to send cases back to the trial court for the seemingly obligatory trial. This step-child treatment of the summary judgment instrument arose out of concern for preserving a litigant's right to a jury trial and a mistake in understanding the purpose behind the summary judgment procedure. Courts seemed to buy into the idea that if a litigant had properly pled a cause of action and been able to withstand rule 12(b)(6) scrutiny it seemed unfair to deprive the litigant of their chance before a jury. Certainly any shred of doubt concerning the adequacy of a plaintiff's claims were resolved against the grant of summary judgment. In reviewing summary judgment motions, courts also often required a defendant to affirmatively negate the plaintiff's claims through its own evidence. That is, the defendant was required to prove a negative and using a standard that said that all inferences were found in favor of the claims and that any claim with a genuine issue of material fact was worthy of a jury trial. This was a tall order in most cases and resulted in few summary judgments being granted or upheld.

> *"This was the unkindest cut of all."*
>
> William Shakespeare, *Julius Caesar* (act 3, sc. 2).

The U.S. Supreme Court revolutionized summary judgment practice with its seminal decision in *Celotex* in 1986.[13] No discussion of summary judgment practice would be complete without mention of this case because it established the correct focus for federal courts and, by example, it has established the analysis employed by most state courts as well. The case itself was a personal injury asbestos lawsuit in which the plaintiff sued 15 different manufacturers of asbestos-containing products. One of the defendants moved for summary judgment arguing that the plaintiff had no sufficient evidence that the decedent was exposed to that defendant's product. After the trial court's grant of summary judgment, the issue on appeal was whether the defendant could move for summary judgment without offering its own evidence negating its liability. The Court of Appeals believed the summary judgment was improper but the Supreme Court reversed. The Supreme Court clarified that the purpose behind summary

---

[13]*Celotex Corp. v. Catrett*, 477 U.S. 317 (1986).

judgments was to save time on unnecessary trials.

In essence, the Court explained that it was silly to put a greater burden on a movant under rule 56 than the movant would have at trial. Applying different standards misses the point behind summary judgment practice–the purpose being to weed out factually inadequate claims for which no jury determination is needed. That is, the court's goal in deciding a summary judgment motion is to spot in advance of trial those claims or defenses for which a directed verdict would likely be granted at trial after the party with the burden of proof on the issue rested. Why go through with the time and ordeal of trial only to have the matter taken away from the jury on a directed verdict motion? If we can spot with confidence these inadequately supported claims and defenses during the pretrial stages, it is much more efficient to do so now rather than later. And the responding party is itself in no worse shape having their claim or defense rejected now rather than during trial. Theoretically, with this new recognition of the correct summary judgment burden, you might easily imagine a world where summary judgment practice completely displaces directed verdict motions–that is, all of the claims/defenses lacking sufficient evidentiary support could be eliminated during pretrial so that only adequate claims/defense would ever see the light of a courtroom for trial. This theory is accurate but has not proven to be entirely true for several reasons. One may be that a party is not required to move for summary judgment. Another might be that the summary judgment record may contain different evidence than that presented later during a trial.

Some summary judgment motions present pure questions of law. For example, may a non-client sue a lawyer for legal malpractice? The plaintiff's complaint might admit that she was not a client of the defendant lawyer but argue that the lawyer still owed her a professional duty of care that was breached. Of course, this claim could be challenged through assertion of a rule 12(b)(6) motion to dismiss for failure to state a claim. If the law says that only clients can sue lawyers and the plaintiff fails to allege an attorney-client relationship with the defendant, she has failed to state a claim. Even if the plaintiff's evidence supports every factual allegation of the complaint (e.g., that the lawyer really did act carelessly and this caused harm toward the non-client plaintiff) if the law simply does not provide for a cause of action in that situation the claims may be dismissed as a matter of law. This would be a proper 12(b)(6) motion if filed in lieu of or with the answer. If the defendant were to wait to assert this legal defect until after the filing of her answer, technically she could either move for judgment on the pleadings (rule 12(c)) or summary judgment. In this instance, the nomenclature of the motion is immaterial because the court need only decide a legal question to determine the merits of the motion. In any event, in these situations involving pure legal questions, there is no confusion surrounding the movant's summary judgment burden because the material facts are not disputed by the motion.

But in summary judgment motions attacking an opponent's evidentiary proof, exactly what is the movant's burden in moving for the summary judgment? To answer this question, you must place over your analytical eyes your trial spectacles and imagine what the trial in the matter will look like. This is true because the answer to the issue of burden depends upon who will have the burden of proof regarding the matter at issue during the imagined trial. Thus, if a defendant is moving for summary judgment on the ground that there is inadequate evidence as to one element of the plaintiff's cause of action–say damages–the defendant/movant need offer no evidence in support of its motion because, at trial, the defendant need not offer any evidence negating that element of the plaintiff's case. The defendant has no duty to prove a negative. At trial, if the plaintiff were to rest without offering sufficient evidence by which a rational jury might find damages, the defendant is entitled to a directed verdict. The defendant's only burden in moving for summary judgment is the same–to point out the evidentiary defect the plaintiff has on an element of her claim. When the movant has demonstrated such a weakness, the burden is on the plaintiff to come forward with sufficient evidence in support of the disputed element of its claim to demonstrate that, at trial, a rational jury hearing this evidence might find in favor of the claimant on that disputed element.

On the other hand, if the movant is seeking summary judgment on its own pled claim or defense, the movant has the duty to demonstrate that the evidence on that issue is so overwhelmingly in favor of the claim/defense that no rational jury could find otherwise. These are, in essence, the same rule 50(a) directed verdict standards that the trial could would employ during trial upon hearing the evidence in support of the claim/defense. When summary judgment practice is considered in this light, there is a beautiful symmetry between summary judgment pretrial practice and directed verdict trial practice. This summary judgment burden can be illustrated by this chart.

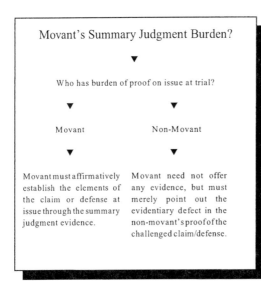

With this understand of the moving party's evidentiary burden in mind, let's consider further the standard the court should apply under rule 56 in deciding on the motion. Rule 56 states in part:

(a) FOR CLAIMANT: A party seeking to recover upon a claim, counterclaim, or cross-claim or to obtain a declaratory judgment may, at any time after the expiration of 20 days from the commencement of the action or after service of a motion for summary judgment by the adverse party, move with or without supporting affidavits for a summary judgment in the party's favor upon all or any part thereof.

(b) FOR DEFENDING PARTY: A party against whom a claim, counterclaim, or cross-claim is asserted or a declaratory judgment is sought may, at any time, move with or without supporting affidavits for a summary judgment in the party's favor as to all or any part thereof.

(c) MOTION AND PROCEEDINGS THEREON. The motion shall be served at least 10 days before the time fixed for the hearing. The adverse party prior to the day of the hearing may serve opposing affidavits. The judgment sought shall be rendered forthwith if the pleadings, depositions, answers to interrogatories, and admissions on file, together with the affidavits, if any, show that there is no genuine issue as to any material fact and that the answering party is entitled to a judgment as a matter of law. A summary judgment, interlocutory in character, may be rendered on the issue of liability alone although there is a genuine issue as to the amount of damages.

These provisions make clear that any litigant, whether a claimant or a defending party, can move for summary judgment. The ultimate standard is the same–whether or not there exists any genuine issue of material fact and, if not, whether the movant is entitled to judgment as a matter of law. How does the court decide if there is any genuine issue of material fact? For this we go back to the discussion of burdens and directed verdict motions from above. When there is sufficient evidence of a claim so that a rational jury might be able to find in favor of the claimant (the rule 50(a) directed verdict standard), then a genuine issue of material fact exist on the claim. A summary judgment for the defendant would be improper. If the moving party is the one having the burden of proof at trial–because the issue is either the movant's own claim or affirmative defense–then the only way the court can conclude that there is no genuine issue of material fact is when the movant's summary judgment proffer of evidence is so conclusively that a rational jury could only find for the moving part on that claim or defense. This quoted passage also makes it clear that in ruling on a motion for summary judgment–when looking to see if there is any genuine issue of material fact–the court looks at all proper summary judgment evidence filed by both the movant and the respondent. While the moving party may file summary judgment evidence it finds helpful to either establishing its own claim or refuting the respondent's claim, the respondent is then free to file its own summary judgment evidence in an attempt to demonstrate that there is enough disputed evidence to create a genuine issue of material fact.

a. Practice

In terms of timing, rule 56 allows a party defending a claim to file a motion for summary at any time. A claimant must wait until at least 20 days after commencing the lawsuit to move for summary judgment establishing its own claim–this is to permit the filing of the defendant's initial answer first. The timing issue is of tremendous strategic importance. If you move too soon, the responding party can either ask the court to overrule the motion because discovery is needed to prepare a response or else ask the court to defer ruling on the motion until the necessary discovery is complete. Of course, the longer you wait before moving for summary judgment, the less you benefit from the early adjudication of the matter and more time and money you spend in the pretrial litigation.

If you are using summary judgment offensively–to establish your own claim or defense–you likely will want to wait until you get some discovery back from the opponent which conceded the necessary facts you need to establish your claim/defense. Deposition testimony or responses to requests for admission are often used for this purpose. Imagine a breach of contract case where your client has sued the defendant for failure to make payment on a promissory note. You might send out some early requests for admission asking the defendant to admit to the authenticity of the promissory note, to admit their signature is genuine, and to admit that they failed to make a required payment by a certain date. If they have admitted each of these facts, you can then consider moving for summary judgment on their breach of contract. If the claim cannot be fully adjudicated at this time–perhaps because they have raised some affirmative defense not dealt with by your motion–the court can enter what is called "partial summary judgment" as to that issue resolved by your motion.[14]

If you are defending a claim, you probably want to wait until the plaintiff has had a sufficient opportunity to take discovery from you before you consider filing a rule 56 motion. It does not really make sense to file a *Celotex*-style "no evidence" motion with your answer saying the plaintiff has insufficient evidence to prove her claim before the plaintiff has had any chance to take discovery. In fact, filing the motion at this premature date likely only serves to accelerate the plaintiff's taking of your client's deposition and service of written discovery

---

[14]Rule 56(d).

requests. If the plaintiff has not yet served you with any discovery or notices of deposition, you should consider waiting further until such time as the court will conclude that the plaintiff had enough time. Ideally, if you could wait until the discovery deadline in the court-issued scheduling order has passed, there would be little chance of the court deciding your motion was premature.

Because both rule 12(b)(6) and 56 can be used to seek early dismissal of a plaintiff's claim, it is useful to compare and contrast the two devices to appreciate the practical differences in application between them. Consider the following differences:

Topic	Rule 12(b)(6)	Rule 56 MSJ
Timing?	Must be filed prior to or with the answer.	Should defer filing until after the respondent has had sufficient time to obtain formal discovery.
Standard?	A pleading standard. Has the plaintiff pled the law and facts sufficient to demonstrate a possible claim?	An evidentiary standard. Does the party with the burden of proof at trial have enough evidence by which a rational jury might find in their favor on that issue?
Purpose?	To avoid unnecessary pretrial litigation (e.g., discovery) on a claim doomed from the start.	To avoid unnecessary trials when the material facts on a claim/defense are so one-sided that a jury's services are not needed.

	Rule 12(b)(6)	Rule 56 MSJ
Use of evidence?	No extra-pleading evidence is to be offered with the motion or considered by the court. Court considers only the "four corners" of the claimant's pleading.	Yes, because the court is engaged in a search for evidence. The parties are to file evidence with their motion and/or response for the court's analysis and preview of what the trial evidence might look like.
Who can use?	Is only used defensively by a party against whom a claim has been asserted. Used to defeat that claim.	Can be used by both claimants and defendants to establish/refute a cause of action or to establish/refute an affirmative defense.
Court's acceptance and willingness to grant?	Disfavored device that should be used sparingly because the claimant is being deprived of all pretrial opportunities to establish their claim.	Well accepted and favored by most courts today as a valuable tool to maximize adjudicative efficiency.
Relief?	Courts typically permit an opportunity to re-plead the claim unless this would be futile. Only when the claimant still cannot cure the pleading deficiencies does entry of final judgment usually occur.	Courts enter judgment on the claim/defense established or refuted. If this resolves the entire case, the summary judgment is a final judgment in the case.

b. Drafting Motions for Summary Judgment and Responses

Motions for summary judgment are governed by all of the general rules on motions and pleadings discussed at the beginning of this chapter. They must have a caption, state the basis for the motion, articulate the specific relief requested, be signed pursuant to rule 11 (representing the good faith basis for the motion), be signed pursuant to rule 5 (evidencing service on all counsel), and be supported by a legal memorandum either incorporated within the body of the motion of by separate brief (as per local rule requirements).

Beyond these general requirements, what else should be considered by the advocate drafting a persuasive motion for summary judgment? Consider these suggestions:

- An introduction should be offered that gives context to the motion by (a) explaining generally what the case is about and who the movant and respondent parties are and (b) identifying the particular claims/defenses that the motion is either attacking or seeking to establish as a matter of law. While such introductions are helpful to many pretrial motions, they are essential to creating a motion that is coherent and persuasive.

- The motion should state up front what the grounds are for the motion. For example, the motion might state that "defendant seeks summary judgment on plaintiff's product liability claim because the summary judgment evidence attached to this motion demonstrates that defendant did not ever sell the product or otherwise introduce it into the stream of commerce." You need not be argumentative (yet) just informative, clear and concise.

- The motion should acknowledge and restate the appropriate standard governing summary judgment practice, taking into account whether the movant has the burden of proof on the matter in question, and preferably using either Supreme Court or other controlling authority (cases from the forum's governing circuit or State supreme court).

- The motion should then recite the undisputed facts that support entry of the motion or, in the alternative, state the lack of evidence the respondent has on their claim/defense being attacked by the motion. As part of the recitation of facts, the motion should attach the evidence relied upon and in the recitation should contain specific citations to the relevant exhibit number or page number containing each fact stated. For example, the motion might state that "Plaintiff admitted in her deposition that she did not purchase the product in question from the defendant and that she has no personal knowledge that the defendant ever sold the product in question to anyone else. (*See* excerpt from deposition of Plaintiff attached at A-14 line 27.)

- A section of argument and authorities should, logically, follow the factual discussion. This should explain the substantive law governing the claim or defense at issue, typically citing the elements of that claim/defense and other legal requirements regarding proof of that matter. Counsel need to be careful when citing cases in a summary judgment brief that the cases they cite apply in the summary judgment context–for example, it may be unwise for a litigant to cite in support of a summary judgment a case discussing the issues in a different procedural context. This portion of the submission is actually the "brief" or "memorandum of law" which, as mentioned before, might either be incorporated into the motion itself or filed as a separate instrument depending upon local practice or the local rules of court. Our Local Rules indicate the brief should be incorporate into the motion or response rather than filed separately.[15]

- The motion should conclude by reminding the court what claim has been established or refuted.

- The motion should conclude with the specific request for relief–some entry of full or partial judgment establishing or rejecting a particular claim or defense.

- Counsel must remember to sign the motion and certificate of serv ice. If local rules require a conference with opposing counsel before filing this motion, this needs to occur and be referenced in a certificate of conference as well. Many courts do not require such a conference concerning dispositive motions like rule 56 motions for summary judgment. Our Local Rules specifically exempt from the conference requirement these motions.

Counsel also needs to make sure they are aware of local rules governing the maximum length of motions. This is particularly true of motions for summary judgment because they tend to be longer on average than most other type of motions. Our Local Rules indicate that motions should be no longer than 25 pages in length, including the signature page.

The nature and form of the summary judgment evidence is worthy of special consideration. Because summary judgment practice is designed avoid unnecessary trials by capturing a snapshot of what the trial might entail, it only

---

[15]Local Rule 3.01(a)-(b).

makes sense that summary judgment evidence must be evidence that would be admissible at a trial. For the most part, any objections to your opponent's evidence you might lodge at trial should be also lodged at the summary judgment stage. When drafting your motion, therefore, you need to exercise caution to offer the attached evidence in admissible form. This means that, for example, affidavits must demonstrate they are based upon personal knowledge and either be sworn to before a notary public or affirmed under penalty of perjury. Affidavits must also be made in good faith or else can be stricken by the trial judge and the party filing the affidavit be made to pay the other's costs in responding to it.[16] Deposition answers must not contain hearsay and each and every document attached to the motion must be authenticated and, if necessary, have any applicable hearsay exception to its admissibility established by the summary judgment evidence. The only perceptible difference between summary judgment evidence and trial evidence is that no live testimony is heard in summary judgment practice–instead the parties must file transcripts from depositions testimony of witnesses or sworn affidavits. Depositions may or may not be offered into evidence at trial–this is governed by rule 32–and affidavits are typically considered hearsay at trial. Beyond these few differences, most of the evidentiary objections available to counsel at trial are also applicable to scrutinizing evidence tendered as part of a summary judgment motion or response.

c. Responding

Technically, you do not always have to file any opposition to a motion for summary judgment. If the movant is trying to establish their own claim by summary judgment, they have a high burden to establish. Even if you file no controverting evidence, they still may not have satisfied the showing needed to prevail. In other words, there is no de facto default form of summary judgment in this scenario. However, if the movant is attacking an element of your cause of action, as under *Celotex*, and you fail to respond with an offer of summary judgment evidence sufficient to at least create a fact issue on that element, your failure gives the court grounds to grant the motion. This dichotomy is somewhat academic, of course, because as an advocate you will always want to avail yourself of the opportunity to respond and point out deficiencies in your adversary's motion even if you need not as a technical matter.

In terms of preparing your response to a motion for summary judgment, you might consider the following strategies, or a combination of them:

- Ask for more time As stated earlier, rule 56(f) permits an advocate to avoid a response when there is good reason for the advocate to not yet be

---

[16]Fed. R. Civ. P. 56(g).

in a position to garner evidence to oppose the motion. This provision states that "the court may refuse the application for judgment or may order a continuance to permit affidavits to be obtained or depositions to be taken or discovery to be had or may make such other order as is just." This approach works best when the motion has been filed early in the litigation. The later in the case the motion has been filed the weaker your contention will be that you need more time for discovery.

- Object to evidence Another tactic is to scrutinize carefully each bit of summary judgment evidence the movant has filed with the court to determine whether it is admissible or not. Look for affidavits that state conclusions rather than facts or purport to offer testimony without personal knowledge of the events. Consider whether deposition excerpts have been unfairly "cut and paste" in a manner that is misleading. Look at each document attached to the motion for issues of authenticity and hearsay. A common mistake made by summary judgment movants is to fail to "prove up" documents they attach to their motion. If you spot objectionable evidence–and this happens frequently–you should include with your response either written objections or even a separate motion to strike the objectionable portions of the summary judgment evidence proffered.

- Proffer your own evidence You need not allow your opponent to dictate all of the evidentiary components of the summary judgment record. You should file evidence either supporting your own claim/defense or attacking the claim/defense of your opponent–as the case may be–through a combination of your opponent's interrogatories and responses to requests for admission, through deposition excerpts, through authenticated documents and through affidavits. If nothing else, your own client can frequently be a source of affidavit testimony that may be sufficient to create a genuine issue of material fact. But be careful in drafting affidavits for signature by your client or other affiliated persons–these are frequently a source for heated cross-examination at trial or scrutiny in depositions. If you are helping to draft any such affidavits, as you should, be sure only to include facts the affiant personally knows, stick to the facts and avoid conclusions and opinions (unless the affiant is an expert witness) and make sure the assertions are true. Destroying your client's credibility in an attempt to avoid partial summary judgment would be a good example of winning the battle at the expense of the war.

- Dispute the law Even if the facts are fairly undisputed you can still argue about whether the movant is entitled to judgment as a matter of law. How do you argue the law? This is what you began doing on the first day of law school. Perhaps your opponent's interpretation of controlling cases is incorrect or maybe your opponent has failed to cite other contrary authorities. Arguing about the application of even settled law to a certain set of facts is something that lawyers are good at doing. Unless the application of the law to the summary judgment evidence establishes the movant's entitlement to judgment as a matter of law, their motion should be denied. When this happens in the face of undisputed facts, it also suggests this might be a good occasion for you to consider a cross-motion for summary judgment (on the same facts) asking the court to rule in your client's favor instead. You can incorporate such a cross-motion into your response if you are relying upon the same facts and legal arguments, for sake of efficiency. If you do this, just be sure to give your document an accurate and complete title, such as: "Defendant's Response to Plaintiff's Motion for Summary Judgment and Cross-Motion for Summary Judgment."

- <u>Cockroach defense</u> Trial lawyers sometimes refer to a cockroach defense that desperate advocates resort to in hard cases. That is, when both the facts and the law cut against your client, the cockroach defense suggests that you simply "crawl all over" your opponent's case and try to distract the judge or jury from finding merit in their case. It  may involve attempted application of each of the foregoing strategies in drafting your response. Some might consider this to be a form of "muddying the picture." One anonymous federal district judge told his law clerks, for example, that they should presume in any response to a summary judgment motion that is more than one inch thick that "surely there is a genuine issue of material fact in there somewhere." Be careful when employing the cockroach defense because you don't want to be accused of violating rule 11 in any of your assertions. You must at least offer good faith arguments even if you think they are probable losers. Also, if you find yourself employing the cockroach defense, it would be a good idea to broach settlement with your opponent prior to the court's ruling or any hearing on the matter. We will discuss this more in the next chapter on Settlement.

d. Arguing

Our prior discussion in this chapter on oral advocacy at motion hearings is equally applicable to summary judgment hearings. In addition to those comments, there are some additional specific strategies you should consider incorporating into your preparation for a summary judgment hearing. If you are the movant, you need to keep your presentation as clear and simple as possible. State up front precisely what you are seeking by way of summary judgment–knocking out plaintiff's fraud claim on the ground that there was no reliance or perhaps establishing defendant's violation of your client's Title VII employment discrimination claim.   As you might imagine, the more claims/defenses covered by a shot-gun motion for summary judgment, the more difficult and confusing the argument will be. This also suggests another strategic consideration when seeking summary judgment–use a piecemeal rifle-shot approach to defeating your opponent's several claims. You can file a series of focused partial summary judgment motions rather than attacking the your adversary's entire case in one motion. This allows the court to stay focused and makes the argument more compelling. If you take this approach, start with the weakest claims and move up from there. After you have explained the scope of your motion, you will need to discuss the law and demonstrate what the undisputed evidence establishes and why your client should prevail. The more factually complex the argument, the better it is to consider a written (or blown-up copy) chronology as a demonstrative aid. In short, you should consider any argument device or aid you can conjure up to simplify the motion and increase your odds of winning. If the court has any confusion, it will likely deny your motion.

As the responding party, you typically have some different primary strategies to consider. If the movant wants to simplify things, doesn't it make sense for you to show how complicated the law and facts actually are? This is one approach, reminiscent of the "cockroach" defense your written submission may have employed. Another idea that may or may not work for your particular circumstance is to simply walk the court through a list of each and every "genuine issue of material fact" that is raised by the summary judgment evidence. Specificity is a powerful aid in this argument–for each disputed issue of fact explain why, under the law, this fact is "material" and then demonstrate where in the summary judgment evidence the factual "dispute" exists. Remember, this is not your closing argument to the jury. To win as the responding party, you are not so much interested in demonstrating what the right factual finding ought to be. Your task is actually simpler than that. You just need to demonstrate that there is work for the jury to do at trial with the evidence–that a rational jury might go either way. This is enough for the court to deny appropriately your adversary's motion for summary judgment. You might wrap up this type of argument with a phrase such as "your Honor, this is a classic case of evidence that points more than one direction. This is a question of fact that the jury is going to have to resolve when this case goes to trial." If the facts are relatively undisputed, your remaining option is to focus your arguments on the law and why the law does not entitled your opponent to judgment on the factual record before the court.

C. DISCOVERY MOTIONS

1. Enforcement of Discovery Obligations

You may recall in our earlier chapters on discovery there was some mention of advocates frequently being involved in discovery disputes. Some of these are simply like quarrels between siblings (advocates) while the parent (judge) is away–they sort themselves out without any judicial intervention. Your opponent goes crazy when you serve your many objections to her requests for production and she calls to complain. You bicker back and forth and finally reach some accommodation in terms of what materials you agree to provide. Or you and your opposing counsel get into a tiff during a deposition you are defending when your opponent gets frustrated with your witness and raises her voice. You threaten to "shut down this deposition and go visit the judge" if she continues. That is the last thing you actually desire to do (you want the thing to really finish once and for all and not give your opponent a two-day recess to think of harder questions) and the last thing opposing counsel wants (she doesn't want the judge to think she's a jerk). So after a ten-minute coffee break and a chance to cool down, you resume the deposition as if nothing ever happened. Such mini-skirmishes are part of the average day for many pretrial advocates. It is nice when you can keep these differences to a minimum and only argue about important matters. But lawyers are people and the more time they spend with each other on discovery matters, the more likely there will be some differences.

Other discovery issues are more likely going to necessitate some judicial intervention of some sort in order to be resolved. When your opponent persists in advancing privilege objections you consider frivolous or refuses to make their client's CEO available for deposition, you may very well need to involve the court in the argument. There are countless examples of the type of discovery disputes that might require a motion and hearing. Most of the prior general discussion on motion practice applies to discovery motions. But there are some nuances to discovery disputes that is worthy of separate brief treatment here.

You have some different options available to you when your opponent fails to appropriately answer your discovery. For example, maybe the defense counsel in your case provided very superficial interrogatory answers or failed to make a complete production of documents in response to your document requests. What are your options for dealing with this situation? Is one option better than the others? What strategic considerations are there in deciding on the best approach to this situation?

In these type of situations the advocate has three primary options to consider and weigh: (a) filing a motion to compel; (b) filing a motion in limine;

and (c) ambushing your opponent at trial with their discovery failure.

1. motion to compel discovery

Motions to compel discovery–the first option–are governed by rule 37 which is a long rule with many subparts. This should tell you something about the frequency that lawyers are involved in discovery motion practice. Subpart (a) of rule 37 discusses motions to compel disclosures, deposition testimony, interrogatory answers, and the production of documents and things. Hmm . . . you may ask why there is no mention here of compelling responses to requests for admission? There is no need to compel such responses because requests for admission are self-effectuating. If your opponent fails to respond, the matters on which admission were sought are deemed admitted. In other words, you would never complain about your opposing party's failure to respond to requests for admission. Further, the only sanction for denying requests for admission that you believe should have been admitted in good faith comes into play only after such underlying fact issues have been resolved–typically after a trial.[17] In any event, the only types of discovery for which you would need to move to compel are covered by rule 37(a).

When the party resisting discovery is another party to your lawsuit, your motion to compel must be filed in the court where the case is pending. If the resisting individual is a non-party (perhaps ignoring a deposition subpoena), you should apply for relief in the court where the discovery was to have been taken.[18] Any motion to compel under rule 37 is expressly required to be preceded by a certification that the movant conferred or made an attempt to confer in "good faith" with the person or party resisting discovery to resolve the matter without court intervention. This mandatory conference is your ticket that gains you access to the court on a discovery dispute. Failure to perform this conference requirement typically results in a summary denial of your motion.

In ruling on a motion to compel, rule 37(a) states that courts shall treat responses or answers that are "evasive or incomplete" as a total "failure to disclose, answer or respond." In other words, cute, tricky discovery responses are treated as not having responded at all and can entitle your adversary to an order compelling discovery.

---

[17]Rule 37(c)(2).

[18]Rule 37(a)(1).

The rule also gives litigants incentive to avoid the courthouse on their discovery disputes. Rule 37(a)(4) discusses sanctions and expenses incurred in discovery motions. In effect, the prevailing party (and sometimes their advocate) is presumed under this provision to be entitled to an award of their expenses incurred (including attorney's fees) in the discovery battle.

> Rule 37's presumption of an award of expenses to the prevailing party is a reaction to the perception of too many discovery disputes being taken to court without reflection, hesitation or any attempt at conciliation.

Whether you are the movant or the respondent you are at risk of such a sanction just for being on the losing end of the engagement. The rule does state that the court can deny such sanction if the court finds your conduct to have been "substantially justified" or that "other circumstances make an award of expenses unjust."[19] This presumption, however, of such an award is unique to discovery motions and is a reaction by the courts to the perception of too many discovery disputes being taken to the court without reflection, hesitation or any attempt at conciliation. The message here to you is to avoid the courthouse on discovery disputes, if possible.

Rather than simply moving to compel discovery, can you be more aggressive and seek so-called "death penalty" sanctions asking the court to strike the opponent's pleadings? Well, you can ask all you want be such sanctions at this point would be error. Rule 37 does authorize such an extreme sanction but not for the mere failure to respond to discovery. It is the act of disobedience of a court's prior order compelling discovery that justifies such a sanction and, even when such disobedience occurs, the court can consider other less sanctions as well.[20] Further, any noncompliance with any court order can subject the offending party to penalties for being in contempt of court. It is not wise to find yourself as the target of an order to "show cause" for why you should not be held in contempt. Talk about being in a triangle of despair.

motion in limine

The next two options for an adversary's failure to provide discovery both stem from the same rule. Rule 37(c) provides that if a party has withheld information, witnesses or documents in response to a prior discovery request, the party may not use or rely upon the withheld information, witnesses, or documents in any subsequent trial, motion, or hearing:

---

[19]Rule 37(a)(4)(A)-(B).

[20]Rule 37(b)(2)(A)-(C).

(1) a party that without substantial justification fails to disclose information required by Rule 26(a) [disclosures] or 26(e)(1) [duty to supplement disclosures], or to amend a prior response to discovery as required by Rule 26(e)(2) [duty to supplement other discovery responses], is not, unless such failure is harmless, permitted to use as evidence at a trial, at a hearing, or on a motion any witness or information not so disclosed. In addition to or in lieu of this sanction, the court, on motion and after affording an opportunity to be heard, may impose other appropriate sanctions. In addition to requiring payment of reasonable expenses, including attorney's fees, caused by the failure, these sanctions may include any of the actions authorized under Rule 37(b)(2)(A), (B), and (C) and may include informing the jury of the failure to make the disclosure.[21]

This rule thus provides for a mandatory exclusion of evidence that should have been disclosed but was not. Further, when a party has attempted to pull out of their litigation bag such surprise evidence the court can also consider the "death penalty" sanctions discussed above as well as telling the jury about the misconduct. You can imagine a jury's reaction to the judge learning over her bench toward the jury, pointing her finger at the defendant and saying something like: "Ladies and gentlemen of the jury. The defendant just attempted to offer into evidence a document that they were require to provide to the plaintiff months ago but chose not to provide in disobedience of the rules of this court. This document may not be considered by you although you may consider the defendant's misconduct in your deliberations."

One of the options available to you when you believe your opponent has failed to produce something in response to discovery is to include make a pretrial motion to exclude such item from evidence at trial. The pretrial motion would be called a "motion in limine" and is commonly used by counsel to keep extremely prejudicial matters from being offered into evidence in front of the jury at trial. If the offending party has failed to produce an item, your chances are extremely good of keeping the item out of evidence. There are two limitations though on this approach. First, if the motion in limine is made too early the other party might be able to cure effectively their earlier non-production. Second, the item that was not produced may only have helped your case and not your opponent's case. The threat of exclusion of an item your opponent would not offer into evidence is no threat at all.

trial by ambush

---

[21]Rule 37(c)(1).

The other way in which the automatic exclusion offered by rule 37(c)(1) can be used to your advantage is simply to remain silent about the lack of discovery until your opponent attempts to use the information or material by offering it into evidence at trial. The court should still sustain your objection, as with the motion in limine approach. The major benefits to this objection-by-ambush are (a) your opponent has no opportunity before trial to cure their mistake; and (b) your opponent will be surprised by the sudden rejection of their evidence and may not be in a position to replace that evidence with some other information or material. If the evidence was crucial to their case, you may have just strategically worked yourself into position to move for a directed verdict. You may have heard (perhaps from us earlier in this book) that the rules of procedure were designed to avoid trials by ambush but this sure seems to resemble an ambush. Yet this rule of automatic exclusion which has occasioned somewhat of an ambush in this circumstance, has a broader good in mind–not permitting counsel to hold on to key evidence only to spring it on their opponent during trial or a hearing. Of course, this strategy only works when you are aware that your opponent has withheld important evidence and intends on relying upon it at trial.

These three options demonstrate that there are several strategic approaches that are each designed as a way for counsel to enforce discovery obligations against their opponent. There is also one other approach; you might think of it as taking the high road. That is, you could just call opposing counsel, indicate you are aware they have withheld some evidence (perhaps inadvertently) and ask them to please provide it to you. This approach is preferred and, in fact, would be required as a first step before filing a motion to compel anyway.

Drafting and Arguing Discovery Motions/Responses

Beyond the general discussion of motion drafting earlier in this chapter, there are a few specific additional matters to bear in mind regarding discovery motions. First, courts do not like discovery motions and so you should avoid filing them, or having them filed against you, unless (a) the discovery dispute has material importance to achieving your client's prize, and (b) you have first tried in good faith through negotiations with opposing counsel to resolve the matter by agreement. Many judges begin discovery hearings by asking both counsel what efforts they made to resolve the dispute on their own. A blank stare in response will not impress the judge.

Second, in addition to several provisions in the rules of civil procedure, most district's local rules have additional specific provisions that pertain to the filing of motions concerning discovery matters. These local rules also echo the requirement for a meaningful conference with opposing counsel before have the audacity to file a discovery motion. What these redundant requirements for a conference reflect is the principle that when you go before a judge on a discovery motion you had better be confident you are the advocate in the white hat or else yo had better be ready to take some abuse from the judge. The local rules also frequently give other instructions regarding the mechanics of preparing discovery motions, such as these examples from our Local Rules:

> A motion to compel discovery . . . shall include quotation in full of each interrogatory, question on deposition, request for admission, or request for production to which the motion is addressed; each of which shall be followed immediately by quotation in full of the objection and grounds therefor as stated by the opposing party; or the answer or response which is asserted to be insufficient, immediately followed by a statement of the reason the motion should be granted. The opposing party shall then respond as required by Rule 3.01(b) of these rules [by written response/brief].[22]

You need to read your local rules carefully and be sure to obey them strictly in preparing or responding to any discovery motion.

With respect to the discovery hearing, you need to be perceived as the reasonable advocate. Your tone and body language will help you if they portray you as cordial and professional. You need to be prepared to give a well grounded answer to any question concerning you or your client's discovery conduct. You also need to avoid, as much as is reasonably possible, attacks on opposing counsel. It is better to let the court draw conclusions that your adversary is unprofessional than for you to show up at court waving your arms and yelling such accusations.

Finally, be prepared for the unexpected and, perhaps, hostile reception you might get from the trial judge. Examples of wacky rulings from trial judges frustrated with advocates' disputes are numerous. One recent example arose in the context of two litigants whose counsel could not agree on the location of the deposition of a corporate representative. They made the mistake of bringing the judge into the midst of their dispute by a "Motion to Designate Location" of the deposition. The judge referred to this issue as the "latest in a series of Gordian knots that the parties have been unable to untangle without enlisting the assistance of the federal courts" and ordered the following relief:

> ORDERED that said Motion is DENIED. Instead, the Court will fashion a new form of alternative dispute resolution, to wit: at 4:00 p.m. on Friday, June 30, 2006, counsel shall convene at a neutral site agreeable to both parties. If counsel cannot agree on a neutral site,

---

[22]Local Rule 3.04(a).

they shall meet on the front steps of the Sam M. Gibbons U.S. Courthouse .... Each lawyer shall be entitled to be accompanied by one paralegal who shall act as an attendant and witness. At that time and location, counsel shall engage in one (1) game of "rock, paper, scissors." The winner of this engagement shall be entitled to select the location for the [rule] 30(b)(6) deposition to be held somewhere in Hillsborough County during the period of July 11-12, 2006. . . .

This order is both humorous and relatively benign. The court was, in effect, telling the advocates that children could do better than they at resolving such petty disputes. Things could have been much worse–rule 37 permits courts to assess sanctions (such as attorney's fees) to either the movant, the respondent, or both in resolving a discovery motion. One wonders if the parties worked together more amicably after receiving this unusual order–perhaps at least they laughed and this caused a thawing of the hostile and apparently unworkable relationship.

D. RULES MATRIX

This table serves as a starting point for additional inquiry into the potential professional responsibility and civil procedure issues that are implicated when drafting and filing pleadings.

Issues Arising During Motions	Applicable Ethical Rule, Federal Rule of Civil Procedure or Local Rule
Duty to service motions, and method of service	**FRCP 5(a)-(b)**
Motion contents generally	**FRCP 7(b)**
Form of motions	**FRCP 10**
Requirement for motions to have a good faith legal and factual basis as well as a legitimate motivation.	**FRCP 11**
Additional requirements concerning the form of motions.	**Local Rule 1.05**
Duty to confer with opposing counsel prior to filing motion.	**FRCP 26, 37; Local Rule 3.01(g)**

No replies to motions generally permitted absent court approval	**Local Rule 3.01(c)**
Court permitted to consider evidence filed with court in ruling on motion.	**FRCP 43**
Prohibition on most ex parte communications by counsel with court.	**Ethical Rule 3.5**
Duty to advise court of contrary controlling authority.	**Ethical Rule 3.3(a)(3)**
Motion for summary judgment procedure and practice.	**FRCP 56**
Enforcement of discovery obligations.	**FRCP 37**

Table 1 - Potential Rules Applicable to Motions

Points To Ponder . . .

1. Which task do you believe you are most skilled at doing–written advocacy or oral advocacy? Is one skill more important to an advocate than another? How can you improve in the area that is not your strongest?

2. In what ways are appellate arguments different from motion arguments to a trial judge? How should this impact your plans for presenting arguments?

3. Does the emergence of summary judgment practice threaten to undermine our jury system for resolving disputes?

4. As an advocate, how do you balance your zealous representation of your client's cause with notions of professionalism in the context of disputes over matters such as the scope of discovery? When does professionalism dictate compromise and when does this go too far?

CHAPTER TEN
SETTLEMENT

" The quality of mercy is not strain'd.
It droppeth as the gentle rain from hea ven
Upon the place beneath.
It is twice blest:
It blesseth him that gives and him that takes. "[1]

A.   *INTRODUCTION*

Most lawsuits settle. This is true, though to a less extent, in the criminal world–where settlements are referred to as "plea bargains"–as the civil world. The most commonly reported statistic shows that 97% of civil cases are either dismissed by the judge on motion or are resolved by settlement. What this means is that if the plaintiff's lawsuit withstands attack by Rule 12(b)(6) motion and Rule 56 motion for summary judgment, the defendant will very likely settle rather than go to trial. While those of you with aspirations of being another Perry Mason or Ben Matlock[2] no doubt find these figures discouraging, you need not have this reaction. As we discussed early in this text, the *threat* of what may happen to a litigant at trial is what fuels and frames settlement negotiations. With their reputation for trial prowess, imagine what great negotiators our fictional heroes, Perry and Ben, would make. Would you want to take a case to court against either of them? Even if you are a pit-bull by nature, would your clients be keen

---

[1] WILLIAM SHAKESPEARE, MERCHANT OF VENICE, act 4, sc. 1.

[2] A survey of "our favorite TV lawyers" revealed America's infatuation with these top legal characters:

Perry Mason	38%
Ben Matlock	29%
Bobby Donnell	16%
Ally McBeal	9%

According to this survey by the website FindLaw, survey respondents picking Perry Mason offered explanations for their choice such as "he seems honest" and that he "would be most likely to win my case."

on going through cross-examination at the hands of such litigation giants? So rather than looking at the rarity of a civil trial as reason to reconsider your calling, you should instead see what terrific power is associated with an advocate's trial prowess and fearlessness at the prospect of facing a jury. The esteem that such advocates demand in the courtroom gives them great leverage in the conference room.

Why do so many civil cases settle? Several factors seem to be behind this phenomenon. First, settlements permit litigants to becomes master of their case destiny and destroy the uncertainty of further litigation. Many a mediator has begun a mediation by telling the parties something like: "Today is your last chance to dictate the outcome for your case. Once you walk away from the settlement table, be prepared to let your fate be decided instead by a jury of people who will know less about this dispute than you do, who care much less about this dispute than you do, and who may, or may not, like you." There is some hyperbole to this–after all, parties can continue to negotiate settlement even during trial–but much truth as well. Litigants can negotiate settlements but not verdicts. Any advocate who has tried a case to final verdict can relate to the feeling of helplessness when the jury files out of the box and into its private room to begin deliberations. This is the first time since the advocate's initial client interview that there is no longer any task the lawyer can do to impact the outcome. The case is literally out of the hands of the advocate (and the client) and in the hands of strangers. There will be little comfort in life's pleasures so long as that jury remains behind closed doors. With each passing hour, each note or question from the jury room, each distant sound of laughter or argument from behind that door, the anxiety level for advocate and client increases. Have they made a mistake not settling the case? Maybe. Maybe not. But they have certainly lost control over the matter.

> *Litigants can negotiate settlements but not verdicts.*

Second, settlements are a rational and efficient means of dealing with the uncertainty of litigation. Business people make decisions every day to hedge the uncertainties of their industry. Lay people take out insurance policies to cut their losses in the event of personal catastrophe or possible liability. Litigants act in much the same rational manner when they perform calculations of the possible lawsuit outcomes and then try to negotiate for a result that they can live with. This is what sparks compromise and leads to settlements. Settlements are also desirable for the related reason that they reduce litigation expenses. Much of the expense of litigation really kicks in during the final pretrial preparation and the actual trial. These often tend to be 18 to 20 hours workdays and, when the lawyer and expert witnesses are billing by the hour, their fees skyrocket fast. Thus, even settlements that occur near the end of the pretrial road can still save a client an enormous sum of money. Further, in cases where the plaintiff's advocate has taken on representation under the terms of a contingency fee agreement, the advocate maximizes her return on the investment of time representing the client by accelerating a final resolution. Settlement not only pushes forward the date of resolution but it ensures at least some recovery by both advocate and client in this scenario. Going to verdict may be an all or nothing proposition for a litigant, while settling affords both parties the chance to walk away content if not ecstatic.

Third, the litigation system encourages settlement. The civil procedure rules instruct both judge and litigant to be thinking about settlement from the beginning of the litigation until the eve of trial. Rule 16(a), dealing with initial and pretrial conferences, expressly states that the judge-led conferences are partly for the purpose of "facilitating the settlement of the case." The early conference of the parties–the prerequisite for doing formal discovery–under Rule 26(f) requires that the parties must consider the "possibilities for a prompt settlement of the case." As will be discussed further below, judges now routinely order the parties to pretrial mediation of their case before allowing them access to a trial. And one of the subjects that arises at all final pretrial conferences–as contemplated by Rule 16(c)(9)–is the topic of "settlement and the use of special procedures to assist in resolving the dispute when authorized by statute or local rule." Judges have been known at hearings to order the parties and counsel into a courthouse conference room to discuss settlement. While no statute, rule of procedure or local rule can actually force a settlement, judges can practically put great pressure on the parties to settle their case. If the judge perceives that the plaintiff is being unreasonable, the judge may threaten to continue a trial setting to some remote future date. If the judge perceives that the defendant is being unreasonable, the judge might comment unfavorably on the defendant's pending motion for summary judgment. The judge might make advance comments concerning anticipated important evidentiary rulings to inject doubts into the minds of both sides. The judge might send the parties back to a second, or third, mandatory mediation session. All of these are discretionary matters, essentially unreviewable by any appellate court, and they each point to the enormous power of the trial judge to impact settlement.

Why does the system strive so hard to encourage settlement? The stress of crowded dockets would make our system of civil litigation crumble if cases did not settle. The time to trial would grow enormously long and the societal cost of paying for more judges, more courthouses and more administrative staff would escalate. With the average time to trial in most jurisdictions being around two years, imagine how much higher that figure would be if even 50% of the cases that now settle went to trial instead. Our current system would not be able to handle those additional pressures if parties did not settle at their current high rates.

All of this is simply to indicate to you the importance that settlements will play during your career as a civil advocate. Given the benefits to litigants, courts, counsel and our system of civil jurisprudence that stem from settlements, perhaps the question to consider is why do *any* cases go to trial? We'll talk about that in the next section.

While there are scant legal rules that govern the settlement process, there are important principles for you to grasp to maximize your ability to achieve your client's prize through settlement. After all, if most of your cases will end in a settlement, doesn't it make some sense to focus upon this as an important part of the pretrial process? This chapter will

"He is no lawyer who cannot take two sides."

Charles Lamb

explore methods of evaluating the settlement value of a case, describe and offer advice concerning the commonly used settlement processes and conclude with a discussion and some examples of the important ingredients in a settlement agreement.

B. CASE EVALUATION

Evaluation of your client's case began during your initial client interview. As you sat and listened to your would-be client's tale, or read through the complaint filed against your client, you began to form a first impression of the relative strength of the client's claim or of the severity of the claim made against your client. These first impressions are no doubt given more concrete form through the subsequent processes of informal and formal discovery, pleadings and motion practice. Your thinking on the merits of the case are refined significantly through your on-going case analysis where you meld your knowledge of the applicable law with the ever-evolving facts presented by the litigation. Sometimes your first impressions turn out to be wrong; more often, they are closer to the final mark.

One aspect of case evaluation is determining when you and your client are in a position to consider entering into settlement discussions. How much more information is needed in a case before your are equipped to settle? How many legal rulings do you need from the court before you can decide? In a perfect world, there would be no uncertainties before you engaged in settlement talks–you would know the absolute truth concerning the facts giving rise to the case and the law's application would be black and white. Of course, you can practically achieve this in litigation by waiting until a final, no-longer-appealable judgment sits on your desk. But at this point we would no longer be discussing settlement but enforcement and collection of a judgment.

We must deal with litigation in the real world and not in a fantasy world of perfect knowledge. During the pretrial phases of a lawsuit, there is no absolute truth. You have testimony that is more credible, in your opinion, than others and documents and other evidence that at least suggests what really happened. But there is often evidence going the other direction and, in any event, the facts are colored by the perspective of each litigant and each advocate. The advocates may also have different ideas as to the contours of the applicable law; the advocate may not even agree on what law is applicable. With all of this uncertainty and differing perspectives, you can imagine why the two (or more) sides in a case often continue to disagree about the proper outcome throughout the pretrial life of hte case. In practice then, how do two sides ever get together to, more or less voluntarily, agree to settle? They each engage in case evaluation that suggests a reasonable range for possible outcomes; this evaluative process then permits settlement when the two sides' estimates for this range overlap. Getting to the point of realization that there is some common ground for a possible settlement and then actually finding that precise promised land of conciliation is what settlement negotiations are all about. But the beginning point is claim evaluation.

Setting aside the theoretical and philosophical, exactly how should a new advocate go about evaluating her client's case? There may be numerous possible constructs advanced in the literature, but claim evaluation at its core involves first the qualitative analysis of a handful of important factors followed by a quantitative analysis using those conclusions weighed against the claims at issue.

Step #1: Qualitative Analysis

Factor	Analysis
Parties	Who are the parties? Are they likeable? Sympathetic? Do they have any relevant prior histories that will be considered by the jury (e.g., prior similar occurrences or criminal histories that will be admissible)? Does the defendant (itself or through insurance) have the financial wherewithal to pay the damage claims?
Undisputed facts (good and bad)	Some background facts are not disputed by the parties. You can consider those facts admitted by the answer as well as admitted in each party's responses to requests for admission. There may be other undisputed information, such as the terms of some controlling documents like a contract between the parties. Do these undisputed facts suggest liability? Do they corroborate any of the damage claims?

Contested facts (good and bad)	There likely are some disputed facts of consequence or else the case is likely ripe for summary judgment disposition. How does the evidence tend to stack up on each of these undisputed facts? Is it likely the jury will find for your client on any of these undisputed facts? You should also consider clusters of facts–facts that are so related that if a jury finds one of these facts in your favor, they are likely to find the other related facts in your favor as well. You need to also consider affirmative defense to the claims–are there contested facts that are likely to be found supporting application of any such defenses? Does a finding in favor of one of the pled defenses constitute a complete or just a partial defense?
Witnesses	Who are the witnesses, both parties and non-parties? How credible is each witness? Are there significant inconsistencies in some witness' testimony? If so, do these inconsistencies relate to matters of great importance or are they trivial? What are the witness' motives for lying? Does a witness' testimony tend to be corroborated by documentary evidence?
Law	The law may be fairly settled on the claims–the elements of a negligence claim and the affirmative defense of comparative fault, for example. Or there may be significant gray areas requiring interpretation or application by the court–whether reliance on a fraudulent representation must be reasonable, for example. Or what constitutes a viable defense to a statutory cause of action. If the court has not yet ruled on these issues, what rulings do you anticipate the judge making?
Judge	Does the judge have some reputation, or has she displayed in your case, some potential for favoring one side's position over the other? How might this impact rulings on summary judgment motions, motion in limine points, evidentiary objections, jury instructions, and directed verdict motions?

Jury	What are the demographics of the area from where your jury will be drawn? Is it a predominantly rural or urban area? Blue collar or white collar? Rich or poor? Educated or uneducated? And how will each of these characteristics impact the jury's reaction to the parties, witnesses, facts, case themes and damage claims?
Actual damages	How significant are the plaintiff's damages? Are any of these damage items undisputed? Has plaintiff exaggerated her injuries? If so, how do you believe a jury will react to the claims? Because of the nature of the incident and the plaintiff's condition (physically, emotionally, economically) will the jury react with sympathy, anger, or ambivalence?
Possible punitive damages	Speaking of angry juries, will the law and the facts permit a submission of punitive damages to the jury? If so, will the jury likely be upset by the defendant's conduct and the plaintiff's injury to be motivated to punish the defendant? How much punishment might be warranted under the circumstances? What is the defendant's net worth relative to the actual damage claims? Or will the jury interpret the punitive damage request as greedy?

In a case seeking damages, all of the above analysis can ultimately be represented in a simple formula: $L \times D = V$ (the likelihood of defendant's liability expressed as a percentage, multiplied by the probable damages equals the likely verdict). The qualitative analysis will ultimately be reduced to percentage chance of the plaintiff obtaining a favorable verdict on liability and then the percentage chances of recovering each of the components of the damages claimed. Application of this formula can be illustrated using a simple example of a case involving a two-car vehicular accident causing property damage and personal injuries to the plaintiff. We start by coming up with a percentage figure representing our best analysis of the likelihood of the jury returning a verdict of liability against the defendant. Next we take each item of damages claimed and reduce that amount by the percentage likelihood of the jury awarding that same amount in damages. After adding all of the likely damage findings together, we simply multiply that total by the percentage chance of the liability finding to come up with our best estimate of the settlement value of the case.

Step #2: Quantitative Analysis

Liability finding against defendant?   ☞ 75% chance

Likely damage finding?
  Property damages ($10,000 x 100%) ☞$10,000
  Past medical ($15,000 x 90%)   ☞$13,500
  Future medical ($5,000 x 50%)   ☞$ 2,500
  Past lost wages ($7,300 x 90%)   ☞$ 6,570
  Future wages ($50,000 x 20%)   ☞$10,000
  Pain and suffering ($250,000 x 30%) ☞$75,000

          Total likely actual damages   ☞$117,570

Liability chance x Likely actual damages=Settlement value
              $117, 570 x 75% = $88,177.50

You should observe that the foregoing analysis can be applied equally well by a claimant or a defendant. Advocates on both sides need to perform their own independent claim evaluation to arrive at some idea of a reasonable settlement value. Dialogue between the client and advocate is essential in perform claim evaluation. Often the client will not have performed this kind of organized analysis and, instead, will just have their own "gut feel" for what the claim is worth and this opinion is normally clouded by their own desires. So often the dialogue is focused upon the advocate injecting some realism to the client's thinking utilizing the sort of qualitative and quantitative analysis illustrated above. Some institutional clients ask their counsel to provide some sort of formal case evaluation including forecasting the percentage likelihood of winning/losing and forecasting a range of possible verdict, perhaps stated as a worst case and best case scenario. Advocates must be sensitive to their client's desire for such information but should be careful to accompany any forecasts with the very true caveat that projections such as these are not very scientific and can, in a given case, prove to be way off the mark. Indeed, some advocates make it a practice of responding to any such request with the somewhat true response that winning any trial is a "50/50" proposition. (One client hearing such forecast stated that they would have saved a lot of money by flipping a coin instead of hiring counsel and engaging in expensive pretrial litigation.)

Given the uncertainties of claim evaluation–since you are essentially engaging in a an attempted prediction of human behavior–it is common to come up with a reasonable settlement "range" rather than one particular settlement amount. Using our analysis from above, you might imagine plaintiff's counsel and defendant's counsel coming up with different ranges for their claim evaluation of a reasonable settlement of the matter. The settlement range reflects the sum a litigant would be willing to consider paying

Plaintiff Claim Evaluation:		Defendant Claim Evaluation:	
High:	$150,000		
	↕	*Likely Settlement*	
		$110,000	High: $110,000
Low:	$100,000	↕	
		$100,000	↕
			Low: $ 75,000

(or accepting) in order to avoid the risks and costs associated with further litigation of the matter. This range should, logically, find its midpoint at the best estimate of the settlement value of the case–how far up and down from that figure a party will consider reasonable will vary by the party and the nuances of the case. As we will discuss further below, however, often one or more of the parties (and even counsel) are not thinking rationally during settlement discussions. One party may be allowing their philosophy, emotions or distaste for their opponent to color their view of the case or undermine their willingness to make any compromise. If this irrational thought prevails, the likelihood of reaching a compromise settlement is very small. On the other hand, among rational litigants, if plaintiff's range is between $100,000 and $150,000 and defendant's range is between $75,000 and $110,000, there is a common area of between $100,000 and $110,000. This would be fertile ground for a possible settlement agreement to come to fruition. Of course, the analysis and conclusions formed by the two counsel is highly sensitive information and they would be unlikely to ever share those candid thoughts with one another directly. This is where different settlement processes are designed to bring the two parties together to increase the likelihood of a settlement.

C. SETTLEMENT NEGOTIATIONS

There are different primary processes used to assist litigants in finding that common ground where settlements occur. We will focus upon the two major processes–private negotiation and mediation.[3]

---

[3]Other procedures can be used to help facilitate a settlement–but these tend to be merely additional evaluative tools that still require either private negotiation or mediation to produce settlement fruit. For example, advocates sometimes will engage in a mock trial before a group of lay people hired to play the role of jury. This can not only help counsel preparing for a trial but can give some guidance on a real jury's likely reaction to the case evidence and themes. As such, a mock trial can aid counsel in claim evaluation in anticipation of settlement talks.

private negotiation

Litigants and their counsel frequently engage in informal settlement discussions. Often this occurs before the filing of any lawsuit. After one party feels aggrieved by another, they frequently will make demand on the other for their losses. One manufacturing business discovering gears it purchased were not exactly to specifications may ask its supplier to take them back. When the supplier refuses, the purchaser may purchase substitute gears from another supplier and then demand the original seller pay for their extra costs. This may lead to some other offer being made, or not. Or imagine a child left unsupervised at a private day-care facility falls off the monkey bars and breaks her arm. The parents of the child may make demand for the day-care to pay for the medical bills. If the aggrieved party cannot be made to feel whole by whatever offers are made by the target, a lawsuit may be filed. In many consumer scenarios, the consumer may complain to a seller about some perceived injustice but may never actually bother to file a lawsuit. The fact is that despite what is portrayed in the popular media, a good many potential legal claims are never actually filed in court. Those that are filed have often been preceded by some form of informal private negotiation that failed to result in a satisfactory agreement.

After the filing of a lawsuit, parties and their counsel commonly engage in some form of informal settlement talks at some point, or many points, during the pretrial process. As mentioned earlier, under the modern rules of civil procedure, it is virtually unthinkable that a case will go to trial without some settlement discussions taking place. Some advocates, often inexperienced, are afraid to be the first to broach the issue of settlement with their adversary for fear of being perceived as weak. Such an attitude is normally unnecessary because initiating settlement discussions only reflects the reality that such negotiations are certain to take place sooner or later anyway. These discussions can actually be initiated even prior to any attempt at formal claim evaluation. Defense counsel, for example, might have a phone call like the following very early in the life of a new case:

Defense counsel: Hello Linda? This is Mike Fox over at Fox and Pickens. I was hired by Acme Gears to answer this case you just filed. I just wanted to introduce myself and let you know I was mailing you our answer today.

Plaintiff counsel: Thanks Mike, I appreciate you calling. I look forward to working with you on this matter.

Defense counsel: Listen, I'm just getting into this matter. Can you give me some idea what you guys are looking for in this case? Is there any chance to short-circuit this lawsuit?

Plaintiff counsel: Hmm. Maybe. Let's have lunch and talk.

These informal conversations might plant the seed that will result in productive settlement talks. Or they might lead to realization that the parties are very far apart in their views of the case merits. This is not bad necessarily. It just means the parties will need to engage in further pretrial litigation before they might be in a position to reevaluate their positions. Often where the parties' view of the case is far apart, it is because the parties each possess different factual information pertaining to the claims. In this way, the process of pleadings and, more importantly, discovery can go a long way toward assisting the litigants in coming up with claim evaluations that are much closer together. The provisions in Rule 16 concerning promoting early dialogue of settlement possibilities reflects the fact that early conversation about this topic, at least at the basic level, can rarely hurt and cause frequently result in an accelerated case resolution with much lower costs for the litigants and the courts.

Where and how should these informal settlement discussions take place? There is, honestly, no right answer. You should find freedom to be creative. Our example of an early dialogue, above, began with a short telephone conversation that opened the door to further discussion and scheduled a face to face meeting between counsel only. These discussions between only the lawyers can be useful because the lawyers can talk without posturing for the benefit of their clients. But sometimes clients will want to be involved directly at any stage of settlement talks. As the advocate, you should encourage your client to use any such time to be productive and not destructive. The parties have already demonstrated an inability, after all, to resolve their dispute without resort to litigation. The last thing the advocate should want to happen is for a settlement discussion to drive the parties further apart through inflamed emotions or an enlargement of the scope of their dispute. One thing you must be careful about in private negotiations, when clients are not involved directly, is that you are vigilant about keeping your client well informed of any offers or demands and that your client consent to any offer before you make it. Excluding the client from having input during these negotiations can result in not only an extremely dissatisfied client but one who may accurately feel that her counsel has acted unethically.[4]

mediation

---

[4] Ethics Rule 1.4 ("Communication) states in subpart (a) that a "lawyer shall (1) promptly inform the client of any decision or circumstance with respect to which the client's informed consent . . . is required by these Rules; (2) reasonably consult with the client about the means by which the client's objectives are to be accomplished; (3) keep the client reasonably informed about the status of the matter . . . ." Subpart (b) also provides that a "lawyer shall explain a matter to the extent reasonably necessary to permit the client to make informed decisions regarding the representation."

Mediation is the semi-formal process of having focused settlement discussions utilizing the assistance of a neutral mediator as a kind of referee to lead and facilitate the discussion. Some non-lawyers confuse mediation and arbitration. Some differences between the two are illustrated below:

	Mediation	Arbitration
Third-party involved?	Utilizes a mediator as a neutral facilitator only. Mediator makes no decisions or findings.	Utilizes one or more arbitrators to play both judge and jury in issuing a decision.
Binding?	Nothing about mediation is binding unless a formal settlement is reached.	Usually is a binding process that results in a final decision that can be enforced, if necessary, by court order.
Discovery available?	There is no formal discovery process involved with the mediation itself. There is only an informal exchange of information.	Arbitration procedures typically involve some procedures for limited formal discovery, similar to under the civil procedure rules.
Court involved?	Mediation can be court-ordered or done at the initiation of the parties alone. It can also occur before, during or after a lawsuit.	Arbitration itself is done independent of the courts. It is viewed as a substitute for traditional litigation. Courts are usually only involved in either ordering enforcement of a prior agreement to arbitrate or enforcement of the final decision of the arbitration panel.

Expense involved?	Most mediations are either a half or full day and the mediators either charge a flat rate or by the hour. The rate frequently is dictated by the amount in controversy or by the judge selecting the mediator. Usually the cost to mediate is fairly nominal compared to the amount in controversy.	Arbitration is designed to be cheaper than formal litigation but many advocates believe it can be just as expensive. Not only does the client need to pay their counsel, but must pay the arbitrators also. Arbitrations can last from a day to many weeks.

As you can deduce from this comparative chart, arbitration is really not a settlement device at all but rather is a form of alternative dispute resolution. It still involves an adjudication of a dispute in a form that takes the resolution out of the parties' hands and instead permits another to impose a result–more similar to traditional litigation than any settlement process. Arbitration as an alternative to the pretrial process described in this text is beyond the scope of our discussion. There are separate courses in law school devoted exclusively to study of the particulars of arbitration.

Mediation, however, is one of the must utilized forms of settlement process throughout the United States today. Many courts expect the litigants to engage in formal mediation at some point prior to trial; often judges will enter orders referring the case to a mediator for mediation to occur by a certain date. And the parties need not wait for a court order. The parties are free to phone a local mediator and schedule their own private mediation session at any time. Or one party can request that the court order mediation. Judges can either select the mediator (usually subject to objection by either party) or advise the litigants to agree on a mediator if possible. *Does it matter who the mediator is?* Yes but perhaps not for the reason you're thinking. Because mediators

> **Two Preliminary Questions:**
>
> 1. **Who** should be your mediator?
>
> 2. **When** should your mediation occur?

have no significant authority over the parties–other than to report to the court whether the parties showed up and participated in mediation–issues of mediator bias are not as significant as you might have believed. At the extreme, mediator bias can be significant if it causes a party or advocate to refrain from frank communications with the mediator. In other words, if the mediator's presence hinders discussion instead of encouraging it, the parties need to find a new mediator. The choice of a mediator can still be significant though. Mediators can provide a valuable service if they encourage the sharing of information, if they can settle down overly emotional participants, and if they can spur creative suggestions for settlement. Some mediators become known for assisting in the settlement of certain types of lawsuits–such as medical malpractice mediators, or construction law mediators. In areas that can call for specialized knowledge or experience, it can save the litigants a lot of time and money to call upon the service of such a specialized mediator as no time is lost trying to educate the mediator on the industry or typical practices. Mediators can also be very helpful at spotting and leading discussion of issues that inevitably arise in certain types of cases. In this sense, choosing a mediator with specialized knowledge can be way for the parties' to obtain some independent assessment of their claim by a third party.

Other than the choice of mediators, the other significant decision concerning the mediation process is the *timing* of the mediation. Some districts have local rules that direct the parties to include in their early case management reports (following their initial 26(f) conference) the parties' positions on when mediation should be scheduled. This raises the issue of whether it is better to schedule mediation early on or later in the case near trial. The early mediation offers the chance to shave off the most cost by facilitating settlement prior to extensive formal discovery, motion practice and trial preparation. On the other hand, by scheduling the mediation later in the pretrial process the parties are almost always in a much better position to engage in knowledgeable claim evaluation. This is because they have had access to a formal sharing of information, listening to the testimony of witnesses and, often, gaining input from the judge on the application of the law to the case through the court's resolution of certain pretrial motions. Further, the closer the case is to trial the greater the incentive on both sets of litigants to settle. Because each case is different, there is no right answer as to the ideal timing for mediation. Sometimes parties are aware of the most significant facts from the inception of the case and the law if fairly clear. It may be that the only significant unknown is how a jury will react to the facts. Such a case might be ideal for a very early mediation. As an advocate, if you are ordered to mediate by a certain date and you are not sure that you and your client are ready, you should engage the mediator and opposing counsel in a discussion about this prior to simply showing up at the mediator's office for the mediation. After all, in most circumstances, everyone has some desire for the mediation to successfully result in a settlement. Litigants are normally thrilled to get a case over with and the mediator loves to report to the court that she has settled yet another case.

Prior to mediation, most mediators will send counsel a report to fill out providing summary information. It might look something like this one.

Confidential Mediation Report

Case name:_____   Mediation date:_____

Name of client and counsel: _____

Court and case no. _____   Date filed:_____

Who will be attending mediation?_____

1.   Describe the nature of the lawsuit, giving a brief summary of the claim and
     defenses:_____
     _____
     _____
     _____

2.   Describe the posture of the case in terms of significant motions heard and
     discovery that has been undertaken:_____
     _____
     _____
     _____

3.   Trial setting:_____

4.   What significant work remains to be done before trial? _____
     _____

5.   Describe any prior settlement discussions, including demands and offers that have
     been made:_____
     _____

6.   Is there anything else I should know before mediation?_____
     _____

These forms may simply be filled out longhand and faxed back to the mediator.
If you want to provide information not requested on the form, you should feel free
to send the mediator a letter. You can also attach a relevant pleading, motion,
deposition, key document or chronology. You just need to remember to keep the
materials very brief–most mediators in a typical case only desire limited
information in advance. If your mediation has special needs–the length, the
amount of time needed for preparation, or other problems you anticipate–you
should telephone the mediator. Remember, this is not a court proceeding so you
are not only permitted but you will be asked to engage in confidential
communications. While such private conversations with a judge would be
unethical, in a mediation setting they are what makes the process work.

Other than providing basic information to the mediator, what else should
you do in advance of the mediation? First, it is essential that you bring the
appropriate client representative to the mediation, not only to have an effective
mediation but to be in compliance with a court order requiring you to mediate.
If you represent an individual, this is a simple enough task. If you represent a

corporate entity, who should come for the corporation? The key is to bring a real decision-maker and not a straw man. You should try to bring the person for the corporation that you report to concerning the case. That person may not have unlimited settlement authority from the corporation–few do in a corporate setting–but if that is the person that would normally recommend a settlement then that is the correct person to have present. If there is a question about significant limitations on that representative's settlement authority, you should arrange for others in the corporate hierarchy to be available by phone during the mediation–get their cell phone number and tell them to be expecting a call. Mediations have been abruptly cancelled because a corporate party showed up without any real decision-maker–this can result in a mediator's report to the court that you have not fulfilled your court-order to participate in mediation. If, despite your best efforts, you are still concerned about having the appropriate person with you at mediation, you should phone the mediator in advanced to discuss the issue and try to reach an understanding that the mediator can live with.

Second, you also should spend some quality time analyzing the merits of the case and considering different possible settlement postures. It is helpful to have discussions with your client in advance about a starting offer, a settlement range, and possible creative settlement solutions you might suggest at the appropriate time in mediation.

> **Preparing for Mediation**
>
> **Report to Mediator**
> ⇓
> **Choose Client Representative**
> ⇓
> **Perform Case Evaluation and Consider Settlement Strategy**
> ⇓
> **Outline Opening Statement**

Third, beyond these administrative and analytical chores, you should spend some time planning your mediation opening statement.

Conducting the Mediation

Because the mediation process itself is not dictated by any rules, the parties and the mediator can select any format they desire. In most typical mediations, however, there are two fundamental aspects: (a) the opening statement and (b) the private caucuses. Both normally take place in either one of the lawyer's offices or, more likely, at the mediators' office.

opening statement

Almost all mediations begin with a joint gathering of the mediator (seated at the head of a conference table) and counsel and the parties sitting on opposite sides of the conference table. There is coffee and soft drinks and, if you are very careful at picking the right mediator, some other snacks available. This part of the process is designed to, literally and figuratively, begin the process of bringing the parties together. It begins with the mediator's comments and then opening statements by the advocates and (if they so desire) the litigants themselves. The mediator's comments include an explanation of the benefits of mediation, a statement concerning the mediator's own effectiveness at mediating[5], and questions to each participant as to their commitment to negotiating in good faith. This is then followed by each advocate, beginning with plaintiff's counsel, giving their opening statement.

The stated purpose of the opening statement is to inform the mediator on what the case is about. However, if this is what was really going on you would not need to do this gathered together; each side could simply talk to the mediator about the case details in advance. The more important purpose behind the opening statement is to let each side, particularly the clients, hear the other advocate describe the strengths of their own case. Opening statements can last from a few minutes to an hour in length–typical opening statement are in the range of ten to fifteen minutes per side. Your goal in giving the opening statement should be to send a message to your opponent that you know your case well (both facts and law), that you are prepared to take the case to trial if necessary, and that you have confidence in your ability to prevail at some level (even if liability is undisputed you might be successful at getting the jury to reject some of the claimant's damages)–all of this is designed to inject doubts in the mind of your opponent and give them incentive to settle through compromise. Some opening statements are so effective that they might cause the opponent to reconsider their original estimates of a reasonable settlement range. If nothing else, an opening statement might give your opponent incentive to at least consider settling for a sum near the limit of their original settlement range.

Topics you might consider including in your opening statement would be:

- Information about your client that, upon hearing, might make a jury sympathetic (plaintiff or defendant);

- A sketch of the background facts, from your client's perspective, often told in the form of a narrative story;

- A recapitulation of the claims or defenses that are really important to the case (the main claims/defenses);

---

[5]Mediators often state in these sessions to be successful at some high rate in helping the parties settle ("more than 90% of the cases I've mediated settle"). Of course, with only 3% of civil cases going to trial anyway, the implications of these mediator statements seem a bit questionable. However, there is no doubt that mediation is an enormously useful tool.

- A summary of the damages incurred and description of some of the proof of those damages, including whether certain components are uncontested;

- Description of your side's case theme (this may be stated or, better, should be woven throughout your statement);

- Your views on some of the weaknesses in your opponent's allegations; and

- Summary of the strengths of your position.

Often counsel conclude their opening statements by advising their opponent that, despite their confidence in their own position, they are at mediation in a good faith desire to settle their differences. This reflects the reality that the opening statements are not being made to convince a judge/jury to impose a verdict but rather to show the other side that if no settlement is reached, it is at least possible that a judge or jury might reject their position. In this regard, the more organized and persuasive your presentation, the more you send the message that you are prepared to take the case to trial if need be and that there is at least a chance the jury will find something about your case appealing. These are both frightening prospects to your opponent. Fear is good.

You should feel free to include whatever you like in your opening statement so long as you remember the purpose behind this aspect of mediation–to drive the parties together and not apart. Opening statements that include emotional outbursts, yelling, and derogatory comments about your opponent are always bad and make the mediator's job of settling a case much more difficult. One of the best opening statements one of your authors ever witnessed was in a case involving a young married man who was paralyzed in a snow skiing accident and sued the ski resort. The defense advocate's opening statement ignored all of the facts in the case. Instead, he advised the plaintiff (and his young wife) that he could empathize with their plight because the advocate's own son had been paralyzed in an accident years earlier. The advocate stated that, regardless of the outcome of the lawsuit, one day both the plaintiff and the advocate's son would get up out of their wheelchairs and walk again due to anticipated medical advances. There was not a single dry eye in that conference room as this dream was shared. The advocate had said nothing about the facts or injecting any doubt into his opponent. But he had miraculously–and sincerely–pulled the parties together by demonstrating that as people they had much in common. That case settled that day because barriers of emotion that had made prior settlement discussions impossible had been broken down through a very creative opening statement. This will not work in every case, but it illustrates that you can be as creative as you would like in trying to bridge the parties' impasse.

Because of the relative informality of the process, both sides may go back and forth making additional comments. Frequently, the mediator may ask follow up questions of counsel. Counsel should feel free to respond to any question by telling the mediator that they would rather save an answer for the private caucus to follow. If there is sensitive information being requested or if you believe that your answer would drive the parties apart, this is the appropriate response to make.

Another important point of deliberation for you prior to the mediation will be deciding whether your client should plan to speak during the opening statement. This is something you need to discuss with your client in advance because the mediator will always ask your client if they would like to do so. Many advocates tell their client to politely decline and for good reason. Clients frequently forget the purpose behind the opening session and may start to point their finger at "the bad guy" and get emotional. Much good will is lost when this occurs. If you think the client speaking directly to the opponent will help in some way, you should discuss with your client what the client should say (and not say) and how they should say it. Encourage your client to practice doing this in front of you before the mediation. Even if the client does speak, the comments should usually be very brief. Sometimes, for example, in a medical malpractice case the doctor will say during the opening session that "even though I do not believe that there was anything wrong with my treatment of you [looking at the plaintiff], I am very sorry about your outcome and what you have been going through and I wish you all the best."

Finally, there are those rare lawsuits where the opening session ought to be abandoned. In some cases the parties have such a history of hostility that there is too much downside to getting them in the same room together. Or the mediation might be the second, or third, negotiating session in the life of that lawsuit. Feel fee when it is appropriate to suggest, in advance, to the mediator that the opening session be eliminated. If both sides agree, this will not be a problem and can reflect wise lawyering.

private caucus

While the opening session may take up to an hour, the rest of the day spent mediating will likely be spent in the private caucuses–this is where the real negotiating begins. After the opening statements, the mediator splits the parties into two (or more if multiple parties with differing interests are involved) groups placed into different conference rooms. The mediator, usually beginning with the plaintiff, will shuffle back and forth between rooms spending time talking to each side and taking settlements offers and demands back and forth. Let's discuss what you should be prepared to take place in these caucus sessions and how to advocate for your client effectively behind closed doors.

When the mediator comes to your conference room for the caucus, she is trying to accomplish several things. First, she is trying to talk to you in private to obtain more of your candid thoughts on the real strengths and weaknesses of your case and your opponent's case. The mediator is not doing this for her own edification; she is trying to use this information to start identifying weaknesses in both sides' positions in order to make all the parties negotiate. In fact, many mediators will simply ask "what is the weakest part of your case?" At this point you have two options: (a) deny all weakness; or (b) be somewhat honest. The problem with option (a) is that you will have no credibility with the mediator and you will start to come across as the unreasonable negotiator. This is not good. Mediators do not spend equal time in both rooms throughout the day. The first caucus or two may be of roughly equivalent length–after that the mediator will spend the most time with the party who the mediator believes is holding up the settlement through stubborn refusal to see the case objectively. Every case has some weak point–not necessarily anything fatal to the claim/defense–just one of those facts that if the advocate could write all of the background on the case, she would change. Maybe the primary weakness in the plaintiff's case is just that the defendant has limited resources to easily pay a large judgment. Yet this is something that needs to be considered at mediation–after all, getting 70 cents on the dollar today is better than a larger paper judgment a year later that may not be fully collectible. Maybe it's that one DWI conviction of the client. Maybe it's that the state supreme court has recently called into doubt the application of a fraud cause of action for a breach of contract scenario.

To be an effective advocate, you should be willing to acknowledge in the private caucus some weakness in your case. Then what? This is where the mediator's second goal from the caucus comes into play. You should begin to point out the many weaknesses in your opponent's case. Here is where you turn your credibility into an asset–begin to point out the biggest problems with your opponent's case and, for each, be prepared to show the mediator the damaging deposition admission or the smoking gun, or the recent appellate decision throwing your opponent's position into question. Have a copy of each of these helpful items so that you can give the material to the mediator to go put in front of your opponent. Help the mediator do her job by giving her the ammunition needed to inject doubts on the part of your opponents in the next conference room.

> **"Demand"**–the amount the claimant requests to be paid in consideration for settling (releasing) her claims.
>
> **"Offer"**–the amount the defendant offers to pay to obtain a full release from the claimant.

The other primary goal of the mediator is to be a catalyst for meaningful negotiations. Many mediators will try to get a feel for the settlement range that each litigant has in mind for the case. Having this information, when you think about it, would make the mediator's job much easier. She would just need to determine if there was any overlap and then suggest this common ground as the basis for a settlement. Why not just share your thoughts on "how far you're willing to go" up or down? Because once the mediator has this information, you have just given up any chance to settle for any better sum. If your top dollar you're willing to pay is $110,000 and you share this, this will suddenly become the starting point in your discussions with the mediator. Most good advocates are careful not to share what their "top" or "bottom" dollar number really is. Yet mediators can still develop a sense of how far you are willing to go to settle the case, and this is okay. When the mediator can at least get a sense for this, she can be more effective in seeing which side might need to show greater flexibility and then begin to focus her efforts on that party.

You should discuss with your client before the mediation what your starting offer or demand should be. As a practical point, the plaintiff's opening demand is typically a figure that is actually higher than the top figure in her reasonable settlement range assessment. And the defendant's opening offer is often less than the bottom of the defendant's reasonable settlement range. Using our prior example, the plaintiff might start with a demand of $175,000 while the defendant might open with an offer of only $25,000. Each side figures that by starting at that point, they maintain maximum flexibility to show good faith "movement" during negotiations without ending up too far above/below their ultimate goal. Some parties take this to a ridiculous extreme–the plaintiff demanding millions (in effect, a grand slam) and the defendant offering nothing (in effect, a surrender). Mediators hate it when litigants begin mediation at such extremes and they will definitely try to talk you out of such a position rather than actually convey it as a serious offer/demand to your opponent. The problem with an extreme opening demand/offer is that it tells the other side that you're not serious about compromising to avoid a trial. If that is true, there is no point in your adversary compromising either and the mediation is effectively dead on arrival. You have just wasted everyone's time. There is nothing to be gained from this "tactic" and you have lost an opportunity to obtain a rational and reasonable result for your client.

On the other hand, you might consider a significant show of good faith by starting at a fairly reasonable place–perhaps the plaintiff in our example demanding $160,000 to start and the defendant offering $60,000. These would constitute serious initial opening bids and would surely cause any mediator to smile. The only downside to this approach is that if you start with a serious number and your opponent does not, you may end up feeling like you are bidding against yourself. This is a particularly appropriate feeling when your opponent comes up $1,000 in its offer for every $20,000 reduction you make on your demand. If you sense this is beginning to happen during the mediation, you need to let the mediator know that you will not continue to negotiate on this basis and that you are "nearing your best offer." You could even tell the mediator that you will refuse to make another offer/demand until your opponent shows some good faith with their next offer/demand. This can be a legitimate position to take.

There are some things that advocates and their clients should simply avoid doing at mediation if they are sincere in their desire to reach a settlement. The following chart offers these summary observations.

Things to Avoid at Mediation

- **Winning a Debate**: You goal is not to "win" at mediation by convincing the mediator that you are right. This is not a trial. And your opponent is not going to just cave in the face of your brilliance. You should aim instead to demonstrate a grounded confidence and to inject doubt in your opponent regarding their own case.

- **Getting Personal**: Personal attacks, hyperbole, heated arguments are things that drive further the wedge between the parties.

- **Holding Back**: To posture your case for the best settlement you need to be willing to play some of your cards at mediation; if you have a great argument or smoking gun you need to consider showing this card. Holding back all of your best ammunition will make trial a certainty.

- **Lying vs. Puffing:** Opinions about the strength of your case are expected and fine. Lying about underlying facts will cause you to either lose credibility or may give rise to a later claim of fraudulent inducement to declare the settlement agreement invalid.

- **Being Unprepared:** You and your client can be unprepared in a number of ways: emotionally, procedurally, factually. All are roadblocks.

The mediation may or may not result in a settlement. If it does not, do not despair too much. Many cases settle after the mediation. The mediation may simply turn out to be the first step in the negotiation process. Keep the lines of communication open with your opponent following the unsuccessful mediation, continue to involve the mediator if it helps, and try to figure out what else you can do during the pretrial stage of the case to bridge the gap between you and your opponent. Perhaps you need to file a partial summary judgment attacking some weakness in your opponent's case or establishing some claim/defense in your own. Maybe you need to designate your star expert witness who you hope will really impress your opponent. Consider your strengths and your opponent's weaknesses and try to see if you highlight these facets of the case to convince your opponent to be more flexible.

Or maybe the problem is you or your client's inflexibility or unrealistic assessment for likely case outcomes. Talk the case over with your colleagues and see if you are being too intransigent. Sometimes it is difficult for the advocate to pause in their advocacy long enough to soberly and objectively reflect on the case and to provide sound counseling to the client. It is so much easier to be a cheerleader than to tell a client that the case is not as good as you had originally thought. But you are a professional and your client deserves not only the best advocacy but also the best counseling. The lawyer also acts as a sort of peacemaker at mediation trying to act in a way that promotes the peaceful resolution of the parties' dispute. Being a good advocate requires a balancing of these hats worn by the lawyer at mediation.

"Doctors . . . still retain a high degree of public confidence because they are perceived as healers. Should lawyers not be healers? Healers, not warriors? Healers, not procurers? Healers, not hired guns?

Warren E. Burger,
Chief Justice, US Supreme Court

If your case settles, either at mediation or during private negotiation, you will need to document the settlement. Not only does a well documented settlement help to ensure its enforcement and diminish later disputes, but many jurisdictions require the settlement of a civil claim to be reduced to writing. For these reasons, mediators will also expect some written memorial of the basic terms of the settlement signed off by the parties and counsel prior to releasing everyone from the mediation session. Such memorial will almost always provide that a more formal and complete settlement agreement will be drafted. Yet the mediation settlement sheet should contain all of the essential terms of the agreement reached in order that the settlement achieved on that day is not put in jeopardy by subsequent disagreements over details proposed in the formal documentation.[6] Let's turn our attention now to the essential terms that should be considered in any settlement.

---

[6]Courts have enforced settlements pursuant to the terms of summary written agreements prepared at mediation. *See e.g., Butler v. Butler*, 622 So.2d 73 (Fla. 2nd DCA 1993).

D.   *SETTLEMENT AGREEMENTS*

A good settlement agreement provides an enforceable mechanism to accurately document the parties' settlement, covers essential topics to avoid unnecessary future disputes and builds in appropriate protections for each advocate's client.   Once the parties have reached a basic understanding of the terms of the settlement, it is time for the careful advocate to begin documenting the settlement.   Settlement agreements are governed by general principles of contract law, which may vary somewhat from jurisdiction to jurisdiction.   You need to be generally familiar with applicable law in your jurisdiction to help you spot any potential problems with a proposed settlement agreement.   There are, however, some general principles and common issues that arise in documenting settlements regardless of your jurisdiction.   Let's review some of these by reference to particular key components of settlement agreements.

Key Provisions

Identification of the Parties

The agreement must accurately and comprehensively identify in its terms the parties intended to be protected and bound by the agreement.   The starting point is with the parties to the lawsuit.   This seems easy enough.   But in many cases there are other individuals and entities that might need to be swept into the coverage offered by the document.   Are there affiliated companies that could have also been conceivably made parties to the lawsuit?   What about the individual employees and officers of the corporate defendant?   Insurers?   If the personal injury plaintiff was a mother and wife, are the possible lost consortium claims of her husband and children also being covered by this agreement, even though never asserted in the Litigation?   If you are the defendant buying your peace, you had better be sure you get what you bargained for.   In drafting the agreement, you should consider be as expansive as possible under the circumstances.

Release–Scope of Claims

What claims exactly are being released?   Will it be only those claims identified so far in the litigation? Any and all claims that the plaintiff might presently have against the defendant? All future claims against the defendant? Are the counterclaims being released as well? Even permissive counterclaims not yet identified?   Are the claimant's claims for attorney's fees also being resolved by the settlement? These are all proper subjects for negotiations–hopefully at the mediation but certainly before finalization in an executed contract. The language of the release can be relatively straightforward yet comprehensive, as with the following example:

RELEASE

The RELEASING PARTIES hereby release the RELEASED PARTIES from any claims or causes of action, whether in tort, contract, or arising under any other substantive law, whether or not existing or known now or which may arise in the future, in any way arising out of or related to the accident that was the subject of the above-referenced lawsuit, including all claims asserted in the Litigation and any other claims that could have been asserted in the Litigation.

Consideration

Exactly what sum is being paid? By whom? To whom? In what form? When? Is the defendant also agreeing to pay the plaintiff's court costs or attorney's fees? If so, is there a sum certain that can be put in the agreement sufficient to cover these amounts? Will there be any future payments? Are there are forms of consideration that are not monetary–maybe an agreement to place a certain document in a former employee's personnel file? An agreement to continue to do business for some length of time? An agreement to return certain confidential records taken by a former employee?

Confidentiality

As a matter of private contract, many settlement agreements are permitted by the law to remain confidential. Of course, both sides may not share the concern for maintaining confidentiality. If you desire the terms to be kept secret, you had better negotiate for such a clause in the agreement.

Indemnification

Are there any possible lien-holders who might own a stake in the lawsuit's outcome? Has the plaintiff ever assigned any portion of the claims to another person or entity? Perhaps the plaintiff has represented that there are no lien-holders or assignees. This representation is helpful, but will the plaintiff stand behind a possible error in this regard? You should consider obtaining a written indemnification from the plaintiff to your client to cover such possibilities.

Entirety of Agreement

The agreement should specify that all terms of the settlement have been included within the body of the settlement agreement and that there have been no oral promises or representations other than what is reflected by the written agreement. It should also say that any modifications to the agreement must be in writing to be enforceable.

Arbitration clause

If there is any dispute about the interpretation or enforcement of the settlement agreement, do the parties desire for those to be resolved in one particular court (maybe the original forum) or would they rather engage in some form of arbitration?

Agreed Judgment or Dismissal

Because there is often already a lawsuit filed when the settlement occurs, something must be done about it. The settlement agreement is not self-effectuating. Therefore, the agreement should specify how the lawsuit will be concluded. Typically it is either dismissed by the plaintiff's own motion or else an agreed judgment is submitted to the court for entry. The judgment might incorporate the terms of the settlement. Usually, however, the agreed judgment is for a "take nothing" judgment against the defendant "with all costs taxed against the party incurring same"–or words to that effect. The only advantage that the agreed judgment offers is some *res judicata* additional protection for the defendant. These principles state that all of the claims that arose out of the same transaction or occurrence complained of by plaintiff in the lawsuit are precluded from ever being reasserted against defendant as a result of the entry of a final judgment in their dispute. Of course, the settlement agreement's release offers this same type of protection. It is an example of "belts and suspenders" duplication–but if a defendant pays a lot of money to settle a case, there is certainly no harm in getting both the contractual (the release) and legal (claim preclusion or *res judicata*) protections. As an agreed disposition of the case termination, the court could not care less what the parties put into the agreed order so long as it results in the case being removed from the court's docket. The order of dismissal or entry of final judgment need not be a lengthy document. It might look like one of the two following examples:

DISMISSAL

IN THE UNITED STATES DISTRICT COURT
FOR THE MIDDLE DISTRICT OF FLORIDA
TAMPA DIVISION

Susan Robinson, et al. §
§
vs. § Case No. A-07-CA-855-JMU
§
Paulson Breweries, et al. §

ORDER OF DISMISSAL

Plaintiffs having appeared before this court, announcing a settlement with Defendants, and requesting that their claims raised in this cause be dismissed with prejudice;

NOW, THEREFORE, it is the ORDER of this Court that all of Plaintiffs' claims in this cause against Defendants should be, and hereby are, DISMISSED WITH PREJUDICE. Costs of court are taxed against the parties incurring same.

Dated this _____ day of _____, 20__.

_____
Presiding Judge

JUDGMENT

IN THE UNITED STATES DISTRICT COURT
FOR THE MIDDLE DISTRICT OF FLORIDA
TAMPA DIVISION

Susan Robinson, et al. §
§
vs. § Case No. A-07-CA-855-JMU
§
Paulson Breweries, et al. §

AGREED FINAL JUDGMENT

Plaintiffs and Defendants appeared and announced that they had settled all claims in this cause. For these reasons, the Court hereby enters JUDGMENT that Plaintiffs take nothing on their claims against Defendants. Further, the court ORDERS that costs of court are taxed against the parties incurring same.

SIGNED this _____ day of _____, 20__.

_____
PRESIDING JUDGE

E. RULES MATRIX

This table serves as a starting point for additional inquiry into the potential professional responsibility and civil procedure issues that are implicated when drafting and filing pleadings.

Issues Arising During Motions	Applicable Ethical Rule, Federal Rule of Civil Procedure or Local Rule
Requirement to discuss possibilities for settlement during initial and final pretrial conferences.	**FRCP 16(a), 16(c)(9)**
Requirement for counsel to discuss the possibility for prompt settlement during mandatory discovery conference.	**FRCP 26(f)**
Advocate's obligation to keep client informed of settlement discussions.	**Ethical Rule 1.4**

Table 1 - Potential Rules Applicable to Settlements

Points To Ponder . . .

1. Taking into account various factors such as litigation expenses, the value of information derived from discovery, and settlement leverage issues, is there a preferred time during the pretrial life of a case to initiate settlement discussions? Does this answer depend at all upon the relative strength of the claims or defenses?

2. What is the greatest value of the mediation procedure over private informal settlement discussions?

3. Given the different roles that an advocate wears during a mediation, how does the advocate decide the right balance to strike between zealous advocacy and client counseling? How does the advocate know where the line is between advocacy and the need to offer sobering counseling to a client?

4. Does the system put too much pressure on litigants to settle? Is something of value lost when litigants settle almost all of their civil disputes and few go to trial?

CHAPTER ELEVEN
TRIAL PREPARATION

"To-morrow, and to-morrow, and to-morrow,
Creeps in this petty pace from day to day,
To the last syllable of recorded time;
And all our yesterdays have lighted fools
The way to dusty death. Out, out, brief candle!
Life's but a walking shadow; a poor player,
That struts and frets his hour upon the stage,
And then is heard no more: it is a tale
Told by an idiot, full of sound and fury,
Signifying nothing. "[1]

A.   FINAL STAGES OF PRETRIAL

How did it come to this? It seems so long ago that you sat down to have your initial client interview. Looking back, it's easy to forget the nervousness you felt when you anticipated meeting your first client. By now, you have talked to that client many times, including conferences at the office and over the telephone–you almost feel like you're related to her. You have stood by the client during her deposition making as many objections as you could spot, you attended your first mediation with her and made a pretty good opening statement (according to the mediator), and you avoided the grant of defendant's motion for summary judgment just a few weeks ago. Despite several recent follow-up conversations with defendant's counsel about settlement, defendant appears unwilling to offer your client more than "nuisance value"–what they call the amount they anticipate spending to defend the case at trial. Unless defendant offers quite a bit more soon, this case appears destined for trial next month. Didn't all of your law school professors tell you that "nobody" actually goes to trial anymore? Didn't you just read something about that thirty or so pages ago? What went wrong?

---

[1] WILLIAM SHAKESPEARE, MACBETH, act 5, sc. 5.

Even though a relatively small percentage of cases go to trial, given the hundreds of thousands of new lawsuits filed every year, that still leaves quite a few that do survive the pretrial process to see the inside of a courtroom. The case may have enough merit to avoid dismissal or summary judgment. Though the parties have discussed settlement, they may just have different enough views on the likely outcome and not quite enough incentive to settle to make a compromise feasible. It is time to quit dreaming of a settlement and face the reality that trial may very well be in your future. You have thirty days until the jury panel strolls into the courtroom for voire dire–jury selection. What can you do during these few remaining weeks of pretrial to maximize your chances of winning at trial? What mandatory steps are you still required to take to avoid getting into trouble with the court? Can you spend this time productively instead of suffering generalized anxiety disorder? Let's take it one step at a time.

The last month before trial can be a busy time for the pretrial advocate. There is no calm before the storm–in many cases it seems some of the most intense work takes place just before you begin the trial. Many an experienced trial lawyer has recognized that much of the stress associated with trials occurs shortly before the trial begins. Lawyers worry about the many exercises of judgment required of them–on issues where there is no right and wrong rule to guide your decision. Do I like my trial theme? What order should I call my witnesses? Lawyers also worry about the many "what if" questions that they anticipate may pop up during trial. What if opposing counsel objects to my cross-examination of the defendant about his prior drug conviction? What if the judge is not inclined to permit my use of this demonstrative exhibit that I spent three hundred dollars having prepared? What if the other side objects to portions of my opening statement as too argumentative? What if I don't have all the witnesses I need to authenticate the documents I intend to introduce at trial? What if my expert witness' vacation prevents him from testifying live? Lawyers also worry during this time about contentious matters that will arise during trial that they cannot even imagine at the moment. Will I be able to react to the unanticipated yet important issue that may spring to life during the middle of trial? These generalized worries about the unknown issue are probably well founded–even the best prepared advocate cannot anticipate every wrinkle that will arise during a trial. With all of these concerns and emotions swirling inside the advocate's head in the days and weeks leading up to trial, it is *almost* a bit of a relief when the judge finally calls the jury panel into the courtroom. In that surreal moment as the potential jurors march single file into the courtroom and look at you for the first time, the realization sinks in that *you are the lawyer*. Really. But we're getting ahead of ourselves.

During this last pretrial period, there are some things you are required to do and other things you should be doing. Rather than simply sit around daydreaming about your opening statement, you should (a) refine your case analysis for trial; (b) double-check on your sources of evidence to avoid surprises;

(c) make your final pretrial disclosures and prepare your joint pretrial statement; and (d) prepare for and participate in the final pretrial conference with the judge. You have worked so hard during the earlier pretrial stages–pleadings, discovery and motions–yet many cases are won and lost during this last month before trial.

Final case analysis

Earlier in this text, we outlined a methodology for your analysis of the case you were just undertaking. As we continued our journey through pleadings, discovery, motions and settlement conferences, we revisited the topic of case analysis frequently. From these many references, you many have realized that case analysis is an on-going process that is never done until the file is closed. Your case analysis evolves in response to (a) changes in the pleadings, (b) your discovery of additional facts derived from both the formal and the informal discovery techniques, (c) actions taken on the case by the presiding judge, and (d) other changes in the case dynamics such as settlements reached between the plaintiff and some of your former co-defendants. During the last pretrial stage, some of your most critical case analysis must occur in order for you to be equipped to present a case at trial that is compelling, cohesive, complete yet not cumbersome.

Litigation files can become cluttered with ideas, miscellaneous facts, additional causes of action or affirmative defenses. Every little idea that pops into counsel's mind during a deposition might begin to take on some life of its own. No outrageous idea is completely discarded during pretrial for fear that it might make the difference between winning and losing at trial. So here is the problem. If you coast into trial aboard this bloated notion of a case, the jury will not be able to understand or appreciate the beauty hidden beneath that clutter. Your final pretrial case analysis, therefore, is the critical time to throw overboard that clutter. Go ahead and dispense with the weak or inconsistent theories, themes and pleadings. It is time to decide which documents are really going to be useful and to commit to those witnesses that really advance the ball. Some duplication of proof can be helpful–some advocate for at least two sources for every important fact you must prove at trial. But the number of sources of proof for each point has its limit–either the judge will begin to limit your redundant witnesses or, after the verdict, you will wish that she had.

> *Advocates must struggle against the clutter that is attracted to their case files and case analysis.*

There was an excellent commentary on the importance of this final pretrial analysis offered by James W. McElhaney a few years ago. He observed how case files become bloated and then offered some tips on eliminating these distractions:

> In part it's the paradox of preparation. Thoughtful, careful lawyers are good at spotting little bits and pieces of law and evidence that might theoretically help the case one way or another. So, they figure out what documents and witnesses they need to nail these things down and then toss them into the legal sausage grinder they call their theory of the case whether they belong there or not.
>
> *   *   *
>
> It takes serious self-discipline to cull out the clutter from a case because the things you have to cut off and pull out are your own ideas–and people like their own ideas.
>
> *   *   *
>
> Most trials are crammed with far too many names, dates, times and places that   really aren't important.   Oh, there are times when precision is essential.   But most of the time, just the month and approximate date are all you need to orient the judge and jury unless the date and time are actually in dispute.[2]

This does not mean that you remove the flesh from your case and go to trial with a bare-bones presentation. But it does mean that you think carefully about having one case theme instead of several. It suggests that you consider dropping causes of action, or affirmative defenses, that are not only redundant, but confusing and of questionable application. And for each witness or document you are thinking about using at trial, you should immediately be able to answer the question–"why am I offering this into evidence and how exactly does it fit in with my case?" Removing clutter from your case allows you to focus upon polishing the really important components instead. It ensures that the jury can appreciate the points you are trying to establish and not get lost or bored. It also requires you to stop being intellectually lazy and refine your own focus[3].

Checking on evidence

You do not want to find out the night before trial that your exhibits are

---

[2] James W. McElhaney, *Diagnosis Clutter: You'll Make Your Case Stronger by Cutting Out What's Unnecessary,* ABA Journal (December 2003).

[3] For a more extensive discussion of trials and case analysis, see the companion text by Charles H. Rose, III entitled *Fundamental Trial Advocacy* (West 2006).

not in order or that you can't reach one of your important witnesses to do some final practice examination. During the last few weeks before trial, you should take care of these administrative matters–you'll be surprised how some of these seemingly minor details can consume your attention and mental capacity when you should instead be focused on more important matters like polishing your opening statement. You might consider incorporating into your final preparation a check-list, which should include some of the following matters:

Trial Preparation Check-List

Evidence

_____ Finalize "order of proof" outline for trial
_____ Select witnesses for trial
_____ Contact each witness and schedule meeting to go over testimony
_____ Prepare topic outline for each direct and cross-examination
_____ Select and mark trial exhibits
_____ Prepare folders for each witness with outline for examination and containing duplicate copies of each exhibit intended to be used with witness
_____ Finalize demonstrative aids–blow-up copies of important documents, chronologies, photographs, etc.
_____ If using video of depositions, have tapes edited

Discovery/Pleadings

_____ Be sure all discovery responses have been supplemented
_____ Be sure final pleadings accurately reflect claims/defenses intended to try
_____ Contact opposing counsel to coordinate assembly of joint pretrial statement
_____ Draft your portion of joint pretrial statement, including making final pretrial disclosures (witnesses, documents, etc)
_____ Prepare proposed jury instructions
_____ Prepare motion in limine
_____ Prepare trial brief, if requested by court or helpful

Miscellaneous

_____ Pull together final version of trial notebook
_____ Outline possible voire dire questions, opening statement, closing argument
_____ Outline possible directed verdict motion/response points
_____ Assemble equipment needed (video, computer, easels, writing tablets, etc)
_____ Select clothes for first day of trial (take to dry cleaners)
_____ Other?

Once you begin to put together this type of check-list, you will quickly appreciate how many details there are to be taken care of before you show up for court. Better to get started on this process as soon as it becomes evident that your case is not going to settle and that trial is imminent.

B.   *PRETRIAL DISCLOSURES & STATEMENT*

Before you can get to trial, you still have a few additional materials you must prepare and serve on opposing counsel and file with the court.

Pretrial disclosures

In our prior chapter on written discovery, we learned about two types of mandatory disclosures required by Rule 26(a)–the initial disclosures and the expert witness disclosures. Rule 26(a)(3) offers the final type of mandatory disclosures–the "pretrial disclosures." This rule requires a party to provide all other parties, and to file with the court, the following information "regarding the evidence that it may present at trial other than solely for impeachment":

(A)   the name, and if not previously provided, the address and telephone number of each witness, separately identifying those whom the party expects to present and those whom the party may call if the need arises;

(B)   the designation of those witnesses whose testimony is expected to be presented by means of a deposition and, if not taken stenographically, a transcript of the pertinent portions of the deposition testimony; and

(C)   an appropriate identification of each document or other exhibit, including summaries of other evidence, separately identifying those which the party expects to offer and those which the party may offer if the need arises.[4]

The same rule goes on to specify that, unless directed otherwise by the court, these pretrial disclosures must be made at least 30 days before trial. Once you are served with your opponent's disclosures, the rule requires you to serve and file a list of any objections you have to those witnesses, exhibits and depositions within fourteen days. Failure to object now can be fatal: "Objections not so disclosed, other than objections under Rules 402 and 403 of the Federal Rules of Evidence,

---

[4]Rule 26(a)(3)(A)-(C).

are waived unless excused by the court for good cause."[5]

Obviously these requirements for pretrial disclosure are designed to avoid trials by ambush. You had better not attempt to call a witness or use a document at trial that is not on your list of disclosures unless the matter utilized is "solely for impeachment." If in doubt, disclose the witness, depositions excerpt or document. You should also be sure that your prior formal written discovery responses have been fully supplemented, as required by Rule 26(e).

By local rules, many federal districts have subsumed this Rule 26(a)(3) requirement for pretrial disclosures into the filing of a joint pretrial statement prepared by counsel for all of the parties. The joint pretrial statement typically incorporates within it these pretrial disclosures, along with other information required of the parties. By appropriately filing the joint pretrial statement, the parties have satisfied their Rule 26(a)(3) duties.

Joint Pretrial Statement

Rule 16(d)-(e) authorizes trial judges to conduct a final pretrial conference and to issue a final pretrial order which "shall control the subsequent course of the action unless modified by subsequent order." In anticipation of this conference, local rules require litigants to prepare a joint pretrial statement. As an example of such requirement, consider our Local Rule 3.06(b)-(c) which prescribes a meeting of counsel to discuss certain topics and to jointly prepare a pretrial statement for filing with the court, as follows:

> (b) In any case in which a final pretrial conference is scheduled by the Court (or in any case in which the Court directs the preparation and filing of a pretrial statement in accordance with this rule, but without scheduling a pretrial conference), it shall be the responsibility of counsel for all parties to meet together no later than ten (10) days before the date of the final pretrial conference (or at such other time as the Court may direct) in a good faith effort to: (1) discuss the possibility of settlement; (2) stipulate to as many facts or issues as possible; (3) examine all exhibits and Rule 5.04 exhibit substitutes or documents and other items of tangible evidence to be offered by any party at trial; (4) exchange the names and addresses of all witnesses; and (5) prepare a pretrial statement in accordance with subsection (c) of this rule.
>
> (c) The pretrial statement shall be filed with the Court no later than three (3) days before the date of the final pretrial conference (or at

---

[5]*Id.*

such other time as the Court may direct), and shall contain: (1) the basis of federal jurisdiction; (2) a concise statement of the nature of the action; (3) a brief, general statement of each party's case; (4) a list of all exhibits and Rule 5.04 exhibit substitutes to be offered at trial with notation of all objections thereto; (5) a list of all witnesses who may be called at trial; (6) a list of all expert witnesses including, as to each such witness, a statement of the subject matter and a summary of the substance of his or her testimony; (7) in cases in which any party claims money damages, a statement of the elements of each such claim and the amount being sought with respect to each such element; (8) a list of all depositions to be offered in evidence at trial (as distinguished from possible use for impeachment), including a designation of the pages and lines to be offered from each deposition; (9) a concise statement of those facts which are admitted and will require no proof at trial, together with any reservations directed to such admissions; (10) a concise statement of applicable principles of law on which there is agreement; (11) a concise statement of those issues of fact which remain to be litigated (without incorporation by reference to prior pleadings and memoranda); (12) a concise statement of those issues of law which remain for determination by the Court (without incorporation by reference to prior pleadings or memoranda); (13) a concise statement of any disagreement as to the application of the Federal Rules of Evidence or the Federal Rules of Civil Procedure; (14) a list of all motions or other matters which require action by the Court; and (15) the signatures of counsel for all parties.

Judges take the requirements for the joint pretrial statement seriously, as so should you. Although the document is referred to as "joint" most of its contents are prepared separately by each litigant's counsel and then merged together into one document. For example, each advocate should prepare their own brief descriptions of the case and separately list their client's exhibits and witnesses. You should draft these portions of the statement carefully. For example, your brief description of the case will not only provide your presiding judge with good background context but many judges will simply read these excerpts to the jury panel at the commencement of jury selection to give them general case information as well. When this is done, your brief case description will be the very first thing the potential jurors hear about your case. Be succinct, clear and incorporate at least a glimpse of your case theme. Where counsel will need to spend some serious time conferring with their opponent is about possible stipulations of fact and identifying the disputed and undisputed issues of fact and law. These lists of disputed facts and law are critical, because they will guide the court in identifying the scope of the trial. They will also likely be incorporated into the final pretrial order–after this all evidentiary objections as to relevancy, for example, will be evaluated against this list of disputed issues. When challenged at trial, unless you can relate your offered evidence to some listed question of disputed fact, your opponent's relevancy objection is likely to be sustained.

Inexperienced advocates often have a difficult time distinguishing between issues of fact and law, and the difference between the two can appear hazy. Your guidepost should be to ask who the decision maker is supposed to be on the particular issue at trial—and resort to the applicable substantive law may be needed to help answer this inquiry. If, for example, the parties dispute whether an element of the plaintiff's cause of action is satisfied by the evidence, this will generally be considered a disputed issue of fact for the jury. If, on the other hand, the parties disagree about whether the law requires proof of something to recover on a claim, this will normally be considered an issue of law for the judge to resolve prior to or during trial. Finally, as you can see by comparing the foregoing example of a joint pretrial statement's contents with the Rule 26(a)(3) disclosures, the pretrial statement is much more extensive and certainly subsumes those final pretrial disclosure obligations entirely. Through compliance with this local rule, counsel will not have to separately worry about making their final pretrial disclosures. In the absence of a local rule mandating the filing of this a statement, however, counsel would still need to comply directly with Rule 26(a)(3). State courts often have similar requirements for pretrial disclosures and some type of pretrial statement, but counsel should check with their local rules in any case well in advance of their trial to ensure they fulfill any requirements.

Counsel need to be reasonable during their meeting to prepare the joint pretrial statement. It would be easy to refuse to make any stipulations, for example. However, as we will discuss in the next section, at the final pretrial conference the court may have some tough questions for counsel about why they are intending to require their opponent to prove what should be an undisputed point. Judges can become impatient with counsel who appear motivated solely by a desire to make their adversary's job unnecessarily difficult. Counsel also need to remember that compliance with their jurisdiction's requirements for preparing and filing pretrial materials is critical to their case–such compliance acts as a sort of ticket providing passage  to the courtroom for trial. Failure to take these requirements seriously can result in some pretty severe sanctions. One very recent example of an order entered against a lawyer who failed to abide by the court's requirements is set forth on the following page.

ORDER

On this date the Court, *sua sponte*, has reviewed this case which is set for trial on Monday, July 30, 2007.

As of this date, Defendant has in no way complied with the Court's scheduling Order concerning the filing of pre-trial documents and has apparently failed to communicate on numerous occasions. Accordingly, it is

ORDERED that upon the trial of this case, Defendant will not be allowed to make an opening statement or call any witnesses, including Defendant, either in person or by deposition, or offer any exhibits.

SIGNED on this 25th day of July, 2007.

_/s/_____
WALTER S. SMITH, JR.
CHIEF UNITED STATES DISTRICT JUDGE

In addition to the joint pretrial statement, most courts in their scheduling orders will provide a deadline near trial for the parties to file a few other items that will be needed to try the case.

Motion in limine

Motions in limine are, by name, nowhere mentioned in the rules of civil procedure yet are so routinely filed as to be expected in virtually every civil trial. The phrase "in limine" literally refers to "at the threshold" of trial. Motions in limine ask the trial court to rule on the admissibility of certain evidence prior to the commencement of the trial and out of the presence of the jury. They are typically filed by litigants asking for an order prohibiting opposing parties and counsel from even mentioning some matter in the presence of the jury–typically based upon the argument that a certain matter is not only inadmissible but would be highly prejudicial if considered by the jury. Occasionally, a litigant might file a motion in limine as to their own evidence asking for an advance ruling that the matter will be admissible, but these type of motions in limine are rare. Examples of common motion in limine subjects are:

- any mention of insurance;
- reference to prior criminal arrests or convictions;
- reference to the amounts of settlements received by the claimant in related litigation;
- any attempt to show or offer into evidence any document not previously disclosed in the litigation;

- any reference to one party's failure to call as a witness at trial someone who is equally available to the other party;
- mention of any previous court orders on matters such as discovery disputes;

The notion behind granting a motion in limine is that the mention of some matter in the presence of the jury might be so inflammatory or prejudicial that even an instruction from the judge to disregard the matter might not cure the error. Trial courts will grant a motion in limine when the judge is not sure that the item in question is admissible and does not want to risk having to order a new trial. Often when the judge is on the fence about a disputed and highly inflammatory piece of evidence, the court will grant the motion in limine and ask that counsel approach the bench at trial before they get into the matter. At this point, the judge will have a much better idea how this disputed evidence fits in with the case and be in a better position to make a definitive ruling on the issue of admissibility.

A motion in limine is best prepared throughout the entire pretrial life of the case rather than pulled together on the eve of trial. For example, as you are sitting in the deposition of your client or other witness, you should be listening for questions that inquire of matters that may be discoverable but not admissible at trial. When these matters strike you as being particularly sensitive, embarrassing, or otherwise prejudicial to your client, you should jot a note in your trial notebook under the tab "motion in limine" and simply keep a running list of such topics. As trial approaches, this list of matters will enable you to draft a fairly comprehensive motion in limine. Failure to keep such a running list of ideas for you motion runs the risk of you forgetting about these matters until your client is seated in the witness box and being cross-examined. Once your adversary asks the question, no matter how fast you get on your feet to object, the jury may be tainted.

Proposed jury instructions

Courts expect counsel to help the court with the drafting of the jury instructions by submitting proposed issues and instructions either before or during trial. The court will either instruct you on when to do this in the scheduling order or during the final pretrial conference. Many judges ask counsel to submit their proposed jury instructions with their joint pretrial statement. How do you know which issues need a proposed jury instruction? Simply look at your list of disputed issues of fact. The job of the jury is to find the facts and they need to be asked proper questions with appropriate instructions to fulfill this mission. Jurors are not simply asked who should win or lose.

Most jurisdictions have some published pattern jury instructions. Many of these are privately written and published and may or may not be accurate–but they are always a good starting place when beginning to draft proposed instructions for your case. Other pattern jury instructions are more authoritative, being drafted by official state bar committees and published by the state bar association or even by the court. For example, the Fifth Circuit (among a number of other circuits) has prepared a book entitled "Pattern Jury Instructions – Civil" published by West based upon a project funded by the Bar Association of the Fifth Circuit Court of Appeals. These instructions are explained in the Forward to that book as follows:

> This work contains general civil jury instructions and special instructions for the most frequently recurring federal question cases. They are illustrative only. they attempt to present the applicable law in language that is precise, clear and brief. Judges are encouraged to modify the instructions or the order in which they are presented to the jury in any manner that will further these goals.

While publications such as these do not create binding forms for judges to blindly adhere to, being drafted by blue-ribbons committees of judges, law professors and prominent attorneys, they are highly respected. There is, in fact if not in law, a presumption that they correctly state the law on a topic. Although your proposed instructions might vary from those offered by the official instructions, you should be prepared to explain to the trial judge any variation between your proposal and the pattern instructions.

The law concerning preservation of error in the submission of jury issues and instructions is quite complex and varies from one jurisdiction to another. That subject is certainly beyond the scope of this pretrial text. As a general proposition, you may be required to submit a proposed issue and instruction on any matter on which you have the burden of proof at trial. Further, you may also be required to submit an alternative instruction on any matter submitted by your opponent to which you lodge an objection.

As with the motion in limine, the best time to commence work on your proposed jury instructions is at the outset of the litigation. It is actually quite useful at the onset of the litigation to at least pull together some potentially applicable pattern instructions and put these in your case notebook. You should refer to these often when drafting discovery and taking depositions. When you are asking your opponent questions in her deposition, wouldn't it be nice to use the same verbiage that the jury is likely to hear from the court at the end of your case? Using the pattern instructions throughout the life of the case simplifies your case and helps to create a consistent approach that the jury can understand.

Trial brief

In some cases, the court will expect counsel to submit trial briefs to the court before the commencement of trial. A trial brief might offer a party's explanation of the case from their perspective and provide a background discussion of the law applicable to their claims/defenses. The brief might also discuss evidence anticipated to be offered in support of the party's case and identify issues of law on which the court might be asked to rule during trial. For example, if a defendant believes they might have a strong possible directed verdict motion, a trial brief would be a good place to highlight that issue for the court. In this manner, the litigant has sensitized the trial judge to the possible evidentiary weakness of their opponent's case so that the court can listen particularly carefully to evidence submitted on that issue. Thus, the trial brief might be a good way to prepare the court for a possibly favorable ruling at trial. Other cases are so routine with primarily disputed issues of fact–the typical traffic accident case–that a trial brief would be unnecessary. If you plan to file a trial brief, either your scheduling order will provide a deadline or you can raise the matter during the final pretrial conference.

C.   *FINAL PRETRIAL CONFERENCE*

Every civil case tried will have some type of final pretrial conference prior to the beginning of the trial. In federal court, the final pretrial conference may occur a few weeks to a month prior to the trial and may be a fairly elaborate conference lasting from 30 minutes to several hours in length. In many state court proceedings, the final pretrial conference may be something that occurs on the morning of trial a few minutes before the jury panel is ushered into the courtroom. What exactly happens at any final pretrial conference depends upon local custom and the preferences of your presiding trial judge.

The possible topics for discussion at a final pretrial conference can be any matter related to the case, from a narrowing of issues of fact and law, the possible amendment of pleadings, obtaining factual admissions, avoiding redundancies in the evidence, arguing and obtaining rulings on issues of law, a resolution of any remaining discovery concerns, the anticipated testimony of witnesses, logistics of dealing with voluminous trial exhibits or use of electronic equipment in the courtroom, the anticipated length of trial, and possible consideration of motions in limine if already filed.[6] Courts also commonly hear arguments in favor of a continuance at final pretrial conferences.

In federal court proceedings, Rule 16(d) states that the final pretrial conference "shall be held as close to the time of trial as reasonable under the circumstances. The participants at any such conference shall formulate a plan for trial, including a program for facilitating the admission of evidence. The conference shall be attended by at least one of the attorneys who will conduct the

---

[6]Rule 16(c) has an even lengthier list. The truth is that any matter relevant to the case can be taken up at this conference. The judge wants an efficient and effective trial and any issue related to obtaining these goals is worthy of being brought up by counsel or the court.

trial for each of the parties and by any unrepresented parties." Rule 16(e) indicates that a pretrial order "shall be entered reciting the action taken . . . [which] shall control the subsequent course of the action . . . ."

Counsel need to know their case well when showing up for the final pretrial conference. They should understand what matters need to be tried to the jury–both why these are in dispute and why they are needed to resolve the claims pled–as well as be prepared to argue for any points of law related to the case. If counsel has any ideas for streamlining the trial, these should be presented during the final pretrial conference. Many courts will "pre-admit" into evidence all marked exhibits to which no written objection has been timely filed prior to the conference. Counsel should also be prepared to discuss the prospects for settling the case–courts never give up on attempts at settling the case. Judges will commonly ask questions such as "Counsel, what is holding up a settlement in this case?" or "Counsel, is there any matter on which you need a ruling that would help the parties with their settlement discussions?" or "Counsel, would another mediation assist you in getting this case resolved?" You should think about your possible answer to questions like these before heading to the courthouse for the final pretrial conference. If a judge feels that one side or the other is being unreasonable in their settlement posture, it is not unheard of for the court to make comments attacking the merits of their case in front of the client to provide some added stimulant for further settlement negotiations. You should prepare your client for this possibility in advance if you are planning to take your client with you.

In terms of the format of the conference, they can range from very formal courtroom proceedings to informal chats in the judge's chambers. This is another area where it is useful for you to inquire about the judge's practices before you attend the final pretrial. Regardless of the format, you should be prepared to appear ready for trial, organized, and thoughtful about the lawsuit. Even in a pretrial conference, you are an advocate for your client and it is time for you to start winning the confidence of the court.

D.   CONCLUSION

At this point, you should be prepared to take a case from client intake to final pretrial conference. You have been given an overview of all of the significant steps you will face–pretrial process should no longer be a mysterious unknown procedure that paralyzes you with doubt. We will end where we started this text–"what is the necessary?" The necessary tasks are simply those that you undertake with a strategic purpose in mind, utilizing pretrial tools to help your client have the best chance possible to achieve her litigation goals. Enjoy the practice of law–it can be one of the most significant and satisfying undertakings of your life.

E.   RULES MATRIX

This table serves as a starting point for additional inquiry into the potential professional responsibility and civil procedure issues that are implicated when drafting and filing pleadings.

Issues Arising During Trial Preparation	Applicable Ethics Rule, Federal Rule of Civil Procedure or Local Rule
Required pretrial disclosures automatically required	**FRCP 26(a)(3)**
Duty to supplement discovery responses	**FRCP 26(e)**
Final pretrial conference and final pretrial order	**FRCP 16(c)-(e)**
Final pretrial statement contents	**Local Rule 3.06(b)-(c)**

Points To Ponder . . .

1. Do you agree with the proposition that the start of a civil trial signals a failure on the part of the parties or their advocates? Can you think of any other reasons why litigants might need to try their dispute?

2. Advocates face great pressure as a trial nears. How does an advocate decide what work is necessary to prepare for trial and what work is being undertaken out of an obsessive desire to avoid mistakes?

3. The advocate faces competing pressures. During a final pretrial conference, the judge will push for settlement, for stipulations, and for agreement on issues of law. The client might bristle at the notion of their advocate conceding any point, no matter how small. How can an advocate balance between zealous advocacy for her client and a desire to please the trial judge?

4. From your review of the entire pretrial process, does there seem to be any particular component most in need of reform? If so, what type of reform would you suggest? What systemic goals would be furthered by this reform?

APPENDIX I
EXCERPTS FROM THE DELAWARE RULES OF
PROFESSIONAL CONDUCT

The following excerpts from the Delaware Rules of Professional Conduct have been heavily edited for brevity and applicability to the specific rules identified in <u>Fundamental Pretrial Advocacy, 1st Edition</u>. The included rules and comments should be helpful to advocates when studying how the rules of professional conduct interact with the pretrial process. In some instances the comments for rules have been removed. In other sections both the rules and their comments were omittedd in their entirety for the sake of brevity and clarity. These rules are a beginning reference point and a refresher of text for those issues identified and discussed in the previous chapters. Before relying upon a final interpretation of the rule in question you should take the time to refer to the rules of professional responsibility for your jurisdiction. The American Bar Association will not provide edited versions of the Model Rules of Professional Conduct so this text has utilized those in the public domain, specifically the Delaware rules. These rules were based almost entirely upon the Model Rules of Professional Conduct promulgated and approved by the American Bar Association.

THE DELAWARE LAWYERS' RULES OF PROFESSIONAL CONDUCT
(Effective July 1, 2003)

Preamble: A lawyer's responsibilities.

[1] A lawyer, as a member of the legal profession, is a representative of clients, an officer of the legal system and a public citizen having special responsibility for the quality of justice.

[2] As a representative of clients, a lawyer performs various functions. As advisor, a lawyer provides a client with an informed understanding of the client's legal rights and obligations and explains their practical implications. As advocate, a lawyer zealously asserts the client's position under the rules of the adversary system. As negotiator, a lawyer seeks a result advantageous to the client but consistent with requirements of honest dealings with others. As an evaluator, a lawyer acts by examining a client's legal affairs and reporting about them to the client or to others.

[3] In addition to these representational functions, a lawyer may serve as a third-party neutral, a nonrepresentational role helping the parties to resolve a dispute or other matter. Some of these Rules apply directly to lawyers who are or have served as third-party neutrals. See, e.g., Rules 1.12 and 2.4. In addition, there are Rules that apply to lawyers who are not active in the practice of law or to practicing lawyers even when they are acting in a nonprofessional capacity. For example, a lawyer who commits fraud in the conduct of a business is subject to discipline for engaging in conduct involving dishonesty, fraud, deceit or misrepresentation. See Rule 8.4.

[4] In all professional functions a lawyer should be competent, prompt and diligent. A lawyer should maintain communication with a client concerning the representation. A lawyer should keep in confidence information relating to representation of a client except so far as disclosure is required or permitted by the Rules of Professional Conduct or other law.

[5] A lawyer's conduct should conform to the requirements of the law, both in professional service to clients and in the lawyer's business and personal affairs. A lawyer should use the law's procedures only for legitimate purposes and not to harass or intimidate others. A lawyer should demonstrate respect for the legal system and for those who serve it, including judges, other lawyers and public officials. While it is a lawyer's duty, when necessary, to challenge the rectitude of official action, it is also a lawyer's duty to uphold legal process.

[6] As a public citizen, a lawyer should seek improvement of the law, access to the legal system, the administration of justice and the quality of service rendered by the legal profession. As a member of a learned profession, a lawyer should cultivate knowledge of the law beyond its use for clients, employ that knowledge in reform of the law and work to strengthen legal education. In addition, a lawyer should further the public's understanding of and confidence in the rule of law and the justice system because legal institutions in a constitutional democracy depend on popular participation and support to maintain their authority. A lawyer should be mindful of deficiencies in the administration of justice and of the fact that the poor, and sometimes persons who are not poor, cannot afford adequate legal assistance. Therefore, all lawyers should devote professional time and resources and use civic influence to ensure equal access to our system of justice for all those who because of economic or social barriers cannot afford or secure adequate legal counsel. A lawyer should aid the legal profession in pursuing these objectives and should help the bar regulate itself in the public interest.

[7] Many of a lawyer's professional responsibilities are prescribed in the Rules of Professional Conduct, as well as substantive and procedural law. However, a lawyer is also guided by personal conscience and the approbation of professional peers. A lawyer should strive to attain the highest level of skill, to improve the law and the legal profession and to exemplify the legal profession's ideals of public

service.

[8] A lawyer's responsibilities as a representative of clients, an officer of the legal system and a public citizen are usually harmonious. Thus, when an opposing party is well represented, a lawyer can be a zealous advocate on behalf of a client and at the same time assume that justice is being done. So also, a lawyer can be sure that preserving client confidences ordinarily serves the public interest because people are more likely to seek legal advice, and thereby heed their legal obligations, when they know their communications will be private.

[9] In the nature of law practice, however, conflicting responsibilities are encountered. Virtually all difficult ethical problems arise from conflict between a lawyer's responsibilities to clients, to the legal system and to the lawyer's own interest in remaining an ethical person while earning a satisfactory living. The Rules of Professional conduct often prescribe terms for resolving such conflicts. Within the framework of these Rules, however, many difficult issues of professional discretion can arise. Such issues must be resolved through the exercise of sensitive professional and moral judgment guided by the basic principles underlying the Rules. These principles include the lawyer's obligation zealously to protect and pursue a client's legitimate interests, within the bounds of the law, while maintaining a professional, courteous and civil attitude toward all persons involved in the legal system.

[10] The legal profession is largely self-governing. Although other professions also have been granted powers of self-government, the legal profession is unique in this respect because of the close relationship between the profession and the processes of government and law enforcement. This connection is manifested in the fact that ultimate authority over the legal profession is vested largely in the courts.

[11] To the extent that lawyers meet the obligations of their professional calling, the occasion for government regulation is obviated. Self-regulation also helps maintain the legal profession's independence from government domination. An independent legal profession is an important force in preserving government under law, for abuse of legal authority is more readily challenged by a profession whose members are not dependent on government for the right to practice.

[12] The legal profession's relative autonomy carries with it special responsibilities of self-government. The profession has a responsibility to assure that its regulations are conceived in the public interest and not in furtherance of parochial or self interested concerns of the bar. Every lawyer is responsible for observance of the Rules of Professional Conduct. A lawyer should also aid in securing their observance by other lawyers. Neglect of these responsibilities compromises the independence of the profession and the public interest which it

serves.

[13] Lawyers play a vital role in the preservation of society. The fulfillment of this role requires an understanding by lawyers of their relationship to our legal system. The Rules of Professional Conduct, when properly applied, serve to define that relationship.

SCOPE

[14] The Rules of Professional Conduct are rules of reason. They should be interpreted with reference to the purposes of legal representation and of the law itself. Some of the Rules are imperatives, cast in the terms "shall" or "shall not." These define proper conduct for purposes of professional discipline. Others, generally cast in the term "may," are permissive and define areas under the Rules in which the lawyer has discretion to exercise professional judgment. No disciplinary action should be taken when the lawyer chooses not to act or acts within the bounds of such discretion. Other Rules define the nature of relationships between the lawyer and others. The Rules are thus partly obligatory and disciplinary and partly constitutive and descriptive in that they define a lawyer's professional role. Many of the Comments use the term "should." Comments do not add obligations to the Rules but provide guidance for practicing in compliance with the Rules.

[15] The Rules presuppose a larger legal context shaping the lawyer's role. That context includes court rules and statutes relating to matters of licensure, laws defining specific obligations of lawyers and substantive and procedural law in general. The Comments are sometimes used to alert lawyers to their responsibilities under such other law.

[16] Compliance with the Rules, as with all law in an open society, depends primarily upon understanding and voluntary compliance, secondarily upon reenforcement by peer and public opinion and finally, when necessary, upon enforcement through disciplinary proceedings. The Rules do not, however, exhaust the moral and ethical considerations that should inform a lawyer, for no worthwhile human activity can be completely defined by legal rules. The Rules simply provide a framework for the ethical practice of law.

[17] Furthermore, for purposes of determining the lawyer's authority and responsibility, principles of substantive law external to these Rules determine whether a client-lawyer relationship exists. Most of the duties flowing from the client-lawyer relationship attach only after the client has requested the lawyer to render legal services and the lawyer has agreed to do so. But there are some duties, such as that of confidentiality under Rule 1.6, that attach when the lawyer agrees to consider whether a client-lawyer relationship shall be established. See Rule

1.18. Whether a client-lawyer relationship exists for any specific purpose can depend on the circumstances and may be a question of fact.

[18] Under various legal provisions, including constitutional, statutory and common law, the responsibilities of government lawyers may include authority concerning legal matters that ordinarily reposes in the client in private client-lawyer relationships. For example, a lawyer for a government agency may have authority on behalf of the government to decide upon settlement or whether to appeal from an adverse judgment. Such authority in various respects is generally vested in the attorney general and the state's attorney in state government, and their federal counterparts, and the same may be true of other government law officers. Also, lawyers under the supervision of these officers may be authorized to represent several government agencies in intragovernmental legal controversies in circumstances where a private lawyer could not represent multiple private clients. These Rules do not abrogate any such authority.

[19] Failure to comply with an obligation or prohibition imposed by a Rule is a basis for invoking the disciplinary process. The Rules presuppose that disciplinary assessment of a lawyer's conduct will be made on the basis of the facts and circumstances as they existed at the time of the conduct in question and in recognition of the fact that a lawyer often has to act upon uncertain or incomplete evidence of the situation. Moreover, the Rules presuppose that whether or not discipline should be imposed for a violation, and the severity of a sanction, depend on all the circumstances, such as the willfulness and seriousness of the violation, extenuating factors and whether there have been previous violations.

[20] Violation of a Rule should not itself give rise to a cause of action against a lawyer nor should it create any presumption in such a case that a legal duty has been breached. In addition, violation of a Rule does not necessarily warrant any other nondisciplinary remedy, such as disqualification of a lawyer in pending litigation. The rules are designed to provide guidance to lawyers and to provide a structure for regulating conduct through disciplinary agencies. They are not designed to be a basis for civil liability. Furthermore, the purpose of the Rules can be subverted when they are invoked by opposing parties as procedural weapons. The fact that a Rule is a just basis for a lawyer's self-assessment, or for sanctioning a lawyer under the administration of a disciplinary authority, does not imply that an antagonist in a collateral
proceeding or transaction has standing to seek enforcement of the Rule.

[21] The Comment accompanying each Rule explains and illustrates the meaning and purpose of the Rule. The Preamble and this note on Scope provide general orientation. The Comments are intended as guides to interpretation, but the text of each rule is authoritative.

Rule 1.0. Terminology

(a) "Belief" or "believes" denotes that the person involved actually supposed the fact in question to be true. A person's belief may be inferred from circumstances.

(b) "Confirmed in writing," when used in reference to the informed consent of a person, denotes informed consent that is given in writing by the person or a writing that a lawyer promptly transmits to the person confirming an oral informed consent. See paragraph (e) for the definition of "informed consent." If it is not feasible to obtain or transmit the writing at the time the person gives informed consent, then the lawyer must obtain or transmit it within a reasonable time thereafter.

(c) "Firm" or "law firm" denotes a lawyer or lawyers in a law partnership, professional corporation, sole proprietorship or other association authorized to practice law; or lawyers employed in a legal services organization or the legal department of a corporation or other organization.

(d) "Fraud" or "fraudulent" denotes conduct that is fraudulent under the substantive or procedural law of the applicable jurisdiction and has a purpose to deceive.

(e) "Informed consent" denotes the agreement by a person to a proposed course of conduct after the lawyer has communicated adequate information and explanation about the material risks of and reasonably available alternatives to the proposed course of conduct.

(f) "Knowingly," "known," or "knows" denotes actual knowledge of the fact in question. A person's knowledge may be inferred from circumstances.
(g) "Partner" denotes a member of a partnership, a shareholder in a law firm organized as a professional corporation, or a member of an association authorized to practice law.

(h) "Reasonable" or "reasonably" when used in relation to conduct by a lawyer denotes the conduct of a reasonably prudent and competent lawyer.

(i) "Reasonable belief" or "reasonably believes" when used in reference to a lawyer denotes that the lawyer believes the matter in question and that the circumstances are such that the belief is reasonable.

(j) "Reasonably should know" when used in reference to a lawyer denotes that a lawyer of reasonable prudence and competence would ascertain the matter in question.

(k) "Screened" denotes the isolation of a lawyer from any participation in a matter through the timely imposition of procedures within a firm that are reasonably adequate under the circumstances to protect information that the isolated lawyer is obligated to protect under these Rules or other law.

(l) "Substantial" when used in reference to degree or extent denotes a material matter of clear and weighty importance.

(m) "Tribunal" denotes a court, an arbitrator in a binding arbitration proceeding or a legislative body, administrative agency or other body acting in an adjudicative capacity. A legislative body, administrative agency or other body acts in an adjudicative capacity when a neutral official, after the presentation of evidence or legal argument by a party or parties, will render a binding legal judgment directly affecting a party's interests in a particular matter.

(n) "Writing" or "written" denotes a tangible or electronic record of a communication or representation, including handwriting, typewriting, printing, photostating, photography, audio or video recording and e-mail. A "signed" writing includes an electronic sound, symbol or process attached to or logically associated with a writing and executed or adopted by a person with the intent to sign the writing.

Rule 1.1. Competence

A lawyer shall provide competent representation to a client. Competent representation requires the legal knowledge, skill, thoroughness and preparation reasonably necessary for the representation.

Rule 1.2. Scope of representation

(a) Subject to paragraphs (c) and (d), a lawyer shall abide by a client's decisions concerning the objectives of representation and, as required by Rule 1.4, shall consult with the client as to the means by which they are to be pursued. A lawyer may take such action on behalf of the client as is impliedly authorized to carry out the representation. A lawyer shall abide by a client's decision whether to settle a matter. In a criminal case, the lawyer shall abide by the client's decision, after consultation with the lawyer, as to a plea to be entered, whether to waive jury trial and whether the client will testify.

(b) A lawyer's representation of a client, including representation by appointment, does not constitute an endorsement of the client's political, economic, social or moral views or activities.

(c) A lawyer may limit the scope of the representation if the limitation is reasonable under the circumstances and the client gives informed consent.

(d) A lawyer shall not counsel a client to engage, or assist a client, in conduct that the lawyer knows is criminal or fraudulent, but a lawyer may discuss the legal consequences of any proposed course of conduct with a client and may counsel or assist a client to make a good faith effort to determine the validity, scope, meaning or application of the law.

Rule 1.3. Diligence
A lawyer shall act with reasonable diligence and promptness in representing a client.

Rule 1.4. Communication

(a) A lawyer shall:
(1) promptly inform the client of any decision or circumstance with respect to which the client's informed consent, as defined in Rule 1.0(e), is required by these Rules; (2) reasonably consult with the client about the means by which the client's objectives are to be accomplished; (3) keep the client reasonably informed about the status of the matter; (4) promptly comply with reasonable requests for information; and (5) consult with the client about any relevant limitation on the lawyer's conduct when the lawyer knows that the client expects assistance not permitted by the Rules of Professional Conduct or other law.

(b) A lawyer shall explain a matter to the extent reasonably necessary to permit the client to make informed decisions regarding the representation.

Rule 1.5. Fees.

(a) A lawyer shall not make an agreement for, charge, or collect an unreasonable fee or an unreasonable amount for expenses. The factors to be considered in determining the reasonableness of a fee include the following:

(1) the time and labor required, the novelty and difficulty of the questions involved, and the skill requisite to perform the legal service properly;
(2) the likelihood, if apparent to the client, that the acceptance of the particular employment will preclude other employment by the lawyer;
(3) the fee customarily charged in the locality for similar legal services;
(4) the amount involved and the results obtained; (5) the time limitations imposed by the client or by the circumstances;

(6) the nature and length of the professional relationship with the client;

(7) the experience, reputation, and ability of the lawyer or lawyers performing the services; and

(8) whether the fee is fixed or contingent.

(b) The scope of the representation and the basis or rate of the fee and expenses for which the client will be responsible shall be communicated to the client, preferably in writing, before or within a reasonable time after commencing the representation, except when the lawyer will charge a regularly represented client on the same basis or rate. Any changes in the basis or rate of the fee or expenses shall also be communicated to the client.

(c) A fee may be contingent on the outcome of the matter for which the service is rendered, except in a matter in which a contingent fee is prohibited by paragraph (d) or other law. A contingent fee agreement shall be in a writing signed by the client and shall state the method by which the fee is to be determined, including the percentage or percentages that shall accrue to the lawyer in the event of settlement, trial or appeal; litigation and other expenses to be deducted from the recovery; and whether such expenses are to be deducted before or after the contingent fee is calculated. The agreement must clearly notify the client of any expenses for which the client will be liable whether or not the client is the prevailing party. Upon conclusion of a contingent fee matter, the lawyer shall provide the client with a written statement stating the outcome of the matter and, if there is a recovery, showing the remittance to the client and the method of its determination.

(d) A lawyer shall not enter into an arrangement for, charge, or collect:

(1) any fee in a domestic relations matter, the payment or amount of which is contingent upon the securing of a divorce or upon the amount of alimony or support, or property settlement in lieu thereof; or

(2) a contingent fee for representing a defendant in a criminal case.

(e) A division of fee between lawyers who are not in the same firm may be made only if:

(1) the client is advised in writing of and does not object to the participation of all the lawyers involved; and

(2) the total fee is reasonable.

(f) A lawyer may require the client to pay some or all of the fee in advance of the lawyer undertaking the representation, provided that:

(1) The lawyer shall provide the client with a written statement that the fee is refundable if it is not earned,

(2) The written statement shall state the basis under which the fees shall be considered to have been earned, whether in whole or in part, and

(3) All unearned fees shall be retained in the lawyer's trust account, with statement of the fees earned provided to the client at the time such funds are withdrawn from the trust account.

COMMENT

[1] *Reasonableness of fee and expenses.* -- Paragraph (a) requires that lawyers charge fees that are reasonable under the circumstances. The factors specified in (1) through (8) are not exclusive. Nor will each factor be relevant in each instance. Paragraph (a) also requires that expenses for which the client will be charged must be reasonable. A lawyer may seek reimbursement for the cost of services performed in-house, such as copying, or for other expenses incurred inhouse, such as telephone charges, either by charging a reasonable amount to which the client has agreed in advance or by charging an amount that reasonably reflects the cost incurred by the lawyer.

[2] *Basis or rate of fee.* -- When the lawyer has regularly represented a client, they ordinarily will have evolved an understanding concerning the basis or rate of the fee and the expenses for which the client will be responsible. In a new client-lawyer relationship, however, an understanding as to fees and expenses must be promptly established. Generally, it is desirable to furnish the client with at least a simple memorandum or copy of the lawyer's customary fee arrangements that states the general nature of the legal services to be provided, the basis, rate or total amount of the fee and whether and to what extent the client will be responsible for any costs, expenses or disbursements in the course of the representation. A written statement concerning the terms of the engagement reduces the possibility of misunderstanding.

[3] Contingent fees, like any other fees, are subject to the reasonableness standard of paragraph (a) of this Rule. In determining whether a particular contingent fee is reasonable, or whether it is reasonable to charge any form of contingent fee, a lawyer must consider the factors that are relevant under the circumstances. Applicable law may impose limitations on contingent fees, such as a ceiling on the percentage allowable, or may require a lawyer to offer clients an alternative basis for the fee. Applicable law also may apply to situations other than a contingent fee, for example, government regulations regarding fees in certain tax matters.

[4] *Terms of payment.* -- A lawyer may require advance payment of a fee, but is obliged to return any unearned portion. See Rule 1.16(d). A lawyer may accept property in payment for services, such as an ownership interest in an enterprise, providing this does not involve acquisition of a proprietary interest in the cause of action or subject matter of the litigation contrary to Rule 1.8(i). However, a fee paid in property instead of money maybe subject to the requirements of Rule 1.8(a) because such fees often have the essential qualities of a business transaction with the client.

[5] An agreement may not be made whose terms might induce the lawyer improperly to curtail services for the client or perform them in a way contrary to the client's interest. For example, a lawyer should not enter into an agreement whereby services are to be provided only up to a stated amount when it is foreseeable that more extensive services probably will be required, unless the situation is adequately explained to the client. Otherwise, the client might have to bargain for further assistance in the midst of a proceeding or transaction. However, it is proper to define the extent of services in light of the client's ability to pay. A lawyer should not exploit a fee arrangement based primarily on hourly charges by using wasteful procedures.

[6] *Prohibited contingent fees.* -- Paragraph (d) prohibits a lawyer from charging a contingent fee in a domestic relations matter when payment is contingent upon the securing of a divorce or upon the amount of alimony or support or property settlement to be obtained. This provision does not preclude a contract for a contingent fee for legal representation in connection with the recovery of post-judgment balances due under support, alimony or other financial orders because such contracts do not implicate the same policy concerns.

[7] *Division of fee.* -- A division of fee is a single billing to a client covering the fee of two or more lawyers who are not in the same firm. A division of fee facilitates association of more than one lawyer in a matter in which neither alone could serve the client as well, and most often is used when the fee is contingent and the division is between a referring lawyer and a trial specialist. Paragraph (e) permits the lawyers to divide a fee without regard to whether the division is in proportion to the services each lawyer renders or whether each lawyer assumes responsibility for the representation as a whole, so long as the client is advised in writing and does not object, and the total fee is reasonable. It does not require disclosure to the client of the share that each lawyer is to receive. Contingent fee agreements must be in a writing signed by the client and must otherwise comply with paragraph (c) of this Rule. A lawyer should only refer a matter to a lawyer whom the referring lawyer reasonably believes is competent to handle the matter. See Rule 1.1.

[8] Paragraph (e) does not prohibit or regulate division of fees to be received in the future for work done when lawyers were previously associated in a law firm.

[9] *Advance fees.* -- A lawyer may require that a client pay a fee in advance of completing the work for the representation. All fees paid in advance are refundable until earned. Until such time as that fee is earned, that fee must be held in the attorney's trust account. An attorney who accepts an advance fee must provide the client with a written statement that the fee is refundable if not earned and how the fee will be considered earned. When the fee is earned and the money is withdrawn from the attorney's trust account, the client must be notified and a statement

provided.

[10] Some smaller fees--such as those less than $2500.00--may be considered earned in whole upon some identified event, such as upon commencement of the attorney's work on that matter or the attorney's appearance on the record. However, a fee considered to be "earned upon commencement of the attorney's work on the matter" is not the same as a fee "earned upon receipt." The former requires that the attorney actually begin work whereas the latter is dependent only upon payment by the client. In a criminal defense matter, for example, a smaller fee--such as a fee under $2500.00--may be considered earned upon entry of the attorney's appearance on the record or at the initial consultation at which substantive, confidential information has been communicated which would preclude the attorney from representation of another potential client (e.g. a co-defendant). Nevertheless, all fees must be reasonable such that even a smaller fee
might be refundable, in whole or in part, if it is not reasonable under the circumstances.

[11] As a general rule, larger advance fees--such as those over $2500.00--will not be considered earned upon one specific event. Therefore, the attorney must identify the manner in which the fee will be considered earned and make the appropriate disclosures to the client at the outset of the representation. The written statement must include a reasonable method of determining fees earned at a given time in the representation. One method might be calculation of fees based upon an agreed upon hourly rate. If an hourly rate is not utilized, the attorney is required to identify certain events which will trigger earned fees. For example, in a criminal defense matter, an attorney might identify events such as entry of appearance, arraignment, certain motions, case review, and trial as the events which might trigger certain specified earned fees and deduction of those fees from the attorney trust account. Likewise, in a domestic matter, an attorney
might identify such events as entry of appearance, drafting petition, attendance at mediation conference, commissioner's hearing, pre-trial conference, and judge's hearing as triggering events for purposes of earning fees. It might be reasonable for an attorney to provide that a certain percentage of this fee will be considered earned on a monthly basis, for any work performed in that month, or upon the completion of an identified portion of the work. Nevertheless, all fees must be reasonable such that even a fee considered earned in full per the written statement provided to the client might be refundable, in whole or in part, if it is not reasonable under the circumstances.

[12] In contrast to the general rule, a larger advance fee may, under certain circumstances, be earned upon one specific event. For example, this fee or a large portion thereof could become earned upon an attorney's initial consultation with a client in a bankruptcy matter at which substantive, confidential information has been communicated which would preclude the attorney from representation of

another potential client (e.g. the client's creditors). In this context, the attorney must provide a clear written statement that the fee, or a portion thereof, is earned at time of consultation as compensation for this lost opportunity. Likewise, a criminal defense attorney might outline in the written agreement that the entire fee becomes earned upon conclusion of the matter--in the case of negotiation and acceptance of a plea agreement prior to trial. Both of these examples are tempered, however, by the reasonableness requirement set forth above.

[13] It is not acceptable for an attorney to hold earned fees in the attorney trust account. See Rule 1.15(a). This is commingling. Once fees are earned, those fees must be withdrawn from the attorney trust account. Typically, it is acceptable to draw down earned fees from an attorney trust account on a monthly or some other reasonable periodic basis. Similarly, monthly/periodic statements are considered an acceptable method of notifying one's clients that earned fees have been withdrawn from a trust account. For those attorneys earning fees on a percentage basis, wherein the fee would be considered earned upon the completion of an identified portion of the work, a statement to that effect upon completion of that work would satisfy this requirement.

[14] *Disputes over fees.* -- If a procedure has been established for resolution of fee disputes, such as an arbitration or mediation procedure established by the bar, the lawyer must comply with the procedure when it is mandatory, and, even when it is voluntary, the lawyer should conscientiously consider submitting to it. Law may prescribe a procedure for determining a lawyer's fee, for example, in representation of an executor or administrator, a class or a person entitled to a reasonable fee as part of the measure of damages. The lawyer entitled to such a fee and a lawyer representing another party concerned with the fee should comply with the prescribed procedure.

Rule 1.6. Confidentiality of information

(a) A lawyer shall not reveal information relating to the representation of a client unless the client gives informed consent, the disclosure is impliedly authorized in order to carry out the representation, or the disclosure is permitted by paragraph (b).

(b) A lawyer may reveal information relating to the representation of a client to the extent the lawyer reasonably believes necessary: (1) to prevent reasonably certain death or substantial bodily harm; (2) to prevent the client from committing a crime or fraud that is reasonably certain to result in substantial injury to the financial interests or property of another and in furtherance of which the client has used or is using the lawyer's services; (3) to prevent, mitigate, or rectify substantial injury to the financial interests or property of another that is reasonably certain to result or has resulted from the client's commission of a crime or fraud in furtherance of which the client has used the lawyer's services; (4) to secure legal advice about the lawyer's compliance with these Rules; (5) to establish a claim or defense on behalf of the lawyer in a controversy between the lawyer and the client, to establish a defense to a criminal charge or civil claim against the lawyer based upon conduct in which the client was involved, or to respond to allegations in any proceeding concerning the lawyer's representation of the client; or (6) to comply with other law or a court order.

COMMENT

[1] This Rule governs the disclosure by a lawyer of information relating to the representation of a client during the lawyer's representation of the client. See Rule 1.18 for the lawyer's duties with respect to information provided to the lawyer by a prospective client, Rule 1.9(c)(2) for the lawyer's duty not to reveal information relating to the lawyer's prior representation of a former client and Rules 1.8(b) and 1.9(c)(1) for the lawyer's duties with respect to the use of such information to the disadvantage of clients and former clients.

[2] A fundamental principle in the client-lawyer relationship is that, in the absence of the client's informed consent, the lawyer must not reveal information relating to the representation. See Rule 1.0(e) for the definition of informed consent. This contributes to the trust that is the hallmark of the client-lawyer relationship. The client is thereby encouraged to seek legal assistance and to communicate fully and frankly with the lawyer even as to embarrassing or legally damaging subject matter. The lawyer needs this information to represent the client effectively and, if necessary, to advise the client to refrain from wrongful conduct. Almost without exception, clients come to lawyers in order to determine their rights and what is, in the complex of laws and regulations, deemed to be legal and correct. Based upon experience, lawyers know that almost all clients follow the advice given, and the law is upheld.

[3] The principle of client-lawyer confidentiality is given effect by related bodies of law: the attorney-client privilege, the work product doctrine and the rule of confidentiality established in professional ethics. The attorney-client privilege and work product doctrine apply in judicial and other proceedings in which a lawyer may be called as a witness or otherwise required to produce evidence concerning a client. The rule of client-lawyer confidentiality applies in situations other than those where evidence is sought from the lawyer through compulsion of law. The confidentiality rule, for example, applies not only to matters communicated in confidence by the client but also to all information relating to the representation, whatever its source. A lawyer may not disclose such information except as authorized or required by the Rules of Professional Conductor other law. See also

Scope.

[4] Paragraph (a) prohibits a lawyer from revealing information relating to the representation of a client. This prohibition also applies to disclosures by a lawyer that do not in themselves reveal protected information but could reasonably lead to the discovery of such information by a third person. A lawyer's use of a hypothetical to discuss issues relating to the representation is permissible so long as there is no reasonable likelihood that the listener will be able to ascertain the identity of the client or the situation involved.

[5] *Authorized disclosure.* -- Except to the extent that the client's instructions or special circumstances limit that authority, a lawyer is impliedly authorized to make disclosures about a client when appropriate in carrying out the representation. In some situations, for example, a lawyer may be impliedly authorized to admit a fact that cannot properly be disputed or to make a disclosure that facilitates a satisfactory conclusion to a matter. Lawyers in a firm may, in the course of the firm's practice, disclose to each other information relating to a client of the firm, unless the client has instructed that particular information be confined to specified lawyers.

[6] *Disclosure adverse to client.* -- Although the public interest is usually best served by a strict rule requiring lawyers to preserve the confidentiality of information relating to the representation of their clients, the confidentiality rule is subject to limited exceptions. Paragraph (b)(1) recognizes the overriding value of life and physical integrity and permits disclosure reasonably necessary to prevent reasonably certain death or substantial bodily harm. Such harm is reasonably certain to occur if it will be suffered imminently or if there is a present and substantial threat that a person will suffer such harm at a later date if the lawyer fails to take action necessary to eliminate the threat. Thus, a lawyer who knows that a client has accidentally discharged toxic waste into a town's water supply may reveal this information to the authorities if there is a present and substantial risk that a person who drinks the water will contract a life-threatening or debilitating disease and the lawyer's disclosure is necessary to eliminate the threat or reduce the number of victims.

[7] Paragraph (b)(2) is a limited exception to the rule of confidentiality that permits the lawyer to reveal information to the extent necessary to enable affected persons or appropriate authorities to prevent the client from committing a crime or a fraud, as defined in Rule 1.0(d), that is reasonably certain to result in substantial injury to the financial or property interests of another and in furtherance of which the client has used or is using the lawyer's services. Such a
serious abuse of the client-lawyer relationship by the client forfeits the protection of this Rule. The client can, of course, prevent such disclosure by refraining from the wrongful conduct. Although paragraph (b)(2) does not require the lawyer to

reveal the client's misconduct, the lawyer may not counsel or assist the client in conduct the lawyer knows is criminal or fraudulent. See Rule 1.2(d). See also Rule 1.16 with respect to the lawyer's obligation or right to withdraw from the representation of the client in such circumstances. Where the client is an organization, the lawyer may be in doubt whether contemplated conduct will actually be carried out by the organization. Where necessary to guide conduct in connection with this Rule, the lawyer may make inquiry within the organization as indicated in Rule 1.13(b).

[8] Paragraph (b)(3) addresses the situation in which the lawyer does not learn of the client's crime or fraud until after it has been consummated. Although the client no longer has the option of preventing disclosure by refraining from the wrongful conduct, there will be situations in which the loss suffered by the affected person can be prevented, rectified or mitigated. In such situations, the lawyer may disclose information relating to the representation to the extent necessary to enable the affected persons to prevent or mitigate reasonably certain losses or to attempt to recoup their losses. Disclosure is not permitted under paragraph (b)(3) when a person who has committed a crime or fraud thereafter employs a lawyer for representation concerning that offense if that lawyer's services were not used in the initial crime or fraud; disclosure would be permitted, however, if the lawyer's services are used to commit a further crime or fraud, such as the crime of obstructing justice. While applicable law may provide that a completed act is regarded for some purposes as a continuing offense, if commission of the initial act has already occurred without the use of the lawyer's services, the lawyer does not have discretion under this paragraph to use or disclose the client's information.

[9] A lawyer's confidentiality obligations do not preclude a lawyer from securing confidential legal advice about the lawyer's personal responsibility to comply with these Rules. In most situations, disclosing information to secure such advice will be impliedly authorized for the lawyer to carry out the representation. Even when the disclosure is not impliedly authorized, paragraph (b)(2) permits such disclosure because of the importance of a lawyer's compliance with the Rules of Professional Conduct.

[10] Where a legal claim or disciplinary charge alleges complicity of the lawyer in a client's conduct or other misconduct of the lawyer involving representation of the client, the lawyer may respond to the extent the lawyer reasonably believes necessary to establish a defense. The same is true with respect to a claim involving the conduct or representation of a former client. Such a charge can arise in a civil, criminal, disciplinary or other proceeding and can be based on a wrong allegedly committed by the lawyer against the client or on a wrong alleged by a third person, for example, a person claiming to have been defrauded by the lawyer and client acting together. The lawyer's right to respond arises when an assertion of such complicity has been made. Paragraph (b)(5) does not require the

lawyer to await the commencement of an action or proceeding that charges such complicity, so that the defense may be established by responding
directly to a third party who has made such an assertion. The right to defend also applies, of course, where a proceeding has been commenced.

[11] A lawyer entitled to a fee is permitted by paragraph (b)(5) to prove the services rendered in an action to collect it. This aspect of the rule expresses the principle that the beneficiary of a fiduciary relationship may not exploit it to the detriment of the fiduciary.

[12] Other law may require that a lawyer disclose information about a client. Whether such a law supersedes Rule 1.6 is a question of law beyond the scope of these rules. When disclosure of information relating to the representation appears to be required by other law, the lawyer must discuss the matter with the client to the extent required by Rule 1.4. If, however, the other law supersedes this Rule and requires disclosure, paragraph (b)(6) permits the lawyer to make
such disclosures as are necessary to comply with the law. See, e.g., *29 DEL. CODE ANN. § 9007A(c)* (which provides that an attorney acting as guardian ad litem for a child in child welfare proceedings shall have the "duty of confidentiality to the child unless the disclosure is necessary to protect the child's best interests").

[13] Paragraph (b)(6) also permits compliance with a court order requiring a lawyer to disclose information relating to a client's representation. If a lawyer is called as a witness to give testimony concerning a client or is otherwise ordered to reveal information relating to the client's representation, however, the lawyer must, absent informed consent of the client to do otherwise, assert on behalf of the client all nonfrivolous claims that the information sought is protected against disclosure by the attorney-client privilege or other applicable law. In the event of an adverse ruling, the lawyer must consult with the client about the possibility of appeal to the extent required by Rule 1.4. Unless review is sought, however, paragraph (b)(6) permits the lawyer to comply with the court's order.

[14] Paragraph (b) permits disclosure only to the extent the lawyer reasonably believes the disclosure is necessary to accomplish one of the purposes specified. Where practicable, the lawyer should first seek to persuade the client to take suitable action to obviate the need for disclosure. In any case, a disclosure adverse to the client's interest should be no greater than the lawyer reasonably believes necessary to accomplish the purpose. If the disclosure will be made in connection with a judicial proceeding, the disclosure should be made in a manner that limits access to the information to the tribunal or other persons having a need to know it and appropriate protective orders or other arrangements should be sought by the lawyer to the fullest extent practicable.

[15] Paragraph (b) permits but does not require the disclosure of information

relating to a client's representation to accomplish the purposes specified in paragraphs (b)(1) through (b)(6). In exercising the discretion conferred by this Rule, the lawyer may consider such factors as the nature of the lawyer's relationship with the client and with those who might be injured by the client, the lawyer's own involvement in the transaction and factors that may extenuate the conduct in question. A lawyer's decision not to disclose as permitted by paragraph (b) does not violate this Rule. Disclosure may be required, however, by other Rules. Some Rules require disclosure only if such disclosure would be permitted by paragraph (b). See Rules 1.2(d), 4.1(b), 8.1 and 8.3. Rule 3.3, on the other hand, requires disclosure in some circumstances regardless of whether such disclosure is permitted by this Rule. See Rule 3.3(c).

[16] *Acting competently to preserve confidentiality.* -- A lawyer must act competently to safeguard information relating to the representation of a client against inadvertent or unauthorized disclosure by the lawyer or other persons who are participating in the representation of the client or who are subject to the lawyer's supervision. See Rules 1.1, 5.1 and 5.3.

[17] When transmitting a communication that includes information relating to the representation of a client, the lawyer must take reasonable precautions to prevent the information from coming into the hands of unintended recipients.
This duty, however, does not require that the lawyer use special security measures if the method of communication affords a reasonable expectation of privacy. Special circumstances, however, may warrant special precautions. Factors to be considered in determining the reasonableness of the lawyer's expectation of confidentiality include the sensitivity of the information and the extent to which the privacy of the communication is protected by law or by a confidentiality agreement. A client may require the lawyer to implement special security measures not required by this Rule or may give informed consent to the use of a means of communication that would otherwise be prohibited by this Rule.

[18] *Former client.* -- The duty of confidentiality continues after the client-lawyer relationship has terminated. See Rule 1.9(c)(2). See Rule 1.9(c)(1) for the prohibition against using such information to the disadvantage of the former client.

Rule 1.7. Conflict of interest: Current clients

(a) Except as provided in paragraph (b), a lawyer shall not represent a client if the representation involves a concurrent conflict of interest. A concurrent conflict of interest exists if: (1) the representation of one client will be directly adverse to another client; or (2) there is a significant risk that the representation of one or more clients will be materially limited by the lawyer's responsibilities to another client, a former client or a third person or by a personal interest of the lawyer.

(b) Notwithstanding the existence of a concurrent conflict of interest under paragraph (a), a lawyer may represent a client if: (1) the lawyer reasonably believes that the lawyer will be able to provide competent and diligent representation to each affected client; (2) the representation is not prohibited by law; (3) the representation does not involve the assertion of a claim by one client against another client represented by the lawyer in the same litigation or other proceeding before a tribunal; and (4) each affected client gives informed consent, confirmed in writing.

Rule 1.8. Conflict of interest: Current clients: Specific rules

(a) A lawyer shall not enter into a business transaction with a client or knowingly acquire an ownership, possessory, security or other pecuniary interest adverse to a client unless: (1) the transaction and terms on which the lawyer acquires the interest are fair and reasonable to the client and are fully disclosed and transmitted in writing to the client in a manner that can be reasonably understood by the client; (2) the client is advised in writing of the desirability of seeking and is given a reasonable opportunity to seek the advice of independent legal counsel on the transaction; and (3) the client gives informed consent, in a writing signed by the client, to the essential terms of the transaction and the lawyer's role in the transaction, including whether the lawyer is representing the client in the transaction.

(b) A lawyer shall not use information relating to representation of a client to the disadvantage of the client unless the client gives informed consent, except as permitted or required by these Rules.

(c) A lawyer shall not solicit any substantial gift from a client, including a testamentary gift, or prepare on behalf of a client an instrument giving the lawyer or a person related to the lawyer any substantial gift unless the lawyer or other recipient of the gift is related to the client. For purposes of this paragraph, related persons include a spouse, child, grandchild, parent, grandparent or other relative or individual with whom the lawyer or the client maintains a close, familial relationship.

(d) Prior to the conclusion of representation of a client, a lawyer shall not make or negotiate an agreement giving the lawyer literary or media rights to a portrayal or account based in substantial part on information relating to the representation.

(e) A lawyer shall not provide financial assistance to a client in connection with pending or contemplated litigation, except that: (1) a lawyer may advance court costs and expenses of litigations, the repayment of which may be contingent on the outcome of the matter; and (2) a lawyer representing an indigent client may pay court costs and expenses of litigation on behalf of the client.

(f) A lawyer shall not accept compensation for representing a client from one other than the client unless: (1) the client gives informed consent; (2) there is no interference with the lawyer's independence of professional judgment or with the client-lawyer relationship; and (3) information relating to representation of a client is protected as required by Rule 1.6.

(g) A lawyer who represents two or more clients shall not participate in making an aggregate settlement of the claims of or against the clients, or in a criminal case an aggregated agreement as to guilty or nolo contendere pleas, unless each client gives informed consent, in a writing signed by the client. The lawyer's disclosure shall include the existence and nature of all the claims or pleas involved and of the participation of each person in the settlement.

(h) A lawyer shall not: (1) make an agreement prospectively limiting the lawyer's liability to a client for malpractice unless the client is independently represented in making the agreement; or (2) settle a claim or potential claim for such liability with an unrepresented client or former client unless that person is advised in writing of the desirability of seeking and is given a reasonable opportunity to seek the advice of independent legal counsel in connection therewith.

(i) A lawyer shall not acquire a proprietary interest in the cause of action or subject matter of litigation the lawyer is conducting for a client, except that the lawyer may: (1) acquire a lien authorized by law to secure the lawyer's fee or expenses; and (2) contract with a client for a reasonable contingent fee in a civil case.

(j) A lawyer shall not have sexual relations with a client unless a consensual sexual relationship existed between them when the client-lawyer relationship commenced.

(k) While lawyers are associated in a firm, a prohibition in the foregoing paragraphs (a) through (i) that applies to any one of them shall apply to all of them.

Rule 1.9. Duties to former clients

(a) A lawyer who has formerly represented a client in a matter shall not thereafter represent another person in the same or a substantially related matter in which that person's interests are materially adverse to the interests of the former client unless the former client gives informed consent, confirmed in writing.

(b) A lawyer shall not knowingly represent a person in the same or a substantially related matter in which a firm with which the lawyer formerly was associated had previously represented a client: (1) whose interests are materially adverse to that person; and (2) about whom the lawyer had acquired information protected by Rules 1.6 and 1.9(c) that is material to the matter; unless the former client gives informed consent, confirmed in writing.

(c) A lawyer who has formerly represented a client in a matter or whose present or former firm has formerly represented a client in a matter shall not thereafter:
(1) use information relating to the representation to the disadvantage of the former client except as these Rules would permit or require with respect to a client, or when the information has become generally known; or (2) reveal information relating to the representation except as these Rules would permit or require with respect to a client.

Rule 1.10. Imputation of conflicts of interest: General rule

(a) Except as otherwise provided in this rule, while lawyers are associated in a firm, none of them shall knowingly represent a client when any one of them practicing alone would be prohibited from doing so by Rules 1.7 or 1.9, unless the prohibition is based on a personal interest of the prohibited lawyer and does not present a significant risk of materially limiting the representation of the client by the remaining lawyers in the firm.

(b) When a lawyer has terminated an association with a firm, the firm is not prohibited from thereafter representing a person with interests materially adverse to those of a client represented by the formerly associated lawyer and not currently represented by the firm, unless: (1) the matter is the same or substantially related to that in which the formerly associated lawyer represented the client; and (2) any lawyer remaining in the firm has information protected by Rules 1.6 and 1.9(c) that is material to the matter.

(c) When a lawyer becomes associated with a firm, no lawyer associated in the firm shall knowingly represent a client in a matter in which that lawyer is disqualified under Rule 1.9 unless: (1) the personally disqualified lawyer is timely screened from any participation in the matter and is apportioned no part of the fee therefrom; and (2) written notice is promptly given to the affected former client.

(d) A disqualification prescribed by this rule may be waived by the affected client under the conditions stated in Rule 1.7.

(e) The disqualification of lawyers associated in a firm with former or current government lawyers is governed by Rule 1.11.

Rule 1.11. Special conflicts of interest for former and current government officers and employees

(a) Except as law may otherwise expressly permit, a lawyer who has formerly served as a public officer or employee of the government: (1) is subject to Rule 1.9(c); and (2) shall not otherwise represent a client in connection with a matter in which the lawyer participated personally and substantially as a public officer or employee, unless the appropriate government agency gives its informed consent, confirmed in writing, to the representation.

(b) When a lawyer is disqualified from representation under paragraph (a), no lawyer in a firm with which that lawyer is associated may knowingly undertake or continue representation in such a matter unless: (1) the disqualified lawyer is timely screened from any participation in the matter and is apportioned no part of the fee therefrom; and (2) written notice is promptly given to the appropriate government agency to enable it to ascertain compliance with the provisions of this rule.

(c) Except as law may otherwise expressly permit, a lawyer having information that the lawyer knows is confidential government information about a person acquired when the lawyer was a public officer or employee, may not represent a private client whose interests are adverse to that person in a matter in which the information could be used to the material disadvantage of that person. As used in this Rule, the term "confidential government information" means information that has been obtained under governmental authority and which, at the time this Rule is applied, the government is prohibited by law from disclosing to the public or has a legal privilege not to disclose and which is not otherwise available to the public. A firm with which that lawyer is associated may undertake or continue representation in the matter only if the disqualified lawyer is timely screened from any participation in the matter and is apportioned no part of the fee therefrom.

(d) Except as law may otherwise expressly permit, a lawyer currently serving as a public officer or employee: (1) is subject to Rules 1.7 and 1.9; and (2) shall not: (i) participate in a matter in which the lawyer participated personally and substantially while in private practice or nongovernmental employment, unless the appropriate government agency gives its informed consent, confirmed in writing; or (ii) negotiate for private employment with any person who is involved as a party or as lawyer for a party in a matter in which the lawyer is participating personally and substantially, except that a lawyer serving as a law clerk to a judge, other adjudicative officer or arbitrator may negotiate for private employment as permitted by Rule 1.12(b) and subject to the conditions stated in Rule 1.12(b).

(e) As used in this Rule, the term "matter" includes: (1) any judicial or other proceeding, application, request for a ruling or other determination, contract, claim, controversy, investigation, charge, accusation, arrest or other particular matter involving a specific party or parties, and (2) any other matter covered by the conflict of interest rules of the appropriate government agency.

Rule 1.12. Former judge, arbitrator, mediator or other third-party neutral

(a) Except as stated in paragraph (d), a lawyer shall not represent anyone in connection with a matter in which the lawyer participated personally and substantially as a judge or other adjudicative officer or law clerk to such a person or as an arbitrator, mediator or other third-party neutral, unless all parties to the proceeding give informed consent, confirmed in writing.

(b) A lawyer shall not negotiate for employment with any person who is involved as a party or as lawyer for a party in a matter in which the lawyer is participating personally and substantially as a judge or other adjudicative officer or as an arbitrator, mediator or other third-party neutral. A lawyer serving as a law clerk to a judge or other adjudicative officer may negotiate for employment with a party or lawyer involved in a matter in which the clerk is participating personally and substantially, but only after the lawyer has notified the judge or other adjudicative officer.

(c) If a lawyer is disqualified by paragraph (a), no lawyer in a firm with which that lawyer is associated may knowingly undertake or continue representation in the matter unless: (1) the disqualified lawyer is timely screened from any participation in the matter and is apportioned no part of the fee therefrom; and
(2) written notice is promptly given to the parties and any appropriate tribunal to enable them to ascertain compliance with the provisions of this rule.

(d) An arbitrator selected as a partisan of a party in a multimember arbitration panel is not prohibited from subsequently representing that party.

Rule 1.13. Organization as client

(a) A lawyer employed or retained by an organization represents the organization acting through its duly authorized constituents.

(b) If a lawyer for an organization knows that an officer, employee or other person associated with the organization is engaged in action, intends to act or refuses to act in a matter related to the representation that is a violation of a legal obligation to the organization, or a violation of law which reasonably might be imputed to the organization, and is likely to result in substantial injury to the organization, the lawyer shall proceed as is reasonably necessary in the best interest of the organization. In determining how to proceed, the lawyer shall give due consideration to the seriousness of the violation and its consequences, the scope and nature of the lawyer's representation, the responsibility in the organization and the apparent motivation of the person involved, the policies of the organization concerning such matters and any other relevant considerations. Any measures taken shall be designed to minimize disruption of the organization and the risk of revealing information relating to the representation to persons outside the organization. Such measures may include among others: (1) asking for reconsideration of the matter; (2) advising that a separate legal opinion on the matter be sought for presentation to appropriate authority in the organization; and (3) referring the matter to higher authority in the organization, including, if warranted by the seriousness of the matter, referral to the highest authority that can act on behalf of the organization as determined by applicable law.

(c) If, despite the lawyer's efforts in accordance with paragraph (b), the highest authority that can act on behalf of the organization insists upon action, or a refusal to act, that is clearly a violation of law and is likely to result in substantial injury to the organization, the lawyer may resign in accordance with Rule 1.16.

(d) In dealing with an organization's directors, officers, employees, members, shareholders or other constituents, a lawyer shall explain the identity of the client when the lawyer knows or reasonably should know that the organization's interests are adverse to those of the constituents with whom the lawyer is dealing.

(e) A lawyer representing an organization may also represent any of its directors, officers, employees, members, shareholders or other constituents, subject to the provisions of Rule 1.7. If the organization's consent to the dual representation is required by Rule 1.7, the consent shall be given by an appropriate official of the organization other than the individual who is to be represented, or by the shareholders.

Rule 1.14. Client with diminished capacity

(a) When a client's capacity to make adequately considered decisions in connection with a representation is diminished, whether because of minority, mental impairment or for some other reason, the lawyer shall, as far as reasonably possible, maintain a normal client-lawyer relationship with the client.

(b) When the lawyer reasonably believes that the client has diminished capacity, is at risk of substantial physical, financial or other harm unless action is taken and cannot adequately act in the client's own interest, the lawyer may take reasonably necessary protective action, including consulting with individuals or entities that have the ability to take action to protect the client and, in appropriate cases, seeking the appointment of a guardian ad litem, conservator or guardian.

(c) Information relating to the representation of a client with diminished capacity is protected by Rule 1.6. When taking protective action pursuant to paragraph (b), the lawyer is impliedly authorized under Rule 1.6(a) to reveal information about the client, but only to the extent reasonably necessary to protect the client's interests.

Rule 1.15. Safekeeping property

(a) A lawyer shall hold property of clients or third persons that is in a lawyer's possession in connection with a representation separate from the lawyer's own property. Funds shall be kept in a separate account maintained in the state where the lawyer's office is situated, or elsewhere with the consent of the client or third person. Funds of the lawyer that are reasonably sufficient to pay bank charges may be deposited therein; however, such amount may not exceed $ 500 and must be separately stated and accounted for in the same manner as clients' funds deposited therein. Other property shall be identified as such and appropriately safeguarded. Complete records of such account funds and other property shall be kept by the lawyer and shall be preserved for a period of five years after the completion of the events that they record.

(b) Upon receiving funds or other property in which a client or third person has an interest, a lawyer shall promptly notify the client or third person. Except as stated in this Rule or otherwise permitted by law or by agreement with the ient, a lawyer shall promptly deliver to the client or third person any funds or other property that the client or third person is entitled to receive and, upon request by the client or third person, shall promptly render a full accounting regarding such property.

(c) When in the course of representation a lawyer is in possession of property in which both the lawyer and another person claim interests, the property shall be kept separate by the lawyer until there is an accounting and severance of their interests. If a dispute arises concerning their respective interests, the portion in dispute shall be kept separate by the lawyer until the dispute is resolved.

(d) A lawyer engaged in the private practice of law must maintain financial books and records on a current basis, and shall preserve the books and records for at least five years following the completion of the year to which they relate, or, as to fiduciary books and records, five years following the completion of that fiduciary obligation. The maintenance of books and records must conform with the following provisions:

(1) All bank statements, cancelled checks, and duplicate deposit slips relating to fiduciary and non-fiduciary accounts must be preserved.

(2) Bank accounts and related statements, checks, deposit slips, and other documents maintained for fiduciary funds must be specifically designated as "Trust Account" or "Escrow Account," and must be used only for funds held in a fiduciary capacity.

(3) Bank accounts and related statements, checks, deposit slips, and other documents maintained for non-fiduciary funds must be specifically designated as "Attorney Business Account" or "Attorney Operating Account," and must be used only for funds held in a non-fiduciary capacity. A lawyer in the private practice of law shall maintain a nonfiduciary
account for general operating purposes, and the account shall be separate from any of the lawyer's personal or other accounts.

(4) All records relating to property other than cash received by a lawyer in a fiduciary capacity shall be maintained and preserved. The records must describe with specificity the identity and location of such property.

(5) All billing records reflecting fees charged and other billings to clients or other parties must be maintained and preserved.

(6) Cash receipts and cash disbursement journals must be maintained and preserved for each bank account for the purpose of recording fiduciary and non-fiduciary transactions. A lawyer using a manual system for such purposes must total and balance the transaction columns on a monthly basis.

(7) A monthly reconciliation for each bank account, matching totals from the cash receipts and cash disbursement journals with the ending check register balance, must be performed. The reconciliation procedures, however, shall not be required for lawyers using a computer accounting system or a general ledger.

(8) The check register balance for each bank account must be reconciled monthly to the bank statement balance.

(9) With respect to all fiduciary accounts:
(A) A subsidiary ledger must be maintained and preserved with a separate account for each client or third party in which cash receipts and cash disbursement transactions and monthly balances are recorded.
(B) Monthly listings of client or third party balances must be prepared showing the name and balance of each client or third party, and the total of all balances.
(C) No funds disbursed for a client or third party must be in excess of funds received from that client or third party. If, however, through error funds disbursed

for a client or third party exceed funds received from that client or third party, the lawyer shall transfer funds from the non-fiduciary account in a timely manner to cover the excess disbursement.

(D) The reconciled total cash balance must agree with the total of the client or third party balance listing. There shall be no unidentified client or third party funds. The bank reconciliation for a fiduciary account is not complete unless there is agreement with the total of client or third party accounts.

(E) If a check has been issued in an attempt to disburse funds, but remains outstanding (that is, the check has not cleared the trust or escrow bank account) six months or more from the date it was issued, a lawyer shall promptly take steps to contact the payee to determine the reason the check was not deposited by the payee, and shall issue a replacement check, as necessary and appropriate. With regard to abandoned or unclaimed trust funds, a lawyer shall comply with requirements of Supreme Court Rule 73.

(F) No funds of the lawyer shall be placed in or left in the account except as provided in Rule 1.15(a).

(G) When a separate real estate bank account is maintained for settlement transactions, and when client or third party funds are received but not yet disbursed, a listing must be prepared on a monthly basis showing the name of the client or third party, the balance due to each client or third party, and the total of all such balances. The total must agree with the reconciled cash balance.

(10) If a lawyer maintains financial books and records using a computer system, the lawyer must cause to be printed each month a hard copy of all monthly journals, ledgers, reports, and reconciliations, and must review and preserve the documents in the same manner as other financial records described in this Rule.

(e) A lawyer's financial books and records must be subject to examination by the auditor for the Lawyers' Fund for Client Protection, for the purpose of verifying the accuracy of a certificate of compliance filed each year by the lawyer pursuant to Supreme Court Rule 69. The examination must be conducted so as to preserve, insofar as is consistent with these Rules, the confidential nature of the lawyer's books and records. If the lawyer's books and records are not located in Delaware, the lawyer may have the option either to produce the books and records at the lawyer's office in Delaware or to produce the books and records at the location outside of Delaware where they are ordinarily located. If the production occurs outside of Delaware, the lawyer shall pay any additional expenses incurred by the auditor for the purposes of an examination.

(f) A lawyer holding client funds must initially and reasonably determine whether the funds should or should not be placed in an interest-bearing depository account for the benefit of the client. In making such a determination, the lawyer must consider the financial interests of the client, the costs of establishing and maintaining the account, any tax reporting procedures or requirements, the nature of the transaction involved, the likelihood of delay in the relevant proceedings, whether the funds are of a nominal amount, and whether the funds are expected to be held by the lawyer for a short period of time. A lawyer must at reasonable intervals consider whether changed circumstances would warrant a different determination with respect to the deposit of client funds. Except as provided in these Rules, interest earned on client funds placed into an interest-bearing depository account for the benefit of the client (less any deductions for service charges or other fees of the depository institution) shall belong to the client whose funds are deposited, and the lawyer shall have no right or claim to such interest.

(g) A lawyer holding client funds who has reasonably determined, pursuant to subsection (f) of this Rule, that such funds need not be deposited into an interest-bearing depository account for the benefit of the client must maintain a pooled interest-bearing depository account for the deposit of the funds; provided, however, that this requirement shall not apply to a lawyer who either has obtained inactive status pursuant to Supreme Court Rule 69(d), or has obtained a Certificate of Retirement pursuant to Supreme Court Rule 69(f), or has formally elected to opt out of this requirement in accordance with the procedure set forth below in subparagraph (k).

(h) A lawyer who maintains such a pooled account shall comply with the following:

(1) The account shall include only client's funds which are nominal amount or are expected to be held for a short period of time.

(2) No interest from such an account shall be made available to a lawyer or law firm.

(3) Lawyers or law firms depositing client funds in a pooled interest-bearing account under this paragraph (h) [(g)] shall direct the depository institution:
(a) To remit interest, net any service charges or fees, as computed in accordance with the institution's standard accounting practice, at least quarterly, to the Delaware Bar Foundation; and (b) To transmit with each remittance to the Delaware Bar Foundation a statement showing the name of the lawyer or law firm on whose accounting remittance is sent and the rate of interest applied; with a copy of statement to be transmitted to the lawyer or law firm by the Delaware Bar Foundation.

(i) The funds transmitted to the Delaware Bar Foundation shall be available for distribution for the following purposes:
(1) To improve the administration of justice;
(2) To provide and to enhance the delivery of legal services to the poor;
(3) To support law related education;

(4) For each other purposes that serve the public interest.

The Delaware Bar Foundation shall recommend for the approval of the Supreme Court of the State of Delaware, such distributions as it may deem appropriate. Distributions shall be made only upon the Court's approval.

(j) Lawyers or law firms, depositing client funds in a pooled interest-bearing depository account under this paragraph shall not be required to advise the client of such deposit or of the purposes to which the interest accumulated by reason of such deposits is to be directed.

(k) The procedure available for opting out of the requirement to maintain pooled interest-bearing accounts are as follows:

(1) Prior to December 15, 1983, a lawyer wishing to decline to maintain a pooled interest-bearing account[s] described in this paragraph for any calendar year may do so by submitting a Notice of Declination in writing to the Clerk of the Supreme Court *ab initio* or before December 15 of the preceding calendar year. Any such submission shall remain effective, unless revoked and need not be renewed for any ensuing year.
(2) Any lawyer who has not filed a Notice of Declination on or before December 15, 1983, may elect not to maintain a pooled interest-bearing depository account for client funds as required and instead to maintain a pooled depository account for such funds that does not bear interest or that bears interest solely for the benefit of the clients who deposited the funds by certifying that the lawyer or law firm opts out of the obligation to comply with the requirements by timely submission of the Annual Registration Statement required by Supreme Court Rule 69(b)(i). Any such certification shall release the lawyer or law firm submitting it from participation effective as of the date that the certification is submitted and it shall remain effective until revoked as set forth below without need for renewal for any ensuing year.
(3) Notwithstanding the foregoing provisions of this subparagraph, any lawyer or law firm may petition the Court at any time and, for good cause shown, may be granted leave to opt out of the obligation to comply with the mandatory requirements of this paragraph.

(l) An election to opt out of the obligation to comply with paragraph (h) hereof may be revoked at any time upon the opening by a non-participating lawyer or law firm of a pooled interest-bearing account as previously described and due notification thereof to the Court Administrator of the Supreme Court pursuant to Supreme Court Rule 69(g).

(m) A lawyer should exercise good faith judgment in determining initially, whether funds of a client are of such nominal amount or are expected to be held by the lawyer for such a short period of time that the funds should not be placed in an interest-bearing depository account for the benefit of the client. The lawyer should also consider such other facts as:

(1) The cost of establishing and maintaining the account, service charges, accounting fees, and tax reporting procedures;

(2) The nature of the transactions(s) involved; and

(3) The likelihood of delay in the relevant proceedings. A lawyer should review at reasonable intervals whether changed circumstances require further action respecting the deposit of client funds.

(n) A lawyer shall not disburse Fiduciary Funds from his or her attorney trust account(s) unless the funds deposited in the account to be disbursed are good funds as hereinafter defined. "Good funds" shall mean:

(1) cash;

(2) electronic fund ("wire") transfer;

(3) certified check;

(4) bank cashier's check or treasurer's check;

(5) U.S. Treasury or State of Delaware Treasury check;

(6) Check drawn on a separate trust or escrow account of an attorney engaged in the private practice of law in the State of Delaware held in a fiduciary capacity, including his or her client's funds;

(7) Check of an insurance company that is authorized by the Insurance Commissioner of Delaware to transact insurance business in Delaware;

(8) Check in an amount no greater than $ 10,000.00;

(9) Check greater than $ 10,000.00, which has been actually and finally collected and may be drawn against under federal or state banking regulations then in effect;

(10) Check drawn on an escrow account of a real estate broker licensed by the state of Delaware up to the limit of guarantee provided per transaction by statute.

COMMENT

[1] A lawyer should hold property of others with the care required of a professional fiduciary. Securities should be kept in a safe deposit box, except when some other form of safekeeping is warranted by special circumstances. All property which is the property of clients or third persons should be kept separate from the lawyer's business and personal property and, if monies, in one or more trust accounts. Separate trust accounts may be warranted when administering estate monies or acting in similar fiduciary capacities.

[2] Lawyers often receive funds from third parties from which the lawyer's fee will be paid. If there is risk that the client may divert the funds without paying the fee, the lawyer is not required to remit the portion from which the fee is to be paid. However, a lawyer may not hold funds to coerce a client into accepting the lawyer's contention. The disputed portion of the funds should be kept in trust and the lawyer should suggest means for prompt resolution of the dispute, such as arbitration. The

undisputed portion of the funds shall be promptly distributed.

[3] Third parties, such as a client's creditors, may have just claims against funds or other property in a lawyer's custody. A lawyer may have a duty under applicable law to protect such third-party claims against wrongful interference by the client, and accordingly may refuse to surrender the property to the client. However, a lawyer should not unilaterally assume to arbitrate a dispute between the client and the third party.

[4] The obligations of a lawyer under this Rule are independent of those arising from activity other than rendering legal services. For example, a lawyer who serves as an escrow agent is governed by the applicable law relating to fiduciaries even though the lawyer does not render legal services in the transaction.

[5] The extensive provisions contained in Rule 1.15(d) represent the financial recordkeeping requirements that Delaware lawyers must follow when engaged in the private practice of law. These provisions are also reflected in a certificate of compliance that is included in each lawyer's registration statement, filed annually pursuant to Delaware Supreme Court Rule 69.

[6] Compliance with these provisions provides the necessary level of control to safeguard client and third party funds, as well as the lawyer's operating funds. When these recordkeeping procedures are not performed on a prompt and timely basis, there will be a loss of control by the lawyer, resulting in insufficient safeguards over client and other property.

[7] Some of the essential financial recordkeeping issues for Delaware lawyers under this Rule include the following:
(a) Segregation of funds. Improper commingling occurs when the lawyer's funds are deposited in an account intended for the holding of client and third party funds, or when client funds are deposited in an account intended for the holding of the lawyer's funds. The only exception is found in Rule 1.15(a), which allows a lawyer to maintain $500 of the lawyer's funds in the fiduciary account in order to cover possible bank service charges. Keeping an accurate account of each client's funds is more difficult if client funds are combined with the lawyer's own funds. The requirement of separate bank accounts for lawyer funds and non-lawyer funds, with separate bookkeeping procedures for each, is intended to avoid commingling.
(b) Deposits of legal fees. Unearned legal fees are the property of the client until earned, and therefore must be deposited into the lawyer's fiduciary account. Legal fees must be withdrawn from the fiduciary account and transferred to the operating or business account promptly upon being earned, to avoid improper commingling. The monthly listing of client and third party funds in the fiduciary account should therefore be carefully reviewed in order to determine whether any earned legal fees remain in the account.

(c) Identity of property. The identity and location of client funds and other property must be maintained at all times. Accordingly, every cash receipt and disbursement transaction in the fiduciary account must be specifically identified by the name of the client or third party. If financial books and records are maintained in the manner, the resultant control should ensure that there are no unidentified funds in the lawyer's possession.

(d) Disbursement of funds. Funds due to clients or third parties must be disbursed without unnecessary delay. The monthly listing of client funds in the fiduciary account should therefore be reviewed carefully in order to determine whether any balances due to clients or third parties remain in the account.

(e) Negative balances. The disbursement of client or third party funds in an amount greater than the amount being held for such client or third party results in a negative balance in the fiduciary account. This should never occur when the proper controls are in place. However, if a negative balance occurs by mistake or oversight, the lawyer must make a timely transfer of funds from the operating account to the fiduciary account in order to cover the excess disbursement and cure the negative balance. Such mistakes can be avoided by making certain that the client balance sufficiently covers a potential disbursement prior to making the actual disbursement.

(f) Reconciliations. Reconciled cash balances in the fiduciary accounts must agree with the totals of client balances held. Only by performing a reconciliation procedure will the lawyer be assured that the cash balance in the fiduciary account exactly covers the balance of client and third party funds that the lawyer is holding.

(g) Real estate accounts. Bank accounts used exclusively for real estate settlement transactions are fiduciary accounts, and are therefore subject to the same recordkeeping requirements as other such accounts, except that cash receipts and cash disbursements journals are not required.

[8] Illustrations of some of the accounting terms that Delaware lawyers need to be aware of, as used in this Rule, include the following:

(a) Financial books and records include all paper documents or computer files in which fiduciary and non-fiduciary transactions are individually recorded, balanced, reconciled, and totalled. Such records include cash receipts and cash disbursements journals, general and subsidiary journals, periodic reports, monthly reconciliations, listings, and so on.

(b) The cash receipts journal is a monthly listing of all deposits made during the month and identified by date, source name, and amount, and in distribution columns, the nature of the funds received, such as "fee income" or "advance from client," and so on. Such a journal is maintained for each bank account.

(c) The cash disbursements journal is a listing of all check payments made during the month and identified by date, payee name, check number, and amount, and in distribution columns, the nature of funds disbursed, such as "rent" or "payroll," and so on. Such a journal is maintained for each bank account. Cash receipts and cash disbursement records may be maintained in one consolidated journal.

(d) Totals and balances refer to the procedures that the lawyer needs to perform when using a manual system for accounting purposes, in order to ensure that the totals in the monthly cash receipts and cash disbursements journal are correct. The cash and distribution columns must be added up for each month, then the total cash received or disbursed must be compared with the total of all of the distribution columns.

(e) The ending check register balance is the accumulated net cash balance of all deposits, check payments, and adjustments for each bank account. This balance will not normally agree with the bank balance appearing on the end-of month bank statement because deposits and checks may not clear with the bank until the next statement period. This is why a reconciliation is necessary.

(f) The reconciled monthly cash balance is the bank balance conformed to the check register balance by taking into account the items recorded in the check register which have not cleared the bank. For example:

Account balance, per bank

statement $2,000.00

Add -- deposits in transit

(deposits in check register that do

not appear on bank statement) $1,500.00

Less -- outstanding checks

(checks entered in check register that do

not appear on bank statement) (1,800.00)

Reconciled cash balance $1,700.00

(g) The general ledger is a yearly record in which all of a lawyer's transactions are recorded and grouped by type, such as cash received, cash disbursed, fee income, funds due to clients, and so on. Each type of transaction recorded in the general ledger is also summarized as an aggregate balance. For example, the ledger shows cash balances for each bank account which represent the accumulation of the beginning balance, all of the deposits in the period, and all of the checks issued in the period.

(h) The subsidiary ledger is the list of transactions shown by each individual client or third party, with the individual balances of each (as contrasted to the general ledger, which lists the total balances in an aggregate amount "due to clients"). The total of all of the individual client and third party balances in the subsidiary ledger should agree with the total account balance in the general ledger.

(i) A variance occurs in a reconciliation procedure when two figures which should agree do not in fact agree. For example, a variance occurs when the reconciled cash balance in a fiduciary account does not agree with the total of client and third party funds that the lawyer is actually holding.

[9] Accrued interest on client and other funds in a lawyer's possession is not the property of the lawyer, but is generally considered to be the property of the owner of the principal. An exception to this legal principle relates to nominal amounts of interest on principal. A lawyer must reasonably determine if the transactional or

other costs of tracking and transferring such interest to the owners of the principal are greater than the amount of the interest itself. The lawyer's proper determination along these lines will result in the lawyer's depositing of fiduciary funds into an interest-bearing account for the benefit of the owners of the principal, or into a pooled interest-bearing account. If funds are deposited into a pooled account, the interest is to be transferred (with some exception) to the Delaware Bar Foundation pursuant to the Delaware Supreme Court's Interest On Lawyer Trust Accounts Program ("IOLTA").

[10] Implicit in the principles underlying Rule 1.15 is the strict prohibition against the misappropriation of client or third party funds. Misappropriation of fiduciary funds is clearly a violation of the lawyer's obligation to safeguard client and other funds. Moreover, intentional or knowing misappropriation may also be a violation Rule 8.4(b) (criminal conduct in the form of theft) and Rule 8.4(c) (general dishonest or deceptive conduct). Intentional or knowing misappropriation is considered to be one of the most serious acts of professional misconduct in which a lawyer can engage, and typically results in severe disciplinary sanctions.

[11] Misappropriation includes any unauthorized taking by a lawyer of client or other property, even for benign reasons or where there is an intent to replenish such funds. Although misappropriation by mistake, neglect, or recklessness is not as serious as intentional or knowing misappropriation, it can nevertheless result in severe disciplinary sanctions. See, e.g. *Matter of Figliola, Del. Supr., 652 A.2d 1071, 1076-78 (1995)*.

Rule 1.15A. Trust account overdraft notification

(a) Attorney accounts designated as "Trust Account" or "Escrow Account" pursuant to Rule 1.15(d)(2) shall be maintained only in financial institutions approved by the Lawyers' Fund for Client Protection (the "Fund"). A financial institution may not be approved as a depository for attorney trust and escrow accounts unless it shall have filed with the Fund an agreement, in a form provided by the Fund, to report to the Office of Disciplinary Counsel ("ODC") in the event any instrument in properly payable form is presented against an attorney trust or escrow account containing insufficient funds, irrespective of whether or not the instrument is honored.

(b) The Supreme Court may establish rules governing approval and termination of approved status for financial institutions and the Fund shall annually publish a list of approved financial institutions. No trust or escrow account shall be maintained in any financial institution that does not agree to make such reports. Any such agreement shall apply to all branches of the financial institution and shall not be canceled except upon thirty (30) days notice in writing to the Fund.

(c) The overdraft notification agreement shall provide that all reports made by the financial institution shall be in the following format:

(1) In the case of a dishonored instrument, the report shall be identical to the overdraft notice customarily forwarded to the depositor, and shall include a copy of the dishonored instrument to the ODC no later than seven (7) calendar days following a request for the copy by the ODC.

(2) In the case of instruments that are presented against insufficient funds, but which instruments are honored, the report shall identify the financial institution, the attorney or law firm, the account number, the date of presentation for payment, and the date paid, as well as the amount of the overdraft created thereby.

(d) Reports shall be made simultaneously with, and within the time provided by law for, notice of dishonor. If an instrument presented against insufficient funds is honored, then the report shall be made within seven (7) calendar days of the date of presentation for payment against insufficient funds.

(e) Every attorney practicing or admitted to practice in this jurisdiction shall, as a condition thereof, be conclusively deemed to have consented to the reporting and production requirements mandated by this rule.

(f) Nothing herein shall preclude a financial institution from charging a particular attorney or law firm for the reasonable costs of producing the reports and records required by this rule.

(g) The terms used in this section are defined as follows:

(1) "Financial institution" includes banks, savings and loan associations, credit unions, savings banks and any other business or persons which accept for deposit funds held in trust by attorneys.

(2) "Properly payable" refers to an instrument which, if presented in the normal course of business, is in a form requiring payment under the laws of Delaware.

(3) "Notice of dishonor" refers to the notice which a financial institution is required to give, under the laws of Delaware, upon presentation of an instrument which the institution dishonors.

(h) Every attorney practicing or admitted to practice in this jurisdiction shall designate every account into which attorney trust or escrow funds are deposited either as a "Rule 1.15A Attorney Trust Account" or as a "Rule 1.15A Attorney Escrow Account".

Rule 1.16. Declining or terminating representation

(a) Except as stated in paragraph (c), a lawyer shall not represent a client or, where representation has commenced, shall withdraw from the representation of a client if: (1) the representation will result in violation of the rules of professional conduct or other law; (2) the lawyer's physical or mental condition materially impairs the lawyer's ability to represent the client; or (3) the lawyer is discharged.

(b) Except as stated in paragraph (c), a lawyer may withdraw from representing a client if: (1) withdrawal can be accomplished without material adverse effect on the interests of the client; (2) the client persists in a course of action involving the lawyer's services that the lawyer reasonably believes is criminal or fraudulent; (3) the client has used the lawyer's service to perpetrate a crime or fraud; (4) a client insists upon taking action that the lawyer considers repugnant or with which the lawyer has a fundamental disagreement; (5) the client fails substantially to fulfill an obligation to the lawyer regarding the lawyer's services and has been given reasonable warning that the lawyer will withdraw unless the obligation is fulfilled; (6) the representation will result in an unreasonable financial burden on the lawyer or has been rendered unreasonably difficult by the client; or (7) other good cause for withdrawal exists.

(c) A lawyer must comply with applicable law requiring notice to or permission of a tribunal when terminating a representation. When ordered to do so by a tribunal, a lawyer shall continue representation notwithstanding good cause for terminating the representation.

(d) Upon termination of representation, a lawyer shall take steps to the extent reasonably practicable to protect a client's interests, such as giving reasonable notice to the client, allowing time for employment of other counsel, surrendering papers and property to which the client is entitled and refunding any advance payment of fee or expense that has not been earned or incurred. The lawyer may retain papers relating to the client to the extent permitted by other law.

COMMENT

[1] A lawyer should not accept representation in a matter unless it can be performed competently, promptly, without improper conflict of interest and to completion. Ordinarily, a representation in a matter is completed when the agreedupon assistance has been concluded. See Rules 1.2(c) and 6.5. See also Rule 1.3, Comment [4].

[2] *Mandatory Withdrawal.* -- A lawyer ordinarily must decline or withdraw from representation if the client demands that the lawyer engage in conduct that is illegal or violates the Rules of Professional Conduct or other law. The lawyer is not obliged to decline or withdraw simply because the client suggests such a course of conduct; a client may make such a suggestion in the hope that a lawyer will not be constrained by a professional obligation.

[3] When a lawyer has been appointed to represent a client, withdrawal ordinarily requires approval of the appointing authority. See also Rule 6.2. Similarly, court approval or notice to the court is often required by applicable law before a lawyer withdraws from pending litigation. Difficulty may be encountered if withdrawal is based on the client's demand that the lawyer engage in unprofessional conduct. The court may request an explanation for the withdrawal, while the lawyer may be bound to keep confidential the facts that would constitute such an explanation. The lawyer's statement that professional considerations require termination of the representation ordinarily should be accepted as sufficient. Lawyers should be mindful of their obligations to both clients and the court under Rules 1.6 and 3.3.

[4] *Discharge.* -- A client has a right to discharge a lawyer at any time, with or without cause, subject to liability for payment for the lawyer's services. Where future dispute about the withdrawal may be anticipated, it may be advisable to prepare a written statement reciting the circumstances.

[5] Whether a client can discharge appointed counsel may depend on applicable law. A client seeking to do so should be given a full explanation of the consequences. These consequences may include a decision by the appointing authority that appointment of successor counsel is unjustified, thus requiring self-representation by the client.

[6] If the client has severely diminished capacity, the client may lack the legal capacity to discharge the lawyer, and in any event the discharge may be seriously adverse to the client's interests. The lawyer should make special effort to help the client consider the consequences and may take reasonably necessary protective action as provided in Rule 1.14.

[7] *Optional Withdrawal.* -- A lawyer may withdraw from representation in some circumstances. The lawyer has the option to withdraw if it can be accomplished without material adverse effect on the client's interests. Withdrawal is also justified if the client persists in a course of action that the lawyer reasonably believes is criminal or fraudulent, for a lawyer is not required to be associated with such conduct even if the lawyer does not further it. Withdrawal is also permitted if the lawyer's services were misused in the past even if that would materially prejudice the client. The lawyer may also withdraw where the client insists on taking action that the lawyer considers repugnant or with which the lawyer has a fundamental disagreement.

[8] A lawyer may withdraw if the client refuses to abide by the terms of an agreement relating to the representation, such as an agreement concerning fees or court costs or an agreement limiting the objectives of the representation.

[9] *Assisting the Client upon Withdrawal.* -- Even if the lawyer has been unfairly

discharged by the client, a lawyer must take all reasonable steps to mitigate the consequences to the client. The lawyer may retain papers as security for a fee only to the extent permitted by law. See Rule 1.15.

Rule 1.17. Sale of law practice - omitted

Rule 1.18. Duties to prospective client

(a) A person who discusses with a lawyer the possibility of forming a client-lawyer relationship with respect to a matter is a prospective client.

(b) Even when no client-lawyer relationship ensues, a lawyer who has had discussions with a prospective client shall not use or reveal information learned in the consultation, except as Rule 1.9 would permit with respect to information of a former client.

(c) A lawyer subject to paragraph (b) shall not represent a client with interests materially adverse to those of a prospective client in the same or a substantially related matter if the lawyer received information from the prospective client that could be significantly harmful to that person in the matter, except as provided in paragraph (d). If a lawyer is disqualified from representation under this paragraph, no lawyer in a firm with which that lawyer is associated may knowingly undertake or continue representation in such a matter, except as provided in paragraph (d).

(d) When the lawyer has received disqualifying information as defined in paragraph (c), representation is permissible if: (1) both the affected client and the prospective client have given informed consent, confirmed in writing, or: (2) the lawyer who received the information took reasonable measures to avoid exposure to more disqualifying information than was reasonably necessary to determine whether to represent the prospective client; and (i) the disqualified lawyer is timely screened from any participation in the matter and is apportioned no part of the fee therefrom; and (ii) written notice is promptly given to the prospective client.

Rule 2.1. Advisor

In representing a client, a lawyer shall exercise independent professional judgment and render candid advice. In rendering advice, a lawyer may refer not only to law but to other considerations, such as moral, economic, social and political factors, that may be relevant to the client's situation.

Rule 2.2. Intermediary (Deleted)

Rule 2.3. Evaluation for use by third persons - omitted

Rule 2.4. Lawyer serving as third-party neutral

(a) A lawyer serves as a third-party neutral when the lawyer assists two or more persons who are not clients of the lawyer to reach a resolution of a dispute or other matter that has arisen between them. Service as a third-party neutral may include service as an arbitrator, a mediator or in such other capacity as will enable the lawyer to assist the parties to resolve the matter.

(b) A lawyer serving as a third-party neutral shall inform unrepresented parties that the lawyer is not representing them. When the lawyer knows or reasonably should know that a party does not understand the lawyer's role in the matter, the lawyer shall explain the difference between the lawyer's role as a third-party neutral and a lawyer's role as one who represents a client.

Rule 3.1. Meritorious claims and contentions

A lawyer shall not bring or defend a proceeding, or assert or controvert an issue therein, unless there is a basis in law and fact for doing so that is not frivolous, which includes a good faith argument for an extension, modification or reversal of existing law. A lawyer for the defendant in a criminal proceeding, or the respondent in a proceeding that could result in incarceration, may nevertheless so defend the proceeding as to require that every element of the case be established.

Rule 3.2. Expediting litigation

A lawyer shall make reasonable efforts to expedite litigation consistent with the interests of the client.

COMMENT

[1] Dilatory practices bring the administration of justice into disrepute. Although there will be occasions when a lawyer may properly seek a postponement for personal reasons, it is not proper for a lawyer to routinely fail to expedite litigation solely for the convenience of the advocates. Nor will a failure to expedite be

reasonable if done for the purpose of frustrating an opposing party's attempt to obtain rightful redress or repose. It is not a justification that similar conduct is often tolerated by the bench and bar. The question is whether a competent lawyer acting in good faith would regard the course of action as having some substantial purpose other than delay. Realizing financial or other benefit from otherwise improper delay in litigation is not a legitimate interest of the client.

Rule 3.3. Candor toward the tribunal

(a) A lawyer shall not knowingly: (1) make a false statement of fact or law to a tribunal or fail to correct a false statement of material fact or law previously made to the tribunal by the lawyer; (2) fail to disclose to the tribunal legal authority in the controlling jurisdiction known to the lawyer to be directly adverse to the position of the client and not disclosed by opposing counsel; or (3) offer evidence that the lawyer knows to be false. If a lawyer, the lawyer's client, or a witness called by the lawyer, has offered material evidence and the lawyer comes to know of its falsity, the lawyer shall take reasonable remedial measures, including, if necessary, disclosure to the tribunal. A lawyer may refuse to offer evidence, other than the testimony of a defendant in a criminal matter, that the lawyer reasonably believes is false.

(b) A lawyer who represents a client in an adjudicative proceeding and who knows that a person intends to engage, is engaging or has engaged in criminal or fraudulent conduct related to the proceeding shall take reasonable remedial measures, including, if necessary, disclosure to the tribunal.

(c) The duties stated in paragraph (a) and (b) continue to the conclusion of the proceeding, and apply even if compliance requires disclosure of information otherwise protected by Rule 1.6.

(d) In an ex parte proceeding, a lawyer shall inform the tribunal of all material facts known to the lawyer which will enable the tribunal to make an informed decision, whether or not the facts are adverse.

COMMENT

[1] This Rule governs the conduct of a lawyer who is representing a client in the proceedings of a tribunal. See Rule 1.0(m) for the definition of "tribunal." It also applies when the lawyer is representing a client in an ancillary proceeding conducted pursuant to the tribunal's adjudicative authority, such as a deposition. Thus, for example, paragraph (a)(3) requires a lawyer to take reasonable remedial measures if the lawyer comes to know that a client who is testifying in a deposition has offered evidence that is false.

[2] This Rule sets forth the special duties of lawyers as officers of the court to avoid conduct that undermines the integrity of the adjudicative process. A lawyer acting as an advocate in an adjudicative proceeding has an obligation to present the client's case with persuasive force. Performance of that duty while maintaining confidences of the client, however, is qualified by the advocate's duty of candor to the tribunal. Consequently, although a lawyer in an adversary proceeding is not required to present an impartial exposition of the law or to vouch for the evidence submitted in a cause, the lawyer must not allow the tribunal to be misled by false statements of law or fact or evidence that the lawyer knows to be false.

[3] *Representations by a Lawyer.* -- An advocate is responsible for pleadings and other documents prepared for litigation, but is usually not required to have personal knowledge of matters asserted therein, for litigation documents ordinarily present assertions by the client, or by someone on the client's behalf, and not assertions by the lawyer. Compare Rule 3.1. However, an assertion purporting to be on the lawyer's own knowledge, as in an affidavit by the lawyer or in a statement in open court, may properly be made only when the lawyer knows the assertion is true or believes it to be true on the basis of a reasonably diligent inquiry. There are circumstances where failure to make a disclosure is the equivalent of an affirmative misrepresentation. The obligation prescribed in Rule 1.2(d) not to counsel a client to commit or assist the client in committing a fraud applies in litigation. Regarding compliance with Rule 1.2(d), see the Comment to that Rule. See also the comment to Rule 8.4(b).

[4] *Legal Argument.* -- Legal argument based on a knowingly false representation of law constitutes dishonesty toward the tribunal. A lawyer is not required to make a disinterested exposition of the law, but must recognize the existence of pertinent legal authorities. Furthermore, as stated in paragraph (a)(2), an advocate has a duty to disclose directly adverse authority in the controlling jurisdiction that has not been disclosed by the opposing party. The underlying concept is that legal argument is a discussion seeking to determine the legal premises properly applicable to the case.

[5] *Offering Evidence.* -- Paragraph (a)(3) requires that the lawyer refuse to offer evidence that the lawyer knows to be false, regardless of the client's wishes. This duty is premised on the lawyer's obligation as an officer of the court to prevent the trier of fact from being misled by false evidence. A lawyer does not violate this Rule if the lawyer offers the evidence for the purpose of establishing its falsity.
[6] If a lawyer knows that the client intends to testify falsely or wants the lawyer to introduce false evidence, the lawyer should seek to persuade the client that the evidence should not be offered. If the persuasion is ineffective and the lawyer continues to represent the client, the lawyer must refuse to offer the false evidence. If only a portion of a witness's testimony will be false, the lawyer may call the witness to testify but may not elicit or otherwise permit the witness to present the

testimony that the lawyer knows is false.

[7] The duties stated in paragraphs (a) and (b) apply to all lawyers, including defense counsel in criminal cases. In some jurisdictions, however, courts have required counsel to present the accused as a witness or to give a narrative statement if the accused so desires, even if counsel knows that the testimony or statement will be false. The obligation of the advocate under the Rules of Professional Conduct is subordinate to such requirements. See also Comment [9].

[8] The prohibition against offering false evidence only applies if the lawyer knows that the evidence is false. A lawyer's reasonable belief that evidence is false does not preclude its presentation to the trier of fact. A lawyer's knowledge that evidence is false, however, can be inferred from the circumstances. See Rule 1.0(f). Thus, although a lawyer should resolve doubts about the veracity of testimony or other evidence in favor of the client, the lawyer cannot ignore an obvious falsehood.

[9] Although paragraph (a)(3) only prohibits a lawyer from offering evidence the lawyer knows to be false, it permits the lawyer to refuse to offer testimony or other proof that the lawyer reasonably believes is false. Offering such proof may reflect adversely on the lawyer's ability to discriminate in the quality of evidence and thus impair the lawyer's effectiveness as an advocate. Because of the special protections historically provided criminal defendants, however, this Rule does not permit a lawyer to refuse to offer the testimony of such a client where the lawyer reasonably believes but does not know that the testimony will be false. Unless the lawyer knows the testimony will be false, the lawyer must honor the client's decision to testify. See also Comment [7].

[10] *Remedial Measures.* -- Having offered material evidence in the belief that it was true, a lawyer may subsequently come to know that the evidence is false. Or, a lawyer may be surprised when the lawyer's client, or another witness called by the lawyer, offers testimony the lawyer knows to be false, either during the lawyer's direct examination or in response to cross-examination by the opposing lawyer. In such situations or if the lawyer knows of the falsity of testimony elicited from the client during a deposition, the lawyer must take reasonable remedial measures. In such situations, the advocate's proper course is to remonstrate with the client confidentially, advise the client of the lawyer's duty of candor to the tribunal and seek the client's cooperation with respect to the withdrawal or correction of the false statements or evidence. If that fails, the advocate must take further remedial action. If withdrawal from the representation is not permitted or will not undo the effect of the false evidence, the advocate must make such disclosure to the tribunal as is reasonably necessary to remedy the situation, even if doing so requires the lawyer to reveal information that otherwise would be protected by Rule 1.6. It is for the tribunal then to determine what should

be done -- making a statement about the matter to the trier of fact, ordering a mistrial or perhaps nothing.

[11] The disclosure of a client's false testimony can result in grave consequences to the client, including not only a sense of betrayal but also loss of the case and perhaps a prosecution for perjury. But the alternative is that the lawyer cooperate in deceiving the court, thereby subverting the truth-finding process which the adversary system is designed to implement. See Rule 1.2(d). Furthermore, unless it is clearly understood that the lawyer will act upon the duty to disclose the existence of false evidence, the client can simply reject the lawyer's advice to reveal the false evidence and insist that the lawyer keep silent. Thus the client could in effect coerce the lawyer into being a party to fraud on the court.

[12] *Preserving Integrety of Adjunctive Process.* -- Lawyers have a special obligation to protect a tribunal against criminal or fraudulent conduct that undermines the integrity of the adjudicative process, such as bribing, intimidating or otherwise unlawfully communicating with a witness, juror, court official or other participant in the proceeding, unlawfully destroying or concealing documents or other evidence or failing to disclose information to the tribunal when required by law to do so. Thus, paragraph (b) requires a lawyer to take reasonable remedial measures, including disclosure if necessary, whenever the lawyer knows that a person, including the lawyer's client, intends to engage, is engaging or has engaged in criminal or fraudulent conduct related to the proceeding.

[13] *Duration of Obligation.* -- A practical time limit on the obligation to rectify false evidence or false statements of law and fact has to be established. The conclusion of the proceeding is a reasonably definite point for the termination of the obligation. A proceeding has concluded within the meaning of this Rule when a final judgment in the proceeding has been affirmed on appeal or the time for review has passed.

[14] *Ex parte Proceedings.* --] Ordinarily, an advocate has the limited responsibility of presenting one side of the matters that a tribunal should consider in reaching a decision; the conflicting position is expected to be presented by the opposing party. However, in any ex parte proceeding, such as an application for a temporary restraining order, there is no balance of presentation by opposing advocates. The object of an ex parte proceeding is nevertheless to yield a substantially just result. The judge has an affirmative responsibility to accord the absent party just consideration. The lawyer for the represented party has the correlative duty to make disclosures of material facts known to the lawyer and that the lawyer reasonably believes are necessary to an informed decision.

[15] *Withdrawal.* -- Normally, a lawyer's compliance with the duty of candor imposed by this rule does not require that the lawyer withdraw from the

representation of a client whose interests will be or have been adversely affected by the lawyer's disclosure. The lawyer may, however, be required by Rule 1.16(a) to seek permission of the tribunal to withdraw if the lawyer's compliance with this Rule's duty of candor results in such an extreme deterioration of the client-lawyer relationship that the lawyer can no longer competently represent the client. Also see Rule 1.16(b) for the circumstances in which a lawyer will be permitted to seek a tribunal's permission to withdraw. In connection with a request for permission to withdraw that is premised on a client's misconduct, a lawyer may reveal information relating to the representation only to the extent reasonably necessary to comply with this Rule or as otherwise permitted by Rule 1.6.

Rule 3.4. Fairness to opposing party and counsel

A lawyer shall not:

(a) unlawfully obstruct another party's access to evidence or unlawfully alter, destroy or conceal a document or other material having potential evidentiary value. A lawyer shall not counsel or assist another person to do any such act;

(b) falsify evidence, counsel or assist a witness to testify falsely, or offer an inducement to a witness that is prohibited by law.

(c) knowingly disobey an obligation under the rules of a tribunal, except for an open refusal based on an assertion that no valid obligation exists;

(d) in pretrial procedure, make a frivolous discovery request or fail to make reasonably diligent efforts to comply with a legally proper discovery request by an opposing party;

(e) in trial, allude to any matter that the lawyer does not reasonably believe is relevant or that will not be supported by admissible evidence, assert personal knowledge of facts in issue except when testifying as a witness, or state a personal opinion as to the justness of a cause, the credibility of a witness, the culpability of a civil litigant or the guilt or innocence of an accused; or

(f) request a person other than a client to refrain from voluntarily giving relevant information to another party unless: (1) the person is a relative or an employee or other agent of a client; and (2) the lawyer reasonably believes that the person's interests will not be adversely affected by refraining from giving such information.

COMMENT

[1] The procedure of the adversary system contemplates that the evidence in a case is to be marshalled competitively by the contending parties. Fair competition in the adversary system is secured by the prohibitions against destruction or concealment of evidence, improperly influencing witnesses, obstructive tactics in discovery procedure, and the like.

[2] Documents and other items of evidence are often essential to establish a claim or defense. Subject to evidentiary privileges, the right of an opposing party, including the government, to obtain evidence through discovery or subpoena is an important procedural right. The exercise of that right can be frustrated if relevant material is altered, concealed or destroyed. Applicable law in many jurisdictions makes it an offense to destroy material for purpose of impairing its availability in a pending proceeding or one whose commencement can be foreseen. Falsifying evidence is also generally a criminal offense. Paragraph (a) applies to evidentiary material generally, including computerized information. Applicable law may permit a lawyer to take temporary possession of physical evidence of client crimes for the purpose of conducting a limited examination that will not alter or destroy material characteristics of the evidence. In such a case, applicable law may require the lawyer to turn the evidence over to the police or other prosecuting authority, depending on the circumstances.

[3] With regard to paragraph (b), it is not improper to pay a witness's expenses or to compensate an expert witness on terms permitted by law. The common law rule in most jurisdictions is that it is improper to pay an occurrence witness any fee for testifying and that it is improper to pay an expert witness a contingent fee.

[4] Paragraph (f) permits a lawyer to advise employees of a client to refrain from giving information to another party, for the employees may identify their interests with those of the client. See also Rule 4.2.

Rule 3.5. Impartiality and decorum of the tribunal

A lawyer shall not:

(a) seek to influence a judge, juror, prospective juror or other official by means prohibited by law;

(b) communicate or cause another to communicate ex parte with such a person or members of such person's family during the proceeding unless authorized to do so by law or court order; or

(c) communicate with a juror or prospective juror after discharge of the jury unless the communication is permitted by court rule;

(d) engage in conduct intended to disrupt a tribunal or engage in undignified or discourteous conduct that is degrading to a tribunal.

COMMENT

[1] Many forms of improper influence upon a tribunal are proscribed by criminal law. Others are specified in the ABA Model Code of Judicial Conduct, with which an advocate should be familiar. A lawyer is required to void contributing to a violation of such provisions.

[2] During a proceeding a lawyer may not communicate or cause another to communicate ex parte with persons serving in an official capacity in the proceeding, such as judges, masters or jurors, or with members of such person's family, unless authorized to do so by law or court order. Furthermore, a lawyer shall not conduct or cause another to conduct a vexatious or harassing investigation of such persons or their family members.

[3] A lawyer may not communicate with a juror or prospective juror after the jury has been discharged unless permitted by court rule. The lawyer may not engage in improper conduct during the communication.

[4] The advocate's function is to present evidence and argument so that the cause may be decided according to law. Refraining from abusive or obstreperous conduct is a corollary of the advocate's right to speak on behalf of litigants. A lawyer may stand firm against abuse by a judge but should avoid reciprocation; the judge's default is no justification for similar dereliction by an advocate. An advocate can present the cause, protect the record for subsequent review and preserve professional integrity by patient firmness no less effectively than by belligerence or theatrics.

[5] The duty to refrain from disruptive, undignified or discourteous conduct applies to any proceeding of a tribunal, including a deposition. See Rule 1.0(m).

Rule 3.6. Trial publicity

(a) A lawyer who is participating or has participated in the investigation or litigation of a matter shall not make an extrajudicial statement that the lawyer knows or reasonably should know will be disseminated by means of public communication and will have a substantial likelihood of materially prejudicing an adjudicative proceeding in the matter.

(b) Notwithstanding paragraph (a), a lawyer may state: (1) the claim, offense or defense involved and, except when prohibited by law, the identity of the persons involved; (2) information contained in a public record; (3) that an investigation of a matter is in progress; (4) the scheduling or result of any step in litigation; (5) a request for assistance in obtaining evidence and information necessary thereto; (6) a warning of danger concerning the behavior of a person involved, when there is reason to believe that there exists the likelihood of substantial harm to an individual or to the public interest; and (7) in a criminal case, in addition to subparagraphs (1) through (6): (i) the identity, residence, occupation and family status of the accused; (ii) if the accused has not been apprehended, information necessary to aid in apprehension of that person; (iii) the fact, time and place of arrest; and (iv) the identity of investigating and arresting officers or agencies and the length of the investigation.

(c) Notwithstanding paragraph (a), a lawyer may make a statement that a reasonable lawyer would believe is required to protect a client from the substantial undue prejudicial effect of recent publicity not initiated by the lawyer or the lawyer's client. A statement made pursuant to this paragraph shall be limited to such information as is necessary to mitigate the recent adverse publicity.

(d) No lawyer associated in a firm or government agency with a lawyer subject to paragraph (a) shall make a statement prohibited by paragraph (a).

COMMENT

[1] It is difficult to strike a balance between protecting the right to a fair trial and safeguarding the right of free expression. Preserving the right to a fair trial necessarily entails some curtailment of the information that may be disseminated about a party prior to trial, particularly where trial by jury is involved. If there were no such limits, the result would be the practical nullification of the protective effect of the rules of forensic decorum and the exclusionary rules of evidence. On the other hand, there are vital social interests served by the free dissemination of information about events having legal consequences and about legal proceedings themselves. The public has a right to know about threats to its safety and measures aimed at assuring its security. It also has a legitimate interest in the conduct of judicial proceedings, particularly in matters of general public concern. Furthermore, the subject matter of legal proceedings is often of direct significance in debate and deliberation over questions of public policy.

[2] Special rules of confidentiality may validly govern proceedings in juvenile, domestic relations and mental disability proceedings, and perhaps other types of litigation. Rule 3.4(c) requires compliance with such Rules.

[3] The Rule sets forth a basic general prohibition against a lawyer's making statements that the lawyer knows or should know will have a substantial likelihood

of materially prejudicing an adjudicative proceeding. Recognizing that the public value of informed commentary is great and the likelihood of prejudice to a proceeding by the commentary of a lawyer who is not involved in the proceeding is small, the rule applies only to lawyers who are, or who have been involved in the investigation or litigation of a case, and their associates.

[4] Paragraph (b) identifies specific matters about which a lawyer's statements would not ordinarily be considered to present a substantial likelihood of material prejudice, and should not in any event be considered prohibited by the general prohibition of paragraph (a). Paragraph (b) is not intended to be an exhaustive listing of the subjects upon which a lawyer may make a statement, but statements on other matters may be subject to paragraph (a).

[5] There are, on the other hand, certain subjects which are more likely than not to have a material prejudicial effect on a proceeding, particularly when they refer to a civil matter triable to a jury, a criminal matter, or any other proceeding that could result in incarceration. These subjects relate to: (1) the character, credibility, reputation or criminal record of a party, suspect in a criminal investigation or witness, or the identity of a witness, or the expected testimony of a party of witness; (2) in a criminal case or proceeding that could result in incarceration, the possibility of a plea of guilty to the offense or the existence or contents of any confession, admission, or statement given by a defendant or suspect or that person's refusal or failure to make a statement; (3) the performance or results of any examination or test or the refusal or failure of a person to submit to an examination or test, or the identity or nature of physical evidence expected to be presented; (4) any opinion as to the guilt or innocence of a defendant or suspect in a criminal case or proceeding that could result in incarceration; (5) information that the lawyer knows or reasonably should know is likely to be inadmissible as evidence in a trial and that would, if disclosed, create a substantial risk of prejudicing an impartial trial; or (6) the fact that a defendant has been charged with a crime, unless there is included therein a statement explaining that the charge is merely an accusation and that the defendant is presumed innocent until and unless proven guilty.

[6] Another relevant factor in determining prejudice is the nature of the proceeding involved. Criminal jury trials will be most sensitive to extrajudicial speech. Civil trials may be less sensitive. Non-jury hearings and arbitration proceedings may be even less affected. The Rule will still place limitations on prejudicial comments in these cases, but the likelihood of prejudice may be different depending on the type of proceeding.

[7] Finally, extrajudicial statements that might otherwise raise a question under this Rule may be permissible when they are made in response to statements made publicly by another party, another party's lawyer, or third persons, where a

reasonable lawyer would believe a public response is required in order to avoid prejudice to the lawyer's client. When prejudicial statements have been publicly made by others, responsive statements may have the salutary effect of lessening any resulting adverse impact on the adjudicative proceeding. Such responsive statements should be limited to contain only such information as is necessary to mitigate undue prejudice created by the statements made by others.

[8] See Rule 3.8(f) for additional duties of prosecutors in connection with extrajudicial statements about criminal proceedings.

Rule 3.7. Lawyer as witness
(a) A lawyer shall not act as advocate at a trial in which the lawyer is likely to be a necessary witness unless: (1) the testimony relates to an uncontested issue; (2) the testimony relates to the nature and value of legal services rendered in the case; or (3) disqualification of the lawyer would work substantial hardship on the client.

(b) A lawyer may act as advocate in a trial in which another lawyer in the lawyer's firm is likely to be called as a witness unless precluded from doing so by Rule 1.7 or Rule 1.9.

COMMENT

[1] Combining the roles of advocate and witness can prejudice the tribunal and the opposing party and can also involve a conflict of interest between the lawyer and client.

[2] *Advocate-Witness Rule.* -- The tribunal has proper objection when the trier of fact may be confused or misled by a lawyer serving as both advocate and witness. The opposing party has proper objection where the combination of roles may prejudice that party's rights in the litigation. A witness is required to testify on the basis of personal knowledge, while an advocate is expected to explain and comment on evidence given by others. It may not be clear whether a statement by an advocate-witness should be taken as proof or as an analysis of the proof.

[3] To protect the tribunal, paragraph (a) prohibits a lawyer from simultaneously serving as advocate and necessary witness except in those circumstances specified in paragraphs (a)(1) through (a)(3). Paragraph (a)(1) recognizes that if the testimony will be uncontested, the ambiguities in the dual role are purely theoretical. Paragraph (a)(2) recognizes that where the testimony concerns the extent and value of legal services rendered in the action in which the testimony is offered, permitting the lawyers to testify avoids the need for a second trial with new counsel to resolve that issue. Moreover, in such a situation the judge has firsthand

knowledge of the matter in issue; hence, there is less dependence on the adversary process to test the credibility of the testimony.

[4] Apart from these two exceptions, paragraph (a)(3) recognizes that a balancing is required between the interests of the client and those of the tribunal and the opposing party. Whether the tribunal is likely to be misled or the opposing party is likely to suffer prejudice depends on the nature of the case, the importance and probable tenor of the lawyer's testimony, and the probability that the lawyer's testimony will conflict with that of other witnesses. Even if there is risk of such prejudice, in determining whether the lawyer should be disqualified, due regard must be given to the effect of disqualification on the lawyer's client. It is relevant that one or both parties could reasonably foresee that the lawyer would probably be a witness. The conflict of interest principles stated in Rules 1.7, 1.9 and 1.10 have no application to this aspect of the problem.

[5] Because the tribunal is not likely to be misled when a lawyer acts as advocate in a trial in which another lawyer in the lawyer's firm will testify as a necessary witness, paragraph (b) permits the lawyer to do so except in situations involving a conflict of interest.

[6] *Conflict of Interest.* -- In determining if it is permissible to act as advocate in a trial in which the lawyer will be a necessary witness, the lawyer must also consider that the dual role may give rise to a conflict of interest that will require compliance with Rules 1.7 or 1.9. For example, if there is likely to be substantial conflict between the testimony of the client and that of the lawyer, the representation involves a conflict of interest that requires compliance with Rule 1.7. This would be true even though the lawyer might not be prohibited by paragraph (a) from simultaneously serving as advocate and witness because the lawyer's disqualification would work a substantial hardship on the client. Similarly, a lawyer who might be permitted to simultaneously serve as an advocate and a witness by paragraph (a)(3) might be precluded from doing so by Rule 1.9. The problem can arise whether the lawyer is called as a witness on behalf of the client or is called by the opposing party. Determining whether or not such a conflict exists is primarily the responsibility of the lawyer involved. If there is a conflict of interest, the lawyer must secure the client's informed consent, confirmed in writing. In some cases, the lawyer will be precluded from seeking the client's consent. See Rule 1.7. See Rule 1.0(b) for the definition of "confirmed in writing" and Rule 1.0(e) for the definition of "informed consent."

[7] Paragraph (b) provides that a lawyer is not disqualified from serving as an advocate because a lawyer with whom the lawyer is associated in a firm is precluded from doing so by paragraph (a). If, however, the testifying lawyer would also be disqualified by Rule 1.7 or Rule 1.9 from representing the client in the matter, other lawyers in the firm will be precluded from representing the client by

Rule 1.10 unless the client gives informed consent under the conditions stated in Rule 1.7.

Rule 3.8. Special responsibilities of a prosecutor

The prosecutor in a criminal case shall:

(a) refrain from prosecuting a charge that the prosecutor knows is not supported by probable cause;

(b) make reasonable efforts to assure that the accused has been advised of the right to, and the procedure for obtaining, counsel and has been given reasonable opportunity to obtain counsel;

(c) not seek to obtain from an unrepresented accused a waiver of important pretrial rights, such as the right to a preliminary hearing;

(d) make timely disclosure to the defense of all evidence or information known to the prosecutor that tends to negate the guilt of the accused or mitigates the offense, and, in connection with sentencing, disclose to the defense and to the tribunal all unprivileged mitigating information known to the prosecutor, except when the prosecutor is relieved of this responsibility by a protective order of the tribunal;

(e) not subpoena a lawyer in a grand jury or other criminal proceeding to present evidence about a past or present client unless the prosecutor reasonably believes: (1) the information sought is not protected from disclosure by any applicable privilege; (2) the evidence sought is essential to the successful completion of an ongoing investigation or prosecution; and (3) there is no other feasible alternative to obtain the information;

(f) except for statements that are necessary to inform the public of the nature and extent of the prosecutor's action and that serve a legitimate law enforcement purpose, refrain from making extrajudicial comments that have a substantial likelihood of heightening public condemnation of the accused and exercise reasonable care to prevent investigators, law enforcement personnel, employees or other persons assisting or associated with the prosecutor in a criminal case from making an extrajudicial statement that the prosecutor would be prohibited from making under Rule 3.6 or this Rule.

COMMENT

[1] A prosecutor has the responsibility of a minister of justice and not simply that of an advocate. This responsibility carries with it specific obligations to see that

the defendant is accorded procedural justice and that guilt is decided upon the basis of sufficient evidence. Precisely how far the prosecutor is required to go in this direction is a matter of debate and varies in different jurisdictions. Many jurisdictions have adopted the ABA Standards of Criminal Justice Relating to the Prosecution Function, which in turn are the product of prolonged and careful deliberation by lawyers experienced in both criminal prosecution and defense. Applicable law may require other measures by the prosecutor and knowing disregard of those obligations or a systematic abuse of prosecutorial discretion could constitute a violation of Rule 8.4.

[2] In some jurisdictions, a defendant may waive a preliminary hearing and thereby lose a valuable opportunity to challenge probable cause. Accordingly, prosecutors should not seek to obtain waivers of preliminary hearings or other important pretrial rights from unrepresented accused persons. Paragraph (c) does not apply, however, to an accused appearing pro se with the approval of the tribunal. Nor does it forbid the lawful questioning of an uncharged suspect who has knowingly waived the rights to counsel and silence.

[3] The exception in paragraph (d) recognizes that a prosecutor may seek an appropriate protective order from the tribunal if disclosure of information to the defense could result in substantial harm to an individual or to the public interest.

[4] Paragraph (e) is intended to limit the issuance of lawyer subpoenas in grand jury and other criminal proceedings to those situations in which there is a genuine need to intrude into the client-lawyer relationship.

[5] Paragraph (f) supplements Rule 3.6, which prohibits extra judicial statements that have a substantial likelihood of prejudicing an adjudicatory proceeding. In the context of a criminal prosecution, a prosecutor's extrajudicial statement can create the additional problem of increasing public condemnation of the accused. Although the announcement of an indictment, for example, will necessarily have severe consequences for the accused, a prosecutor can, and should, avoid comments that have no legitimate law enforcement purpose and have a substantial likelihood of increasing public opprobrium of the accused. Nothing in this Comment is intended to restrict the statements which a prosecutor may make which comply with Rule 3.6(b) or 3.6(c).

[6] Like other lawyers, prosecutors are subject to Rules 5.1 and 5.3, which relate to responsibilities regarding lawyers and nonlawyers who work for or are associated with the lawyer's office. Paragraph (f) reminds the prosecutor of the importance of these obligations in connection with the unique dangers of improper extrajudicial statements in a criminal case. In addition, paragraph (f) requires a prosecutor to exercise reasonable care to prevent persons assisting or associated with the prosecutor from making improper extrajudicial statements, even when

such persons are not under the direct supervision of the prosecutor. Ordinarily, the reasonable care standard will be satisfied if the prosecutor issues the appropriate cautions to law-enforcement personnel and other relevant individuals.

Rule 3.9. Advocate in nonadjudicative proceedings - omitted

Rule 4.3. Dealing with unrepresented person

In dealing on behalf of a client with a person who is not represented by counsel, a lawyer shall not state or imply that the lawyer is disinterested. When the lawyer knows or reasonably should know that the unrepresented person misunderstands the lawyer's role in the matter, the lawyer shall make reasonable efforts to correct the misunderstanding. The lawyer shall not give legal advice to an unrepresented person, other than the advice to secure counsel, if the lawyer knows or reasonably should know that the interests of such a person are or have a reasonable possibility of being in conflict with the interests of the client.

COMMENT

[1] An unrepresented person, particularly one not experienced in dealing with legal matters, might assume that a lawyer is disinterested in loyalties or is a disinterested authority on the law even when the lawyer represents a client. In order to avoid a misunderstanding, a lawyer will typically need to identify the lawyer's client and, where necessary, explain that the client has interests opposed to those of the unrepresented person. For misunderstandings that sometimes arise when a lawyer for an organization deals with an unrepresented constituent, see Rule 1.13(d).

[2] The Rule distinguishes between situations involving unrepresented persons whose interests may be adverse to those of the lawyer's client and those in which the person's interests are not in conflict with the client's. In the former situation, the possibility that the lawyer will compromise the unrepresented person's interests is so great that the Rule prohibits the giving of any advice, apart from the advice to obtain counsel. Whether a lawyer is giving impermissible advice may depend on the experience and sophistication of the unrepresented person, as well as the setting in which the behavior and comments occur. This Rule does not prohibit a lawyer from negotiating the terms of a transaction or settling a dispute with an unrepresented person. So long as the lawyer has explained that the lawyer represents an adverse party and is not representing the person, the lawyer may inform the person of the terms on which the lawyer's client will enter into an agreement or settle a matter, prepare documents that require the person's signature and explain the lawyer's own view of the meaning of the document or the lawyer's view of the underlying legal obligations.

Rule 4.4. Respect for rights of third persons

(a) In representing a client, a lawyer shall not use means that have no substantial purpose other than to embarrass, delay or burden a third person, or use methods of obtaining evidence that violate the legal rights of such a person.

(b) A lawyer who receives a document relating to the representation of the lawyer's client and knows or reasonably should know that the document was inadvertently sent shall promptly notify the sender.

COMMENT

[1] Responsibility to a client requires a lawyer to subordinate the interests of others to those of the client, but that responsibility does not imply that a lawyer may disregard the rights of third persons. It is impractical to catalogue all such rights, but they include legal restrictions on methods of obtaining evidence from third persons and unwarranted intrusions into privileged relationships, such as the client-lawyer relationship.

[2] Paragraph (b) recognizes that lawyers sometimes receive documents that were mistakenly sent or produced by opposing parties or their lawyers. If a lawyer knows or reasonably should know that a such a document was sent inadvertently, then this Rule requires the lawyer to promptly notify the sender in order to permit that person to take protective measures. Whether the lawyer is required to take additional steps, such as returning the original document, is a matter of law beyond the scope of these Rules, as is the question of whether the privileged status of a document has been waived. Similarly, this Rule does not address the legal duties of a lawyer who receives a document that the lawyer knows or reasonably should know may have been wrongfully obtained by the sending person. For purposes of this Rule, "document" includes e-mail or other electronic modes of transmission subject to being read or put into readable form.

[3] Some lawyers may choose to return a document unread, for example, when the lawyer learns before receiving the document that it was inadvertently sent to the wrong address. Where a lawyer is not required by applicable law to do so, the decision to voluntarily return such a document is a matter of professional judgment ordinarily reserved to the lawyer. See Rules 1.2 and 1.4.

Rule 5.1. Responsibilities of partners, managers, and supervisory lawyers

(a) A partner in a law firm, and a lawyer who individually or together with other lawyers possesses comparable managerial authority in a law firm, shall make reasonable efforts to ensure that the firm has in effect measures giving reasonable assurance that all lawyers in the firm conform to the Rules of Professional Conduct.

(b) A lawyer having direct supervisory authority over another lawyer shall make reasonable efforts to ensure that the other lawyer conforms to the Rules of Professional Conduct.

(c) A lawyer shall be responsible for another lawyer's violation of the Rules of Professional Conduct if: (1) the lawyer orders or, with knowledge of the specific conduct, ratifies the conduct involved; or (2) the lawyer is a partner or has comparable managerial authority in the law firm in which the other lawyer practices, or has direct supervisory authority over the other lawyer, and knows of the conduct at a time when its consequences can be avoided or mitigated but fails to take reasonable remedial action.

Rule 5.3. Responsibilities regarding non-lawyer assistants

With respect to a nonlawyer employed or retained by or associated with a lawyer:

(a) a partner in a law firm, and a lawyer who individually or together with other lawyers possesses comparable managerial authority in a law firm, shall make reasonable efforts to ensure that the firm has in effect measures giving reasonable assurance that the person's conduct is compatible with the professional obligations of the lawyer;
(b) a lawyer having direct supervisory authority over the nonlawyer shall make reasonable efforts to ensure that the person's conduct is compatible with the professional obligations of the lawyer; and

(c) a lawyer shall be responsible for conduct of such a person that would be a violation of the Rules of Professional Conduct if engaged in by a lawyer if: (1) the lawyer orders or, with the knowledge of the specific conduct, ratifies the conduct involved; or (2) the lawyer is a partner or has comparable managerial authority in the law firm in which the person is employed, or has direct supervisory authority over the person, and knows of the conduct at a time when its consequences can be avoided or mitigated but fails to take reasonable remedial action.

Rule 5.4. Professional independence of a lawyer

(a) A lawyer or law firm shall not share legal fees with a nonlawyer, except that: (1) an agreement by a lawyer with the lawyer's firm, partner, or associate may provide for the payment of money, over a reasonable period of time after the lawyer's death, to the lawyer's estate or to one or more specified persons; (2) a lawyer who undertakes to complete unfinished legal business of a deceased lawyer may pay to the estate of the deceased lawyer that proportion of the total compensation which fairly represents the services rendered by the deceased lawyer; (3) a lawyer who purchases the practice of a deceased, disabled, or disappeared lawyer may, pursuant to the provisions of Rule 1.17, pay to the estate or other representative of that lawyer the agreed-upon purchase price; (4) a lawyer or law firm may include nonlawyer employees in a compensation or retirement plan, even though the plan is based in whole or in part on a profit-sharing arrangement; and (5) a lawyer may share court-awarded legal fees with a nonprofit organization that employed, retained or recommended employment of the lawyer in the matter.

(b) A lawyer shall not form a partnership with a nonlawyer if any of the activities of the partnership consist of the practice of law.

(c) A lawyer shall not permit a person who recommends, employs, or pays the lawyer to render legal services for another to direct or regulate the lawyer's professional judgment in rendering such legal services.

(d) A lawyer shall not practice with or in the form of a professional corporation or association authorized to practice law for a profit, if: (1) a nonlawyer owns any interest therein, except that a fiduciary representative of the estate of a lawyer may hold the stock or interest of the lawyer for a reasonable time during administration; (2) a nonlawyer is a corporate director or officer thereof or occupies the position of similar responsibility in any form of association other than a corporation; or (3) a nonlawyer has the right to direct or control the professional judgment of a lawyer

Rule 5.5. Unauthorized practice of law; multijurisdictional practice of law - omitted

---

Rule 5.6. Restrictions on right to practice - omitted

Rule 5.7. Responsibilities regarding law-related services - omitted

---

Rule 6.1. Voluntary pro bono publico service - omitted

Rule 6.2. Accepting appointments

A lawyer shall not seek to avoid appointment by a tribunal to represent a person except for good cause, such as:

(a) representing the client is likely to result in violation of the Rules of Professional Conduct or other law;

(b) representing the client is likely to result in an unreasonable financial burden on the lawyer; or

(c) the client or the cause is so repugnant to the lawyer as to be likely to impair the client-lawyer relationship or the lawyer's ability to represent the client.

Rule 6.3. Membership in legal services organization - omitted

---

Rule 6.4. Law reform activities affecting client interests - omitted

---

Rule 6.5. Non-profit and court-annexed limited legal-service programomitted

---

Rule 7.1. Communications concerning a lawyer's services - omitted

---

Rule 7.2. Advertising - omitted

Rule 7.3. Direct contact with prospective clients - omitted

Rule 7.4. Communication of fields of practice and specialization - omitted

---

Rule 7.5. Firm names and letterheads - omitted

Rule 8.1. Bar admission and disciplinary matters

An applicant for admission to the bar, or a lawyer in connection with a bar admission application or in connection with a disciplinary matter, shall not:

(a) knowingly make a false statement of material fact; or

(b) fail to disclose a fact necessary to correct a misapprehension known by the person to have arisen in the matter, or knowingly fail to respond to a lawful demand for information from an admission or disciplinary authority, except that this rule does not require disclosure of information otherwise protected by Rule 1.6.

Rule 8.2. Judicial and legal officials

(a) A lawyer shall not make a statement that the lawyer knows to be false or with reckless disregard as to its truth or falsity concerning the qualifications or integrity of a judge, adjudicatory officer or public legal officer, or a candidate for election or appointment to judicial or legal office.

(b) A lawyer who is a candidate for judicial office shall comply with the applicable provisions of the Code of Judicial Conduct.

Rule 8.3. Reporting professional misconduct

(a) A lawyer who knows that another lawyer has committed a violation of the rules of Professional Conduct that raises a substantial question as to that lawyer's honesty, trustworthiness or fitness as a lawyer in other respects, shall inform the appropriate professional authority.

(b) A lawyer who knows that a judge has committed a violation of applicable rules of judicial conduct that raises a substantial question as to the judge's fitness for office shall inform the appropriate authority.

(c) This Rule does not require disclosure of information otherwise protected by rule 1.6.

(d) Notwithstanding anything in this or other of the rules to the contrary, the relationship between members of either (i) the Lawyers Assistance Committee of the Delaware State Bar Association and counselors retained by the Bar Association, or (ii) the Professional Ethics Committee of the Delaware State Bar Association, or (iii) the Fee dispute Conciliation and Mediation Committee of the Delaware State Bar Association, or (iv) the Professional Guidance Committee of the Delaware State Bar Association, and a lawyer or a judge shall be the same as that of attorney and client.

Rule 8.4. Misconduct

It is professional misconduct for a lawyer to:

(a) violate or attempt to violate the Rules of Professional Conduct, knowingly assist or induce another to do so or do so through the acts of another;

(b) commit a criminal act that reflects adversely on the lawyer's honesty, trustworthiness or fitness as a lawyer in other respects;

(c) engage in conduct involving dishonesty, fraud, deceit or misrepresentation;

(d) engage in conduct that is prejudicial to the administration of justice;

(e) state or imply an ability to influence improperly a government agency or official or to achieve results by means that violate the Rules of Professional Conduct or other law; or

(f) knowingly assist a judge or judicial officer in conduct that is a violation of applicable rules of judicial conduct or other law.

APPENDIX II
RULES OF CIVIL PROCEDURE FOR THE UNITED STATES DISTRICT COURT
Effective September 16, 1938, as amended to December 1, 2006

The following excerpts are from the federal rules of civil procedure and are valid as of December 31, 2006.

I. SCOPE OF RULES—ONE FORM OF ACTION

Rule 1. Scope and Purpose of Rules

These rules govern the procedure in the United States district courts in all suits of a civil nature whether cognizable as cases at law or in equity or in admiralty, with the exceptions stated in Rule 81. They shall be construed and administered to secure the just, speedy, and inexpensive determination of every action.

(As amended Dec. 29, 1948, eff. Oct. 20, 1949; Feb. 28, 1966, eff. July 1, 1966; Apr. 22, 1993, eff. Dec. 1, 1993.)

Rule 2. One Form of Action

There shall be one form of action to be known as ''civil action.''

II. COMMENCEMENT OF ACTION; SERVICE OF PROCESS, PLEADINGS, MOTIONS, AND ORDERS

Rule 3. Commencement of Action

A civil action is commenced by filing a complaint with the court.

Rule 4. Summons

(a) FORM. The summons shall be signed by the clerk, bear the seal of the court, identify the court and the parties, be directed to the defendant, and state the name and address of the plaintiff's attorney or, if unrepresented, of the plaintiff. It shall also state the time within which the defendant must appear and defend, and notify the defendant that failure to do so will result in a judgment by default against the defendant for the relief demanded in the complaint. The court may allow a summons to be amended.

(b) ISSUANCE. Upon or after filing the complaint, the plaintiff may present a summons to the clerk for signature and seal. If the summons is in proper form, the clerk shall sign, seal, and issue it to the plaintiff for service on the defendant. A summons, or a copy of the summons if addressed to multiple defendants, shall be issued for each defendant to be served.

(c) SERVICE WITH COMPLAINT; BY WHOM MADE.

(1) A summons shall be served together with a copy of the complaint. The plaintiff is responsible for service of a summons and complaint within the time allowed under subdivision (m) and shall furnish the person effecting service with the necessary copies of the summons and complaint.

(2) Service may be effected by any person who is not a party and who is at least 18 years of age. At the request of the plaintiff, however, the court may direct that service be effected by a United States marshal, deputy United States marshal, or other person or officer specially appointed by the court for that purpose. Such an appointment must be made when the plaintiff is authorized to proceed in forma pauperis pursuant to 28 U.S.C. § 1915 or is authorized to proceed as a seaman under 28 U.S.C. § 1916.

(d) WAIVER OF SERVICE; DUTY TO SAVE COSTS OF SERVICE; REQUEST TO WAIVE.

(1) A defendant who waives service of a summons does not thereby waive any objection to the venue or to the jurisdiction of the court over the person of the defendant.

(2) An individual, corporation, or association that is subject to service under subdivision (e), (f), or (h) and that receives notice of an action in the manner provided in this paragraph has a duty to avoid unnecessary costs of serving the summons. To avoid costs, the plaintiff may notify such a defendant of the commencement of the action and request that the defendant waive service of a summons. The notice and request (A) shall be in writing and shall be addressed

directly to the defendant, if an individual, or else to an officer or managing or general agent (or other agent authorized by appointment or law to receive service of process) of a defendant subject to service under subdivision (h); (B) shall be dispatched through first-class mail or other reliable means; (C) shall be accompanied by a copy of the complaint and shall identify the court in which it has been filed; (D) shall inform the defendant, by means of a text prescribed in an official form promulgated pursuant to Rule 84, of the consequences of compliance and of a failure to comply with the request; (E) shall set forth the date on which the request is sent; (F) shall allow the defendant a reasonable time to return the waiver, which shall be at least 30 days from the date on which the request is sent, or 60 days from that date if the defendant is addressed outside any judicial district of the United States; and (G) shall provide the defendant with an extra copy of the notice and request, as well as a prepaid means of compliance in writing. If a defendant located within the United States fails to comply with a request for waiver made by a plaintiff located within the United States, the court shall impose the costs subsequently incurred in effecting service on the defendant unless good cause for the failure be shown.

(3) A defendant that, before being served with process, timely returns a waiver so requested is not required to serve an answer to the complaint until 60 days after the date on which the request for waiver of service was sent, or 90 days after that date if the defendant was addressed outside any judicial district of the United States.

(4) When the plaintiff files a waiver of service with the court, the action shall proceed, except as provided in paragraph (3), as if a summons and complaint had been served at the time of filing the waiver, and no proof of service shall be required.

(5) The costs to be imposed on a defendant under paragraph (2) for failure to comply with a request to waive service of a summons shall include the costs subsequently incurred in effecting service under subdivision (e), (f), or (h), together with the costs, including a reasonable attorney's fee, of any motion required to collect the costs of service.

(e) SERVICE UPON INDIVIDUALS WITHIN A JUDICIAL DISTRICT OF THE UNITED STATES. Unless otherwise provided by federal law, service upon an individual from whom a waiver has not been obtained and filed, other than an infant or an incompetent person, may be effected in any judicial district of the United States: (1) pursuant to the law of the state in which the district court is located, or in which service is effected, for the service of a summons upon the defendant in an action brought in the courts of general jurisdiction of the State; or (2) by delivering a copy of the summons and of the complaint to the individual personally or by leaving copies thereof at the individual's dwelling house or usual

place of abode with some person of suitable age and discretion then residing therein or by delivering a copy of the summons and of the complaint to an agent authorized by appointment or by law to receive service
of process.

(f) SERVICE UPON INDIVIDUALS IN A FOREIGN COUNTRY. Unless otherwise provided by federal law, service upon an individual from whom a waiver has not been obtained and filed, other than an infant or an incompetent person, may be effected in a place not within any judicial district of the United States: (1) by any internationally agreed means reasonably calculated to give notice, such as those means authorized by the Hague Convention on the Service Abroad of Judicial and Extrajudicial Documents; or (2) if there is no internationally agreed means of service or the applicable international agreement allows other means of service, provided that service is reasonably calculated to give notice: (A) in the manner prescribed by the law of the foreign country for service in that country in an action in any of its courts of general jurisdiction; or (B) as directed by the foreign authority in response to a letter interrogatory or letter of request; or (C) unless prohibited by the law of the foreign country, by (i) delivery to the individual personally of a copy of the summons and the complaint; or (ii) any form of mail requiring a signed receipt, to be addressed and dispatched by the clerk of the court to the party to be served; or (3) by other means not prohibited by international agreement as may be directed by the court.

(g) SERVICE UPON INFANTS AND INCOMPETENT PERSONS. Service upon an infant or an incompetent person in a judicial district of the United States shall be effected in the manner prescribed by the law of the state in which the service is made for the service of summons or other like process upon any such defendant in an action brought in the courts of general jurisdiction of that state. Service upon an infant or an incompetent person in a place not within any judicial district of the United States shall be effected in the manner prescribed by paragraph (2)(A) or (2)(B) of subdivision (f) or by such means as the court may direct.

(h) SERVICE UPON CORPORATIONS AND ASSOCIATIONS. Unless otherwise provided by federal law, service upon a domestic or foreign corporation or upon a partnership or other unincorporated association that is subject to suit under a common name, and from which a waiver of service has not been obtained and filed, shall be effected: (1) in a judicial district of the United States in the manner
prescribed for individuals by subdivision (e)(1), or by delivering a copy of the summons and of the complaint to an officer, a managing or general agent, or to any other agent authorized by appointment or by law to receive service of process and, if the agent is one authorized by statute to receive service and
the statute so requires, by also mailing a copy to the defendant, or (2) in a place not within any judicial district of the United States in any manner prescribed for

individuals by subdivision (f) except personal delivery as provided in paragraph (2)(C)(I) thereof.

(i) SERVING THE UNITED STATES, ITS AGENCIES, CORPORATIONS, OFFICERS, OR EMPLOYEES.

(1) Service upon the United States shall be effected (A) by delivering a copy of the summons and of the complaint to the United States attorney for the district in which the action is brought or to an assistant United States attorney or clerical employee designated by the United States attorney in a writing filed with the clerk of the court or by sending a copy of the summons and of the complaint by registered or certified mail addressed to the civil process clerk at the office of the United States attorney and (B) by also sending a copy of the summons and of the complaint by registered or certified mail to the Attorney General of the United States at Washington, District of Columbia, and (C) in any action attacking the validity of an order of an officer or agency of the United States not made a party, by also sending a copy of the summons and of the complaint by registered or certified mail to the officer or agency. (2)(A) Service on an agency or corporation of the United States, or an officer or employee of the United States sued only in an official capacity, is effected by serving the United States in the manner prescribed by Rule 4(i)(1) and by also sending a copy of the summons and complaint by registered or certified mail to the officer, employee, agency, or corporation. (B) Service on an officer or employee of the United States sued in an individual capacity for acts or omissions occurring in connection with the performance of duties on behalf of the United States—whether or not the officer or employee is sued also in an official capacity—is effected by serving the United States in the manner prescribed by Rule 4(i)(1) and by serving the officer or employee in the manner prescribed by Rule 4(e), (f), or (g).

(j) SERVICE UPON FOREIGN, STATE, OR LOCAL GOVERNMENTS.

(1) Service upon a foreign state or a political subdivision, agency, or instrumentality thereof shall be effected pursuant to 28 U.S.C. § 1608.

(2) Service upon a state, municipal corporation, or other governmental organization subject to suit shall be effected by delivering a copy of the summons and of the complaint to its chief executive officer or by serving the summons and complaint in the manner prescribed by the law of that state for the service of summons or other like process upon any such defendant.

(k) TERRITORIAL LIMITS OF EFFECTIVE SERVICE.

(1) Service of a summons or filing a waiver of service is effective to establish jurisdiction over the person of a defendant (A) who could be subjected to the

jurisdiction of a court of general jurisdiction in the state in which the district court is located, or (B) who is a party joined under Rule 14 or Rule 19 and is served at a place within a judicial district of the United States and not more than 100 miles from the place from which the summons issues, or (C) who is subject to the federal interpleader jurisdiction under 28 U.S.C. § 1335, or (D) when authorized by a statute of the United States.

(2) If the exercise of jurisdiction is consistent with the Constitution and laws of the United States, serving a summons or filing a waiver of service is also effective, with respect to claims arising under federal law, to establish personal jurisdiction over the person of any defendant who is not subject to the jurisdiction of the courts of general jurisdiction of any state.

(*l*) PROOF OF SERVICE. If service is not waived, the person effecting service shall make proof thereof to the court. If service is made by a person other than a United States marshal or deputy United States marshal, the person shall make affidavit thereof. Proof of service in a place not within any judicial district of the United States shall, if effected under paragraph (1) of subdivision (f), be made pursuant to the applicable treaty or convention, and shall, if effected under paragraph (2) or (3) thereof, include a receipt signed by the addressee or other evidence of delivery to the addressee satisfactory to the court. Failure to make proof of service does not affect the validity of the service. The court may allow proof of service to be amended.

(m) TIME LIMIT FOR SERVICE. If service of the summons and complaint is not made upon a defendant within 120 days after the filing of the complaint, the court, upon motion or on its own initiative after notice to the plaintiff, shall dismiss the action without prejudice as to that defendant or direct that service be effected within a specified time; provided that if the plaintiff shows good cause for the failure, the court shall extend the time for service for an appropriate period. This subdivision does not apply to service in a foreign country pursuant to subdivision (f) or (j)(1).

(n) SEIZURE OF PROPERTY; SERVICE OF SUMMONS NOT FEASIBLE.

(1) If a statute of the United States so provides, the court may assert jurisdiction over property. Notice to claimants of the property shall then be sent in the manner provided by the statute or by service of a summons under this rule.
(2) Upon a showing that personal jurisdiction over a defendant cannot, in the district where the action is brought, be obtained with reasonable efforts by service of summons in any manner authorized by this rule, the court may assert jurisdiction over any of the defendant's assets found within the district by seizing the assets under the circumstances and in the manner provided by the law of the state in which the district court is located.

(As amended Jan. 21, 1963, eff. July 1, 1963; Feb. 28, 1966, eff. July 1, 1966; Apr. 29, 1980, eff. Aug. 1, 1980; Jan. 12, 1983, eff. Feb. 26, 1983; Mar. 2, 1987, eff. Aug. 1, 1987; Apr. 22, 1993, eff. Dec. 1, 1993; Apr. 17, 2000, eff. Dec. 1, 2000.)

Rule 4.1. Service of Other Process

(a) GENERALLY. Process other than a summons as provided in Rule 4 or subpoena as provided in Rule 45 shall be served by a United States marshal, a deputy United States marshal, or a person specially appointed for that purpose, who shall make proof of service as provided in Rule 4(*l*). The process may be served anywhere within the territorial limits of the state in which the district court is located, and, when authorized by a statute of the United States, beyond the territorial limits of that state.

(b) ENFORCEMENT OF ORDERS: COMMITMENT FOR CIVIL CONTEMPT. An order of civil commitment of a person held to be in contempt of a decree or injunction issued to enforce the laws of the United States may be served and enforced in any district. Other orders in civil contempt proceedings shall be served in the state in which the court issuing the order to be enforced is located or elsewhere within the United States if not more than 100 miles from the place at which the order to be enforced was issued.

(As added Apr. 22, 1993, eff. Dec. 1, 1993.)

Rule 5. Service and Filing of Pleadings and Other Papers

(a) SERVICE: WHEN REQUIRED. Except as otherwise provided in these rules, every order required by its terms to be served, every pleading subsequent to the original complaint unless the court otherwise orders because of numerous defendants, every paper relating to discovery required to be served upon a party unless the court otherwise orders, every written motion other than one which may be heard ex parte, and every written notice, appearance, demand, offer of judgment, designation of record on appeal, and similar paper shall be served upon each of the parties. No service need be made on parties in default for failure to appear except that pleadings asserting new or additional claims for relief against them shall be served upon them in the manner provided for service of summons in Rule 4. In an action begun by seizure of property, in which no person need be or is named as defendant, any service required to be made prior to the filing of an answer, claim, or appearance shall be made upon the person having custody or possession of the property at the time of its seizure.

(b) MAKING SERVICE.

(1) Service under Rules 5(a) and 77(d) on a party represented by an attorney is made on the attorney unless the court orders service on the party.

(2) Service under Rule 5(a) is made by: (A) Delivering a copy to the person served by: (i) handing it to the person; (ii) leaving it at the person's office with a clerk or other person in charge, or if no one is in charge leaving it in a conspicuous place in the office; or (iii) if the person has no office or the office is closed, leaving it at the person's dwelling house or usual place of abode with someone of suitable age and discretion residing there. (B) Mailing a copy to the last known address of the person served. Service by mail is complete on mailing. (C) If the person served has no known address, leaving a copy with the clerk of the court. (D) Delivering a copy by any other means, including electronic means, consented to in writing by the person served. Service by electronic means is complete on transmission; service by other consented means is complete when the person making service delivers the copy to the agency designated to make delivery. If authorized by local rule, a party may make service under this subparagraph (D) through the court's transmission facilities.
(3) Service by electronic means under Rule 5(b)(2)(D) is not effective if the party making service learns that the attempted service did not reach the person to be served.

(c) SAME: NUMEROUS DEFENDANTS. In any action in which there are unusually large numbers of defendants, the court, upon motion or of its own initiative, may order that service of the pleadings of the defendants and replies thereto need not be made as between the defendants and that any cross-claim, counterclaim, or matter constituting an avoidance or affirmative defense contained therein shall be deemed to be denied or avoided by all other parties and that the filing of any such pleading and service thereof upon the plaintiff constitutes due notice of it to the parties. A copy of every such order shall be served upon the parties in such manner and form as the court directs.

(d) FILING; CERTIFICATE OF SERVICE. All papers after the complaint required to be served upon a party, together with a certificate of service, must be filed with the court within a reasonable time after service, but disclosures under Rule 26(a)(1) or (2) and the following discovery requests and responses must not be filed until they are used in the proceeding or the court orders filing: (I) depositions, (ii) interrogatories, (iii) requests for documents or to permit entry upon land, and (iv) requests for admission.

(e) FILING WITH THE COURT DEFINED. The filing of papers with the court as required by these rules shall be made by filing them with the clerk of court, except that the judge may permit the papers to be filed with the judge, in which event the judge shall note thereon the filing date and forthwith transmit them to the office of the clerk. A court may by local rule permit or require papers to be filed, signed, or verified by electronic means that are consistent with technical standards, if any, that the Judicial Conference of the United States establishes. A local rule may require filing by electronic means only if reasonable exceptions are allowed. A paper filed by electronic means in compliance with a local rule constitutes a written paper for the purpose of applying these rules. The clerk shall not refuse to accept for filing any paper presented for that purpose solely because it is not presented in proper form as required by these rules or any local rules or practices.

(As amended Jan. 21, 1963, eff. July 1, 1963; Mar. 30, 1970, eff. July 1, 1970; Apr. 29, 1980, eff. Aug. 1, 1980; Mar. 2, 1987, eff. Aug. 1, 1987; Apr. 30, 1991, eff. Dec. 1, 1991; Apr. 22, 1993, eff. Dec. 1, 1993; Apr. 23, 1996, eff. Dec. 1, 1996; Apr. 17, 2000, eff. Dec. 1, 2000; Apr. 23, 2001, eff. Dec. 1, 2001; Apr. 12, 2006, eff. Dec. 1, 2006.)

Rule 5.1. Constitutional Challenge to a Statute—Notice, Certification, and Intervention

(a) NOTICE BY A PARTY. A party that files a pleading, written motion, or other paper drawing into question the constitutionality of a federal or state statute must promptly: (1) file a notice of constitutional question stating the question and identifying the paper that raises it, if: (A) a federal statute is questioned and neither the United States nor any of its agencies, officers, or employees is a party in an official capacity, or (B) a state statute is questioned and neither the state nor any of its agencies, officers, or employees is a party in an official capacity; and (2) serve the notice and paper on the Attorney General of the United States if a federal statute is challenged—or on the state attorney general if a state statute is challenged—either by certified or registered mail or by sending it to an electronic address designated by the attorney general for this purpose.

(b) CERTIFICATION BY THE COURT. The court must, under 28 U.S.C. § 2403, certify to the Attorney General of the United States that there is a constitutional challenge to a federal statute, or certify to the state attorney general that there is a constitutional challenge to a state statute.

(c) INTERVENTION; FINAL DECISION ON THE MERITS. Unless the court sets a later time, the attorney general may intervene within 60 days after the notice of constitutional question is filed or after
the court certifies the challenge, whichever is earlier. Before the time to intervene expires, the court may reject the constitutional challenge, but may not enter a final judgment holding the statute unconstitutional.

(d) NO FORFEITURE. A party's failure to file and serve the notice, or the court's failure to certify, does not forfeit a constitutional claim or defense that is otherwise timely asserted.

(As added Apr. 12, 2006, eff. Dec. 1, 2006.)

Rule 6. Time

(a) COMPUTATION. In computing any period of time prescribed or allowed by these rules, by the local rules of any district court, by order of court, or by any applicable statute, the day of the act, event, or default from which the designated period of time begins to run shall not be included. The last day of the period so computed shall be included, unless it is a Saturday, a Sunday, or a legal holiday, or, when the act to be done is the filing of a paper in court, a day on which weather or other conditions have made the office of the clerk of the district court inaccessible, in which event the period runs until the end of the next day which is not one of the aforementioned days. When the period of time prescribed or allowed is less than 11 days, intermediate Saturdays, Sundays, and legal holidays shall be excluded in the computation. As used in this rule and in Rule 77(c), "legal holiday" includes New Year's Day, Birthday of Martin Luther King, Jr., Washington's Birthday, Memorial Day, Independence Day, Labor Day, Columbus Day, Veterans Day, Thanksgiving Day, Christmas Day, and any other day appointed as a holiday by the President or the Congress of the United States, or by the state in which the district court is held.

(b) ENLARGEMENT. When by these rules or by a notice given thereunder or by order of court an act is required or allowed to be done at or within a specified time, the court for cause shown may at any time in its discretion (1) with or without motion or notice order the period enlarged if request therefor is made before the expiration of the period originally prescribed or as extended by a previous order, or (2) upon motion made after the expiration of the specified period permit the act to be done where the failure to act was the result of excusable neglect; but it may not extend the time for taking any action under Rules 50(b) and (c)(2), 52(b), 59(b), (d) and (e), and 60(b), except to the extent and under the conditions stated in them.

[(c) UNAFFECTED BY EXPIRATION OF TERM.] (Rescinded Feb. 28, 1966, eff. July 1, 1966)

(d) FOR MOTIONS—AFFIDAVITS. A written motion, other than one which may be heard ex parte, and notice of the hearing thereof shall be served not later than 5 days before the time specified for the hearing, unless a different period is fixed by these rules or by order of the court. Such an order may for cause shown be made on ex parte application. When a motion is supported by affidavit, the affidavit shall be served with the motion; and, except as otherwise provided in Rule 59(c), opposing affidavits may be served not later than 1 day before the hearing, unless the court permits them to be served at some other time.

(e) ADDITIONAL TIME AFTER CERTAIN KINDS OF SERVICE. Whenever a party must or may act within a prescribed period after service and service is made under Rule 5(b)(2)(B), (C), or (D), 3 days are added after the prescribed period would otherwise expire under subdivision (a).

(As amended Dec. 27, 1946, eff. Mar. 19, 1948; Jan. 21, 1963, eff. July 1, 1963; Feb. 28, 1966, eff. July 1, 1966; Dec. 4, 1967, eff. July 1, 1968; Mar. 1, 1971, eff. July 1, 1971; Apr. 28, 1983, eff. Aug. 1, 1983; Apr. 29, 1985, eff. Aug. 1, 1985; Mar. 2, 1987, eff. Aug. 1, 1987; Apr. 26, 1999, eff. Dec. 1, 1999; Apr. 23, 2001, eff. Dec. 1, 2001; Apr. 25, 2005, eff. Dec. 1, 2005.)

III. PLEADINGS AND MOTIONS

Rule 7. Pleadings Allowed; Form of Motions

(a) PLEADINGS. There shall be a complaint and an answer; a reply to a counterclaim denominated as such; an answer to a cross-claim, if the answer contains a cross-claim; a third-party complaint, if a person who was not an original party is summoned under the provisions of Rule 14; and a third-party answer, if a third-party complaint is served. No other pleading shall be allowed, except that the court may order a reply to an answer or a third-party answer.

(b) MOTIONS AND OTHER PAPERS.

(1) An application to the court for an order shall be by motion which, unless made during a hearing or trial, shall be made in writing, shall state with particularity the grounds therefor, and shall set forth the relief or order sought. The requirement of writing is fulfilled if the motion is stated in a written notice of the hearing of the motion.

(2) The rules applicable to captions and other matters of form of pleadings apply to all motions and other papers provided for by these rules.

(3) All motions shall be signed in accordance with Rule 11.

(c) DEMURRERS, PLEAS, ETC., ABOLISHED. Demurrers, pleas, and exceptions for insufficiency of a pleading shall not be used.

(As amended Dec. 27, 1946, eff. Mar. 19, 1948; Jan. 21, 1963, eff. July 1, 1963; Apr. 28, 1983, eff. Aug. 1, 1983.)

Rule 7.1. Disclosure Statement

(a) WHO MUST FILE: NONGOVERNMENTAL CORPORATE PARTY. A nongovernmental corporate party to an action or proceeding in a district court must file two copies of a statement that identifies any parent corporation and any publicly held corporation that owns 10% or more of its stock or states that there is no such corporation.

(b) TIME FOR FILING; SUPPLEMENTAL FILING. A party must: (1) file the Rule 7.1(a) statement with its first appearance, pleading, petition, motion, response, or other request addressed to the court, and (2) promptly file a supplemental statement upon any change in the information that the statement requires.

(As added Apr. 29, 2002, eff. Dec. 1, 2002.)

Rule 8. General Rules of Pleading

(a) CLAIMS FOR RELIEF. A pleading which sets forth a claim for relief, whether an original claim, counterclaim, cross-claim, or third-party claim, shall contain (1) a short and plain statement of the grounds upon which the court's jurisdiction depends, unless the court already has jurisdiction and the claim needs no new grounds of jurisdiction to support it, (2) a short and plain statement of the claim showing that the pleader is entitled to relief, and (3) a demand for judgment for the relief the pleader seeks. Relief in the alternative or of several different types may be demanded.

(b) DEFENSES; FORM OF DENIALS. A party shall state in short and plain terms the party's defenses to each claim asserted and shall admit or deny the averments upon which the adverse party relies. If a party is without knowledge or information sufficient to form a belief as to the truth of an averment, the party shall so state and this has the effect of a denial. Denials shall fairly meet the substance of the averments denied. When a pleader intends in good faith to deny only a part or a qualification of an averment, the pleader shall specify so much of it as is true and material and shall deny only the remainder. Unless the pleader intends in good faith to controvert all the averments of the preceding pleading, the pleader may make denials as specific denials of designated averments or paragraphs or may generally deny all the averments except such designated averments or paragraphs as the pleader expressly admits; but, when the pleader does so intend to controvert all its averments, including averments of the grounds upon which the court's jurisdiction depends, the pleader may do so by general denial subject to the obligations set forth in Rule 11.

(c) AFFIRMATIVE DEFENSES. In pleading to a preceding pleading, a party shall set forth affirmatively accord and satisfaction, arbitration and award, assumption of risk, contributory negligence, discharge in bankruptcy, duress, estoppel, failure of consideration, fraud, illegality, injury by fellow servant, laches, license, payment, release, res judicata, statute of frauds, statute of limitations, waiver, and any other matter constituting an avoidance or affirmative defense. When a party has mistakenly designated a defense as a counterclaim or a counterclaim as a defense, the court on terms, if justice so requires, shall treat the pleading as if there had been a proper designation.

(d) EFFECT OF FAILURE TO DENY. Averments in a pleading to which a responsive pleading is required, other than those as to the amount of damage, are admitted when not denied in the responsive pleading. Averments in a pleading to which no responsive pleading is required or permitted shall be taken as denied or avoided.

(e) PLEADING TO BE CONCISE AND DIRECT; CONSISTENCY.

(1) Each averment of a pleading shall be simple, concise, and direct. No technical forms of pleading or motions are required.

(2) A party may set forth two or more statements of a claim or defense alternately or hypothetically, either in one count or defense or in separate counts or defenses. When two or more statements are made in the alternative and one of them if made independently would be sufficient, the pleading is not made insufficient by the insufficiency of one or more of the alternative statements. A party may also state as many separate claims or defenses as the party has regardless of consistency and whether based on legal, equitable, or maritime grounds. All statements shall be made subject to the obligations set forth in Rule 11.

(f) CONSTRUCTION OF PLEADINGS. All pleadings shall be so construed as to do substantial justice.

(As amended Feb. 28, 1966, eff. July 1, 1966; Mar. 2, 1987, eff. Aug. 1, 1987.)

Rule 9. Pleading Special Matters

(a) CAPACITY. It is not necessary to aver the capacity of a party to sue or be sued or the authority of a party to sue or be sued in a representative capacity or the legal existence of an organized association of persons that is made a party, except to the extent required to show the jurisdiction of the court. When a party desires to raise an issue as to the legal existence of any party or the capacity of any party to sue or be sued or the authority of a party to sue or be sued in a representative capacity, the party desiring to raise the issue shall do so by specific negative averment, which shall include such supporting particulars as are peculiarly within the pleader's knowledge.

(b) FRAUD, MISTAKE, CONDITION OF THE MIND. In all averments of fraud or mistake, the circumstances constituting fraud or mistake shall be stated with particularity. Malice, intent, knowledge, and other condition of mind of a person may be averred generally.

(c) CONDITIONS PRECEDENT. In pleading the performance or occurrence of conditions precedent, it is sufficient to aver generally that all conditions precedent have been performed or have occurred. A denial of performance or occurrence shall be made specifically and with particularity.

(d) OFFICIAL DOCUMENT OR ACT. In pleading an official document or official act it is sufficient to aver that the document was issued or the act done in compliance with law.

(e) JUDGMENT. In pleading a judgment or decision of a domestic or foreign court, judicial or quasi-judicial tribunal, or of a board or officer, it is sufficient to aver the judgment or decision without setting forth matter showing jurisdiction to render it.

(f) TIME AND PLACE. For the purpose of testing the sufficiency of a pleading, averments of time and place are material and shall be considered like all other averments of material matter.

(g) SPECIAL DAMAGE. When items of special damage are claimed, they shall be specifically stated.

(h) ADMIRALTY AND MARITIME CLAIMS. A pleading or count setting forth a claim for relief within the admiralty and maritime jurisdiction that is also within the jurisdiction of the district court on some other ground may contain a statement identifying the claim as an admiralty or maritime claim for the purposes of Rules 14(c), 38(e), and 82, and the Supplemental Rules for Admiralty or Maritime Claims and Asset Forfeiture Actions. If the claim is cognizable only in admiralty, it is an admiralty or maritime claim for those purposes whether so identified or not. The amendment of a pleading to add or withdraw an identifying statement is governed by the principles of Rule 15. A case that includes an admiralty or maritime claim within this subdivision is an admiralty case within 28 U.S.C. § 1292(a)(3).

(As amended Feb. 28, 1966, eff. July 1, 1966; Dec. 4, 1967, eff. July 1, 1968; Mar. 30, 1970, eff. July 1, 1970; Mar. 2, 1987, eff. Aug. 1, 1987; Apr. 11, 1997, eff. Dec. 1, 1997; Apr. 12, 2006, eff. Dec. 1, 2006.)

Rule 10. Form of Pleadings

(a) CAPTION; NAMES OF PARTIES. Every pleading shall contain a caption setting forth the name of the court, the title of the action, the file number, and a designation as in Rule 7(a). In the complaint the title of the action shall include the names of all the parties, but in other pleadings it is sufficient to state the name of the first party on each side with an appropriate indication of other parties.

(b) PARAGRAPHS; SEPARATE STATEMENTS. All averments of claim or defense shall be made in numbered paragraphs, the contents of each of which shall be limited as far as practicable to a statement of a single set of circumstances; and a paragraph may be referred to by number in all succeeding pleadings. Each claim founded upon a separate transaction or occurrence and each defense other than denials shall be stated in a separate count or defense whenever a separation facilitates the clear presentation of the matters set forth.

(c) ADOPTION BY REFERENCE; EXHIBITS. Statements in a pleading may be adopted by reference in a different part of the same pleading or in another pleading or in any motion. A copy of any written instrument which is an exhibit to a pleading is a part thereof for all purposes.

Rule 11. Signing of Pleadings, Motions, and Other Papers; Representations to Court; Sanctions

(a) SIGNATURE. Every pleading, written motion, and other paper shall be signed by at least one attorney of record in the attorney's individual name, or, if the party is not represented by an attorney, shall be signed by the party. Each paper shall state the signer's address and telephone number, if any. Except when otherwise specifically provided by rule or statute, pleadings need not be verified or accompanied by affidavit. An unsigned paper shall be stricken unless omission of the signature is corrected promptly after being called to the attention of the attorney or party.

(b) REPRESENTATIONS TO COURT. By presenting to the court (whether by signing, filing, submitting, or later advocating) a pleading, written motion, or other paper, an attorney or unrepresented party is certifying that to the best of the person's knowledge, information, and belief, formed after an inquiry reasonable under the circumstances,—

(1) it is not being presented for any improper purpose, such as to harass or to

cause unnecessary delay or needless increase in the cost of litigation;

(2) the claims, defenses, and other legal contentions therein are warranted by existing law or by a nonfrivolous argument for the extension, modification, or reversal of existing law or the establishment of new law;

(3) the allegations and other factual contentions have evidentiary support or, if specifically so identified, are likely to have evidentiary support after a reasonable opportunity for further investigation or discovery; and

(4) the denials of factual contentions are warranted on the evidence or, if specifically so identified, are reasonably based on a lack of information or belief.

(c) SANCTIONS. If, after notice and a reasonable opportunity to respond, the court determines that subdivision (b) has been violated, the court may, subject to the conditions stated below, impose an appropriate sanction upon the attorneys, law firms, or parties that have violated subdivision (b) or are responsible for the violation.

(1) *How Initiated.*

(A) *By Motion.* A motion for sanctions under this rule shall be made separately from other motions or requests and shall describe the specific conduct alleged to violate subdivision (b). It shall be served as provided in Rule 5, but shall not be filed with or presented to the court unless, within 21 days after service of the motion (or such other period as the court may prescribe), the challenged paper, claim, defense, contention, allegation, or denial is not withdrawn or appropriately corrected. If warranted, the court may award to the party prevailing on the motion the reasonable expenses and attorney's fees incurred in presenting or opposing the motion. Absent exceptional circumstances, a law firm shall be held jointly responsible for violations committed by its partners, associates, and employees.

(B) *On Court's Initiative.* On its own initiative, the court may enter an order describing the specific conduct that appears to violate subdivision (b) and directing an attorney, law firm, or party to show cause why it has not violated subdivision (b) with respect thereto.

(2) *Nature of Sanction; Limitations.* A sanction imposed for violation of this rule shall be limited to what is sufficient to deter repetition of such conduct or comparable conduct by others similarly situated. Subject to the limitations in subparagraphs (A) and (B), the sanction may consist of, or include, directives of a nonmonetary nature, an order to pay a penalty into court, or, if imposed on motion and warranted for effective deterrence, an order directing payment to the movant of some or all of the reasonable attorneys' fees and other expenses incurred as a direct result of the violation.

(A) Monetary sanctions may not be awarded against a represented party for a violation of subdivision (b)(2).

(B) Monetary sanctions may not be awarded on the court's initiative unless the court issues its order to show cause before a voluntary dismissal or settlement of the claims made by or against the party which is, or whose attorneys are, to be sanctioned.

(3) *Order.* When imposing sanctions, the court shall describe the conduct determined to constitute a violation of this rule and explain the basis for the sanction imposed.

(d) INAPPLICABILITY TO DISCOVERY. Subdivisions (a) through (c) of this rule do not apply to disclosures and discovery requests, responses, objections, and motions that are subject to the provisions of Rules 26 through 37.

(As amended Apr. 28, 1983, eff. Aug. 1, 1983; Mar. 2, 1987, eff. Aug. 1, 1987; Apr. 22, 1993, eff. Dec. 1, 1993.)

Rule 12. Defenses and Objections—When and How Presented—By Pleading or Motion—Motion for Judgment on the Pleadings

(a) WHEN PRESENTED.

(1) Unless a different time is prescribed in a statute of the United States, a defendant shall serve an answer (A) within 20 days after being served with the summons and complaint, or (B) if service of the summons has been timely waived on request under Rule 4(d), within 60 days after the date when the request for waiver was sent, or within 90 days after that date if the defendant was addressed outside any judicial district of the United States.

(2) A party served with a pleading stating a cross-claim against that party shall serve an answer thereto within 20 days after being served. The plaintiff shall serve a reply to a counterclaim in the answer within 20 days after service of the answer, or, if a reply is ordered by the court, within 20 days after service of the order, unless the order otherwise directs.

(3)(A) The United States, an agency of the United States, or an officer or employee of the United States sued in an official capacity, shall serve an answer to the complaint or crossclaim—or a reply to a counterclaim—within 60 days after the United States attorney is served with the pleading asserting the claim. (B) An officer or employee of the United States sued in an individual capacity for acts or omissions occurring in connection with the performance of duties on behalf of the United States shall serve an answer to the complaint or cross-claim—or a reply to a counterclaim—within 60 days after service on the officer or employee, or service on the United States attorney, whichever is later.

(4) Unless a different time is fixed by court order, the service of a motion permitted under this rule alters these periods of time as follows: (A) if the court denies the motion or postpones its disposition until the trial on the merits, the responsive pleading shall be served within 10 days after notice of the court's action; or (B) if the court grants a motion for a more definite statement, the responsive pleading shall be served within 10 days after the service of the more definite statement.

(b) HOW PRESENTED. Every defense, in law or fact, to a claim for relief in any pleading, whether a claim, counterclaim, cross-claim, or third-party claim, shall be asserted in the responsive pleading thereto if one is required, except that the following defenses may at the option of the pleader be made by motion: (1) lack of jurisdiction over the subject matter, (2) lack of jurisdiction over the person, (3) improper venue, (4) insufficiency of process, (5) insufficiency of service of process, (6) failure to state a claim upon which relief can be granted, (7) failure to join a party under Rule 19. A motion making any of these defenses shall be made before pleading if a further pleading is permitted. No defense or objection is waived by being joined with one or more other defenses or objections in a responsive pleading or motion. If a pleading sets forth a claim for relief to which the adverse party is not required to serve a responsive pleading, the adverse party may assert at the trial any defense in law or fact to that claim for relief. If, on a motion asserting the defense numbered (6) to dismiss for failure of the pleading to state a claim upon which relief can be granted, matters outside the pleading are presented to and not excluded by the court, the motion shall be treated as one for summary judgment and disposed of as provided in Rule 56, and all parties shall be given reasonable opportunity to present all material made pertinent to such a motion by Rule 56.

(c) MOTION FOR JUDGMENT ON THE PLEADINGS. After the pleadings are closed but within such time as not to delay the trial, any party may move for judgment on the pleadings. If, on a motion for judgment on the pleadings, matters outside the pleadings are presented to and not excluded by the court, the motion shall be treated as one for summary judgment and disposed of as provided in Rule 56, and all parties shall be given reasonable opportunity to present all material made pertinent to such a motion by Rule 56.

(d) PRELIMINARY HEARINGS. The defenses specifically enumerated (1)–(7) in subdivision (b) of this rule, whether made in a pleading or by motion, and the motion for judgment mentioned in subdivision (c) of this rule shall be heard and determined before trial on application of any party, unless the court orders that the hearing and determination thereof be deferred until the trial.

(e) MOTION FOR MORE DEFINITE STATEMENT. If a pleading to which a responsive pleading is permitted is so vague or ambiguous that a party cannot reasonably be required to frame a responsive pleading, the party may move for a more definite statement before interposing a responsive pleading. The motion shall point out the defects complained of and the details desired. If the motion is granted and the order of the court is not obeyed within 10 days after notice of the order or within such other time as the court may fix, the court may strike the pleading to which the motion was directed or make such order as it deems just.

(f) MOTION TO STRIKE. Upon motion made by a party before responding to a pleading or, if no responsive pleading is permitted by these rules, upon motion made by a party within 20 days after the service of the pleading upon the party or upon the court's own initiative at any time, the court may order stricken from any pleading any insufficient defense or any redundant, immaterial, impertinent, or scandalous matter.

(g) CONSOLIDATION OF DEFENSES IN MOTION. A party who makes a motion under this rule may join with it any other motions herein provided for and then available to the party. If a party makes a motion under this rule but omits therefrom any defense or objection then available to the party which this rule permits to be raised by motion, the party shall not thereafter make a motion based on the defense or objection so omitted, except a motion as provided in subdivision (h)(2) hereof on any of the grounds there stated.

(h) WAIVER OR PRESERVATION OF CERTAIN DEFENSES.

(1) A defense of lack of jurisdiction over the person, improper venue, insufficiency of process, or insufficiency of service of process is waived (A) if omitted from a motion in the circumstances described in subdivision (g), or (B) if it is neither made by motion under this rule nor included in a responsive pleading or an amendment thereof permitted by Rule 15(a) to be made as a matter of course.

(2) A defense of failure to state a claim upon which relief can be granted, a defense of failure to join a party indispensable under Rule 19, and an objection of failure to state a legal defense to a claim may be made in any pleading permitted or ordered under Rule 7(a), or by motion for judgment on the pleadings, or at the trial on the merits.

(3) Whenever it appears by suggestion of the parties or otherwise that the court lacks jurisdiction of the subject matter, the court shall dismiss the action.

(As amended Dec. 27, 1946, eff. Mar. 19, 1948; Jan. 21, 1963, eff. July 1, 1963; Feb. 28, 1966, eff. July 1, 1966; Mar. 2, 1987, eff. Aug. 1, 1987; Apr. 22, 1993, eff. Dec. 1, 1993; Apr. 17, 2000, eff. Dec. 1, 2000.)

Rule 13. Counterclaim and Cross-Claim

(a) COMPULSORY COUNTERCLAIMS. A pleading shall state as a counterclaim any claim which at the time of serving the pleading the pleader has against any opposing party, if it arises out of the transaction or occurrence that is the subject matter of the opposing party's claim and does not require for its adjudication the presence of third parties of whom the court cannot acquire jurisdiction. But the pleader need not state the claim if (1) at the time the action was commenced the claim was the subject of another pending action, or (2) the opposing party brought suit upon the claim by attachment or other process by which the court did not acquire jurisdiction to render a personal judgment on that claim, and the pleader is not stating any counterclaim under this Rule 13.

(b) PERMISSIVE COUNTERCLAIMS. A pleading may state as a counterclaim any claim against an opposing party not arising out of the transaction or occurrence that is the subject matter of the opposing party's claim.

(c) COUNTERCLAIM EXCEEDING OPPOSING CLAIM. A counterclaim may or may not diminish or defeat the recovery sought by the opposing party. It may claim relief exceeding in amount or different in kind from that sought in the pleading of the opposing party.

(d) COUNTERCLAIM AGAINST THE UNITED STATES. These rules shall not be construed to enlarge beyond the limits now fixed by law the right to assert counterclaims or to claim credits against the United States or an officer or agency thereof.

(e) COUNTERCLAIM MATURING OR ACQUIRED AFTER PLEADING. A claim which either matured or was acquired by the pleader after serving a pleading may, with the permission of the court, be presented as a counterclaim by supplemental pleading.

(f) OMITTED COUNTERCLAIM. When a pleader fails to set up a counterclaim through oversight, inadvertence, or excusable neglect, or when justice requires, the pleader may by leave of court set up the counterclaim by amendment.

(g) CROSS-CLAIM AGAINST CO-PARTY. A pleading may state as a cross-claim any claim by one party against a co-party arising out of the transaction or occurrence that is the subject matter either of the original action or of a counterclaim therein or relating to any property that is the subject matter of the original action. Such cross-claim may include a claim that the party against whom it is asserted is or may be liable to the cross-claimant for all or part of a claim asserted in the action against the crossclaimant.

(h) JOINDER OF ADDITIONAL PARTIES. Persons other than those made parties to the original action may be made parties to a counterclaim or cross-claim in accordance with the provisions of Rules 19 and 20.

(i) SEPARATE TRIALS; SEPARATE JUDGMENTS. If the court orders separate trials as provided in Rule 42(b), judgment on a counterclaim or cross-claim may be rendered in accordance with the terms of Rule 54(b) when the court has jurisdiction so to do, even if the claims of the opposing party have been dismissed or otherwise disposed of.

(As amended Dec. 27, 1946, eff. Mar. 19, 1948; Jan. 21, 1963, eff. July 1, 1963; Feb. 28, 1966, eff. July 1, 1966; Mar. 2, 1987, eff. Aug. 1, 1987.)

Rule 14. Third-Party Practice

(a) WHEN DEFENDANT MAY BRING IN THIRD PARTY. At any time after commencement of the action a defending party, as a third party plaintiff, may cause a summons and complaint to be served upon a person not a party to the action who is or may be liable to the third-party plaintiff for all or part of the plaintiff's claim against the third-party plaintiff. The third-party plaintiff need not obtain leave to make the service if the third-party plaintiff files the third-party complaint not later than 10 days after serving the original answer. Otherwise the third-party plaintiff must obtain leave on motion upon notice to all parties to the action. The person served with the summons and third-party complaint, hereinafter called the third-party defendant, shall make any defenses to the third-party plaintiff's claim as provided in Rule 12 and any counterclaims against the third-party plaintiff and cross-claims against other third-party defendants as provided in Rule 13. The third-party defendant may assert against the plaintiff any defenses which the third-party plaintiff has to the plaintiff's claim. The third-party defendant may also assert any claim against the plaintiff arising out of the transaction or occurrence that is the subject matter of the plaintiff's claim against the third-party plaintiff. The plaintiff may assert any claim against the third party defendant arising out of the transaction or occurrence that is the subject matter of the plaintiff's claim against the third party plaintiff, and the third-party defendant thereupon shall assert any defenses as provided in Rule 12 and any counterclaims and cross-claims as provided in Rule 13. Any party may move to strike the third-party claim, or for its severance or separate trial. A third-party defendant may proceed under this rule against any person not a party to the action who is or may be liable to the third-party defendant for all or part of the claim made in the action against the third-party defendant. The third-party complaint, if within the admiralty and maritime jurisdiction, may be in rem against a vessel, cargo, or other property subject to admiralty or maritime process in rem, in which case references in this rule to the summons include the warrant of arrest, and references to the third-party plaintiff or defendant include, where appropriate, a person who asserts a right under Supplemental Rule C(6)(a)(1) in the property arrested.

(b) WHEN PLAINTIFF MAY BRING IN THIRD PARTY. When a counterclaim is asserted against a plaintiff, the plaintiff may cause a third party to be brought in under circumstances which under this rule would entitle a defendant to do so.

(c) ADMIRALTY AND MARITIME CLAIMS. When a plaintiff asserts an admiralty or maritime claim within the meaning of Rule 9(h), the defendant or person who asserts a right under Supplemental Rule C(6)(a)(1), as a third-party plaintiff, may bring in a third-party defendant who may be wholly or partly liable, either to the plaintiff or to the third-party plaintiff, by way of remedy over, contribution, or otherwise on account of the same transaction, occurrence, or series of transactions or occurrences. In such a case the third party plaintiff may also demand judgment against the third-party defendant in favor of the plaintiff, in which event the third-party defendant shall make any defenses to the claim of the plaintiff as well as to that of the third-party plaintiff in the manner provided in Rule 12 and the action shall proceed as if the plaintiff had commenced it against the third-party defendant as well as the third party plaintiff.

(As amended Dec. 27, 1946, eff. Mar. 19, 1948; Jan. 21, 1963, eff. July 1, 1963; Feb. 28, 1966, eff. July 1, 1966; Mar. 2, 1987, eff. Aug. 1, 1987; Apr. 17, 2000, eff. Dec. 1, 2000; Apr. 12, 2006, eff. Dec. 1, 2006.)

Rule 15. Amended and Supplemental Pleadings

(a) AMENDMENTS. A party may amend the party's pleading once as a matter of course at any time before a responsive pleading is served or, if the pleading is one to which no responsive pleading is permitted and the action has not been placed upon the trial calendar, the party may so amend it at any time within 20 days after it is served. Otherwise a party may amend the party's pleading only by leave of court or by written consent of the adverse party; and leave shall be freely given when justice so requires. A party shall plead in response to an amended pleading within the time remaining for response to the original pleading or within 10 days after service of the amended pleading, whichever period may be the longer, unless the court otherwise orders.

(b) AMENDMENTS TO CONFORM TO THE EVIDENCE. When issues not raised by the pleadings are tried by express or implied consent of the parties, they shall be treated in all respects as if they had been raised in the pleadings. Such amendment of the pleadings as may be necessary to cause them to conform to the evidence and to raise these issues may be made upon motion of any party at any time, even after judgment; but failure so to amend does not affect the result of the trial of these issues. If evidence is objected to at the trial on the ground that it is not within the issues made by the pleadings, the court may allow the pleadings to be amended and shall do so freely when the presentation of the merits of the action will be subserved thereby and the objecting party fails to satisfy the court that the admission of such evidence would prejudice the party in maintaining the party's action or defense upon the merits. The court may grant a continuance to enable the objecting party to meet such evidence.

(c) RELATION BACK OF AMENDMENTS. An amendment of a pleading relates back to the date of the original pleading when (1) relation back is permitted by the law that provides the statute of limitations applicable to the action, or (2) the claim or defense asserted in the amended pleading arose out of the conduct, transaction, or occurrence set forth or attempted to be set forth in the original pleading, or (3) the amendment changes the party or the naming of the party against whom a claim is asserted if the foregoing provision (2) is satisfied and, within the period provided by Rule 4(m) for service of the summons and complaint, the party to be brought in by amendment (A) has received such notice of the institution of the action that the party will not be prejudiced in maintaining a defense on the merits, and (B) knew or should have known that, but for a mistake concerning the identity of the proper party, the action would have been brought against the party. The delivery or mailing of process to the United States Attorney, or United States Attorney's designee, or the Attorney General of the United States, or an agency or officer who would have been a proper defendant if named, satisfies the requirement of subparagraphs (A) and (B) of this paragraph (3) with respect to the United States or any agency or officer thereof to be brought into the action as a defendant.

(d) SUPPLEMENTAL PLEADINGS. Upon motion of a party the court may, upon reasonable notice and upon such terms as are just, permit the party to serve a supplemental pleading setting forth transactions or occurrences or events which have happened since the date of the pleading sought to be supplemented. Permission may be granted even though the original pleading is defective in its statement of a claim for relief or defense. If the court deems it advisable that the adverse party plead to the supplemental pleading, it shall so order, specifying the time therefor.

(As amended Jan. 21, 1963, eff. July 1, 1963; Feb. 28, 1966, eff. July 1, 1966; Mar. 2, 1987, eff. Aug. 1, 1987; Apr. 30, 1991, eff. Dec. 1, 1991; Dec. 9, 1991; Apr. 22, 1993, eff. Dec. 1, 1993.)

Rule 16. Pretrial Conferences; Scheduling; Management

(a) PRETRIAL CONFERENCES; OBJECTIVES. In any action, the court may in its discretion direct the attorneys for the parties and any unrepresented parties to appear before it for a conference or conferences before trial for such purposes as (1) expediting the disposition of the action; (2) establishing early and continuing control so that the case will not be protracted because of lack of management; (3) discouraging wasteful pretrial activities; (4) improving the quality of the trial through more thorough preparation, and; (5) facilitating the settlement of the case.

(b) SCHEDULING AND PLANNING. Except in categories of actions exempted by district court rule as inappropriate, the district judge, or a magistrate judge when authorized by district court rule, shall, after receiving the report from the parties under Rule 26(f) or after consulting with the attorneys for the parties and any unrepresented parties by a scheduling conference, telephone, mail, or other suitable means, enter a scheduling order that limits the time (1) to join other parties and to amend the pleadings; (2) to file motions; and (3) to complete discovery. The scheduling order also may include (4) modifications of the times for disclosures under Rules 26(a) and 26(e)(1) and of the extent of discovery to be permitted; (5) provisions for disclosure or discovery of electronically stored information; (6) any agreements the parties reach for asserting claims of privilege or of protection as trial-preparation material after production; (7) the date or dates for conferences before trial, a final pretrial conference, and trial; and (8) any other matters appropriate in the circumstances of the case. The order shall issue as soon as practicable but in any event within 90 days after the appearance of a defendant and within 120 days after the complaint has been served on a defendant. A schedule shall not be modified except upon a showing of good cause and by leave of the district judge or, when authorized by local rule, by a magistrate judge.

(c) SUBJECTS FOR CONSIDERATION AT PRETRIAL CONFERENCES. At any conference under this rule consideration may be given, and the court may take appropriate action, with respect to (1) the formulation and simplification of the issues, including the elimination of frivolous claims or defenses; (2) the necessity or desirability of amendments to the pleadings; (3) the possibility of obtaining admissions of fact and of documents which will avoid unnecessary proof, stipulations regarding the authenticity of documents, and advance rulings from the court on the admissibility of evidence; (4) the avoidance of unnecessary proof and of cumulative evidence, and limitations or restrictions on the use of testimony under Rule 702 of the Federal Rules of Evidence; (5) the appropriateness and timing of summary adjudication under Rule 56; (6) the control and scheduling of discovery, including orders affecting disclosures and discovery pursuant to Rule 26 and Rules 29 through 37; (7) the identification of witnesses and documents, the need and schedule for filing and exchanging pretrial briefs, and the date or dates for further conferences and for trial; (8) the advisability of referring matters to a magistrate judge or master; (9) settlement and the use of special procedures to assist in resolving the dispute when authorized by statute or local rule; (10) the form and substance of the pretrial order; (11) the disposition of pending motions; (12) the need for adopting special procedures for managing potentially difficult or protracted actions that may involve complex issues, multiple parties, difficult legal questions, or unusual proof problems; (13) an order for a separate trial pursuant to Rule 42(b) with respect to a claim, counterclaim, cross-claim, or third-party claim, or with respect to any particular issue in the case; (14) an order directing a party or parties to present evidence early in the trial with respect to a manageable issue that could, on the evidence, be the basis for a judgment as a matter of law under Rule 50(a) or a judgment on partial findings under Rule 52(c); (15) an order establishing a reasonable limit on the time allowed for presenting evidence; and

(16) such other matters as may facilitate the just, speedy, and inexpensive disposition of the action. At least one of the attorneys for each party participating in any conference before trial shall have authority to enter into stipulations and to make admissions regarding all matters that the participants

may reasonably anticipate may be discussed. If appropriate, the court may require that a party or its representative be present or reasonably available by telephone in order to consider possible settlement of the dispute.

(d) FINAL PRETRIAL CONFERENCE. Any final pretrial conference shall be held as close to the time of trial as reasonable under the circumstances. The participants at any such conference shall formulate a plan for trial, including a program for facilitating the admission of evidence. The conference shall be attended by at least one of the attorneys who will conduct the trial for each of the parties and by any unrepresented parties.

(e) PRETRIAL ORDERS. After any conference held pursuant to this rule, an order shall be entered reciting the action taken. This order shall control the subsequent course of the action unless modified by a subsequent order. The order following a final pretrial conference shall be modified only to prevent manifest injustice.

(f) SANCTIONS. If a party or party's attorney fails to obey a scheduling or pretrial order, or if no appearance is made on behalf of a party at a scheduling or pretrial conference, or if a party or party's attorney is substantially unprepared to participate in the conference, or if a party or party's attorney fails to participate in good faith, the judge, upon motion or the judge's own initiative, may make such orders with regard thereto as are just, and among others any of the orders provided in Rule 37(b)(2)(B), (C), (D). In lieu of or in addition to any other sanction, the judge shall require the party or the attorney representing the party or both to pay the reasonable expenses incurred because of any noncompliance with this rule, including attorney's fees, unless the judge finds

that the noncompliance was substantially justified or that other circumstances make an award of expenses unjust.

(As amended Apr. 28, 1983, eff. Aug. 1, 1983; Mar. 2, 1987, eff. Aug. 1, 1987;

Apr. 22, 1993, eff. Dec. 1, 1993; Apr. 12, 2006, eff. Dec. 1, 2006.)

IV. PARTIES

Rule 17. Parties Plaintiff and Defendant; Capacity

(a) REAL PARTY IN INTEREST. Every action shall be prosecuted in the name of the real party in interest. An executor, administrator, guardian, bailee, trustee of an express trust, a party with whom or in whose name a contract has been made for the benefit of another, or a party authorized by statute may sue in that person's own name without joining the party for whose benefit the action is brought; and when a statute of the United States so provides, an action for the use or benefit of another shall be brought in the name of the United States. No action shall be dismissed on the ground that it is not prosecuted in the name of the real party in interest until a reasonable time has been allowed after objection
for ratification of commencement of the action by, or joinder or substitution of, the real party in interest; and such ratification, joinder, or substitution shall have the same effect as if the action had been commenced in the name of the real party in interest.

(b) CAPACITY TO SUE OR BE SUED. The capacity of an individual, other than one acting in a representative capacity, to sue or be sued shall be determined by the law of the individual's domicile. The capacity of a corporation to sue or be sued shall be determined by the law under which it was organized. In all other cases capacity to sue or be sued shall be determined by the law of the state in which the district court is held, except (1) that a partnership or other unincorporated association, which has no such capacity by the law of such state, may sue or be sued in its common name for the purpose of enforcing for or against it a substantive right existing under the Constitution or laws of the United States, and (2) that the capacity of a receiver appointed by a court of the United States to sue or be sued in a court of the United States is governed by Title 28, U.S.C., Sections 754 and 959(a).

(c) INFANTS OR INCOMPETENT PERSONS. Whenever an infant or incompetent person has a representative, such as a general guardian, committee, conservator, or other like fiduciary, the representative may sue or defend on behalf of the infant or incompetent person. An infant or incompetent person who does not have a duly appointed representative may sue by a next friend or by a
guardian ad litem. The court shall appoint a guardian ad litem for an infant or incompetent person not otherwise represented in an action or shall make such other order as it deems proper for the protection of the infant or incompetent person.

(As amended Dec. 27, 1946, eff. Mar. 19, 1948; Dec. 29, 1948, eff. Oct. 20,

1949; Feb. 28, 1966, eff. July 1, 1966; Mar. 2, 1987, eff. Aug. 1, 1987; Apr. 25, 1988, eff. Aug. 1, 1988; Nov. 18, 1988.)

Rule 18. Joinder of Claims and Remedies

(a) JOINDER OF CLAIMS. A party asserting a claim to relief as an original claim, counterclaim, cross-claim, or third-party claim, may join, either as independent or as alternate claims, as many claims, legal, equitable, or maritime, as the party has against an opposing party.

(b) JOINDER OF REMEDIES; FRAUDULENT CONVEYANCES. Whenever a claim is one heretofore cognizable only after another claim has been prosecuted to a conclusion, the two claims may be joined in a single action; but the court shall grant relief in that action only in accordance with the relative substantive rights of the parties. In particular, a plaintiff may state a claim for money and a claim to have set aside a conveyance fraudulent as to that plaintiff,
without first having obtained a judgment establishing the claim for money.

(As amended Feb. 28, 1966, eff. July 1, 1966; Mar. 2, 1987, eff. Aug. 1, 1987.)

Rule 19. Joinder of Persons Needed for Just Adjudication

(a) PERSONS TO BE JOINED IF FEASIBLE. A person who is subject to service of process and whose joinder will not deprive the court of jurisdiction over the subject matter of the action shall be joined as a party in the action if (1) in the person's absence complete relief cannot be accorded among those already parties, or (2) the person claims an interest relating to the subject of the action
and is so situated that the disposition of the action in the person's absence may (i) as a practical matter impair or impede the person's ability to protect that interest or (ii) leave any of the persons already parties subject to a substantial risk of incurring double, multiple, or otherwise inconsistent obligations by reason of the claimed interest. If the person has not been so joined, the court shall order that the person be made a party. If the person should join as a plaintiff but refuses to do so, the person may be made a defendant, or, in a proper case, an involuntary plaintiff. If the joined party objects to venue and joinder of that party would render the venue of the action improper, that party shall be dismissed from the action.

(b) DETERMINATION BY COURT WHENEVER JOINDER NOT FEASIBLE.

If a person as described in subdivision (a)(1)–(2) hereof cannot be made a party, the court shall determine whether in equity and good conscience the action should proceed among the parties before it, or should be dismissed, the absent person being thus regarded as indispensable. The factors to be considered by the court include: first, to what extent a judgment rendered in the person's absence might be prejudicial to the person or those already parties; second, the extent to which, by protective provisions in the judgment, by the shaping of relief, or other measures, the prejudice can be lessened or avoided; third, whether a judgment rendered in the person's absence will be adequate; fourth, whether the plaintiff will have an adequate remedy if the action is dismissed for nonjoinder.

(c) PLEADING REASONS FOR NONJOINDER. A pleading asserting a claim for relief shall state the names, if known to the pleader, of any persons as described in subdivision (a)(1)–(2) hereof who are not joined, and the reasons why they are not joined.

(d) EXCEPTION OF CLASS ACTIONS. This rule is subject to the provisions of Rule 23.

(As amended Feb. 28, 1966, eff. July 1, 1966; Mar. 2, 1987, eff. Aug. 1, 1987.)

Rule 20. Permissive Joinder of Parties

(a) PERMISSIVE JOINDER. All persons may join in one action as plaintiffs if they assert any right to relief jointly, severally, or in the alternative in respect of or arising out of the same transaction, occurrence, or series of transactions or occurrences and if any question of law or fact common to all these persons will arise in the action. All persons (and any vessel, cargo or other property subject to admiralty process in rem) may be joined in one action as defendants if there is asserted against them jointly, severally, or in the alternative, any right to relief in respect of or arising out of the same transaction, occurrence, or series of transactions or occurrences and if any question of law or fact common to all defendants will arise in the action. A plaintiff or defendant need not be interested in obtaining or defending against all the relief demanded. Judgment may be given for one or more of the plaintiffs according to their respective rights to relief, and against one or more defendants according to their respective liabilities.

(b) SEPARATE TRIALS. The court may make such orders as will prevent a party from being embarrassed, delayed, or put to expense by the inclusion of a party against whom the party asserts no claim and who asserts no claim against the party, and may order separate trials or make other orders to prevent delay or prejudice.

(As amended Feb. 28, 1966, eff. July 1, 1966; Mar. 2, 1987, eff. Aug. 1, 1987.)

Rule 21. Misjoinder and Non-Joinder of Parties

Misjoinder of parties is not ground for dismissal of an action. Parties may be dropped or added by order of the court on motion of any party or of its own initiative at any stage of the action and on such terms as are just. Any claim against a party may be severed and proceeded with separately.

Rule 22. Interpleader

(1) Persons having claims against the plaintiff may be joined as defendants and required to interplead when their claims are such that the plaintiff is or may be exposed to double or multiple liability. It is not ground for objection to the joinder that the claims of the several claimants or the titles on which their claims depend do not have a common origin or are not identical but are adverse to and independent of one another, or that the plaintiff avers that the plaintiff is not liable in whole or in part to any or all of the claimants. A defendant exposed to similar liability may obtain such interpleader by way of cross-claim or counterclaim. The provisions of this rule supplement and do not in any way limit the joinder of parties permitted in Rule 20. (2) The remedy herein provided is in addition to and in no way supersedes or limits the remedy provided by Title 28, U.S.C., §§ 1335, 1397, and 2361. Actions under those provisions shall be conducted in accordance with these rules.

(As amended Dec. 29, 1948, eff. Oct. 20, 1949; Mar. 2, 1987, eff. Aug. 1, 1987.)

Rule 23. Class Actions

(a) PREREQUISITES TO A CLASS ACTION. One or more members of a class may sue or be sued as representative parties on behalf of all only if (1) the class is so numerous that joinder of all members is impracticable, (2) there are questions of law or fact common to the class, (3) the claims or defenses of the representative parties are typical of the claims or defenses of the class, and (4) the representative parties will fairly and adequately protect the interests of the class.

(b) CLASS ACTIONS MAINTAINABLE. An action may be maintained as a class action if the prerequisites of subdivision (a) are satisfied, and in addition: (1) the prosecution of separate actions by or against individual members of the class would create a risk of (A) inconsistent or varying adjudications with respect to individual members of the class which would establish incompatible standards of conduct for the party opposing the class, or (B) adjudications with respect to individual members of the class which would as a practical matter be dispositive of the interests of the other members not parties to the adjudications or substantially impair or impede their ability to protect their interests; or (2) the party opposing the class has acted or refused to act on grounds generally applicable to the class, thereby making appropriate final injunctive relief or corresponding declaratory relief with respect to the class as a whole; or (3) the court finds that the questions of law or fact common to the members of the class predominate over any questions affecting only individual members, and that a class action is superior to other available methods for the fair and efficient adjudication of the controversy. The matters pertinent to the findings include: (A) the interest of members of the class in individually controlling the prosecution or defense of separate actions; (B) the extent and nature of any litigation concerning the controversy already commenced by or against members of the class; (C) the desirability or undesirability of concentrating the litigation of the claims in the particular forum; (D) the difficulties likely to be encountered in the management of a class action.

(c) DETERMINING BY ORDER WHETHER TO CERTIFY A CLASS ACTION; APPOINTING CLASS COUNSEL; NOTICE AND MEMBERSHIP IN CLASS; JUDGMENT; MULTIPLE CLASSES AND SUBCLASSES.

(1)(A) When a person sues or is sued as a representative of a class, the court must—at an early practicable time—determine by order whether to certify the action as a class action. (B) An order certifying a class action must define the class and the class claims, issues, or defenses, and must appoint class counsel under Rule 23(g). (C) An order under Rule 23(c)(1) may be altered or amended before final judgment. (2)(A) For any class certified under Rule 23(b)(1) or (2), the court may direct appropriate notice to the class. (B) For any class certified under Rule 23(b)(3), the court must direct to class members the best notice practicable under the circumstances, including individual notice to all members who can be identified through reasonable effort. The notice must concisely and clearly state in plain, easily understood language:

- the nature of the action,
- the definition of the class certified,
- the class claims, issues, or defenses,
- that a class member may enter an appearance through counsel if the member so desires,
- that the court will exclude from the class any member who requests exclusion, stating when and how members may elect to be excluded, and
- the binding effect of a class judgment on class members under Rule 23(c)(3).

(3) The judgment in an action maintained as a class action under subdivision (b)(1) or (b)(2), whether or not favorable to the class, shall include and describe those whom the court finds to be members of the class. The judgment in an action maintained as a class action under subdivision (b)(3), whether or not favorable to the class, shall include and specify or describe those to whom the notice provided

in subdivision (c)(2) was directed, and who have not requested exclusion, and whom the court finds to be members of the class.

(4) When appropriate (A) an action may be brought or maintained as a class action with respect to particular issues, or (B) a class may be divided into subclasses and each subclass treated as a class, and the provisions of this rule shall then be construed and applied accordingly.

(d) ORDERS IN CONDUCT OF ACTIONS. In the conduct of actions to which this rule applies, the court may make appropriate orders: (1) determining the course of proceedings or prescribing measures to prevent undue repetition or complication in the presentation of evidence or argument; (2) requiring, for the protection of the members of the class or otherwise for the fair conduct of the action, that notice be given in such manner as the court may direct to some or all of the members of any step in the action, or of the proposed extent of the judgment, or of the opportunity of members to signify whether they consider the representation fair and adequate, to intervene and present claims or defenses, or otherwise to come into the action; (3) imposing conditions on the representative parties or on intervenors; (4) requiring that the pleadings be amended to eliminate therefrom allegations as to representation of absent persons, and that the action proceed accordingly; (5) dealing with similar procedural matters. The orders may be combined with an order under Rule 16, and may be altered or amended as may be desirable from time to time.

(e) SETTLEMENT, VOLUNTARY DISMISSAL, OR COMPROMISE.

(1)(A) The court must approve any settlement, voluntary dismissal, or compromise of the claims, issues, or defenses of a certified class. (B) The court must direct notice in a reasonable manner to all class members who would be bound by a proposed settlement, voluntary dismissal, or compromise. (C) The court may approve a settlement, voluntary dismissal, or compromise that would bind class members only after a hearing and on finding that the settlement, voluntary dismissal, or compromise is fair, reasonable, and adequate.

(2) The parties seeking approval of a settlement, voluntary dismissal, or compromise under Rule 23(e)(1) must file a statement identifying any agreement made in connection with the proposed settlement, voluntary dismissal, or compromise.

(3) In an action previously certified as a class action under Rule 23(b)(3), the court may refuse to approve a settlement unless it affords a new opportunity to request exclusion to individual class members who had an earlier opportunity to request exclusion but did not do so.

(4)(A) Any class member may object to a proposed settlement, voluntary dismissal, or compromise that requires court approval under Rule 23(e)(1)(A). (B) An objection made under Rule 23(e)(4)(A) may be withdrawn only with the court's approval.

(f) APPEALS. A court of appeals may in its discretion permit an appeal from an order of a district court granting or denying class action certification under this rule if application is made to it within ten days after entry of the order. An appeal does not stay proceedings in the district court unless the district judge or the court of appeals so orders.

(g) CLASS COUNSEL.
(1) *Appointing Class Counsel.* (A) Unless a statute provides otherwise, a court that certifies a class must appoint class counsel. (B) An attorney appointed to serve as class counsel must fairly and adequately represent the interests of the class. (C) In appointing class counsel, the court (i) must consider:
• the work counsel has done in identifying or investigating potential claims in the action,
• counsel's experience in handling class actions, other complex litigation, and claims of the type asserted in the action,
• counsel's knowledge of the applicable law, and
• the resources counsel will commit to representing the class;
(ii) may consider any other matter pertinent to counsel's ability to fairly and adequately represent the interests of the class;
(iii) may direct potential class counsel to provide information on any subject pertinent to the appointment and to propose terms for attorney fees and nontaxable costs; and
(iv) may make further orders in connection with the appointment.

(2) *Appointment Procedure.* (A) The court may designate interim counsel to act on behalf of the putative class before determining whether to certify the action as a class action. (B) When there is one applicant for apointment as class counsel, the court may appoint that applicant only if the applicant is adequate under Rule 23(g)(1)(B) and (C). If more than one adequate applicant seeks appointment as class counsel, the court must appoint the applicant best able to represent the interests of the class. (C) The order appointing class counsel may include provisions about the award of attorney fees or nontaxable costs under Rule 23(h).

(h) ATTORNEY FEES AWARD. In an action certified as a class action, the court may award reasonable attorney fees and nontaxable costs authorized by law or by agreement of the parties as follows:

(1) *Motion for Award of Attorney Fees.* A claim for an award of attorney fees and nontaxable costs must be made by motion under Rule 54(d)(2), subject to the provisions of this subdivision, at a time set by the court. Notice of the motion must

be served on all parties and, for motions by class counsel, directed to class members in a reasonable manner.

(2) *Objections to Motion.* A class member, or a party from whom payment is sought, may object to the motion.

(3) *Hearing and Findings.* The court may hold a hearing and must find the facts and state its conclusions of law on the motion under Rule 52(a).

(4) *Reference to Special Master or Magistrate Judge.* The court may refer issues related to the amount of the award to a special master or to a magistrate judge as provided in Rule 54(d)(2)(D).

(As amended Feb. 28, 1966, eff. July 1, 1966; Mar. 2, 1987, eff. Aug. 1, 1987; Apr. 24, 1998, eff. Dec. 1, 1998; Mar. 27, 2003, eff. Dec. 1, 2003.)

Rule 23.1. Derivative Actions by Shareholders - Omitted

Rule 23.2. Actions Relating to Unincorporated Associations

Rule 24. Intervention

(a) INTERVENTION OF RIGHT. Upon timely application anyone shall be permitted to intervene in an action: (1) when a statute of the United States confers an unconditional right to intervene; or (2) when the applicant claims an interest relating to the property or transaction which is the subject of the action and the applicant is so situated that the disposition of the action may as a practical matter impair or impede the applicant's ability to protect that interest,
unless the applicant's interest is adequately represented by existing parties.

(b) PERMISSIVE INTERVENTION. Upon timely application anyone may be permitted to intervene in an action: (1) when a statute of the United States confers a conditional right to intervene; or (2) when an applicant's claim or defense and the main action have a question of law or fact in common. When a party to an action relies for ground of claim or defense upon any statute or executive order administered by a federal or state governmental officer or agency or upon any regulation, order, requirement, or agreement issued or made pursuant to the statute or executive order, the officer or agency upon timely application may be permitted to intervene in the action. In exercising its discretion the court shall consider whether the intervention will unduly delay or prejudice the adjudication of the rights of the original parties.

(c) PROCEDURE. A person desiring to intervene shall serve a motion to intervene upon the parties as provided in Rule 5. The motion shall state the grounds therefor and shall be accompanied by a pleading setting forth the claim or defense for which intervention is sought. The same procedure shall be followed when a statute of the United States gives a right to intervene.

(As amended Dec. 27, 1946, eff. Mar. 19, 1948; Dec. 29, 1948, eff. Oct. 20, 1949; Jan. 21, 1963, eff. July 1, 1963; Feb. 28, 1966, eff. July 1, 1966; Mar. 2, 1987, eff. Aug. 1, 1987; Apr. 30, 1991, eff. Dec. 1, 1991; Apr. 12, 2006, eff. Dec. 1, 2006.)

Rule 25. Substitution of Parties

(a) DEATH.

(1) If a party dies and the claim is not thereby extinguished, the court may order substitution of the proper parties. The motion for substitution may be made by any party or by the successors or representatives of the deceased party and, together with the notice of hearing, shall be served on the parties as provided in Rule 5 and upon persons not parties in the manner provided in Rule 4 for the service of a summons, and may be served in any judicial district. Unless the motion for substitution is made not later than 90 days after the death is suggested upon the record by service of a statement of the fact of the death as provided herein for the service of the motion, the action shall be dismissed as to the deceased party.

(2) In the event of the death of one or more of the plaintiffs or of one or more of the defendants in an action in which the right sought to be enforced survives only to the surviving plaintiffs or only against the surviving defendants, the action does not abate. The death shall be suggested upon the record and the action shall proceed in favor of or against the surviving parties.

(b) INCOMPETENCY. If a party becomes incompetent, the court upon motion served as provided in subdivision (a) of this rule may allow the action to be continued by or against the party's representative.

(c) TRANSFER OF INTEREST. In case of any transfer of interest, the action may be continued by or against the original party, unless the court upon motion directs the person to whom the interest is transferred to be substituted in the action or joined with the original party. Service of the motion shall be made as provided in subdivision (a) of this rule.

(d) PUBLIC OFFICERS; DEATH OR SEPARATION FROM OFFICE.

(1) When a public officer is a party to an action in his official capacity and during

its pendency dies, resigns, or otherwise ceases to hold office, the action does not abate and the officer's successor is automatically substituted as a party. Proceedings following the substitution shall be in the name of the substituted party, but any misnomer not affecting the substantial rights of the parties shall be disregarded. An order of substitution may be entered at any time, but the omission to enter such an order shall not affect the substitution.

(2) A public officer who sues or is sued in an official capacity may be described as a party by the officer's official title rather than by name; but the court may require the officer's name to be added.

(As amended Dec. 29, 1948, eff. Oct. 20, 1949; Apr. 17, 1961, eff. July 19, 1961; Jan. 21, 1963, eff. July 1, 1963; Mar. 2, 1987, eff. Aug. 1, 1987.)

V. DEPOSITIONS AND DISCOVERY

Rule 26. General Provisions Governing Discovery; Duty of Disclosure

(a) REQUIRED DISCLOSURES; METHODS TO DISCOVER ADDITIONAL MATTER.

(1) *Initial Disclosures.* Except in categories of proceedings specified in Rule 26(a)(1)(E), or to the extent otherwise stipulated or directed by order, a party must, without awaiting a discovery request, provide to other parties: (A) the name and, if known, the address and telephone number of each individual likely to have discoverable information that the disclosing party may use to support its claims or defenses, unless solely for impeachment, identifying the subjects of the information; (B) a copy of, or a description by category and location of, all documents, electronically stored information, and tangible things that are in the possession, custody, or control of the party and that the disclosing party may use to support its claims or defenses, unless solely for impeachment; (C) a computation of any category of damages claimed by the disclosing party, making available for inspection and copying as under Rule 34 the documents or other evidentiary material, not privileged or protected from disclosure, on which such computation is based, including materials bearing on the nature and extent of injuries suffered; and (D) for inspection and copying as under Rule 34 any insurance agreement under which any person carrying on an insurance business may be liable to satisfy part or all of a judgment which may be entered in the action or to indemnify or reimburse for payments made to satisfy the judgment. (E) The following categories of proceedings are exempt from initial disclosure under Rule 26(a)(1):

(i) an action for review on an administrative record;

(ii) a forfeiture action in rem arising from a federal statute;

(iii) a petition for habeas corpus or other proceeding to challenge a criminal conviction or sentence;

(iv) an action brought without counsel by a person in custody of the United States, a state, or a state subdivision;

(v) an action to enforce or quash an administrative summons or subpoena;

(vi) an action by the United States to recover benefit payments;

(vii) an action by the United States to collect on a student loan guaranteed by the United States;

(viii) a proceeding ancillary to proceedings in other courts; and

(ix) an action to enforce an arbitration award.

These disclosures must be made at or within 14 days after the Rule 26(f) conference unless a different time is set by stipulation or court order, or unless a party objects during the conference that initial disclosures are not appropriate in the circumstances of the action and states the objection in the Rule 26(f) discovery plan. In ruling on the objection, the court must determine what disclosures—if any—are to be made, and set the time for disclosure. Any party first served or otherwise joined after the Rule 26(f) conference must make these disclosures within 30 days after being served or joined unless a different time is set by stipulation or court order. A party must make its initial disclosures based on the information then reasonably available to it and is not excused from making its disclosures because it has not fully completed its investigation of the case or because it challenges the sufficiency of another party's disclosures or because another party has not made its disclosures.

(2) *Disclosure of Expert Testimony.*

(A) In addition to the disclosures required by paragraph (1), a party shall disclose to other parties the identity of any person who may be used at trial to present evidence under Rules 702, 703, or 705 of the Federal Rules of Evidence.

(B) Except as otherwise stipulated or directed by the court, this disclosure shall, with respect to a witness who is retained or specially employed to provide expert testimony in the case or whose duties as an employee of the party regularly involve giving expert testimony, be accompanied by a written report prepared and signed by the witness. The report shall contain a complete statement of all opinions to be expressed and the basis and reasons therefor; the data or other information considered by the witness in forming the opinions; any exhibits to be used as a summary of or support for the opinions; the qualifications of the witness, including a list of all publications authored by the witness within the preceding ten years; the compensation to be paid for the study and testimony; and a listing of any other cases in which the witness has testified as an expert at trial or by deposition within the preceding four years.

(C) These disclosures shall be made at the times and in the sequence directed by the court. In the absence of other directions from the court or stipulation by the parties, the disclosures shall be made at least 90 days before the trial date or the date the case is to be ready for trial or, if the evidence is intended solely to contradict or rebut evidence on the same subject matter identified by another party under paragraph (2)(B), within 30 days after the disclosure made by the other party. The parties shall supplement these disclosures when required under subdivision (e)(1).

(3) *Pretrial Disclosures.* In addition to the disclosures required by Rule 26(a)(1) and (2), a party must provide to other parties and promptly file with the court the following information regarding the evidence that it may present at trial other than solely for impeachment:

(A) the name and, if not previously provided, the address and telephone number of each witness, separately identifying those whom the party expects to present and those whom the party may call if the need arises;

(B) the designation of those witnesses whose testimony is expected to be presented by means of a deposition and, if not taken stenographically, a transcript of the pertinent portions of the deposition testimony; and

(C) an appropriate identification of each document or other exhibit, including summaries of other evidence, separately identifying those which the party expects to offer and those which the party may offer if the need arises. Unless otherwise directed by the court, these disclosures must be made at least 30 days before trial. Within 14 days thereafter, unless a different time is specified by the court, a party may serve and promptly file a list disclosing (i) any objections to the use under Rule 32(a) of a deposition designated by another party under Rule 26(a)(3)(B), and (ii) any objection, together with the grounds therefor, that may be made to the admissibility of materials identified under Rule 26(a)(3)(C). Objections not so disclosed, other than objections under Rules 402 and 403 of the Federal Rules of Evidence, are waived unless excused by the court for good cause.

(4) *Form of Disclosures.* Unless the court orders otherwise, all disclosures under Rules 26(a)(1) through (3) must be made in writing, signed, and served.

(5) *Methods to Discover Additional Matter.* Parties may obtain discovery by one or more of the following methods: depositions upon oral examination or written questions; written interrogatories; production of documents or things or permission to enter upon land or other property under Rule 34 or 45(a)(1)(C), for inspection and other purposes; physical and mental examinations; and requests for admission.

(b) DISCOVERY SCOPE AND LIMITS. Unless otherwise limited by order of the court in accordance with these rules, the scope of discovery is as follows:

(1) *In General.* Parties may obtain discovery regarding any matter, not privileged, that is relevant to the claim or defense of any party, including the existence, description, nature, custody, condition, and location of any books, documents, or other tangible things and the identity and location of persons having knowledge of any discoverable matter. For good cause, the court may order discovery of any matter relevant to the subject matter involved in the action. Relevant information need not be admissible at the trial if the discovery appears reasonably calculated to lead to the discovery of admissible evidence. All discovery is subject to the limitations imposed by Rule 26(b)(2)(i), (ii), and (iii).

(2) *Limitations.*

(A) By order, the court may alter the limits in these rules on the number of depositions and interrogatories or the length of depositions under Rule 30. By order or local rule, the court may also limit the number of requests under Rule 36.

(B) A party need not provide discovery of electronically stored information from sources that the party identifies as not reasonably accessible because of undue burden or cost. On motion to compel discovery or for a protective order, the party from whom discovery is sought must show that the information is not reasonably accessible because of undue burden or cost. If that showing is made, the court may nonetheless order discovery from such sources if the requesting party shows good cause, considering the limitations of Rule 26(b)(2)(C). The court may specify conditions for the discovery.

(C) The frequency or extent of use of the discovery methods otherwise permitted under these rules and by any local rule shall be limited by the court if it determines that: (i) the discovery sought is unreasonably cumulative or duplicative, or is obtainable from some other source that is more convenient, less burdensome, or less expensive; (ii) the party seeking discovery has had ample opportunity by discovery in the action to obtain the information sought; or (iii) the burden or expense of the proposed discovery outweighs its likely benefit, taking into account the needs of the case, the amount in controversy, the parties' resources, the importance of the issues at stake in the litigation, and the importance of the proposed discovery in resolving the issues. The court may act upon its own initiative after reasonable notice or pursuant to a motion under Rule 26(c).

(3) *Trial Preparation: Materials.* Subject to the provisions of subdivision (b)(4) of this rule, a party may obtain discovery of documents and tangible things otherwise discoverable under subdivision (b)(1) of this rule and prepared in anticipation of litigation or for trial by or for another party or by or for that other party's representative (including the other party's attorney, consultant, surety, indemnitor, insurer, or agent) only upon a showing that the party seeking discovery has substantial need of the materials in the preparation of the party's

case and that the party is unable without undue hardship to obtain the substantial equivalent of the materials by other means. In ordering discovery of such materials when the required showing has been made, the court shall protect against disclosure of the mental impressions, conclusions, opinions, or legal theories of an attorney or other representative of a party concerning the litigation. A party may obtain without the required showing a statement concerning the action or its subject matter previously made by that party. Upon request, a person not a party may obtain without the required showing a statement concerning the action or its subject matter previously made by that person. If the request is refused, the person may move for a court order. The provisions of Rule 37(a)(4) apply to the award of expenses incurred in relation to the motion. For purposes of this paragraph, a statement previously made is (A) a written statement signed or otherwise adopted or approved by the person making it, or (B) a stenographic, mechanical, electrical, or other recording, or a transcription thereof, which is a substantially verbatim recital of an oral statement by the person making it and contemporaneously recorded.

(4) *Trial Preparation: Experts.*
(A) A party may depose any person who has been identified as an expert whose opinions may be presented at trial. If a report from the expert is required under subdivision (a)(2)(B), the deposition shall not be conducted until after the report is provided.

(B) A party may, through interrogatories or by deposition, discover facts known or opinions held by an expert who has been retained or specially employed by another party in anticipation of litigation or preparation for trial and who is not expected to be called as a witness at trial only as provided in Rule 35(b) or upon a showing of exceptional circumstances under which it is impracticable for the party seeking discovery to obtain facts or opinions on the same subject by other means.

(C) Unless manifest injustice would result, (i) the court shall require that the party seeking discovery pay the expert a reasonable fee for time spent in responding to discovery under this subdivision; and (ii) with respect to discovery obtained under subdivision (b)(4)(B) of this rule the court shall require the party seeking discovery to pay the other party a fair portion of the fees and expenses reasonably incurred by the latter party in obtaining facts and opinions from the expert.

(5) *Claims of Privilege or Protection of Trial-Preparation Materials.*
(A) Information Withheld. When a party withholds information otherwise discoverable under these rules by claiming that it is privileged or subject to protection as trial preparation material, the party shall make the claim expressly and shall describe the nature of the documents, communications, or things not

produced or disclosed in a manner that, without revealing information itself privileged or protected, will enable other parties to assess the applicability of the privilege or protection.

(B) Information Produced. If information is produced in discovery that is subject to a claim of privilege or of protection as trial-preparation material, the party making the claim may notify any party that received the information of the claim and the basis for it. After being notified, a party must promptly return, sequester, or destroy the specified information and any copies it has and may not use or disclose the information until the claim is resolved. A receiving party may promptly present the information to the court under seal for a determination of the claim. If the receiving party disclosed the information before being notified, it must take reasonable steps to retrieve it. The producing party must preserve the information until the claim is resolved.

(c) PROTECTIVE ORDERS. Upon motion by a party or by the person from whom discovery is sought, accompanied by a certification that the movant has in good faith conferred or attempted to confer with other affected parties in an effort to resolve the dispute without court action, and for good cause shown, the court in which the action is pending or alternatively, on matters relating to a deposition, the court in the district where the deposition is to be taken may make any order which justice requires to protect a party or person from annoyance, embarrassment, oppression, or undue burden or expense, including one or more of the following: (1) that the disclosure or discovery not be had; (2) that the disclosure or discovery may be had only on specified terms and conditions, including a designation of the time or place; (3) that the discovery may be had only by a method of discovery other than that selected by the party seeking discovery; (4) that certain matters not be inquired into, or that the scope of the disclosure or discovery be limited to certain matters; (5) that discovery be conducted with no one present except persons designated by the court; (6) that a deposition, after being sealed, be opened only by order of the court; (7) that a trade secret or other confidential research, development, or commercial information not be revealed or be revealed only in a designated way; and (8) that the parties simultaneously file specified documents or information enclosed in sealed envelopes to be opened as directed by the court. If the motion for a protective order is denied in whole or in part, the court may, on such terms and conditions as are just, order that any party or other person provide or permit discovery. The provisions of Rule 37(a)(4) apply to the award of expenses incurred in relation to the motion.

(d) TIMING AND SEQUENCE OF DISCOVERY. Except in categories of proceedings exempted from initial disclosure under Rule 26(a)(1)(E), or when authorized under these rules or by order or agreement of the parties, a party may not seek discovery from any source before the parties have conferred as required by Rule 26(f). Unless the court upon motion, for the convenience of parties and witnesses and in the interests of justice, orders otherwise, methods of discovery may be used in any sequence, and the fact that a party is conducting discovery, whether by deposition or otherwise, does not operate to delay any other party's discovery.

(e) SUPPLEMENTATION OF DISCLOSURES AND RESPONSES. A party who has made a disclosure under subdivision (a) or responded to a request for discovery with a disclosure or response is under a duty to supplement or correct the disclosure or response to include information thereafter acquired if ordered by the court or in the following circumstances:

(1) A party is under a duty to supplement at appropriate intervals its disclosures under subdivision (a) if the party learns that in some material respect the information disclosed is incomplete or incorrect and if the additional or corrective information has not otherwise been made known to the other parties during the discovery process or in writing. With respect to testimony of an expert from whom a report is required under subdivision (a)(2)(B) the duty extends both to information contained in the report and to information provided through a deposition of the expert, and any additions or other changes to this information shall be disclosed by the time the party's disclosures under Rule 26(a)(3) are due.

(2) A party is under a duty seasonably to amend a prior response to an interrogatory, request for production, or request for admission if the party learns that the response is in some material respect incomplete or incorrect and if the additional or corrective information has not otherwise been made known to the other parties during the discovery process or in writing.

(f) CONFERENCE OF PARTIES; PLANNING FOR DISCOVERY. Except in categories of proceedings exempted from initial disclosure under Rule 26(a)(1)(E) or when otherwise ordered, the parties must, as soon as practicable and in any event at least 21 days before a scheduling conference is held or a scheduling order is due under Rule 16(b), confer to consider the nature and basis of their claims and defenses and the possibilities for a prompt settlement or resolution of the case, to make or arrange for the disclosures required by Rule 26(a)(1), to discuss any issues relating to preserving discoverable information, and to develop a proposed discovery plan that indicates the parties' views and proposals concerning:

(1) what changes should be made in the timing, form, or requirement for disclosures under Rule 26(a), including a statement as to when disclosures under Rule 26(a)(1) were made or will be made;

(2) the subjects on which discovery may be needed, when discovery should be completed, and whether discovery should be conducted in phases or be limited to or focused upon particular issues;

(3) any issues relating to disclosure or discovery of electronically stored information, including the form or forms in which it should be produced;

(4) any issues relating to claims of privilege or of protection as trial-preparation material, including—if the parties agree on a procedure to assert such claims after production—whether to ask the court to include their agreement in an order;

(5) what changes should be made in the limitations on discovery imposed under these rules or by local rule, and what other limitations should be imposed; and

(6) any other orders that should be entered by the court under Rule 26(c) or under Rule 16(b) and (c). The attorneys of record and all unrepresented parties that have appeared in the case are jointly responsible for arranging the conference, for attempting in good faith to agree on the proposed discovery plan, and for submitting to the court within 14 days after the conference a written report outlining the plan. A court may order that the parties or attorneys attend the conference in person. If necessary to comply with its expedited schedule for Rule 16(b) conferences, a court may by local rule (i) require that the conference between the parties occur fewer than 21 days before the scheduling conference is held or a scheduling order is due under Rule 16(b), and (ii) require that the written report outlining the discovery plan be filed fewer than 14 days after the conference between the parties, or excuse the parties from submitting a written report and permit them to report orally on their discovery plan at the Rule 16(b) conference.

(g) SIGNING OF DISCLOSURES, DISCOVERY REQUESTS, RESPONSES, AND OBJECTIONS.

(1) Every disclosure made pursuant to subdivision (a)(1) or subdivision (a)(3) shall be signed by at least one attorney of record in the attorney's individual name, whose address shall be stated. An unrepresented party shall sign the disclosure and state the party's address. The signature of the attorney or party constitutes a certification that to the best of the signer's knowledge, information, and belief, formed after a reasonable inquiry, the disclosure is complete and correct as of the time it is made.

(2) Every discovery request, response, or objection made by a party represented by an attorney shall be signed by at least one attorney of record in the attorney's individual name, whose address shall be stated. An unrepresented party shall sign the request, response, or objection and state the party's address. The signature of the attorney or party constitutes a certification that to the best of the signer's knowledge, information, and belief, formed after a reasonable inquiry, the request, response, or objection is: (A) consistent with these rules and warranted by existing law or a good faith argument for the extension, modification, or reversal of existing law; (B) not interposed for any improper purpose, such as to harass or

to cause unnecessary delay or needless increase in the cost of litigation; and (C) not unreasonable or unduly burdensome or expensive, given the needs of the case, the discovery already had in the case, the amount in controversy, and the importance of the issues at stake in the litigation.

If a request, response, or objection is not signed, it shall be stricken unless it is signed promptly after the omission is called to the attention of the party making the request, response, or objection, and a party shall not be obligated to take any action with respect to it until it is signed.

(3) If without substantial justification a certification is made in violation of the rule, the court, upon motion or upon its own initiative, shall impose upon the person who made the certification, the party on whose behalf the disclosure, request, response, or objection is made, or both, an appropriate sanction, which may include an order to pay the amount of the reasonable expenses incurred because of the violation, including a reasonable attorney's fee.

(As amended Dec. 27, 1946, eff. Mar. 19, 1948; Jan. 21, 1963, eff. July 1, 1963; Feb. 28, 1966, eff. July 1, 1966; Mar. 30, 1970, eff. July 1, 1970; Apr. 29, 1980, eff. Aug. 1, 1980; Apr. 28, 1983, eff. Aug. 1, 1983; Mar. 2, 1987, eff. Aug. 1, 1987; Apr. 22, 1993, eff. Dec. 1, 1993; Apr. 17, 2000, eff. Dec. 1, 2000; Apr. 12, 2006, eff. Dec. 1, 2006.)

Rule 27. Depositions Before Action or Pending Appeal

(a) BEFORE ACTION.

(1) *Petition.* A person who desires to perpetuate testimony regarding any matter that may be cognizable in any court of the United States may file a verified petition in the United States district court in the district of the residence of any expected adverse party. The petition shall be entitled in the name of the petitioner and shall show: 1, that the petitioner expects to be a party to an action cognizable in a court of the United States but is presently unable to bring it or cause it to be brought, 2, the subject matter of the expected action and the petitioner's interest therein, 3, the facts which the petitioner desires to establish by the proposed testimony and the reasons for desiring to perpetuate it, 4, the names or a description of the persons the petitioner expects will be adverse parties and their addresses so far as known, and 5, the names and addresses of the persons to be examined and the substance of the testimony which the petitioner expects to elicit from each, and shall ask for an order authorizing the petitioner to take the depositions of the persons to be examined named in the petition, for the purpose of perpetuating their testimony.

(2) *Notice and Service.* At least 20 days before the hearing date, the petitioner

must serve each expected adverse party with a copy of the petition and a notice stating the time and place of the hearing. The notice may be served either inside or outside the district or state in the manner provided in Rule 4. If that service cannot be made with due diligence on an expected adverse party, the court may order service by publication or otherwise. The court must appoint an attorney to represent persons not served in the manner provided by Rule 4 and to cross-examine the deponent if an unserved person is not otherwise represented. Rule 17(c) applies if any expected adverse party is a minor or is incompetent.

(3) *Order and Examination*. If the court is satisfied that the perpetuation of the testimony may prevent a failure or delay of justice, it shall make an order designating or describing the persons whose depositions may be taken and specifying the subject matter of the examination and whether the depositions shall be taken upon oral examination or written interrogatories. The depositions may then be taken in accordance with these rules; and the court may make orders of the character provided for by Rules 34 and 35. For the purpose of applying these rules to depositions for perpetuating testimony, each reference therein to the court in which the action is pending shall be deemed to refer to the court in which the petition for such deposition was filed.

(4) *Use of Deposition*. If a deposition to perpetuate testimony is taken under these rules or if, although not so taken, it would be admissible in evidence in the courts of the state in which it is taken, it may be used in any action involving the same subject matter subsequently brought in a United States district court, in accordance with the provisions of Rule 32(a).

(b) PENDING APPEAL. If an appeal has been taken from a judgment of a district court or before the taking of an appeal if the time therefor has not expired, the district court in which the judgment was rendered may allow the taking of the depositions of witnesses to perpetuate their testimony for use in the event of further proceedings in the district court. In such case the party who desires to perpetuate the testimony may make a motion in the district court for leave to take the depositions, upon the same notice and service thereof as if the action was pending in the district court. The motion shall show (1) the names and addresses of persons to be examined and the substance of the testimony which the party expects to elicit from each; (2) the reasons for perpetuating their testimony. If the court finds that the perpetuation of the testimony is proper to avoid a failure or delay of justice, it may make an order allowing the depositions to be taken and may make orders of the character provided for by Rules 34 and 35, and thereupon the depositions may be taken and used in the same manner and under the same conditions as are prescribed in these rules for depositions taken in actions pending in the district court.

(c) PERPETUATION BY ACTION. This rule does not limit the power of a court to entertain an action to perpetuate testimony.

(As amended Dec. 27, 1946, eff. Mar. 19, 1948; Dec. 29, 1948, eff. Oct. 20, 1949; Mar. 1, 1971, eff. July 1, 1971; Mar. 2, 1987, eff. Aug. 1, 1987; Apr. 25, 2005, eff. Dec. 1, 2005.)

Rule 28. Persons Before Whom Depositions May Be Taken

(a) WITHIN THE UNITED STATES. Within the United States or within a territory or insular possession subject to the jurisdiction of the United States, depositions shall be taken before an officer authorized to administer oaths by the laws of the United States or of the place where the examination is held, or before a person appointed by the court in which the action is pending. A person so appointed has power to administer oaths and take testimony. The term officer as used in Rules 30, 31 and 32 includes a person appointed by the court or designated by the parties under Rule 29.

(b) IN FOREIGN COUNTRIES. Depositions may be taken in a foreign country (1) pursuant to any applicable treaty or convention, or (2) pursuant to a letter of request (whether or not captioned a letter rogatory), or (3) on notice before a person authorized to administer oaths in the place where the examination is held, either by the law thereof or by the law of the United States, or (4) before a person commissioned by the court, and a person so commissioned shall have the power by virtue of the commission to administer any necessary oath and take testimony. A commission or a letter of request shall be issued on application and notice and on terms that are just and appropriate. It is not requisite to the issuance of a commission or a letter of request that the taking of the deposition in any other manner is impracticable or inconvenient; and both a commission and a letter of request may be issued in proper cases. A notice or commission may designate the person before whom the deposition is to be taken either by name or descriptive title. A letter of request may be addressed "To the Appropriate Authority in [here name the country]." When a letter of request or any other device is used pursuant to any applicable treaty or convention, it shall be captioned in the form prescribed by that treaty or convention. Evidence obtained in response to a letter of request need not be excluded merely because it is not a verbatim transcript, because the testimony was not taken under oath, or because of any similar departure from the requirements for depositions taken within the United States under these rules.

(c) DISQUALIFICATION FOR INTEREST. No deposition shall be taken before a person who is a relative or employee or attorney or counsel of any of the parties, or is a relative or employee of such attorney or counsel, or is financially interested in the action.

(As amended Dec. 27, 1946, eff. Mar. 19, 1948; Jan. 21, 1963, eff. July 1, 1963; Apr. 29, 1980, eff. Aug. 1, 1980; Mar. 2, 1987, eff. Aug. 1, 1987; Apr. 22, 1993, eff. Dec. 1, 1993.)

Rule 29. Stipulations Regarding Discovery Procedure

Unless otherwise directed by the court, the parties may by written stipulation (1) provide that depositions may be taken before any person, at any time or place, upon any notice, and in any manner and when so taken may be used like other depositions, and (2) modify other procedures governing or limitations placed upon discovery, except that stipulations extending the time provided in Rules 33, 34, and 36 for responses to discovery may, if they would interfere with any time set for completion of discovery, for hearing of a motion, or for trial, be made only with the approval of the court.

(As amended Mar. 30, 1970, eff. July 1, 1970; Apr. 22, 1993, eff. Dec. 1, 1993.)

Rule 30. Depositions Upon Oral Examination

(a) WHEN DEPOSITIONS MAY BE TAKEN; WHEN LEAVE REQUIRED.

(1) A party may take the testimony of any person, including a party, by deposition upon oral examination without leave of court except as provided in paragraph (2). The attendance of witnesses may be compelled by subpoena as provided in Rule 45.

(2) A party must obtain leave of court, which shall be granted to the extent consistent with the principles stated in Rule 26(b)(2), if the person to be examined is confined in prison or if, without the written stipulation of the parties, (A) a proposed deposition would result in more than ten depositions being taken under this rule or Rule 31 by the plaintiffs, or by the defendants, or by third-party defendants; (B) the person to be examined already has been deposed in the case; or (C) a party seeks to take a deposition before the time specified in Rule 26(d) unless the notice contains a certification, with supporting facts, that the person to be examined is expected to leave the United States and be unavailable for examination in this country unless deposed before that time.

(b) NOTICE OF EXAMINATION: GENERAL REQUIREMENTS; METHOD OF RECORDING; PRODUCTION OF DOCUMENTS AND THINGS; DEPOSITION OF ORGANIZATION; DEPOSITION BY TELEPHONE.

(1) A party desiring to take the deposition of any person upon oral examination shall give reasonable notice in writing to every other party to the action. The notice shall state the time and place for taking the deposition and the name and

address of each person to be examined, if known, and, if the name is not known, a general description sufficient to identify the person or the particular class or group to which the person belongs. If a subpoena duces tecum is to be served on the person to be examined, the designation of the materials to be produced as set forth in the subpoena shall be attached to, or included in, the notice.

(2) The party taking the deposition shall state in the notice the method by which the testimony shall be recorded. Unless the court orders otherwise, it may be recorded by sound, sound-and-visual, or stenographic means, and the party taking the deposition shall bear the cost of the recording. Any party may arrange for a transcription to be made from the recording of a deposition taken by nonstenographic means.

(3) With prior notice to the deponent and other parties, any party may designate another method to record the deponent's testimony in addition to the method specified by the person taking the deposition. The additional record or transcript shall be made at that party's expense unless the court otherwise orders.

(4) Unless otherwise agreed by the parties, a deposition shall be conducted before an officer appointed or designated under Rule 28 and shall begin with a statement on the record by the officer that includes (A) the officer's name and business address; (B) the date, time, and place of the deposition; (C) the name of the deponent; (D) the administration of the oath or affirmation to the deponent; and (E) an identification of all persons present. If the deposition is recorded other than stenographically, the officer shall repeat items (A) through (C) at the beginning of each unit of recorded tape or other recording medium. The appearance or demeanor of deponents or attorneys shall not be distorted through camera or sound-recording techniques. At the end of the deposition, the officer shall state on the record that the deposition is complete and shall set forth any stipulations made by counsel concerning the custody of the transcript or recording and the exhibits, or concerning other pertinent matters.

(5) The notice to a party deponent may be accompanied by a request made in compliance with Rule 34 for the production of documents and tangible things at the taking of the deposition. The procedure of Rule 34 shall apply to the request.

(6) A party may in the party's notice and in a subpoena name as the deponent a public or private corporation or a partnership or association or governmental agency and describe with reasonable particularity the matters on which examination is requested. In that event, the organization so named shall designate one or more officers, directors, or managing agents, or other persons who consent to testify on its behalf, and may set forth, for each person designated, the matters on which the person will testify. A subpoena shall advise a non-party organization of its duty to make such a designation. The persons so

designated shall testify as to matters known or reasonably available to the organization. This subdivision (b)(6) does not preclude taking a deposition by any other procedure authorized in these rules.

(7) The parties may stipulate in writing or the court may upon motion order that a deposition be taken by telephone or other remote electronic means. For the purposes of this rule and Rules 28(a), 37(a)(1), and 37(b)(1), a deposition taken by such means is taken in the district and at the place where the deponent is to answer questions.

(c) EXAMINATION AND CROSS-EXAMINATION; RECORD OF EXAMINATION; OATH; OBJECTIONS.

Examination and cross-examination of witnesses may proceed as permitted at the trial under the provisions of the Federal Rules of Evidence except Rules 103 and 615. The officer before whom the deposition is to be taken shall put the witness on oath or affirmation and shall personally, or by someone acting under the officer's direction and in the officer's presence, record the testimony of the witness. The testimony shall be taken stenographically or recorded by any other method authorized by subdivision (b)(2) of this rule. All objections made at the time of the examination to the qualifications of the officer taking the deposition, to the manner of taking it, to the evidence presented, to the conduct of any party, or to any other aspect of the proceedings shall be noted by the officer upon the record of the deposition; but the examination shall proceed, with the testimony being taken subject to the objections. In lieu of participating in the oral examination, parties may serve written questions in a sealed envelope on the party taking the deposition and the party taking the deposition shall transmit them to the officer, who shall propound them to the witness and record the answers verbatim.

(d) SCHEDULE AND DURATION; MOTION TO TERMINATE OR LIMIT EXAMINATION.

(1) Any objection during a deposition must be stated concisely and in a non-argumentative and non-suggestive manner. A person may instruct a deponent not to answer only when necessary to preserve a privilege, to enforce a limitation directed by the court, or to present a motion under Rule 30(d)(4).

(2) Unless otherwise authorized by the court or stipulated by the parties, a deposition is limited to one day of seven hours. The court must allow additional time consistent with Rule 26(b)(2) if needed for a fair examination of the deponent or if the deponent or another person, or other circumstance, impedes or delays the examination.

(3) If the court finds that any impediment, delay, or other conduct has frustrated the fair examination of the deponent, it may impose upon the persons responsible

an appropriate sanction, including the reasonable costs and attorney's fees incurred by any parties as a result thereof.

(4) At any time during a deposition, on motion of a party or of the deponent and upon a showing that the examination is being conducted in bad faith or in such manner as unreasonably to annoy, embarrass, or oppress the deponent or party, the court in which the action is pending or the court in the district where the deposition is being taken may order the officer conducting the examination to cease forthwith from taking the deposition, or may limit the scope and manner of the taking of the deposition as provided in Rule 26(c). If the order made terminates the examination, it may be resumed thereafter only upon the order of the court in which the action is pending. Upon demand of the objecting party or deponent, the taking of the deposition must be suspended for the time necessary
to make a motion for an order. The provisions of Rule 37(a)(4) apply to the award of expenses incurred in relation to the motion.

(e) REVIEW BY WITNESS; CHANGES; SIGNING. If requested by the deponent or a party before completion of the deposition, the deponent shall have 30 days after being notified by the officer that the transcript or recording is available in which to review the transcript or recording and, if there are changes in form or substance, to sign a statement reciting such changes and the reasons given by the deponent for making them. The officer shall indicate in the certificate prescribed by subdivision (f)(1) whether any review was requested and, if so, shall append any changes made by the deponent during the period allowed.

(f) CERTIFICATION AND DELIVERY BY OFFICER; EXHIBITS; COPIES.

(1) The officer must certify that the witness was duly sworn by the officer and that the deposition is a true record of the testimony given by the witness. This certificate must be in writing and accompany the record of the deposition. Unless otherwise ordered by the court, the officer must securely seal the deposition in an envelope or package indorsed with the title of the action and marked "Deposition of [here insert name of witness]" and must promptly send it to the attorney who arranged for the transcript or recording, who must store
it under conditions that will protect it against loss, destruction, tampering, or deterioration. Documents and things produced for inspection during the examination of the witness, must, upon the request of a party, be marked for identification and annexed to the deposition and may be inspected and copied by any party, except that if the person producing the materials desires to retain them the person may (A) offer copies to be marked for identification and annexed to the deposition and to serve thereafter as originals if the person affords to all parties fair opportunity to verify the copies by comparison with the originals, or (B) offer the originals to be marked for identification, after giving to each party an opportunity to inspect and copy them, in which event the materials may then be

used in the same manner as if annexed to the deposition.

Any party may move for an order that the original be annexed to and returned with the deposition to the court, pending final disposition of the case.

(2) Unless otherwise ordered by the court or agreed by the parties, the officer shall retain stenographic notes of any deposition taken stenographically or a copy of the recording of any deposition taken by another method. Upon payment of reasonable charges therefor, the officer shall furnish a copy of the transcript or other recording of the deposition to any party or to the deponent.

(3) The party taking the deposition shall give prompt notice of its filing to all other parties.

(g) FAILURE TO ATTEND OR TO SERVE SUBPOENA; EXPENSES.

(1) If the party giving the notice of the taking of a deposition fails to attend and proceed therewith and another party attends in person or by attorney pursuant to the notice, the court may order the party giving the notice to pay to such other party the reasonable expenses incurred by that party and that party's attorney in attending, including reasonable attorney's fees.

(2) If the party giving the notice of the taking of a deposition of a witness fails to serve a subpoena upon the witness and the witness because of such failure does not attend, and if another party attends in person or by attorney because that party expects the deposition of that witness to be taken, the court may order the party giving the notice to pay to such other party the reasonable expenses incurred by that party and that party's attorney in attending, including reasonable attorney's fees.

(As amended Jan. 21, 1963, eff. July 1, 1963; Mar. 30, 1970, eff. July 1, 1970; Mar. 1, 1971, eff. July 1, 1971; Nov. 20, 1972, eff. July 1, 1975; Apr. 29, 1980, eff. Aug. 1, 1980; Mar. 2, 1987, eff. Aug. 1, 1987; Apr. 22, 1993, eff. Dec. 1, 1993; Apr. 17, 2000, eff. Dec. 1, 2000.)

Rule 31. Depositions Upon Written Questions

(a) SERVING QUESTIONS; NOTICE.

(1) A party may take the testimony of any person, including a party, by deposition upon written questions without leave of court except as provided in paragraph (2). The attendance of witnesses may be compelled by the use of subpoena as provided in Rule 45.

(2) A party must obtain leave of court, which shall be granted to the extent consistent with the principles stated in Rule 26(b)(2), if the person to be examined

is confined in prison or if, without the written stipulation of the parties, (A) a proposed deposition would result in more than ten depositions being taken under this rule or Rule 30 by the plaintiffs, or by the defendants, or by third-party defendants; (B) the person to be examined has already been deposed in the case; or (C) a party seeks to take a deposition before the time specified in Rule 26(d).

(3) A party desiring to take a deposition upon written questions shall serve them upon every other party with a notice stating (1) the name and address of the person who is to answer them, if known, and if the name is not known, a general description sufficient to identify the person or the particular class or group to which the person belongs, and (2) the name or descriptive title and address of the officer before whom the deposition is to be taken. A deposition upon written questions may be taken of a public or private corporation or a partnership or association or governmental agency in accordance with the provisions of Rule 30(b)(6).

(4) Within 14 days after the notice and written questions are served, a party may serve cross questions upon all other parties. Within 7 days after being served with cross questions, a party may serve redirect questions upon all other parties. Within 7 days after being served with redirect questions, a party may serve recross questions upon all other parties. The court may for cause shown enlarge or shorten the time.

(b) OFFICER TO TAKE RESPONSES AND PREPARE RECORD. A copy of the notice and copies of all questions served shall be delivered by the party taking the deposition to the officer designated in the notice, who shall proceed promptly, in the manner provided by Rule 30(c), (e), and (f), to take the testimony of the witness in response to the questions and to prepare, certify, and file or mail the deposition, attaching thereto the copy of the notice and the questions received by the officer.

(c) NOTICE OF FILING. When the deposition is filed the party taking it shall promptly give notice thereof to all other parties.

(As amended Mar. 30, 1970, eff. July 1, 1970; Mar. 2, 1987, eff. Aug. 1, 1987; Apr. 22, 1993, eff. Dec. 1, 1993.)

Rule 32. Use of Depositions in Court Proceedings

(a) USE OF DEPOSITIONS. At the trial or upon the hearing of a motion or an interlocutory proceeding, any part or all of a deposition, so far as admissible under the rules of evidence applied as though the witness were then present and testifying, may be used against any party who was present or represented at the taking of the deposition or who had reasonable notice thereof, in accordance with any of the following provisions:

(1) Any deposition may be used by any party for the purpose of contradicting or impeaching the testimony of deponent as a witness, or for any other purpose permitted by the Federal Rules of Evidence.

(2) The deposition of a party or of anyone who at the time of taking the deposition was an officer, director, or managing agent, or a person designated under Rule 30(b)(6) or 31(a) to testify on behalf of a public or private corporation, partnership or association or governmental agency which is a party
may be used by an adverse party for any purpose.

(3) The deposition of a witness, whether or not a party, may be used by any party for any purpose if the court finds: (A) that the witness is dead; or (B) that the witness is at a greater distance than 100 miles from the place of trial or hearing, or is out of the United States, unless it appears that the absence of the witness was procured by the party offering the deposition; or (C) that the witness is unable to attend or testify because of age, illness, infirmity, or imprisonment; or
(D) that the party offering the deposition has been unable to procure the attendance of the witness by subpoena; or (E) upon application and notice, that such exceptional circumstances exist as to make it desirable, in the interest of justice and with due regard to the importance of presenting the testimony of witnesses orally in open court, to allow the deposition to be used. A deposition taken without leave of court pursuant to a notice under Rule 30(a)(2)(C) shall not be used against a party who demonstrates that, when served with the notice, it was unable through the exercise of diligence to obtain counsel to represent it at the taking of the deposition; nor shall a deposition be used against a party who, having received less than 11 days notice of a deposition, has promptly upon receiving such notice filed a motion for a protective order under Rule 26(c)(2) requesting that the deposition not be held or be held at a different time or place and such motion is pending at the time the deposition is held.

(4) If only part of a deposition is offered in evidence by a party, an adverse party may require the offeror to introduce any other part which ought in fairness to be considered with the part introduced, and any party may introduce any other parts. Substitution of parties pursuant to Rule 25 does not affect the right to use depositions previously taken; and, when an action has been brought in any court of the United States or of any State and another action involving the same subject matter is afterward brought between the same parties or their representatives or successors in interest, all depositions lawfully taken and duly filed in the former action may be used in the latter as if originally taken therefor. A deposition previously taken may also be used as permitted by the Federal Rules of Evidence.

(b) OBJECTIONS TO ADMISSIBILITY. Subject to the provisions of Rule 28(b) and subdivision (d)(3) of this rule, objection may be made at the trial or hearing to receiving in evidence any deposition or part thereof for any reason which would require the exclusion of the evidence if the witness were then present and testifying.

(c) FORM OF PRESENTATION. Except as otherwise directed by the court, a party offering deposition testimony pursuant to this rule may offer it in stenographic or nonstenographic form, but, if in nonstenographic form, the party shall also provide the court with a transcript of the portions so offered. On request of any party in a case tried before a jury, deposition testimony offered other than for impeachment purposes shall be presented in nonstenographic form, if available, unless the court for good cause orders otherwise.

(d) EFFECT OF ERRORS AND IRREGULARITIES IN DEPOSITIONS.

(1) *As to Notice.* All errors and irregularities in the notice for taking a deposition are waived unless written objection is promptly served upon the party giving the notice.

(2) *As to Disqualification of Officer.* Objection to taking a deposition because of disqualification of the officer before whom it is to be taken is waived unless made before the taking of the deposition begins or as soon thereafter as the disqualification becomes known or could be discovered with reasonable diligence.

(3) *As to Taking of Deposition.* (A) Objections to the competency of a witness or to the competency, relevancy, or materiality of testimony are not waived by failure to make them before or during the taking of the deposition, unless the ground of the objection is one which might have been obviated or removed if presented at that time. (B) Errors and irregularities occurring at the oral examination in the manner of taking the deposition, in the form of the questions or answers, in the oath or affirmation, or in the conduct of parties, and errors of any kind which might be obviated, removed, or cured if promptly presented, are waived unless seasonable objection thereto is made at the taking of the deposition. (C) Objections to the form of written questions submitted under Rule 31 are waived unless served in writing upon the party propounding them within the time allowed for serving the succeeding cross or other questions and within 5 days after service of the last questions authorized.

(4) *As to Completion and Return of Deposition.* Errors and irregularities in the manner in which the testimony is transcribed or the deposition is prepared, signed, certified, sealed, indorsed, transmitted, filed, or otherwise dealt with by the officer under Rules 30 and 31 are waived unless a motion to suppress the deposition or some part thereof is made with reasonable promptness after such defect is, or with

due diligence might have been, ascertained.

(As amended Mar. 30, 1970, eff. July 1, 1970; Nov. 20, 1972, eff. July 1, 1975; Apr. 29, 1980, eff. Aug. 1, 1980; Mar. 2, 1987, eff. Aug. 1, 1987; Apr. 22, 1993, eff. Dec. 1, 1993.)

Rule 33. Interrogatories to Parties

(a) AVAILABILITY. Without leave of court or written stipulation, any party may serve upon any other party written interrogatories, not exceeding 25 in number including all discrete subparts, to be answered by the party served or, if the party served is a public or private corporation or a partnership or association or governmental agency, by any officer or agent, who shall furnish such information as is available to the party. Leave to serve additional interrogatories shall be granted to the extent consistent with the principles of Rule 26(b)(2). Without leave of court or written stipulation, interrogatories may not be served before the time specified in Rule 26(d).

(b) ANSWERS AND OBJECTIONS.

(1) Each interrogatory shall be answered separately and fully in writing under oath, unless it is objected to, in which event the objecting party shall state the reasons for objection and shall answer to the extent the interrogatory is not objectionable.

(2) The answers are to be signed by the person making them, and the objections signed by the attorney making them.

(3) The party upon whom the interrogatories have been served shall serve a copy of the answers, and objections if any, within 30 days after the service of the interrogatories. A shorter or longer time may be directed by the court or, in the absence of such an order, agreed to in writing by the parties subject to Rule 29.

(4) All grounds for an objection to an interrogatory shall be stated with specificity. Any ground not stated in a timely objection is waived unless the party's failure to object is excused by the court for good cause shown.

(5) The party submitting the interrogatories may move for an order under Rule 37(a) with respect to any objection to or other failure to answer an interrogatory.

(c) SCOPE; USE AT TRIAL. Interrogatories may relate to any matters which can be inquired into under Rule 26(b)(1), and the answers may be used to the extent permitted by the rules of evidence. An interrogatory otherwise proper is not necessarily objectionable merely because an answer to the interrogatory involves

an opinion or contention that relates to fact or the application of law
to fact, but the court may order that such an interrogatory need not be answered
until after designated discovery has been completed or until a pre-trial conference
or other later time.

(d) OPTION TO PRODUCE BUSINESS RECORDS. Where the answer to an
interrogatory may be derived or ascertained from the business records, including
electronically stored information, of the party upon whom the interrogatory has
been served or from an examination, audit or inspection of such business records,
including a compilation, abstract or summary thereof, and the burden of deriving
or ascertaining the answer is substantially the same for the party serving the
interrogatory as for the party served, it is a sufficient answer to such interrogatory
to specify the records from which the answer may be derived or ascertained and
to afford to the party serving the interrogatory reasonable opportunity to examine,
audit or inspect such records and to make copies, compilations, abstracts, or
summaries. A specification shall be in sufficient detail to permit the interrogating
party to locate and to identify, as readily as can the party served, the records from
which the answer may be ascertained.

(As amended Dec. 27, 1946, eff. Mar. 19, 1948; Mar. 30, 1970, eff. July 1, 1970;
Apr. 29, 1980, eff. Aug. 1, 1980; Apr. 22, 1993, eff. Dec. 1, 1993; Apr. 12,
2006, eff. Dec. 1, 2006.)

Rule 34. Production of Documents, Electronically Stored Information, and Things and Entry Upon Land for Inspection and Other Purposes

(a) SCOPE. Any party may serve on any other party a request (1) to produce and
permit the party making the request, or someone acting on the requestor's behalf,
to inspect, copy, test, or sample any designated documents or electronically stored
information—including writings, drawings, graphs, charts, photographs, sound
recordings, images, and other data or data compilations stored in any medium
from which information can be obtained—translated, if necessary, by the
respondent into reasonably usable form, or to inspect, copy, test, or sample any
designated tangible things which constitute or contain matters within the scope of
Rule 26(b) and which are in the possession, custody or control of the party upon
whom the request is served; or (2) to permit entry upon designated
land or other property in the possession or control of the party upon whom the
request is served for the purpose of inspection and measuring, surveying,
photographing, testing, or sampling the property or any designated object or
operation thereon, within the scope of Rule 26(b).

(b) PROCEDURE. The request shall set forth, either by individual item or by
category, the items to be inspected, and describe each with reasonable

particularity. The request shall specify a reasonable time, place, and manner of making the inspection and performing the related acts. The request may specify the form or forms in which electronically stored information is to be produced. Without leave of court or written stipulation, a request may not be served before the time specified in Rule 26(d). The party upon whom the request is served shall serve a written response within 30 days after the service of the request. A shorter or longer time may be directed by the court or, in the absence of such an order, agreed to in writing by the parties, subject to Rule 29. The response shall state, with respect to each item or category, that inspection and related activities will be permitted as requested, unless the request is objected to, including an objection to the requested form or forms for producing electronically stored information, stating the reasons for the objection. If objection is made to part of an item or category, the part shall be specified and inspection permitted of the remaining parts. If objection is made to the requested form or forms for producing electronically stored information—or if no form was specified in the request—the responding party must state the form or forms it intends to use. The party submitting the request may move for an order under Rule 37(a) with respect to any objection to or other failure to respond to the request or any part thereof, or any failure to permit inspection as requested. Unless the parties otherwise agree, or the court otherwise orders: (i) a party who produces documents for inspection shall produce them as they are kept in the usual course of business or shall organize and label them to correspond with the categories in the request; (ii) if a request does not specify the form or forms for producing electronically stored information, a responding party must produce the information in a form or forms in which it is ordinarily maintained or in a form or forms that are reasonably usable; and (iii) a party need not produce the same electronically stored information in more than one form.

(c) PERSONS NOT PARTIES. A person not a party to the action may be compelled to produce documents and things or to submit to an inspection as provided in Rule 45.

(As amended Dec. 27, 1946, eff. Mar. 19, 1948; Mar. 30, 1970, eff. July 1, 1970; Apr. 29, 1980, eff. Aug. 1, 1980; Mar. 2, 1987, eff. Aug. 1, 1987; Apr. 30, 1991, eff. Dec. 1, 1991; Apr. 22, 1993, eff. Dec. 1, 1993; Apr. 12, 2006, eff. Dec. 1, 2006.)

Rule 35. Physical and Mental Examinations of Persons

(a) ORDER FOR EXAMINATION. When the mental or physical condition (including the blood group) of a party or of a person in the custody or under the legal control of a party, is in controversy, the court in which the action is pending may order the party to submit to a physical or mental examination by a suitably licensed or certified examiner or to produce for examination the person in the party's custody or legal control. The order may be made only on motion for good cause shown and upon notice to the person to be examined and to all parties and shall specify the time, place, manner, conditions, and scope of the examination and the person or persons by whom it is to be made.

(b) REPORT OF EXAMINER.

(1) If requested by the party against whom an order is made under Rule 35(a) or the person examined, the party causing the examination to be made shall deliver to the requesting party a copy of the detailed written report of the examiner setting out the examiner's findings, including results of all tests made, diagnoses and conclusions, together with like reports of all earlier examinations of the same condition. After delivery the party causing the examination shall be entitled upon request to receive from the party against whom the order is made a like report of any examination, previously or thereafter made, of the same condition, unless, in the case of a report of examination of a person not a party, the party shows that the party is unable to obtain it. The court on motion may make an order against a party requiring delivery of a report on such terms as are just, and if an examiner fails or refuses to make a report the court may exclude the examiner's testimony if offered at trial.

(2) By requesting and obtaining a report of the examination so ordered or by taking the deposition of the examiner, the party examined waives any privilege the party may have in that action or any other involving the same controversy, regarding the testimony of every other person who has examined or may thereafter examine the party in respect of the same mental or physical condition.

(3) This subdivision applies to examinations made by agreement of the parties, unless the agreement expressly provides otherwise. This subdivision does not preclude discovery of a report of an examiner or the taking of a deposition of the examiner in accordance with the provisions of any other rule.

(As amended Mar. 30, 1970, eff. July 1, 1970; Mar. 2, 1987, eff. Aug. 1, 1987; Nov. 18, 1988; Apr. 30, 1991, eff. Dec. 1, 1991.)

Rule 36. Requests for Admission

(a) REQUEST FOR ADMISSION. A party may serve upon any other party a written request for the admission, for purposes of the pending action only, of the truth of any matters within the scope of Rule 26(b)(1) set forth in the request that relate to statements or opinions of fact or of the application of law to fact, including the genuineness of any documents described in the request. Copies of documents shall be served with the request unless they have been or are otherwise furnished or made available for inspection and copying. Without leave of court or written stipulation, requests for admission may not be served before the time specified in Rule 26(d). Each matter of which an admission is requested shall be separately set forth. The matter is admitted unless, within 30 days after service of the request, or within such shorter or longer time as the court may allow or as the parties may agree to in writing, subject to Rule 29, the party to whom the request is directed serves upon the party requesting the admission a written answer or objection addressed to the matter, signed by the party or by the

party's attorney. If objection is made, the reasons therefor shall be stated. The answer shall specifically deny the matter or set forth in detail the reasons why the answering party cannot truthfully admit or deny the matter. A denial shall fairly meet the substance of the requested admission, and when good faith requires that a party qualify an answer or deny only a part of the matter of which an admission is requested, the party shall specify so much of it as is true and qualify or deny the remainder. An answering party may not give lack of information or knowledge as a reason for failure to admit or deny unless the party states that the party has made reasonable inquiry and that the information

known or readily obtainable by the party is insufficient to enable the party to admit or deny. A party who considers that a matter of which an admission has been requested presents a genuine issue for trial may not, on that ground alone, object to the request; the party may, subject to the provisions of Rule 37(c), deny the matter or set forth reasons why the party cannot admit or deny it. The party who has requested the admissions may move to determine the sufficiency of the answers or objections. Unless the court determines that an objection is justified, it shall order that an answer be served. If the court determines that an answer does not comply with the requirements of this rule, it may order either

that the matter is admitted or that an amended answer be served. The court may, in lieu of these orders, determine that final disposition of the request be made at a pre-trial conference or at a designated time prior to trial. The provisions of Rule 37(a)(4) apply to the award of expenses incurred in relation to the motion.

(b) EFFECT OF ADMISSION. Any matter admitted under this rule is conclusively established unless the court on motion permits withdrawal or amendment of the admission. Subject to the provision of Rule 16 governing amendment of a pre-trial order, the court may permit withdrawal or amendment when the presentation of the merits of the action will be subserved thereby and the party who obtained the admission fails to satisfy the court that withdrawal or amendment will prejudice that party in maintaining the action or defense on the merits. Any admission made by a party under this rule is for the purpose of the pending action only and is not an admission for any other purpose nor may it be used against the party in any other proceeding.

(As amended Dec. 27, 1946, eff. Mar. 19, 1948; Mar. 30, 1970, eff. July 1, 1970; Mar. 2, 1987, eff. Aug. 1, 1987; Apr. 22, 1993, eff. Dec. 1, 1993.)

Rule 37. Failure to Make Disclosures or Cooperate in Discovery; Sanctions

(a) MOTION FOR ORDER COMPELLING DISCLOSURE OR DISCOVERY. A party, upon reasonable notice to other parties and all persons affected thereby, may apply for an order compelling disclosure or discovery as follows:

(1) *Appropriate Court.* An application for an order to a party shall be made to the court in which the action is pending. An application for an order to a person who is not a party shall be made to the court in the district where the discovery is being, or is to be, taken.

(2) *Motion.* (A) If a party fails to make a disclosure required by Rule 26(a), any other party may move to compel disclosure and for appropriate sanctions. The motion must include a certification that the movant has in good faith conferred or attempted to confer with the party not making the disclosure in an effort to secure the disclosure without court action. (B) If a deponent fails to answer a question propounded or submitted under Rules 30 or 31, or a corporation or other entity fails to make a designation under Rule 30(b)(6) or 31(a), or a party fails to answer an interrogatory submitted under Rule 33, or if a party, in response to a request for inspection submitted under Rule 34, fails to respond
that inspection will be permitted as requested or fails to permit inspection as requested, the discovering party may move for an order compelling an answer, or a designation, or an order compelling inspection in accordance with the request. The motion must include a certification that the movant has in good faith conferred or attempted to confer with the person or party failing to make
the discovery in an effort to secure the information or material without court action. When taking a deposition on oral examination, the proponent of the question may complete or adjourn the examination before applying for an order.

(3) *Evasive or Incomplete Disclosure, Answer, or Response.* For purposes of this subdivision an evasive or incomplete disclosure, answer, or response is to be treated as a failure to disclose, answer, or respond.

(4) *Expenses and Sanctions.* (A) If the motion is granted or if the disclosure or requested discovery is provided after the motion was filed, the court shall, after affording an opportunity to be heard, require the party or deponent whose conduct necessitated the motion or the party or attorney advising such conduct
or both of them to pay to the moving party the reasonable expenses incurred in making the motion, including attorney's fees, unless the court finds that the motion was filed without the movant's first making a good faith effort to obtain the disclosure or discovery without court action, or that the opposing party's nondisclosure, response, or objection was substantially justified, or that other circumstances make an award of expenses unjust. (B) If the motion is denied, the

court may enter any protective order authorized under Rule 26(c) and shall, after affording an opportunity to be heard, require the moving party or the attorney filing the motion or both of them to pay to the party or deponent who opposed the motion the reasonable expenses incurred in opposing the motion, including attorney's fees, unless the court finds that the making of the motion was substantially justified or that other circumstances make an award of expenses unjust. (C) If the motion is granted in part and denied in part, the court may enter any protective order authorized under Rule 26(c) and may, after affording an opportunity to be heard, apportion the reasonable expenses incurred in relation to the motion among the parties and persons in a just manner.

(b) FAILURE TO COMPLY WITH ORDER.

(1) *Sanctions by Court in District Where Deposition Is Taken.* If a deponent fails to be sworn or to answer a question after being directed to do so by the court in the district in which the deposition is being taken, the failure may be considered a contempt of that court.

(2) *Sanctions by Court in Which Action Is Pending.* If a party or an officer, director, or managing agent of a party or a person designated under Rule 30(b)(6) or 31(a) to testify on behalf of a party fails to obey an order to provide or permit discovery, including an order made under subdivision (a) of this rule or Rule 35, or if a party fails to obey an order entered under Rule 26(f), the court in which the action is pending may make such orders in regard to the failure as are just, and among others the following: (A) An order that the matters regarding which the order was made or any other designated facts shall be taken to be established for the purposes of the action in accordance with the claim of the party obtaining the order; (B) An order refusing to allow the disobedient party to support or oppose designated claims or defenses, or prohibiting that party from introducing designated matters in evidence; (C) An order striking out pleadings or parts thereof, or staying further proceedings until the order is obeyed, or dismissing the action or proceeding or any part thereof, or rendering a judgment by default against the disobedient party; (D) In lieu of any of the foregoing orders or in addition thereto, an order treating as a contempt of court the failure to obey any orders except an order to submit to a physical or mental examination; (E) Where a party has failed to comply with an order under Rule 35(a) requiring that party to produce another for examination, such orders as are listed in paragraphs (A), (B), and (C) of this subdivision, unless the party failing to comply shows that that party is unable to produce such person for examination. In lieu of any of the foregoing orders or in addition thereto, the court shall require the party failing to obey the order or the attorney advising that party or both to pay the reasonable expenses, including attorney's fees, caused by the failure, unless the court finds that the failure was substantially justified or that other circumstances make an award of expenses unjust.

(c) FAILURE TO DISCLOSE; FALSE OR MISLEADING DISCLOSURE; REFUSAL TO ADMIT.

(1) A party that without substantial justification fails to disclose information required by Rule 26(a) or 26(e)(1), or to amend a prior response to discovery as required by Rule 26(e)(2), is not, unless such failure is harmless, permitted to use as evidence at a trial, at a hearing, or on a motion any witness or information not so disclosed. In addition to or in lieu of this sanction, the court, on motion and after affording an opportunity to be heard, may impose other appropriate sanctions. In addition to requiring payment of reasonable expenses, including attorney's fees, caused by the failure, these sanctions may include any of the actions authorized under Rule 37(b)(2)(A), (B), and (C) and may include informing the jury of the failure to make the disclosure.

(2) If a party fails to admit the genuineness of any document or the truth of any matter as requested under Rule 36, and if the party requesting the admissions thereafter proves the genuineness of the document or the truth of the matter, the requesting party may apply to the court for an order requiring the other party to pay the reasonable expenses incurred in making that proof, including reasonable attorney's fees. The court shall make the order unless it finds that (A) the request was held objectionable pursuant to Rule 36(a), or (B) the admission sought was of no substantial importance, or (C) the party failing to admit had reasonable ground to believe that the party might prevail on the matter, or (D) there was other good reason for the failure to admit.

(d) FAILURE OF PARTY TO ATTEND AT OWN DEPOSITION OR SERVE ANSWERS TO INTERROGATORIES OR RESPOND TO REQUEST FOR INSPECTION.

If a party or an officer, director, or managing agent of a party or a person designated under Rule 30(b)(6) or 31(a) to testify on behalf of a party fails (1) to appear before the officer who is to take the deposition, after being served with a proper notice, or (2) to serve answers or objections to interrogatories submitted under Rule 33, after proper service of the interrogatories, or (3) to serve a written response to a request for inspection submitted under Rule 34, after proper service of the request, the court in which the action is pending on motion may make such orders in regard to the failure as are just, and among others it may take any action authorized under subparagraphs (A), (B), and (C) of subdivision (b)(2) of this rule. Any motion specifying a failure under clause (2) or (3) of this subdivision shall include a certification that the movant has in good faith conferred or attempted to confer with the party failing to answer or respond in an effort to obtain such answer or response without court action. In lieu of any order or in addition thereto, the court shall require the party failing to act or the attorney advising that party or both to pay the reasonable expenses, including attorney's fees, caused by the failure unless the court finds that the failure was substantially justified or that other circumstances make an award of expenses unjust. The failure to act described in this subdivision may not be excused on the ground that the discovery sought is objectionable unless the party failing to act has a pending motion for a protective order as provided by Rule 26©.

[(e) SUBPOENA OF PERSON IN FOREIGN COUNTRY.] (Abrogated Apr. 29, 1980, eff. Aug. 1, 1980)

(f) ELECTRONICALLY STORED INFORMATION. Absent exceptional circumstances, a court may not impose sanctions under these rules on a party for failing to provide electronically stored information lost as a result of the routine, good-faith operation of an electronic information system.

(g) FAILURE TO PARTICIPATE IN THE FRAMING OF A DISCOVERY PLAN. If a party or a party's attorney fails to participate in good faith in the development and submission of a proposed discovery plan as required by Rule 26(f), the court may, after opportunity for hearing, require such party or attorney to pay to any other party the reasonable expenses, including attorney's fees, caused by the failure.

(As amended Dec. 29, 1948, eff. Oct. 20, 1949; Mar. 30, 1970, eff. July 1, 1970; Apr. 29, 1980, eff. Aug. 1, 1980; Oct. 21, 1980, eff. Oct. 1, 1981; Mar. 2, 1987, eff. Aug. 1, 1987; Apr. 22, 1993, eff. Dec. 1, 1993; Apr. 17, 2000, eff. Dec. 1, 2000; Apr. 12, 2006, eff. Dec. 1, 2006.)

VI. TRIALS

Rule 38. Jury Trial of Right - omitted

Rule 39. Trial by Jury or by the Court - omitted

Rule 40. Assignment of Cases for Trial - omitted

Rule 41. Dismissal of Actions

(a) VOLUNTARY DISMISSAL: EFFECT THEREOF.

(1) *By Plaintiff; by Stipulation.* Subject to the provisions of Rule 23(e), of Rule 66, and of any statute of the United States, an action may be dismissed by the plaintiff without order of court (i) by filing a notice of dismissal at any time before

service by the adverse party of an answer or of a motion for summary judgment, whichever first occurs, or (ii) by filing a stipulation of dismissal signed by all parties who have appeared in the action. Unless otherwise stated in the notice of dismissal or stipulation, the dismissal is without prejudice, except that a notice of dismissal operates as an adjudication upon the merits when filed by a plaintiff who has once dismissed in any court of the United States or of any state an action based on or including the same claim.

(2) *By Order of Court.* Except as provided in paragraph (1) of this subdivision of this rule, an action shall not be dismissed at the plaintiff's instance save upon order of the court and upon such terms and conditions as the court deems proper. If a counterclaim has been pleaded by a defendant prior to the service upon the defendant of the plaintiff's motion to dismiss, the action shall not be dismissed against the defendant's objection unless the counterclaim can remain pending for independent adjudication by the court. Unless otherwise specified in the order, a dismissal under this paragraph is without prejudice.

(b) INVOLUNTARY DISMISSAL: EFFECT THEREOF. For failure of the plaintiff to prosecute or to comply with these rules or any order of court, a defendant may move for dismissal of an action or of any claim against the defendant. Unless the court in its order for dismissal otherwise specifies, a dismissal under this subdivision and any dismissal not provided for in this rule, other than a dismissal for lack of jurisdiction, for improper venue, or for failure to join a party under Rule 19, operates as an adjudication upon the merits.

(c) DISMISSAL OF COUNTERCLAIM, CROSS-CLAIM, OR THIRD-PARTY CLAIM. The provisions of this rule apply to the dismissal of any counterclaim, cross-claim, or third-party claim. A voluntary dismissal by the claimant alone pursuant to paragraph (1) of subdivision (a) of this rule shall be made before a responsive pleading is served or, if there is none, before the introduction of evidence at the trial or hearing.

(d) COSTS OF PREVIOUSLY-DISMISSED ACTION. If a plaintiff who has once dismissed an action in any court commences an action based upon or including the same claim against the same defendant, the court may make such order for the payment of costs of the action previously dismissed as it may deem proper and may stay the proceedings in the action until the plaintiff has complied with the order.

(As amended Dec. 27, 1946, eff. Mar. 19, 1948; Jan. 21, 1963, eff. July 1, 1963; Feb. 28, 1966, eff. July 1, 1966; Dec. 4, 1967, eff. July 1, 1968; Mar. 2, 1987, eff. Aug. 1, 1987; Apr. 30, 1991, eff. Dec. 1, 1991.)

Rule 42. Consolidation; Separate Trials

(a) CONSOLIDATION. When actions involving a common question of law or fact are pending before the court, it may order a joint hearing or trial of any or all the matters in issue in the actions; it may order all the actions consolidated; and it may make such orders concerning proceedings therein as may tend to avoid unnecessary costs or delay.

(b) SEPARATE TRIALS. The court, in furtherance of convenience or to avoid prejudice, or when separate trials will be conducive to expedition and economy, may order a separate trial of any claim, cross-claim, counterclaim, or third-party claim, or of any separate issue or of any number of claims, cross-claims, counterclaims, third-party claims, or issues, always preserving inviolate the right of trial by jury as declared by the Seventh Amendment to the Constitution or as given by a statute of the United States.

(As amended Feb. 28, 1966, eff. July 1, 1966.)

Rule 43. Taking of Testimony - omitted

Rule 44. Proof of Official Record - omitted

Rule 44.1. Determination of Foreign Law - omitted

Rule 45. Subpoena - omitted

Rule 46. Exceptions Unnecessary - omitted

Rule 47. Selection of Jurors - omitted

Rule 48. Number of Jurors—Participation in Verdict - omitted

Rule 49. Special Verdicts and Interrogatories - omitted

Rule 50. Judgment as a Matter of Law in Jury Trials; Alternative Motion for

New Trial; Conditional Rulings - omitted

Rule 51. Instructions to Jury; Objections; Preserving a Claim of Error - omitted

---

Rule 52. Findings by the Court; Judgment on Partial Findings - omitted

---

Rule 53. Masters - omitted

VII. JUDGMENT

Rule 54. Judgments; Costs - omitted

Rule 55. Default

(a) ENTRY. When a party against whom a judgment for affirmative relief is sought has failed to plead or otherwise defend as provided by these rules and that fact is made to appear by affidavit or otherwise, the clerk shall enter the party's default.

(b) JUDGMENT. Judgment by default may be entered as follows:

(1) *By the Clerk.* When the plaintiff's claim against a defendant is for a sum certain or for a sum which can by computation be made certain, the clerk upon request of the plaintiff and upon affidavit of the amount due shall enter judgment for that amount and costs against the defendant, if the defendant has been defaulted for failure to appear and is not an infant or incompetent person.

(2) *By the Court.* In all other cases the party entitled to a judgment by default shall apply to the court therefor; but no judgment by default shall be entered against an infant or incompetent person unless represented in the action by a general guardian, committee, conservator, or other such representative who has appeared therein. If the party against whom judgment by default is sought has appeared in the action, the party (or, if appearing by representative, the party's representative) shall be served with written notice of the application for judgment at least 3 days prior to the hearing on such application. If, in order to enable the

court to enter judgment or to carry it into effect, it is necessary to take an account or to determine the amount of damages or to establish the truth of any averment by evidence or to make an investigation of any other matter, the court may conduct such hearings or order such references as it deems necessary and proper and shall accord a right of trial by jury to the parties when and as required by any statute of the United States.

(c) SETTING ASIDE DEFAULT. For good cause shown the court may set aside an entry of default and, if a judgment by default has been entered, may likewise set it aside in accordance with Rule 60(b).

(d) PLAINTIFFS, COUNTERCLAIMANTS, CROSS-CLAIMANTS. The provisions of this rule apply whether the party entitled to the judgment by default is a plaintiff, a third-party plaintiff, or a party who has pleaded a cross-claim or counterclaim. In all cases a judgment by default is subject to the limitations of Rule 54(c).

(e) JUDGMENT AGAINST THE UNITED STATES. No judgment by default shall be entered against the United States or an officer or agency thereof unless the claimant establishes a claim or right to relief by evidence satisfactory to the court.

(As amended Mar. 2, 1987, eff. Aug. 1, 1987.)

Rule 56. Summary Judgment

(a) FOR CLAIMANT. A party seeking to recover upon a claim, counterclaim, or cross-claim or to obtain a declaratory judgment may, at any time after the expiration of 20 days from the commencement of the action or after service of a motion for summary judgment by the adverse party, move with or without supporting affidavits for a summary judgment in the party's favor upon all or any part thereof.

(b) FOR DEFENDING PARTY. A party against whom a claim, counterclaim, or cross-claim is asserted or a declaratory judgment is sought may, at any time, move with or without supporting affidavits for a summary judgment in the party's favor as to all or any part thereof.

(c) MOTION AND PROCEEDINGS THEREON. The motion shall be served at least 10 days before the time fixed for the hearing. The adverse party prior to the day of hearing may serve opposing affidavits. The judgment sought shall be rendered forthwith if the pleadings, depositions, answers to interrogatories, and admissions on file, together with the affidavits, if any, show that there is no genuine issue as to any material fact and that the moving party is entitled to a judgment as a matter of law. A summary judgment, interlocutory in character, may be rendered on the issue of liability alone although there is a genuine issue as to the amount of damages.

(d) CASE NOT FULLY ADJUDICATED ON MOTION. If on motion under this rule judgment is not rendered upon the whole case or for all the relief asked and a trial is necessary, the court at the hearing of the motion, by examining the pleadings and the evidence before it and by interrogating counsel, shall if practicable ascertain what material facts exist without substantial controversy and what material facts are actually and in good faith controverted. It shall thereupon make an order specifying the facts that appear without substantial controversy, including the extent to which the amount of damages or other relief is not in controversy, and directing such further proceedings in the action as are just. Upon the trial of the action the facts so specified shall be deemed established, and the trial shall be conducted accordingly.

(e) FORM OF AFFIDAVITS; FURTHER TESTIMONY; DEFENSE REQUIRED.

Supporting and opposing affidavits shall be made on personal knowledge, shall set forth such facts as would be admissible in evidence, and shall show affirmatively that the affiant is competent to testify to the matters stated therein. Sworn or certified copies of all papers or parts thereof referred to in an affidavit shall be attached thereto or served therewith. The court may permit affidavits to be supplemented or opposed by depositions, answers to interrogatories, or further affidavits. When a motion for summary judgment is made and supported as provided in this rule, an adverse party may not rest upon the mere allegations or denials of the adverse party's pleading, but the adverse party's response, by affidavits or as otherwise provided in this rule, must set forth specific facts showing that there is a genuine issue for trial. If the adverse party does not so respond, summary judgment, if appropriate, shall be entered against the adverse party.

(f) WHEN AFFIDAVITS ARE UNAVAILABLE. Should it appear from the affidavits of a party opposing the motion that the party cannot for reasons stated present by affidavit facts essential to justify the party's opposition, the court may refuse the application for judgment or may order a continuance to permit affidavits to be obtained or depositions to be taken or discovery to be had or may make such other order as is just.

(g) AFFIDAVITS MADE IN BAD FAITH. Should it appear to the satisfaction of the court at any time that any of the affidavits presented pursuant to this rule are presented in bad faith or solely for the purpose of delay, the court shall forthwith order the party employing them to pay to the other party the amount of the reasonable expenses which the filing of the affidavits caused the other party to incur, including reasonable attorney's fees, and any offending party or attorney may be adjudged guilty of contempt.

(As amended Dec. 27, 1946, eff. Mar. 19, 1948; Jan. 21, 1963, eff. July 1, 1963; Mar. 2, 1987, eff. Aug. 1, 1987.)

Rule 57. Declaratory Judgments - omitted

Rule 58. Entry of Judgment - omitted

Rule 59. New Trials; Amendment of Judgments

(a) GROUNDS. A new trial may be granted to all or any of the parties and on all or part of the issues (1) in an action in which there has been a trial by jury, for any of the reasons for which new trials have heretofore been granted in actions at law in the courts of the United States; and (2) in an action tried without a jury, for any of the reasons for which rehearings have heretofore been
granted in suits in equity in the courts of the United States. On a motion for a new trial in an action tried without a jury, the court may open the judgment if one has been entered, take additional testimony, amend findings of fact and conclusions of law or make new findings and conclusions, and direct the entry of a new judgment.

(b) TIME FOR MOTION. Any motion for a new trial shall be filed no later than 10 days after entry of the judgment.

(c) TIME FOR SERVING AFFIDAVITS. When a motion for new trial is based on affidavits, they shall be filed with the motion. The opposing party has 10 days after service to file opposing affidavits, but that period may be extended for up to 20 days, either by the court for good cause or by the parties' written stipulation. The court may permit reply affidavits.

(d) ON COURT'S INITIATIVE; NOTICE; SPECIFYING GROUNDS. No later than 10 days after entry of judgment the court, on its own, may order a new trial for any reason that would justify granting one on a party's motion. After giving the parties notice and an opportunity to be heard, the court may grant a timely motion for a new trial for a reason not stated in the motion. When granting a new trial on its own initiative or for a reason not stated in a motion, the court shall specify the grounds in its order.

(e) MOTION TO ALTER OR AMEND JUDGMENT. Any motion to alter or amend a judgment shall be filed no later than 10 days after entry of the judgment.

(As amended Dec. 27, 1946, eff. Mar. 19, 1948; Feb. 28, 1966, eff. July 1, 1966; Apr. 27, 1995, eff. Dec. 1, 1995.)

Rule 60. Relief From Judgment or Order

(a) CLERICAL MISTAKES. Clerical mistakes in judgments, orders or other parts of the record and errors therein arising from oversight or omission may be corrected by the court at any time of its own initiative or on the motion of any party and after such notice, if any, as the court orders. During the pendency of an appeal, such mistakes may be so corrected before the appeal is docketed in the appellate court, and thereafter while the appeal is pending may be so corrected with leave of the appellate court.

(b) MISTAKES; INADVERTENCE; EXCUSABLE NEGLECT; NEWLY DISCOVERED EVIDENCE; FRAUD, ETC. On motion and upon such terms as are just, the court may relieve a party or a party's legal representative from a final judgment, order, or proceeding for the following reasons: (1) mistake, inadvertence, surprise, or excusable neglect; (2) newly discovered evidence which by due diligence could not have been discovered in time to move for a new trial under Rule 59(b); (3) fraud (whether heretofore denominated intrinsic or extrinsic), misrepresentation, or other misconduct of an adverse party; (4) the judgment is void; (5) the judgment has been satisfied, released, or discharged, or a prior judgment upon which it is based has been reversed or otherwise vacated, or it is no longer equitable that the judgment should have prospective application; or (6) any other reason justifying relief from the operation of the judgment. The motion shall be made within a reasonable time, and for reasons (1), (2), and (3) not more than one year after the judgment, order, or proceeding was entered or taken. A motion under this subdivision (b) does not affect the finality of a judgment or suspend its operation. This rule does not limit the power of a court to entertain an independent action to relieve a party from a judgment, order, or proceeding, or to grant relief to a defendant not actually personally notified as provided in Title 28, U.S.C., § 1655, or to set aside a judgment for fraud upon the court. Writs of coram nobis, coram vobis, audita querela, and bills of review and bills in the nature of a bill of review, are abolished, and the procedure for obtaining any relief from a judgment shall be by motion as prescribed in these rules or by an independent action.

(As amended Dec. 27, 1946, eff. Mar. 19, 1948; Dec. 29, 1948, eff. Oct. 20, 1949; Mar. 2, 1987, eff. Aug. 1, 1987.)

Rule 61. Harmless Error

No error in either the admission or the exclusion of evidence and no error or defect in any ruling or order or in anything done or omitted by the court or by any of the parties is ground for granting a new trial or for setting aside a verdict or for vacating, modifying, or otherwise disturbing a judgment or order, unless refusal to take such action appears to the court inconsistent with substantial justice. The court at every stage of the proceeding must is regard any error or defect in the proceeding which does not affect the substantial rights of the parties.

Rule 62. Stay of Proceedings To Enforce a Judgment

(a) AUTOMATIC STAY; EXCEPTIONS—INJUNCTIONS, RECEIVERSHIPS, AND PATENT ACCOUNTINGS. Except as stated herein, no execution shall issue upon a judgment nor shall proceedings be taken for its enforcement until the expiration of 10 days after its entry. Unless otherwise ordered by the court, an interlocutory or final judgment in an action for an injunction or in a receivership action, or a judgment or order directing an accounting in an action for infringement of letters patent, shall not be stayed during the period after its entry and until an appeal is taken or during the pendency of an appeal. The provisions of subdivision (c) of this rule govern the suspending, modifying, restoring, or granting of an injunction during the pendency of an appeal.

(b) STAY ON MOTION FOR NEW TRIAL OR FOR JUDGMENT. In its discretion and on such conditions for the security of the adverse party as are proper, the court may stay the execution of or any proceedings to enforce a judgment pending the disposition of a motion for a new trial or to alter or amend a judgment made pursuant to Rule 59, or of a motion for relief from a judgment or order made pursuant to Rule 60, or of a motion for judgment in accordance with a motion for a directed verdict made pursuant to Rule 50, or of a motion for amendment to the findings or for additional findings made pursuant to Rule 52(b).

(c) INJUNCTION PENDING APPEAL. When an appeal is taken from an interlocutory or final judgment granting, dissolving, or denying an injunction, the court in its discretion may suspend, modify, restore, or grant an injunction during the pendency of the appeal upon such terms as to bond or otherwise as it considers proper for the security of the rights of the adverse party. If the judgment appealed from is rendered by a district court of three judges specially constituted pursuant to a statute of the United States, no such order shall be made except (1) by such court sitting in open court or (2) by the assent of all the judges of such court evidenced by their signatures to the order.

(d) STAY UPON APPEAL. When an appeal is taken the appellant by giving a supersedeas bond may obtain a stay subject to the exceptions contained in subdivision (a) of this rule. The bond may be given at or after the time of filing the notice of appeal or of procuring the order allowing the appeal, as the case may be. The stay is effective when the supersedeas bond is approved by the court.

(e) STAY IN FAVOR OF THE UNITED STATES OR AGENCY THEREOF. When an appeal is taken by the United States or an officer or agency thereof or by direction of any department of the Government of the United States and the operation or enforcement of the judgment is stayed, no bond, obligation, or other security shall be required from the appellant.

(f) STAY ACCORDING TO STATE LAW. In any state in which a judgment is a lien upon the property of the judgment debtor and in which the judgment debtor is entitled to a stay of execution, a judgment debtor is entitled, in the district court held therein, to such stay as would be accorded the judgment debtor had the action been maintained in the courts of that state.

(g) POWER OF APPELLATE COURT NOT LIMITED. The provisions in this rule do not limit any power of an appellate court or of a judge or justice thereof to stay proceedings during the pendency of an appeal or to suspend, modify, restore, or grant an injunction during the pendency of an appeal or to make any order appropriate to preserve the status quo or the effectiveness of the judgment subsequently to be entered.

(h) STAY OF JUDGMENT AS TO MULTIPLE CLAIMS OR MULTIPLE PARTIES. When a court has ordered a final judgment under the conditions stated in Rule 54(b), the court may stay enforcement of that judgment until the entering of a subsequent judgment or judgments and may prescribe such conditions as are necessary to secure the benefit thereof to the party in whose favor the judgment is entered.

(As amended Dec. 27, 1946, eff. Mar. 19, 1948; Dec. 29, 1948, eff. Oct. 20, 1949; Apr. 17, 1961, eff. July 19, 1961; Mar. 2, 1987, eff. Aug. 1, 1987.)

Rule 63. Inability of a Judge to Proceed - ommited

VIII. PROVISIONAL AND FINAL REMEDIES

Rule 64. Seizure of Person or Property - omitted

Rule 65. Injunctions

(a) PRELIMINARY INJUNCTION.

(1) *Notice*. No preliminary injunction shall be issued without notice to the adverse party.

(2) *Consolidation of Hearing With Trial on Merits*. Before or after the commencement of the hearing of an application for a preliminary injunction, the court may order the trial of the action on the merits to be advanced and consolidated with the hearing of the application. Even when this consolidation is not ordered, any evidence received upon an application for a preliminary injunction which would be admissible upon the trial on the merits becomes part of the record on the trial and need not be repeated upon the trial. This subdivision (a)(2) shall be so construed and applied as to save to the parties any rights they may have to trial by jury.

(b) TEMPORARY RESTRAINING ORDER; NOTICE; HEARING; DURATION. A temporary restraining order may be granted without written or oral notice to the adverse party or that party's attorney only if (1) it clearly appears from specific facts shown by affidavit or by the verified complaint that immediate and irreparable injury, loss, or damage will result to the applicant before the adverse party or that party's attorney can be heard in opposition, and (2) the applicant's attorney certifies to the court in writing the efforts, if any, which have been made to give the notice and the reasons supporting the claim that notice should not be required. Every temporary restraining order granted without notice shall be indorsed with the date and hour of issuance; shall be filed forthwith in the clerk's office and entered of record; shall define the injury and state why it is irreparable and why the order was granted without notice; and shall expire by its terms within such time after entry, not to exceed 10 days, as the court fixes, unless within the time so fixed the order, for good cause shown, is extended for a like period or unless the party against whom the order is directed consents that it may be extended for a longer period. The reasons for the extension shall be entered of record. In case a temporary restraining order is granted without notice, the motion for a preliminary injunction shall be set down for hearing at the earliest possible time and takes precedence of all matters except older matters of the same character; and when the motion comes on for hearing the party who obtained the temporary restraining order shall proceed with the application for a preliminary injunction and, if the party does not do so, the court shall dissolve the temporary restraining order. On 2 days' notice to the
party who obtained the temporary restraining order without notice or on such shorter notice to that party as the court may prescribe, the adverse party may appear and move its dissolution or modification and in that event the court shall proceed to hear and determine such motion as expeditiously as the ends of justice require.

(c) SECURITY. No restraining order or preliminary injunction shall issue except upon the giving of security by the applicant, in such sum as the court deems proper, for the payment of such costs and damages as may be incurred or suffered by any party who is found to have been wrongfully enjoined or restrained. No such security shall be required of the United States or of an officer or agency thereof. The provisions of Rule 65.1 apply to a surety upon a bond or undertaking under this rule.

(d) FORM AND SCOPE OF INJUNCTION OR RESTRAINING ORDER. Every order granting an injunction and every restraining order shall set forth the reasons for its issuance; shall be specific in terms; shall describe in reasonable detail, and not by reference to the complaint or other document, the act or acts sought to be restrained; and is binding only upon the parties to the action, their officers, agents, servants, employees, and attorneys, and upon those persons in active concert or participation with them who receive actual notice of the order by personal service or otherwise.

(e) EMPLOYER AND EMPLOYEE; INTERPLEADER; CONSTITUTIONAL CASES. These rules do not modify any statute of the United States relating to temporary restraining orders and preliminary injunctions in actions affecting employer and employee; or the provisions of Title 28, U.S.C., § 2361, relating to preliminary injunctions in actions of interpleader or in the nature of interpleader; or Title 28, U.S.C., § 2284, relating to actions required by Act of Congress to be heard and determined by a district court of three judges.

(f) COPYRIGHT IMPOUNDMENT. This rule applies to copyright impoundment proceedings.

Repealed and reenacted as 28 U.S.C. §§ 572a and 2043 by Public Law 97–258, §§ 2(g)(3)(B), (4)(E), 5(b), Sept. 13, 1982, 96 Stat. 1061, 1068. (As amended Dec. 27, 1946, eff. Mar. 19, 1948; Dec. 29, 1948, eff. Oct. 20, 1949; Feb. 28, 1966, eff. July 1, 1966; Mar. 2, 1987, eff. Aug. 1, 1987; Apr. 23, 2001, eff. Dec. 1, 2001.)

Rule 65.1. Security: Proceedings Against Sureties - omitted

Rule 66. Receivers Appointed by Federal Courts - omitted

Rule 67. Deposit in Court - omitted

Rule 68. Offer of Judgment - omitted

Rule 69. Execution - omitted

Rule 70. Judgment for Specific Acts; Vesting Title - omitted

Rule 71. Process in Behalf of and Against Persons Not Parties - omitted

---

IX. SPECIAL PROCEEDINGS

Rule 71A. Condemnation of Property - omitted

Rule 72. Magistrate Judges; Pretrial Orders

(a) NONDISPOSITIVE MATTERS. A magistrate judge to whom a pretrial matter not dispositive of a claim or defense of a party is referred to hear and determine shall promptly conduct such proceedings as are required and when appropriate enter into the record a written order setting forth the disposition of the matter. Within 10 days after being served with a copy of the magistrate judge's order, a party may serve and file objections to the order; a party may not thereafter assign as error a defect in the magistrate judge's order to which objection was not timely made. The district judge to whom the case is assigned shall consider such objections and shall modify or set aside any portion of the magistrate judge's order found to be clearly erroneous or contrary to law.

(b) DISPOSITIVE MOTIONS AND PRISONER PETITIONS. A magistrate judge assigned without consent of the parties to hear a pretrial matter dispositive of a claim or defense of a party or a prisoner petition challenging the conditions of confinement shall promptly conduct such proceedings as are required. A record shall be made of all evidentiary proceedings before the magistrate judge, and a record may be made of such other proceedings as the magistrate judge deems necessary. The magistrate judge shall enter into the record a recommendation for disposition of the matter, including proposed findings of fact when appropriate. The clerk shall forthwith mail copies to all parties. A party objecting to the recommended disposition of the matter shall promptly arrange for the transcription of the record, or portions of it as all parties may agree upon or the magistrate judge deems sufficient, unless the district judge otherwise directs. Within 10 days after being served with a copy of the recommended disposition, a party may serve and file specific, written objections to the proposed findings and recommendations. A party may respond to another party's objections within 10 days after being served with a copy thereof. The district judge to whom the case is assigned shall make a de novo determination upon the record, or after additional evidence, of any portion of the magistrate judge's disposition to which specific written objection has been made in accordance with this rule. The district judge may accept, reject, or modify the recommended decision, receive further evidence, or recommit the matter to the magistrate judge with instructions.

(As added Apr. 28, 1983, eff. Aug. 1, 1983; amended Apr. 30, 1991, eff. Dec. 1, 1991; Apr. 22, 1993, eff. Dec. 1, 1993.)

Rule 73. Magistrate Judges; Trial by Consent and Appeal - omitted

---

[Rule 74. Method of Appeal From Magistrate Judge to District Judge Under Title 28, U.S.C. § 636(c)(4) and Rule 73(d)] (Abrogated Apr. 11, 1997, eff. Dec. 1, 1997)

[Rule 75. Proceedings on Appeal From Magistrate Judge to District Judge Under Rule 73(d)] (Abrogated Apr. 11, 1997, eff. Dec. 1, 1997)

[Rule 76. Judgment of the District Judge on the Appeal Under Rule 73(d) and Costs] (Abrogated Apr. 11, 1997, eff. Dec. 1, 1997)

X. DISTRICT COURTS AND CLERKS

Rule 77. District Courts and Clerks

(a) DISTRICT COURTS ALWAYS OPEN. The district courts shall be deemed always open for the purpose of filing any pleading or other proper paper, of issuing and returning mesne and final process, and of making and directing all interlocutory motions, orders, and rules.

(b) TRIALS AND HEARINGS; ORDERS IN CHAMBERS. All trials upon the merits shall be conducted in open court and so far as convenient in a regular court room. All other acts or proceedings may be done or conducted by a judge in chambers, without the attendance of the clerk or other court officials and at any place either within or without the district; but no hearing, other than one ex parte, shall be conducted outside the district without the consent of all parties affected thereby.

(c) CLERK'S OFFICE AND ORDERS BY CLERK. The clerk's office with the clerk or a deputy in attendance shall be open during business hours on all days except Saturdays, Sundays, and legal holidays, but a district court may provide by local rule or order that its clerk's office shall be open for specified hours on Saturdays or particular legal holidays other than New Year's Day, Birthday of Martin Luther King, Jr., Washington's Birthday, Memorial Day, Independence Day, Labor Day, Columbus Day, Veterans Day, Thanksgiving Day, and Christmas Day. All motions and applications in the clerk's office for issuing mesne process, for issuing final process to enforce and execute judgments, for entering defaults or judgments by default, and for other proceedings which do not require allowance or order of the court are grantable of course by the clerk; but the clerk's action may be suspended or altered or rescinded by the court upon cause shown.

(d) NOTICE OF ORDERS OR JUDGMENTS. Immediately upon the entry of an order or judgment the clerk shall serve a notice of the entry in the manner provided for in Rule 5(b) upon each party who is not in default for failure to appear, and shall make a note in the docket of the service. Any party may in addition serve a notice of such entry in the manner provided in Rule 5(b) for the service of papers. Lack of notice of the entry by the clerk does not affect the time to appeal or relieve or authorize the court to relieve a party for failure to appeal within the time allowed, except as permitted in Rule 4(a) of the Federal Rules of Appellate Procedure.

(As amended Dec. 27, 1946, eff. Mar. 19, 1948; Jan. 21, 1963, eff. July 1, 1963; Dec. 4, 1967, eff. July 1, 1968; Mar. 1, 1971, eff. July 1, 1971; Mar. 2, 1987, eff. Aug. 1, 1987; Apr. 30, 1991, eff. Dec. 1, 1991; Apr. 23, 2001, eff. Dec. 1, 2001.)

Rule 78. Motion Day

Unless local conditions make it impracticable, each district court shall establish regular times and places, at intervals sufficiently frequent for the prompt dispatch of business, at which motions requiring notice and hearing may be heard and disposed of; but the judge at any time or place and on such notice, if any, as the judge considers reasonable may make orders for the advancement, conduct, and hearing of actions. To expedite its business, the court may make provision by rule or order for the submission and determination of motions without oral hearing upon brief written statements of reasons in support and opposition.

(As amended Mar. 2, 1987, eff. Aug. 1, 1987.)

Rule 79. Books and Records Kept by the Clerk and Entries Therein - omitted

Rule 80. Stenographer; Stenographic Report or Transcript as Evidence - omitted

---

XI. GENERAL PROVISIONS

Rule 81. Applicability in General

(a) TO WHAT PROCEEDINGS APPLICABLE.

(1) These rules do not apply to prize proceedings in admiralty governed by Title 10, U.S.C., §§ 7651–7681. They do apply to proceedings in bankruptcy to the extent provided by the Federal Rules of Bankruptcy Procedure.

(2) These rules are applicable to proceedings for admission to citizenship, habeas corpus, and quo warranto, to the extent that the practice in such proceedings is not set forth in statutes of the United States, the Rules Governing Section 2254 Cases, or the Rules Governing Section 2255 Proceedings, and has heretofore conformed to the practice in civil actions.

(3) In proceedings under Title 9, U.S.C., relating to arbitration, or under the Act of May 20, 1926, ch. 347, § 9 (44 Stat. 585), U.S.C., Title 45, § 159, relating to boards of arbitration of railway labor disputes, these rules apply only to the extent that matters of procedure are not provided for in those statutes. These rules apply to proceedings to compel the giving of testimony or production of documents in accordance with a subpoena issued by an officer or agency of the United States under any statute of the United States except as otherwise provided by statute or by rules of the district court or by order of the court in the proceedings.

(4) These rules do not alter the method prescribed by the Act of February 18, 1922, ch. 57, § 2 (42 Stat. 388), U.S.C., Title 7, § 292; or by the Act of June 10, 1930, ch. 436, § 7 (46 Stat. 534), as amended, U.S.C., Title 7, § 499g(c), for instituting proceedings in the United States district courts to review orders of the Secretary of Agriculture; or prescribed by the Act of June 25, 1934, ch. 742, § 2 (48 Stat. 1214), U.S.C., Title 15, § 522, for instituting proceedings to review orders of the Secretary of the Interior; or prescribed by the Act of February 22, 1935, ch. 18, § 5 (49 Stat. 31), U.S.C., Title 15, § 715d(c), as extended, for instituting proceedings to review orders of petroleum control boards; but the conduct of such proceedings in the district courts shall be made to conform to these rules so far as applicable.

(5) These rules do not alter the practice in the United States district courts

prescribed in the Act of July 5, 1935, ch. 372, §§ 9 and 10 (49 Stat. 453), as amended, U.S.C., Title 29, §§ 159 and 160, for beginning and conducting proceedings to enforce orders of the National Labor Relations Board; and in respects not covered by those statutes, the practice in the district courts shall conform to these rules so far as applicable.

(6) These rules apply to proceedings for enforcement or review of compensation orders under the Longshoremen's and Harbor Workers' Compensation Act, Act of March 4, 1927, c. 509, §§ 18, 21 (44 Stat. 1434, 1436), as amended, U.S.C., Title 33, §§ 918, 921, except to the extent that matters of procedure are provided for in that Act. The provisions for service by publication and for answer in proceedings to cancel certificates of citizenship under the Act of June 27, 1952, c. 477, Title III, c. 2, § 340 (66 Stat. 260), U.S.C., Title 8, § 1451, remain in effect.

[(7)] (Abrogated Apr. 30, 1951, eff. Aug. 1, 1951)

(b) SCIRE FACIAS AND MANDAMUS. The writs of scire facias and mandamus are abolished. Relief heretofore available by mandamus or scire facias may be obtained by appropriate action or by appropriate motion under the practice prescribed in these rules.

(c) REMOVED ACTIONS. These rules apply to civil actions removed to the United States district courts from the state courts and govern procedure after removal. Repleading is not necessary unless the court so orders. In a removed action in which the defendant has not answered, the defendant shall answer or present the other defenses or objections available under these rules within 20 days after the receipt through service or otherwise of a copy of the initial pleading setting forth the claim for relief upon which the action or proceeding is based, or within 20 days after the service of summons upon such initial pleading, then filed, or within 5 days after the filing of the petition for removal, whichever period is longest. If at the time of removal all necessary pleadings have been served, a party entitled to trial by jury under Rule 38 shall be accorded it, if the party's demand therefor is served within 10 days after the petition for removal is filed if the party is the petitioner, or if not the petitioner within 10 days after service on the party of the notice of filing the petition. A party who, prior to removal, has made an express demand for trial by jury in accordance with state law, need not make a demand after removal. If state law applicable in the court from which the case is removed does not require the parties to make express demands in order to claim trial by jury, they need not make demands after removal unless the court directs that they do so within a specified time if they desire to claim trial by jury. The court may make this direction on its own motion and shall do so as a matter of course at the request of any party. The failure of a party to make demand as directed constitutes a waiver by that party of trial by jury.

[(d) DISTRICT OF COLUMBIA; COURTS AND JUDGES.] (Abrogated Dec. 29, 1948, eff. Oct. 20, 1949)

(e) LAW APPLICABLE. Whenever in these rules the law of the state in which the district court is held is made applicable, the law applied in the District of Columbia governs proceedings in the United States District Court for the District of Columbia. When the word "state" is used, it includes, if appropriate, the District of Columbia. When the term "statute of the United States" is used, it includes, so far as concerns proceedings in the United States District Court for the District of Columbia, any Act of Congress locally applicable to and in force in the District of Columbia. When the law of a state is referred to, the word "law" includes the statutes of that state and the state judicial decisions construing them.

(f) REFERENCES TO OFFICER OF THE UNITED STATES. Under any rule in which reference is made to an officer or agency of the United States, the term "officer" includes a district director of internal revenue, a former district director or collector of internal revenue, or the personal representative of a deceased district director or collector of internal revenue.

(As amended Dec. 28, 1939, eff. Apr. 3, 1941; Dec. 27, 1946, eff. Mar. 19, 1948; Dec. 29, 1948, eff. Oct. 20, 1949; Apr. 30, 1951, eff. Aug. 1, 1951; Jan. 21, 1963, eff. July 1, 1963; Feb. 28, 1966, eff. July 1, 1966; Dec. 4, 1967, eff. July 1, 1968; Mar. 1, 1971, eff. July 1, 1971; Mar. 2, 1987, eff. Aug. 1, 1987; Apr. 23, 2001, eff. Dec. 1, 2001; Apr. 29, 2002, eff. Dec. 1, 2002.)

Rule 82. Jurisdiction and Venue Unaffected

These rules shall not be construed to extend or limit the jurisdiction of the United States district courts or the venue of actions therein. An admiralty or maritime claim within the meaning of Rule 9(h) shall not be treated as a civil action for the purposes of Title 28, U.S.C., §§ 1391–1392.

(As amended Dec. 29, 1948, eff. Oct. 20, 1949; Feb. 28, 1966, eff. July 1, 1966; Apr. 23, 2001, eff. Dec. 1, 2001.)

Rule 83. Rules by District Courts; Judge's Directives

(a) LOCAL RULES.

(1) Each district court, acting by a majority of its district judges, may, after giving appropriate public notice and an opportunity for comment, make and amend rules governing its practice. A local rule shall be consistent with—but not duplicative

of—Acts of Congress and rules adopted under 28 U.S.C. §§ 2072 and 2075, and shall conform to any uniform numbering system prescribed by the Judicial Conference of the United States. A local rule takes effect on the date specified by the district court and remains in effect unless amended by the court or abrogated by the judicial council of the circuit. Copies of rules and amendments shall, upon their promulgation, be furnished to the judicial council and the Administrative Office of the United States Courts and be made available to the public.

(2) A local rule imposing a requirement of form shall not be enforced in a manner that causes a party to lose rights because of a nonwillful failure to comply with the requirement.

(b) PROCEDURES WHEN THERE IS NO CONTROLLING LAW. A judge may regulate practice in any manner consistent with federal law, rules adopted under 28 U.S.C. §§ 2072 and 2075, and local rules of the district. No sanction or other disadvantage may be imposed for noncompliance with any requirement not in federal law, federal rules, or the local district rules unless the alleged violator has been furnished in the particular case with actual notice of the requirement.

(As amended Apr. 29, 1985, eff. Aug. 1, 1985; Apr. 27, 1995, eff. Dec. 1, 1995.)

Rule 84. Forms - omitted

Rule 85. Title

These rules may be known and cited as the Federal Rules of Civil Procedure.

Rule 86. Effective Date

(a) 1 [EFFECTIVE DATE OF ORIGINAL RULES.] These rules will take effect on the day which is 3 months subsequent to the adjournment of the second regular session of the 75th Congress, but if that day is prior to September 1, 1938, then these rules will take effect on September 1, 1938. They govern all proceedings in actions brought after they take effect and also all further proceedings in actions then pending, except to the extent that in the opinion of
the court their application in a particular action pending when the rules take effect would not be feasible or would work injustice, in which event the former procedure applies.

(b) EFFECTIVE DATE OF AMENDMENTS. The amendments adopted by the Supreme Court on December 27, 1946, and transmitted to the Attorney General on January 2, 1947, shall take effect on the day which is three months subsequent to the adjournment of the first regular session of the 80th Congress, but, if that day is prior to September 1, 1947, then these amendments shall take effect on September 1, 1947. They govern all proceedings in actions brought after they take effect and also all further proceedings in actions then pending, except to the extent that in the opinion of the court their application in a particular action pending when the amendments take effect would not be feasible or would work injustice, in which event the former procedure applies.

(c) EFFECTIVE DATE OF AMENDMENTS. The amendments adopted by the Supreme Court on December 29, 1948, and transmitted to the Attorney General on December 31, 1948, shall take effect on the day following the adjournment of the first regular session of the 81st Congress.

(d) EFFECTIVE DATE OF AMENDMENTS. The amendments adopted by the Supreme Court on April 17, 1961, and transmitted to the Congress on April 18, 1961, shall take effect on July 19, 1961. They govern all proceedings in actions brought after they take effect and also all further proceedings in actions then pending, except to the extent that in the opinion of the court their application in a particular action pending when the amendments take effect would not be feasible or would work injustice, in which event the former procedure applies.

(e) EFFECTIVE DATE OF AMENDMENTS. The amendments adopted by the Supreme Court on January 21, 1963, and transmitted to the Congress on January 21, 1963, shall take effect on July 1, 1963. They govern all proceedings in actions brought after they take effect and also all further proceedings in actions then pending, except to the extent that in the opinion of the court their application in a particular action pending when the amendments take effect would not be feasible or would work injustice, in which event the former procedure applies.

(As amended Dec. 27, 1946, eff. Mar. 19, 1948; Dec. 29, 1948, eff. Oct. 20, 1949; Apr. 17, 1961, eff. July 19, 1961; Jan. 21 and Mar. 18, 1963, eff. July 1, 1963.)

RULE 3.01 MOTIONS; BRIEFS AND HEARINGS

(a) In a motion or other application for an order, the movant shall include a concise statement of the precise relief requested, a statement of the basis for the request, and a memorandum of legal authority in support of the request, all of which the movant shall include in a single document not more than twenty-five (25) pages.

(b) Each party opposing a motion or application shall file within ten (10) days after service of the motion or application a response that includes a memorandum of legal authority in opposition to the request, all of which the respondent shall include in a document not more than twenty (20) pages.

(c) No party shall file any reply or further memorandum directed to the motion or response allowed in (a) and (b) unless the Court grants leave.

(d) A motion requesting leave to file either a motion in excess of twenty-five (25) pages, a response in excess of twenty (20) pages, or a reply or further memorandum shall not exceed three (3) pages, shall specify the length of the proposed filing, and shall not include, as an attachment or otherwise, the proposed motion, response, reply, or other paper.

(e) Motions of an emergency nature may be considered and determined by the Court at any time, in its discretion (see also, Rule 4.05). The unwarranted designation of a motion as an emergency motion may result in the imposition of sanctions.

(f) All applications to the Court (i) requesting relief in any form, or (ii) citing authorities or presenting argument with respect to any matter awaiting decision, shall be made in writing (except as provided in Rule 7(b) of the Federal Rules of Civil Procedure) in accordance with this rule and in appropriate form pursuant to Rule 1.05; and, unless invited or directed by the presiding judge, shall not be addressed or presented to the Court in the form of a letter or the like. All pleadings and papers to be filed shall be filed with the Clerk of the Court and not with the judge thereof, except as provided by Rule 1.03(c) of these Rules.

(g) Before filing any motion in a civil case, except a motion for injunctive relief, for judgment on the pleadings, for summary judgment, to dismiss or to permit maintenance of a class action, to dismiss for failure to state a claim upon which relief can be granted, or to involuntarily dismiss an action, the moving party shall confer with counsel for the opposing party in a good faith effort to resolve the issues raised by the motion, and shall file with the motion a statement (1) certifying that the moving counsel has conferred with opposing counsel and (2) stating whether counsel agree on the resolution of the motion. A certification to the effect that opposing counsel was unavailable for a conference before filing a motion is insufficient to satisfy the parties' obligation to confer. The moving party retains the duty to contact opposing counsel expeditiously after filing and to supplement the motion promptly with a statement certifying whether or to what extent the parties have resolved the issue(s) presented in the motion. If the interested parties agree to all or part of the relief sought in any motion, the caption of the motion shall include the word "unopposed," "agreed," or "stipulated" or otherwise succinctly inform the reader that, as to all or part of the requested relief, no opposition exists.

(h) All dispositive motions must be so designated in the caption of the motion. All dispositive motions which are not decided within one hundred and eighty (180) days of the responsive filing (or the expiration of the time allowed for its filing under the local rules) shall be brought to the attention of the district judge by the movant by filing a "Notice To the Court" within ten days after the time for deciding the motion has expired. Movant shall file an additional "Notice To The Court" after the expiration of each and every additional thirty day period during which the motion remains undecided. Movant shall provide the Chief Judge of the Middle District with a copy of each and every "Notice To The Court" which movant is required to file under this rule.

(i) The use of telephonic hearings and conferences is encouraged, whenever possible, particularly when counsel are located in different cities.

(j) Motions and other applications will ordinarily be determined by the Court on the basis of the motion papers and briefs or legal memoranda; provided, however, the Court may allow oral argument upon the written request of any interested party or upon the Court's own motion. Requests for oral argument shall accompany the motion, or the opposing brief or legal memorandum, and shall estimate the time required for argument. All hearings on motions shall be noticed by the Clerk, as directed by the judge assigned to the case, either on regular motion days if practicable (pursuant to Rule 78, Fed.R.Civ.P.), or at such other times as the Court shall direct.

APPENDIX III
LOCAL RULES OF COURT, THE UNITED STATES MIDDLE DISTRICT OF FLORIDA

The following excerpts are valid as of May 31, 2006.

CHAPTER ONE -ADMINISTRATION OF COURT BUSINESS:

RULE 1.01 SCOPE AND CONSTRUCTION OF RULES

(a) These rules, made pursuant to the authority of 28 U.S.C. Section 2071, Rule 83, Fed.R.Civ.P., and Rule 57, Fed.R.Cr.P., shall apply to all proceedings in this Court, whether civil or criminal, unless specifically provided to the contrary or necessarily restricted by inference from the context. The Court may prescribe by administrative order procedures for electronic filing and related matters in civil and criminal cases. The administrative order shall govern, notwithstanding these rules, which otherwise will govern to the extent not inconsistent with the administrative order.

(b) These rules are intended to supplement and complement the Federal Rules of Civil Procedure, the Federal Rules of Criminal Procedure, and other controlling statutes and rules of Court. They shall be applied, construed and enforced to avoid inconsistency with other governing statutes and rules of court, and shall be employed to provide fairness and simplicity in procedure, to avoid technical and unjustified delay, and to secure just, expeditious and inexpensive determination of all proceedings.

(c) The Court may suspend application and enforcement of these rules, in whole or in part, in the interests of justice in individual cases by written order. When a judge of this Court in a specific case issues any order which is not consistent with these rules, such order shall constitute a suspension of the rules with respect to the case only, and only to the extent that such order is inconsistent with the rules.

(d) In all circumstances in which these rules, the Federal Rules of Civil Procedure, the Federal Rules of Criminal Procedure, other rules as prescribed by the Supreme

Court of the United States, or any statute of the United States, or the Federal Common Law, do not apply, the practices, pleadings, forms and modes of proceedings then existing in like causes in the Courts of the State of Florida shall be followed.

RULE 1.02 DIVISIONS OF THE COURT - OMITTED

RULE 1.03 DOCKETING AND ASSIGNMENT OF CASES

(a) Upon the filing of the initial paper or pleading in any case the Clerk shall docket the proceeding as a civil, criminal or miscellaneous action. Each case or proceeding shall be given a six-part docket number, which includes: (1) the one-digit number indicating the division of the Court; (2) the two-digit number indicating the year in which the proceeding is initiated; (3) the code indicating the docket to which the case is assigned; (4) the sequence number of the case or proceeding; (5) a designation consisting of a letter or series of letters disclosing the division in which the proceeding is pending; and (6) the code indicating the judge to whom the case is assigned (the code shall conform to the code assigned by the Administrative Office of the United States Courts) followed by the initials of the magistrate judge to whom the case is assigned.

(b) Each case, upon the filing of the initial paper or pleading, shall be assigned by the Clerk to an individual judge of the Court who shall thereafter be the presiding judge with respect to that cause. Individual assignment of cases within each Division shall be made at random or by lot in such proportions as the judges of the Court from time to time direct. Neither the Clerk nor any member of his staff shall have any power or discretion in determining the judge to whom any case is assigned. The method of assignment shall be designed to prevent anyone from choosing the judge to whom a case is to be assigned, and all persons shall conscientiously refrain from attempting to circumvent this rule.

(c) No application for any order of court shall be made until the case or controversy in which the matter arises has been docketed and assigned by the Clerk as prescribed by subsection

(b) of this rule, and then only to the judge to whom the case has been assigned; provided, however: (1) When no case has previously been initiated, docketed and assigned, emergency applications arising during days or hours that the Clerk's Office is closed may be submitted to any available judge resident in the appropriate Division, or, if no judge is available in the Division, to any other judge in the District, but the case shall then be docketed and assigned by the Clerk on the next business day and shall thereafter be conducted by the judge to whom it is assigned in accordance with subsection (b) of this rule. (2) When the judge to whom a case has been assigned is temporarily unavailable due to illness, absence or prolonged engagement in other judicial business, emergency applications arising in the case may be made to the other resident judge in the Division or, if more than one, to the judge who is junior in commission in that Division. If no other judge is available in the Division such applications may be made to any other available judge in the District.

(d) The judge to whom any case is assigned may, at any time, reassign the case to any other consenting judge for any limited purpose or for all further purposes.

(e) The Clerk shall accept for filing all prisoner cases filed with or without the required filing fee or application to proceed in forma pauperis. However, a prisoner case will be subject to dismissal by the Court, sua sponte, if the filing fee is not paid or if the application is not filed within 30 days of the commencement of the action.

RULE 1.04 SIMILAR OR SUCCESSIVE CASES; DUTY OF COUNSEL

(a) Whenever a case, once docketed and assigned, is terminated by any means and is thereafter refiled without substantial change in issues or parties, it shall be assigned, or reassigned if need be, to the judge to whom the original case was assigned. Whenever a second or subsequent case seeking post conviction or other relief by petition for writ of habeas corpus is filed by the same petitioner involving the same conviction, it shall be assigned, or reassigned if need be, to the same judge to whom the original case was assigned. All motions under 28 U.S.C. Section 2255 shall be assigned to the judge to whom the original criminal case was assigned.

(b) **TRANSFER OF RELATED CASES BEFORE TWO OR MORE JUDGES**. If cases assigned to different judges are related because of either a common question of fact or any other prospective duplication in the prosecution or resolution of the cases, a party may move to transfer any related case to the judge assigned to the first-filed among the related cases. The moving party shall file a notice of filing the motion to transfer, including a copy of the motion to transfer, in each related case. The proposed transferor judge shall dispose of the motion to transfer but shall grant the motion only with the consent of the transferee judge. If the transferee judge determines that the same magistrate judge should preside in some or all respects in some or all of the related cases, the Clerk shall assign the magistrate judge assigned to the first-filed among the affected cases to preside in that respect in those cases.

(c) **CONSOLIDATION OF RELATED CASES BEFORE ONE JUDGE**. If cases assigned to a judge are related because of either a common question of law or fact or any other prospective duplication in the prosecution or resolution of the cases, a party may move to consolidate the cases for any or all purposes in accord with Rule 42.Fed.R.Civ.P., or Rule 13, Fed.R.Cr.P. The moving party shall file a notice of filing the motion to consolidate, including a copy of the motion to consolidate, in each related case. If the presiding judge determines that the same magistrate judge should preside in some or all respects in some or all of the consolidated cases, the Clerk shall assign the magistrate judge assigned to the first-filed among the affected cases to preside in that respect in those cases.

(d) All counsel of record in any case have a continuing duty promptly to inform the Court and counsel of the existence of any other case within the purview of this rule, as well as the existence of any similar or related case or proceeding pending before any other court or administrative agency. Counsel shall notify the Court by filing and serving a **"Notice of Pendency of Related Actions"** that identifies and describes any related case.

RULE 1.05 FORM OF PLEADINGS; GENERAL REQUIREMENTS

(a) Although a quotation of three (3) lines or more may be single-spaced and indented and a footnote shall be single-spaced in no smaller than ten-point type, all pleadings and other papers tendered by counsel for filing shall be typewritten, double-spaced, in at least twelve-point type, and, if filed on paper, shall be on opaque, unglazed, white paper eight and one-half inches wide by eleven inches long (8 ½ x 11), with one and one-fourth inch top, bottom and left margins and a one to one and one-fourth inch right margin. Only one side of the paper may be used.

(b) All pleadings, motions, briefs, applications, and orders tendered by counsel for filing shall contain on the first page a caption as prescribed by Rule 10(a), Fed.R.Civ.P., and in addition thereto shall state in the title the name and designation of the party (as Plaintiff or Defendant or the like) in whose behalf the paper is submitted.

(c) The first pleading filed on behalf of any party or parties represented by counsel shall be signed by at least one attorney in his individual name with the designation **"Trial Counsel"**, or the equivalent. Thereafter, until seasonable notice to the contrary is filed with the Court and served upon opposing counsel, such attorney shall be the person responsible for the case with full authority, individually, to conduct all proceedings including trial.

(d) All pleadings, motions, briefs, applications and other papers tendered by counsel for filing shall be signed personally by counsel as required by Rule 11, Fed.R.Civ.P. Immediately under every signature line, additional information shall be given as indicated in the example below:

(Signature of Counsel)
Typed Name of Counsel
Florida Bar Identification Number (if admitted to practice in Florida)
Firm or Business Name
Mailing Address
City, State, Zip Code
Telephone Number
Facsimile Phone Number (if available)
E-mail address

(e) The Clerk is authorized and directed to require a complete and executed AO Form JS44, Civil Cover Sheet, which shall accompany each civil case as a condition to the filing thereof. State and federal prisoners, aNd other persons filing civil cases *pro se* are exempt from the requirements of this subsection.

RULE 1.06 FORM OF PLEADINGS; SPECIAL REQUIREMENTS

(a) If demand for jury trial is contained within a pleading pursuant to Rule 38(b), Fed.R.Civ.P., the title of the pleading shall include the words "**And Demand for Jury Trial**" or the equivalent.

(b) If a pleading contains a prayer for injunctive relief pursuant to Rule 65, Fed.R.Civ.P., the title of the pleading shall include the words "**Injunctive Relief Sought**" or the equivalent. (See also Rules 4.05 and 4.06.)

(c) To enable the Court to comply with the provisions of 28 U.S.C. Section 2284, in any case which a party believes may require a three-judge district court, the words, "**Three-Judge District Court Requested**" or the equivalent shall be included within the title of the first pleading filed by that party. If a three-judge district court is convened all subsequent pleading, motions, briefs, applications and orders shall be tendered for filing in quadruplicate (the original and three copies).

(d) To enable the Court to comply with 28 U.S.C. Section 2403, in any case to which the United States or any agency, officer or employee thereof is not a party, any party who shall draw into question the constitutionality of any Act of Congress affecting the public interest shall forthwith so notify the Clerk in writing, stating the title of the case, its docket number, the Act of Congress in question and the grounds upon which it is assailed.

RULE 1.07 PREPARATION, SERVICE AND RETURN OF PROCESS; SERVICE OF PLEADINGS SUBSEQUENT TO ORIGINAL COMPLAINT

(a) Counsel shall prepare all process and present it to the Clerk for certification.

(b) When service of process has been effected but no appearance or response is made within the time and manner provided by Rule 12, Fed.R.Civ.P., the party effecting service shall promptly apply to the Clerk for entry of default pursuant to Rule 55(a), Fed.R.Civ.P., and shall then proceed without delay to apply for a judgment pursuant to Rule 55(b), Fed.R.Civ.P., failing which the case shall be subject to dismissal sixty (60) days after such service without notice and without prejudice; provided, however, such time may be extended by order of the Court on reasonable application with good cause shown.

(c) Service of a pleading or paper subsequent to the original complaint may be made by transmitting it by facsimile to the attorney's or party's office with a cover sheet containing the sender's name, firm, address, telephone number, and facsimile number, and the number of pages transmitted. When service is made by facsimile, a copy shall also be served by any other method permitted by Rule 5, Fed. R. Civ. P. Service by delivery after 5:00 p.m. shall be deemed to have been made on the next business day.

RULE 1.08 INTEGRITY OF FILES AND RECORDS

(a) No person, other than the Clerk or his authorized deputies, shall insert or delete, or deface, or make any entry or correction by interlineation or otherwise, in, from or upon any file or other record of the Court unless expressly permitted or ordered to do so by the Court.

(b) Court files or other papers or records in the possession of the Clerk may be removed from the Clerk's Office only upon written permission or order of the Court which shall specify the time within which the same shall be returned.

RULE 1.09 FILING UNDER SEAL

(a) Unless filing under seal is authorized by statute, rule, or order, a party seeking to file under seal any paper or other matter in any civil case shall file and serve a motion, the title of which includes the words "Motion to Seal" and which includes (i) an identification and description of each item proposed for sealing; (ii) the reason that filing each item is necessary; (iii) the reason that sealing each item is necessary; (iv) the reason that a means other than sealing is unavailable or unsatisfactory to preserve the interest advanced by the movant in support of the seal; (v) a statement of the proposed duration of the seal; and (vi) a memorandum of legal authority supporting the seal. The movant shall not file or otherwise tender to the Clerk any item proposed for sealing unless the Court has granted the motion required by this section. No settlement agreement shall be sealed absent extraordinary circumstances, such as the preservation of national security, protection of trade secrets or other valuable proprietary information, protection of especially vulnerable persons including minors or persons with disabilities, or protection of non-parties without either the opportunity or ability to protect themselves. Every order sealing any item pursuant this section shall state the particular reason the seal is required.

(b) If filing under seal is authorized by statute, rule, or order (including an order requiring or permitting a seal and obtained pursuant to (a) of this rule), a party seeking to file under seal any paper or other matter in any civil case shall file and serve a motion, the title of which includes the words "Motion to Seal Pursuant to [Statute, Rule, or Order]" and which includes (i) a citation to the statute, rule, or order authorizing the seal; (ii) an identification and description of each item submitted for sealing; (iii) a statement of the proposed duration of the seal; and (iv) a statement establishing that the items submitted for sealing are within the identified statute, rule, or order the movant cites as authorizing the seal. The movant shall submit to the Clerk along with a motion under this section each item proposed for sealing. Every order sealing any item pursuant to this section shall state the particular reason the seal is required and shall identify the statute, rule, or order authorizing the seal.

(c) Unless otherwise ordered by the Court for good cause shown, no order sealing any item pursuant to this section shall extend beyond one year, although a seal is renewable by a motion that complies with (b) of this rule, identifies the expiration of the seal, and is filed before the expiration of the seal.

(d) The Clerk shall return to the movant any matter for which sealing is denied.

CHAPTER THREE: MOTIONS, DISCOVERY & PRETRIAL PROCEEDINGS

RULE 3.01 MOTIONS; BRIEFS AND HEARINGS

(a) In a motion or other application for an order, the movant shall include a concise statement of the precise relief requested, a statement of the basis for the request, and a memorandum of legal authority in support of the request, all of which the movant shall include in a single document not more than twenty-five

(25) pages.

(b) Each party opposing a motion or application shall file within ten (10) days after service of the motion or application a response that includes a memorandum of legal authority in opposition to the request, all of which the respondent shall include in a document not more than twenty (20) pages.

(c) No party shall file any reply or further memorandum directed to the motion or response allowed in (a) and (b) unless the Court grants leave.

(d) A motion requesting leave to file either a motion in excess of twenty-five (25) pages, a response in excess of twenty (20) pages, or a reply or further memorandum shall not exceed three (3) pages, shall specify the length of the proposed filing, and shall not include, as an attachment or otherwise, the proposed motion, response, reply, or other paper.

(e) Motions of an emergency nature may be considered and determined by the Court at any time, in its discretion (see also, Rule 4.05). The unwarranted designation of a motion as an emergency motion may result in the imposition of sanctions.

(f) All applications to the Court (i) requesting relief in any form, or (ii) citing authorities or presenting argument with respect to any matter awaiting decision, shall be made in writing (except as provided in Rule 7(b) of the Federal Rules of Civil Procedure) in accordance with this rule and in appropriate form pursuant to Rule 1.05; and, unless invited or directed by the presiding judge, shall not be addressed or presented to the Court in the form of a letter or the like. All pleadings and papers to be filed shall be filed with the Clerk of the Court and not with the judge thereof, except as provided by Rule 1.03(c) of these Rules.

(g) Before filing any motion in a civil case, except a motion for injunctive relief, for judgment on the pleadings, for summary judgment, to dismiss or to permit maintenance of a class action, to dismiss for failure to state a claim upon which relief can be granted, or to involuntarily dismiss an action, the moving party shall confer with counsel for the opposing party in a good faith effort to resolve the issues raised by the motion, and shall file with the motion a statement (1) certifying that the moving counsel has conferred with opposing counsel and (2) stating whether counsel agree on the resolution of the motion. A certification to the effect that opposing counsel was unavailable for a conference before filing a motion is insufficient to satisfy the parties' obligation to confer. The moving party retains the duty to contact opposing counsel expeditiously after filing and to supplement the motion promptly with a statement certifying whether or to what extent the parties have resolved the issue(s) presented in the motion. If the interested parties agree to all or part of the relief sought in any motion, the caption of the motion shall include the word "unopposed," "agreed," or "stipulated" or otherwise succinctly inform the reader that, as to all or part of the requested relief, no opposition exists.

(h) All dispositive motions must be so designated in the caption of the motion. All dispositive motions which are not decided within one hundred and eighty (180) days of the responsive filing (or the expiration of the time allowed for its filing under the local rules) shall be brought to the attention of the district judge by the movant by filing a "Notice To the Court" within ten days after the time for deciding the motion has expired. Movant shall file an additional "Notice To The Court" after the expiration of each and every additional thirty day period during which the motion remains undecided. Movant shall provide the Chief Judge of the Middle District with a copy of each and every "Notice To The Court" which movant is required to file under this rule.

(i) The use of telephonic hearings and conferences is encouraged, whenever possible, particularly when counsel are located in different cities.

(j) Motions and other applications will ordinarily be determined by the Court on the basis of the motion papers and briefs or legal memoranda; provided, however, the Court may allow oral argument upon the written request of any interested party or upon the Court's own motion. Requests for oral argument shall accompany the motion, or the opposing brief or legal memorandum, and shall estimate the time required for argument. All hearings on motions shall be noticed by the Clerk, as directed by the judge assigned to the case, either on regular motion days if practicable (pursuant to Rule 78, Fed.R.Civ.P.), or at such other times as the Court shall direct.

RULE 3.02 NOTICE OF DEPOSITIONS

Unless otherwise stipulated by all interested parties pursuant to Rule 29, Fed.R.Civ.P., and excepting the circumstances governed by Rule 30(a), Fed.R.Civ.P., a party desiring to take the deposition of any person upon oral examination shall give at least ten (10) days notice in writing to every other party to the action and to the deponent (if the deponent is not a party).

RULE 3.03 WRITTEN INTERROGATORIES; FILING OF DISCOVERY MATERIAL; EXCHANGE OF DISCOVERY REQUEST BY COMPUTER DISK

(a) Written interrogatories shall be so prepared and arranged that a blank space shall be provided after each separately numbered interrogatory. The space shall be reasonably calculated to enable the answering party to insert the answer within the space.

(b) The original of the written interrogatories and a copy shall be served on the party to whom the interrogatories are directed, and copies on all other parties. No copy of the written interrogatories shall be filed with the Court by the party propounding them. The answering party shall use the original of the written interrogatories for his answers and objections, if any; and the original shall be returned to the party propounding the interrogatories with copies served upon all other parties. The interrogatories as answered or objected to shall not be filed with the Court as a matter of course, but may later be filed by any party in whole or in part if necessary to presentation and consideration of a motion to compel, a motion for summary judgment, a motion for injunctive relief, or other similar proceedings.

(c) Notices of the taking of oral depositions shall not be filed with the Court as a matter of course (except as necessary to presentation and consideration of motions to compel); and transcripts of oral depositions shall not be filed unless and until requested by a party or ordered by the Court.

(d) Requests for the production of documents and other things, matters disclosed pursuant to Fed. R. Civ. P. 26, and requests for admission, and answers and responses thereto, shall not be filed with the Court as a matter of course but may later be filed in whole or in part if necessary to presentation and consideration of a motion to compel, a motion for summary judgment, a motion for injunctive relief, or other similar proceedings.

(e) Litigants' counsel should utilize computer technology to the maximum extent possible in all phases of litigation *i.e.*, to serve interrogatories on opposing counsel with a copy of the questions on computer disk in addition to the required printed copy.

RULE 3.04 MOTIONS TO COMPEL AND FOR PROTECTIVE ORDER

(a) A motion to compel discovery pursuant to Rule 36 or Rule 37, Fed.R.Civ.P., shall include quotation in full of each interrogatory, question on deposition, request for admission, or request for production to which the motion is addressed; each of which shall be followed immediately by quotation in full of the objection and grounds therefor as stated by the opposing party; or the answer or response which is asserted to be insufficient, immediately followed by a statement of the reason the motion should be granted. The opposing party shall then respond as required by Rule 3.01(b) of these rules.

(b) For the guidance of counsel in preparing or opposing contemplated motions for a protective order pursuant to Rule 26(c), Fed.R.Civ.P., related to the place of taking a party-litigant's deposition, or the deposition of the managing agent of a party, it is the general policy of the Court that a non-resident plaintiff may reasonably be deposed at least once in this District during the discovery stages of the case; and that a non-resident defendant who intends to be present in person at trial may reasonably be deposed at least once in this District either during the discovery stages of the case or within a week prior to trial as the circumstances seem to suggest. Otherwise, depositions of parties should usually be taken as in the case of other witnesses pursuant to Rule 45(d), Fed.R.Civ.P.. A non-resident, within the meaning of this rule, is a person residing outside the State of Florida.

RULE 3.05 CASE MANAGEMENT

(a) As soon as practicable after the filing of any civil action, the Clerk shall designate the case for future management on one of three tracks. The Clerk will notify the Plaintiff of such designation and the Plaintiff must then serve that notice upon all other parties. However, in cases governed by Rule 4.02, the Clerk will notify the party effecting removal, as specified in Rule 4.02(b), who then must serve that notice upon all other parties. The presiding judge may thereafter direct at any time that a case be redesignated from one track to a different track.

(b) Cases shall be designated by the Clerk to their appropriate tracks as follows:

(1) The following categories of proceedings are Track One Cases: (A) an action for review on an administrative record; (B) a petition for habeas corpus or other proceeding to challenge a criminal conviction or sentence; (C) an action brought without counsel by a person in custody of the United States, a state, or a state subdivision; (D) an action to enforce or quash an administrative summons or subpoena; (E) an action by the United States to recover benefit payments; (F) an action by the United States to collect on a student loan guaranteed by the United States; (G) a proceeding ancillary to proceedings in other courts; and (H) an action to enforce an arbitration award.

(2) Track Two cases shall include all cases not designated as Track One Cases, and not within the definition of Track Three Cases as hereafter stated. Track Two Cases will normally consist of non-complex actions which will require a trial, either jury or non-jury, absent earlier settlement or disposition by summary judgment or some other means.

(3) Track Three Cases shall include those cases involving class action or antitrust claims, securities litigation, mass disaster or other complex tort cases, or those actions presenting factual or legal issues arising from the presence of

multiple parties or multiple claims portending extensive discovery procedures or numerous legal issues such that the management techniques recommended in the current edition of the Manual For Complex Litigation should be considered and applied as appropriate to the circumstances of the case. Track Three Cases shall also include any action so imminently affecting the public interest (e.g. legislative redistricting, school desegregation, voting rights) as to warrant heightened judicial attention or expedited treatment.

(c) The following procedures shall apply depending upon the Track to which a case has been designated:

(1) Track One Cases - -(A) Government foreclosure or recovery cases, motions to withdraw references to the Bankruptcy Court, and proceedings under 28 USC § 2255 will normally be managed by the presiding District Judge pursuant to notices or orders entered by the Judge, or by the Clerk under the Court's direction, in each such case. (B) Other Track One cases will normally be referred at the time of filing to the Magistrate Judges for management by them in accordance with other provisions of these local rules or standing orders entered in each Division of the Court governing the duties and responsibilities of the Magistrate Judges. Such cases will then be managed by them pursuant to notices or orders entered by the Magistrate Judge, or by the Clerk under the Court's direction, in each such case.

(2) Track Two Cases - - (A) All Rule 12, F. R. Civ. P., motions will be promptly considered by the Court and will normally be decided within sixty (60) days after receipt of the last paper directed to the motion. (B) Counsel and any unrepresented party shall meet within 60 days after service of the complaint upon any defendant, or the first appearance of any defendant, regardless of the pendency of any undecided motions, for the purpose of preparing and filing a Case Management Report in the form prescribed below. Unless the Court orders otherwise, parties represented by counsel are permitted, but are not required, to attend the case management meeting. The Case Management Report must be filed within 14 days after the meeting. Unless otherwise ordered by the Court, a party may not seek discovery from any source before the meeting. (C) The Case Management Report shall include: (I) The date(s) and time(s) of the meetings of the parties and the identity of the persons present. (ii) A date by which the parties have agreed to prediscovery disclosures of core information, either voluntarily or as may be required by the Federal Rules of Civil Procedure or other provisions of these rules, and a detailed description of the information
scheduled for disclosure. (iii) A discovery plan which shall include a detailed description of the discovery each party intends to pursue (requests for admission, requests for production or inspection, written interrogatories, oral depositions), the time during which each form of discovery will be pursued, the proposed date for completion of discovery, and such other matters relating to discovery as the parties may agree upon (e.g., handling of confidential information, limits on the number

or length of depositions, assertion of privileges). (iv) A final date for the filing of all motions for leave to file third party claims or to join other parties and specification of a final date for the filing of any motions for summary judgment. (v) A statement concerning the intent of the parties regarding alternative dispute resolution (settlement negotiations, court annexed arbitration under Chapter Eight or court annexed mediation under Chapter Nine of these rules), and specification of a date by which the parties will either report to the court concerning prospective settlement or apply for an order invoking arbitration or mediation. (vi) A date by which the parties will be ready for a final pretrial conference and subsequent trial. (vii) The signature of all counsel and all unrepresented parties either in a single document or duplicate originals. (viii) A statement assessing the need for a preliminary pretrial conference before entry of a Case Management and Scheduling Order. (D) Upon receipt of the Case Management Report the court will either (I) schedule a preliminary pretrial conference to further discuss the content of the report and the subjects enumerated in Rule 16, F.R.Civ.P., before the entry of a Case Management and Scheduling Order, or (ii) enter a Case Management and Scheduling Order. The Case Management and Scheduling Order will establish a discovery plan and a schedule of dates including the dates of a final pretrial conference and trial (or specify dates after which a pretrial conference or trial may be scheduled on twenty (20) days' notice). (E) It is the goal of the court that a trial will be conducted in all Track Two Cases within two years after the filing of the complaint, and that most such cases will be tried within one year after the filing of the complaint. A motion to amend any pleading or a motion for continuance of any pretrial conference, hearing, or trial is distinctly disfavored after entry of the Case Management and Scheduling Order.

(3) Track Three Cases - -(A) The provisions of subsections (c)(2)(A),(B) and (c)(I)-(vii) of this rule shall apply to all Track Three Cases. (B) Upon receipt of the Case Management Report, if not sooner in some cases, the Court will schedule and conduct a preliminary pretrial conference to discuss with the parties the content of the report and the subjects enumerated in Rule 16, F.R.Civ.P., before the entry of a Case Management and Scheduling Order. (C) The Case Management and Scheduling Order will establish a discovery plan and will also schedule such additional preliminary pretrial conferences as may seem necessary as well as a final pretrial conference and trial (or specify dates after which a pretrial conference or trial may be scheduled on twenty (20) days' notice). (D) It is the goal of the court that a trial will be conducted in all Track Three Cases within three years after the filing of the complaint, and that most such cases will be tried within two (2) years after the filing of the complaint or on an acutely accelerated schedule if the public interest requires. A motion to amend any pleading or to continue any pretrial conference, hearing or trial is severely disfavored because, in light of the need for special judicial attention, counsel should prosecute or defend a Track Three Case only if able to accommodate the scheduling demands.

(d) The disclosures required by Fed.R.Civ.P. 26 (including the initial disclosures specified in Rule 26(a)(1)) shall be made in Track Two and Track Three Cases in the time and manner required by that rule unless otherwise ordered by the Court or stipulated by the parties. If the parties stipulate not to exchange initial disclosures, the Court may order the parties to exchange similar information pursuant to Fed.R.Civ.P.16. Track One Cases are exempt from the initial disclosures provisions of Rule 26(a)(1).

RULE 3.06 FINAL PRETRIAL PROCEDURES

(a) Final pretrial conferences may be scheduled by the Court pursuant to Rule 16(d), Fed.R.Civ.P., in any civil case on not less than twenty (20) days notice.

(b) In any case in which a final pretrial conference is scheduled by the Court (or in any case in which the Court directs the preparation and filing of a pretrial statement in accordance with this rule, but without scheduling a pretrial conference), it shall be the responsibility of counsel for all parties to meet together no later than ten (10) days before the date of the final pretrial conference (or at such other time as the Court may direct) in a good faith effort to: (1) discuss the possibility of settlement; (2) stipulate to as many facts or issues as possible; (3) examine all exhibits and Rule 5.04 exhibit substitutes or documents and other items of tangible evidence to be offered by any party at trial; (4) exchange the names and addresses of all witnesses; and (5) prepare a pretrial statement in accordance with subsection (c) of this rule.

(c) The pretrial statement shall be filed with the Court no later than three (3) days before the date of the final pretrial conference (or at such other time as the Court may direct), and shall contain: (1) the basis of federal jurisdiction; (2) a concise statement of the nature of the action; (3) a brief, general statement of each party's case; (4) a list of all exhibits and Rule 5.04 exhibit substitutes to be offered at trial with notation of all objections thereto; (5) a list of all witnesses who may be called at trial; (6) a list of all expert witnesses including, as to each such witness, a statement of the subject matter and a summary of the substance of his or her testimony; (7) in cases in which any party claims money damages, a statement of the elements of each such claim and the amount being sought with respect to each such element; (8) a list of all depositions to be offered in evidence at trial (as distinguished from possible use for impeachment), including a designation of the pages and lines to be offered from each deposition; (9) a concise statement of those facts which are admitted and will require no proof at trial, together with any reservations directed to such admissions; (10) a concise statement of applicable principles of law on which there is agreement; (11) a concise statement of those issues of fact which remain to be litigated (without incorporation by reference to prior pleadings and memoranda); (12) a concise statement of those issues of law which remain for determination by the Court (without incorporation by reference to prior pleadings or memoranda); (13) a concise statement of any disagreement as to the application of the Federal Rules of Evidence or the Federal Rules of Civil Procedure; (14) a list of all motions or other matters which require action by the Court; and (15) the signatures of counsel for all parties.

(d) If a final pretrial conference is scheduled by the Court, lead trial counsel for each party shall attend.

(e) All pleadings filed by any party prior to filing of the pretrial statement shall be deemed to be merged therein, or in any subsequent pretrial order entered by the Court. The pretrial statement and the pretrial order, if any, will control the course of the trial and may not be amended except by order of the Court in the furtherance of justice. If new evidence or witnesses are discovered after filing of the pretrial statement, the party desiring to use the same shall immediately notify opposing counsel and the Court, and such use shall be permitted only by order of the Court in the furtherance of justice.

RULE 3.07 MARKING AND LISTING EXHIBITS

(a) In advance of trial and, when reasonable, in advance of evidentiary hearing, counsel for each party in any case shall obtain from the Clerk (or from an outside source in the format utilized by the Clerk or in a format approved by the presiding judge), tabs or labels. These tabs or labels shall be used for the marking and identification of each exhibit proposed to be offered in evidence
or otherwise tendered to any witness during trial and evidentiary hearing and for the marking and identification of photographs and reductions proposed to be offered with exhibits in accordance with Rule 5.04. Counsel shall identify a photograph or reduction offered with an exhibit with the number identifying the exhibit.

(b) Upon marking exhibits, counsel shall also prepare a list of such exhibits, in sequence, with a descriptive notation sufficient to identify each separate numbered exhibit. Counsel shall furnish copies of the list to opposing counsel and three copies to the Court at the commencement of trial and, when reasonable, at the commencement of evidentiary hearing. (See also Rules 5.03 and 5.04.)

RULE 3.08 NOTICE OF SETTLEMENTS; DISMISSAL

(a) It shall be the duty of all counsel to immediately notify the Court upon the settlement of any case.

(b) When notified that a case has been settled and for purposes of administratively closing the file, the Court may order that a case be dismissed subject to the right of any party to move the Court within sixty (60) days thereafter (or within such other period of time as the Court may specify) for the purpose of entering a stipulated form of final order or judgment; or, on good cause shown, to reopen the case for further proceedings.

RULE 3.09 CONTINUANCES

(a) No trial, hearing or other proceeding shall be continued upon stipulation of counsel alone, but a continuance may be allowed by order of the Court for good cause shown.

(b) Failure to complete discovery procedures within the time established pursuant to Rule 3.05 of these rules shall not constitute cause for continuance unless such failure or inability is brought to the attention of the Court at least sixty (60) days in advance of any scheduled trial date and is not the result of lack of diligence in pursuing such discovery.

(c) Except for good cause shown, no continuance shall be granted on the ground that a party or witness has not been served with process or a subpoena, as the case might be, unless the moving party, at least five (5) days before the return date, has delivered the papers to be served to the Marshal (or other appropriate person) for that purpose.

(d) Motions to continue trial must be signed by the attorney of record who shall certify that the moving party has been informed of the motion and has consented to it.

RULE 3.10 FAILURE TO PROSECUTE: DISMISSAL

(a) Whenever it appears that any case is not being diligently prosecuted the Court may, on motion of any party or on its own motion, enter an order to show cause why the case should not be dismissed, and if no satisfactory cause is shown, the case may be dismissed by the Court for want of prosecution.

CHAPTER FOUR- SPECIAL RULES:

OMITTED WITH THE EXCEPTION OF:

RULE 4.02 REMOVAL OF CASES FROM STATE COURT

(a) All cases removed to this Court from the courts of the State of Florida shall be docketed and assigned, in accordance with Rule 1.03 of these rules, in the Division encompassing the county of the State in which the case was pending.

(b) The party effecting removal shall file with the notice of removal a true and legible copy of all process, pleadings, orders, and other papers or exhibits of every kind, including depositions, then on file in the state court.

(c) When a case is removed to this Court with pending motions on which briefs or legal memoranda have not been submitted, the moving party shall file and serve a supporting brief within ten (10) days after the removal in accordance with Rule 3.01(a) of these rules, and the party or parties opposing the motion shall then comply with Rule 3.01(b) of these rules.

CHAPTER SIX - UNITED STATES MAGISTRATE JUDGES

OMITTED

CHAPTER SEVEN - ADMIRALTY AND MARITIME RULES

OMITTED

CHAPTER EIGHT - COURT ANNEXED ARBITRATION

OMITTED

CHAPTER NINE - COURT ANNEXED MEDIATION

OMITTED

INDEX